Windows 3: A Developer's Guide

Windows 3: A Developer's Guide

Jeffrey M. Richter

 **M&T Books**
A Division of M&T Publishing, Inc.
501 Galveston Drive
Redwood City, CA 94063

Limits of Liability and Disclaimer of Warranty
The Author and Publisher of this book have used their best efforts in preparing this book and the programs contained in it. These efforts include the development, research, and testing of the theories and programs to determine their effectiveness.

The Author and Publisher make no warranty of any kind, expressed or implied, with regard to these programs or the documentation contained in this book. The Author and Publisher shall not be liable in any event for incidental or consequential damages in connection with, or arising out of, the furnishing, performance, or use of these programs.

Library of Congress Cataloging-in-Publication Data

Richter, Jeffrey
    Windows 3: a developer's guide / Jeffrey Richter
        p.   cm.
    Includes index.
    ISBN 1-55851-162-8 (book only)
    ISBN 1-55851-164-4 (book/disk)
    1. Microsoft Windows (Computer program) 2. C (Computer programming language) 3. Computer software—Development. I. Title.
QA76.76.W56R54 1991
005.4'3—dc20   90-24597
94 93 92 91   4 3 2 1   CIP

All products, names, and services are trademarks or registered trademarks of their respective companies.

Cover Design: Lauren Smith Designs	**Cover Illustration**: Christine Mortensen
Technical Editor: Bruce P. Gage	**Project Editor**: Linda Comer

To Donna Murray
for all the great times we spent
together over the years

Contents

Acknowledgments

I would like to thank the following people, for without their assistance you would be staring at the palm of your hand right now.

To Donna Murray for proofreading every chapter, making suggestions, discussing various implementations for the sample applications, and playing that popular game, "Stump the Author." I hope your knowledge of Presentation Manager won't hurt you when you look for a job as a Windows programmer.

To my parents, Arlene and Sylvan, who bought me my first computer (a TRS-80 Model I). Actually, they were afraid that I would use the computer for a week and then toss it in the closet next to the chemistry set. Thank you for all the love and support you've given me over the years.

To Susan Ramee for all the effort and discussions on getting the figures, diagrams, and icons (especially the icons) just right.

To Elvira Peretsman for her assistance with the MDI Sample Application and for brightening my every day with a new wardrobe.

To Larry Hackett for assistance with the bitmap and icon processing. I hope you'll save the X-rated bitmaps for my next book.

To Tony Spica for giving me my first C language lessons some six or seven years ago. Maybe now you'll use Windows for pawnshop programs.

To Bruce Gage of Kuvera Associates in Redmond, WA, for doing the technical review of this book.

And to Linda Comer at M&T Books for the time and effort she invested in creating this book, especially the marathon days and evenings toward the end.

Introduction

It wasn't until Microsoft Windows Version 3.0 was introduced on May 22, 1990, that graphical computing finally took the IBM-PC family of computers by storm. There are many reasons for Windows 3.0's success: the improved interface, the improved memory management, and the abundance of applications being developed and distributed for Windows. While it's true that Windows 3.0 sports some impressive technical features, I believe it owes most of its success to the third-party companies that have devoted their time and money to producing Windows applications. After all, people don't buy operating environments; they buy applications that help them do their work more efficiently.

Microsoft, realizing this, set up a "Windows Prerelease" program. This program was designed to give serious Windows developers the ability to design and use Windows 3.0 almost a full year before its commercial release. This means that a large number of commercial applications could be announced the same day as Windows 3.0. Without these third-party products, the demand for Windows wouldn't be as high as it is today.

Of course, the Windows operating environment itself offers many new improvements over the conventional DOS system. Users no longer have to close one application before using another, and data can be shared between applications. Applications have a consistent appearance that makes them easy to use. But an operating environment that affords so much capability is bound to make the applications developer's job more difficult.

Before designing any Windows application, examine existing programs closely. New Windows applications are hitting the market almost every day. While many of these applications are good, some are poorly designed and implemented. It doesn't take long for a user to figure out which are poorly designed. For example, some applications all but ignore the IBM SAA/CUA guide that's included with the Windows SDK. All Windows applications must follow this specification. While it does leave room for subjective interpretation, some things are specified explicitly. For example, menu items in the File and Edit menus must appear in a specific order. Also, hot keys should have the same meanings across applications. For example, users expect that Alt-V will open the View menu. If your application also has a Verify menu, keep the Alt-V for the View menu and use another letter to open the Verify menu.

I've also seen a number of applications that incorrectly organize the child controls in dialog boxes. It's easy to forget that a user may prefer to use a keyboard instead of a mouse. After designing your dialog boxes, test them using a keyboard. Child controls are created in the order in which they appear in the dialog-box template and not by their location on the screen. When the user presses the Tab key, Windows gives focus to the next control containing the *WS_TABSTOP* style. If the controls aren't created in the correct order, they will appear to gain focus in an almost random fashion.

When you're designing a Windows application, pay attention to small details like these. These concepts are stressed throughout this book.

Windows 3: A Developer's Guide is for the experienced Windows 3.0 developer who wants to gain insight into some of this complicated environment's most powerful features. Every chapter contains at least one programming example that demonstrates the concepts presented. Some of these programs are complete applications that may be used unmodified, while others show how to combine various Windows features to produce a result greater than the sum of its parts. Many of the applications contain code sections or modules that isolate some of the more fundamental concepts. These isolated sections are usually general enough that you can include them in your own Windows applications without modification. All the explanations and source-code examples are geared toward designing and implementing applications that will someday become commercial products.

Before You Get Started

To compile and experiment with the sample applications in this book, you must have the following:

- The Windows 3.0 run-time system
- The Windows 3.0 Software Development Kit (SDK)
- Microsoft C 6.0

The variable names are preceded by one of the standard prefixes explained on page xxii of the *Microsoft Windows Programmer's Reference*, Volume 1. However, I use the *b* prefix to represent bytes instead of Boolean values and the *f* prefix to represent Boolean values instead of bit flag values. This is the notation recommended for OS/2 Presentation Manager programming.

All global variables are prefixed by a single underscore character. This makes functions easier to understand because any variable not preceded by an underscore is either a parameter to the function or an auto or static local variable.

When a function is declared, a space appears immediately before the opening parenthesis. For example:

```
int FunctionName (int nX, int nY) { }
   ^ space character
```

However, when calls to this function are made, the space is not used:

```
nZ = FunctionName(nX, nY);
   ^ no space character
```

The reason for doing this is so you can easily locate a function declaration in a source module. By asking your program editor to search for "FunctionName " (notice the trailing space), it will find the function itself rather than calls to the function.

Why This Book Is For You

This book is for the Windows 3.0 developer who wants to explore this intricate operating environment in detail. While there are many books about Microsoft Windows programming, most simply discuss the basic features, capabilities, and resources Windows offers. This book covers some of the more advanced and powerful features of Windows that receive little or no mention in the other books. It also demonstrates how to combine the basic Windows building blocks to create complete applications.

Each topic presented gives insights into Windows' inner workings, followed by sample source code demonstrating the implementation details. Having this understanding will enable you to exploit the facilities offered by Windows, making your applications more robust and efficient. The goal of this book is to give you the tools and knowledge you need to develop professional Windows applications.

CHAPTER 1

Anatomy of a Window

The window class, which controls a window's appearance and behavior, plays a central role in Windows programming. It must be explicitly defined before any windows can be created.

The process of defining a class in Windows is called *registering the class*. Registering a class does not create any windows. However, once the class is defined any number of windows can be created.

Applications may register many window classes. Windows maintains knowledge of these classes until the registering application terminates or explicitly unregisters the class.

Registering a Window Class

To create a window class, you must write a window procedure, initialize a *WNDCLASS* structure, and call the *RegisterClass* function. The most important members of the *WNDCLASS* structure are:

- *lpszClassName*. The name given to the class.

- *lpfnWndProc*. The address of the procedure that performs operations for windows of the class.

- *hInstance*. The handle or owner of the application or dynamic link library (DLL) that registered the class.

The remaining members of the *WNDCLASS* structure define default attributes for windows of the class.

When a window class is no longer needed, the *UnregisterClass* function should be called to remove the class from memory. All windows must be destroyed before their class is unregistered. Windows automatically unregisters window classes when the owning application or DLL terminates.

Class Types

There are three types of window classes: system global, application global, and application local.

System Global Classes. System global classes are registered by Windows when you start up the environment. Windows defines all the window procedures for these classes internally, initializes the *WNDCLASS* structure for each of them, and calls *RegisterClass*—all before Program Manager appears on the screen. System global classes are unregistered only when Windows terminates. This means that all these classes are available the entire time Windows is running.

To use these classes, call *CreateWindow* or *CreateWindowEx* and pass it the class name of the type of window you wish to create. Below is a list of the system global classes you can use in your applications:

BUTTON	COMBOBOX	EDIT	LISTBOX
MDICLIENT	SCROLLBAR	STATIC	

Although these classes are frequently referred to as *child controls*, they are no different from classes that you register yourself.

Windows also registers a number of window classes that are used implicitly by applications. Windows automatically creates instances of these window classes as needed. For example, when you call the *DialogBox* or *CreateDialog* function,

Windows creates a dialog-box window and all the child controls are created as children of this window. Windows also creates a caption window when your application is minimized. The text that appears below your application's icon is painted in a caption window that Windows created implicitly when the application was minimized.

Application Global Classes. Application global classes are registered by an application or, more often, a DLL. DLLs usually include class registration in their initialization code and unregister the classes at termination. This means that window classes registered in DLLs are only available while the DLL is running.

Once a class is registered, any application can create windows of that class. Custom controls that you create yourself should be registered as application global classes. For example, you might design a window class called SPIN for use in two applications. By registering the class in a DLL as application global, you can ensure that both applications can create windows of the SPIN class.

To register a class as application global, include the *CS_GLOBALCLASS style* flag when initializing the *style* member of the *WNDCLASS* structure.

Application Local Classes. Application local classes are registered by your application for its sole use. Applications cannot create windows based on application local classes registered by other applications. These classes are available from the time they are registered to the time they are unregistered, or until all instances of the registering application terminate.

A class is registered as application local by default; the *CS_GLOBALCLASS* flag is omitted when the style member of the *WNDCLASS* structure is initialized.

Window Classes with the Same Name. It's possible for different applications to register window classes with the same name. When an application is creating a window, Windows first tries to match the class name with local window classes registered by the same application. If a matching application local class cannot be found, Windows searches for an application global class with the same name. Finally, if an application global class cannot be found, Windows searches the system global window classes.

Because Windows uses this order to locate classes, defining an application local class called EDIT would cause all EDIT windows created by your application (including those in your dialog-box templates) to be of the application local class and not of the Windows system global class. This scheme also allows two applications to register SPIN classes and be guaranteed that windows created in each application are based on their respective SPIN classes.

The following table summarizes the results of calling *RegisterClass* when an application attempts to register a window class having the same name as a previously registered class.

	How the class was previously registered:			
Application wants to register the new class as:	System Global	Application Global	Application Local, same application	Application Local, different application
Application Global	TRUE	FALSE	FALSE	TRUE
Application Local	TRUE	FALSE	FALSE	TRUE

It would be logical to assume that an application local class could override an application global class. However, Windows does not allow this, as it would break compatibility with previous versions of Windows.

The Parts of a Window Class

The first step in registering a window class is to initialize the members of *WNDCLASS*. Here is a description of some of these members:

- *lpszClassName*

  The *lpszClassName* member of *WNDCLASS* indicates the name of the window class. When you ask Windows to create a window of a certain class, it compares the class name of each registered class with the class name of the window you wish to create. If a matching registered class can be found, Windows creates the window and returns its window handle. If there is no registered class with the name you specified, Windows returns NULL.

- *hInstance*

  The *hInstance* member of *WNDCLASS* identifies the owner or creator of the window class. For an application, this value is passed to the *WinMain* function. For DLLs, the information is passed to the *LibEntry* function. This value lets Windows automatically unregister the class when all instances of its creator terminate.

- *lpfnWndProc*

  The *lpfnWndProc* member of *WNDCLASS* specifies the procedure that defines the behavior for all windows of the class. When something happens or is requested of the window, the window procedure is called and passed a message describing the event that occurred or the service that needs to be performed. The procedure then performs some operation to satisfy the request.

  Windows supplies a default window procedure called *DefWindowProc*. The messages processed by this procedure deal with the behavior of the window's system menu and nonclient area. The complete list of recognized messages can be found on page 1-20 of the *Microsoft Windows Programmer's Reference*, Volume 1. The table also describes, for each message, the operations *DefWindowProc* will perform. These operations are what Microsoft has defined as "standard" behavior for windows.

It's possible to set the *lpfnWndProc* member of *WNDCLASS* to *DefWindowProc* before registering the class. This will register a window class that has default, or standard, behavior. However, the window can never do anything more or different, so there's little point.

• *style*

The *style* member of the *WNDCLASS* structure specifies some of the behavioral aspects for windows of the class. WINDOWS.H defines the valid class styles that can be used to register a class. The list appears below:

Class style	WINDOWS.H identifier	ID value
Painting	CS_VREDRAW	0x0001
	CS_HREDRAW	0x0002
	CS_OWNDC	0x0020
	CS_CLASSDC	0x0040
	CS_PARENTDC	0x0080
	CS_SAVEBITS	0x0800
	CS_BYTEALIGNCLIENT	0x1000
	CS_BYTEALIGNWINDOW	0x2000
Input conversions	CS_KEYCVTWINDOW	0x0004
	CS_DBLCLKS	0x0008
	CS_NOKEYCVT	0x0100
	CS_NOCLOSE	0x0200

Class style	WINDOWS.H identifier	ID value
Class type	*CS_GLOBALCLASS*	0x4000

- The Remaining Members

The remaining members of the *WNDCLASS* structure are *cbClsExtra*, *cbWndExtra*, *hIcon*, *hCursor*, *hbrBackground*, and *lpszMenuName*. These members describe the default attributes and behavior that windows of the registered class should have.

How Windows Stores Window Classes Internally

When you call *RegisterClass*, Windows allocates a block of memory to store information about the class. The block contains all the information specified in *WNDCLASS* plus the class name and menu name, so the original strings need not be retained by the application. Windows extends the size of the block by the number of bytes you specified in the *cbClsExtra* member and initializes these bytes to zero.

These additional bytes are reserved for your application's use, and Windows does not use them at all. The information stored in the extra bytes is available to every window based on the registered class. The management of these extra bytes is left entirely up to the programmer. Figure 1-1 shows how a window class may be represented internally.

Windows contains functions that allow you to retrieve and modify the information in the class structure after the class has been registered. These functions are described in this section.

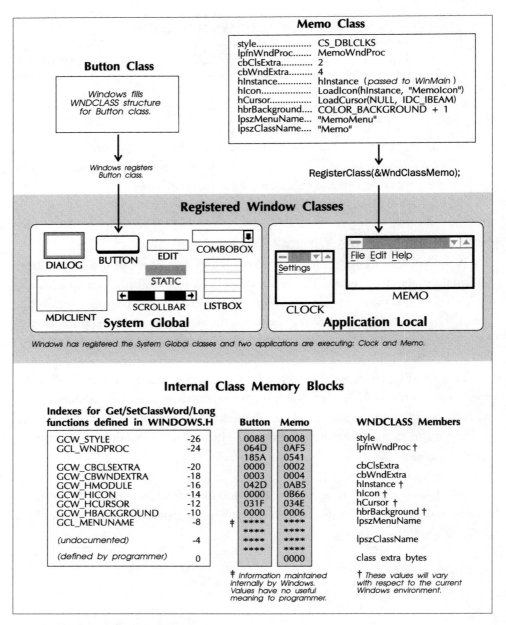

Figure 1-1. Using window classes.

GetClassInfo can be used to fill a *WNDCLASS* structure with information about a previously registered class. However, this function will not set the *lpszMenuName*, *lpszClassName*, and *hInstance* members of the *WNDCLASS* structure. In addition, it cannot return the contents of the class extra bytes. Windows does not supply an inverse function to *GetClassInfo* that lets you change all the class information in one call. What differentiates this function from the remaining class functions is that it does not require a handle to an existing window to access the data.

GetClassLong and *GetClassWord* allow you to retrieve the individual members of the window class structure. To get any of the class information, you must supply a handle to an existing window that was created from the class you are interested in and an offset into the window class data structure. WINDOWS.H defines the offsets for all the elements in the window class structure. The list appears below:

Class element	WINDOWS.H identifier	Offset
Style	*GCW_STYLE*	−26
Window procedure	*GCL_WNDPROC*	−24
Class extra bytes	*GCW_CBCLSEXTRA*	−20
Window extra bytes	*GCW_CBWNDEXTRA*	−18
Owner's instance	*GCW_HMODULE*	−16
Icon	*GCW_HICON*	−14
Cursor	*GCW_HCURSOR*	−12
Brush background	*GCW_HBRBACKGROUND*	−10
Menu name	*GCL_MENUNAME*	−8
Class name	(undefined)	−4
Start of class extra bytes	(programmer-defined)	0

SetClassLong and *SetClassWord* allow you to change the individual members of the window class structure. To alter any of the class information, you must supply a handle to an existing window that was created from the class you are interested in, an offset into the window class data structure, and the desired new value. The

WINDOWS.H identifiers listed above for *GetClassLong* and *GetClassWord* should be used for these functions as well.

Note that *SetClassLong*, *SetClassWord*, *GetClassLong*, and *GetClassWord* do not check parameters for validity. To prevent errors, always use the manifest constants defined in WINDOWS.H to access class elements. If you're accessing the extra bytes associated with the class, use caution. It's up to you to make sure an invalid index is never passed to these functions. Appendix C presents a method of accessing the class extra bytes that will ensure only valid indexes are used.

The most common reason for changing the window class structure is to change window attributes before creating a new window. The *SetClassLong* and *SetClassWord* functions are inconvenient because they require a handle to a window of the desired class. Windows offers no satisfactory solution to this problem. To change an attribute of the window class structure, you must create a window of the desired class, call *SetClassLong* or *SetClassWord*, destroy the window, and create a new window of the same class.

Here is an example of how you could change all EDIT windows so that the mouse cursor will be an up-arrow instead of an I-beam:

```
// Create a window from the "EDIT" style
hWndEdit = CreateWindow("EDIT", "", WS_OVERLAPPED, 0, 0, 0, 0,
    NULL, NULL, hInstance, 01);
// Change the cursor handle to that of the up-arrow
SetClassWord(hWndEdit, GCW_HCURSOR,
    LoadCursor(NULL, IDC_UPARROW));
// Destroy the edit window
DestroyWindow(hWndEdit);
// From this point on, all edit windows will use an
// up-arrow instead of the I-beam mouse cursor
```

Because Windows always refers to the window class structure when it's going to display a cursor, the up-arrow will appear for EDIT windows that have already been created as well as those that will be created in the future. Note that because EDIT is a system global class, this affects EDIT windows created by other applications as well as your own.

Creating and Destroying Window Instances

Windows are created by calling *CreateWindow* or *CreateWindowEx* with the name of the desired window class. This function sends several messages to the window procedure associated with the window class.

When *CreateWindow(Ex)* sends the *WM_NCCREATE* message to the window procedure, it's usually passed on to *DefWindowProc. DefWindowProc* allocates the block of memory used internally to describe this window instance, sets the window's caption, and initializes the scroll-bar values. The block of memory contains some information that is copied from the internal window class structure and some information from the parameters passed to *CreateWindow(Ex)*. If sufficient memory is not available for this memory block, *DefWindowProc* returns NULL.

When *CreateWindow(Ex)* sends the *WM_NCCREATE* message and NULL is returned, it stops sending messages to the window procedure and returns a NULL window handle to the caller. The return code of *WM_NCCREATE* is the only value *CreateWindow(Ex)* will examine to determine if halting the window-creation process is necessary.

During the creation of a window, *CreateWindow(Ex)* sends a *WM_CREATE* message (after the *WM_NCCREATE* message) so that any window-specific initialization may be performed. If you desire that the window not be created if initialization fails, place your initialization code in the processing of *WM_NCCREATE*. Most initialization requires that the window's memory block be available; calling *DefWindowProc* before performing your own initialization will ensure this. The following code is an example:

```
BOOL fOk;
  .
  .
  .
case WM_NCCREATE:
   fOk = (BOOL) DefWindowProc(hWnd, wMsg, wParam, lParam);
      if (!fOk) {
          lResult = 0;
          break;
   }
   hMem = GlobalAlloc(GMEM_MOVEABLE, BUFFERSIZE);
   if (hMem == NULL) {
      // Free block allocated by previous call to DefWindowProc
      DefWindowProc(hWnd, WM_NCDESTROY, 0, 0l);
      lResult = 0;
      break;
   }
   SetClassWord(hWnd, GWW_DATA, hMem);
   lResult = 1;
   break;

case WM_DESTROY:
   // Free block of memory created during WM_NCCREATE message
   GlobalFree(GetClassWord(hWnd, GWW_DATA));
   break;
  .
  .
  .
return(lResult);
```

Because the internal block was allocated before our own initialization, we must explicitly free the block if we are going to halt the creation of the window. We free the block by having *DefWindowProc* process the *WM_NCDESTROY* message.

This code fragment also demonstrates how *WM_DESTROY* should be used to perform window cleanup. In this example, the global memory allocated by *WM_NCCREATE* is freed.

Window Styles

CreateWindow's third parameter is the style of the window. As mentioned earlier, class style information affects all windows based on the class. Style information can also be specified for an individual instance of a class. The style parameter is a 32-bit value in which the high 16 bits specify style information that applies to all windows. WINDOWS.H defines styles that can be used for all windows. The list appears below:

Window style	WINDOWS.H identifier	ID value
Type	WS_OVERLAPPED	0x00000000L
	WS_POPUP	0x80000000L
	WS_CHILD	0x40000000L
Initial state	WS_MINIMIZE	0x20000000L
	WS_VISIBLE	0x10000000L
	WS_DISABLED	0x08000000L
	WS_MAXIMIZE	0x01000000L
Appearance	WS_CLIPSIBLINGS	0x04000000L
	WS_CLIPCHILDREN	0x02000000L
	WS_CAPTION	0x00C00000L
	WS_BORDER	0x00800000L
	WS_DLGFRAME	0x00400000L
	WS_THICKFRAME	0x00040000L
	WS_HSCROLL	0x00100000L
	WS_VSCROLL	0x00200000L
	WS_SYSMENU	0x00080000L
Capabilities	WS_MINIMIZEBOX	0x00020000L
	WS_MAXIMIZEBOX	0x00010000L
Input focus sequence	WS_GROUP	0x00020000L
	WS_TABSTOP	0x00010000L

Note that the *WS_CAPTION* style is a combination of *WS_BORDER* and *WS_DLGFRAME*. Because a window cannot have both the *WS_BORDER* and *WS_DLGFRAME* styles, Windows interprets both bits being on as the *WS_CAPTION* style.

Also note that the *WS_MINIMIZEBOX* and *WS_MAXIMIZEBOX* styles have identical values to the *WS_GROUP* and *WS_TABSTOP* identifiers. Windows treats these bits as *WS_GROUP* and *WS_TABSTOP* when the window is part of a dialog box to determine the input focus sequence. However, if the window is not part of a dialog box, Windows treats these bits as *WS_MINIMIZEBOX* and *WS_MAXIMIZEBOX*.

The low 16 bits of the window style parameter are specific to each class of window and have no meaning to Windows. Microsoft has specified which styles apply to each of the system global classes. These can be combined with the window styles listed above to give greater control over the behavior of a window. WINDOWS.H defines the styles that can be used with each of the system global classes. Notice that each style for a class begins with a unique prefix.

System global class	Style prefix
DIALOG	*DS_*
BUTTON	*BS_*
COMBOBOX	*CBS_*
EDIT	*ES_*
LISTBOX	*LBS_*
MDICLIENT	(none)
SCROLLBAR	*SBS_*
STATIC	*SS_*

*DS_* styles are specified in the *STYLE* line for a dialog-box template. Windows knows to use these styles when the *DialogBox* or *CreateDialog* function implicitly creates the dialog-box window.

When examining the values for these identifiers in WINDOWS.H, you will notice that many of the values repeat. For example, *BS_DEFPUSHBUTTON* and *SS_CENTER* both have a value of 0x0001. This does not cause a problem because only the window procedure associated with the class will see these style bits. Each class will interpret the bits differently.

A window procedure can retrieve style information by using the *GetWindowLong* function. Once the styles are retrieved, the procedure can *AND* the style with a particular identifier to see if the style is on or off. This information can be used to modify the behavior of the window.

Beginning with Windows 3.0, Microsoft added two new styles that can affect a window. To create a window using these new styles, you use *CreateWindowEx* instead of *CreateWindow*. The first parameter to *CreateWindowEx* represents the extended window styles. Like the window style value, the extended window style value is 32 bits long. WINDOWS.H defines the valid extended window styles. The list appears below:

Extended window style	WINDOWS.H identifier	ID value
Appearance	*WS_EX_DLGMODALFRAME*	0x80000000L
Communication	*WS_EX_NOPARENTNOTIFY*	0x40000000L

When you create a window using *CreateWindow*, the extended styles are considered to have a value of 0x00000000L.

How Windows Stores Window Instances Internally

The *CreateWindow* function can only create windows from a registered class. If Windows finds a class registered with the same name as the one requested, it allocates a block of memory to store information about the individual window. The block contains some of the information in the window class structure and some of the information that was passed to the *CreateWindow* function. Windows extends the size of the block by the number of bytes specified by the *cbWndExtra* value in the window class structure and initializes these bytes to zero.

Every window instance receives its own set of extra bytes. Like the class extra bytes, these are available solely for your application's use.

Figure 1-2 shows an example of how a window structure may be represented internally. Windows contains functions that allow you to retrieve and modify the information in the window structure after the window has been created. These functions are described in the following paragraphs.

The *GetClassName* function retrieves the class name that was used to create the window.

The *GetWindowLong* and *GetWindowWord* functions allow you to retrieve the individual members of the window structure. To get any of the window information, you must supply a window handle and an offset into the window data structure. WINDOWS.H defines the offsets for all the elements in the window structure. The list appears below:

Window element	WINDOW.H identifier	Offset
Extended style	*GWL_EXSTYLE*	−20
Style	*GWL_STYLE*	−16
ID	*GWW_ID*	−12
(undocumented)	(undocumented)	−10
Parent	*GWW_HWNDPARENT*	−8
Instance	*GWW_HINSTANCE*	−6
Window procedure	*GWL_WNDPROC*	−4
Start of window extra bytes	(programmer-defined)	0

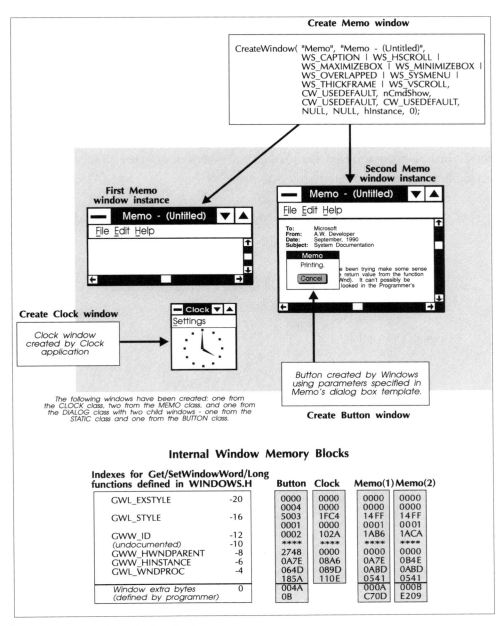

Figure 1-2. Creating window instances.

The *SetWindowLong* and *SetWindowWord* functions let you change individual members of the window structure. To alter this information, you must supply a window handle, an offset into the window data structure, and the desired new value. The WINDOWS.H identifiers listed earlier for *GetWindowLong* and *GetWindowWord* should be used for these functions as well.

The most common reason for changing the window structure is to store new values in the extra bytes. Here is an example of how you could keep track of how long an application has been running.

- Step 1: Define an ID to be used for referencing the window extra bytes:

```
#define GWL_STARTTIME    (0)
```

- Step 2: Register the class, making sure that four extra window bytes will be reserved for every window of this class:

```
WNDCLASS wc;
.
.
.
wc.cbWndExtra = 4;
RegisterClass(&wc);
```

- Step 3: When the window is created, initialize the window extra bytes to the Windows system time:

```
case WM_CREATE:
  SetWindowLong(hWnd, GWL_STARTTIME, GetTickCount());
  break;
```

- Step 4: Determine the total time the application has been running:

```
DWORD dwSecondsRunning;
    .
    .
    .
dwSecondsRunning = (GetTickCount() -
    GetWindowLong(hWnd, GWL_CREATTIME)) / 1000;
```

Window Properties

Window properties give the programmer another way to associate data with windows. Properties are extremely useful if you want to associate data with an instance for a class that you did not register yourself. If you didn't register the window class yourself, you don't know how many extra bytes were specified in the *WNDCLASS* structure. Although you can retrieve this information with *GetClassInfo*, you can be sure that if extra bytes were allocated they are being used by the window procedure that operates on this class. Using these extra bytes for your own purpose would surely interfere with the behavior of this window.

Properties allow you to associate data with a window by using a string name instead of modifying the information stored in the internal window structure. Only 16-bit values may be associated with a property. Because Windows must store property string names with a window, properties are slower to use and require more memory than window extra bytes.

Windows supplies four functions to manipulate properties of a window:

- The *SetProp* function associates a property with a window.
- The *RemoveProp* function removes a property associated with a window.
- The *GetProp* function retrieves the property associated with a window.
- The *EnumProps* function retrieves the list of all properties associated with a window.

The following is an example of how you could acquire some information in a modal dialog box and return that information to the caller.

Step 1: The caller allocates memory for the information that will be retrieved by the modal dialog box:

```
#define MAX_USERS_NAME_LEN (30)
 .
 .
 .
hMem = LocalAlloc(LMEM_MOVEABLE | LMEM_ZEROINIT,
   MAX_USERS_NAME_LEN + 1);
lpfnDlgProc = MakeProcInstance(hInstance, UserNameDlgProc);
DialogBoxParam(hInstance, "USERNAME", hWnd,
   lpfnDlgProc, (LONG) hMem);
FreeProcInstance(lpfnDlgProc);
// The local memory block will contain the user's name
 .
 .
 .
```

Step 2: The dialog-box procedure associates the memory handle with the dialog-box window:

```
case WM_INITDIALOG:
   // The lParam contains the last parameter value passed to
   // DialogBoxParam. This is the handle to the local block of
   // memory.
   SetProp(hDlg, "Memory", (LOCALHANDLE) lParam);
   // Perform any other initialization for the dialog box
   .
   .
   .
```

Step 3: The dialog box will fill the block of memory when the user clicks OK:

```
case IDOK:
   hMem = GetProp(hDlg, "Memory");
   npszName = LocalLock(hMem);
   GetDlgItemText(hDlg, ID_USERNAMEEDITBOX,
      (LONG) (LPSTR) npszName, MAX_USERS_NAME_LEN);
```

```
LocalUnlock(hMem);
  .
  .
  .
EndDialog(hDlg, IDOK);
break;
```

Step 4: When the dialog box is destroyed, the property must be removed:

```
case WM_DESTROY:
  RemoveProp(hDlg, "Memory");
  break;
```

Window Messages

Windows are passive workers. When a manager (the user or Windows) requires that work be done, it sends a message to the window procedure instructing it to perform the work. The type of work to be done is specified by the message. When more information is needed to carry out the task, the *wParam* and *lParam* parameters relay the additional information. Window procedures have many alternatives for handling window messages:

1. Pass the message to *DefWindowProc*. This has the effect described on page 1-20 of the *Microsoft Windows Programmer's Reference*. Any message not recognized by *DefWindowProc* is ignored and zero is returned.

2. Process the message. This is usually accomplished by including a *case* statement for the message in your window procedure. Any operation may be performed. An appropriate value should be returned.

3. Process the message and call *DefWindowProc* (in either order). This is usually accomplished by including a *case* statement for the message in your window procedure. However, the code for the *case* includes an explicit call to *DefWindowProc*. This executes the operations defined by *DefWindowProc* as well as any additional actions you may desire.

4. Ignore the message. No action is to be performed when the window procedure receives this message. An appropriate value should be returned.

Kinds of Messages. Window messages are sent as unsigned integer values in the range of 0x0000 to 0xFFFF. Microsoft Windows divides this range into four sections:

Message range	Section description
0x0000 to *WM_USER* - 1	All standard window messages. This includes all messages that begin with the *WM_* prefix.
WM_USER to 0x7FFF	Class-defined integer messages.
0x8000 to 0xBFFF	Messages reserved for Windows.
0xC000 to 0xFFFF	System-defined string messages. This includes all message numbers returned by the *RegisterWindowMessage* function.

Note that *WM_USER* is defined in WINDOWS.H to be 0x0400.

Class-Defined Integer Messages. You can create messages that perform operations specific to a class of windows. Suppose you created an INFO window that maintained a block of memory and allowed other windows access to that block. You could create a class-specific message for the INFO window; when it received the message, it would return the handle of the block of memory. The list of class-specific messages should be placed in a header file, INFO.H. This file should be included by all windows that will send messages to INFO windows. INFO.H should look like this:

```
#define IM_GETMEMORY (WM_USER + 0)
```

In the file that contains the window procedure for an INFO window, INFO.C, the following code fragment should exist:

```
#include "INFO.H"
  .
  .
  .
case IM_GETMEMORY:
   lResult = GetWindowWord(hWnd, GWW_MEMORYHANDLE);
   break;
  .
  .
  .
return(lResult);
```

Class-defined messages should only be sent to windows of the class that defines the messages. Sending a class-defined message to a window of another class will have an unpredictable effect or the wrong effect.

WINDOWS.H defines class-specific messages that can be sent to most of the system global classes. Notice that each message begins with a unique prefix.

System global class	Message prefix
DIALOG	DM_
BUTTON	BM_
COMBOBOX	CB_
EDIT	EM_
LISTBOX	LB_
MDICLIENT	(none)
SCROLLBAR	(none)
STATIC	(none)

System-Defined String Messages. You create system-defined string messages when you wish to send a message and are unsure of the receiving window's class. When you register a system-defined message, you are telling the Windows environment that there is a new "standard" message that any window can recognize.

We add a new system message by calling *RegisterWindowMessage*. This function accepts a character string and returns a numeric value in the range of 0xC000 to 0xFFFF. If another call to *RegisterWindowMessage* is placed with the same character string, Windows returns the same value that was returned the first time. Because of this, different windows will be using the same integer value to represent the same type of message.

All applications that wish to use these new messages should call *RegisterWindowMessage* during initialization. Once a window message has been registered, it remains in existence during the entire Windows session. This is because Windows has no function to unregister a window message.

Sneaking a Peek at Windows

Voyeur, a sample application discussed here, is a tool that demonstrates most of the concepts explained in this chapter. Voyeur's client area shows all the information associated with a window on the screen. The user instructs Voyeur to begin peering into windows by selecting one of the two peer options on the system menu. At this point, the mouse cursor changes into a pair of eyes that can be positioned anywhere on the screen. When the cursor enters a window, a frame is drawn around the window and Voyeur updates its dialog box with information about the window.

Figure 1-3 shows Voyeur in action. In this example, Voyeur is displaying the information for the Main group window of Program Manager. Because Voyeur's window is so large, Voyeur's menu options are part of the system menu instead of in a separate menu bar. For convenience, Voyeur interprets the class styles, window styles, and extended window styles and fills list boxes with the appropriate style's text name. The actual hexadecimal value of the styles is given above the list box. Also, the class extra bytes and window extra bytes are shown in list boxes.

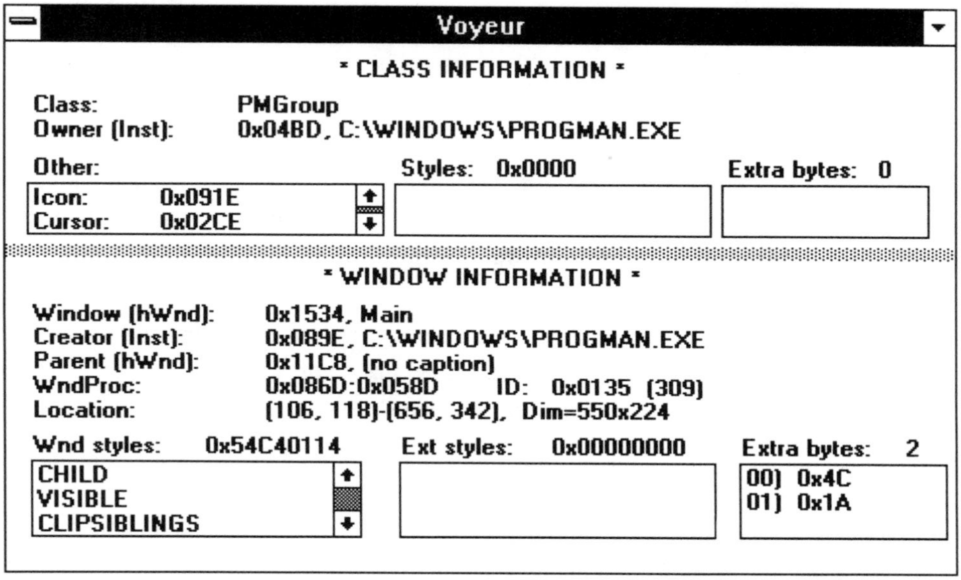
Voyeur
* CLASS INFORMATION *
Class: PMGroup
Owner (Inst): 0x04BD, C:\WINDOWS\PROGMAN.EXE
Other:
Styles: 0x0000
Extra bytes: 0
Icon: 0x091E
Cursor: 0x02CE
* WINDOW INFORMATION *
Window (hWnd): 0x1534, Main
Creator (Inst): 0x089E, C:\WINDOWS\PROGMAN.EXE
Parent (hWnd): 0x11C8, (no caption)
WndProc: 0x086D:0x058D ID: 0x0135 (309)
Location: (106, 118)-(656, 342), Dim=550x224
Wnd styles: 0x54C40114
Ext styles: 0x00000000
Extra bytes: 2
CHILD
VISIBLE
CLIPSIBLINGS
00) 0x4C
01) 0x1A

Figure 1-3. Voyeur displaying information for the Main group window of Program Manager.

Voyeur adds three options to the system menu:

- "Peer into window" changes the mouse cursor into a pair of eyes and allows the user to examine different windows by positioning the cursor on them. As the cursor is moved, Voyeur determines which window is under the cursor and updates the information in Voyeur's dialog box.

- "Drop back and peer" is identical to "Peer into window" with one small exception. Due to Voyeur's size, it will often cover other windows on the screen. The "Drop back and peer" instruction puts Voyeur in the background; other windows rise to the top. After you have selected a window to examine by clicking the left mouse button, Voyeur will force itself to the top of the screen. This allows a clear view of Voyeur without having to move any windows out of the way.

- "About" displays Voyeur's About box. The box shows the last date and time the program was compiled.

Voyeur's Initialization. Voyeur first registers a window class for its main window and then tries to create the main window. The window procedure for the main window does all of its initialization with the *WM_NCCREATE* method described in the "Creating and Destroying Window Instances" section earlier in this chapter. It's a good place to use this method because Voyeur cannot be used if its dialog box cannot be created. In this case, *WinMain* would see NULL returned from the *CreateWindow* call and would terminate the program. The *WM_NCCREATE* message can be found in the *VoyeurAppWndProc* function.

Voyeur now creates the modeless dialog box that will display information to the user. This is done using the VOYEUR template in the VOYEUR.DLG file. Once the dialog box has been created, Voyeur's main window changes its size so that it fits snugly around the dialog box:

```
GetWindowRect(hWnd, &rc);
GetWindowRect(_hWndStats, &rcStatDlg);
MoveWindow(hWnd, rc.left, rc.top,
   rcStatDlg.right - rcStatDlg.left,
   rcStatDlg.bottom - rcStatDlg.top +
   GetSystemMetrics(SM_CYCAPTION), FALSE);
```

This gives the impression that the dialog box is the client area of Voyeur, when in fact it's a modeless dialog box covering the main window's client area. Since the *CreateWindow* call to create the Voyeur window uses *CW_USEDEFAULT* to specify the location of the window, Windows may place the window anywhere on the user's screen. Using the *MoveWindow* function with the values in *rc.left* and *rc.top* as the origin will not change Voyeur's screen position.

Note that we must take into consideration the height of a caption bar when changing the height of Voyeur's main window. This is done by adding the height of a caption bar to the height of the modeless dialog box. The height of a caption bar can be obtained by using

```
GetSystemMetrics(SM_CYCAPTION)
```

Normally, dialog boxes are able to move independently of their parents. This is not desirable for Voyeur. If the user moves the Voyeur window, the modeless dialog box should move with the window. This again gives the impression that Voyeur is one window and not made up of two independent windows. You can make the dialog box move with the main window by changing the *STYLE* line in the template for the dialog box.

If you refer to the VOYEUR.DLG file, you will see the line

```
STYLE WS_VISIBLE | WS_CHILD
```

By default, the dialog editor gives dialog boxes the *WS_POPUP* style. By manually changing *WS_POPUP* to *WS_CHILD*, we force Windows to move the dialog box with the main window.

While we are looking at the template for the dialog box, notice the line

```
FONT 8, "Helv"
```

This tells Windows that all the children in the dialog box should use the 8-point Helvetica font. This font is smaller than the system font, which Windows normally uses for dialog boxes. Because of the smaller font, Voyeur takes up less screen space.

The remainder of the initialization involves adding options to Voyeur's system menu. Options to be added to a system menu must have identifier values of less than 0xF000. Windows sends a *WM_SYSCOMMAND* message to the window procedure when an option from the system menu has been selected. The *wParam* variable contains the menu identifier of the selected option. Windows uses the bottom four bits of *wParam* internally. When you define option identifiers to be used in the system menu, select values that contain zeros in the last four bits.

Initializing the Statistics Dialog Box. When *VoyeurAppWndProc* calls the *CreateDialog* function, a *WM_INITDIALOG* message is sent to the dialog-box procedure, *VoyeurDlgProc*. This gives the dialog box a chance to do its initialization. The only initialization that needs to be performed is the setting of a tab stop in the "Other" list box that appears in the Class Information section of the dialog box.

Take a look at the "Other" list box in Figure 1-3. You will notice that all the data fields are left-justified within the box. If Windows used a fixed-pitch font, it would be easy to pad each heading with spaces so that the data would be left-justified. However, Windows 3.0 uses a proportionally spaced font, which makes left-justifying the data much more difficult. We solve this problem by setting a tab stop within the list box and embedding tab characters in the strings. For a list box to process tabs, it must have the *LBS_USETABSTOPS* style specified in the dialog-box template.

To determine the correct location for the tab stop, we must first calculate the number of pixels required to display the widest heading. The *GetTextExtent* function examines a string and returns its dimensions in pixels—the width in the low word and the height in the high word. The first parameter to *GetTextExtent* is the handle to a device context (HDC), obtained by calling the *GetDC* function. The *GetTextExtent* function uses the font currently selected in the device context when determining the dimensions of the string. Naturally, a string will be wider using a 36-point font than the same text displayed in a 12-point font.

The *LB_SETTABSTOPS* message sets the position of a tab stop in a list box. The *wParam* value indicates the number of tab stops to be set. The *lParam* value is a far pointer to an array of integers. This array contains the list of tab-stop settings. Tab-stop settings are not in pixels, but in dialog units. Dialog units are always based on the system font, not the font that the dialog box or individual control is using. Believe it or not, this makes things easier for us because we do not have to get a handle for the font used by the list box and select it into the device context before calling *GetTextExtent*.

Once we get the width (in pixels) of the largest heading that can appear in the list box by cycling through all the headings, we must convert this number into dialog units. The line

```
wTabStop = 4 + wMaxTextLen / (LOWORD(GetDlgBaseUnits()) / 4);
```

does just that. The *GetDlgBaseUnits* function returns the number of pixels needed to make up four horizontal dialog units in the low word and the number of pixels needed to make up eight vertical dialog units in the high word. Since we are only interested in the width, or horizontal units, *LOWORD(GetDlgBaseUnits()) / 4* is the number of pixels in one horizontal dialog unit. If we then divide the number of pixels required for the largest heading by this value, we get the number of horizontal dialog units required for the longest heading. Finally, we add four horizontal dialog units to give us some space between the headings and the data.

This may seem like an awful lot of trouble—and it is! The tab stop's position could have been determined by calculating its value ahead of time or even using trial-and-error methods. But the contents of the list box probably would not have lined up correctly on a monitor with a different resolution. Also, if we changed a heading or added a field, we would have to recalculate the tab stop.

Device independence is one of Windows' most powerful features, but it isn't automatic. Paying attention to this kind of detail makes a good application better.

Once the tab stop has been set by calling

```
SendMessage(hWndOtherBox, LB_SETTABSTOPS, 1,
   (LONG) (INT FAR *) &wTabStop);
```

it will stay in effect for the life of the list box.

Peering into Windows. Voyeur starts tracking the mouse and updating its dialog box after you have chosen "Peer into window." A *WM_SYSCOMMAND* message is sent to *VoyeurAppWndProc*. The code looks like this:

```
case IDM_PEERINTOWINDOW:
   SetCapture(hWnd);
   SetCursor(LoadCursor(_hInstance, "Eyes"));
   hWndLastSubject = NULL;
   break;
```

First we tell Windows that all mouse messages should be sent to *VoyeurAppWndProc* no matter where the mouse is. Then we load the "Eyes" cursor from the resource section of the program file and make it the mouse cursor. This gives the user a visual indication that Voyeur is functioning. Finally a static variable, *hWndLastSubject*, is initialized to NULL. This tells Voyeur that no window has been passed over by the mouse yet.

The *hWndLastSubject* variable contains the handle of the window that Voyeur was just looking at. This is because:

1. Voyeur can reduce flicker and increase program speed if the mouse moves within the same window. Since the window's information is already displayed in Voyeur's dialog box, there is no need to update it.

2. When the mouse cursor is positioned over a different window from *hWndLastSubject*, Voyeur must remove the frame it placed around the previous window.

The "Drop back and peer" option forces Voyeur to go behind all other windows on the screen. This allows any windows originally hidden by Voyeur to appear above it. This feature is useful because it allows access to windows that you might not otherwise be able to pass the mouse cursor over.

Windows maintains a list of all windows in the system. This is called the *window manager's list*. In addition to width and height, a window also has a position describing how close it is to the top of the screen. This front-to-back position is called the window's *z-order*, named for the z-axis of a three-dimensional coordinate system. The topmost window on the screen is the one at the top of the window manager's list. When painting the screen, Windows uses the z-order to clip display output. This guarantees that windows closer to the top of the window manager's list will not be overwritten by windows closer to the bottom of the list.

When the user clicks on an application's caption bar, Windows forces that window to the top of the window manager's list and activates the application. When this application's window is moved to the top of the window manager's list, all of its child windows and owned pop-up windows (including dialog boxes) are also moved to the top of the list. As you can see, windows can change their position on this list very easily. Programs can use the *SetWindowPos* function to alter the z-order maintained by the window manager's list.

The second parameter to *SetWindowPos* is used to change the z-order of the window. Normally, this parameter indicates the handle of the window behind which this window should be positioned. However, if this parameter is NULL or 1, the window is positioned at the top or bottom, respectively, of the window manager's list. The line

```
SetWindowPos(hWnd, 1, 0, 0, 0, 0, SWP_NOMOVE | SWP_NOSIZE);
```

causes Voyeur's application window and modeless dialog-box window to be positioned at the bottom of the window manager's list. Any windows originally hidden by Voyeur will be closer to the top of the screen and will automatically be sent *WM_NCPAINT* and *WM_PAINT* messages by Windows to be redrawn. The *SWP_NOMOVE* and *SWP_NOSIZE* flags cause the position and size parameters to be ignored.

The execution of the *SetWindowPos* function above is the only difference between the "Peer into window" and "Drop back and peer" menu options.

Any time an application processes the *WM_SYSCOMMAND* message, it must do all the processing for any menu items the application has appended to the system menu and not pass these messages on to *DefWindowProc*. Also, for any "standard" system menu options, *WM_SYSCOMMAND* messages must be passed to *DefWindowProc*. The only exception to this rule is if we trap a "standard" menu item and perform some special processing before or instead of passing it to *DefWindowProc*.

Updating the Dialog Box. All windows normally receive *WM_MOUSEMOVE* messages only when the mouse cursor passes through the client area of the window. However, it's possible for a window to "steal" all the mouse messages from other windows and have Windows direct them to a particular window procedure. This is done with the *SetCapture* function. When Voyeur calls *SetCapture(hWnd)* during the *IDM_PEERINTOWINDOW* case of the *WM_SYSCOMMAND* message, it tells Windows that all mouse messages (*WM_LBUTTONDOWN*, *WM_LBUTTONUP*, *WM_LBUTTONDBLCLK*, *WM_MOUSEMOVE*, and so on), regardless of the mouse-cursor position, should be directed to the window procedure for the window specified by the *hWnd* parameter to *SetCapture*.

The *GetCapture* function can determine the handle of the window that currently has capture. Normally no window has capture, and the *GetCapture* function returns NULL. Because Voyeur should not update its dialog box if mouse capture has not been set to Voyeur's main window, we simply break out of the *switch* statement:

```
case WM_MOUSEMOVE:
   if (GetCapture(hWnd) == NULL) break;
```

In fact, whenever *GetCapture* is called from within a mouse message (in this case, *WM_MOUSEMOVE*), the only return values possible are NULL and the window handle passed to the window procedure, *hWnd*. This is because the window procedure would never receive a mouse message if another window had captured the mouse.

If *GetCapture* doesn't return NULL, we must determine which window the mouse cursor is over. The value in the *lParam* parameter for a *WM_MOUSEMOVE* message is the location (in device units) of the mouse. These coordinates are relative to Voyeur's client area. The *ClientToScreen* function can be used to convert the value of *lParam* into coordinates relative to the entire screen:

```
ClientToScreen(hWnd, &MAKEPOINT(lParam));
```

Now we can call the *WindowFromPoint* function to determine the handle of the window below the mouse cursor:

```
hWndSubject = WindowFromPoint(MAKEPOINT(lParam));
```

The *WindowFromPoint* function returns NULL if the mouse isn't over a window. Next, we check to see if the task that created the window is the same as Voyeur's task. This prevents the viewing of window and class information for any windows created by Voyeur.

If the mouse cursor is over a child window, the *WindowFromPoint* function returns the handle of the child's parent instead of the handle of the child window. To obtain the handle for the child window, we must use the *ChildWindowFromPoint* function:

```
ScreenToClient(hWndSubject, &MAKEPOINT(lParam));
hWndChild = ChildWindowFromPoint(hWndSubject, MAKEPOINT(lParam));
```

Notice that the point in *lParam* must be converted again, this time so it is relative to the client area of the child's parent. If the point passed to *ChildWindowFromPoint*

35

is outside the parent window's area, the return value is NULL. If the point is not over a child, the function will return the handle to the parent. If the function returns a valid window handle, this window is now our new subject.

If the window happens to be the same as our last subject, then the information in the dialog box will be the same as before and no further actions need to be taken. Otherwise, we remove the frame around the previous window and draw a frame around our new window. Both actions are done by calling *DrawWindowFrame*. *SetClassInfo* and *SetWindowInfo* are called to fill the dialog box with information relevant to our new window. Finally, we save our new window handle in the static variable *hWndLastSubject*.

Freezing the Dialog-Box Information. After choosing a window, the user can freeze the class and window information by clicking the left mouse button. When Voyeur gets a *WM_LBUTTONUP* message, it removes any frame around the most recently passed-over window and releases the mouse capture. The line

```
BringWindowToTop(hWnd);
```

tells Windows to bring Voyeur and its dialog box back to the top of the window manager's list. (Remember that if the user had selected "Drop back and peer" from the system menu, Voyeur would be placed behind all other windows.) This function causes Voyeur to return to the top so that the information can easily be seen by the user. If the "Peer into window" option was chosen, Voyeur was already the topmost window and bringing it to the top again doesn't do anything. We could have used

```
SetWindowPos(hWnd, NULL, 0, 0, 0, 0, SWP_NOMOVE | SWP_NOSIZE);
```

to accomplish the same operation.

Recall that Voyeur changed the mouse cursor to a pair of eyes after the user selected one of the "Peer" options from the system menu. If the mouse has not been captured, Windows sends a *WM_SETCURSOR* message to a window procedure whenever the mouse moves within the window. The *DefWindowProc* function will automatically change the mouse cursor back to the cursor selected when the window's class was registered. For this reason, the mouse cursor will not maintain the shape of the eyes once we call the *ReleaseCapture* function. This is the desired behavior.

Drawing a Frame Around the Window. Voyeur's *DrawWindowFrame* function draws a frame around any window whose handle is passed to it. This function also removes the frame.

The main requirement for drawing a frame around a window is that the frame must be visible. This may sound obvious, but in a graphical environment where a window can be any color or combination of colors, what color do you choose? The best answer is whatever color the window is not. In other words, the frame should be drawn in the inverse color of the screen. This guarantees that the frame will be visible.

This has an added advantage for us. If we draw the frame again in the same location, the screen will be restored to its original colors. This has the effect of removing the frame. That way, one function can be used to draw and remove the window's frame.

The code for *DrawWindowFrame* looks like this:

```
void NEAR PASCAL DrawWindowFrame (HWND hWnd) {
   HDC hDC;
   RECT rc;
   HPEN hPen;

   GetWindowRect(hWnd, &rc);
   hDC = GetWindowDC(hWnd);
   SetROP2(hDC, R2_NOT);
   hPen = CreatePen(PS_INSIDEFRAME, 3 *
      GetSystemMetrics(SM_CXBORDER), RGB(0, 0, 0));
   SelectObject(hDC, hPen);
```

```
SelectObject(hDC, GetStockObject(NULL_BRUSH));
Rectangle(hDC, 0, 0, rc.right - rc.left, rc.bottom - rc.top);
ReleaseDC(hWnd, hDC);
DeleteObject(hPen);
}
```

This function first retrieves the rectangle (in screen coordinates) of the desired window. Next, we obtain a device context for the entire window using the *GetWindowDC* function. With the device context returned from this function, Windows gives us permission to write anywhere within the area occupied by the window. If we had used the *GetDC* function, Windows would only allow us to write in the client area of the window.

Before drawing a rectangle around the window, we must prepare the device context by specifying that drawing with the pen should yield the inverse of the screen color. This is done by setting the *ROP2* value to *R2_NOT*. Next, we create a thick pen so that our frame will be easily seen. We specify a pen style of *PS_INSIDEFRAME* so Windows will draw the frame within the window's area. The width of the pen is specified as three times the width of a nonsizeable window frame. This means it should look fine on any monitor.

The last parameter to the *CreatePen* function specifies the pen's color. Because the *ROP2* value is set to *R2_NOT*, the pen's color won't actually be used when the frame is drawn. For this reason the color may be any value. I arbitrarily selected black.

Because the *Rectangle* function fills the rectangle with the brush currently selected in the device context, we must select a *NULL_BRUSH*. This will let us draw a frame without obscuring the remaining contents of the window.

We draw the frame by calling *Rectangle*. Because the coordinates are relative to the device context, the top left corner of the rectangle is point (0, 0). The lower right corner is (width of window, height of window).

The remainder of the function releases the device context and deletes the pen. Note that the order of these lines is important. A device context must have handles to existing objects within it at all times. If we deleted the pen before releasing the device context, Windows would crash with a fatal exit. Once the device context has been released, the pen may be deleted.

Setting the Class and Window Information. *SetClassInfo* accepts a handle to the modeless dialog box and a handle to the window whose class information is displayed. *GetClassName* can be used to obtain the name of the class of the window. Once we have the class name, calling *GetClassInfo* fills a *WNDCLASS* structure with the rest of the information needed for the display. The *GetClassInfo* function requires the instance handle of the creator of the window class so Windows can distinguish between two application local classes having the same name but created by different applications. The handle of the application that registered the window class can be obtained from:

```
GetClassWord(hWnd, GCW_HMODULE)
```

After calling the *GetClassInfo* function, we execute the following line:

```
WndClass.hInstance = GetClassWord(hWnd, GCW_HMODULE);
```

because the *GetClassInfo* function does not fill in the *hInstance* member of the *WNDCLASS* structure.

The *GetModuleFileName* function retrieves the name of the executable file that registered the class:

```
GetModuleFileName(WndClass.hInstance, szText, sizeof(szText));
```

This function will return the full path of a file associated with the task handle that is passed in.

The remainder of the *SetClassInfo* function formats the strings for display and sets them in the dialog box. Because each static box maintains the information most recently placed in it, the repainting of Voyeur's client area is the responsibility of the static windows. This way, our application never has to worry about processing *WM_PAINT* messages. Voyeur is also designed so that the location of text in the window is left entirely up to the dialog-box template. If we wish to move things around at a later time or add more information, this scheme is very flexible.

Filling the "Extra bytes:" list box is a small problem because Windows does not offer a *GetClassByte* function. We must call *GetClassWord* repeatedly, incrementing the offset by one each time and appending the value in the *LOBYTE* of each returned word into the list box.

When Voyeur fills the contents of a list box, it sends a *WM_SETREDRAW* message to the list box with *wParam* set to FALSE. For example:

```
SendDlgItemMessage(hDlg, ID_CLASSOTHERBOX, WM_SETREDRAW, FALSE,
    0);
```

This tells the list box not to update its window while entries are being added or deleted. Normally, list boxes update their windows immediately as their contents are changed. By turning redraw off, we ensure that the list boxes don't flicker on the screen and make Voyeur's display of information significantly faster. After all the new entries have been added to the list box, Voyeur sends another *WM_SETREDRAW* message to the list box with *wParam* set to TRUE. This tells the list box that it's now OK for it to repaint the window. However, the list box does not automatically force a repaint when it receives this message. To force the contents of the list box to be updated, Voyeur must call *InvalidateRect*.

SetWindowInfo is similar to *SetClassInfo*. Most of its information is retrieved by the *GetWindowWord* and *GetWindowLong* functions. *GetWindowText* gets the captions of the window (and its parent, if it exists). Once again, *GetModuleFileName* gets the name of the executable file that created the window. The instance handle passed to *GetModuleFileName* is the handle of the task that created the window. This is obtained by calling *GetWindowWord* and passing it the *GWW_HINSTANCE* offset. The location and dimensions of the window are determined by calling *GetWindowRect*.

Filling the window "Extra bytes:" list box is the same as filling the class extra bytes list box. Since all windows of a class must have the same number of window extra bytes, this value is retrieved by calling *GetClassWord* and passing it the *GCW_CBWNDEXTRA* offset.

When the "Wnd styles:" list box is being filled, only the top 16 bits of the value returned by

```
GetWindowLong(hWnd, GWL_STYLE);
```

are examined. Remember, the bottom 16 bits are window-class specific. Voyeur cannot determine the meaning of these bits for the selected window.

Filling the Style List Boxes. Because Voyeur has three style list boxes—class styles, window styles, and extended window styles—it's useful to have one function that is general enough to fill all three. *FillStyleBox* accepts a handle to the appropriate list box, a pointer to an array of *STYLELIST* structures, and a *DWORD* representing the style bits to be checked. Each *STYLELIST* structure contains a value for the style and a text string that should appear if that style bit is on. These style arrays are declared as follows:

```
typedef struct { DWORD dwID; char *szName; } STYLELIST;

STYLELIST _ClassStyle[] = {
    { CS_VREDRAW,            "VREDRAW"               },
    { CS_HREDRAW,            "HREDRAW"               },
```

```
        .
        .
        .
    { CS_GLOBALCLASS,              "GLOBALCLASS"              },
    { 0,                          NULL                       }
};

STYLELIST _WindowStyles[] = {
    { WS_POPUP,                   "POPUP"                    },
    { WS_CHILD,                   "CHILD"                    },
        .
        .
        .
    { WS_TABSTOP,                 "TABSTOP, MAXIMIZEBOX"     },
    { 0,                          NULL                       }
};

STYLELIST _ExtWindowStyles[] = {
    { WS_EX_DLGMODALFRAME,        "DLGMODALFRAME"            },
    { WS_EX_NOPARENTNOTIFY,       "NOPARENTNOTIFY"           },
    { 0,                          NULL                       }
};
```

This method is very general and easily expanded to accommodate styles that future versions of Windows might offer. Unfortunately, it does have some drawbacks. For example, an overlapped window is denoted by having no window style bits on. Voyeur will display an empty list box for this window instead of having "*OVERLAPPED*" in the list box. Styles represented by multiple bits are not displayed. For example, a window created with the *WS_CAPTION* style will be represented by "*BORDER*" and "*DLGFRAME*" in the list box instead of "*CAPTION*." Finally, Voyeur cannot determine if bit 17 of the window style's *DWORD* means *WS_TABSTOP* or *WS_MAXIMIZEBOX*. This is also true for bit 18, *WS_GROUP* or *WS_MINIMIZEBOX*. For this reason, Voyeur displays both styles when applicable.

The Voyeur application, presented in Listings 1-1 through 1-7, illustrates the window attribute information.

Figure 1-4. VOYEUR.ICO.

EYES.CUR

Figure 1-5. Voyeur eyes cursor icon for window peering.

Listing 1-1. VOYEUR.C application source module.

```
/*******************************************************************
Module name: Voyeur.C
Programmer : Jeffrey M. Richter
*******************************************************************/

#include "..\nowindws.h"
#undef NOCOLOR
#undef NOCTLMGR
#undef NOGDI
#undef NOKERNEL
#undef NOLSTRING
#undef NOMB
#undef NOMENUS
#undef NOMINMAX
#undef NOMSG
#undef NORASTEROPS
#undef NOSHOWWINDOW
```

```
#undef NOSYSMETRICS
#undef NOUSER
#undef NOWINOFFSETS
#undef NOWINMESSAGES
#undef NOWINSTYLES
#include <windows.h>

#include "voyeur.h"

char _szAppName[] = "Voyeur";

HANDLE _hInstance = NULL; // our instance handle
HWND _hWndStats = NULL;

#define IDM_PEERINTOWINDOW      (0x0110)   // Must be < 0xF000
                                          // (GetSystemMenu)
#define IDM_DROPBACKANDPEER     (0x0120)   // Must be < 0xF000
#define IDM_ABOUT               (0x0130)   // Must be < 0xF000


typedef struct { DWORD dwID; char *szName; } STYLELIST;

STYLELIST _ClassStyles[] = {
    { CS_VREDRAW,           "VREDRAW"           },
    { CS_HREDRAW,           "HREDRAW"           },
    { CS_KEYCVTWINDOW,      "KEYCVTWINDOW"      },
    { CS_DBLCLKS,           "DBLCLKS"           },
    // Windows 2.x
    { 0x0010,               "OEMCHARS"          },
    { CS_OWNDC,             "OWNDC"             },
    { CS_CLASSDC,           "CLASSDC"           },
    { CS_PARENTDC,          "PARENTDC"          },
    { CS_NOKEYCVT,          "NOKEYCVT"          },
    { CS_NOCLOSE,           "NOCLOSE"           },
    { CS_SAVEBITS,          "SAVEBITS"          },
    { CS_BYTEALIGNCLIENT,   "BYTEALIGNCLIENT"   },
    { CS_BYTEALIGNWINDOW,   "BYTEALIGNWINDOW"   },
    { CS_GLOBALCLASS,       "GLOBALCLASS"       },
    { 0,                    NULL                }
};
```

44

```
STYLELIST _WindowStyles[] = {
    { WS_POPUP,            "POPUP"                      },
    { WS_CHILD,            "CHILD"                      },
    { WS_MINIMIZE,         "MINIMIZE"                   },
    { WS_VISIBLE,          "VISIBLE"                    },
    { WS_DISABLED,         "DISABLED"                   },
    { WS_CLIPSIBLINGS,     "CLIPSIBLINGS"               },
    { WS_CLIPCHILDREN,     "CLIPCHILDREN"               },
    { WS_MAXIMIZE,         "MAXIMIZE"                   },
    { WS_BORDER,           "BORDER"                     },
    { WS_DLGFRAME,         "DLGFRAME"                   },
    { WS_VSCROLL,          "VSCROLL"                    },
    { WS_HSCROLL,          "HSCROLL"                    },
    { WS_SYSMENU,          "SYSMENU"                    },
    { WS_THICKFRAME,       "THICKFRAME"                 },
    { WS_GROUP,            "GROUP, MINIMIZEBOX"         },
    { WS_TABSTOP,          "TABSTOP, MAXIMIZEBOX"       },
    { 0,                   NULL                         }
};

STYLELIST _ExtWindowStyles[] = {
    { WS_EX_DLGMODALFRAME,     "DLGMODALFRAME"          },
    { WS_EX_NOPARENTNOTIFY,    "NOPARENTNOTIFY"         },
    { 0,                       NULL                     }
};


typedef enum {
    CIH_ICON, CIH_CURSOR, CIH_BACKGROUND, CIH_WNDPROC, CIH_MENU,
        CIH_END
} CLASSINFOHEAD;

char *szClassInfoHeading[] = {
    "Icon: ",
    "Cursor: ",
    "Backgrnd: ",
    "WndProc: ",
    "Menu: ",
    NULL
};
```

```
BOOL NEAR PASCAL RegisterAppWndClass (HANDLE hInstance);
BOOL FAR PASCAL AboutProc (HWND hDlg, WORD wMsg, WORD wParam,
   LONG lParam);
BOOL FAR PASCAL ForcePeer (HWND hDlg, WORD wMsg, WORD wParam,
   LONG lParam);
LONG FAR PASCAL VoyeurAppWndProc (HWND hWnd, WORD wMsg,
   WORD wParam, LONG lParam);


// ***************************************************************
int PASCAL WinMain (HANDLE hInstance, HANDLE hPrevInstance,
      LPSTR lpszCmdLine, int nCmdShow) {
   MSG msg;
   HWND hWnd;

   _hInstance = hInstance;

   if (hPrevInstance == NULL)
      if (!RegisterAppWndClass(hInstance))
         return(0);

   hWnd = CreateWindow(_szAppName, _szAppName,
      WS_OVERLAPPED | WS_VISIBLE | WS_CLIPCHILDREN | WS_CAPTION |
      WS_SYSMENU | WS_MINIMIZEBOX, CW_USEDEFAULT, nCmdShow,
      CW_USEDEFAULT, CW_USEDEFAULT, NULL, NULL, hInstance, 0);

   if (hWnd == NULL) return(0);

   while (GetMessage(&msg, NULL, 0, 0)) {
      if (!IsDialogMessage(_hWndStats, &msg)) {
         TranslateMessage(&msg);
         DispatchMessage(&msg);
      }
   }

   return(0);
}
```

```
// ****************************************************************
// This function registers Voyeur's main window

BOOL NEAR PASCAL RegisterAppWndClass (HANDLE hInstance) {
   WNDCLASS WndClass;

   WndClass.style              = 0;
   WndClass.lpfnWndProc        = VoyeurAppWndProc;
   WndClass.cbClsExtra         = 0;
   WndClass.cbWndExtra         = 0;
   WndClass.hInstance          = hInstance;
   WndClass.hIcon              = LoadIcon(hInstance, _szAppName);
   WndClass.hCursor            = LoadCursor(NULL, IDC_ARROW);
   WndClass.hbrBackground      = COLOR_WINDOW + 1;
   WndClass.lpszMenuName       = NULL;
   WndClass.lpszClassName      = _szAppName;
   return(RegisterClass(&WndClass));
}



// ****************************************************************
// This function processes all messages sent to the modeless
// dialog box

BOOL FAR PASCAL VoyeurDlgProc (HWND hDlg, WORD wMsg, WORD wParam,
      LONG lParam) {
   BOOL fProcessed = TRUE;
   WORD wTextLen, wMaxTextLen = 0, wTabStop;
   NPSTR szHeading; HDC hDC;
   CLASSINFOHEAD ClassInfoHead;
   HWND hWndOtherBox;

   switch (wMsg) {
      case WM_INITDIALOG:
         // Determine where to place tab stop in list box
         hWndOtherBox = GetDlgItem(hDlg, ID_CLASSOTHERBOX);
         hDC = GetDC(hWndOtherBox);
```

```
        for (ClassInfoHead = 0; ClassInfoHead != CIH_END;
              ClassInfoHead++) {
          szHeading = szClassInfoHeading[ClassInfoHead];

          // Get length (in pixels) of heading
          wTextLen = LOWORD(GetTextExtent(hDC, szHeading,
              lstrlen(szHeading)));

          // Find heading with maximum length
          wMaxTextLen = max(wMaxTextLen, wTextLen);
        }
        ReleaseDC(hWndOtherBox, hDC);

        // Convert pixels into dialog units
        wTabStop = 4 + wMaxTextLen /
            (LOWORD(GetDialogBaseUnits()) / 4);

        // Set tab-stop position in list box. Note: list box must
        // have LBS_USETABSTOPS style in dialog-box template.
        SendMessage(hWndOtherBox, LB_SETTABSTOPS, 1,
            (LONG) (WORD FAR *) &wTabStop);

        fProcessed = FALSE;
        break;

    default:
        fProcessed = FALSE;
        break;
    }

  return(fProcessed);
}


// ****************************************************************
// This function fills a list box with the text names of the
// styles. It is used for the class styles, window styles, and
// extended window styles.
```

```
void NEAR PASCAL FillStyleBox (HWND hListBox, STYLELIST Styles[],
    DWORD dwStyleFlags) {
  int x;

  // Turn off redraw so that the list box will not flicker every
  // time an entry is added to it. This also makes updating much
  // faster.
  SendMessage(hListBox, WM_SETREDRAW, FALSE, 0);

  // Empty the list box
  SendMessage(hListBox, LB_RESETCONTENT, 0, 0);

  for (x = 0; Styles[x].szName != NULL; x++) {

     if (Styles[x].dwID & dwStyleFlags) {
        // If the style bit is set, add the style text to the
        // list box
        SendMessage(hListBox, LB_ADDSTRING, 0,
           (LONG) (LPSTR) Styles[x].szName);
     }
  }

  // Turn redraw back on
  SendMessage(hListBox, WM_SETREDRAW, TRUE, 0);

  // Force redraw of list box so screen shows proper information
  InvalidateRect(hListBox, NULL, TRUE);
}


// *****************************************************************
// This function sets all the static and list-box windows with the
// class information about the passed-in window (hWnd)

void NEAR PASCAL SetClassInfo (HWND hDlg, HWND hWnd) {
  char szText[100], szBuf[100];
  WNDCLASS WndClass;
  WORD x;
```

```
// Get the class name of the window
GetClassName(hWnd, szBuf, sizeof(szBuf));
SetDlgItemText(hDlg, ID_CLASSNAME, szBuf);

// Fill a WNDCLASS structure
GetClassInfo(GetClassWord(hWnd, GCW_HMODULE), szBuf,
    &WndClass);
WndClass.hInstance = GetClassWord(hWnd, GCW_HMODULE);

// Get the module name of the application that registered
// this class
GetModuleFileName(WndClass.hInstance, szText, sizeof(szText));
wsprintf(szBuf, "0x%04X, %s", WndClass.hInstance, (LPSTR)
    szText);
SetDlgItemText(hDlg, ID_OWNER, szBuf);


// Fill the "Other" list box with information from WNDCLASS
// structure
SendDlgItemMessage(hDlg, ID_CLASSOTHERBOX, WM_SETREDRAW, FALSE,
    0);
SendDlgItemMessage(hDlg, ID_CLASSOTHERBOX, LB_RESETCONTENT, 0,
    0);

wsprintf(szBuf, "%s\t0x%04X",
    (LPSTR) szClassInfoHeading[CIH_ICON], WndClass.hIcon);
SendDlgItemMessage(hDlg, ID_CLASSOTHERBOX, LB_ADDSTRING, 0,
    (LONG) (LPSTR) szBuf);

wsprintf(szBuf, "%s\t0x%04X",
    (LPSTR) szClassInfoHeading[CIH_CURSOR], WndClass.hCursor);
SendDlgItemMessage(hDlg, ID_CLASSOTHERBOX, LB_ADDSTRING, 0,
    (LONG) (LPSTR) szBuf);

wsprintf(szBuf, "%s\t0x%04X",
    (LPSTR) szClassInfoHeading[CIH_BACKGROUND],
    WndClass.hbrBackground);
SendDlgItemMessage(hDlg, ID_CLASSOTHERBOX, LB_ADDSTRING, 0,
    (LONG) (LPSTR) szBuf);
```

```
wsprintf(szBuf, "%s\t0x%04X:0x%04X",
   (LPSTR) szClassInfoHeading[CIH_WNDPROC],
   HIWORD(WndClass.lpfnWndProc), LOWORD((LONG)
   WndClass.lpfnWndProc));
SendDlgItemMessage(hDlg, ID_CLASSOTHERBOX, LB_ADDSTRING, 0,
   (LONG) (LPSTR) szBuf);

wsprintf(szBuf, "%s\t0x%04X:0x%04X",
   (LPSTR) szClassInfoHeading[CIH_MENU],
   HIWORD(WndClass.lpszMenuName), LOWORD((LONG)
   WndClass.lpszMenuName));
SendDlgItemMessage(hDlg, ID_CLASSOTHERBOX, LB_ADDSTRING, 0,
   (LONG) (LPSTR) szBuf);

SendDlgItemMessage(hDlg, ID_CLASSOTHERBOX, WM_SETREDRAW, TRUE,
   0);
InvalidateRect(GetDlgItem(hDlg, ID_CLASSOTHERBOX), NULL, TRUE);

// Fill in all the "Class style" information
wsprintf(szBuf, "0x%04X", WndClass.style);
SetDlgItemText(hDlg, ID_CLASSSTYLE, szBuf);

// Fill the "Class style" list box with information from
// WndClass.style
FillStyleBox(GetDlgItem(hDlg, ID_CLASSSTYLEBOX),_ClassStyles,
   WndClass.style);


// Fill in all the "Class extra bytes" information
wsprintf(szBuf, "%d", WndClass.cbClsExtra);
SetDlgItemText(hDlg, ID_CBCLSEXTRA, szBuf);

// Fill the "Class extra bytes" list box
SendDlgItemMessage(hDlg, ID_CBCLSEXTRABOX, WM_SETREDRAW, FALSE,
   0);
SendDlgItemMessage(hDlg, ID_CBCLSEXTRABOX, LB_RESETCONTENT, 0,
   0);
```

```
   for (x = 0; x < (WORD) WndClass.cbClsExtra; x++) {
     wsprintf(szBuf, "%02d) 0x%02X", x, LOBYTE(GetClassWord(hWnd,
         x)));
     SendDlgItemMessage(hDlg, ID_CBCLSEXTRABOX, LB_ADDSTRING, 0,
         (LONG) (LPSTR) szBuf);
   }

   SendDlgItemMessage(hDlg, ID_CBCLSEXTRABOX, WM_SETREDRAW, TRUE,
       0);

   // Force redraw of "Class extra bytes" list box
   InvalidateRect(GetDlgItem(hDlg, ID_CBCLSEXTRABOX), NULL, TRUE);
}


// *****************************************************************
// This function sets all the static and list-box windows with the
// window information about the passed-in window (hWnd)

void NEAR PASCAL SetWindowInfo (HWND hDlg, HWND hWnd) {
   char szText[100], szBuf[100];
   HANDLE hInstance;
   FARPROC lpfnWndProc;
   HWND hWndParent;
   RECT rc;
   WORD x, cbWndExtra;

   // Get caption of "peered" window
   if (GetWindowText(hWnd, szText, sizeof(szText)) == 0)
       lstrcpy(szText, "(no caption)");
   wsprintf(szBuf, "0x%04X, %s", hWnd, (LPSTR) szText);
   SetDlgItemText(hDlg, ID_WINDOW, szBuf);

   // Get module name of application that created this window
   hInstance = GetWindowWord(hWnd, GWW_HINSTANCE);
   if (GetModuleFileName(hInstance, szText, sizeof(szText)) == 0)
       lstrcpy(szText, "(no module name)");
   wsprintf(szBuf, "0x%04X, %s", hInstance, (LPSTR) szText);
   SetDlgItemText(hDlg, ID_CREATOR, szBuf);
```

```
// If window has a parent, get the parent's information
hWndParent = GetParent(hWnd);
if (hWndParent == NULL)
   lstrcpy(szBuf, "(no parent window)");
else {
   if (GetWindowText(hWndParent, szText, sizeof(szText)) == 0)
      lstrcpy(szText, "(no caption)");
   wsprintf(szBuf, "0x%04X, %s", hWndParent, (LPSTR) szText);
}
SetDlgItemText(hDlg, ID_PARENT, szBuf);

// Get address of window's window procedure
lpfnWndProc = (FARPROC) GetWindowLong(hWnd, GWL_WNDPROC);
wsprintf(szBuf, "0x%04X:0x%04X",
   HIWORD(lpfnWndProc), LOWORD((LONG) lpfnWndProc));
SetDlgItemText(hDlg, ID_WNDPROC, szBuf);

// Get window's ID
wsprintf(szBuf, "0x%04X (%d)", GetWindowWord(hWnd, GWW_ID),
   GetWindowWord(hWnd, GWW_ID));
SetDlgItemText(hDlg, ID_ID, szBuf);

// Get screen coordinates of window
// Show (left, top)-(right, bottom), Dim=Width x Height
GetWindowRect(hWnd, &rc);
wsprintf(szBuf, "(%d, %d)-(%d, %d), Dim=%dx%d",
   rc.left, rc.top, rc.right, rc.bottom,
   rc.right - rc.left, rc.bottom - rc.top);
SetDlgItemText(hDlg, ID_LOCATION, szBuf);


// Fill in all the "Window style" information
wsprintf(szBuf, "0x%08lX", GetWindowLong(hWnd, GWL_STYLE));
SetDlgItemText(hDlg, ID_WNDSTYLES, szBuf);

// Fill the "Window style" list box
FillStyleBox(GetDlgItem(hDlg, ID_WNDSTYLESBOX),
   _WindowStyles, GetWindowLong(hWnd, GWL_STYLE));
```

```
    // Fill in all the "Extended window style" information
    wsprintf(szBuf, "0x%08lX", GetWindowLong(hWnd, GWL_EXSTYLE));
    SetDlgItemText(hDlg, ID_WNDEXTSTYLES, szBuf);

    // Fill the "Extended window style" list box
    FillStyleBox(GetDlgItem(hDlg, ID_WNDEXTSTYLESBOX),
      _ExtWindowStyles, GetWindowLong(hWnd, GWL_EXSTYLE));


    // Fill in all the "Window extra byte" information
    cbWndExtra = GetClassWord(hWnd, GCW_CBWNDEXTRA);
    wsprintf(szBuf, "%d", cbWndExtra);
    SetDlgItemText(hDlg, ID_CBWNDEXTRA, szBuf);

    // Fill the "Window extra bytes" list box
    SendDlgItemMessage(hDlg, ID_CBWNDEXTRABOX, WM_SETREDRAW, FALSE,
      0);
    SendDlgItemMessage(hDlg, ID_CBWNDEXTRABOX, LB_RESETCONTENT, 0,
      0);

    for (x = 0; x < cbWndExtra; x++) {
      wsprintf(szBuf, "%02d) 0x%02X", x,
        LOBYTE(GetWindowWord(hWnd, x)));
      SendDlgItemMessage(hDlg, ID_CBWNDEXTRABOX, LB_ADDSTRING, 0,
        (LONG) (LPSTR) szBuf);
    }

    SendDlgItemMessage(hDlg, ID_CBWNDEXTRABOX, WM_SETREDRAW, TRUE,
      0);

    // Force redraw of "Window extra bytes" list box
    InvalidateRect(GetDlgItem(hDlg, ID_CBWNDEXTRABOX), NULL, TRUE);
}

// ****************************************************************
// This function draws a frame around a given window. The frame is
// drawn in the inverse screen color. This allows a second call to
// this function to restore the screen display to its original
// appearance.
```

```
void NEAR PASCAL DrawWindowFrame (HWND hWnd) {
    HDC hDC;
    RECT rc;
    HPEN hPen;

    // Retrieve location of window on screen
    GetWindowRect(hWnd, &rc);

    // Get a device context that allows us to write anywhere within
    // the window. NOTE: GetDC would only allow us to write in the
    // window's client area.
    hDC = GetWindowDC(hWnd);

    // To guarantee that the frame will be visible, tell Windows to
    // draw the frame using the inverse screen color
    SetROP2(hDC, R2_NOT);

    // Create a pen that is three times the width of a nonsizeable
    // border. The color will not be used to draw the frame, so its
    // value could be anything. PS_INSIDEFRAME tells windows that
    // the entire frame should be enclosed within the window.
    hPen = CreatePen(PS_INSIDEFRAME, 3 * GetSystemMetrics
        (SM_CXBORDER), RGB(0, 0, 0));
    SelectObject(hDC, hPen);

    // We must select a NULL brush so that the contents of the
    // window will not be covered
    SelectObject(hDC, GetStockObject(NULL_BRUSH));

    // Draw the frame. Because the device context is relative to
    // the window, the top left corner is (0, 0) and the lower
    // right corner is (width of window, height of window).
    Rectangle(hDC, 0, 0, rc.right - rc.left, rc.bottom - rc.top);

    ReleaseDC(hWnd, hDC);

    // We can only destroy the pen AFTER we have released the
    // device context because the DC must have valid "tools" in it
    // at all times
    DeleteObject(hPen);
}
```

```
// ****************************************************************
// This function processes all messages sent to Voyeur's main
// window

LONG FAR PASCAL VoyeurAppWndProc (HWND hWnd, WORD wMsg,
      WORD wParam, LONG lParam) {
   BOOL fOk, fCallDefProc = FALSE;
   LONG lResult = 0;
   HMENU hMenu;
   RECT rc, rcStatDlg;
   FARPROC fpProc;
   HWND hWndSubject, hWndChild;
   static HWND hWndLastSubject = NULL;

   switch (wMsg) {

      case WM_NCCREATE:
         // Allow Windows to allocate memory for window
         fOk = (BOOL) DefWindowProc(hWnd, wMsg, wParam, lParam);

         if (!fOk) {
            // Windows couldn't create the window; return
            lResult = 0;
            break;
         }

         // Try to create modeless dialog box
         _hWndStats = CreateDialog(_hInstance, "VOYEUR", hWnd,
            MakeProcInstance(VoyeurDlgProc, _hInstance));

         if (_hWndStats == NULL) {

            // If modeless dialog box couldn't be created, tell
            // Windows to free memory for window and return
            DefWindowProc(hWnd, WM_NCDESTROY, 0, 0);
            lResult = 0;
            break;
         }
```

```
    // Change Voyeur's window dimensions so that it exactly
    // surrounds the modeless dialog box. Voyeur's position
    // on the screen should not be altered.
    GetWindowRect(hWnd, &rc);
    GetWindowRect(_hWndStats, &rcStatDlg);
    MoveWindow(hWnd, rc.left, rc.top,
       rcStatDlg.right - rcStatDlg.left,
       rcStatDlg.bottom - rcStatDlg.top +
       GetSystemMetrics(SM_CYCAPTION), FALSE);

    // Get handle to Voyeur's system menu
    hMenu = GetSystemMenu(hWnd, 0);

    // Append separator bar and two options
    AppendMenu(hMenu, MF_SEPARATOR, 0, 0);
    AppendMenu(hMenu, MF_STRING,
       IDM_PEERINTOWINDOW, "&Peer into window");
    AppendMenu(hMenu, MF_STRING,
       IDM_DROPBACKANDPEER, "&Drop back and peer");

    // Append separator bar and "About..." option
    AppendMenu(hMenu, MF_SEPARATOR, 0, 0);
    AppendMenu(hMenu, MF_STRING, IDM_ABOUT, "A&bout...");
    DrawMenuBar(hWnd);

    lResult = 1;      // Window has been created OK
    break;

case WM_DESTROY:
    PostQuitMessage(0);
    break;

case WM_SYSCOMMAND:
    // Any menu option selected from Voyeur's system menu

    // Any options that we appended to system menu should be
    // processed by Voyeur and NOT passed to DefWindowProc

    switch (wParam & 0xfff0) {
```

```
     case IDM_ABOUT:
        // Display Voyeur's About box
        fpProc = MakeProcInstance(AboutProc, _hInstance);
        DialogBox(_hInstance, "About", hWnd, fpProc);
        FreeProcInstance(fpProc);
        break;


     case IDM_DROPBACKANDPEER:
        // Send Voyeur's window to back of window manager's
        // list. This causes any windows that are overlapped
        // by Voyeur to become visible. This allows these
        // windows to be "peered" into.
        SetWindowPos(hWnd, 1, 0, 0, 0, 0, SWP_NOMOVE |
           SWP_NOSIZE);

        // Fall through to IDM_PEERINTOWINDOW


     case IDM_PEERINTOWINDOW:
        // Force all mouse messages to arrive at this window
        // procedure
        SetCapture(hWnd);

        // Change the mouse cursor to a pair of eyes. This
        // provides a visual indication to the user that
        // Voyeur is in "peer" mode.
        SetCursor(LoadCursor(_hInstance, "Eyes"));

        // Set the window handle of the last viewed window to
        // NULL
        hWndLastSubject = NULL;
        break;

  default:
     // Any options that we do not process should be passed
     // to DefWindowProc
     fCallDefProc = TRUE;
     break;
  }
  break;
```

```
case WM_MOUSEMOVE:
    // If we don't have capture, we shouldn't do anything
    if (GetCapture() == NULL)
        break;

    // lParam contains the mouse location relative to
    // Voyeur's client area

    // Convert the location to screen coordinates
    ClientToScreen(hWnd, &MAKEPOINT(lParam));

    // Get the window handle of the window under the mouse
    // cursor
    hWndSubject = WindowFromPoint(MAKEPOINT(lParam));

    // If mouse isn't over a window, return
    if (hWndSubject == NULL) break;

    // If window was created by Voyeur, ignore it
    if (GetWindowTask(hWndSubject) == GetCurrentTask())
        break;

    // Convert the mouse location into client coordinates
    // relative to the window under the mouse cursor
    ScreenToClient(hWndSubject, &MAKEPOINT(lParam));

    // Get the window handle of the child window under the
    // mouse cursor
    hWndChild = ChildWindowFromPoint(hWndSubject,
        MAKEPOINT(lParam));

    // If point is over a child, our subject is the child
    // window
    if (hWndChild != NULL)
        hWndSubject = hWndChild;

    // If our new subject is the same as our last subject,
    // there is no need to update our display
    if (hWndLastSubject == hWndSubject)
        break;
```

```
      // If this is not our first window being viewed, remove
      // the frame surrounding the previously viewed window
      if (hWndLastSubject != NULL)
         DrawWindowFrame(hWndLastSubject);

      UpdateWindow(hWndSubject);

      // Draw a frame around our new window
      DrawWindowFrame(hWndSubject);

      // Fill our status box with the subject window's class
      // information
      SetClassInfo(_hWndStats, hWndSubject);

      // Fill our status box with the subject window's window
      // information
      SetWindowInfo(_hWndStats, hWndSubject);

      hWndLastSubject = hWndSubject;
      break;


   case WM_LBUTTONUP:
      // If we don't have capture, we shouldn't do anything
      if (GetCapture() != hWnd)
         break;

      // If we never "peered" into a window, we don't have to
      // remove its surrounding frame
      if (hWndLastSubject != NULL)
         DrawWindowFrame(hWndLastSubject);

      // Allow other applications to receive mouse messages
      ReleaseCapture();

      // Force Voyeur to appear on top of all other windows
      BringWindowToTop(hWnd);

      break;
```

```
         default:
            fCallDefProc = TRUE; break;
      }

   if (fCallDefProc)
      lResult = DefWindowProc(hWnd, wMsg, wParam, lParam);

   return(lResult);
}

// ************************************************************
// This function processes all messages sent to the About dialog
// box

BOOL FAR PASCAL AboutProc (HWND hDlg, WORD wMsg, WORD wParam, LONG
      lParam) {
   char szBuffer[100];
   BOOL fProcessed = TRUE;

   switch (wMsg) {

      case WM_INITDIALOG:
         // Set version static window to have date and time of
         // compilation
         wsprintf(szBuffer, "%s at %s", (LPSTR) __DATE__, (LPSTR)
            __TIME__);
         SetWindowText(GetDlgItem(hDlg, ID_VERSION), szBuffer);
          break;

      case WM_COMMAND:
         switch (wParam) {
            case IDOK: case IDCANCEL:
               if (HIWORD(lParam) == BN_CLICKED)
                  EndDialog(hDlg, wParam);
               break;

            default:
               break;
         }
         break;
```

```
    default:
        fProcessed = FALSE; break;
  }
  return(fProcessed);
}
```

Listing 1-2. VOYEUR.H application header file.

```
/***********************************************************
Module name: Voyeur.H
Programmer : Jeffrey M. Richter
***********************************************************/

#include "dialog.h"
```

Listing 1-3. DIALOG.H (dialog-box template defines).

```
#define ID_CBCLSEXTRA          105
#define ID_CBCLSEXTRABOX       106
#define ID_CBWNDEXTRA          118
#define ID_CBWNDEXTRABOX       119
#define ID_CLASSNAME           100
#define ID_CLASSOTHERBOX       102
#define ID_CLASSSTYLE          103
#define ID_CLASSSTYLEBOX       104
#define ID_CREATOR             108
#define ID_ID                  112
#define ID_LOCATION            113
#define ID_NUMPROPS            140
#define ID_OWNER               101
#define ID_PARENT              110
#define ID_TASK                109
#define ID_VERSION             200
#define ID_WINDOW              107
#define ID_WINDOWHANDLE        121
#define ID_WNDEXTSTYLES        116
#define ID_WNDEXTSTYLESBOX     117
```

```
#define ID_WNDPROC              111
#define ID_WNDPROPBOX           141
#define ID_WNDSTYLES            114
#define ID_WNDSTYLESBOX         115
#define IDOK                    1
```

Listing 1-4. VOYEUR.RC application resource file.

```
/*********************************************
Module name: Voyeur.RC
Programmer : Jeffrey M. Richter
*********************************************/

#include <windows.h>

#include   "voyeur.h"
#include   "dialog.h"
#include   "voyeur.dlg"

Voyeur     ICON     MOVEABLE DISCARDABLE Voyeur.Ico
Eyes       CURSOR   MOVEABLE DISCARDABLE Eyes.Cur
```

Listing 1-5. VOYEUR.DLG dialog-box templates.

```
ABOUT DIALOG LOADONCALL MOVEABLE DISCARDABLE 16, 20, 126, 92
CAPTION "About Voyeur"
STYLE WS_BORDER | WS_CAPTION | WS_DLGFRAME | WS_SYSMENU |
      WS_VISIBLE | WS_POPUP
BEGIN
  CONTROL "Voyeur", -1, "static", SS_ICON | WS_CHILD, 4, 16, 18,
      21
  CONTROL "Voyeur", -1, "static", SS_CENTER | WS_CHILD, 22, 8,
      100, 12
  CONTROL "Written by:", -1, "static", SS_CENTER | WS_CHILD, 22,
      20, 100, 12
  CONTROL "Jeffrey M. Richter", -1, "static", SS_CENTER |
      WS_CHILD, 22, 32, 100, 12
```

```
    CONTROL "Version date:", -1, "static", SS_CENTER | WS_CHILD,
        22, 48, 100, 12
    CONTROL "", ID_VERSION, "static", SS_CENTER | WS_CHILD, 22, 60,
        100, 12
    CONTROL "&OK", IDOK, "button", BS_DEFPUSHBUTTON | WS_TABSTOP |
        WS_CHILD, 40, 76, 44, 12
END

VOYEUR DIALOG LOADONCALL MOVEABLE DISCARDABLE 0, 0, 280, 17
FONT 8, "Helv"
STYLE WS_VISIBLE | WS_CHILD
BEGIN
    CONTROL "* CLASS INFORMATION *", -1, "static", SS_CENTER |
        WS_CHILD, 0, 4, 280, 8
    CONTROL "Class:", -1, "static", SS_LEFT | WS_CHILD, 8, 16,
        28, 8
    CONTROL "", ID_CLASSNAME, "static", SS_LEFT | WS_CHILD, 68,
        16, 172, 8
    CONTROL "Owner (Inst):", -1, "static", SS_LEFT | WS_CHILD, 8,
        24, 72, 8
    CONTROL "", ID_OWNER, "static", SS_LEFT | WS_CHILD, 68, 24,
        172, 8
    CONTROL "Other:", -1, "static", SS_LEFT | WS_CHILD, 8, 36, 32,
        8
    CONTROL "", ID_CLASSOTHERBOX, "listbox", LBS_USETABSTOPS |
        WS_BORDER | WS_VSCROLL | WS_TABSTOP | WS_CHILD, 7, 46,
        104, 26
    CONTROL "Styles:", -1, "static", SS_LEFT | WS_CHILD, 116, 36,
        28, 8
    CONTROL "", ID_CLASSSTYLE, "static", SS_LEFT | WS_CHILD, 144,
        36, 32, 8
    CONTROL "", ID_CLASSSTYLEBOX, "listbox", WS_BORDER | WS_VSCROLL
        | WS_CHILD, 115, 46, 92, 26
    CONTROL "Extra bytes:", -1, "static", SS_LEFT | WS_CHILD, 212,
        36, 48, 8
    CONTROL "", ID_CBCLSEXTRA, "static", SS_LEFT | WS_CHILD, 256,
        36, 16, 8
    CONTROL "", ID_CBCLSEXTRABOX, "listbox", WS_BORDER | WS_VSCROLL
        | WS_CHILD, 211, 46, 60, 26
    CONTROL "", -1, "static", SS_GRAYRECT | WS_CHILD, 0, 66, 280, 4
```

```
CONTROL "* WINDOW INFORMATION *", -1, "static", SS_CENTER |
    WS_CHILD, 0, 72, 280, 8
CONTROL "Window (hWnd):", -1, "static", SS_LEFT | WS_CHILD, 8
    84, 68, 8
CONTROL "", ID_WINDOW, "static", SS_LEFT | WS_CHILD, 76, 84,
    184, 8
CONTROL "Creator (Inst):", -1, "static", SS_LEFT | WS_CHILD, 8,
    92, 68, 8
CONTROL "", ID_CREATOR, "static", SS_LEFT | WS_CHILD, 76, 92,
    184, 8
CONTROL "Parent (hWnd):", -1, "static", SS_LEFT | WS_CHILD, 8,
    100, 68, 8
CONTROL "", ID_PARENT, "static", SS_LEFT | WS_CHILD, 76, 100,
    184, 8
CONTROL "WndProc:", -1, "static", SS_LEFT | WS_CHILD, 8, 108,
    48, 8
CONTROL "", ID_WNDPROC, "static", SS_LEFT | WS_CHILD, 76, 108,
    64, 8
CONTROL "ID:", -1, "static", SS_LEFT | WS_CHILD, 144, 108, 16,
    8
CONTROL "", ID_ID, "static", SS_LEFT | WS_CHILD, 160, 108, 84,
    8
CONTROL "Location:", -1, "static", SS_LEFT | WS_CHILD, 8, 116,
    36, 8
CONTROL "", ID_LOCATION, "static", SS_LEFT | WS_CHILD, 76, 116,
    184, 8
CONTROL "Wnd styles:", -1, "static", SS_LEFT | WS_CHILD, 8,
    128, 48, 8
CONTROL "", ID_WNDSTYLES, "static", SS_LEFT | WS_CHILD, 58,
    128, 52, 8
CONTROL "", ID_WNDSTYLESBOX, "listbox", WS_BORDER | WS_VSCROLL
    | WS_CHILD, 8, 138, 96, 34
CONTROL "Ext styles:", -1, "static", SS_LEFT | WS_CHILD, 116,
    128, 44, 8
CONTROL "", ID_WNDEXTSTYLES, "static", SS_LEFT | WS_CHILD, 160,
    128, 48, 8
CONTROL "", ID_WNDEXTSTYLESBOX, "listbox", WS_BORDER |
    WS_VSCROLL | WS_CHILD, 116, 138, 92, 34
CONTROL "Extra bytes:", -1, "static", SS_LEFT | WS_CHILD, 216,
    128, 48, 8
```

```
    CONTROL "", ID_CBWNDEXTRA, "static", SS_LEFT | WS_CHILD, 264,
        128, 12, 8
    CONTROL "", ID_CBWNDEXTRABOX, "listbox", WS_BORDER | WS_VSCROLL
        | WS_CHILD, 216, 138, 60, 34
END
```

Listing 1-6. VOYEUR.DEF application definitions file.

```
; Module name: Voyeur.DEF
; Programmer : Jeffrey M. Richter

NAME            Voyeur
DESCRIPTION     'Voyeur: Window Examination Application'
STUB            'WinStub.exe'
EXETYPE         WINDOWS
CODE            MOVEABLE DISCARDABLE PRELOAD
DATA            MOVEABLE MULTIPLE PRELOAD
HEAPSIZE        1024
STACKSIZE       4096
EXPORT
    VoyeurAppWndProc
    VoyeurDlgProc
    AboutProc
```

Listing 1-7. MAKEFILE for Voyeur application.

```
#*********************************************************
#Module name: MAKEFILE
#Programmer : Jeffrey M. Richter
#*********************************************************

PROG = Voyeur
MODEL = S
CFLAGS = -A$(MODEL) -D_WINDOWS -Gcsw2 -W4 -Zlepid -Od
LFLAGS = /NOE/BA/A:16/M/CO/LI/F
LIBS = $(MODEL)nocrt + libw
```

```
M1 = $(PROG).obj

ICONS = $(PROG).ico
BITMAPS =
CURSORS = Eyes.cur
RESOURCES = $(ICONS) $(BITMAPS) $(CURSORS)

.SUFFIXES: .rc

.rc.res:
   rc -r $*.rc

$(PROG).Exe: $(M1) $(PROG).Def $(PROG).Res
   link $(LFLAGS) @<<$(PROG).lnk
$(M1)
$(PROG), $(PROG), $(LIBS), $(PROG)
<<
   rc $(PROG).Res

$(PROG).obj:   $*.c $*.h dialog.h

$(PROG).res:   $*.rc $*.h $*.dlg dialog.h $(RESOURCES)
```

CHAPTER 2

Subclassing and Superclassing Windows

The Microsoft Windows Software Development Kit (SDK) supplies a number of ready-to-use window classes, including LISTBOX, COMBOBOX, EDIT, and so on. These controls are intended to be general enough for use in any application. Sometimes, however, you may wish that one of the controls had slightly different behavior.

One solution to this problem is to design your own control from scratch. This is usually a significant task. It would be nice if Microsoft distributed the source code for controls so that we could modify their behavior. However, since Microsoft does not make the source code available, we cannot do this. Window subclassing and superclassing come to the rescue and save us from reinventing the wheel.

Subclassing and superclassing can also be used on your own window classes, including application windows and custom controls that you create. You can also modify the behavior of applications written by others through subclassing and superclassing.

How Window Subclassing Works

When registering a window class, you fill the members of the *WNDCLASS* structure and pass the structure to the *RegisterClass* function. The address of the window procedure is set using the *lpfnWndProc* member of the structure. This procedure processes messages pertaining to all instances of windows of this class.

The window procedure must be declared as *FAR PASCAL* and be listed in the *EXPORTS* section of your .DEF file. However, you do not have to make a procedural instance of this function by calling *MakeProcInstance*; Windows does that automatically when you call *RegisterClass*. The resulting procedural-instance address is stored in the block of memory associated with the registered class.

Whenever a new window is created, Windows allocates a block of memory containing information specific to that window. The value of *lpfnWndProc* is copied from the block of memory for the window class into the block of memory allocated for the newly created window. When a message is dispatched to a window procedure (Figure 2-1), Windows examines the value of the window procedure in the window's memory block and calls the function whose address is stored there. Windows does not examine the window class memory block when dispatching a message to a window.

To subclass a window, you change the window procedure address in the window's memory block to point to a new window procedure. Because the address is changed in one window's memory block, it does not affect any other windows created from the same class.

If Windows did not give each window instance its own copy of the window procedure address, then changing the address would alter the behavior of all windows in the class. If this were the case, subclassing a single EDIT control so that it would no longer accept letters would cause EDIT controls in all applications to stop accepting letters. This is certainly not desirable.

Once you have told Windows the procedural-instance address of your own window procedure, all messages destined for the window will be sent to your own window procedure. Your procedure must look exactly like a standard window procedure. In other words, it must have an identical prototype:

```
LONG FAR PASCAL WndSubClassProc (HWND hWnd, WORD wMsg,
  WORD wParam, LONG lParam);
```

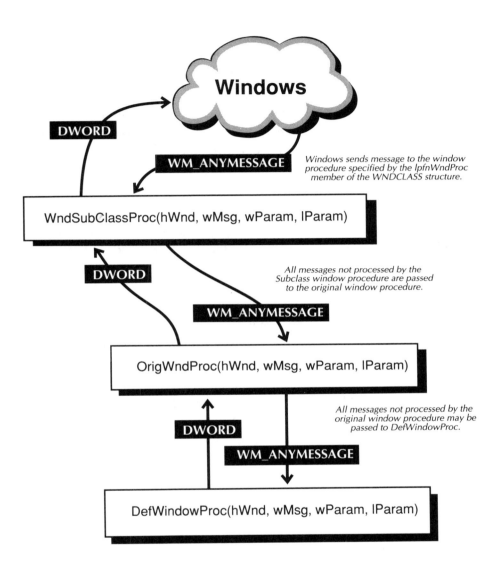

Figure 2-1. Window subclassing.

Once the message destined for the original window procedure has been sent to your procedure, you may do one of the following:

1. Pass it on to the original procedure. This is done for most messages. The reason for subclassing is usually to alter the behavior of a window only slightly. For this reason, most messages will be passed to the original procedure so that the default behavior for this class of window be performed.

2. Stop the message from being passed to the original procedure. For example, if you wanted an EDIT control to stop accepting letters, you would examine *WM_CHAR* messages, check to see if the *wParam* value is between A and Z or a and z, and, if so, return from the *WndSubClassProc* function. If *wParam* is any other character, you would pass the message to the original window procedure for EDIT controls.

3. Alter the message before sending it. If you want a COMBOBOX to accept only uppercase characters, examine each *WM_CHAR* message and convert the key to uppercase before passing the message to the original procedure.

Here is an example of how to subclass a window:

```
// Prototype for forward reference
LONG FAR PASCAL EditSubClassProc (HWND, WORD, WORD, LONG);

FARPROC _fpOrigWndProc;
.
.
.
int WinMain (HANDLE hInstance, HANDLE hPrevInstance,
     LPSTR szCmdLine, int nCmdShow) {
  FARPROC fpEditSubClassProc;
  HWND hWndEdit;
  .
  .
  .
```

```
    hWndEdit = CreateWindow("EDIT", "", WS_CHILD,
        10, 20, 100, 16, hWndParent, NULL, hInstance, OL);

    // Save address of the original window's window procedure
    _fpOrigWndProc = GetWindowLong(hWndEdit, GWL_WNDPROC);

    // Bind data segment with calls to EditSubClassProc
    fpEditSubClassProc =
        MakeProcInstance(hInstance, EditSubClassProc);

    // Set new address for window procedure
    SetWindowLong(hWndEdit, GWL_WNDPROC, fpEditSubClassProc);

    // All messages destined for hWndEdit will be sent to
    // EditSubClassProc
}
.
.
.

LONG FAR PASCAL EditSubClassProc (HWND hWnd, WORD wMsg,
        WORD wParam, LONG lParam) {
    LONG lResult = 0;
    BOOL fCallOrigWndProc = TRUE;
    switch (wMsg) {
        .
        .
        .
    }
    if (fCallOrigWndProc)
        lResult = CallWindowProc(_fpOrigWndProc, hWnd, wMsg,
            wParam, lParam);

    return(lResult);
}
```

The only information required to subclass a window is its window handle.

The function you write to intercept messages is identical in form to a window procedure. The only difference is that you pass the messages to the original window procedure instead of calling *DefWindowProc*. Your function must be declared *FAR PASCAL* and must be listed in the *EXPORTS* section of your .DEF file. This time, however, you must call *MakeProcInstance* yourself and pass the address of the procedural instance into *SetWindowLong* to change the address of the window procedure. To have the original window perform its normal operations for a particular message, you must use the *CallWindowProc* function. This function is passed the address of the original window procedure, the window handle (*hWnd*), the message (*wMsg*), and the two data elements (*wParam* and *lParam*).

When your window subclass procedure is called, the data segment register is set so that it points to your application's data segment. This allows you to modify or reference your own static and global variables while the *EditSubClassProc* function is being processed. When you call the *CallWindowProc* function, the first parameter is the procedural-instance address you obtained from the *GetWindowLong* call. By calling this address, you set the data segment to the one associated with the application that registered the subclassed window's class.

Note that you can subclass a subclassed window. If this is the case, calling the procedural instance of the first subclassing function will set the data segment to its proper value. In all cases, each procedure will use its own data segment properly. This ensures that no application can use or modify another application's data area.

What is a Procedural Instance?

A procedural instance is a small block of code that binds a data segment with a function's address. Because Windows is a multitasking environment, many applications may be running simultaneously. Each instance of an application has its own data segment.

Let's say two windows from different applications are side by side on the desktop. When the windows receive messages, the responses may include altering global or static variables or updating references to literal strings. All these items are in the application's data segment. Since the user may easily switch from using the first application to the second, there must be a way to set the *DS* register every time a message is sent to a window procedure. You do this by making a procedural-instance address of the window procedure.

The *MakeProcInstance* function accepts two parameters. The first is the address of the procedure to be made into a procedural instance; the second is the handle to the application whose data segment is to be bound to the procedure's address. *MakeProcInstance* allocates a block of memory that contains some assembly language instructions to do the following:

1. Set the *AX* register to the segment (in real mode) or selector (in protected mode) associated with the application's data segment.

2. Call the address specified by the first parameter to *MakeProcInstance*.

The address returned by *MakeProcInstance* is that of the procedural instance. Calling this address is just like calling the function directly except that the data segment is guaranteed to be correct. (As stated earlier, the procedural instance sets the *AX* register to the application's data segment, not the *DS* register. The responsibility for setting the *DS* register to the *AX* register is left to the function.) When the linker sees a function listed in the *EXPORTS* section of the .DEF file, it modifies the prolog and epilog code for that function. The prolog code becomes:

1. Push the current value of the *DS* register on the stack.
2. Copy the contents of the *AX* register into the *DS* register.

Now references to data will be within the application's own data segment. The epilog code for the function becomes:

1. Pop the original value of the *DS* register off the stack and into the *DS* register.

One caveat: An *EXPORT*ed function must always be called by using a procedural instance. Because an *EXPORT*ed function always sets the *DS* register to the value of the *AX* register upon entry, calling the function directly will not ensure that the *AX* register is set to the proper data segment. You will crash Windows (in real mode) or generate a global protection violation (in protected mode).

It should also be noted that when the *MakeProcInstance* function creates a procedural instance, the memory block that is created is flagged as *FIXED*. This way, your application can maintain the address of the block at all times and does not have to worry about Windows moving the block to another location. The address returned from *MakeProcInstance* is always valid.

Limitations Imposed by Window Subclassing

Suppose we would like to further restrict our EDIT control subclass to accept only a certain range of numbers. We are not familiar with the way an EDIT control uses its extra class and window bytes, so we cannot use these bytes for storing information about the valid data range. Because subclassing requires that a window instance already exist before we can subclass it, increasing the number of class or window extra bytes is also impossible. The best way to associate data with a subclassed window is by using window properties, as explained in Chapter 1.

Of course, if you know how the window class uses its class and window extra bytes, it's OK to use them for yourself. You should, however, try to think ahead to how the subclassed class may change. Such changes may prevent your subclass window procedure from working correctly.

Finally, you can add your own user messages to a subclassed window if you approach the task carefully. An example: If we examine WINDOWS.H, we discover that the highest used BUTTON class-specific message is *BM_SETSTYLE*, defined as *WM_USER + 4*. We do not know if Microsoft has defined some other, internal messages for the BUTTON class that do not appear in the WINDOWS.H file. If we added our own user message starting at *WM_USER + 5*, it could conflict with an undocumented message recognized by the BUTTON class. Actually, choosing any value—*WM_USER + 500*, for example—would be tempting fate. The only way to solve this problem is by using the *RegisterWindowMessage* function described in Chapter 1.

The Program Manager Restore Program

In my Windows environment, I have checked the "Minimize on Use" option that appears on the Options menu in Program Manager. This tells Program Manager to turn itself into an icon whenever I use it to launch an application. When the application terminates, Program Manager remains an icon.

Because the only action I can do now is open Program Manager, it would be convenient if Program Manager could detect that it is the only application running and restore itself automatically. The Program Manager Restore program demonstrates how this function can be added to Program Manager via window subclassing.

Program Manager Restore doesn't create any windows of its own; it subclasses Program Manager's window and just waits for messages. Program Manager Restore also demonstrates how to add new menu items to an existing or already running application by appending "About PM Restore..." and "Remove PM Restore" to Program Manager's Options menu.

Note: Subclassing a window for a class created by someone else can cause your application to fail when the company releases new versions of its application. Because Program Manager Restore subclasses Microsoft's Program Manager application, it is possible that Program Manager Restore will not function with future versions of Program Manager.

Program Manager Restore assumes that Program Manager is the shell application of Windows. This is specified by the *SHELL=PROGMAN.EXE* line in the

SYSTEM.INI file. By default, all Windows installations set up Program Manager as the shell application. If your Windows setup has a different application from the Windows shell, the Program Manager Restore application will not work.

How Program Manager Restore Works

Windows sends notification messages to windows when something has happened. One of these is *WM_ACTIVATEAPP*, which is sent to the main window of the currently active application to notify it that it is being deactivated. The message is also sent to the main window of the application being activated. The *wParam* parameter associated with the *WM_ACTIVATEAPP* message can be examined to determine whether the application is being activated or deactivated.

When you terminate an application, Windows makes another application active. Since Program Manager is always running, Windows could make it the active application. If this happens, Program Manager receives a *WM_ACTIVATEAPP* message. Program Manager Restore, which has subclassed Program Manager, intercepts the *WM_ACTIVATEAPP* message before Program Manager sees it.

Program Manager Restore first determines whether Windows is activating or deactivating Program Manager. If Program Manager is being deactivated, Program Manager Restore does not process the message; it's passed to Program Manager.

If Windows is activating Program Manager, Program Manager Restore determines whether any other applications are running. If at least one other application is running, Program Manager Restore does nothing and simply passes the *WM_ACTIVATEAPP* message to Program Manager's original window procedure.

If no other applications are running, Program Manager Restore calls the *ShowWindow* function, which tells Program Manager to restore itself to its last "opened" size. The *WM_ACTIVATEAPP* message is then passed to Program Manager.

The *WinMain* Function

For reasons that will be discussed later, Program Manager Restore will crash Windows if it's running in real mode with expanded memory. To guarantee that this doesn't happen, a check is performed:

```
dwWinFlags = GetWinFlags();
if ((dwWinFlags & WF_LARGEFRAME) ||
   (dwWinFlags & WF_SMALLFRAME)) {
  MessageBox(GetFocus(),
     "PM Restore cannot run with EMS memory.",
     _szAppName, MB_OK | MB_SYSTEMMODAL);
  return(FALSE);
}
```

The *GetWinFlags* function reports what processors are in the computer and the mode in which Windows is running. Depending on the memory configuration, Windows will treat expanded memory as either small frame or large frame. If either of these flags is set, Windows is using expanded memory and Program Manager Restore terminates without installing itself.

Because it doesn't make sense to run multiple instances of Program Manager Restore, *hPrevInstance* is checked. If it's not NULL, Program Manager Restore is not installed. The Program Manager Restore application then stores its task handle in a global variable:

```
HANDLE _PMRestoreTask;
 .
 .
 .
  _PMRestoreTask = GetCurrentTask();
```

When Windows executes an instance of an application, each instance is assigned a unique task-instance handle. *GetCurrentTask* returns the task-instance handle of the currently executing task. When the Program Manager Restore application calls *GetCurrentTask*, Windows returns the task-instance handle of the Program Manager

Restore application. This handle is used later so the user can remove Program Manager Restore from memory. (The procedure for doing this is explained later in this section.) For a complete discussion of tasks and their instance handles, see Chapter 6.

To subclass Program Manager and add menu items to it, we must retrieve its window handle by calling *FindWindow:*

```
_hWndPM = FindWindow(_szPMClass, NULL);
```

The first parameter is the class name of the window we are looking for (or NULL to find windows matching any class). The second parameter is the caption of that window (or NULL to match any caption). At first, you might think we should use the caption and specify NULL for the window class because we can see that the caption of Program Manager on the screen is "Program Manager" (Figure 2-2) and don't know what Microsoft used as the class name for the window. However, we can easily change the caption of Program Manager by maximizing one of its child windows. If we maximize the Main group (Figure 2-3), the caption changes to "Program Manager - [Main]." If we had tried to locate Program Manager with

```
_hWndPM = FindWindow(NULL, "Program Manager");
```

_hWndPM would be NULL because a window would not exist with the specified caption.

So the best way to get Program Manager's window handle is to specify its class name. I discovered the class name by using the Spy application that comes with the Windows SDK. I ran Spy, selecting the "Window..." option under the Window menu and positioning the mouse cursor over Program Manager's caption. Spy's dialog box revealed the class name (PROGMAN) of Program Manager. The Voyeur application presented in Chapter 1 could also be used to retrieve the class name of Program Manager's window.

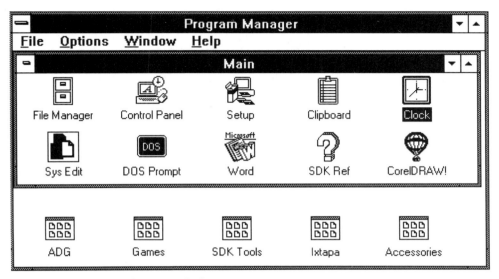

Figure 2-2. Program Manager window.

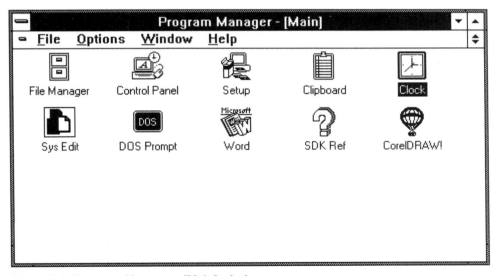

Figure 2-3. Program Manager - [Main] window.

The *FindWindow* function can be extremely useful for locating windows to subclass. It has one drawback, however: if multiple windows of the same class exist and have the same caption, *FindWindow* will only locate the first one and its handle. Because it is possible to execute only one instance of Program Manager, Program Manager Restore can use *FindWindow* without any chance of retrieving the wrong handle.

Notice that the return value of *FindWindow* is checked to see if Program Manager could, in fact, be found. If _*hWndPM* is NULL, Program Manager could not be found. This occurs if you set up your system so that Program Manager Restore automatically executes every time you start Windows by specifying

```
LOAD=PMRest.EXE
```

in the WIN.INI file. When Windows begins, any applications listed on the *LOAD=* and *RUN=* lines in the WIN.INI file are started first, before Program Manager.

To overcome this problem, Program Manager Restore tries to invoke Program Manager by calling the *WinExec* function. Another attempt is made at getting Program Manager's window handle. If we are unsuccessful this time, Program Manager Restore cannot subclass Program Manager. It notifies the user and terminates.

After Windows has executed all the applications listed in the *LOAD=* and *RUN=* lines of the WIN.INI file, the shell application is executed. In our case, this would be Program Manager, except that it's already running. Fortunately, Microsoft designed Program Manager so that it only allows one instance of itself to execute. Otherwise, our Windows session would start with two Program Managers.

Changing Program Manager's Menus. Once we have the window handle of Program Manager, we can easily add new menu items to it. But first we must choose menu ID values that do not conflict with any of the values already selected by Microsoft for Program Manager menu options.

Spy can determine the ID values of all Program Manager menu options. Windows sends the *WM_SYSCOMMAND* message to a window procedure when the user has selected a menu option from a system menu (this includes the system menu of Multiple Document Interface, or MDI, children). Windows sends the *WM_COMMAND* message to a window procedure when the user has selected a menu option from a nonsystem menu. Because we will be adding our menu options to Program Manager's nonsystem menu, we must determine all the menu IDs assigned by Microsoft for use by that menu and select values that do not conflict.

I used Spy to examine *WM_COMMAND* messages passed to Program Manager's window procedure. I selected each option in turn and recorded the *wParam* values, resulting in this table:

Menu item	Hex	Decimal
File menu		
New...	0x0065	101
Open	0x0066	102
Move...	0x0067	103
Copy...	0x0068	104
Delete	0x0069	105
Properties...	0x006A	106
Run...	0x006B	107
Exit Windows...	0x006C	108
Options menu		
Auto Arrange	0x00C9	201
Minimize on Use	0x00CA	202

Menu item	Hex	Decimal
Window menu		
Cascade	0x012D	301
Tile	0x012E	302
Arrange Icons	0x012F	303
Group Window 1	0x0130	304
.	.	.
.	.	.
.	.	.
Group Window 9	0x0138	312
More Windows...	0x0139	313
Help menu		
Index	0x0385	901
Keyboard	0x001E	30
Basic Skills	0x001F	31
Commands	0x0020	32
Procedures	0x0021	33
Glossary	0x0022	34
Using Help	0x0386	902
About Program Manager...	0x0387	903

Note that in an MDI application, Windows maintains the list of MDI child windows in the Window menu on behalf of the programmer. The programmer tells Windows the ID value of the first MDI child window. Windows will assign ID values in ascending order (incrementing each ID by one) to all MDI child windows created after the first. Each of the program group windows in Program Manager is an MDI child window. The first program group window will have an ID value of 0x0130, the second, 0x0131, and so on.

Now that we have this information, we just have to select menu IDs that do not conflict. I have selected a value of 4444 for *IDM_PMRESTOREABOUT* and a value of 4445 for *IDM_PMRESTOREREMOVE*. Since we want to append the new option to the menu that contains the "Auto Arrange" option, we must locate that menu and get its handle. At first, you might think that we could use

```
hMenu = GetSubMenu(GetMenu(_hWndPM), 1);
```

but this will not work if an MDI child window is maximized. The system menu for the MDI child becomes the first pop-up menu in the application's menu bar. Because of this, the line of code above will return to us the menu handle of the File menu. By setting the code up in a loop and checking the first menu option in each pop-up to see if its menu ID is *IDM_AUTO_ARRANGE* (0xC9), we will be sure to add our option to the correct pop-up menu.

We now subclass Program Manager as follows:

```
// Save window function for Program Manager in global variable
_fpOrigPMProc = (FARPROC) GetWindowLong(_hWndPM, GWL_WNDPROC);
// Set new window function for Program Manager
SetWindowLong(_hWndPM, GWL_WNDPROC,
    (LONG) MakeProcInstance((FARPROC) PMSubClass, hInstance));
```

This step saves the address of Program Manager's original window procedure in a global variable so it can be used in the call to the *CallWindowProc* function that appears at the end of the *PMSubClass* function. Passing this procedural instance address into *SetWindowLong* causes the subclassing to take effect.

When Program Manager Restore is executed from Program Manager after Windows is up and running, Program Manager will be minimized as usual if "Minimize on Use" is checked in the Options menu. Program Manager Restore will not restore Program Manager to its original size because the active application has not changed. The following call:

```
PostMessage(_hWndPM, WM_SYSCOMMAND, SC_RESTORE, 0);
```

forces Program Manager back to its restored state.

Finally, we want Program Manager Restore to relinquish control to Windows without terminating. We do this by entering a message loop. If Program Manager Restore did terminate, Windows would try to call a subclass function that is no longer in memory whenever a new message is sent to Program Manager.

At this point, Program Manager Restore has been initialized, Program Manager has been subclassed, and three new menu items have been added to Program Manager's menu. On the desktop, the only visual indication that everything has been performed successfully is the new menu items appearing under the Options menu of Program Manager.

The *PMSubClass* Function and Message Trapping

Since we wish to affect Program Manager in a very small way and not change the bulk of its behavior, our subclass function only intercepts two messages. *WM_ACTIVATEAPP* is intercepted so that Program Manager Restore can perform the restore operation. *WM_COMMAND* is intercepted so that we can pop up our own About box and allow the user to remove Program Manager Restore from memory.

This is the code associated with the *WM_ACTIVATEAPP* message:

```
case WM_ACTIVATEAPP:
   if (wParam == 0) break;
   if (!IsIconic(hWnd)) break;
   fpProc = MakeProcInstance(AnyAppsRunning, _hInstance);
   fAnyWindowsUp = (EnumWindows(fpProc, 0l) == 0);
   FreeProcInstance(fpProc);
   if (fAnyWindowsUp) break;
   ShowWindow(hWnd, SW_RESTORE);
   break;
```

If Program Manager is being deactivated or is not an icon, it will not need to be restored to its "open" size. That's why we perform the tests in the first two *if* conditions. Then we must discover whether any other applications are running. We ask Windows to enumerate all the parent windows on the screen by passing each window's handle to the specified callback function.

EnumWindows calls the specified procedural instance once for each parent window. The callback function has the option of continuing the enumeration or halting it. If the return value from *EnumWindows* is zero, our callback function saw a window from another running application and halted the enumeration. Program Manager will not be restored.

If the enumeration continues to completion, no other applications are running and we call the *ShowWindow* function to pop Program Manager back to its open state.

Here's the code associated with the *WM_COMMAND* message:

```
case WM_COMMAND:
   switch (wParam) {
   .
   .
   .
   case IDM_PMRESTOREABOUT:
      fpProc = MakeProcInstance(AboutProc, _hInstance);
      DialogBox(_hInstance, "About", hWnd, fpProc);
      FreeProcInstance(fpProc);
      fCallOrigProc = FALSE;
      break;

   case IDM_PMRESTOREREMOVE:
      // Stop window subclassing by putting back the address of
      // the original window procedure
      SetWindowLong(hWnd, GWL_WNDPROC, (LONG) _fpOrigPMProc);

      // Get menu handle to Program Manager's Options menu
      hMenu = GetMenu(hWnd);
```

```
// Remove the bottom two menu options
RemoveMenu(hMenu, IDM_PMRESTOREABOUT, MF_BYCOMMAND);
RemoveMenu(hMenu, IDM_PMRESTOREREMOVE, MF_BYCOMMAND);

// Get number of top-level menu items
nTopLevelMenuNum = GetMenuItemCount(hMenu) - 1;
while (nTopLevelMenuNum) {
    // Get handle to pop-up menu
    hMenuPopup = GetSubMenu(hMenu, nTopLevelMenuNum);
    // Is first option in pop-up menu IDM_AUTO_ARRANGE?
    if (IDM_AUTO_ARRANGE == GetMenuItemID(hMenuPopup, 0)) {
        // Remove separator bar
        RemoveMenu(hMenuPopup,
            GetMenuItemCount(hMenuPopup) - 1,
            MF_BYPOSITION);
        break;                              // Stop check menus
    }
    nTopLevelMenuNum--;                     // Try next menu
}
DrawMenuBar(hWnd);                          // Update new menu bar
// Post a WM_QUIT message to our application to remove it
// from memory
PostAppMessage(_PMRestoreTask, WM_QUIT, 0, 0);
break;

default:
    break;
```

The subclass function will intercept *WM_COMMAND* messages each time a menu item is selected from within Program Manager. If the *wParam* is *IDM_PM-RESTOREABOUT*, Program Manager Restore will display our About dialog box. Notice that after the About box is closed, we set *fCallOrigProc* to FALSE. This will prevent us from calling the original window procedure and telling it that a menu item was selected since Program Manager never expects a *wParam* value of 4444. If we allowed this message to be processed by the original window procedure, the results would be unpredictable.

When *wParam* is *IDM_PMRESTOREREMOVE*, the user has requested that the Program Manager Restore application terminate and remove itself from memory. Program Manager Restore does this by setting Program Manager's window bytes back to the original *WndProc* address. The three menu items that were appended to Program Manager are then removed. Finally, the *PostAppMessage* function is called, instructing Program Manager Restore that it should terminate:

```
PostAppMessage(_PMRestoreTask, WM_QUIT, 0, 0);
```

PostAppMessage is similar to *PostMessage* except that its first parameter is a task-instance handle instead of a window handle. When this function is called, Windows places the specified message in the application queue identified by the first parameter. In this case, the *WM_QUIT* message is placed in Program Manager Restore's application queue. The *GetMessage* function in Program Manager Restore's *WinMain* function will retrieve the *WM_QUIT* message. Just before *GetMessage* returns, it checks to see if the message being returned is *WM_QUIT*. If it is, *GetMessage* returns zero, causing the *while* loop to terminate. Once the loop has terminated, Program Manager Restore returns to Windows and is removed from memory.

When a message is dispatched to a window procedure, Windows sets the current task to the application that registered the window's class. If we were to call the *GetCurrentTask* function here, it would not return the task-instance handle of Program Manager Restore. This is why Program Manager Restore's task-instance handle had to be saved earlier in a global variable. For a complete discussion of tasks, refer to Chapter 6.

For all other values of *wParam* associated with the *WM_COMMAND* message, the message is just passed to the original window procedure and handled normally. The other messages are not intercepted and are passed to the original window procedure.

The *AnyAppsRunning* Function

The Windows function *EnumWindows* calls *AnyAppsRunning* once for each parent window. If the window handle passed to this function is the handle for the desktop, a window associated with Program Manager, or an invisible window, we don't care about it and continue with the window enumeration. If it is not one of these, it must be a window for an application. At this point we stop the enumeration and *EnumWindows* returns zero, telling *PMSubClass* that another application is running and not to restore Program Manager.

Running Program Manager Restore

To run the program, start Windows and execute PMREST.EXE like any other Windows application. You could also place PMREST.EXE in the *LOAD=* line of your WIN.INI file to make it load automatically whenever you start Windows. Once invoked, Program Manager Restore stays active during your entire Windows session. The only way to remove or disable Program Manager Restore is by terminating Windows or selecting "Remove PM Restore" from Program Manager's Options menu.

Program Manager Restore and Expanded Memory (EMS)

Windows places an application's code segments in EMS memory if the machine is in real mode and has expanded memory. If a message is sent to a window in another application, the code for the subclass function is not mapped into an EMS page frame. Windows attempts to jump to the subclass function's address and crashes. This means Program Manager Restore will not function properly in a machine with EMS memory.

To solve this problem, we must place the code for the subclass function in a DLL with fixed code segments. This keeps the code below the EMS bank line and guarantees that it is accessible at all times.

Listings 2-1 through 2-7, the Program Manager Restore application, illustrate window subclassing.

Listing 2-1. PMREST.C application source module.

```
/******************************************************************
Module name: PMRest.C
Programmer : Jeffrey M. Richter
******************************************************************/

#include "..\nowindws.h"
#undef NOCTLMGR
#undef NOKERNEL
#undef NOMB
#undef NOMENUS
#undef NOMSG
#undef NOSHOWWINDOW
#undef NOSYSCOMMANDS
#undef NOUSER
#undef NOWINOFFSETS
#undef NOWINMESSAGES
#include <windows.h>

#include "pmrest.h"

// menu IDs from Program Manager's menu
#define IDM_AUTO_ARRANGE (0xC9)
#define IDM_PMRESTOREABOUT (4444)
#define IDM_PMRESTOREREMOVE (4445)

char _szAppName[] = "Program Manager Restore";

// class name of the Program Manager window
char _szPMClass[] = "PROGMAN";

// address for original window procedure
FARPROC _fpOrigPMProc = NULL;

// window handle of Program Manager
HWND _hWndPM = NULL;

// our instance handle
HANDLE _hInstance = NULL;
```

```
// our task handle
HANDLE _PMRestoreTask = NULL;

// forward reference to subclass function
LONG FAR PASCAL PMSubClass (HWND, WORD, WORD, LONG);

int PASCAL WinMain (HANDLE hInstance, HANDLE hPrevInstance,
      LPSTR lpszCmdLine, int cmdShow) {
   MSG msg;
   DWORD dwWinFlags;
   HMENU hMenu, hMenuPopup;
   int nTopLevelMenuNum;

   dwWinFlags = GetWinFlags();
   if ((dwWinFlags & WF_LARGEFRAME) ||
      (dwWinFlags & WF_SMALLFRAME)) {
         MessageBox(GetFocus(), "PM Restore cannot run with EMS
            memory.", _szAppName, MB_OK | MB_SYSTEMMODAL);
         return(FALSE);
   }

   // Don't allow second instance of "PMRest" to run
   if (hPrevInstance != NULL) {
      MessageBox(GetFocus(), "Application already running.",
         _szAppName, MB_OK | MB_SYSTEMMODAL);
      return(FALSE);
   }

   // Get our data-instance handle and store it in a global
   // variable
   _hInstance = hInstance;

   // Get task-instance handle and store it in a global variable
   _PMRestoreTask = GetCurrentTask();


   // Find window handle of Program Manager. Do not specify a
   // caption because Program Manager's caption changes depending
   // on whether a group is maximized or not.
   _hWndPM = FindWindow(_szPMClass, NULL);
```

```
if (_hWndPM == NULL) {

   // If Program Manager's window couldn't be found, try to
   // execute the Program Manager application. This happens if
   // PMREST.EXE is in the LOAD= line of the WIN.INI file.
   WinExec("ProgMan", SW_SHOW);
   _hWndPM = FindWindow(_szPMClass, NULL);


   // If we still can't find Program Manager, we can't subclass
   // it and must terminate
   if (_hWndPM == NULL) {
      MessageBox(GetFocus(), "Cannot find Program Manager.",
         _szAppName, MB_OK);
      return(FALSE);
   }
}

// Get handle to Program Manager's Options menu
hMenu = GetMenu(_hWndPM);

// Get number of top-level menu items
nTopLevelMenuNum = GetMenuItemCount(hMenu) - 1;
while (nTopLevelMenuNum) {

   // Get handle to pop-up menu
   hMenuPopup = GetSubMenu(hMenu, nTopLevelMenuNum);

   // Is the first option in the pop-up menu IDM_AUTO_ARRANGE?
   if (IDM_AUTO_ARRANGE == GetMenuItemID(hMenuPopup, 0)) {

      // Add a separator bar and "About PM Restore..." option
      // to this menu
      AppendMenu(hMenuPopup, MF_SEPARATOR, 0, 0);
      AppendMenu(hMenuPopup, MF_ENABLED | MF_STRING,
         IDM_PMRESTOREABOUT, "A&bout PM Restore...");
      AppendMenu(hMenuPopup, MF_ENABLED | MF_STRING,
         IDM_PMRESTOREREMOVE, "&Remove PM Restore");

      break;            // Stop check menus
```

```
      }
    nTopLevelMenuNum--; // Try next menu
  }

  DrawMenuBar(_hWndPM);   // Update the new menu bar

  // Save current window function for Program Manager in a
  // global variable
  _fpOrigPMProc = (FARPROC) GetWindowLong(_hWndPM, GWL_WNDPROC);

  // Set new window function for Program Manager
  SetWindowLong(_hWndPM, GWL_WNDPROC,
    (LONG) MakeProcInstance((FARPROC) PMSubClass, hInstance));

  // Running PMRest.EXE will minimize Program Manager if
  // "Minimize on Use" is selected in Program Manager's
  // Options menu. Since there will not be an application
  // switch, our subclassing will not restore Program Manager
  // automatically, so we must do it.
  PostMessage(_hWndPM, WM_SYSCOMMAND, SC_RESTORE, 0);


  // Begin message loop. This is so that our application doesn't
  // terminate. If we terminated, our subclass function would be
  // removed from memory. When Windows tried to call it, it would
  // jump to garbage.
  while (GetMessage(&msg, NULL, 0, 0)) DispatchMessage(&msg);

  return(0);
}


// function to process About box
BOOL FAR PASCAL AboutProc (HWND hDlg, WORD wMsg, WORD wParam,
    LONG lParam) {
  char szBuffer[100];
  BOOL fProcessed = TRUE;

  switch (wMsg) {
```

```
    case WM_INITDIALOG:
      // Set version static window to have date and time of
      // compilation
      wsprintf(szBuffer, "%s at %s", (LPSTR) __DATE__,
        (LPSTR) __TIME__);
      SetWindowText(GetDlgItem(hDlg, ID_VERSION), szBuffer);
      break;

    case WM_COMMAND:
      switch (wParam) {
        case IDOK: case IDCANCEL:
          if (HIWORD(lParam) == BN_CLICKED)
            EndDialog(hDlg, wParam);
          break;

        default:
          break;
      }
      break;

    default:
      fProcessed = FALSE; break;
  }
  return(fProcessed);
}


// forward reference to function called by EnumWindows
BOOL FAR PASCAL AnyAppsRunning (HWND, LONG);


// Subclass function for Program Manager. Any messages for Program
// Manager window come here before reaching the original window
// function.
LONG FAR PASCAL PMSubClass (HWND hWnd, WORD wMsg, WORD wParam,
    LONG lParam) {
  FARPROC fpProc;
  BOOL fAnyWindowsUp, fCallOrigProc = TRUE;
  LONG lResult = 0L;
  HMENU hMenu, hMenuPopup;
  int nTopLevelMenuNum;
```

```
    switch (wMsg) {

  case WM_ACTIVATEAPP:
    // Program Manager is being either activated or deactivated

    if (wParam == 0) break;       // PM is being deactivated
    if (!IsIconic(hWnd)) break;   // PM isn't an icon

    // Program Manager is being made active and is an icon. We
    // have to check to see if any other applications are
    // running.
    fpProc = MakeProcInstance(AnyAppsRunning, _hInstance);
    fAnyWindowsUp = (EnumWindows(fpProc, 0l) == 0);
    FreeProcInstance(fpProc);

    // If the enumeration was stopped prematurely, there must be
    // at least one other application running
    if (fAnyWindowsUp) break;

    // No other applications are running; restore Program
    // Manager to "open" state
    ShowWindow(hWnd, SW_RESTORE);
    break;

  case WM_COMMAND:
    switch (wParam) {

    case IDM_PMRESTOREABOUT:
      // Our added menu option to display "About PM Restore..."
      // was chosen
      fpProc = MakeProcInstance(AboutProc, _hInstance);
      DialogBox(_hInstance, "About", hWnd, fpProc);
      FreeProcInstance(fpProc);

      // Don't pass this message to original Program Manager
      // window procedure because it wouldn't know what to do
      // with it
      fCallOrigProc = FALSE;
      break;
```

```
case IDM_PMRESTOREREMOVE:
   // Stop window subclassing by putting back the address of
   // the original window procedure
   SetWindowLong(hWnd, GWL_WNDPROC, (LONG) _fpOrigPMProc);

   // Get menu handle to Program Manager's "Options" menu
   hMenu = GetMenu(hWnd);
   RemoveMenu(hMenu, IDM_PMRESTOREABOUT, MF_BYCOMMAND);
   RemoveMenu(hMenu, IDM_PMRESTOREREMOVE, MF_BYCOMMAND);

   // Get number of top-level menu items
   nTopLevelMenuNum = GetMenuItemCount(hMenu) - 1;
   while (nTopLevelMenuNum) {

      // Get handle to pop-up menu
      hMenuPopup = GetSubMenu(hMenu, nTopLevelMenuNum);

      // Is the first option in the pop-up menu
      // IDM_AUTO_ARRANGE?
      if (IDM_AUTO_ARRANGE ==
         GetMenuItemID(hMenuPopup, 0)) {

         // Remove separator bar
         RemoveMenu(hMenuPopup, GetMenuItemCount(hMenuPopup)
            - 1, MF_BYPOSITION);

         break;              // Stop check menus
      }
      nTopLevelMenuNum--;   // Try next menu
   }

   DrawMenuBar(hWnd);       // Update the new menu bar


   // Post a WM_QUIT message to our application to remove it
   // from memory
   PostAppMessage(_PMRestoreTask, WM_QUIT, 0, 0);
   break;

default:                    // Pass other WM_COMMAND's to
   break                    // original procedure
```

```
        }
      break;

   default:            // Pass other messages to original procedure
      break;

   }

   if (fCallOrigProc) {
      // Call original window procedure and return the result to
      // whoever sent this message to Program Manager
      lResult = CallWindowProc(_fpOrigPMProc, hWnd, wMsg, wParam,
         lParam);
   }

   return(lResult);
}


// Windows' callback function to determine if any windows exist
// that should stop us from restoring Program Manager
BOOL FAR PASCAL AnyAppsRunning (HWND hWnd, LONG lParam) {
   GetCurrentTask();

   // If window is the window's desktop, continue enumeration
   if (hWnd == GetDesktopWindow())
      return(1);

   // If the window is invisible (hidden), continue enumeration
   if (!IsWindowVisible(hWnd))
      return(1);

   // If window is associated with Program Manager, continue
   // enumeration
   if (GetWindowTask(_hWndPM) == GetWindowTask(hWnd))
      return(1);

   // Any other type of window, stop enumeration
   return(0);
}
```

Listing 2-2. PMREST.H application header module.

```
/***************************************************************
Module name: PMRest.H
Programmer : Jeffrey M. Richter
***************************************************************/

#include "dialog.h"
```

Listing 2-3. DIALOG.H (dialog-box template defines).

```
#define ID_VERSION   (100)
```

Listing 2-4. PMREST.RC application resource file.

```
/***************************************************************
Module name: PMRest.RC
Programmer : Jeffrey M. Richter
***************************************************************/

#include <windows.h>

#include   "pmrest.h"
#include   "dialog.h"
#include   "pmrest.dlg"

PM_Rest    ICON  MOVEABLE DISCARDABLE PMRest.Ico
```

Listing 2-5. PMREST.DLG dialog-box templates.

```
ABOUT DIALOG LOADONCALL MOVEABLE DISCARDABLE 16, 20, 126, 92
CAPTION "About Program Manager Restore"
STYLE WS_BORDER | WS_CAPTION | WS_DLGFRAME | WS_SYSMENU |
   WS_VISIBLE | WS_POPUP
```

```
BEGIN
   CONTROL "PM_Rest", -1, "static", SS_ICON | WS_CHILD, 4, 16, 18,
      21
   CONTROL "Program Manager Restore", -1, "static", SS_CENTER |
      WS_CHILD, 22, 8, 100, 12
   CONTROL "Written by:", -1, "static", SS_CENTER | WS_CHILD, 22,
      20, 100, 12
   CONTROL "Jeffrey M. Richter", -1, "static", SS_CENTER |
      WS_CHILD, 22, 32, 100, 12
   CONTROL "Version date:", -1, "static", SS_CENTER | WS_CHILD,
      22, 48, 100, 12
   CONTROL "", ID_VERSION, "static", SS_CENTER | WS_CHILD, 22, 60,
      100, 12
   CONTROL "&OK", IDOK, "button", BS_DEFPUSHBUTTON | WS_TABSTOP |
      WS_CHILD, 40, 76, 44, 12
END
```

Listing 2-6. PMREST.DEF definitions file.

```
; Module name: PMRest.DEF
; Programmer : Jeffrey M. Richter

NAME            PMRest
DESCRIPTION     'Program Manager Restore Application'
STUB            'WinStub.exe'
EXETYPE         WINDOWS
CODE            MOVEABLE NONDISCARDABLE PRELOAD
DATA            MOVEABLE MULTIPLE PRELOAD
HEAPSIZE        1024
STACKSIZE       4096
EXPORTS
   PMSubClass
   AnyAppsRunning
   AboutProc
```

Listing 2-7. MAKEFILE for PMRest application.

```
#*****************************************************************
#Module name: MAKEFILE
#Programmer : Jeffrey M. Richter
#*****************************************************************

PROG = PMRest
MODEL = S
CFLAGS = -A$(MODEL) -D_WINDOWS -Gcsw2 -W4 -Zlepid -Od
LFLAGS = /NOE/BA/A:16/M/CO/LI/F
LIBS = $(MODEL)nocrt + libw

M1 = $(PROG).obj

ICONS = $(PROG).ico
BITMAPS =
CURSORS =
RESOURCES = $(ICONS) $(BITMAPS) $(CURSORS)

.SUFFIXES: .rc

.rc.res:
    rc -r $*.rc

$(PROG).Exe: $(M1) $(PROG).Def $(PROG).Res
    link $(LFLAGS) @<<$(PROG).lnk
$(M1)
$(PROG), $(PROG), $(LIBS), $(PROG)
<<
    rc $(PROG).Res

$(PROG).obj:    $*.c $*.h dialog.h

$(PROG).res:    $*.rc $*.h $*.dlg dialog.h $(RESOURCES)
```

Figure 2-4. PMREST.ICO.

How Window Superclassing Works

Window superclassing is similar to window subclassing. The idea is that messages intended for the window procedure of the original class are routed to a different procedure that you supply. At the bottom of this procedure, the message is passed to the original window procedure instead of *DefWindowProc*. This is done by calling the *CallWindowProc* function.

Superclassing alters the behavior of an existing window class. This window class is called the *base class*. The base is usually a system global class like BUTTON or COMBOBOX, but it may be any window class.

When you superclass a window class, you must register a new window class with Windows. The *lpfnWndProc* member of the *WNDCLASS* structure points to your superclass window procedure. When a message is dispatched to the superclassed window (Figure 2-5), Windows examines the memory block for the window and calls the superclass window procedure. After the superclass window procedure processes the message, it passes the message to the window procedure associated with the base class.

Many more steps are necessary to create a superclass than to subclass a window. The process of superclassing a window begins with a call to the *GetClassInfo* function, passing it the name of the desired base class. This fills a *WNDCLASS* structure with most of the statistics regarding the base class.

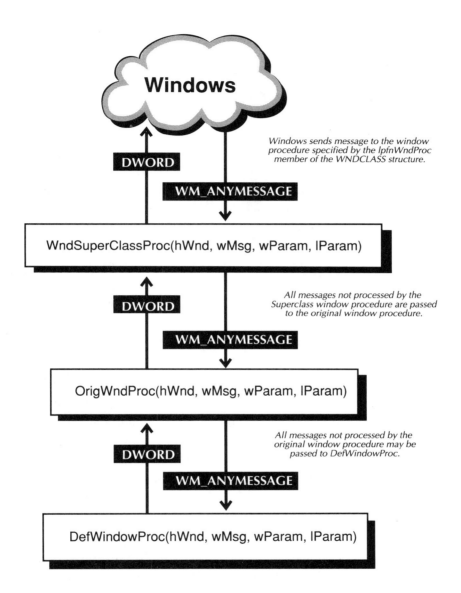

Figure 2-5. Window superclassing.

This *WNDCLASS* structure serves as a starting point for the new window class. The next step is to give the new class a name. This is done by setting the *lpszClassName* member to the new name for the class. The value of the *hInstance* member should be set to the value of *hInstance* that was passed to *WinMain* when the application that is registering the superclass was invoked, since this new class is being registered by your application.

It is important to save the value of the original *lpfnWndProc* member (usually in a global variable). This value is the address of the base class window procedure. This variable will be used later in the superclass window procedure as the first parameter to the *CallWindowProc* function. The *lpfnWndProc* member of the *WNDCLASS* structure is then set to the address of the superclass window procedure. This procedure must be declared *FAR PASCAL* and listed in the *EXPORTS* section of the .DEF file. However, you don't need to make a procedural instance for this function because the *RegisterClass* function will do that automatically.

Because a new window class is going to be registered, you can increase the values of the *cbClsExtra* and *cbWndExtra* members of the *WNDCLASS* structure. These additional bytes may be used by your superclass function. This is a big advantage of superclassing over subclassing. But be careful when using the class or window extra bytes for a superclassed window class. The base class window procedure was written with the assumption that the class extra bytes from zero to *cbClsExtra*-1 and the window extra bytes from zero to *cbWndExtra*-1 are for its own use. The superclass window procedure must not access the class and window extra bytes within these ranges unless it knows exactly how they are used by the base class.

If the superclass window procedure is going to add class and window extra bytes, it must save the original values of the *cbClsExtra* and *cbWndExtra* members of the *WNDCLASS* structure, usually in global variables, before changing the values of those members. When the superclass window procedure wants to access any of the window extra bytes, it must add the original value of *cbWndExtra* to the index so that it does not reference the window extra bytes used by the base class. Here is an example of how to prepare and access additional window bytes added to the superclass:

```
// Global variables to save the number of class extra bytes,
// window extra bytes, and the window procedure address of the
// LISTBOX base class
int _cbClsExtraOrig;
int _cbWndExtraOrig;
FARPROC _lpfnWndProcOrig;

// Index into window extra bytes where LISTBOX data can be found
#define GWW_LISTBOXDATA    (_cbWndExtraOrig + 0)
  .
  .
  .
BOOL RegisterSuperClass (void) {
   WNDCLASS WndClass;
   // Fill WNDCLASS structure with information about
   // LISTBOX class
   GetClassInfo(NULL, "LISTBOX", &WndClass);

   // Save the information we need later in global variables
   _cbClsExtraOrig = WndClass.cbClsExtra;
   _cbWndExtraOrig = WndClass.cbWndExtra;
   _lpfnWndProcOrig = WndClass.lpfnWndProc;

     .
     .
     .
   // Add two window extra bytes to account for our LISTBOX data
   WndClass.cbWndExtra += 2;

   // Register the new window class
   return(RegisterClass(&WndClass));
}
  .
  .
  .
```

```
LONG FAR PASCAL LBSuperClsWndProc (HWND hWnd, WORD wMsg,
    WORD wParam, LONG lParam) {
  int wListBoxData;
    .
    .
    .
  // Retrieve the LISTBOX data from the window extra bytes
  wListBoxData = GetWindowWord(hWnd, GWW_LISTBOXDATA);
    .
    .
    .
  // Call base class window procedure for remainder of processing
  return(CallWindowProc(_lpfnWndProcOrig, hWnd, wMsg,
    wParam, lParam));
}
```

Of course, it is possible to associate data with a superclassed window via window properties as explained in Chapter 1. However, it is always better to store information in window extra bytes because properties require more data space and take longer to operate.

The *lpszMenuName* member of *WNDCLASS* may also be changed to give the new class a new menu. If a new menu is used, the IDs for the menu options should correspond with the IDs in the "standard" menu for the base class. This is not necessary if the superclass window procedure processes the *WM_COMMAND* message in its entirety and does not pass this message to the base class window procedure.

The remaining members of the *WNDCLASS* structure—*style*, *hIcon*, *hCursor*, and *hbrBackground*—may be changed in any way you desire. For example, if you want your new window class to use a different mouse cursor or a different icon, change the *hCursor* and *hIcon* members of the *WNDCLASS* structure accordingly.

Finally, call the *RegisterClass* function to notify Windows of the new class. This will let you create new windows of this class.

The main difference between subclassing and superclassing is that subclassing alters the behavior of an existing window, while superclassing alters the behavior of an existing window class. It is better to use superclassing when you wish to change the operation of many windows. This is because it is easier to register a new class, give it a new name, and create windows of this new class than it is to create all the desired windows and use the *SetWindowLong* function to change the address of their window procedures.

The most common use for superclassing is for a dialog box that has many controls. When a dialog box is created, the dialog-box manager goes through the dialog-box template and creates windows based on each *CONTROL* line in the template. If the template contains several LISTBOX windows that require altered behavior, it is much easier to specify NEWLISTBOX in the *CONTROL* line of the template. With window subclassing, the dialog-box manager would have to create all the LISTBOX windows before you could subclass these windows, one at a time, during the processing of the *WM_INITDIALOG* message.

Another advantage of superclassing is that the superclass window procedure gets to perform its own initialization for the window. This is because Windows knows about the superclass window procedure from the class memory block before a window is created. When the window is created, the superclass window procedure receives the *WM_NCCREATE* and *WM_CREATE* messages. During the processing of these messages, the superclass window procedure may initialize its class or window extra bytes or do any other processing it desires.

Both of these messages should be passed to the base class window procedure, whether the superclass window procedure processes them or not. As explained in Chapter 1, Windows allocates the memory block required for each window in response to *WM_NCCREATE*. Since the superclass window procedure does not call the *DefWindowProc* function directly, Windows will not be able to create the memory block. By passing the *WM_NCCREATE* message to the base class procedure, we ensure that *DefWindowProc* will eventually be called. The *WM_CREATE* message should be passed to the base class window procedure so it can perform any necessary initialization.

You can add your own user messages for a superclassed window class using *RegisterWindowMessage*. The same rules apply to superclassed window classes as to subclassed windows.

The following table summarizes the differences between window subclassing and superclassing.

Subclassing	Superclassing
Not recommended if many windows need to have altered behavior.	Recommended if many windows need to have altered behavior.
No new window class is registered.	A new window class must be registered.
Subclass function may not use any class or window extra bytes.	Superclass function may use class and window extra bytes.
Subclassing can only be done with existing windows.	Superclassing can only be done with existing window classes.
Subclassed windows cannot intercept the window's initialization messages (*WM_NCCREATE* and *WM_CREATE*).	Superclassed windows can intercept the window's initialization messages (*WM_NCCREATE* and *WM_CREATE*).

An Example of Window Superclassing

The sample program that demonstrates window superclassing, NOALPHA.EXE, creates a window that contains nothing but a menu bar. The one option on this menu bar evokes a dialog box that contains several windows. Two of these windows are of the NOALPHA class, a superclass based on the system global EDIT class. The

NOALPHA class behaves just like an EDIT window except that it does not accept lowercase or uppercase letters. In fact, when the user tries to type a letter into a NOALPHA window, the computer beeps, notifying the user that letters are not allowed.

A window created using the NOALPHA superclass can restrict input to a programmer-specified range of values. A new window message is registered that allows an application using a NOALPHA window to change the legal range of values. Another new message is registered that allows an application using a NOALPHA window to check to see if the value in the window is within the legal range.

The source code for this example is split between two source files: NOALPHA.C and SUPERCLS.C.

The Window Superclassing Package: SUPERCLS.C

SUPERCLS.C contains source code that could easily be incorporated into your own applications. The functions in this module help you manipulate any class and window extra bytes that you may add when superclassing a window class.

Some of the information obtained from the base class must be used when processing superclassed windows, including the number of class and window extra bytes and the address of the base class window procedure. Instead of storing this information in global variables, the *RegisterSuperClass* function in SUPERCLS.C adds eight bytes to the class extra bytes and stores the information there. This is a much cleaner method for working with superclasses.

The prototype for the *RegisterSuperClass* function is:

```
BOOL FAR PASCAL RegisterSuperClass (LPWNDCLASS WndClass,
  LONG (FAR PASCAL *lpfnSCWndProc)(),
  int cbClsAdditional, int cbWndAdditional);
```

The first parameter is a pointer to a *WNDCLASS* structure. This structure should have been set using *GetClassInfo*. The calling function should update any necessary members, with the exception of *cbClsExtra*, *cbWndExtra*, and *lpfnWndProc*. These values are the remaining ones passed to the *RegisterSuperClass* function. The *lpfnSCWndProc* parameter should be the address of the superclass window procedure. Remember that this address should not be a procedural instance. The remaining two parameters are the number of *additional* class and window extra bytes that the superclass would like to add.

Next, we save the base class values of the *cbClsExtra*, *cbWndExtra*, and *lpfnWndProc* members in temporary variables. Then we increment the *cbClsExtra* member by the value in the *cbClsAdditional* parameter plus eight. The eight bytes at the end will hold the base class's *cbClsExtra*, *cbWndExtra*, and *lpfnWndProc* data. We then increment *cbWndExtra* by the value of the *cbWndAdditional* parameter. Finally, we set *lpfnWndProc* to the value of *lpfnSCWndProc*.

Now that the *WNDCLASS* structure has been updated, we register the window class using *RegisterClass*. If the class is registered successfully, we must now set the last eight class extra bytes to the values that were saved in the temporary variables. Unfortunately, Windows doesn't offer a way to alter a class's extra bytes without first having a handle to a window of the desired class. Here is the solution to this problem:

RegisterSuperClass saves the base class values of the *cbClsExtra*, *cbWndExtra*, and *lpfnWndProc* members of *WNDCLASS* in global variables. The *cbClsExtra*, *cbWndExtra*, and *lpfnWndProc* members are initialized as described above, and the new class is registered by calling *RegisterClass*. Setting the last eight class extra bytes requires a window of the new class to be created first so that its handle can be passed to the *SetClassWord* and *SetClassLong* functions.

While the window is being created, Windows sends *WM_GETMINMAXINFO*, *WM_NCCREATE*, *WM_NCCALCSIZE*, and *WM_CREATE* messages (in that order) to the superclass window procedure. At the bottom of the superclass window procedure is the following:

```
CallWindowProc((FARPROC) GetBCWndProc(hWnd), hWnd, wMsg, wParam,
    lParam);
```

When this line is executed during the first message, *WM_GETMINMAXINFO*, the *GetBCWndProc* function is called. This function, in SUPERCLS.C, returns the address of the base class window procedure from the window's class extra bytes. However, the class extra bytes have not yet been initialized and still contain zeros. When the *GetBCWndProc* function retrieves the address of the base class window procedure, the address will be 0x0000:0x0000. If this is the case, the value in the global variable *_lpfnBCWndProc* is returned. This value is the address of the base window procedure.

SetSuperClassInfo should be called as soon as possible during the creation of the new window (for example, while the *WM_GETMINMAXINFO*, *WM_NCCREATE,* or *WM_CREATE* message is being processed). This function takes the values stored in the three global variables, *_cbBCClsExtra*, *_cbBCWndExtra*, and *_lpfnBCWndProc*, and sets them into the appropriate class extra bytes. Your superclass window procedure should not alter any class or window extra bytes until after *SetSuperClassInfo* has been called.

If the call to *SetSuperClassInfo* occurs during *WM_GETMINMAXINFO*, the *GetBCWndProc* function will never see NULL returned from the *GetClassLong* function. However, Windows sends the *WM_GETMINMAXINFO* message whenever the size of the window will change. Because the *WM_NCCREATE* and *WM_CREATE* messages are only sent once during the lifetime of a window, it is better to place the call to *SetSuperClassInfo* in one of these two messages. Notice that

SetSuperClassInfo first checks to see if the class extra bytes have already been set by comparing the address of the base class window procedure with NULL. If this address is not NULL, the function returns immediately.

The following table shows the contents of the class extra bytes after *SetSuperClassInfo* has been called. The Example column shows the index into the class extra bytes if the base class required two extra class bytes and the superclass required four additional class bytes.

Offset	Example	Contents
The *GCW_* and *GCL_* defines in WINDOWS.H (all have negative offset)	*GCW_STYLE* (-26) to -1	All the class information contained in the *WNDCLASS* structure.
0 to *cbClsExtra* - 1 (retrieved from the *GetClassInfo* call)	0 to 1	All the class extra bytes needed by the base class.
cbClsExtra to (*cbClsExtra* + *cbClsAdditional* - 1)	2 to 5	All the class extra bytes needed by the superclass.
(*cbClsExtra* + *cbClsAdditional*) to (*cbClsExtra* + *cbClsAdditional* + 1)	6 to 7	The number of window extra bytes needed by base class. Used by functions in SUPERCLS.C.
(*cbClsExtra* + *cbClsAdditional* + 2) to (*cbClsExtra* + *cbClsAdditional* + 3)	8 to 9	The number of class extra bytes needed by base class. Used by functions in SUPERCLS.C.
(*cbClsExtra* + *cbClsAdditional* + 4) to (*cbClsExtra* + *cbClsAdditional* + 7)	10 to 13	The address of the base window procedure. Used by *GetBCWndProc* function in SUPERCLS.C.

If the call to *CreateWindow* in the *RegisterSuperClass* function returns NULL, the new class is unregistered using the *UnregisterClass* function and FALSE is returned to the application. If the window is created, the class extra bytes have been initialized and the window may be destroyed using the *DestroyWindow* function.

The *CalcClassByteIndex* function is only used by other functions in this module. It's declared as

```
static int NEAR PASCAL CalcClassByteIndex (HWND hWnd, int nIndex);
```

This function accepts a window handle to a superclassed window and an index into the class extra bytes. This index is zero-based and allows us to ignore any class extra bytes needed by the base class. If the specified index is negative, it refers to information that is part of the *WNDCLASS* structure. If the number is greater than or equal to zero, it refers to class bytes that are needed by the superclass window procedure. The index into the class extra bytes for the superclassed extra bytes is calculated by retrieving the number of class extra bytes required by the base class and adding it to the *nIndex* parameter. The new value of *nIndex* is the index that should be used with the *Get/SetClassWord/Long* functions for class extra bytes associated with the superclassed window.

CalcWindowByteIndex is identical to *CalcClassByteIndex* except that it calculates the index into the window extra bytes. The new value of *nIndex* is the index that should be used with the *Get/SetWindowWord/Long* functions for window extra bytes associated with the superclassed window.

The remaining functions (*SetSCClassWord*, *GetSCClassWord*, *SetSCClassLong*, *GetSCClassLong*, *SetSCWindowWord*, *GetSCWindowWord*, *SetSCWindowLong*, and *GetSCWindowLong*) are used by the application whenever any class or window extra bytes must be referenced. These functions prevent the calling application from altering the class and window extra bytes of the base class window procedure.

The Application Program: NOALPHA.C

Initializing the Application. NoAlpha's initialization code registers its application window class (NOALPHAAPP) and the superclass window class (NOALPHA). The *RegisterNoAlphaWndClass* function simply fills a *WNDCLASS* structure by calling the *GetClassInfo* function, using EDIT as the base class. The *lpszClassName* and *hInstance* members of the *WNDCLASS* structure are modified to point to NOALPHA and the value of the *hInstance* parameter, respectively. The NOALPHA class does not change any of the other members of the *WNDCLASS* structure. However, when you create other superclasses you may change these values.

Because *RegisterNoAlphaWndClass* uses functions from SUPERCLS.C, the *cbClsExtra*, *cbWndExtra*, and *lpfnWndProc* members need not be changed. The desired values are passed to *RegisterSuperClass*, which fixes up the *WNDCLASS* structure and calls *RegisterClass* on behalf of the application.

When the call to *RegisterSuperClass* returns, the *WNDCLASS* structure contains all the appropriate values for the superclassed window class. The return value from *RegisterSuperClass* is returned to the caller of the *RegisterNoAlphaWndClass* function.

The new superclass (NOALPHA) requires no additional class extra bytes. However, it does use four additional window extra bytes. These two words contain the low and high values representing the valid range for numbers in the NOALPHA window. We want to let applications send messages to the NOALPHA window to set the valid range and to return a Boolean indicating whether the value in the window is within the valid range. Because NOALPHA is a superclass, it would not be prudent to create messages based on the *WM_USER* method. The only way we can guarantee that message values do not conflict with any other message values is by using *RegisterWindowMessage*.

After the NOALPHA superclass is registered, the NOALPHA class-specific messages "ValidRange" and "SetRange" are defined and their values saved in global variables:

```
_ValidRangeMsg = RegisterWindowMessage("ValidRange");
_SetRangeMsg = RegisterWindowMessage("SetRange");
```

If another instance of this application is running, neither the application window class nor the NOALPHA superclass should be registered. However, this new instance of the application needs to be aware of the values for the "ValidRange" and "SetRange" messages. The source code demonstrates two ways these values may be obtained.

The first method calls *RegisterWindowMessage*, passing it the same message string used for the first instance of the application. Windows remembers the value that was returned when the message was first registered and returns the same value. (Once a window message has been registered, Windows remembers its value for the entire session, even if all instances of the application terminate.)

The second method calls *GetInstanceData*. This function retrieves data from another instance's data segment. The first parameter is the instance handle of the application that contains the source data. The second parameter is the offset into the data segment where the desired information begins. This parameter is also the offset into the application's own data segment where the information should be stored. The last parameter is the number of bytes to be copied. Because the second parameter is an offset into both the source and destination application's data segments, the instance handle of the source application should be just another instance of the same application making the *GetInstanceData* call. The offset into the data segment must be the address of a global variable.

The line

```
GetInstanceData(hPrevInstance, (NPSTR) &_ValidRangeMsg,
    sizeof(_ValidRangeMsg))
```

tells Windows to use the data segment of the previously running instance of the application and copy its value for the global variable _ValidRangeMsg.

The Superclass Window Procedure. *NoAlphaWndProc* is the superclass window procedure. All messages destined for a window of the NOALPHA class are directed to this function. The first thing this function does is determine if the message is one of the two NOALPHA class-specific messages ("SetRange" or "ValidRange"). Because the values of these messages must be obtained from variables, *case* statements cannot be used. Checking for these messages must be done with *if* statements. If the message is "SetRange," the lowest value in the range is in the low word of the *lParam* parameter and the highest value is in the high word.

The *SetSCWindowWord* function in SUPERCLS.C changes the window extra bytes to reflect the new valid range:

```
#define NOALPHA_CBWNDEXTRA      (4)
#define GSCWW_LOVALUE           (0)
#define GSCWW_HIVALUE           (2)
    .
    .
    .
SetSCWindowWord(hWnd, GSCWW_LOVALUE, LOWORD(lParam));
SetSCWindowWord(hWnd, GSCWW_HIVALUE, HIWORD(lParam));
```

Because this message is our own, it should not be passed to the base window procedure. If this message were passed to the base window procedure, that procedure should ignore the message anyway.

If the message is "ValidRange," the text of the NOALPHA window is copied to a buffer and converted to an integer:

```
GetWindowText(hWnd, szValue, sizeof(szValue));
nValue = atoi(szValue);
```

The low and high values are retrieved from the window extra bytes:

```
nLoValue = GetSCWindowWord(hWnd, GSCWW_LOVALUE);
nHiValue = GetSCWindowWord(hWnd, GSCWW_HIVALUE);
```

and the result of the message processing is the result of *nLoValue <= nValue <= nHiValue*:

```
lResult = (nLoValue <= nValue) && (nValue <= nHiValue);
```

Since this message is our own, it should not be passed to the base window procedure.

The remaining messages can be processed using the familiar *switch-case* construct.

Remember that the superclass function in SUPERCLS.C requires a call to *SetSuperClassInfo* in one of the window initialization messages (*WM_GETMIN-MAXINFO, WM_NCCREATE,* or *WM_CREATE*). Because *WM_GETMINMAX-INFO* messages are sent to a window frequently, it is usually best to place the *SetSuperClassInfo* call in one of the other two messages. Because it is also better to place this call as early in the lifetime of a window as possible, I chose to place it in the *WM_NCCREATE* message. Although *NoAlphaWndProc* processes *WM_NC-CREATE* , this message must be passed to the base class window procedure.

The *WM_CREATE* message initializes the two window extra words so that the default low range of legal values is -32,767 and the default high range is +32,767. If this were not done, the default range would be from zero to zero.

The *WM_CHAR* message checks the value of the *wParam* parameter to determine if a letter was pressed. If a letter was pressed, the base window procedure should not be called. This prohibits the message from ever being seen by the EDIT class's window procedure and guarantees that no letters will ever appear in a NOALPHA window. The *MessageBeep* function notifies the user that an illegal key has been pressed.

Any other messages destined for the NOALPHA window are passed directly to the base class window procedure for default or standard EDIT window processing:

```
CallWindowProc((FARPROC) GetBCWndProc(hWnd), hWnd, wMsg,
   wParam, 1Param));
```

The call to the *GetBCWndProc* function (found in the SUPERCLS.C module) looks into the class extra bytes and retrieves the address of the base class window procedure.

The Dialog-Box Function. *DlgProc* processes all messages for the dialog box shown in Figure 2-6. During the *WM_INITDIALOG* message, the valid range for the two NOALPHA windows is set:

```
SendDlgItemMessage(hDlg, ID_NOALPHA1, _SetRangeMsg,
   0, MAKELONG(100, 200));
SendDlgItemMessage(hDlg, ID_NOALPHA2, _SetRangeMsg,
   0, MAKELONG(-300, 100));
```

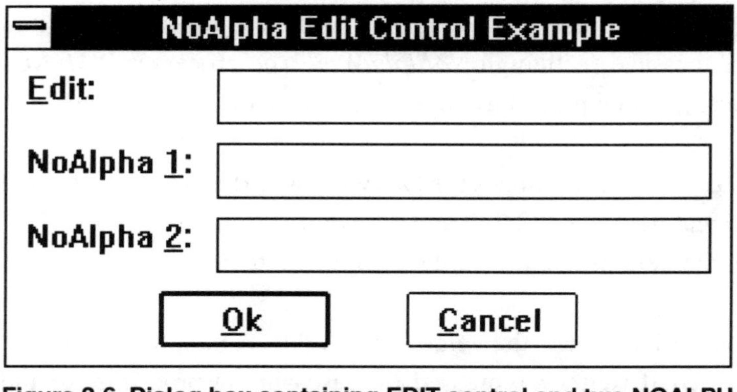

Figure 2-6. Dialog box containing EDIT control and two NOALPHA controls.

When a *BN_CLICKED* message is received from the "Ok" button, a message is sent to the first NOALPHA window to assess whether the entered value is within the legal range:

```
fOk = SendDlgItemMessage(hWnd, ID_NOALPHA1, _ValidRangeMsg, 0, 0);
```

If the value is not in the legal range, the *MessageBox* function displays a notice to that effect. The *SetFocus* function changes the input focus to the first NOALPHA window so that the user can correct the value.

If the window contains a valid value, the second NOALPHA window is checked in the same fashion. Only when the user has entered legal values in both NOALPHA windows is the *EndDialog* function called, closing the dialog box.

The NoAlpha edit control application, shown in Listings 2-8 through 2-16, demonstrates window superclassing.

Figure 2-7. NOALPHA.ICO.

Listing 2-8. NOALPHA.C application source module.

```
/****************************************************************
Module name: NoAlpha.C
Programmer : Jeffrey M. Richter
****************************************************************/

#include "..\nowindws.h"
#undef NOCOLOR
#undef NOCTLMGR
#undef NOKERNEL
#undef NOMB
#undef NOMENUS
#undef NOMSG
#undef NOSHOWWINDOW
#undef NOUSER
#undef NOWINOFFSETS
#undef NOWINMESSAGES
#undef NOWINSTYLES
#include <windows.h>

#include <stdlib.h>

#include "supercls.h"
#include "noalpha.h"

char _szAppName[] = "NoAlphaApp";

HANDLE _hInstance = NULL; // our instance handle

// ****************************************************************
// message number of our message to be sent to superclass window
// proc
WORD _SetRangeMsg = WM_NULL, _ValidRangeMsg = WM_NULL;

// forward reference to various functions
BOOL NEAR PASCAL RegisterAppWndClass (HANDLE hInstance);
BOOL NEAR PASCAL RegisterNoAlphaWndClass (HANDLE hInstance);
BOOL FAR PASCAL AboutProc (HWND, WORD, WORD, LONG);
```

```
BOOL FAR PASCAL DlgProc (HWND, WORD, WORD, LONG);
LONG FAR PASCAL NoAlphaAppWndProc (HWND, WORD, WORD, LONG);

// *****************************************************************
int PASCAL WinMain (HANDLE hInstance, HANDLE hPrevInstance,
      LPSTR lpszCmdLine, int cmdShow) {
   MSG msg;
   HWND hWnd;

   _hInstance = hInstance;

   if (hPrevInstance == NULL) { // first instance of NOALPHA
                                // running

      // Register NOALPHA's main window's class
      if (!RegisterAppWndClass(hInstance))
         return(0);

      // Register the NOALPHA class. This is a superclass based on
      // the standard Window's EDIT control.
      if (!RegisterNoAlphaWndClass(hInstance))
         return(0);

      // Register two new window messages called "ValidRange" and
      // "SetRange." If these messages have been registered
      // before, Windows returns the same values that were
      // returned the first time these messages were registered.
      _ValidRangeMsg = RegisterWindowMessage("ValidRange");
      _SetRangeMsg = RegisterWindowMessage("SetRange");

   } else {       // Another instance of this application is running

      // Demonstrated here are two different ways of getting the
      // values of the two NOALPHA-specific messages:

      // Get the value associated with message "ValidRange."
      // Because this message has been previously registered,
      // Windows just returns the same value that was returned the
      // first time RegisterWindowMessage was called.
      _ValidRangeMsg = RegisterWindowMessage("ValidRange");
```

```
        // Get the value associated with the message "SetRange."
        // Because this is a global variable and another instance
        // of this application is running, we can use the
        // GetInstanceData function to retrieve the value for this
        // message.
        GetInstanceData(hPrevInstance, (NPSTR) &_ValidRangeMsg,
          sizeof(_ValidRangeMsg));
    }

    // Create NOALPHA's application window
    hWnd = CreateWindow(_szAppName, _szAppName,
       WS_OVERLAPPEDWINDOW, CW_USEDEFAULT, SW_SHOW,
       CW_USEDEFAULT, CW_USEDEFAULT, NULL, NULL, hInstance, 0);

    if (hWnd == NULL) return(0);
    ShowWindow(hWnd, cmdShow);
    UpdateWindow(hWnd);

    while (GetMessage(&msg, NULL, 0, 0)) {
       TranslateMessage(&msg);
       DispatchMessage(&msg);
    }
    return(0);
}


// ***************************************************************
// This function registers NOALPHA's application window
BOOL near pascal RegisterAppWndClass (HANDLE hInstance) {
    WNDCLASS WndClass;

    WndClass.style          = 0;
    WndClass.lpfnWndProc    = NoAlphaAppWndProc;
    WndClass.cbClsExtra     = 0;
    WndClass.cbWndExtra     = 0;
    WndClass.hInstance      = hInstance;
    WndClass.hIcon          = LoadIcon(hInstance, _szAppName);
    WndClass.hCursor        = LoadCursor(NULL, IDC_ARROW);
    WndClass.hbrBackground  = COLOR_WINDOW + 1;
    WndClass.lpszMenuName   = _szAppName;
```

```
   WndClass.lpszClassName = _szAppName;
   return(RegisterClass(&WndClass));
}


// ****************************************************************
// This function processes all messages sent to NOALPHA's
// application window

LONG FAR PASCAL NoAlphaAppWndProc (HWND hWnd, WORD wMsg,
      WORD wParam, LONG lParam) {
   BOOL fCallDefProc = FALSE;
   LONG lResult = 0;
   FARPROC fpDlgProc;

   switch (wMsg) {
      case WM_DESTROY:
         PostQuitMessage(0);
         break;

      case WM_COMMAND:
         switch (wParam) {
         case IDM_ABOUT:
            fpDlgProc = MakeProcInstance(AboutProc, _hInstance);
            DialogBox(_hInstance, "About", hWnd, fpDlgProc);
            FreeProcInstance(fpDlgProc);
            break;

         case IDM_DIALOGBOX:
            fpDlgProc = MakeProcInstance(DlgProc, _hInstance);
            DialogBox(_hInstance, "DlgBox", hWnd, fpDlgProc);
            FreeProcInstance(fpDlgProc);
            break;

         default:
            break;
         }
         break;

      default:
         fCallDefProc = TRUE; break;
   }
```

```
    if (fCallDefProc)
       lResult = DefWindowProc(hWnd, wMsg, wParam, lParam);

    return(lResult);
}

// ****************************************************************
// This function processes all messages sent to the About dialog
// box

BOOL FAR PASCAL AboutProc (HWND hDlg, WORD wMsg, WORD wParam,
       LONG lParam) {
    char szBuffer[100];
    BOOL fProcessed = TRUE;

    switch (wMsg) {

       case WM_INITDIALOG:
          // Set version static window to have date and time of
          // compilation
          wsprintf(szBuffer, "%s at %s", (LPSTR) __DATE__,
             (LPSTR) __TIME__);
          SetWindowText(GetDlgItem(hDlg, ID_VERSION), szBuffer);
          break;

       case WM_COMMAND:
          switch (wParam) {
             case IDOK:
             case IDCANCEL:
                if (HIWORD(lParam) == BN_CLICKED)
                   EndDialog(hDlg, wParam);
                break;

             default:
                break;
          }
          break;
```

```
      default:
         fProcessed = FALSE; break;
   }
   return(fProcessed);
}

// *************************************************************
// This function processes all messages sent to NOALPHA's dialog
// box

BOOL FAR PASCAL DlgProc (HWND hDlg, WORD wMsg, WORD wParam,
      LONG lParam) {
   BOOL fProcessed = TRUE, fInRange;

   switch (wMsg) {
      case WM_INITDIALOG:
         // Set valid range in both NOALPHA controls
         SendDlgItemMessage(hDlg, ID_NOALPHA1, _SetRangeMsg, 0,
            MAKELONG(100, 200));

         SendDlgItemMessage(hDlg, ID_NOALPHA2, _SetRangeMsg, 0,
            MAKELONG(-300, 100));
         break;

      case WM_COMMAND:
         switch (wParam) {
            case IDOK:
               if (HIWORD(lParam) != BN_CLICKED) break;

               // Send message to first NOALPHA control to see if
               // its value is in range
               fInRange = (BOOL)
                  SendDlgItemMessage(hDlg, ID_NOALPHA1,
                  _ValidRangeMsg, 0, 0l);

               if (!fInRange) {
                  // Display error message to user
                  MessageBox(hDlg, "Value is out of range.",
                     _szAppName, MB_OK);
```

```
                    // Set focus to NOALPHA control so user can
                    // change its value
                    SetFocus(GetDlgItem(hDlg, ID_NOALPHA1));
                     break;
                  }

                  // Send message to second NOALPHA control to see if
                  // its value is in range
                  fInRange = (BOOL)
                     SendDlgItemMessage(hDlg, ID_NOALPHA2,
                     _ValidRangeMsg, 0, 01);

                  if (!fInRange) {
                     // Display error message to user
                     MessageBox(hDlg, "Value is out of range.",
                        _szAppName, MB_OK);

                     // Set focus to NOALPHA control so user can
                     // change its value
                     SetFocus(GetDlgItem(hDlg, ID_NOALPHA2));
                      break;
                  }

                  EndDialog(hDlg, wParam);
                  break;

               case IDCANCEL:
                  EndDialog(hDlg, wParam);
                  break;
            }

      default:
         fProcessed = FALSE; break;
   }
   return(fProcessed);
}
```

```c
// ***************************************************************
// window words for the NOALPHA superclass
#define NOALPHA_CBCLSEXTRA (0)

#define NOALPHA_CBWNDEXTRA (4)
#define GSCWW_LOVALUE      (0)
#define GSCWW_HIVALUE      (2)

LONG FAR PASCAL NoAlphaWndProc (HWND hWnd, WORD wMsg, WORD wParam,
   LONG lParam);

// ***************************************************************
// This function registers the NOALPHA class. This is a
// superclassed class based on the standard Windows EDIT control.
BOOL near pascal RegisterNoAlphaWndClass (HANDLE hInstance) {
   WNDCLASS WndClass;

   // Retrieve current class information for EDIT system global
   // class
   GetClassInfo(NULL, "EDIT", &WndClass);

   // Our new class should have a new name
   WndClass.lpszClassName = "NoAlpha";
   WndClass.hInstance = hInstance;

   // The following WNDCLASS members are not changed for NOALPHA:
   // style, hIcon, hCursor, hbrBackground, lpszMenuName

   // Register the new window class
   return(RegisterSuperClass(
      &WndClass,              // address of WNDCLASS structure
      NoAlphaWndProc,         // address of superclass window proc
      NOALPHA_CBCLSEXTRA,     // number of additional class extra
                              // bytes
      NOALPHA_CBWNDEXTRA      // number of additional window extra
                              // bytes
      ));
}
```

```
// *************************************************************
// This function processes all messages sent to NOALPHA windows

LONG FAR PASCAL NoAlphaWndProc (HWND hWnd, WORD wMsg, WORD wParam,
     LONG lParam) {
   LONG lResult = 0L;
   BOOL fCallBaseClassWndProc = TRUE;
   char szValue[10];
   int nValue, nLoValue, nHiValue;

   // Check if message is the registered message: "SetRange"
   if (wMsg == _SetRangeMsg) {

      // Change window extra bytes to reflect new valid range
      SetSCWindowWord(hWnd, GSCWW_LOVALUE, LOWORD(lParam));
      SetSCWindowWord(hWnd, GSCWW_HIVALUE, HIWORD(lParam));

      // Message should not be passed to base class window
      // procedure
      fCallBaseClassWndProc = FALSE;
   }

   // Check if message is the registered message: "ValidRange"
   if (wMsg == _ValidRangeMsg) {

      // Get value in NOALPHA window
      GetWindowText(hWnd, szValue, sizeof(szValue));

      // Convert number to integer
      nValue = atoi(szValue);

      // Retrieve valid range from window extra bytes
      nLoValue = GetSCWindowWord(hWnd, GSCWW_LOVALUE);
      nHiValue = GetSCWindowWord(hWnd, GSCWW_HIVALUE);

      // Determine if user's value is within legal range
      lResult = (nLoValue <= nValue) && (nValue <= nHiValue);

      // Message should not be passed to base class window proc
      fCallBaseClassWndProc = FALSE;
   }
```

```
switch (wMsg) {
   case WM_NCCREATE:
      // Set the last eight class extra bytes to have
      // information about the base class
      SetSuperClassInfo(hWnd);
      break;

   case WM_CREATE:
      // By default, set valid range to -32767 to + 32767
      SetSCWindowWord(hWnd, GSCWW_LOVALUE, -32767);
      SetSCWindowWord(hWnd, GSCWW_HIVALUE, +32767);
      break;

   case WM_CHAR:
      // Prohibit message from being sent to base window
      // procedure if wParam is a letter
      if (wParam >= 'A' && wParam <= 'Z') fCallBaseClassWndProc
         = FALSE;
      if (wParam >= 'a' && wParam <= 'z') fCallBaseClassWndProc
         = FALSE;

      // If message is a letter, notify user that key is
      // illegal for a NOALPHA window by beeping
      if (fCallBaseClassWndProc == FALSE) MessageBeep(0);
      break;

   default:        // Pass other messages to base class window
      break;        // procedure

}

if (fCallBaseClassWndProc) {
   // Call the base class window procedure and return its
   // result to the caller
   lResult =
      CallWindowProc((FARPROC) GetBCWndProc(hWnd),
      hWnd, wMsg, wParam, lParam);
}

return(lResult);
}
```

Listing 2-9. NOALPHA.H application header module.

```
/*******************************************************************
Module name: NoAlpha.H
Programmer : Jeffrey M. Richter
*******************************************************************/

#include "dialog.h"

#define IDM_DIALOGBOX    (100)
#define IDM_ABOUT        (101)
```

Listing 2-10. NOALPHA.RC application resource file.

```
/*******************************************************************
Module name: NoAlpha.RC
Programmer : Jeffrey M. Richter
*******************************************************************/

#include <windows.h>

#include "noalpha.h"

#include "dialog.h"
#include "noalpha.dlg"

NoAlphaApp  ICON  MOVEABLE DISCARDABLE NoAlpha.Ico

NoAlphaApp MENU
BEGIN
   MENUITEM "See NoAlpha class...", IDM_DIALOGBOX
   MENUITEM "A&bout!", IDM_ABOUT
END
```

Listing 2-11. NOALPHA.DLG dialog-box templates.

```
DLGBOX DIALOG LOADONCALL MOVEABLE DISCARDABLE 8, 26, 152, 68
CAPTION "NoAlpha Edit Control Example"
```

```
STYLE WS_BORDER | WS_CAPTION | WS_DLGFRAME | WS_SYSMENU |
   WS_VISIBLE | WS_POPUP
BEGIN
   CONTROL "&Edit:", -1, "static", SS_LEFT | WS_CHILD, 4, 4, 32,
      12
   CONTROL "", ID_EDIT, "edit", ES_LEFT | WS_BORDER | WS_TABSTOP |
      WS_CHILD, 44, 4, 104, 12
   CONTROL "NoAlpha &1:", -1, "static", SS_LEFT | WS_CHILD, 4, 20,
      40, 12
   CONTROL "", ID_NOALPHA1, "noalpha", 0 | WS_BORDER | WS_TABSTOP
      | WS_CHILD, 44, 20, 104, 12
   CONTROL "NoAlpha &2:", -1, "static", SS_LEFT | WS_CHILD, 4, 36,
      40, 12
   CONTROL "", ID_NOALPHA2, "noalpha", 0 | WS_BORDER | WS_TABSTOP
      | WS_CHILD, 44, 36, 104, 12
   CONTROL "&Ok", IDOK, "button", BS_DEFPUSHBUTTON | WS_TABSTOP |
      WS_CHILD, 32, 52, 36, 12
   CONTROL "&Cancel", IDCANCEL, "button", BS_PUSHBUTTON |
      WS_TABSTOP | WS_CHILD, 84, 52, 36, 12
END

ABOUT DIALOG LOADONCALL MOVEABLE DISCARDABLE 16, 20, 126, 92
CAPTION "About NoAlpha"
STYLE WS_BORDER | WS_CAPTION | WS_DLGFRAME | WS_SYSMENU |
   WS_VISIBLE | WS_POPUP
BEGIN
   CONTROL "NoAlphaApp", -1, "static", SS_ICON | WS_CHILD, 4, 16,
      18, 21
   CONTROL "NoAlpha", -1, "static", SS_CENTER | WS_CHILD, 22, 8,
      100, 12
   CONTROL "Written by:", -1, "static", SS_CENTER | WS_CHILD, 22,
      20, 100, 12
   CONTROL "Jeffrey M. Richter", -1, "static", SS_CENTER |
      WS_CHILD, 22, 32, 100, 12
   CONTROL "Version date:", -1, "static", SS_CENTER | WS_CHILD,
      22, 48, 100, 12
   CONTROL "", ID_VERSION, "static", SS_CENTER | WS_CHILD, 22, 60,
      100, 12
   CONTROL "&OK", IDOK, "button", BS_DEFPUSHBUTTON | WS_TABSTOP |
      WS_CHILD, 40, 76, 44, 12
END
```

Listing 2-12. NOALPHA.DEF definitions file.

```
; Module name: NoAlpha.DEF
; Programmer : Jeffrey M. Richter

NAME            NoAlpha
DESCRIPTION     'NoAlpha: "EDIT" Superclass Application'
STUB            'WinStub.exe'
EXETYPE         WINDOWS
CODE            MOVEABLE DISCARDABLE PRELOAD
DATA            MOVEABLE MULTIPLE PRELOAD
HEAPSIZE        1024
STACKSIZE       4096
EXPORTS
    AboutProc
    DlgProc
    NoAlphaAppWndProc
    NoAlphaWndProc
```

Listing 2-13. DIALOG.H (dialog-box template defines).

```
#define ID_EDIT       (100)
#define ID_NOALPHA1   (101)
#define ID_NOALPHA2   (102)
#define ID_VERSION    (200)
```

Listing 2-14. MAKEFILE for NoAlpha application.

```
#*****************************************************************
#Module name: MAKEFILE
#Programmer : Jeffrey M. Richter
#*****************************************************************

PROG = NoAlpha
MODEL = S
CFLAGS = -A$(MODEL) -D_WINDOWS -Gcsw2 -W4 -Zlepid -Od
LFLAGS = /NOE/BA/A:16/M/CO/LI/F
```

132

```
LIBS = $(MODEL)libcew + libw

M1 = $(PROG).obj SuperCls.obj

ICONS = $(PROG).ico
BITMAPS =
CURSORS =
RESOURCES = $(ICONS) $(BITMAPS) $(CURSORS)

.SUFFIXES: .rc

.rc.res:
   rc -r $*.rc

$(PROG).Exe: $(M1) $(PROG).Def $(PROG).Res
   link $(LFLAGS) @<<$(PROG).lnk
$(M1)
$(PROG), $(PROG), $(LIBS), $(PROG)
<<
   rc $(PROG).Res

$(PROG).obj:    $*.c $*.h dialog.h SuperCls.h
SuperCls.obj:   $*.c $*.h

$(PROG).res:    $*.rc $*.h $*.dlg dialog.h $(RESOURCES)
```

Listing 2-15. SUPERCLS.C window superclassing source module.

```
/*******************************************************************
Module name: SuperCls.C
Programmer : Jeffrey M. Richter
*******************************************************************/

#include "..\nowindws.h"
#undef NOUSER
#undef NOWINOFFSETS
#include <windows.h>

#include "supercls.h"
```

```
// Offsets of base class values from the high end of the class
// extra bytes
#define BCWNDPROCINDEX    (sizeof(FARPROC))
#define CBBCCLSEXTRAINDEX (sizeof(FARPROC) + sizeof(int))
#define CBBCWNDEXTRAINDEX (sizeof(FARPROC) + sizeof(int) + \
   sizeof(int))

#define MINCBCLSADDTIONAL (sizeof(FARPROC) + sizeof(int) + \
   sizeof(int))

static LONG (FAR PASCAL *_lpfnBCWndProc)();
static int _cbBCClsExtra, _cbBCWndExtra;

BOOL FAR PASCAL RegisterSuperClass (LPWNDCLASS WndClass,
     LONG (FAR PASCAL *lpfnSCWndProc)(), int cbClsAdditional,
     int cbWndAdditional) {
  HWND hWnd;
  _lpfnBCWndProc = WndClass->lpfnWndProc;
  _cbBCClsExtra = WndClass->cbClsExtra;
  _cbBCWndExtra = WndClass->cbWndExtra;

  WndClass->cbClsExtra += cbClsAdditional + MINCBCLSADDTIONAL;
  WndClass->cbWndExtra += cbWndAdditional;
  WndClass->lpfnWndProc = lpfnSCWndProc;
  if (!RegisterClass(WndClass)) return(FALSE);
  hWnd = CreateWindow(WndClass->lpszClassName, "", 0, 0, 0, 0, 0,
     NULL, NULL, WndClass->hInstance, 0);

  if (hWnd == NULL) {
    UnregisterClass(WndClass->lpszClassName,
       WndClass->hInstance);
     return(FALSE);
  }

  DestroyWindow(hWnd);
  return(TRUE);
}
```

```
void FAR PASCAL SetSuperClassInfo (HWND hWnd) {
   WORD cbClsTotal = GetClassWord(hWnd, GCW_CBCLSEXTRA);
   DWORD dwBCWndProc = GetWindowLong(hWnd, cbClsTotal -
      BCWNDPROCINDEX);
   if (dwBCWndProc != NULL) return;
   SetClassLong(hWnd, cbClsTotal - BCWNDPROCINDEX,
      (LONG) _lpfnBCWndProc);
   SetClassWord(hWnd, cbClsTotal - CBBCCLSEXTRAINDEX,
      _cbBCClsExtra);
   SetClassWord(hWnd, cbClsTotal - CBBCWNDEXTRAINDEX,
      _cbBCWndExtra);
}


DWORD FAR PASCAL GetBCWndProc (HWND hWnd) {
   DWORD dwBCWndProc;
   int nIndex = GetClassWord(hWnd, GCW_CBCLSEXTRA) -
      BCWNDPROCINDEX;
   dwBCWndProc = GetClassLong(hWnd, nIndex);
   if (dwBCWndProc != NULL) return(dwBCWndProc);
   return((DWORD) _lpfnBCWndProc);
}


//********************************************************************
// Function used internally by the Get/SetClassWord/Long
// functions
static int NEAR PASCAL CalcClassByteIndex (HWND hWnd, int nIndex)
   {
   int cbBCClsExtraIndex, cbBCClsExtra;

   // If nIndex is negative, it points to internal window
   // memory block; same index should be returned
   if (nIndex < 0) return(nIndex);

   // Retrieve index into class extra bytes for the number of
   // class extra bytes used by the base class
   cbBCClsExtraIndex =
      GetClassWord(hWnd, GCW_CBCLSEXTRA) - CBBCCLSEXTRAINDEX;

   // Retrieve number of class extra bytes used by the base class
   cbBCClsExtra = GetClassWord(hWnd, cbBCClsExtraIndex);
```

```
   // Return desired index + number of class extra bytes used by
   // the base class
   return(nIndex + cbBCClsExtra);
}


// Function used internally by the Get/SetWindowWord/Long
// functions
static int NEAR PASCAL CalcWindowByteIndex (HWND hWnd, int nIndex)
   {
   int cbBCWndExtraIndex, cbBCWndExtra;

   // If nIndex is negative, it points to internal window
   // memory block; same index should be returned
   if (nIndex < 0) return(nIndex);

   // Retrieve index into class extra bytes for the number of
   // window extra bytes used by the base class
   cbBCWndExtraIndex =
      GetClassWord(hWnd, GCW_CBCLSEXTRA) - CBBCWNDEXTRAINDEX;

   // Retrieve number of window extra bytes used by the base class
   cbBCWndExtra = GetClassWord(hWnd, cbBCWndExtraIndex);

   // Return desired index + number of window extra bytes used by
   // the base class
   return(nIndex + cbBCWndExtra);
}


//******************************************************************
// The four Get/SetClassWord/Long functions

WORD FAR PASCAL SetSCClassWord (HWND hWnd, int nIndex,
      WORD wNewWord) {
   nIndex = CalcClassByteIndex(hWnd, nIndex);
   return(SetClassWord(hWnd, nIndex, wNewWord));
}

WORD FAR PASCAL GetSCClassWord (HWND hWnd, int nIndex) {
   nIndex = CalcClassByteIndex(hWnd, nIndex);
   return(GetClassWord(hWnd, nIndex));
}
```

```
DWORD FAR PASCAL SetSCClassLong (HWND hWnd, int nIndex,
      DWORD dwNewLong) {
   nIndex = CalcClassByteIndex(hWnd, nIndex);
   return(SetClassLong(hWnd, nIndex, dwNewLong));
}

DWORD FAR PASCAL GetSCClassLong (HWND hWnd, int nIndex) {
   nIndex = CalcClassByteIndex(hWnd, nIndex);
   return(GetClassLong(hWnd, nIndex));
}

//****************************************************************
// The four Get/SetWindowWord/Long functions

WORD FAR PASCAL SetSCWindowWord (HWND hWnd, int nIndex,
      WORD wNewWord) {
   nIndex = CalcWindowByteIndex(hWnd, nIndex);
   return(SetWindowWord(hWnd, nIndex, wNewWord));
}

WORD FAR PASCAL GetSCWindowWord (HWND hWnd, int nIndex) {
   nIndex = CalcWindowByteIndex(hWnd, nIndex);
   return(GetWindowWord(hWnd, nIndex));
}

DWORD FAR PASCAL SetSCWindowLong (HWND hWnd, int nIndex,
      DWORD dwNewLong) {
   nIndex = CalcWindowByteIndex(hWnd, nIndex);
   return(SetWindowLong(hWnd, nIndex, dwNewLong));
}

DWORD FAR PASCAL GetSCWindowLong (HWND hWnd, int nIndex) {
   nIndex = CalcWindowByteIndex(hWnd, nIndex);
   return(GetWindowLong(hWnd, nIndex));
}
```

Listing 2-16. SUPERCLS.H window superclassing header module.

```
/**************************************************************
Module name: SuperCls.h
Programmer : Jeffrey M. Richter
**************************************************************/

BOOL  FAR PASCAL RegisterSuperClass (LPWNDCLASS WndClass,
      LONG (FAR PASCAL *lpfpSCWndProc)(),
      int cbClsAdditional, int cbWndAdditional);

void  FAR PASCAL SetSuperClassInfo (HWND hWnd);

DWORD FAR PASCAL GetBCWndProc (HWND hWnd);

WORD  FAR PASCAL SetSCClassWord (HWND hWnd, int nIndex,
      WORD wNewWord);
WORD  FAR PASCAL GetSCClassWord (HWND hWnd, int nIndex);
DWORD FAR PASCAL SetSCClassLong (HWND hWnd, int nIndex,
      DWORD dwNewLong);
DWORD FAR PASCAL GetSCClassLong (HWND hWnd, int nIndex);

WORD  FAR PASCAL SetSCWindowWord (HWND hWnd, int nIndex,
      WORD wNewWord);
WORD  FAR PASCAL GetSCWindowWord (HWND hWnd, int nIndex);
DWORD FAR PASCAL GetSCWindowLong (HWND hWnd, int nIndex);
DWORD FAR PASCAL SetSCWindowLong (HWND hWnd, int nIndex,
      DWORD dwNewLong);
```

CHAPTER 3

Dialog-Box Techniques

Dialog boxes are a consistent, convenient way for applications to request information from the user. The dialog editor that comes with the Windows SDK makes it easy to design dialog boxes. It relieves the programmer of responsibility for many tedious details, such as calculating window locations for controls. The dialog editor can also be used by nonprogrammers, allowing much of the application's interface to be designed by other members of a design team.

The Voyeur application in Chapter 1 uses a dialog box to display information to the user. Much of the work was done by the dialog-box mechanism, and less by the application. Since the information fields were handled by the dialog mechanism, we can move them around to improve the application's appearance without rewriting any of the program code.

This chapter discusses various techniques for working with dialog boxes. Here's a brief preview of the dialog-box techniques we'll discuss:

- The *SetWindowPos* dialog box lets the programmer to create new controls and add them to a dialog box after it has been displayed. The programmer can also use this technique to alter the tab-stop order of the controls.

- The Options >> dialog box seems to be appearing more and more often in commercial applications. It presents a dialog box to the user, but some of the controls are not shown. When the "Options >>" button is selected, the dialog box expands and the user gains access to the remaining controls. For an example of this type of dialog box, open the Windows Control Panel application and select Printers. In the Printers dialog box is a button marked "Add Printer >>." If this button is pressed, the dialog box expands to include the controls necessary to add printers to the Windows environment.

- The *modalless* dialog box is a cross between a modal dialog box and a modeless dialog box. It allows the programmer to display what appears to be a modal dialog box to the user. However, when the user closes the dialog box, the box is not destroyed...and neither are the settings the user selected. This lets the programmer retrieve the settings via standard Windows Applications Programming Interface (API) functions.

- The *dynamic* dialog box allows the programmer to create a dialog-box template at run time. This is useful for database applications and applications similar to the SDK's Dialog Editor.

All the techniques discussed in this chapter are demonstrated by the dialog-techniques application, DLGTECH.EXE. This application consists of four C modules. The first, DLGTECH.C, contains the *WinMain* function, initialization code for the application, and the window procedure for the main window. The dialog-box function demonstrating the *SetWindowPos* technique is also contained in DLGTECH.C.

The remaining source files contain dialog-box functions as well as functions necessary for supporting the demonstrated technique. A header file also exists for each file. The header file contains all the prototypes for the support functions. The following are the techniques and the files in which they're implemented:

The Options >> technique: DLG-OPTS.C and DLG-OPTS.H
The modalless dialog-box technique: DLG-MDLS.C and DLG-MDLS.H
The dynamic dialog-box technique: DLG-DYNA.C and DLG-DYNA.H

The *SetWindowPos* Dialog Box

The window manager maintains an internal list of every existing window. When the dialog-box manager creates child controls, they are inserted one by one into the list. For operations that affect the windows of a dialog box, Windows consults the list. If the dialog box is hidden, for example, all of its children are likewise hidden. The same is true if the dialog box is destroyed.

When the user presses the Tab key within a dialog box, Windows searches through the window manager's list for children of the dialog box, locates the child that has focus, and searches forward for the next child window that has the *WS_TABSTOP* style set. Change the order of the windows in the window manager's list and you've changed the tab-stop order.

Figure 3-1 shows the dialog box for the *SetWindowPos* example.

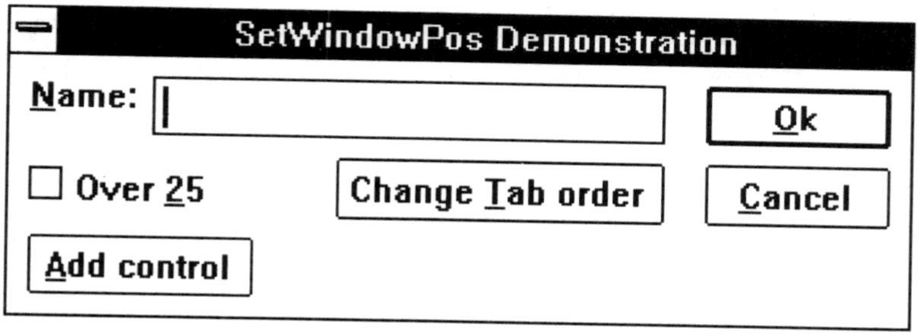

Figure 3-1. The *SetWindowPos* dialog box.

This dialog box is created from the following template (from the file DLGTECH.DLG):

```
SETWINDOWPOS DIALOG LOADONCALL MOVEABLE DISCARDABLE 8, 29, 176, 52
CAPTION "SetWindowPos Demonstration"
STYLE WS_BORDER | WS_CAPTION | WS_DLGFRAME | WS_SYSMENU | WS_POPUP
BEGIN
    CONTROL "&Name:", ID_NAMETEXT, "static", SS_LEFT | WS_CHILD,
        4, 4, 24, 8
```

```
CONTROL "", ID_NAME, "edit", ES_LEFT | WS_BORDER | WS_GROUP |
    WS_TABSTOP | WS_CHILD, 28, 4, 100, 12
CONTROL "Over &25", ID_OVER25, "button", BS_AUTOCHECKBOX |
    WS_GROUP | WS_TABSTOP | WS_CHILD, 4, 20, 40, 12
CONTROL "Change &Tab order", ID_CHANGETABORDER, "button",
    BS_PUSHBUTTON | WS_GROUP | WS_TABSTOP | WS_CHILD, 64,
    20, 64, 12
CONTROL "&Add control", ID_ADDCONTROL, "button", BS_PUSHBUTTON
    | WS_GROUP | WS_TABSTOP | WS_CHILD, 4, 36, 44, 12
CONTROL "&Ok", IDOK, "button", BS_DEFPUSHBUTTON | WS_GROUP |
    WS_TABSTOP | WS_CHILD, 136, 4, 36, 12
CONTROL "&Cancel", IDCANCEL, "button", BS_PUSHBUTTON | WS_GROUP
    | WS_TABSTOP | WS_CHILD, 136, 20, 36, 12
END
```

Because Windows creates the controls in the order in which they are listed in the template, pressing the Tab key while the EDIT control has focus will shift the focus to the "Over 25" CHECKBOX control. The following code, taken from the *SWPDlgProc* function in DLGTECH.C, shows how *SetWindowPos* can alter the sequence of these controls. It executes when the user selects the "Change Tab order" button.

```
case ID_CHANGETABORDER:
   if (HIWORD(lParam) != BN_CLICKED)
      break;

   SetWindowPos(GetDlgItem(hDlg, ID_OVER25),
      GetDlgItem(hDlg, ID_NAMETEXT),
      0, 0, 0, 0, SWP_NOMOVE | SWP_NOSIZE);

   SetWindowPos(GetDlgItem(hDlg, ID_NAMETEXT),
      GetDlgItem(hDlg, ID_OVER25),
      0, 0, 0, 0, SWP_NOMOVE | SWP_NOSIZE);

   SetFocus(GetNextDlgTabItem(hDlg, LOWORD(lParam), 0));
   EnableWindow(LOWORD(lParam), FALSE);
   break;
```

In the window manager's list, the controls are in the following order (by ID): *ID_NAMETEXT*, *ID_NAME*, *ID_OVER25*. The first call to *SetWindowPos* changes this order so that the control identified by *ID_OVER25* is placed after the control identified by *ID_NAMETEXT*, resulting in a new tab order: *ID_NAMETEXT*, *ID_OVER25*, *ID_NAME*. The second call to *SetWindowPos* places the control identified by *ID_NAMETEXT* after the control identified by *ID_OVER25*. The final order is *ID_OVER25*, *ID_NAMETEXT*, *ID_NAME*. Pressing the Tab key while the "Over 25" check box has focus will shift the focus to the EDIT control.

The "Change Tab order" button was the last control to have focus. We should set the focus to some other control in the dialog box by calling the *SetFocus* function. The call to *GetNextDlgTabItem* tells Windows to search through the window manager's list and find the next (or previous) control that has the *WS_TABSTOP* style.

The *Windows Programmer's Reference* states that *GetNextDlgTabItem* searches for the previous control if the third parameter is zero and the next control if this parameter is nonzero. This is incorrect; the description of the third parameter is backwards. To search for the next control with the *WS_TABSTOP* style, the third parameter must be zero.

Finally, the code disables the "Change Tab order" button so that the user cannot select this option again.

You might be thinking that this is a cute thing to know but really isn't useful. I agree. But by building on this concept, we can dynamically add controls to a dialog box after it has been created. When the "Add control" button is pressed, the following code in the *SWPDlgProc* function executes:

```
case ID_ADDCONTROL:
   if (HIWORD(lParam) != BN_CLICKED)
      break;
```

```
wDlgWidth = LOWORD(GetDialogBaseUnits());
wDlgHeight = HIWORD(GetDialogBaseUnits());

hWndControl = CreateWindow("scrollbar", "",
    SBS_HORZ | WS_CHILD | WS_TABSTOP | WS_GROUP,
    (64 * wDlgWidth) / 4, (36 * wDlgHeight) / 8,
    (64 * wDlgWidth) / 4, (12 * wDlgHeight) / 8,
    hDlg, ID_SCROLLBAR, _hInstance, 0);

SetWindowPos(hWndControl, LOWORD(lParam),
    0, 0, 0, 0, SWP_NOMOVE | SWP_NOSIZE | SWP_SHOWWINDOW);

SetFocus(GetNextDlgTabItem(hDlg, LOWORD(lParam), 0));

EnableWindow(LOWORD(lParam), FALSE);
break;
```

Here's how it works:

First, we retrieve the number of pixels used for the horizontal and vertical dialog units using the *GetDialogBaseUnits* function.

Next, we create a new control with *CreateWindow*. The style parameter should have the same values that the dialog editor would have used. For example, the *WS_CHILD* style must be specified. If the control is to be a tab stop, specify the *WS_TABSTOP* style.

The top left coordinate for the control is relative to the top left corner of the dialog box's client area. *CreateWindow* expects the window's coordinates in screen units. To convert the dialog-box units into screen units, we modify the results of *GetDialogBaseUnits* as shown in the listing.

The control's parent window is the handle to the dialog box. When you create a child control with the *CreateWindow* function, the parameter after the parent window is the ID value that the child should have. After the child control has been

144

created, the window is inserted into the window manager's list using the *SetWindow-Pos* function. Remember that the placement of the control affects how the Tab key changes the order in which controls gain focus.

Because the "Add control" button received focus when the user selected it, we must change the focus to another control. This button is also disabled in this demonstration so that the user cannot select it again.

The Options Dialog Box

Any new application involves a learning curve for the user. To help a user learn, the application can initially "hide" some of its functionality. Then, as the user becomes more adept, the program can reveal its advanced features. Many modern applications offer this kind of handholding.

For example, Microsoft Word for Windows and Microsoft Excel offer "Short Menus" and "Full Menus" options. The "Short Menus" option hides some of the advanced features from the user. When the user is more confident and familiar with the program, the "Full Menus" option is ready to allow full access to the program's features.

This feature tiering can also be applied to dialog boxes. When the user selects the "Print..." option from the File menu in Word for Windows, the dialog box in Figure 3-2 appears.

This dialog box displays everything most users may ever need to print documents. When the user has advanced and needs to do some fine-tuning, Word for Windows allows easy access to additional printing options via the "Options >>" button. When this button is selected, the dialog box expands to show the remaining options (Figure 3-3).

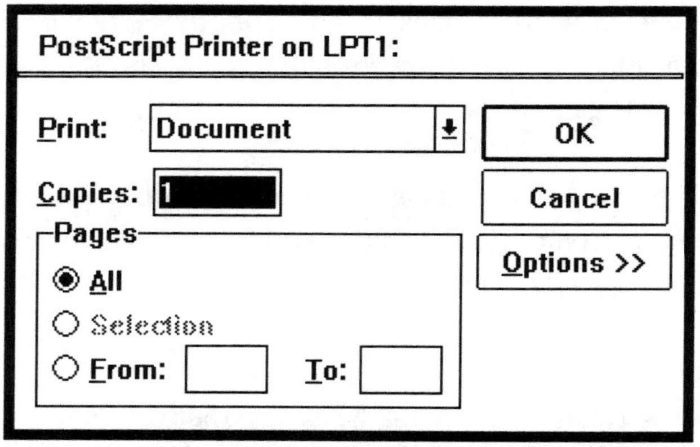

```
┌─────────────────────────────────────────────────┐
│  ┌────────────────────────────────────────────┐  │
│  │ PostScript Printer on LPT1:                │  │
│  ├────────────────────────────────────────────┤  │
│  │                                            │  │
│  │ Print:   ┌─────────────────┬───┐  ┌──────┐ │  │
│  │          │ Document        │ ↓ │  │  OK  │ │  │
│  │          └─────────────────┴───┘  └──────┘ │  │
│  │ Copies: ┌────────────┐             ┌──────┐ │  │
│  │         │ 1          │             │Cancel│ │  │
│  │ ┌Pages──┴────────────┘             └──────┘ │  │
│  │ │                                 ┌────────┐│  │
│  │ │ ◉ All                           │Options>>││  │
│  │ │ ○ Selection                     └────────┘│  │
│  │ │ ○ From: ┌──────┐   To: ┌──────┐           │  │
│  │ │         └──────┘       └──────┘           │  │
│  └────────────────────────────────────────────┘  │
└─────────────────────────────────────────────────┘
```

Figure 3-2. Word for Windows printer dialog box before "Options >>" button is pressed.

The next few pages describe how to implement a dialog box that contains this type of functionality. The source code for this example can be found in DLG-OPTS.C and DLG-OPTS.H (presented at the end of this chapter).

Designing the Dialog Box. The first step is to design the dialog box using the Dialog Editor supplied with the Windows SDK. Create the dialog box so that it contains all the controls. The upper left portion of the dialog box should contain the controls that will always be displayed. This is called the *default area* because it is the part of the dialog box that is always shown by default.

Once the entire dialog box has been laid out, add a STATIC control called the *default area control*. Change the style of this control so that it is a black rectangle. This will allow you to identify it easily while you work with the dialog box. The identifier assigned to this control will be used by the functions contained in the DLG-OPTS.C file and therefore must be unique.

Position the default area control so that its lower right corner is where you want the lower right corner of the default area to be. Figure 3-4 shows the final dialog box.

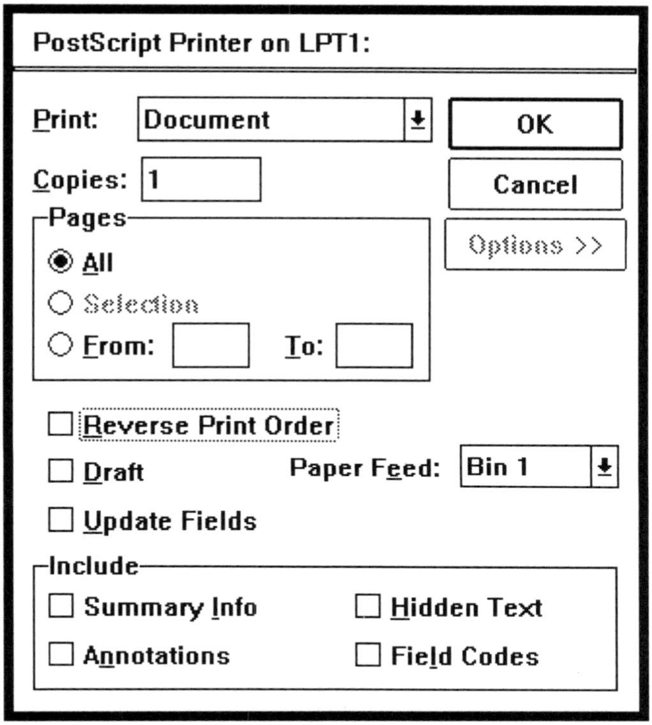

PostScript Printer on LPT1:

Print: | Document | [▼]   OK

Copies: | 1 | Cancel

Pages
◉ All   Options >>
○ Selection
○ From: [   ]   To: [   ]

☐ Reverse Print Order
☐ Draft   Paper Feed: | Bin 1 | [▼]
☐ Update Fields

Include
☐ Summary Info   ☐ Hidden Text
☐ Annotations   ☐ Field Codes

Figure 3-3. Word for Windows dialog box after "Options >>" button is pressed.

The Dialog-Box Function. The function that processes this dialog box is called *OptionsDlgProc.* It can be found in DLGTECH.C. The code is shown below:

```
BOOL FAR PASCAL OptionsDlgProc (HWND hDlg, WORD wMsg, WORD wParam,
    LONG lParam) {
  BOOL fProcessed = TRUE;

  switch (wMsg) {

    case WM_INITDIALOG:
      ShowArea(TRUE, hDlg, GetDlgItem(hDlg, ID_DEFAULTBOX));
      break;
```

```
    case WM_COMMAND:

        switch (wParam) {
            case IDOK:
            case IDCANCEL:
                EndDialog(hDlg, wParam);
                break;


            case ID_OPTIONS:
                if (HIWORD(lParam) != BN_CLICKED)
                    break;

                ShowArea(FALSE, hDlg, GetDlgItem(hDlg,
                    ID_DEFAULTBOX));

                // The ShowArea(FALSE, ...) function enables all
                // windows outside the "default" area. Any windows
                // that should be disabled must be explicitly
                // disabled here. Note that the status of the win-
                // dows within the default area is NOT changed.

                SetFocus(GetNextDlgTabItem(hDlg,
                    LOWORD(lParam), 0));
                EnableWindow(LOWORD(lParam), FALSE);
                break;

            default:
                fProcessed = FALSE;
                break;
        }
        break;

    default:
        fProcessed = FALSE;
        break;
    }
    return(fProcessed);
}
```

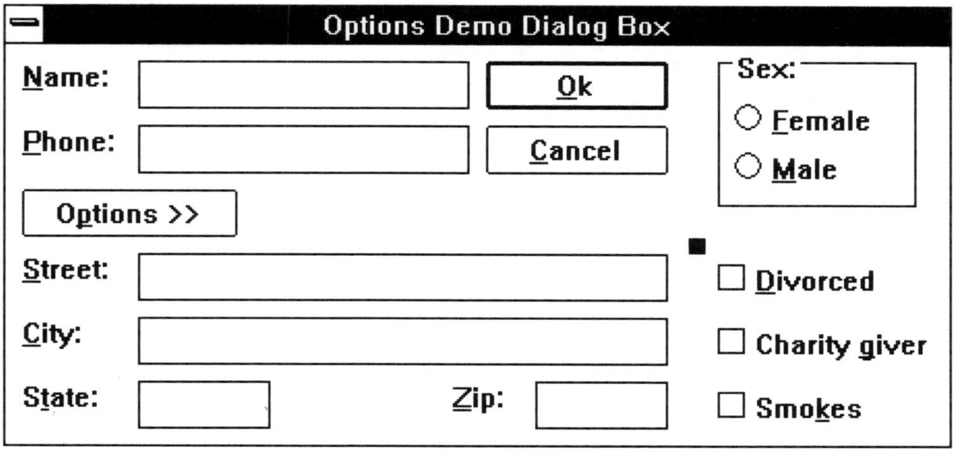

Figure 3-4. Options Demo dialog box.

When *OptionsDlgProc* receives the *WM_INITDIALOG* message, all the child controls have been created but the dialog box has not yet been displayed. Here's the prototype for the *ShowArea* function:

```
void FAR PASCAL ShowArea (BOOL fShowDefAreaOnly, HWND hDlg,
    HWND hWndDefArea);
```

When we call *ShowArea* and pass TRUE as the first parameter, the dialog box is shrunk so that its lower right corner is the same as the lower right corner of the default area control. *ShowArea* disables all the controls that appear to the right of or below the default area control. This function also hides the default area control so the black rectangle is not visible to the user.

When the user presses the Tab key, Windows sets the window focus to the next enabled control that has the *WS_TABSTOP* style. Although shrinking the dialog box clips the controls beyond the default area, they are still enabled. A clipped control could get focus, but the user would not be able to see it. By disabling these controls, *ShowArea* ensures that the Tab key will allow the user to traverse only the controls in the default area.

This time, *ShowArea* is called when the user selects the "Options >>" button with the first parameter set to FALSE. The function restores the dialog box to its original size and enables the controls outside the default area, allowing the user to access them by pressing the Tab key. Of course, the user may also select these controls with the mouse.

Sometimes you will want some of the controls to remain disabled. *ShowArea* cannot determine which specific controls you may want to enable or disable. For this reason, you must explicitly disable any controls in the options area after the call to *ShowArea*.

Once the additional controls are available to the user, focus is set to the next control after the "Options >>" button; the button is then disabled so it cannot be selected again.

The *ShowArea* Function. The main purpose of *ShowArea* is to expand or shrink the dialog box. If the *fShowDefAreaOnly* parameter is TRUE, the dialog box is shrunk. If *fShowDefAreaOnly* is FALSE, the dialog box is expanded to show all of its controls.

When the dialog box is shrunk, all the controls outside the default area control must be disabled. This is done by calling *EnumChildWindows*:

```
#define ENABLECHILDREN    (0x80000000L)
#define DISABLECHILDREN   (0x00000000L)
 .
 .
 .
GetWindowRect(hWndDefArea, &rcDefArea);

fpProc = MakeProcInstance(EnableChildrenInOptionArea, _hInstance);
EnumChildWindows(hDlg, fpProc,
   (fShowDefAreaOnly ? DISABLECHILDREN : ENABLECHILDREN) |
   MAKELONG(rcDefArea.right, rcDefArea.bottom));
FreeProcInstance(fpProc);
```

The first parameter is the handle of the dialog box whose children are to be enumerated, and the second parameter is the procedural instance of the *Enable-ChildrenInOptionArea* function. The last parameter is a long value. The low word contains the coordinate of the right edge of the default area control, and the high word contains the coordinate of the bottom edge. We can tell *EnableChildrenInOptionArea* whether to enable or disable the controls by setting the high bit of this long. If the high bit is one, the controls should be enabled.

When *ShowArea* is called via the *WM_INITDIALOG* message, the dialog box has been created (though not displayed) full size. The original width and height of the dialog box must be saved so that it can be restored to this size later. It would be convenient if we could use the window extra bytes associated with the dialog box, but—because we do not know how these bytes are used—they should not be altered. However, we can convert the width and height values to a string and then save the contents of the string in the default area control. Here's the code that does the job:

```
// Turns a style ON for a window
#define SetWindowStyle(hWnd, Style) \
    SetWindowLong(hWnd, GWL_STYLE, Style | \
    GetWindowLong(hWnd, GWL_STYLE));

// Turns a style OFF for a window
#define ResetWindowStyle(hWnd, Style) \
    SetWindowLong(hWnd, GWL_STYLE, ~Style & \
    GetWindowLong(hWnd, GWL_STYLE));
     .
     .
     .
wsprintf(szDlgDims, "%05u %05u",
    rcDlg.right - rcDlg.left, rcDlg.bottom - rcDlg.top);

ResetWindowStyle(hWndDefArea, SS_BLACKRECT);
SetWindowStyle(hWndDefArea, SS_LEFT);
SetWindowText(hWndDefArea, szDlgDims);
```

Since the default area control is not visible, it will not display the information it contains. The *ResetWindowStyle* and *SetWindowStyle* macros turn off the *SS_BLACKRECT* style and turn on the *SS_LEFT* style of this control. If this were not done, the default window control would ignore the *SetWindowText* call.

After the width and height are saved, the dialog box is resized:

```
SetWindowPos(hDlg, NULL, 0, 0,
    rcDefArea.right - rcDlg.left, rcDefArea.bottom - rcDlg.top,
    SWP_NOZORDER | SWP_NOMOVE);
```

and the default area control is hidden:

```
ShowWindow(hWndDefArea, SW_HIDE);
```

When *ShowArea* is called upon receipt of a *BN_CLICKED* notification from the "Options >>" button, the controls outside the dialog box must be enabled and the dialog box restored to its full size. The controls are enabled using the code explained above. Here's how the dialog box is restored to its full size:

```
GetWindowText(hWndDefArea, szDlgDims, sizeof(szDlgDims));

SetWindowPos(hDlg, NULL, 0, 0,
    atoi(szDlgDims), atoi(szDlgDims + 6),
    SWP_NOZORDER | SWP_NOMOVE);
```

First, the text associated with the default area control is retrieved. Remember, this string was set during processing of the *WM_INITDIALOG* message. It contains the width and height of the full-size dialog box. The numbers in the string must be converted to integers using *atoi*.

The *EnableChildrenInOptionArea* function is called once for each child control in the dialog box. Here's the code to do that:

152

```
#define ENABLECHILDREN      (0x80000000L)
.
.
.
BOOL FAR PASCAL EnableChildrenInOptionArea (HWND hWnd,
     LONG lParam) {
  RECT rc;
  BOOL fEnable = (lParam & ENABLECHILDREN) != 0;
  lParam &= ~ENABLECHILDREN;

  GetWindowRect(hWnd, &rc);

  if ((rc.right >= (int) LOWORD(lParam)) || (rc.bottom >=
     (int) HIWORD(lParam)))
     EnableWindow(hWnd, fEnable);

  return(1);
}
```

This function can determine whether the child controls should be enabled or disabled by checking the high bit of the *lParam* parameter. If the high bit is 1, the child controls should be enabled. Once this has been determined, the high bit is set to zero and the *lParam* parameter contains the lower right coordinate of the default area control.

If the control being enumerated has a right edge greater than the default area control's right edge or a bottom edge greater than or equal to the default area control's bottom edge, the control status is changed.

Finally, this function returns 1 so Windows will continue to enumerate all the child controls.

Modalless Dialog Boxes

Modal dialog boxes are used to request additional information from a user before continuing with an action. When the dialog box is displayed, the user fills in the required information. The user selects the "Ok" button, the dialog box is destroyed, and the user's settings are lost. Most Windows programs save the user's settings in global variables when the "Ok" button is selected.

Windows 3.0 offers the new *DialogBoxParam* and *DialogBoxIndirectParam* functions that can be used to pass the address of a memory block to the dialog-box procedure. The dialog procedure can use this memory block to save the user's settings when the "Ok" button is selected. Since this address is sent to the dialog-box procedure only during the processing of the *WM_INITDIALOG* message, the procedure must somehow save this value.

This section describes a type of dialog box called a *modalless* dialog box. To Windows, this is a modeless dialog box. To the user, it operates like a modal dialog box. To the programmer, it is created and destroyed like a modeless dialog but is displayed and hidden like a modal dialog box.

Because the dialog box is modeless, it exists even when it is not displayed. This allows the application to use Windows API functions to set and retrieve data from the controls in the dialog box.

Working with Modalless Dialog Boxes. Modalless dialog boxes are created by calling the *CreateModalLessDlgBox* function in the DLG-MDLS.C file. During processing of the *WM_CREATE* message in the *AppWndProc* function, the modalless dialog box is created:

```
_hDlgModalLess = CreateModalLessDlgBox(_hInstance, "Modalless",
    hWnd, MakeProcInstance(ModalLessDemoProc, _hInstance), 0);
if (_hDlgModalLess == NULL) {
    MessageBox(hWnd, "Can't create modalless dialog box.",
        _szAppName, MB_OK);
```

```
EnableMenuItem(GetMenu(hWnd), IDM_MODALLESSDEMO, MF_BYCOMMAND |
    MF_GRAYED);
}
break;
```

If the modalless dialog box cannot be created, the application displays a notice to the user and disables the menu item that activates the modalless dialog box demonstration.

The modalless dialog box is destroyed when the *AppWndProc* function processes the *WM_CLOSE* message:

```
if (_hDlgModalLess)
  DestroyModalLessDlgBox(_hDlgModalLess);
fCallDefProc = TRUE;
break;
```

Notice that the *fCallDefProc* variable must be set to TRUE so that the standard processing for *WM_CLOSE* is performed.

Once a modalless dialog box is created, the functions that access it are similar to those for modal dialog boxes. Below is a table showing the modal dialog-box functions and their equivalent modalless dialog-box functions.

Action	Modal Dialog-Box Function	Modalless Dialog-Box Function
Display dialog box	*DialogBox*	*ModalLessDlgBox*
	DialogBoxParam	*ModalLessDlgBox*
Terminate dialog-box usage	*EndDialog*	*EndModalLessDlgBox*

When the application wants the modalless dialog box to be displayed, the *ModalLessDlgBox* function is called:

```
nResult = ModalLessDlgBox(_hDlgModalLess, hWnd, 0);
```

This function requires the window handle to the modalless dialog box, the window handle to the window that is to be disabled, and a long data value. The long value may contain any value the application would like to pass to the modalless dialog box just before the box is displayed. This function will not return to the caller until the modalless dialog-box function has called the *EndModalLessDlgBox* function.

Here's a dialog-box procedure that demonstrates the use of modalless dialog boxes:

```
BOOL FAR PASCAL ModalLessDlgProc (HWND hDlg, WORD wMsg,
    WORD wParam, LONG lParam) {
  BOOL fProcessed = TRUE;

  if (wMsg == RegisterWindowMessage(SZMODALLESSSHOWMSG)) {
    // lParam is the data value passed to ModalLessDlgBox
    // function
    SetDlgItemText(hDlg, ID_NAME, "Default text");
    SetFocus(GetDlgItem(hDlg, ID_NAME));
  }

  switch (wMsg) {
    case WM_INITDIALOG:
      break;

    case WM_COMMAND:
      switch (wParam) {
        case IDOK:
        case IDCANCEL:
          if (HIWORD(lParam) == BN_CLICKED)
            EndModalLessDlgBox(hDlg, wParam);
          break;

        default:
          break;
      }
      break;
```

```
    default:
        fProcessed = FALSE;
        break;
    }
  return(fProcessed);
}
```

When the dialog box is created with *CreateModalLessDlgBox*, a *WM_INIT-DIALOG* message is sent to the dialog-box procedure. This is when any one-time initialization should be performed on the dialog box. Just before the dialog box is displayed (called by the *ModalLessDlgBox* function) it receives a message. This message is represented by the ASCII string defined in the DLG-MDLS.H file *SZMODALLESSSHOWMSG*. This is defined as "*ModalLessShowMsg.*"

When the modalless dialog-box procedure receives a message, it first checks to see if the message is *SZMODALLESSSHOWMSG*. If it is, the necessary actions are performed to prepare the dialog box for display. In our example, default text is placed in the EDIT control, and this control receives the input focus.

EndModalLessDlgBox removes the dialog box from the screen and returns control to the calling application. The first parameter is the handle of the dialog box; the second is the value to be returned to the caller of the *ModalLessDlgBox* function. This function is similar to the *EndDialog* function for modal dialog boxes.

How Modalless Dialog Boxes Work. The DLG-MDLS.H file contains proto-types for all the functions defined in DLG-MDLS.C that may be called from your application. The macro *SZMODALLESSSHOWMSG* is also defined. This message notifies the dialog-box procedure when the dialog box is about to be shown. The functions in DLG-MDLS.C are described below:

- *CreateModalLessDlgBox* creates a modeless dialog box and returns its window handle. It is simply a call to *CreateDialogParam*.

157

- *DestroyModalLessDlgBox* destroys the modeless dialog box created by *CreateModalLessDlgBox*. It is simply a call to *DestroyWindow*.

- *ModalLessDlgBox* displays a modalless dialog box to the user. Like the *DialogBox* and *DialogBoxParam* functions for modal dialog boxes, this function will not return until the modalless dialog box has been closed by a call to *EndModalLessDlgBox* (described later).

The *ModalLessDlgBox* function requires the handle to the modalless dialog box (created via a call to the *CreateModalLessDlgBox* function), the handle of the window to be disabled when this dialog box appears, and a long value that is passed during the *SZMODALLESSSHOWMSG* message loop.

After this function disables the window defined in the second parameter, the *SZMODALLESSSHOWMSG* message is sent to the dialog-box procedure and the dialog box is made visible:

```
nModalLessShowMsg = RegisterWindowMessage(SZMODALLESSSHOWMSG);
SendMessage(hDlg, nModalLessShowMsg, 0, lParam);
ShowWindow(hDlg, SW_SHOW);
```

A message loop must be initiated so control does not immediately return to the calling application:

```
while (!fPropFound) {
   GetMessage(&msg, NULL, 0, 0);
      if (!IsDialogMessage(hDlg, &msg)) {
         TranslateMessage(&msg);
         DispatchMessage(&msg);
      }
   }
   nResult = GetProp(hDlg, _szModalLessResult);
   fPropFound = RemoveProp(hDlg, _szModalLessResult) != NULL;
}
```

A modalless dialog box returns a result by calling *EndModalLessDlgBox*. This function associates a window property with the dialog box. During the message loop, the *GetProp* function is called to see if *EndModalLessDlgBox* has been called. If the value returned by *GetProp* is zero, it means that the property has not yet been associated with the window or that the *nResult* parameter to the *EndModalLessDlgBox* function was zero. We can determine which of these cases it was by calling the *RemoveProp* function. If this function is unable to remove a property with the specified name, NULL is returned. This means that the message loop should not terminate.

If the property was removed, the message loop terminates, the disabled window is enabled, the modalless dialog box is hidden, and the result from the *GetProp* function is returned to the application:

```
EnableWindow(hWndParent, TRUE);
ShowWindow(hDlg, SW_HIDE);
return(nResult);
```

The final function, *EndModalLessDlgBox*, is called from the modalless dialog-box function when the dialog box is to be removed from the screen. The parameters are identical to the parameters for *EndDialog*. Associating the window property with the dialog box notifies the message loop in *ModalLessDlgBox* that *EndModalLessDlgBox* has been called:

```
return(SetProp(hDlg, _szModalLessResult, nResult));
```

However, an attempt to set a property can fail. The return value is zero if the property could not be associated. This means that the dialog cannot be terminated.

Dynamic Dialog Boxes

Sometimes it is necessary to design dialog boxes while the application is running. For example, a database application may allow the user to design the entry form and then create a dialog box based on this form for adding records to the database.

Windows offers four functions for creating dialog boxes at run time. *DialogBoxIndirect* and *DialogBoxIndirectParam* create modal dialog boxes, while *CreateDialogIndirect* and *CreateDialogIndirectParam* create modeless dialog boxes. Dynamic dialog boxes are created by building a dialog template in a global memory block and passing this memory block to one of the functions.

Volume 2 of the *Windows Programmer's Reference* describes the three data structures necessary for building dialog-box templates in memory: *DLGTEMPLATE*, *FONTINFO*, and *DLGITEMTEMPLATE*. If you search through the WINDOWS.H file, you won't find any of these structures defined; you must define them yourself. All these structures consist of a fixed portion at the beginning and a variable-length portion at the end. While this method conserves memory, it makes dialog-box templates much more difficult to create.

The first data structure, *DLGTEMPLATE*, holds information that applies to the entire dialog box. This structure must appear at the beginning of the memory block in the following format:

```
typedef struct {
    long dtStyle;
    BYTE dtItemCount;
    int dtX;
    int dtY;
    int dtCX;
    int dtCY;
    // char dtMenuName[];        // variable-length string
    // char dtClassName[];       // variable-length string
    // char dtCaptionText[];     // variable-length string
} DLGTEMPLATE, FAR *LPDLGTEMPLATE;
```

The fixed elements of this data structure describe the dialog box's style, number of controls, position, and dimensions. The variable-length portion of the data structure describes the dialog box's menu name, class name, and caption text. Each of these fields is a zero-terminated string.

The second data structure is *FONTINFO,* which specifies the font Windows should use when drawing text in the dialog box. If the *DS_SETFONT* style is specified in the *DLGTEMPLATE* structure, then the *FONTINFO* structure must appear immediately after *DLGTEMPLATE* in memory. If *DS_SETFONT* is not specified, *FONTINFO* should not appear in the memory block at all. This structure has the following format:

```
typedef struct {
   short int PointSize;
   // char szTypeFace[];          // variable-length string
} FONTINFO, FAR *LPFONTINFO;
```

The fixed element of this data structure is the point size of the font specified in the variable-length part. The typeface name must specify a font that was previously loaded via WIN.INI or the *LoadFont* function.

The third data structure is *DLGITEMTEMPLATE.* This structure must appear for every control that will appear in the dialog-box template. This is the number specified in the *dtItemCount* member of the *DLGTEMPLATE* structure. The first of these structures appears immediately after the *FONTINFO* structure (or after the *DLGTEMPLATE* structure if the *DS_SETFONT* style is not specified). The *DLGITEMTEMPLATE* structure has the following format:

```
typedef struct {
   int dtilX;
   int dtilY;
   int dtilCX;
   int dtilCY;
   int dtilID;
   long dtilStyle;
   // char dtilClass[];     // variable-length string
   // char dtilText[];      // variable-length string
   // BYTE dtilInfo;        // # of bytes in following memory block
   // PTR dtilData;         // variable-length memory block
} DLGITEMTEMPLATE, FAR *LPDLGITEMTEMPLATE;
```

The fixed elements of this structure contain each control's position, dimensions, ID value, and styles. The variable-length elements are zero-terminated strings that hold the control's class name and window text.

The next byte, *dtilInfo*, specifies the number of bytes in the remaining field, *dtilData*. The *dtilData* field is a variable-length block of bytes. When Windows creates the control specified by this *DLGITEMTEMPLATE* structure, it calls the *CreateWindow* function and passes the address to the *dtilData* memory block in the last parameter. The window procedure for this control can examine the *dtilData* bytes while processing the *WM_NCCREATE* and *WM_CREATE* messages. When Windows sends a *WM_NCCREATE* or *WM_CREATE* message to a window procedure, the *lParam* parameter is a pointer to a *CREATESTRUCT* data structure. The address of the *dtilData* bytes is located in the *lpCreateParams* member of this structure.

The *dtilInfo* member is necessary so the functions that create the dialog boxes know how many bytes to skip to get to the beginning of the next *DLGITEMTEMPLATE* structure.

Once the memory block has been initialized (Figure 3-5), one of the dialog-box functions may be called. The functions that create modal dialog boxes accept as their second parameter the handle to this block of memory:

```
int DialogBoxIndirect(HANDLE hInstance, HANDLE hDialogTemplate,
   HWND hWndParent, FARPROC lpDialogFunc);

int DialogBoxIndirectParam(HANDLE hInstance,
   HANDLE hDialogTemplate, HWND hWndParent, FARPROC lpDialogFunc,
   DWORD dwInitParam);
```

When the modal dialog box has been removed, the block of memory may be freed using the *GlobalFree* function.

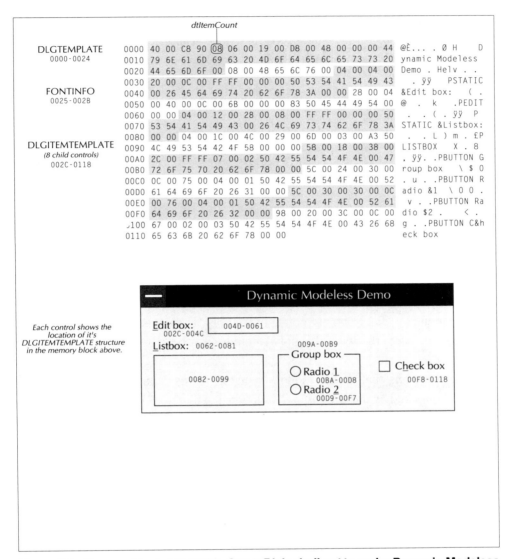

dtItemCount

DLGTEMPLATE
0000-0024

FONTINFO
0025-002B

DLGITEMTEMPLATE
(8 child controls)
002C-0118

```
0000  40 00 C8 90 (08) 06 00 19 00 D8 00 48 00 00 00 44    @È... . Ø H    D
0010  79 6E 61 6D 69 63 20 4D 6F 64 65 6C 65 73 73 20    ynamic Modeless
0020  44 65 6D 6F 00 08 00 48 65 6C 76 00 04 00 04 00    Demo . Helv . .
0030  20 00 0C 00 FF FF 00 00 00 00 50 53 54 41 54 49 43   . ÿÿ   PSTATIC
0040  00 26 45 64 69 74 20 62 6F 78 3A 00 00 28 00 04    &Edit box:  ( .
0050  00 40 00 0C 00 6B 00 00 00 83 50 45 44 49 54 00    @ . k   .PEDIT
0060  00 00 04 00 12 00 28 00 08 00 FF FF 00 00 00 50    . . ( . ÿÿ   P
0070  53 54 41 54 49 43 00 26 4C 69 73 74 62 6F 78 3A    STATIC &Listbox:
0080  00 00 04 00 1C 00 4C 00 29 00 6D 00 03 00 A3 50    . . L ) m . £P
0090  4C 49 53 54 42 4F 58 00 00 00 58 00 18 00 38 00    LISTBOX   X . 8
00A0  2C 00 FF FF 07 00 02 50 42 55 54 54 4F 4E 00 47    , ÿÿ. .PBUTTON G
00B0  72 6F 75 70 20 62 6F 78 00 00 5C 00 24 00 30 00    roup box  \ $ 0
00C0  0C 00 75 00 04 00 01 50 42 55 54 54 4F 4E 00 52    . u . .PBUTTON R
00D0  61 64 69 6F 20 26 31 00 00 5C 00 30 00 30 00 0C    adio &1  \ 0 0 .
00E0  00 76 00 04 00 01 50 42 55 54 54 4F 4E 00 52 61    v . .PBUTTON Ra
00F0  64 69 6F 20 26 32 00 00 98 00 20 00 3C 00 0C 00    dio &2 .   < .
0100  67 00 02 00 03 50 42 55 54 54 4F 4E 00 43 26 68    g . .PBUTTON C&h
0110  65 63 6B 20 62 6F 78 00 00                         eck box
```

Each control shows the location of it's DLGITEMTEMPLATE structure in the memory block above.

Dynamic Modeless Demo

Edit box:
002C-004C   004D-0061

Listbox: 0062-0081   009A-00B9
                              ┌─ Group box ─┐
                              ⊙ Radio 1
          0082-0099   00BA-00D8   □ Check box
                              ⊙ Radio 2   00F8-0118
                                00D9-00F7

Figure 3-5. Memory block used with *CreateDialogIndirect* to make Dynamic Modeless Demo dialog box.

The dialog techniques application demonstrates how to create modal and modeless dialog boxes (the source code for DlgTech appears at the end of this chapter). When the "Dynamic modal demo..." option is chosen, the following code fragment executes:

```
case IDM_DYNAMICMODALDEMO:
   hMem = BuildDynamicDlgBox(FALSE);
   if (hMem == NULL) {
      MessageBox(hWnd, "Insufficient memory.", _szAppName, MB_OK);
   break;
}
fpProc = MakeProcInstance(DynamicDlgProc, _hInstance);
DialogBoxIndirect(_hInstance, hMem, hWnd, fpProc);
FreeProcInstance(fpProc);
GlobalFree(hMem);
break;
```

The *BuildDynamicDlgBox* function in the DLG-DYNA.C file performs all the work to create the dialog-box template in memory. If there is insufficient memory, NULL is returned; otherwise, the global memory handle to the template is returned.

The functions that create modeless dialog boxes require that the block of memory be locked by the *GlobalLock* function and that the address be passed as the second parameter:

```
int CreateDialogIndirect(HANDLE hInstance, LPSTR lpDialogTemplate,
   HWND hWndParent, FARPROC lpDialogFunc);

int CreateDialogIndirectParam(HANDLE hInstance, LPSTR
   lpDialogTemplate, HWND hWndParent, FARPROC lpDialogFunc,
   DWORD dwInitParam);
```

Once the dialog box has been created, the block of memory may be unlocked and freed using the *GlobalUnlock* and *GlobalFree* functions.

When the "Dynamic modeless demo..." option is chosen in the dialog techniques application, the following code fragment executes:

```
case IDM_DYNAMICMODELESSDEMO:
  if (_hDlgDynamic != NULL) {
    DestroyWindow(_hDlgDynamic);
    _hDlgDynamic = NULL;
    CheckMenuItem(GetMenu(hWnd), wParam,
      MF_BYCOMMAND | MF_UNCHECKED);
    FreeProcInstance(fpProcModeless);
    break;
  }

  hMem = BuildDynamicDlgBox(TRUE);
  if (hMem == NULL) {
    MessageBox(hWnd, "Insufficient memory.", _szAppName, MB_OK);
    break;
  }

  fpProcModeless = MakeProcInstance(DynamicDlgProc, _hInstance);
  _hDlgDynamic = CreateDialogIndirect(_hInstance,
    GlobalLock(hMem), hWnd, fpProcModeless);
  GlobalUnlock(hMem);
  GlobalFree(hMem);
  CheckMenuItem(GetMenu(hWnd), wParam, MF_BYCOMMAND |
    MF_CHECKED);
  break;
```

The _hDlgDynamic_ global variable contains the handle of the modeless dynamic dialog box. If the dialog box does not exist, it is NULL. If the dialog box exists, choosing the "Dynamic modeless demo..." option destroys the dialog box. If the dialog box doesn't exist, this menu option creates it.

The first test in the code above ascertains whether the dialog box already exists. If it does, it is destroyed and _hDlgDynamic_ is set to NULL to indicate that the dialog box may be created again. The menu item "Dynamic modeless demo..." is unchecked to show the user that the dialog box does not exist. Finally, the procedural instance for the dialog-box procedure is freed.

165

If the dialog box does not exist, the template for it is created in memory. If the global handle returned is NULL, the user is notified that there is insufficient memory. If the dialog-box template is created successfully, the memory block is locked and *CreateDialogIndirect* is called with the template's address. Immediately after the dialog box has been created, the memory is unlocked and freed. Finally, the "Dynamic modeless demo..." option is checked to indicate to the user that the dialog box is active.

Building the Dialog-Box Template. *BuildDynamicDlgBox* calls various functions in the DLG-DYNA.C file to create the dialog-box template. The only parameter to this function is a Boolean value, *fModeless*, which specifies whether a modal or modeless dialog box is to be created.

The call to *CreateDlgTemplate* performs the initial memory allocation and fills in the *DLGTEMPLATE* structure at the beginning of the memory block:

```
GLOBALHANDLE FAR PASCAL CreateDlgTemplate(
    LONG dtStyle,
    int dtX, int dtY,        // in dialog-box units
    int dtCX, int dtCY,      // in dialog-box units
    LPSTR dtMenuName,        // "" if no menu
    LPSTR dtClassName,       // "" if standard dialog-box class
    LPSTR dtCaptionText,
    short int PointSize,     // only used if DS_SETFONT style specified
    LPSTR szTypeFace);       // only used if DS_SETFONT style specified
    .
    .
    .
if(fModeless)
    hMem = CreateDlgTemplate(
        WS_BORDER | WS_CAPTION | WS_DLGFRAME |
        WS_SYSMENU | WS_VISIBLE | WS_POPUP | DS_SETFONT,
        6, 25, 216, 72, "", "","Dynamic Modeless Demo",8,"Helv");
else
```

```
hMem = CreateDlgTemplate(
   WS_BORDER | WS_CAPTION | WS_DLGFRAME |
   WS_SYSMENU | WS_VISIBLE | WS_POPUP,
   6, 25, 216, 72, "", "","Dynamic Modal Demo",0,"");
```

Because the *DS_SETFONT* flag is specified when the modeless dialog box is created, the last two parameters (*8* and *"Helv"*) indicate the font that should be used when the dialog box is created. The *DS_SETFONT* flag is not specified for the modal dialog box, so *CreateDlgTemplate* will ignore the last two parameters. The number of controls that will appear in the dialog-box template is not specified to *CreateDlgTemplate*; it is set to zero initially and is incremented with each call to the *AddDlgControl* function.

Once the *DLGTEMPLATE* structure has been placed in the memory block, the individual controls are appended. *BuildDynamicDlgBox* uses the following data structure to create those controls:

```
#define MAXDLGITEMDATA    (10)

struct {
   int x, y, cx, cy, id;
   long Style;
   LPSTR szClass, szText;
   BYTE Info;
   BYTE Data[MAXDLGITEMDATA];
} DynamicDlgBoxData[] = {
   { 4, 4, 32, 12, -1, SS_LEFT, "STATIC", "&Edit box:", 0,
      { 0 } },
   { 40, 4, 64, 12, ID_EDITBOX, ES_LEFT | WS_BORDER | WS_TABSTOP |
      WS_GROUP, "EDIT", "", 0, { 0 } },
   { 4, 18, 40, 8, -1, SS_LEFT, "STATIC", "&Listbox:", 0, { 0 } },
   .
   .
   .
   { 0, 0, 0, 0, 0, 0, NULL, NULL, 0, { 0 } }
};
```

AddDlgControl is called for each item in this data structure, and a new *DLGITEMTEMPLATE* structure is appended to the end of the memory block:

```
// LOWORD = Success(TRUE)/Failure(FALSE), HIWORD=New hMem
DWORD FAR PASCAL AddDlgControl (
    GLOBALHANDLE hMem,         // handle from CreateDlgTemplate or
                               // AddDlgControl
    int dtilX, int dtilY,      // in dialog-box units
    int dtilCX, int dtilCY,    // in dialog-box units
    int dtilID,
    long dtilStyle,            // WS_CHILD is automatically added;
    LPSTR dtilClass,           // may be: "BUTTON", "EDIT", "STATIC",
                               // "LISTBOX", "SCROLLBAR", "COMBOBOX"

    LPSTR dtilText,
    BYTE dtilInfo,             // number of additional data bytes
    LPBYTE dtilData);          // address of additional bytes
.
.
.
for (x = 0; DynamicDlgBoxData[x].szClass != NULL; x++) {
    // Do not add the "Ok" and "Cancel" buttons if a modeless
    // dialog box is being created
    if (fModeless) {
        if (DynamicDlgBoxData[x].id == IDOK ||
            DynamicDlgBoxData[x].id == IDCANCEL)
            continue;
    }

    dwAddDlgControlResult = AddDlgControl(hMem,
        DynamicDlgBoxData[x].x,        DynamicDlgBoxData[x].y,
        DynamicDlgBoxData[x].cx,       DynamicDlgBoxData[x].cy,
        DynamicDlgBoxData[x].id,       DynamicDlgBoxData[x].Style,
        DynamicDlgBoxData[x].szClass,  DynamicDlgBoxData[x].szText,
        DynamicDlgBoxData[x].Info,     DynamicDlgBoxData[x].Data);

    // LOWORD is FALSE if insufficient memory exists
    if (LOWORD(dwAddDlgControlResult) == FALSE) break;
```

```
    // HIWORD is handle to new block of memory
    hMem = HIWORD(dwAddDlgControlResult);
}
```

The "Ok" and "Cancel" buttons are not included in the modeless version of this dialog-box template (they are not usually included in modeless dialog boxes).

After the template has been created successfully, *DoneAddingControls* performs some internal cleanup in the memory block and the memory handle is returned to the application.

Managing the Dialog Templates Memory Block

The functions that manage the block of memory are *CreateDlgTemplate*, *AddDlgControl*, and *DoneAddingControls*.

CreateDlgTemplate performs the initial global memory allocation. This allocation must be large enough to contain a *DLGTEMPLATE* structure and its three variable-length fields: *dtMenuName*, *dtClassName*, and *dtCaptionText*. If the dialog template includes the *DS_SETFONT* style, the memory block must be large enough to include the *FONTINFO* structure, including its variable-length field, *szTypeFace*.

An additional two bytes are included in the size of the memory block. This word contains the number of bytes used in the block so far, letting the *AddDlgControl* function know where to begin appending its *DLGITEMTEMPLATE* structures. After the memory block is allocated, *CreateDlgTemplate* fills the memory block with the values passed in the parameters to the function and the *dtItemCount* member is initialized to zero. The handle to the memory block is then returned to the caller.

AddDlgControl appends new controls to the end of a memory block that was created by *CreateDlgTemplate*. This function first calculates the number of bytes required to contain a *DLGITEMTEMPLATE* structure and its three variable-length fields: *dtilClass*, *dtilText*, and *dtilData*. Before the memory block can be enlarged, this function must determine the number of bytes already used. The Windows *GlobalSize* function cannot be used because Windows sometimes allocates more

169

bytes than requested when satisfying a memory allocation. To solve this problem, the first word in the memory block contains the number of bytes used in the block. This was updated by *CreateDlgTemplate* or a previous call to *AddDlgControl*. Now *AddDlgControl* can add the value in the first word of the block to the number of bytes required by the new control and call *GlobalReAlloc*:

```
wBlockLen += * (WORD FAR *) GlobalLock(hMem);
GlobalUnlock(hMem);
hMemNew = GlobalReAlloc(hMem, wBlockLen, GMEM_MOVEABLE |
   GMEM_ZEROINIT);
```

Because *GlobalReAlloc* does not necessarily return the same memory handle that was passed to it, *AddDlgControl* must notify the calling application of the new handle by returning it.

With the memory block now large enough to hold the additional control, the new *DLGITEMTEMPLATE* structure is appended after the number of bytes used in the block. When a new control is added, the *dtItemCount* member in *DLGTEMPLATE* is incremented. Before the memory block is unlocked, the first word in the block is updated to reflect the total number of bytes now used in the block.

Once the application is done adding controls to the dialog-box template, the *DoneAddingControls* function must be called. This function simply locks the memory block and does a memory move to shift all the information in the block toward the beginning by two bytes. This removes the number-of-bytes-used information. Once this is done, the *AddDlgControl* function may no longer be called for this memory block. The memory block is now in the correct format to be used by the *DialogBoxIndirect(Param)* and *CreateDialogIndirect(Param)* functions.

The dialog techniques application, shown in the following listings, shows how to change the tab order of child controls, add controls to and expand a dialog box, use a modalless dialog box, and create modal and modeless dialog-box templates at run time.

Figure 3-6. DLGTECH.ICO.

Listing 3-1. DLGTECH.C application source module.

```
/*****************************************************************
Module name: DlgTech.C
Programmer : Jeffrey M. Richter
*****************************************************************/

#include "..\nowindws.h"
#undef NOCOLOR
#undef NOCTLMGR
#undef NOGDI
#undef NOKERNEL
#undef NOMB
#undef NOMEMMGR
#undef NOMENUS
#undef NOMSG
#undef NOSHOWWINDOW
#undef NOUSER
#undef NOWINMESSAGES
#undef NOWINOFFSETS
#undef NOWINSTYLES
#include <windows.h>

#include "dlg-opts.h"
#include "dlg-mdls.h"
#include "dlg-dyna.h"
```

```
#include "dlgtech.h"
#include "dialog.h"

char _szAppName[] = "DlgTech";
static HWND _hDlgDynamic = NULL;
static HWND _hDlgModalLess = NULL;

HANDLE _hInstance = NULL;  // our instance handle

BOOL NEAR PASCAL RegisterAppWndClass (HANDLE hInstance);
LONG FAR PASCAL AppWndProc (HWND hWnd, WORD wMsg, WORD wParam,
    LONG lParam);
BOOL FAR PASCAL SWPDlgProc (HWND hDlg, WORD wMsg, WORD wParam,
    LONG lParam);
BOOL FAR PASCAL AboutDlgProc (HWND hDlg, WORD wMsg, WORD wParam,
    LONG lParam);

int PASCAL WinMain (HANDLE hInstance, HANDLE hPrevInstance,
      LPSTR lpszCmdLine, int cmdShow) {
    MSG msg;
    HWND hWnd;

    _hInstance = hInstance;

    if (hPrevInstance == NULL)
      if (!RegisterAppWndClass(hInstance))
        return(0);

    hWnd = CreateWindow(_szAppName, _szAppName,
      WS_OVERLAPPED | WS_VISIBLE | WS_CLIPCHILDREN | WS_CAPTION |
      WS_SYSMENU | WS_MINIMIZEBOX | WS_MAXIMIZEBOX |
      WS_THICKFRAME, CW_USEDEFAULT, SW_SHOW, CW_USEDEFAULT,
      CW_USEDEFAULT, NULL, NULL, hInstance, 0);

    if (hWnd == NULL) return(0);
    ShowWindow(hWnd, cmdShow);
    UpdateWindow(hWnd);
```

```
   while (GetMessage(&msg, NULL, 0, 0)) {
      if (!IsWindow(_hDlgDynamic) ||
          !IsDialogMessage(_hDlgDynamic, &msg)) {
          TranslateMessage(&msg);
          DispatchMessage(&msg);
      }
   }
   return(0);
}

BOOL NEAR PASCAL RegisterAppWndClass (HANDLE hInstance) {
   WNDCLASS WndClass;

   WndClass.style          = 0;
   WndClass.lpfnWndProc    = AppWndProc;
   WndClass.cbClsExtra     = 0;
   WndClass.cbWndExtra     = 0;
   WndClass.hInstance      = hInstance;
   WndClass.hIcon          = LoadIcon(hInstance, _szAppName);
   WndClass.hCursor        = LoadCursor(NULL, IDC_ARROW);
   WndClass.hbrBackground  = COLOR_WINDOW + 1;
   WndClass.lpszMenuName   = _szAppName;
   WndClass.lpszClassName  = _szAppName;
   return(RegisterClass(&WndClass)); }


//**********************************************************************
// This function processes all messages sent to the main window

LONG FAR PASCAL AppWndProc (HWND hWnd, WORD wMsg, WORD wParam,
      LONG lParam) {
   BOOL fCallDefProc = FALSE;
   LONG lResult = 0;
   static FARPROC fpProcModeless;
   FARPROC fpProc;
   GLOBALHANDLE hMem;
   int nResult;
   char szBuf[100], szName[50];
```

```
switch (wMsg) {
  case WM_CREATE:
    _hDlgModalLess =
      CreateModalLessDlgBox(_hInstance, "ModalLess", hWnd,
        MakeProcInstance(ModalLessDlgProc, _hInstance), 0);
    if (_hDlgModalLess == NULL) {
      MessageBox(hWnd, "Can't create modalless dialog box.",
        _szAppName, MB_OK);
      EnableMenuItem(GetMenu(hWnd), IDM_MODALLESSDEMO,
        MF_BYCOMMAND | MF_GRAYED);
    }
    break;

  case WM_CLOSE:
    if (_hDlgModalLess)
      DestroyModalLessDlgBox(_hDlgModalLess);
    fCallDefProc = TRUE;
    break;

  case WM_DESTROY:
    PostQuitMessage(0);
    break;

  case WM_COMMAND:
    switch (wParam) {

    case IDM_OPTIONSDEMO:
      fpProc = MakeProcInstance(OptionsDlgProc, _hInstance);
      DialogBox(_hInstance, "Options", hWnd, fpProc);
      FreeProcInstance(fpProc);
      break;

    case IDM_DYNAMICMODALDEMO:
      hMem = BuildDynamicDlgBox(FALSE);
      if (hMem == NULL) {
        MessageBox(hWnd, "Insufficient memory.",
          _szAppName, MB_OK);
        break;
      }
```

```
   fpProc = MakeProcInstance(DynamicDlgProc, _hInstance);
   DialogBoxIndirect(_hInstance, hMem, hWnd, fpProc);
   FreeProcInstance(fpProc); GlobalFree(hMem);
    break;

case IDM_DYNAMICMODELESSDEMO:
    if (_hDlgDynamic != NULL) {
       DestroyWindow(_hDlgDynamic);
       _hDlgDynamic = NULL;
       CheckMenuItem(GetMenu(hWnd), wParam,
          MF_BYCOMMAND | MF_UNCHECKED);
       FreeProcInstance(fpProcModeless);
        break;
    }

    hMem = BuildDynamicDlgBox(TRUE);
    if (hMem == NULL) {
       MessageBox(hWnd, "Insufficient memory.",
          _szAppName, MB_OK);
        break;
    }

    fpProcModeless = MakeProcInstance(DynamicDlgProc,
       _hInstance);
    _hDlgDynamic = CreateDialogIndirect(_hInstance,
       GlobalLock(hMem), hWnd, fpProcModeless);

    GlobalUnlock(hMem);
    GlobalFree(hMem);
    CheckMenuItem(GetMenu(hWnd), wParam,
       MF_BYCOMMAND | MF_CHECKED);
    break;

case IDM_MODALLESSDEMO:
    nResult = ModalLessDlgBox(_hDlgModalLess, hWnd, 0);
    GetDlgItemText(_hDlgModalLess, ID_NAME, szName,
       sizeof(szName));
    wsprintf(szBuf, "Button: %s, Name: %s",
       (nResult == IDOK) ? (LPSTR) "Ok" : (LPSTR)
       "Cancel", (LPSTR) szName);
```

```
                MessageBox(hWnd, szBuf, _szAppName, MB_OK);
                break;

          case IDM_SETWINDOWPOSDEMO:
                fpProc = MakeProcInstance(SWPDlgProc, _hInstance);
                DialogBox(_hInstance, "SetWindowPos", hWnd, fpProc);
                FreeProcInstance(fpProc);
                break;

          case IDM_ABOUT:
                // Display About box
                fpProc = MakeProcInstance(AboutDlgProc, _hInstance);
                DialogBox(_hInstance, "About", hWnd, fpProc);
                FreeProcInstance(fpProc);
                break;

          default:
                // Any options that we do not process should be passed
                // to DefWindowProc
                fCallDefProc = TRUE;
                break;
          }

          break;

      default:
          fCallDefProc = TRUE; break;
   }

   if (fCallDefProc)
      lResult = DefWindowProc(hWnd, wMsg, wParam, lParam);

   return(lResult);
}

//***************************************************************
// Functions for the SetWindowPos Dialog Box Demonstration

BOOL FAR PASCAL SWPDlgProc (HWND hDlg, WORD wMsg, WORD wParam,
      LONG lParam) {
```

```
BOOL fProcessed = TRUE;
HWND hWndControl;
WORD wDlgWidth, wDlgHeight;
switch (wMsg) {

    case WM_INITDIALOG:
        break;

    case WM_COMMAND:
        switch (wParam) {
            case IDOK:
            case IDCANCEL:
                if (HIWORD(lParam) == BN_CLICKED)
                    EndDialog(hDlg, wParam);
                break;

            case ID_CHANGETABORDER:
                if (HIWORD(lParam) != BN_CLICKED)
                    break;

                // Order is "&Name:", "edit", "Over &25".
                // Move "Over &25" after "&Name:" field.
                SetWindowPos(GetDlgItem(hDlg, ID_OVER25),
                    GetDlgItem(hDlg, ID_NAMETEXT), 0, 0, 0, 0,
                    SWP_NOMOVE | SWP_NOSIZE);

                // Order is "&Name:", "Over &25", "edit".
                // Move "&Name:" after "Over &25" field.
                SetWindowPos(GetDlgItem(hDlg, ID_NAMETEXT),
                    GetDlgItem(hDlg, ID_OVER25), 0, 0, 0, 0,
                    SWP_NOMOVE | SWP_NOSIZE);

                // Order is "Over &25", "&Name:", "edit"

                // Set the focus to the control after this button
                SetFocus(GetNextDlgTabItem(hDlg, LOWORD(lParam),
                    0));

                EnableWindow(LOWORD(lParam), FALSE);
                break;
```

```
            case ID_ADDCONTROL:
                if (HIWORD(lParam) != BN_CLICKED)
                    break;

                wDlgWidth = LOWORD(GetDialogBaseUnits());
                wDlgHeight = HIWORD(GetDialogBaseUnits());

                hWndControl = CreateWindow("scrollbar", "",
                    SBS_HORZ | WS_CHILD | WS_TABSTOP | WS_GROUP,
                    (64 * wDlgWidth) / 4, (36 * wDlgHeight) / 8,
                    (64 * wDlgWidth) / 4, (12 * wDlgHeight) / 8,
                    hDlg, ID_SCROLLBAR, _hInstance, 0);

                SetWindowPos(hWndControl, LOWORD(lParam),
                    0, 0, 0, 0, SWP_NOMOVE | SWP_NOSIZE |
                    SWP_SHOWWINDOW);

                // Set the focus to the control after this button
                SetFocus(GetNextDlgTabItem(hDlg, LOWORD(lParam),
                    0));

                EnableWindow(LOWORD(lParam), FALSE);
                break;

            default:
                break;
        }
        break;

    default:
        fProcessed = FALSE; break;
    }
    return(fProcessed);
}
```

```
//*************************************************************
// Function for the About Box

BOOL FAR PASCAL AboutDlgProc (HWND hDlg, WORD wMsg, WORD wParam,
      LONG lParam) {
   char szBuffer[100];
   BOOL fProcessed = TRUE;

   switch (wMsg) {

      case WM_INITDIALOG:
         // Set version static window to have date and time of
         // compilation
         wsprintf(szBuffer, "%s at %s", (LPSTR) __DATE__,
            (LPSTR) __TIME__);
         SetWindowText(GetDlgItem(hDlg, ID_VERSION), szBuffer);
         break;

      case WM_COMMAND:
         switch (wParam) {
            case IDOK:
            case IDCANCEL:
               if (HIWORD(lParam) == BN_CLICKED)
                  EndDialog(hDlg, wParam);
               break;

            default:
               break;
         }
         break;

      default:
         fProcessed = FALSE;
         break;
   }
   return(fProcessed);
}
```

Listing 3-2. DLGTECH.H application header module.

```
/****************************************************************
Module name: DlgTech.H
Programmer : Jeffrey M. Richter
****************************************************************/

#define IDM_SETWINDOWPOSDEMO    (100)
#define IDM_OPTIONSDEMO         (101)
#define IDM_MODALLESSDEMO       (102)
#define IDM_DYNAMICMODALDEMO    (103)
#define IDM_DYNAMICMODELESSDEMO (104)
#define IDM_ABOUT               (105)
```

Listing 3-3. DLG-OPTS.C Options dialog box source module.

```
/****************************************************************
Module name: Dlg-Opts.C
Programmer : Jeffrey M. Richter
****************************************************************/

#include "..\nowindws.h"
#undef NOCOLOR
#undef NOCTLMGR
#undef NOKERNEL
#undef NOMSG
#undef NOSHOWWINDOW
#undef NOUSER
#undef NOWINMESSAGES
#undef NOWINOFFSETS
#undef NOWINSTYLES
#include <windows.h>

#include <stdlib.h>

#include "dlg-opts.h"

extern HANDLE _hInstance;
```

180

```
// Turns a style ON for a window
#define SetWindowStyle(hWnd, Style) \
   SetWindowLong(hWnd, GWL_STYLE, Style | GetWindowLong(hWnd, \
   GWL_STYLE));

// Turns a style OFF for a window
#define ResetWindowStyle(hWnd, Style) \
   SetWindowLong(hWnd, GWL_STYLE, ~Style & GetWindowLong(hWnd, \
   GWL_STYLE));

#define ENABLECHILDREN (0x80000000L)
#define DISABLECHILDREN (0x00000000L)

BOOL FAR PASCAL EnableChildrenInOptionArea (HWND hWnd,
   LONG lParam);

void FAR PASCAL ShowArea (BOOL fShowDefAreaOnly, HWND hDlg,
      HWND hWndDefArea) {
   FARPROC fpProc;
   RECT rcDlg, rcDefArea;
   char szDlgDims[25];

   // Save original width and height of dialog box
   GetWindowRect(hDlg, &rcDlg);

   // Retrieve coordinates for default area window
   GetWindowRect(hWndDefArea, &rcDefArea);

   // Disable controls outside of default area. Any window whose
   // left edge > rcDefArea.right || right > rcDefArea.bottom.
   fpProc = MakeProcInstance(EnableChildrenInOptionArea,
      _hInstance);
   EnumChildWindows(hDlg, fpProc,
      (fShowDefAreaOnly ? DISABLECHILDREN : ENABLECHILDREN) |
      MAKELONG(rcDefArea.right, rcDefArea.bottom));
   FreeProcInstance(fpProc);

   if (fShowDefAreaOnly) {
      wsprintf(szDlgDims, "%05u %05u",
         rcDlg.right - rcDlg.left, rcDlg.bottom - rcDlg.top);
```

```
    ResetWindowStyle(hWndDefArea, SS_BLACKRECT);
    SetWindowStyle(hWndDefArea, SS_LEFT);
    SetWindowText(hWndDefArea, szDlgDims);

    // Resize dialog box to fit only default area
    SetWindowPos(hDlg, NULL, 0, 0,
      rcDefArea.right - rcDlg.left, rcDefArea.bottom -
      rcDlg.top, SWP_NOZORDER | SWP_NOMOVE);

    // Make sure the default area box is hidden
    ShowWindow(hWndDefArea, SW_HIDE);

  } else {
    GetWindowText(hWndDefArea, szDlgDims, sizeof(szDlgDims));

    // Restore dialog box to its original size
    SetWindowPos(hDlg, NULL, 0, 0,
      atoi(szDlgDims), atoi(szDlgDims + 6),
      SWP_NOZORDER | SWP_NOMOVE);
  }
}


BOOL FAR PASCAL EnableChildrenInOptionArea (HWND hWnd,
    LONG lParam) {
  RECT rc;
  BOOL fEnable = (lParam & ENABLECHILDREN) != 0;
  lParam &= ~ENABLECHILDREN;

  // Calculate rectangle occupied by child window in screen
  // coordinates
  GetWindowRect(hWnd, &rc);

  // NOTE: Right edge of "Default area" window is in
  // LOWORD(lParam). Bottom edge of "Default area" window
  // is in HIWORD(lParam).

  // Enable/disable child if its:
  // right edge is >= the right edge of hWndDefArea.
  // bottom edge is >= the bottom edge of hWndDefArea.
```

```
    if ((rc.right >= (int) LOWORD(lParam)) ||
        (rc.bottom >= (int) HIWORD(lParam)))
        EnableWindow(hWnd, fEnable);

    // Allow enumeration to continue until all windows are checked
    return(1);
}

#ifdef _DEMO
//****************************************************************
// Functions for the ModalLess Dialog Box Demonstration

#include "dialog.h"

BOOL FAR PASCAL OptionsDlgProc (HWND hDlg, WORD wMsg, WORD wParam,
        LONG lParam) {
    BOOL fProcessed = TRUE;

    switch (wMsg) {

        case WM_INITDIALOG:
            // During initialization, before any windows are shown,
            // resize the dialog box so that only the "default"
            // portion is shown
            ShowArea(TRUE, hDlg, GetDlgItem(hDlg, ID_DEFAULTBOX));
            break;

        case WM_COMMAND:
            switch (wParam) {

                case IDOK:
                case IDCANCEL:
                    // Terminate dialog box if user selects the "Ok" or
                    // "Cancel" button
                    EndDialog(hDlg, wParam);
                    break;

                case ID_OPTIONS:
                    if (HIWORD(lParam) != BN_CLICKED)
                        break;
```

```
                    // User selected "Options >>" button; show entire
                    // dialog box
                    ShowArea(FALSE, hDlg, GetDlgItem(hDlg,
                        ID_DEFAULTBOX));

                    // The ShowArea(FALSE, ...) function enables all
                    // windows outside the "default" area. Any windows
                    // that should be disabled must be explicitly
                    // disabled here. Note: the status of the windows
                    // within the "default" area is NOT changed.

                    // Set the focus to the desired control
                    SetFocus(GetNextDlgTabItem(hDlg, LOWORD(lParam),
                        0));

                    // Disable "Options>>" button
                    EnableWindow(LOWORD(lParam), FALSE);
                    break;

                default:
                    fProcessed = FALSE;
                    break;
            }
            break;

        default:
            fProcessed = FALSE;
            break;
    }
    return(fProcessed);
}
#endif
```

Listing 3-4. DLG-OPTS.H Options dialog box header module.

```
/********************************************************************
Module name: Dlg-Opts.H
Programmer : Jeffrey M. Richter
********************************************************************/

void FAR PASCAL ShowArea (BOOL fShowDefAreaOnly, HWND hDlg,
   HWND hWndDefArea);

#ifdef _DEMO
//******************************************************************
// Functions for the "Options >>" Dialog Box Demonstration

BOOL FAR PASCAL OptionsDlgProc (HWND hDlg, WORD wMsg, WORD wParam,
   LONG lParam);
#endif
```

Listing 3-5. DLG-MDLS.C modalless dialog box source module.

```
/********************************************************************
Module name: Dlg-Mdls.C
Programmer : Jeffrey M. Richter
********************************************************************/

#include "..\nowindws.h"
#undef NOCOLOR
#undef NOCTLMGR
#undef NOKERNEL
#undef NOMSG
#undef NOSHOWWINDOW
#undef NOUSER
#undef NOWINMESSAGES
#undef NOWINOFFSETS
#undef NOWINSTYLES
#include <windows.h>

#include "dlg-mdls.h"
```

```
static char _szModalLessResult[] = "ModalLessResult";

HWND FAR PASCAL CreateModalLessDlgBox (HANDLE hInstance,
   LPSTR szTemplateName, HWND hWndParent, FARPROC DialogFunc,
   DWORD lInitParam) {

   return(CreateDialogParam(hInstance, szTemplateName,
      hWndParent, DialogFunc, lInitParam));
}

BOOL FAR PASCAL DestroyModalLessDlgBox (HWND hDlg) {
   return(DestroyWindow(hDlg));
}

int FAR PASCAL ModalLessDlgBox (HWND hDlg, HWND hWndParent,
      LONG lParam) {
   BOOL fPropFound = FALSE;
   int nResult = NULL, nModalLessShowMsg
   MSG msg;

   EnableWindow(hWndParent, FALSE);

   // Register and send the "ModalLessShowMsg" message to the
   // modalless dialog box
   nModalLessShowMsg = RegisterWindowMessage(SZMODALLESSSHOWMSG);
   SendMessage(hDlg, nModalLessShowMsg, 0, lParam);

   // Display the modalless dialog box
   ShowWindow(hDlg, SW_SHOW);

   // Continue the message loop until the "ModalLessResult"
   // property has been associated with the modalless dialog box.
   // This happens when the dialog-box function calls the
   // EndModalLessDlgBox function.

   while (!fPropFound) {
      GetMessage(&msg, NULL, 0, 0);
      if (!IsDialogMessage(hDlg, &msg)) {
         TranslateMessage(&msg);
         DispatchMessage(&msg);
      }
```

```
         // Get value of "ModalLessResult" property. If property does
         // not exist, GetProp returns zero.
         nResult = GetProp(hDlg, _szModalLessResult);

         // Try to remove the property. If RemoveProp returns NULL,
         // the property was never associated with the window and the
         // message loop must continue.
         fPropFound = RemoveProp(hDlg, _szModalLessResult) != NULL;
      }

   EnableWindow(hWndParent, TRUE);

   // Hide the modalless dialog box and return the result to the
   // application
   ShowWindow(hDlg, SW_HIDE);
   return(nResult);
}

BOOL FAR PASCAL EndModalLessDlgBox (HWND hDlg, int nResult) {
   return(SetProp(hDlg, _szModalLessResult, nResult));
}

#ifdef _DEMO
//*****************************************************************
// Functions for the ModalLess Dialog Box Demonstration

#include "dialog.h"

BOOL FAR PASCAL ModalLessDlgProc (HWND hDlg, WORD wMsg,
      WORD wParam, LONG lParam) {
   BOOL fProcessed = TRUE;

   if (wMsg == RegisterWindowMessage(SZMODALLESSSHOWMSG)) {
      // Initialize the EDIT window with some text whenever the
      // dialog box is about to be shown
      SetDlgItemText(hDlg, ID_NAME, "Default text");

      // Make the EDIT window have the focus
      SetFocus(GetDlgItem(hDlg, ID_NAME));
   }
```

```
    switch (wMsg) {
      case WM_INITDIALOG:
         break;

      case WM_COMMAND:
         switch (wParam) {
            case IDOK:
            case IDCANCEL:
               if (HIWORD(lParam) == BN_CLICKED)
                  EndModalLessDlgBox(hDlg, wParam);
               break;

            default:
               break;
         }
         break;

      default:
         fProcessed = FALSE;
         break;
   }
   return(fProcessed);
}
#endif
```

Listing 3-6. DLG-MDLS.H modalless dialog box header module.

```
/****************************************************************
Module name: Dlg-Mdls.H
Programmer : Jeffrey M. Richter
****************************************************************/

#define SZMODALLESSSHOWMSG     "ModalLessShowMsg"

HWND FAR PASCAL CreateModalLessDlgBox (HANDLE hInstance,
     LPSTR szTemplateName,
   HWND hWndParent, FARPROC DialogFunc, DWORD lInitParam);

BOOL FAR PASCAL DestroyModalLessDlgBox (HWND hDlg);
```

```
int  FAR PASCAL ModalLessDlgBox (HWND hDlg, HWND hWndParent,
   LONG lParam);

BOOL FAR PASCAL EndModalLessDlgBox (HWND hDlg, int nResult);

#ifdef _DEMO
//****************************************************************
// Functions for the ModalLess Dialog Box Demonstration

BOOL FAR PASCAL ModalLessDlgProc (HWND hDlg, WORD wMsg,
   WORD wParam, LONG lParam);
#endif
```

Listing 3-7. DLG-DYNA.C dynamic dialog box source module.

```
/****************************************************************
Module name: Dlg-Dyna.C
Programmer : Jeffrey M. Richter
****************************************************************/

#include "..\nowindws.h"
#undef NOCTLMGR
#undef NOKERNEL
#undef NOLSTRING
#undef NOMEMMGR
#undef NOUSER
#undef NOWINMESSAGES
#undef NOWINSTYLES
#include <windows.h>

#include <memory.h>

#include "dlg-dyna.h"

typedef struct {
   long dtStyle;
   BYTE dtItemCount;
   int dtX;
```

```
    int dtY;
    int dtCX;
    int dtCY;
// char dtMenuName[];     // variable-length string
// char dtClassName[];    // variable-length string
// char dtCaptionText[];  // variable-length string
} DLGTEMPLATE, FAR *LPDLGTEMPLATE;

typedef struct {
    short int PointSize;
// char szTypeFace[];     // variable-length string
} FONTINFO, FAR *LPFONTINFO;

typedef struct {
    int   dtilX;
    int   dtilY;
    int   dtilCX;
    int   dtilCY;
    int   dtilID;
    long  dtilStyle;
// char dtilClass[];      // variable-length string
// char dtilText[];       // variable-length string
// BYTE dtilInfo;         // # of bytes in following memory block
// BYTE dtilData;         // variable-length memory block
} DLGITEMTEMPLATE, FAR *LPDLGITEMTEMPLATE;

GLOBALHANDLE FAR PASCAL CreateDlgTemplate(
    LONG dtStyle,
    int dtX, int dtY,     // in dialog-box units
    int dtCX, int dtCY,   // in dialog-box units
    LPSTR dtMenuName,     // "" if no menu
    LPSTR dtClassName,    // "" if standard dialog-box class
    LPSTR dtCaptionText,
    short int PointSize,  // Only used if DS_SETFONT style specified
    LPSTR szTypeFace) {   // Only used if DS_SETFONT style specified

    GLOBALHANDLE hMem;
    WORD wBlockLen, FAR *wNumBytes;
    WORD wMenuNameLen, wClassNameLen, wCaptionTextLen,
        wTypeFaceLen;
```

```
LPSTR szDlgTemplate, szDlgTypeFace;
LPDLGTEMPLATE lpDlgTemplate;
LPFONTINFO lpFontInfo;

// Calculate number of bytes required by following fields:
wMenuNameLen = 1 + lstrlen(dtMenuName);
wClassNameLen = 1 + lstrlen(dtClassName);
wCaptionTextLen = 1 + lstrlen(dtCaptionText);

// Block must be large enough to contain the following:
wBlockLen =
    sizeof(WORD) +          // stores # of bytes used in block
    sizeof(DLGTEMPLATE) +   // # bytes for fixed part of
                            // DLGTEMPLATE
    wMenuNameLen +          // # bytes for menu name
    wClassNameLen +         // # bytes for dialog class name
    wCaptionTextLen;        // # bytes for dialog-box caption

if (dtStyle & DS_SETFONT) {
    // Dialog box uses font other than system font

    // Calculate # of bytes required for typeface name
    wTypeFaceLen = 1 + lstrlen(szTypeFace);

    // Block must be large enough to include font information
    wBlockLen +=
        sizeof(short int) +  // # bytes for font's point size
        wTypeFaceLen;        // # bytes for font typeface name

} else {
    // Dialog box uses the system font
    wTypeFaceLen = 0;

    // Block length does not change
}

// Allocate global block of memory for dialog template
hMem = GlobalAlloc(GMEM_MOVEABLE | GMEM_ZEROINIT, wBlockLen);
if (hMem == NULL) return(hMem);
```

```
// wNumBytes points to beginning of memory block
wNumBytes = (WORD FAR *) GlobalLock(hMem);

// Store in first two bytes the number of bytes used in block
*wNumBytes = (WORD) wBlockLen;

// lpDlgTemplate points to start of DLGTEMPLATE in block
lpDlgTemplate = (LPDLGTEMPLATE) (wNumBytes + 1);

// Set the members of the DLGTEMPLATE structure
lpDlgTemplate->dtStyle = dtStyle;
lpDlgTemplate->dtItemCount = 0;   // Incremented with calls
lpDlgTemplate->dtX = dtX;         // to AddDlgItem
lpDlgTemplate->dtY = dtY;
lpDlgTemplate->dtCX = dtCX;
lpDlgTemplate->dtCY = dtCY;

// szDlgTemplate points to start of variable part of
// DLGTEMPLATE
szDlgTemplate = (LPSTR) (lpDlgTemplate + 1);

// Append menu name, class name, and caption text to the block
_fmemcpy(szDlgTemplate, dtMenuName, wMenuNameLen);
szDlgTemplate += wMenuNameLen;
_fmemcpy(szDlgTemplate, dtClassName, wClassNameLen);
szDlgTemplate += wClassNameLen;
_fmemcpy(szDlgTemplate, dtCaptionText, wCaptionTextLen);
szDlgTemplate += wCaptionTextLen;

if (dtStyle & DS_SETFONT) {
    // Dialog box uses font other than system font

    // lpFontInfo points to start of FONTINFO structure in block
    lpFontInfo = (LPFONTINFO) szDlgTemplate;

    // Set the members of the FONTINFO structure
    lpFontInfo->PointSize = PointSize;

    // szTypeFace points to start of variable part of FONTINFO
    szDlgTypeFace = (LPSTR) (lpFontInfo + 1);
```

```
        // Append the typeface name to the block
        _fmemcpy(szDlgTypeFace, szTypeFace, wTypeFaceLen);
    }

    GlobalUnlock(hMem);
    return(hMem);
}


// LOWORD = Success(TRUE)/Failure(FALSE), HIWORD=New hMem
DWORD FAR PASCAL AddDlgControl (
    GLOBALHANDLE hMem,              // handle from CreateDlgData or
                                   // AddDlgItem
    int dtilX, int dtilY,          // in dialog-box units
    int dtilCX, int dtilCY,        // in dialog-box units
    int dtilID,
    long dtilStyle,                // WS_CHILD is automatically added
    LPSTR dtilClass,               // May be: "BUTTON", "EDIT",
                                   // "STATIC", "LISTBOX",
                                   // "SCROLLBAR", "COMBOBOX"
    LPSTR dtilText,
    BYTE dtilInfo,                 // number of additional data bytes
    LPBYTE dtilData) {             // value passed through
                                   // lpCreateParams field of
                                   // CREATESTRUCT

    GLOBALHANDLE hMemNew;
    WORD wBlockLen, wClassLen, wTextLen, FAR *wNumBytes;
    LPDLGTEMPLATE lpDlgTemplate;
    LPDLGITEMTEMPLATE lpDlgItemTemplate;
    LPSTR szDlgItemTemplate;

    // Calculate number of bytes required by following fields:
    wClassLen = 1 + lstrlen(dtilClass);
    wTextLen = 1 + lstrlen(dtilText);

    // Block must be increased to contain the following:
    wBlockLen =
        sizeof(DLGITEMTEMPLATE) + // # bytes for fixed part of
                                  // DLGITEMTEMPLATE
        wClassLen +               // # bytes for control class
```

```
    wTextLen +                // # bytes for control text
    sizeof(BYTE) +            // 1 byte  for # of dtilInfo bytes
                              // (below)
    dtilInfo;                 // # bytes for extra data

// Guarantee that all controls have WS_CHILD style
dtilStyle |= WS_CHILD;

// Get number of bytes currently in the memory block
wBlockLen += * (WORD FAR *) GlobalLock(hMem);
GlobalUnlock(hMem);

// Increase the size of the memory block to include the new
// dialog item
hMemNew = GlobalReAlloc(hMem, wBlockLen,
   GMEM_MOVEABLE | GMEM_ZEROINIT);
if (hMemNew == NULL)
   return(MAKELONG(FALSE, hMem));

// wNumBytes points to beginning of memory block
wNumBytes = (WORD FAR *) GlobalLock(hMemNew);

// lpDlgTemplate points to start of DLGTEMPLATE in block
lpDlgTemplate = (LPDLGTEMPLATE) (wNumBytes + 1);

// Increment the number of controls in the template
lpDlgTemplate->dtItemCount++;

// lpDlgItemTemplate points to start of new DLGITEMTEMPLATE
// in block. This is at the end of the memory block.
lpDlgItemTemplate = (LPDLGITEMTEMPLATE)
   (((LPSTR) wNumBytes) + *wNumBytes);

// Set the members of the DLGITEMTEMPLATE structure
lpDlgItemTemplate->dtilX = dtilX;
lpDlgItemTemplate->dtilY = dtilY;
lpDlgItemTemplate->dtilCX = dtilCX;
lpDlgItemTemplate->dtilCY = dtilCY;
lpDlgItemTemplate->dtilID = dtilID;
lpDlgItemTemplate->dtilStyle = dtilStyle;
```

```
// szDlgTemplate points to start of variable part
// of DLGITEMTEMPLATE
szDlgItemTemplate = (LPSTR) (lpDlgItemTemplate + 1);

// Append the control's class name, text to the block
_fmemcpy(szDlgItemTemplate, dtilClass, wClassLen);
szDlgItemTemplate += wClassLen;
_fmemcpy(szDlgItemTemplate, dtilText, wTextLen);
szDlgItemTemplate += wTextLen;

// Append the control's dtilInfo member
*szDlgItemTemplate = dtilInfo;
szDlgItemTemplate += sizeof(BYTE);

// Append the control's dtilData member
_fmemcpy(szDlgItemTemplate, dtilData, dtilInfo);
szDlgItemTemplate += dtilInfo;

 // Store in the first two bytes the number of bytes used
// in the block
*wNumBytes = (WORD) (szDlgItemTemplate - (LPSTR) wNumBytes);

GlobalUnlock(hMemNew);
return(MAKELONG(TRUE, hMemNew));
}

void FAR PASCAL DoneAddingControls (GLOBALHANDLE hMem) {
WORD FAR *wNumBytes;

// wNumBytes points to beginning of memory block
wNumBytes = (WORD FAR *) GlobalLock(hMem);

// Move all the bytes in the block down two bytes
_fmemcpy(wNumBytes, wNumBytes + 1, *wNumBytes - 2);
GlobalUnlock(hMem);

// Once this function is executed, no more items can be
// added to the dialog-box template
}
```

```
#ifdef _DEMO
//***************************************************************
// Functions for the Dynamic Modal and Modeless Dialog Box
// Demonstrations

#include "dialog.h"

#define MAXDLGITEMDATA  (10)

struct {
    int x, y, cx, cy, id;
    long Style;
    LPSTR szClass, szText;
    BYTE Info;
    BYTE Data[MAXDLGITEMDATA];

} DynamicDlgBoxData[] = {

    {  4,  4, 32, 12, -1, SS_LEFT, "STATIC", "&Edit box:", 0,
       { 0 } },

    { 40,  4, 64, 12, ID_EDITBOX, ES_LEFT | WS_BORDER | WS_TABSTOP
       | WS_GROUP, "EDIT", "", 0, { 0 } },

    {  4, 18, 40,  8, -1, SS_LEFT, "STATIC", "&Listbox:", 0,
       { 0 } },

    {  4, 28, 76, 41, ID_LISTBOX, LBS_NOTIFY | LBS_SORT |
       LBS_STANDARD | WS_BORDER | WS_VSCROLL | WS_TABSTOP |
       WS_GROUP, "LISTBOX", "", 0, { 0 } },

    { 132,  4, 36, 12, IDOK, BS_DEFPUSHBUTTON | WS_TABSTOP |
       WS_GROUP, "BUTTON", "&Ok", 0, { 0 } },

    { 176,  4, 36, 12, IDCANCEL, BS_PUSHBUTTON | WS_TABSTOP |
       WS_GROUP, "BUTTON", "&Cancel", 0, { 0 } },

    { 88, 24, 56, 44, -1, BS_GROUPBOX | WS_GROUP, "BUTTON",
       "Group box", 0, { 0 } },
```

```
{ 92, 36, 48, 12, ID_RADIO1, BS_RADIOBUTTON | WS_TABSTOP,
   "BUTTON", "Radio &1", 0, { 0 } },

{ 92, 48, 48, 12, ID_RADIO2, BS_RADIOBUTTON | WS_TABSTOP,
   "BUTTON", "Radio &2", 0, { 0 } },

{ 152, 32, 60, 12, ID_CHECKBOX, BS_CHECKBOX | WS_TABSTOP |
   WS_GROUP, "BUTTON", "C&heck box", 0, { 0 } },

{ 0, 0, 0, 0, 0, 0, NULL, NULL, 0, { 0 } }
};

BOOL FAR PASCAL DynamicDlgProc (HWND hDlg, WORD wMsg, WORD wParam,
   LONG lParam) {
  BOOL fProcessed = TRUE;
  switch (wMsg) {

    case WM_INITDIALOG:
       break;

    case WM_COMMAND:
       switch (wParam) {
         case IDOK:
         case IDCANCEL:
           // Although the two pushbuttons for IDOK and
           // IDCANCEL are not included in the modeless
           // version of this dialog box, these options can
           // still come through to here if the user presses
           // the "Enter" or "Esc" key, respectively.

           // In the case of a modeless dialog box, we cannot
           // call the EndDialog() function. We can determine
           // if this window is the modeless one because it
           // does not have the IDOK button within it. In this
           // case, GetDlgItem() below returns NULL.
           if (GetDlgItem(hDlg, IDOK) == NULL)
             break;
```

```
                    if (HIWORD(lParam) == BN_CLICKED)
                        EndDialog(hDlg, wParam);
                    break;

                default:
                    break;
            }
            break;

        default:
            fProcessed = FALSE; break;
    }
    return(fProcessed);
}

GLOBALHANDLE FAR PASCAL BuildDynamicDlgBox (BOOL fModeless) {
    GLOBALHANDLE hMem;
    WORD x;
    DWORD dwAddDlgControlResult;

    // Create the dynamic dialog box header information
    if (fModeless) hMem = CreateDlgTemplate( WS_BORDER | WS_CAPTION
        | WS_DLGFRAME | WS_SYSMENU | WS_VISIBLE | WS_POPUP |
        DS_SETFONT, 6, 25, 216, 72, "", "", "Dynamic Modeless Demo",
        8, "Helv");
    else
        hMem = CreateDlgTemplate( WS_BORDER | WS_CAPTION |
            WS_DLGFRAME | WS_SYSMENU | WS_VISIBLE | WS_POPUP, 6,
            25, 216, 72, "", "", "Dynamic Modal Demo", 0, "");

    if (hMem == NULL)
        return(hMem);

    // Add each of the controls in the DynamicDlgBoxData array
    for (x = 0; DynamicDlgBoxData[x].szClass != NULL; x++) {
```

```
        // Do not add the "Ok" and "Cancel" buttons if a modeless
        // dialog box is being created
        if (fModeless) {
            if (DynamicDlgBoxData[x].id == IDOK ||
                DynamicDlgBoxData[x].id == IDCANCEL)
                continue;
        }

        dwAddDlgControlResult = AddDlgControl(hMem,
            DynamicDlgBoxData[x].x,        DynamicDlgBoxData[x].y,
            DynamicDlgBoxData[x].cx,       DynamicDlgBoxData[x].cy,
            DynamicDlgBoxData[x].id,
            DynamicDlgBoxData[x].Style | WS_VISIBLE,
            DynamicDlgBoxData[x].szClass,
            DynamicDlgBoxData[x].szText,
            DynamicDlgBoxData[x].Info,     DynamicDlgBoxData[x].Data);

        // LOWORD is FALSE if insufficient memory exists
        if (LOWORD(dwAddDlgControlResult) == FALSE) break;

        // HIWORD is handle to new block of memory
        hMem = HIWORD(dwAddDlgControlResult);
    }

    // LOWORD is FALSE if insufficient memory exists; free what
    // we have and return NULL to caller
    if (LOWORD(dwAddDlgControlResult) == FALSE) {
        GlobalFree(hMem);
        hMem = NULL;
    } else {
        // Clean up the dialog box information
        DoneAddingControls(hMem);
    }

    // Return the handle to the dynamic dialog box information
    return(hMem);
}
#endif
```

Listing 3-8. DLG-DYNA.H dynamic dialog box header module.

```
/*******************************************************************
Module name: Dlg-Dyna.H
Programmer : Jeffrey M. Richter
*******************************************************************/

GLOBALHANDLE FAR PASCAL CreateDlgData(
    LONG dtStyle,
    int dtX, int dtY,        // in dialog-box units
    int dtCX, int dtCY,      // in dialog-box units
    LPSTR dtMenuName,        // "" if no menu
    LPSTR dtClassName,       // "" if standard dialog-box class
    LPSTR dtCaptionText,
    short int PointSize,     // Only used if DS_SETFONT style
                             // specified
    LPSTR szTypeFace);       // Only used if DS_SETFONT style
                             // specified

// LOWORD = Success(TRUE)/Failure(FALSE), HIWORD=New hMem
DWORD FAR PASCAL AddDlgItem (
    GLOBALHANDLE hMem,       // handle from CreateDlgData or
                             // AddDlgItem
    int dtilX, int dtilY,    // in dialog-box units
    int dtilCX, int dtilCY,  // in dialog-box units
    int dtilID,
    long dtilStyle,          // (WS_CHILD | WS_VISIBLE) is
                             // automatically added
    LPSTR dtilClass,         // May be: "BUTTON", "EDIT",
                             // "STATIC", "LISTBOX",
                             // "SCROLLBAR", "COMBOBOX"
    LPSTR dtilText,
    BYTE dtilInfo,           // number of additional data bytes
    LPBYTE dtilData);        // value passed through
                             // lpCreateParams field of CREATESTRUCT

void FAR PASCAL DoneAddingControls (
    GLOBALHANDLE hMem);      // handle from CreateDlgData or
                             // AddDlgItem
```

```
#ifdef _DEMO
//*************************************************************
// Functions for the Dynamic Dialog Box Demonstrations

BOOL FAR PASCAL DynamicDlgProc (HWND hDlg, WORD wMsg, WORD wParam,
    LONG lParam);
GLOBALHANDLE FAR PASCAL BuildDynamicDlgBox (BOOL fModeless);
#endif
```

Listing 3-9. DIALOG.H dialog box template defines.

```
#define ID_ADDCONTROL        100
#define ID_CARITY            101
#define ID_CHANGETABORDER    102
#define ID_CHECKBOX          103
#define ID_CITY              104
#define ID_DEFAULTBOX        105
#define ID_DIVORCED          106
#define ID_EDITBOX           107
#define ID_FEMALE            108
#define ID_LISTBOX           109
#define ID_MALE              110
#define ID_NAME              111
#define ID_NAMETEXT          112
#define ID_OPTIONS           113
#define ID_OVER25            114
#define ID_PHONE             115
#define ID_QUEST             116
#define ID_RADIO1            117
#define ID_RADIO2            118
#define ID_SCROLLBAR         119
#define ID_SMOKES            120
#define ID_STATE             121
#define ID_STREET            122
#define ID_VERSION           123
#define ID_XBUTTON           124
#define ID_ZIP               125
#define IDCANCEL             2
#define IDOK                 1
```

Listing 3-10. DLGTECH.RC application resource file.

```
/**************************************************************
Module name: DlgTech.RC
Programmer : Jeffrey M. Richter
**************************************************************/

#include <windows.h>

#include "dlgtech.h"
#include "dialog.h"
#include "dlgtech.dlg"

DlgTech  ICON    MOVEABLE DISCARDABLE DlgTech.Ico

DlgTech  MENU
BEGIN
   POPUP    "&Examples"
     BEGIN
     MENUITEM "&SetWindowPos demo...",  IDM_SETWINDOWPOSDEMO
     MENUITEM "&Options demo...",       IDM_OPTIONSDEMO
     MENUITEM "&ModalLess demo...",     IDM_MODALLESSDEMO
     MENUITEM "&Dynamic modal demo...", IDM_DYNAMICMODALDEMO
     MENUITEM "D&ynamic modeless demo...",
        IDM_DYNAMICMODELESSDEMO
     MENUITEM SEPARATOR
     MENUITEM "A&bout DlgTech...",      IDM_ABOUT
     END
END
```

Listing 3-11. DLGTECH.DLG dialog-box templates.

```
OPTIONS DIALOG LOADONCALL MOVEABLE DISCARDABLE 9, 24, 228, 100
CAPTION "Options Demo Dialog Box"
STYLE WS_BORDER | WS_CAPTION | WS_DLGFRAME | WS_SYSMENU |
   WS_VISIBLE | WS_POPUP
```

```
BEGIN
    CONTROL "&Name:", -1, "static", SS_LEFT | WS_CHILD, 4, 4,
        24, 12
    CONTROL "", ID_NAME, "edit", ES_LEFT | WS_BORDER | WS_GROUP |
        WS_TABSTOP | WS_CHILD, 32, 4, 80, 12
    CONTROL "&Phone:", -1, "static", SS_LEFT | WS_CHILD, 4, 20,
        24, 12
    CONTROL "", ID_PHONE, "edit", ES_LEFT | WS_BORDER | WS_GROUP |
        WS_TABSTOP | WS_CHILD, 32, 20, 80, 12
    CONTROL "&Ok", IDOK, "button", BS_DEFPUSHBUTTON | WS_GROUP |
        WS_TABSTOP | WS_CHILD, 116, 4, 44, 12
    CONTROL "&Cancel", IDCANCEL, "button", BS_PUSHBUTTON | WS_GROUP
        | WS_TABSTOP | WS_CHILD, 116, 20, 44, 12
    CONTROL "O&ptions >>", ID_OPTIONS, "button", BS_PUSHBUTTON |
        WS_GROUP | WS_TABSTOP | WS_CHILD, 4, 36, 52, 12
    CONTROL "", ID_DEFAULTBOX, "static", SS_BLACKRECT | WS_CHILD,
        165, 48, 4, 4
    CONTROL "&Street:", -1, "static", SS_LEFT | WS_CHILD, 4, 52,
        24, 12
    CONTROL "", ID_STREET, "edit", ES_LEFT | WS_BORDER | WS_GROUP |
        WS_TABSTOP | WS_CHILD, 32, 52, 128, 12
    CONTROL "&City:", -1, "static", SS_LEFT | WS_CHILD, 4, 68,
        20, 12
    CONTROL "", ID_CITY, "edit", ES_LEFT | WS_BORDER | WS_GROUP |
        WS_TABSTOP | WS_CHILD, 32, 68, 128, 12
    CONTROL "S&tate:", -1, "static", SS_LEFT | WS_CHILD, 4, 84,
        24, 12
    CONTROL "", ID_STATE, "edit", ES_LEFT | WS_BORDER | WS_GROUP |
        WS_TABSTOP | WS_CHILD, 32, 84, 32, 12
    CONTROL "&Zip:", -1, "static", SS_LEFT | WS_CHILD, 108, 84,
        16, 12
    CONTROL "", ID_ZIP, "edit", ES_LEFT | WS_BORDER | WS_GROUP |
        WS_TABSTOP | WS_CHILD, 128, 84, 32, 12
    CONTROL "Sex:", -1, "button", BS_GROUPBOX | WS_CHILD, 172, 0,
        48, 40
    CONTROL "&Female", ID_FEMALE, "button", BS_AUTORADIOBUTTON |
        WS_TABSTOP | WS_CHILD, 176, 12, 36, 12
    CONTROL "&Male", ID_MALE, "button", BS_AUTORADIOBUTTON |
        WS_TABSTOP | WS_CHILD, 176, 24, 28, 12
```

```
    CONTROL "&Divorced", ID_DIVORCED, "button", BS_AUTOCHECKBOX |
        WS_GROUP | WS_TABSTOP | WS_CHILD, 172, 52, 44, 12
    CONTROL "Charity &giver", ID_CARITY, "button", BS_AUTOCHECKBOX
        | WS_GROUP | WS_TABSTOP | WS_CHILD, 172, 68, 52, 12
    CONTROL "Smo&kes", ID_SMOKES, "button", BS_AUTOCHECKBOX |
        WS_GROUP | WS_TABSTOP | WS_CHILD, 172, 84, 52, 12
END

SETWINDOWPOS DIALOG LOADONCALL MOVEABLE DISCARDABLE 8, 29, 176, 52
CAPTION "SetWindowPos Demonstration"
STYLE WS_BORDER | WS_CAPTION | WS_DLGFRAME | WS_SYSMENU | WS_POPUP
BEGIN
    CONTROL "&Name:", ID_NAMETEXT, "static", SS_LEFT | WS_CHILD, 4,
        4, 24, 8
    CONTROL "", ID_NAME, "edit", ES_LEFT | WS_BORDER | WS_GROUP |
        WS_TABSTOP | WS_CHILD, 28, 4, 100, 12
    CONTROL "Over &25", ID_OVER25, "button", BS_AUTOCHECKBOX |
        WS_GROUP | WS_TABSTOP | WS_CHILD, 4, 20, 40, 12
    CONTROL "Change &Tab order", ID_CHANGETABORDER, "button",
        BS_PUSHBUTTON | WS_GROUP | WS_TABSTOP | WS_CHILD, 64,
        20, 64, 12
    CONTROL "&Add control", ID_ADDCONTROL, "button", BS_PUSHBUTTON
        | WS_GROUP | WS_TABSTOP | WS_CHILD, 4, 36, 44, 12
    CONTROL "&Ok", IDOK, "button", BS_DEFPUSHBUTTON | WS_GROUP |
        WS_TABSTOP | WS_CHILD, 136, 4, 36, 12
    CONTROL "&Cancel", IDCANCEL, "button", BS_PUSHBUTTON | WS_GROUP
        | WS_TABSTOP | WS_CHILD, 136, 20, 36, 12
END

ABOUT DIALOG LOADONCALL MOVEABLE DISCARDABLE 16, 20, 126, 92
CAPTION "About DlgTech"
STYLE WS_BORDER | WS_CAPTION | WS_DLGFRAME | WS_SYSMENU |
    WS_VISIBLE | WS_POPU
BEGIN
    CONTROL "DlgTech", -1, "static", SS_ICON | WS_CHILD, 4, 16,
        18, 21
    CONTROL "DlgTech", -1, "static", SS_CENTER | WS_CHILD, 22, 8,
        100, 12
    CONTROL "Written by:", -1, "static", SS_CENTER | WS_CHILD, 22,
        20, 100, 12
```

```
    CONTROL "Jeffrey M. Richter", -1, "static", SS_CENTER |
      WS_CHILD, 22, 32, 100, 12
    CONTROL "Version date:", -1, "static", SS_CENTER | WS_CHILD,
      22, 48, 100, 12
    CONTROL "", ID_VERSION, "static", SS_CENTER | WS_CHILD, 22, 60,
      100, 12
    CONTROL "&Ok", IDOK, "button", BS_DEFPUSHBUTTON | WS_TABSTOP |
      WS_CHILD, 40, 76, 44, 12
END

MODALLESS DIALOG LOADONCALL MOVEABLE DISCARDABLE 9, 27, 132, 36
CAPTION "ModalLess Dialog Box Demo"
STYLE WS_BORDER | WS_CAPTION | WS_DLGFRAME | WS_SYSMENU | WS_POPUP
BEGIN
    CONTROL "&Name:", -1, "static", SS_LEFT | WS_CHILD, 4, 4,
      24, 12
    CONTROL "", ID_NAME, "edit", ES_LEFT | WS_BORDER | WS_TABSTOP |
      WS_CHILD, 28, 4, 100, 12
    CONTROL "&Ok", IDOK, "button", BS_DEFPUSHBUTTON | WS_TABSTOP |
      WS_CHILD, 24, 20, 36, 12
    CONTROL "&Cancel", IDCANCEL, "button", BS_PUSHBUTTON |
      WS_TABSTOP | WS_CHILD, 72, 20, 36, 12
END
```

Listing 3-12. DLGTECH.DEF application definitions file.

```
; Module name: DlgTech.DEF
; Programmer : Jeffrey M. Richter

NAME         DlgTech
DESCRIPTION  'DlgTech: Dialog techniques Application'
STUB         'WinStub.exe'
EXETYPE      WINDOWS
CODE         MOVEABLE DISCARDABLE PRELOAD
DATA         MOVEABLE MULTIPLE PRELOAD
HEAPSIZE     1024
STACKSIZE    4096
```

```
EXPORTS
    AppWndProc
    OptionsDlgProc
    DynamicDlgProc
    ModalLessDlgProc
    SWPDlgProc
    AboutDlgProc
    EnableChildrenInOptionArea
```

Listing 3-13. MAKEFILE for dialog techniques application.

```
#******************************************************************
#Module name: MAKEFILE
#Programmer : Jeffrey M. Richter
#******************************************************************

PROG = DlgTech
MODEL = S
CFLAGS = -A$(MODEL) -D_WINDOWS -Gcsw2 -W4 -Zlepid -Od -D_DEMO
LFLAGS = /NOE/BA/A:16/M/CO/LI/F
LIBS = $(MODEL)libcew + libw

M1 = $(PROG).obj dlg-dyna.obj dlg-opts.obj dlg-mdls.obj

ICONS = $(PROG).ico
BITMAPS =
CURSORS =
RESOURCES = $(ICONS) $(BITMAPS) $(CURSORS)

.SUFFIXES: .rc

.rc.res:
    rc -r $*.rc

$(PROG).Exe: $(M1) $(PROG).Def $(PROG).Res
    link $(LFLAGS) @<<$(PROG).lnk
```

```
$(M1)
$(PROG), $(PROG), $(LIBS), $(PROG)
<<
   rc $(PROG).Res

$(PROG).obj:    $*.c $*.h dlg-dyna.h dlg-opts.h dlg-mdls.h
dlg-dyna.obj:   $*.c $*.h
dlg-opts.obj:   $*.c $*.h
dlg-mdls.obj:   $*.c $*.h
```

CHAPTER 4

Designing Custom Child Controls

The system global child control classes supplied by Windows provide standard elements of the user interface. Microsoft endowed these controls with many features so they would be suitable for use in almost any application. However, there may be occasions when one of the supplied child controls just doesn't have the features your application requires. The solution is to design and implement your own child controls. These custom controls may be used in dialog boxes or as stand-alone windows.

In this chapter we'll create two custom child controls. The first one, Meter, lets a user know how much of a job has been completed. This type of control is frequently used by installation software to indicate the percentage of the files that have been copied from the floppy disk to the hard drive. In fact, the Setup program used to install Microsoft Windows uses this type of control (see Figure 4-1).

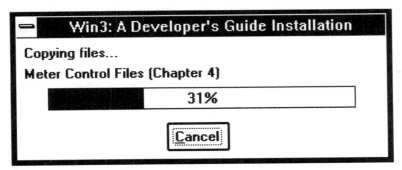

Figure 4-1. Dialog box containing a Meter custom control.

The second control is called a *spin button*. The spin button lets mouse users scroll through a list of values. It is a small window that usually appears just to the right of an edit control. The Microsoft Windows Control Panel application uses several. Spin buttons appear to the right of the date and time fields in Control Panel, as shown in Figure 4-2.

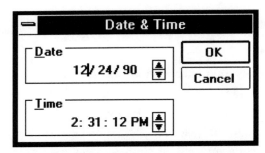

Figure 4-2. Dialog box containing two Spin Button controls.

Rules for Designing Custom Child Controls

Designing custom child controls and designing normal window classes are very similar. It is slightly more difficult to design custom child controls than to design an application's main window because most child controls are designed so that several instances of them may exist at one time.

A child control should be designed with the knowledge that its capabilities will be enhanced in the future. As you write applications, you will hear yourself saying, "I could use that custom child control if it only had (fill in the feature)." You will find that adding the new capabilities to your control for one application will improve the other applications that already use the control. Watch out for overdesigning your custom controls or adding features that you speculate might be useful *someday*. It is much better to start with a simple design and add to it as necessary.

Do not add features to a custom control if the features are required only by a single application. Instead, add the features the application needs by subclassing or superclassing the custom child control.

You can implement your custom control as part of an application or as a DLL. There are two advantages to using a DLL. The first is that all of your applications may use the same control, and the window procedure for the control is only in memory once. The second advantage is that the control can be accessed by the SDK's Dialog Editor application. This allows you to design dialog boxes using your own child control as though it were one of the system global child controls, like LISTBOX and EDIT. Later in this chapter, I'll demonstrate how to use custom child controls in the Dialog Editor.

One of the most important design issues to keep in mind when implementing a custom control is that it should not use any global or static variables. Unlike application windows, child controls are usually created in bunches. Even if several instances of the same application are running, each has its own data segment where global and static variables are stored. This is not true for child controls. Changes made to global and static variables will affect all child controls of a single class, and this is usually not desired. For example, if windows created from the EDIT class stored their text in a global variable, all EDIT windows on the screen would always contain and display the same text.

A custom child control requires a cleanly designed programmatic interface that explains, in detail, all the capabilities of the custom child control and how the programmer can manage the control's actions. Designing the programmer's interface involves creating a list of #*defined* values that should be placed in a header file for the control. Any application that is going to use the custom child control must include this header file.

Each custom child control may have styles specific to the window class. These styles allow the programmer to fine-tune the control's behavior and appearance. A window's style is specified by the *dwStyle* parameter passed to the *CreateWindow* and *CreateWindowEx* functions.

The top 16 bits are used for window styles that are specific to all created windows. These include the *WS_BORDER*, *WS_VISIBLE*, and *WS_POPUP* styles, to name just a few.

The low 16 bits are specific to each class. For example, all the styles specific to the BUTTON class begin with *BS_*, and all the styles specific to the LISTBOX class begin with *LBS_*. When you design a custom child control, you also define the styles that can be used to modify the control's behavior.

Each custom child control may have messages specific to its window class. The first class-specific message should be defined as (*WM_USER* + 0). The next should be (*WM_USER* + 1) and so on. Like the styles, these messages should be listed in the control's header file.

Comments should completely explain what the message does, what the return value means (if anything), and the values of the *wParam* and *lParam* parameters. For example, the *LB_DELETESTRING* message for the LISTBOX class requires that the *wParam* parameter contain the index of the string to be deleted; the *lParam* parameter is not used. The return from this message is the number of strings remaining or *LB_ERR* if an error occurs. If this information is documented as a comment in the custom child control's header file, it will be very easy for the programmer to use this control.

The last part of the programmer's interface is the notification codes sent by the control to its parent when some action takes place. Each code, which may be any value, should be defined in the header file. The control notifies the parent of the action by sending a *WM_COMMAND* message. When the parent receives this message, the *wParam* parameter contains the ID for the child control. The *lParam* parameter contains the notification code in the high word and the child control's window handle in the low word.

To help send notification codes to the parent, the following function may be used:

```
LONG NEAR PASCAL NotifyParent (HWND hWndControl,
    WORD wNotifyCode) {
  LONG lResult;
  lResult = SendMessage(GetParent(hWndControl), WM_COMMAND,
          GetWindowWord(hWndControl, GWW_ID),
          MAKELONG(hWndControl, wNotifyCode));
  return(lResult);
}
```

This function creates the *WM_COMMAND* message with the proper parameters and sends it to the control's parent window. If the notification message requires a return value from the parent, this value is returned to the child. Curiously, the Windows dialog-box manager will always return zero to child controls in response to a *WM_COMMAND* message. (Microsoft may change this in the future.)

Once the programmer's interface has been designed and the control's header file created, you need to determine what information, if any, the custom child control will need internally. For example, each LISTBOX control must remember the number of items in the list, which item is selected, which item is at the top of the box, and other information.

If a small amount of information is common to all instances of the particular custom child control, the class's extra bytes can be used. To store a larger amount of information, a block of memory may be allocated and its handle stored in the class extra bytes.

For information that pertains to each instance of the custom child control, use the window extra bytes. Again, if the amount of information required is large, a block of memory should be allocated and its handle stored in the window extra bytes.

Although it is possible to use window properties to store information, storing the data in the window extra bytes is preferred due to the memory and performance overhead associated with window properties.

Implementing a Meter Control

The Meter control is used when an application is about to begin a lengthy process and wants to notify the user of its progress. The programmer first tells the control how many parts make up the entire job. Then, as the job is processing, the programmer notifies the Meter control after each part has completed. This causes Meter to update its display, which graphically depicts the percentage of the job that is complete.

Designing the Meter Programmer's Interface. The programmer's interface for the Meter control should be designed first. This control has no class-specific styles. However, Meter does define four class-specific window messages:

Message	Description	Returns	wParam	lParam
MM_SETPARTSINJOB	Tells the control how many parts are in the job	N/A	Number of parts in job	Not used
MM_GETPARTSINJOB	Returns the number of parts in the job	Number of parts in job	Not used	Not used
MM_SETPARTSCOMPLETE	Tells the control how many parts of the job have been completed	N/A	Number of completed parts	Not used
MM_GETPARTSCOMPLETE	Returns the number of parts that have been completed	Number of completed parts	Not Used	Not used

An application must initialize a Meter control after creating it by telling it how many parts make up the completed job. For example, if an installation program has 10 files to copy, the program might send a message to the Meter control to tell it that the job is divided into 10 parts:

```
SendDlgItemMessage(hDlg, ID_METER, MM_SETPARTSINJOB, 10, 0);
```

After each part of the job has been performed, the application sends a message to the Meter control telling it how many have been completed. So after each file has been copied from the floppy disk to the hard drive, the application must notify the Meter control:

```
for (nFileNum = 0; nFileNum < 10; nFileNum++) {
   // code to copy file from floppy disk to hard drive
   .
   .
   .
   SendDlgItemMessage(hDlg, ID_METER, MM_SETPARTSCOMPLETE,
      nFileNum + 1, 0);
}
```

After the Meter control receives the *MM_SETPARTSCOMPLETE* message, it computes the percentage of work done and updates its window. For example, after the program has copied the fourth file, Meter determines that four files out of 10 is 40% and redraws its window so that the leftmost 40% of the window is in one color and the rightmost 60% is in another color. The string "40%" is displayed in the center of Meter's window.

Should an application need to know how many parts the job is divided into, the application can send an *MM_GETPARTSINJOB* message:

```
wMaxValue = (WORD) SendDlgItemMessage(hDlg, ID_METER,
   MM_GETPARTSINJOB, 0, 0);
```

Likewise, an application may determine the number of parts of the job that have been completed by using the *MM_GETPARTSCOMPLETE* message:

```
wPartsDone = (WORD) SendDlgItemMessage(hDlg, ID_METER,
    MM_GETPARTSCOMPLETE, 0, 0);
```

Although all the preceding examples have demonstrated how messages would be sent to the Meter control if it were part of a dialog box, any custom child control may be created by using the *CreateWindow* or *CreateWindowEx* function. The Meter control would then be manipulated with the *SendMessage* function instead of *SendDlg-ItemMessage*. The first parameter of the *SendMessage* function must be the window handle of the control.

The Meter control's header file, METER.H, contains all the *#define*s discussed earlier.

Implementing the Meter Control Code. When a custom child control is im– plemented using a DLL, the window class for the control should be registered upon initialization of the library. The following is the code for the *LibMain* function:

```
HANDLE _hInstance = NULL;
.
.
.
BOOL EXPORT LibMain (HANDLE hModule, WORD wDataSeg,
      WORD wHeapSize, LPSTR lpszCmdLine) {
   BOOL fOk;
   _hInstance = hModule;
   if (wHeapSize != 0)
      UnlockData(0);        // Let data segment move

   fOk = RegisterControlClass(hModule);
   return(fOk);              // TRUE if initialization is successful
}
```

Once the control's window class has been registered, any application can create windows of the class. The *RegisterControlClass* function fills the *WNDCLASS* structure and returns the result of the call to *RegisterClass*:

```
static BOOL LOCAL RegisterControlClass (HANDLE hInstance) {
    WNDCLASS wc;
    wc.style            = CS_GLOBALCLASS | CS_HREDRAW | CS_VREDRAW;
    wc.lpfnWndProc      = MeterWndFn;
    wc.cbClsExtra       = 0;
    wc.cbWndExtra       = CBWNDEXTRA;
    wc.hInstance        = hInstance;
    wc.hIcon            = NULL;
    wc.hCursor          = LoadCursor(NULL, IDC_ARROW);
    wc.hbrBackground    = NULL;
    wc.lpszMenuName     = NULL;
    wc.lpszClassName    = _szControlName;
    return(RegisterClass(&wc));
}
```

Although the DLL registers the Meter control class, windows of this class are created by the application. Therefore, the Meter control must be registered as an application global class. This is done by *OR*ing the *CS_GLOBALCLASS* style with any other desired class styles. Failing to use this style will cause the Meter class to be registered as application local, and Windows would not allow any applications to create windows of this class.

Specifying the *CS_HREDRAW* and *CS_VREDRAW* styles causes Windows to invalidate the entire window whenever its size changes. If these styles are not included, Windows does not invalidate any part of the window when the window is made smaller and invalidates only the uncovered area of a window when the window is made larger. Because Meter should be completely redrawn whenever the size of the window is changed, these two styles must be specified. It should be noted, however, that the size of a Meter control, like most controls in a dialog box, does not change after it is created.

Since most custom child controls maintain some internal information, the *cbWndExtra* member of the *WNDCLASS* structure is usually not zero. The Meter control must maintain a value representing the number of parts in the whole job and the number of parts that have been completed. Because each of these values requires a word, four extra bytes are necessary for Meter windows. The *#defines* to access this information are found at the top of the METER.C file:

```
#define CBWNDEXTRA              (4)
#define GWW_PARTSINJOB          (0)
#define GWW_PARTSCOMPLETE       (2)
```

The last member of note in the *WNDCLASS* structure is *hbrBackground*. When *BeginPaint* is called, Windows sends a *WM_ERASEBKGND* message to the window procedure. Normally, window procedures pass this message directly to the *DefWindowProc* function for processing. If the *hbrBackground* member's value is NULL, *DefWindowProc* doesn't paint the window's background and returns zero, indicating that the background has not been erased. Because the *WM_PAINT* message in the Meter control's window procedure draws the window including its background, painting the window is faster if *DefWindowProc* doesn't also have to paint the background. Also, Meter's background color varies depending on the number of parts that have been completed. If *DefWindowProc* were allowed to erase the background, Meter's window would flash because it would first be painted with the background color specified when the class was registered; that color would change when the *WM_PAINT* message redrew the background.

When the DLL that registered the custom child control's window class terminates, the window exit procedure (*WEP*) is called. This procedure removes the custom child control's window class by calling the *UnregisterClass* function. The *WEP* procedure for the Meter control is as follows:

```
int FAR PASCAL WEP (int nSystemExit) {
   switch (nSystemExit) {
      case WEP_SYSTEM_EXIT:               // System is shutting down
         break;
```

```
   case WEP_FREE_DLL:              // Usage count is zero
      break;
   }
 UnregisterClass(_szControlName, _hInstance);
 return(1);                        // Termination successful
}
```

Before the class is unregistered, all windows created from the class must be destroyed. This is the responsibility of the application that created the windows. We will discuss at the end of the chapter how an application loads the DLL and how it tells Windows when it is no longer needed.

A Special Message for Child Controls. Meter's window procedure, *MeterWndFn*, is almost identical to any other window procedure except that it processes one additional message, *WM_GETDLGCODE*. The dialog-box manager periodically sends *WM_GETDLGCODE* messages to windows that are in a dialog box. If the user presses a key while a dialog box is active, the dialog-box manager receives the key. It then sends the *WM_GETDLGCODE* message to the window that currently has the input focus, asking it what type of keys it is interested in receiving. The control must respond by using one of the identifiers defined in WINDOWS.H:

Identifier	Meaning
DLGC_BUTTON	Control can be checked.
DLGC_DEFPUSHBUTTON	Control is a default pushbutton.
DLGC_HASSETSEL	Control processes *EM_SETSEL* messages.
DLGC_RADIOBUTTON	Control is a radio button.
DLGC_STATIC	Control doesn't processes any keys.
DLGC_UNDEFPUSHBUTTON	Control is not a default pushbutton.
DLGC_WANTALLKEYS	Control processes all keys. Same as *DLGC_WANTMESSAGE*.
DLGC_WANTARROWS	Control processes arrow keys.
DLGC_WANTCHARS	Control wants *WM_CHAR* messages.

Identifier	Meaning
DLGC_WANTMESSAGE	Control processes all keys. Same as *DLGC_WANTALLKEYS*.
DLGC_WANTTAB	Control processes the Tab key.

This message allows a control to let the dialog-box manager know which keys it would like to receive. For example, if the EDIT control's window procedure responded to the *WM_GETDLGCODE* message by returning *DLG_WANTALLKEYS*, the Tab key would be sent to the control and the dialog-box manager would not change the input focus to the next control, as would ordinarily be expected.

Because Meter does not process any keystrokes, it simply returns the *DLGC_STATIC* value:

```
BOOL FAR PASCAL MeterWndProc (HWND hDlg, WORD wMsg, WORD wParam,
      LONG lParam) {
   LONG lResult = 0;

   switch (wMsg) {
      case WM_GETDLGCODE:
         lResult = DLGC_STATIC;
         break;
      .
      .
      .
   }
   .
   .
   .

   return(lResult);
}
```

Painting the Meter Control. Most of the work done by the Meter control is in the *WM_PAINT* message. First, the values used by Meter must be retrieved by sending the *MM_GETPARTSINJOB* and *MM_GETPARTSCOMPLETE* messages:

```
wPartsInJob = (WORD) SendMessage(hWnd, MM_GETPARTSINJOB, 0, 01);
wPartsComplete = (WORD) SendMessage(hWnd, MM_GETPARTSCOMPLETE,
    0, 01);
```

These values are retrieved by sending a message to the control instead of accessing the window's extra bytes directly with *GetWindowWord*. If Meter's implementation is someday changed so that these values are stored in a local block of memory, our code to retrieve the values would not have to change; only the processing for the *MM_GETPARTSINJOB* and *MM_GETPARTSCOMPLETE* message would need to be modified. This is good programming practice because it places fewer dependencies in the code.

Now that we have these values, we create a string reflecting the percentage of the job completed:

```
wsprintf(szPercentage, "%d%%", (100 * wPartsComplete) /
    wPartsInJob);
```

The *BeginPaint* function gets a device context for the window. The window's background and text colors are set to what the user has chosen in the Colors section of Control Panel by default:

```
BeginPaint(hWnd, &ps);

SetBkColor(ps.hdc, GetSysColor(COLOR_WINDOW));
SetTextColor(ps.hdc, GetSysColor(COLOR_WINDOWTEXT));
```

Most child controls allow the parent to alter their colors. For example, an application may let the user select a color by presenting three scroll bars: one for the amount of red, one for the amount of green, and one for the amount of blue. Just before each scroll bar is about to paint itself, it allows the parent to alter the colors it will use. This way, the parent could make the scroll bars themselves appear as red, green, and blue.

Child controls let parents alter their colors by sending a *WM_CTLCOLOR* message before the child paints its window. When the parent receives this message, *wParam* contains the handle to the device context the child will use when painting; *lParam* contains the child control's window handle in the low word and an identifier for the control type in the high word. The following identifiers are used to notify the parent of the type of control that is about to begin painting:

WINDOWS.H identifier	WINDOWS.H value	Type of control
CTLCOLOR_BTN	3	BUTTON control
CTLCOLOR_DLG	4	Dialog box
CTLCOLOR_EDIT	1	EDIT control
CTLCOLOR_LISTBOX	2	LISTBOX or COMBOBOX control
CTLCOLOR_SCROLLBAR	5	SCROLLBAR control
CTLCOLOR_STATIC	6	STATIC control

You may define an identifier for your own custom child controls via a *CTLCOLOR_** identifier in the header file for your control. Make sure you select a value that does not conflict with any of the values above. METER.H defines the following identifier for use with the *WM_CTLCOLOR* message:

```
#define CTLCOLOR_METER              (100)
```

By passing the handle to the device context in *wParam*, the parent can use *SetBkColor* and *SetTextColor* to change the color the control will use for painting. The parent also has the option of changing any of the other attributes associated with a device context. When the parent receives a *WM_CTLCOLOR* message, it must

return the handle of a valid brush. If the parent does not trap the *WM_CTL*
message, *DefWindowProc* does not alter anything in the device contex
returns a valid brush handle on behalf of the parent. The code that proc___
WM_PAINT message in the control's window procedure must select this brush into
the device context before painting:

```
HBRUSH hBrush;
.
.
.
hBrush = (HBRUSH) SendMessage(GetParent(hWnd), WM_CTLCOLOR,
    ps.hdc, MAKELONG(hWnd, CTLCOLOR_METER));
SelectObject(ps.hdc, hBrush);
.
.
.
// Paint the window using the DC modified by parent and
// the brush returned by parent
.
.
.
EndPaint(hWnd, &ps);
```

The control's parent is responsible for destroying the brush. Brushes are usually
created by the dialog box during *WM_INITDIALOG* message processing and destroyed during *WM_DESTROY* message processing.

Meter takes the window's background and text colors and displays their inverse
to represent the part of the task that has been completed:

```
dwColor = GetBkColor(ps.hdc);
SetBkColor(ps.hdc, SetTextColor(ps.hdc, dwColor));
```

The left part of the window indicates the percentage of the job complete, while
the right indicates the remaining percentage of the job. In the middle of the window
is the percentage complete, shown as a number. The rectangle that bounds the area
to be drawn in the percent-completed color is calculated as follows:

```
GetClientRect(hWnd, &rcClient);
SetRect(&rcPrcnt, 0, 0, (rcClient.right * wPartsComplete) /
  wPartsInJob, rcClient.bottom);
```

The *ExtTextOut* function draws the left side of the window:

```
SetTextAlign(ps.hdc, TA_CENTER | TA_TOP);
ExtTextOut(ps.hdc, rcClient.right / 2,
  (rcClient.bottom - HIWORD(GetTextExtent(ps.hdc, "X", 1))) / 2,
  ETO_OPAQUE | ETO_CLIPPED, &rcPrcnt,
  szPercentage, lstrlen(szPercentage), NULL);
```

The first parameter is the same as for all functions that perform output: the handle to the device context. The second and third parameters specify the x- and y-coordinates where the string is to be placed. Because the text alignment is set to *TA_CENTER*, the text string will always be displayed centered around the middle of the window (*rcClient.right / 2*). To center the text vertically, the height of a capital letter *X* is subtracted from the height of the window and the result divided by two. The fourth parameter specifies that the background color should be used to fill the rectangle (*ETO_OPAQUE*) and that no text should be drawn outside the clipping rectangle (*ETO_CLIPPED*). The next parameter is the address of the clipping rectangle to be used. The address of the string containing the text and the length of the string are specified next. The final parameter is NULL, indicating that we want Windows to use normal spacing for displaying the text.

The coordinates of the rectangle are now changed to fill in the right part of the window. First, the colors are inverted again:

```
rcPrcnt.left = rcPrcnt.right;
rcPrcnt.right = rcClient.right;

dwColor = GetBkColor(ps.hdc);
SetBkColor(ps.hdc, SetTextColor(ps.hdc, dwColor));
```

ExtTextOut is called again with the same parameters as before. This paints the right part of Meter's window.

224

Let's look at an example. If the job is 50% complete, Meter should display the string "50%" in the center of the window. The left half of the window should be in one color and the right half in a different color. If the background were drawn first and the string placed on top of it, some of the string would be unreadable because the text color would be the same as the background color. The solution: Write the string to the screen twice, first with the clipping rectangle on the left half the window and then with the clipping rectangle on the right. *ExtTextOut* will not allow any text to be written outside the clipping rectangle because of the *ETO_CLIPPED* option. In the case of our string, the first call to *ExtTextOut* draws the five and the left half of the zero. The second call draws the right half of the zero and the percent symbol.

The remaining messages processed by Meter's window procedure are class-specific. *MM_GETPARTSINJOB* and *MM_GETPARTSCOMPLETE* simply place calls to *GetWindowWord* and return the result to the caller. *MM_SETPARTSINJOB* and *MM_SETPARTSCOMPLETE* call *SetWindowWord,* passing it the value in *wParam.* Because a value has changed, making the contents of Meter's window inaccurate, we call *InvalidateRect* so a *WM_PAINT* message for the Meter control will be placed in the application's message queue.

Windows will not examine any window's message queue until the executing application yields control. This happens when the application calls the Windows function *PeekMessage, GetMessage,* or *WaitMessage.* When copying files from the floppy drive to the hard disk, for instance, the application may not yield control to Windows until all the files have been copied. This means the *WM_PAINT* message might not be sent to Meter until all files have been copied. Meter would report "0% complete" until the job was done, then suddenly jump to "100% complete." The user would never see any intermediate progress.

To force Meter to reflect the true percentage complete when the application sends a *MM_SETPARTSINJOB* or *MM_SETPARTSCOMPLETE* message, we must call *UpdateWindow.* This forces Windows to send the *WM_PAINT* message to the window immediately.

The following section, Integrating Custom Child Controls with the Dialog Editor, demonstrates how the Meter control can be added to dialog boxes with the Dialog Editor and how to manipulate Meter controls from your application. Because additional functions are necessary to integrate Meter with the Dialog Editor, the module-definitions file (METER.DEF) and the MAKEFILE appear later in this chapter. The Meter source and header modules appear in Listings 4-1 and 4-2.

Listing 4-1. METER.H DLL header module.

```
/***************************************************************
Module name: Meter.H
Programmer : Jeffrey M. Richter
***************************************************************/

// Meter control sends WM_CTLCOLOR message to parent window with
// the following identifier in the HIWORD of the lParam
#define CTLCOLOR_METER     (100)

// The Meter control has no class-specific window styles

// Meter control's class-specific window messages
#define MM_SETPARTSINJOB        (WM_USER + 0)
#define MM_GETPARTSINJOB        (WM_USER + 1)
#define MM_SETPARTSCOMPLETE     (WM_USER + 2)
#define MM_GETPARTSCOMPLETE     (WM_USER + 3)

// Meter control has no notification codes to send to parent
```

Listing 4-2. METER.C DLL source module.

```
/***************************************************************
Module name: Meter.C
Programmer : Jeffrey M. Richter
***************************************************************/

#include "..\nowindws.h"
#define OEMRESOURCE
```

226

```
#undef NOCOLOR
#undef NOCTLMGR
#undef NODRAWTEXT
#undef NOGDI
#undef NOKERNEL
#undef NOLSTRING
#undef NOMEMMGR
#undef NORASTEROPS
#undef NOUSER
#undef NOVIRTUALKEYCODES
#undef NOWINMESSAGES
#undef NOWINOFFSETS
#undef NOWINSTYLES
#include <windows.h>

#include "meter.h"

HANDLE _hInstance = NULL;
char _szControlName[] = "Meter";

#define CBWNDEXTRA          (4)
#define GWW_PARTSINJOB     (0)
#define GWW_PARTSCOMPLETE  (2)

static short NEAR PASCAL RegisterControlClass (HANDLE hInstance);
LONG FAR PASCAL MeterWndFn (HWND hWnd, WORD wMsg, WORD wParam,
   LONG lParam);

/**** Windows' Dynamic Link Library Initialization Routines ****/

BOOL FAR PASCAL LibMain (HANDLE hModule, WORD wDataSeg,
     WORD wHeapSize, LPSTR lpszCmdLine) {
   BOOL fOk;
   _hInstance = hModule;
   if (wHeapSize != 0) UnlockData(0);     // Let data segment move
   fOk = RegisterControlClass(hModule);
   return(fOk); // Return TRUE if initialization is successful
}
```

```
int FAR PASCAL WEP (int nSystemExit) {
   switch (nSystemExit) {
      case WEP_SYSTEM_EXIT:     // System is shutting down
         break;

      case WEP_FREE_DLL:        // Usage count is zero
         break;
   }
   UnregisterClass(_szControlName, _hInstance);
   return(1);                      // WEP function successful
}

static short NEAR PASCAL RegisterControlClass (HANDLE hInstance) {
   WNDCLASS wc;
   wc.style          = CS_GLOBALCLASS | CS_HREDRAW | CS_VREDRAW;
   wc.lpfnWndProc    = MeterWndFn;
   wc.cbClsExtra     = 0;
   wc.cbWndExtra     = CBWNDEXTRA;
   wc.hInstance      = hInstance;
   wc.hIcon          = NULL;
   wc.hCursor        = LoadCursor(NULL, IDC_ARROW);
   wc.hbrBackground  = NULL;
   wc.lpszMenuName   = NULL;
   wc.lpszClassName  = _szControlName;
   return(RegisterClass(&wc));
}

LONG FAR PASCAL MeterWndFn (HWND hWnd, WORD wMsg, WORD wParam,
      LONG lParam) {
   LONG lResult = 0;
   char szPercentage[10];
   RECT rcClient, rcPrcnt;
   PAINTSTRUCT ps;
   WORD wPartsInJob, wPartsComplete;
   HBRUSH hBrush;
   DWORD dwColor;

   switch (wMsg) {
      case WM_GETDLGCODE:
         lResult = DLGC_STATIC;
         break;
```

```
case WM_CREATE:               // lParam == &CreateStruct
   SendMessage(hWnd, MM_SETPARTSINJOB, 100, 0l);
   SendMessage(hWnd, MM_SETPARTSCOMPLETE, 50, 0);
   break;

case WM_PAINT:
   wPartsInJob = (WORD) SendMessage(hWnd, MM_GETPARTSINJOB,
      0, 0l);
   wPartsComplete = (WORD) SendMessage(hWnd,
      MM_GETPARTSCOMPLETE, 0, 0l);
   if (wPartsInJob == 0) {
      wPartsInJob = 1;
      wPartsComplete = 0;
   }
   wsprintf(szPercentage, "%d%%", (100 * wPartsComplete) /
      wPartsInJob);

   BeginPaint(hWnd, &ps);

   // Set up default foreground and background text colors
   SetBkColor(ps.hdc, GetSysColor(COLOR_WINDOW));
   SetTextColor(ps.hdc, GetSysColor(COLOR_WINDOWTEXT));

   // Send WM_CTLCOLOR message to parent in case parent
   // wants to use a different color in the Meter control
   hBrush = (HBRUSH) SendMessage(GetParent(hWnd),
      WM_CTLCOLOR, ps.hdc, MAKELONG(hWnd, CTLCOLOR_METER));

   // Always use brush returned by parent
   SelectObject(ps.hdc, hBrush);

   SetTextAlign(ps.hdc, TA_CENTER | TA_TOP);

   // Invert the foreground and background colors
   dwColor = GetBkColor(ps.hdc);
   SetBkColor(ps.hdc, SetTextColor(ps.hdc, dwColor));

   // Set rectangle coordinates to include only left
   // percentage of the window
   GetClientRect(hWnd, &rcClient);
```

```
        SetRect(&rcPrcnt, 0, 0, (rcClient.right * wPartsComplete)
          / wPartsInJob, rcClient.bottom);

        // Output the percentage value in the window.
        // Function also paints left part of window.
        ExtTextOut(ps.hdc, rcClient.right / 2,
          (rcClient.bottom - HIWORD(GetTextExtent(ps.hdc,
          "X", 1))) / 2, ETO_OPAQUE | ETO_CLIPPED, &rcPrcnt,
          szPercentage, lstrlen(szPercentage), NULL);

        // Adjust rectangle so that it includes the remaining
        // percentage of the window
        rcPrcnt.left = rcPrcnt.right;
        rcPrcnt.right = rcClient.right;

        // Invert the foreground and background colors
        dwColor = GetBkColor(ps.hdc);
        SetBkColor(ps.hdc, SetTextColor(ps.hdc, dwColor));

        // Output the percentage value a second time in the
        // window. Function also paints right part of window.
        ExtTextOut(ps.hdc, rcClient.right / 2,
          (rcClient.bottom - HIWORD(GetTextExtent(ps.hdc,
          "X", 1))) / 2, ETO_OPAQUE | ETO_CLIPPED, &rcPrcnt,
          szPercentage, lstrlen(szPercentage), NULL);

        EndPaint(hWnd, &ps);
        break;

    case MM_SETPARTSINJOB:
      SetWindowWord(hWnd, GWW_PARTSINJOB, wParam);
      InvalidateRect(hWnd, NULL, FALSE);
      UpdateWindow(hWnd);
      break;

    case MM_GETPARTSINJOB:
      lResult = (LONG) GetWindowWord(hWnd, GWW_PARTSINJOB);
      break;

    case MM_SETPARTSCOMPLETE:
      SetWindowWord(hWnd, GWW_PARTSCOMPLETE, wParam);
```

```
            InvalidateRect(hWnd, NULL, FALSE);
            UpdateWindow(hWnd);
            break;

        case MM_GETPARTSCOMPLETE:
            lResult = (LONG) GetWindowWord(hWnd, GWW_PARTSCOMPLETE);
            break;

        default:
            lResult = DefWindowProc(hWnd, wMsg, wParam, lParam);
            break;
    }
    return(lResult);
}
```

A Homespun Spin Button

Chapter 6 of IBM's *System Application Architecture Common User Access Advanced Interface Design Guide* describes the Spin Button control. Although many of the applications that come with Windows use spin buttons, Microsoft has not designed one as a system global class that can be used by our applications.

A spin button allows the user to cycle through a list of values. It should only be used when the choices are in consecutive order and the user can anticipate the next value. There should always be a default value in the edit field. A spin button is a convenience for mouse users only and never receives the keyboard input focus. Therefore, the EDIT control associated with the spin button should let the user type directly into the field and allow the use of the up and down arrow keys to cycle through the choices.

The programmer must tell the Spin Button control the range of possible values. For example, an application may associate a spin button with a month field. In this case, the application would tell the spin button that the valid range is 1 to 12. The spin button also maintains a value, within the valid range, that indicates the current value. If the month displayed in the edit field is July, the value associated with the spin button is 7.

Designing the Spin Button Programmer's Interface. The first step in designing the programmer's interface for the spin button is deciding what styles, if any, can be specified to modify the behavior of the custom child control. Our spin button supports only one style, *SPNS_WRAP*. By examining the Windows Control Panel application, we see spin buttons behaving in two ways. In the "Date/Time" option, the spin button wraps around when the value reaches a maximum or minimum. For example, if the month is 12 and the spin button is used to increment the month, the value wraps around to the value 1. Similarly, decrementing the month when it is at 1 changes the value to 12.

If you choose the "Desktop" option in the Control Panel, you'll notice that the range associated with the Granularity field is zero to 49 and the value will not wrap. That is, using the spin button to increment the Granularity field when it is at 49 has no effect on the value.

By default, our spin button will not allow wrapping. If the application wishes to create a spin button that does allow wrapping, you must *OR* the *SPNS_WRAP* style with the other window styles when creating the custom child control. The header file, SPIN.H, includes all the styles that can be used when creating a Spin Button control and must be included by applications that use this control. If spin buttons are created in dialog boxes that have been defined in the resource file, this header file must also be included there so that the resource compiler knows the values of any control-specific styles.

The only style available for spin buttons is the "wrap" flag. It is defined in SPIN.H as

```
#define SPNS_WRAP 0x0001L
```

The next part of the programmer's interface is the messages that are to be recognized by the control. The Spin Button control recognizes four messages, which are defined in SPIN.H. The messages and their descriptions are:

Message	Description	Returns	wParam	lParam
SPNM_SETRANGE	Sets the valid range.	N/A	Not used	Bottom of range in the low word. Top of range in the high word.
SPNM_GETRANGE	Gets the valid range.	Bottom of range in low word. Top of range in high word.	Not used	Not used
SPNM_SETCRNTVALUE	Sets the current value.	N/A	New value	Not used
SPNM_GETCRNTVALUE	Gets the current value.	Current value	Not used	Not used
SPNM_SCROLLVALUE	Increments or decrements the current value. The message is sent from the spin button itself. It is not sent from other windows.	N/A	Not used	Not used

It is sometimes necessary for a control to recognize messages that can only be sent from the control itself. For example, the spin button's window procedure sends a *SPNM_SCROLLVALUE* message to itself while the user holds down the mouse button. This message should never be sent from any other window. The message should be placed not in the control's header file but in the file containing the window procedure. It should be defined so that its value will not interfere with the values assigned to messages that may be sent from other windows. For example, defining the *SPNM_SCROLLVALUE* message as

```
#define SPNM_SCROLLVALUE  (WM_USER + 500)
```

leaves room for 500 public class-specific messages, (*WM_USER* + 0) to (*WM_USER* + 499). This should be more than enough. Remember that the values of class-specific messages must be within the range of (*WM_USER* + 0) to 0x7FFF. In WINDOWS.H, *WM_USER* is defined as 0x0400.

The last part of the programmer's interface defines the notification codes that can be sent from the custom child control. Notification codes are always sent via *WM_COMMAND* messages to the control's parent. The notification code *SPNN_VALUECHANGE* sent from a spin button notifies the parent whenever the spin button's value has changed.

Implementing the Spin Button Code. The *LibMain* and *WEP* functions in the spin button's source code are identical to those in Meter. *RegisterControlClass* is also identical, except that the *hbrBackground* member of the *WNDCLASS* structure is set to *COLOR_BTNFACE* + 1. Because of this, the spin button's background will have the same color as a pushbutton.

The Spin Button control must maintain a value representing the valid range as well as the current value. Because the range consists of a low number and a high number, a *DWORD* is required. The current value requires a *WORD*. The spin button also needs to maintain an additional *WORD* value that is used internally. This value is explained later. The *#defines* to access this information are found at the top of the SPIN.C file:

```
#define CBWNDEXTRA          (8)
#define GWL_RANGE           (0)
#define GWW_CRNTVALUE       (4)
#define GWW_TRIANGLEDOWN    (6)
```

Painting the Spin Button Control. The new pushbuttons in Windows 3.0 are complicated to draw because of their three-dimensional effect. To maintain this effect, the *WM_PAINT* message in the window procedure for a pushbutton control does not send *WM_CTLCOLOR* messages to the control's parent. Instead, colors are retrieved by calling *GetSysColor* using the *COLOR_BTNFACE*, *COLOR_BTN-SHADOW*, and *COLOR_BTNTEXT* identifiers. Because spin buttons use the same colors as pushbuttons, the spin button does not send a *WM_CTLCOLOR* message to its parent when processing a *WM_PAINT* message.

The code that processes the spin button's *WM_PAINT* message is shown below:

```
hDC = BeginPaint(hWnd, &ps);
GetClientRect(hWnd, &rc);
x = rc.right / 2;
y = rc.bottom / 2;

// Draw middle separator bar
MoveTo(hDC, 0, y);
LineTo(hDC, rc.right, y);

// Whenever a DC is retrieved, it is created with a WHITE_BRUSH
// by default. We must change this to a BLACK_BRUSH so that we
// can fill the triangles.
SelectObject(hDC, GetStockObject(BLACK_BRUSH));
```

235

```
// Draw top triangle and fill it in
MoveTo(hDC, x, 2);
LineTo(hDC, rc.right - 2, y - 2);
LineTo(hDC, 2, y - 2);
LineTo(hDC, x, 2);
FloodFill(hDC, x, y - 3, RGB(0, 0, 0));

// Draw bottom triangle and fill it in
MoveTo(hDC, 2, y + 2);
LineTo(hDC, rc.right - 2, y + 2);
LineTo(hDC, x, rc.bottom - 2);
LineTo(hDC, 2, y + 2);
FloodFill(hDC, x, y + 3, RGB(0, 0, 0));

EndPaint(hWnd, &ps);
break;
```

When *BeginPaint* is called, Windows repaints the background of the window using the color selected in the *hbrBackground* member of *WNDCLASS* when the class was registered. In this case, this is the color used for button faces, *COLOR_BTNFACE*. The x and y values are calculated to be the middle of the window. The spin button must draw a horizontal bar across the middle of the window and draw the two triangles.

Because the triangles are always drawn in black, *BLACK_BRUSH* is selected into the device context. Once the outline of each triangle has been drawn, a point is selected that is known to be within each triangle, and *FloodFill* fills the triangle with black.

Figure 4-3 shows how the interior of the spin button is drawn.

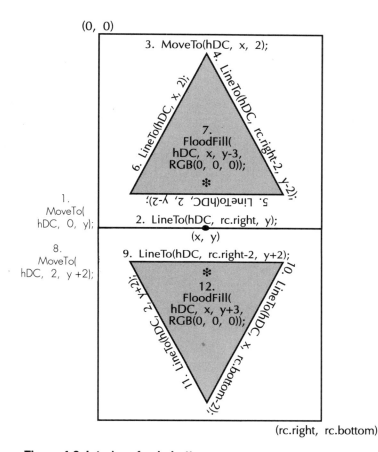

Figure 4-3. Interior of spin button.

Changing a Value with the Spin Button. A *WM_LBUTTONDOWN* message is sent to the spin button's window procedure when the user clicks the mouse. During this procedure, the spin button must determine whether the mouse is over the up-triangle or the down-triangle. This can easily be computed because the *lParam* for a *WM_LBUTTONDOWN* message contains the x- and y- coordinates of the mouse cursor relative to the window's client area:

237

```
typedef enum { TD_NONE, TD_UP, TD_DOWN } TRIANGLEDOWN;
.
.
.
LONG FAR PASCAL SpinWndFn (HWND hWnd, WORD wMsg, WORD wParam,
      LONG lParam) {
  TRIANGLEDOWN TriangleDown;
    .
    .
    .
  case WM_LBUTTONDOWN:
    GetClientRect(hWnd, &rc);
    if ((int) HIWORD(lParam) < rc.bottom / 2) {
        // mouse over up-triangle
        TriangleDown = TD_UP;
        rc.bottom /= 2;
    } else {
        // mouse over down-triangle
        TriangleDown = TD_DOWN;
        rc.top = rc.bottom / 2;
    }
    SetWindowWord(hWnd, GWW_TRIANGLEDOWN, TriangleDown);
    .
    .
    .
}
```

TriangleDown is an enumerated type that represents the triangle the mouse was last over. This value is stored in the window extra bytes for the spin button so that it can be used later by the *SPNM_SCROLLVALUE* message.

Using the updated value in the *RECT* variable, *rc*, we invert the half of the spin button over which the mouse was clicked to indicate to the user that the spin button has been activated:

```
hDC = GetDC(hWnd);
InvertRect(hDC, &rc);
ReleaseDC(hWnd, hDC);
```

We now tackle a common problem faced by many child controls and applications: how to continue scrolling when no messages are entering the window procedure.

Suppose you are marking text in a Notepad-like application by clicking the mouse on the start of the desired text and dragging the mouse below the window. Once the mouse moves below the window, the window no longer receives mouse messages. One way to continue scrolling is by setting a timer when the *WM_LBUTTONDOWN* message is received. This will cause *WM_TIMER* messages to come to your window procedure periodically. With each timer message, the window could be scrolled.

This method has some disadvantages:

1. Other applications are allowed to run while your application is scrolling and your window procedure is waiting for *WM_TIMER* messages. While this may seem like an advantage, the effect to the user is uneven, jerky scrolling. In fact, this may even give the appearance that your application has stopped working completely if another application does not relinquish control for you to receive another *WM_TIMER* message.

2. It requires a timer. Windows allows only 16 timers to be active at any one time. While this is usually sufficient, users should not expect to see an "Out of timers!" message when they want to begin scrolling through their text.

The spin button window procedure for scrolling avoids the problems associated with timers. This method starts a loop that compares the current Windows system time with the time the next event should occur. The system time is retrieved by using the *GetTickCount* function. If the system time is earlier than the event start time, the loop repeats. When the Windows system time is later than the event start time, the event is executed and the new event start time is set to the current Windows system time plus a programmer-defined delay period. The cycle then repeats.

It is important to decide on a time delay between scrolling events. The spin button uses an identifier at the top of its source code:

```
// delay between scrolling events in milliseconds
#define TIME_DELAY        (150)
```

We then calculate the time of the first event by retrieving the current Windows system time and subtracting from it the time delay. This ensures that the scrolling event occurs at least once:

```
dwEventTime = GetTickCount() - TIME_DELAY;
```

The *do...while* loop below will continue to send *SPNM_SCROLLVALUE* messages to the spin button's window procedure, telling it to scroll the button's value until the user has released the left mouse button:

```
do {
    if (dwEventTime > GetTickCount()) continue;
    SendMessage(hWnd, SPNM_SCROLLVALUE, 0, 0l);
    dwEventTime = GetTickCount() + TIME_DELAY;
} while (GetAsyncKeyState(VK_LBUTTON) & 0x8000);
```

The *GetAsyncKeyState* function tests the status of virtual keys. In this case, we test the status of the left mouse button (*VK_LBUTTON*). If the most significant bit of the return value is 1, the virtual key is still held down and the loop continues.

At the top of the loop we check to see if the current Windows system time is later than the event time. If it isn't, no actions are performed and the loop condition is tested again. If the event time has passed, the *SPNM_SCROLLVALUE* message causes the spin button to update its value. After the value has been scrolled, *dwEventTime* is set to the time the next event should occur and the loop continues.

Once the user has released the left mouse button, the Spin Button window must be redrawn to remove the half that is currently inverted:

```
InvalidateRect(hWnd, NULL, TRUE);
```

The *InvalidateRect* function instructs Windows to send a *WM_PAINT* message to the window procedure, redrawing the window in its "normal" state.

Scrolling the Spin Button. The value in the spin button is scrolled while the *SPNM_SCROLLVALUE* message is being processed. This is an internal message that is only sent by the spin button to itself. For this reason, the message is not in the header file, SPIN.H, but is defined at the top the SPIN.C source file (presented at the end of this section):

```
#define SPNM_SCROLLVALUE        (WM_USER + 500)
```

This message is generated at 150-millisecond intervals for as long as the user holds down the left mouse button.

You may notice by experimenting with the spin buttons in the "Date/Time" section of the Control Panel application that the user is able to change the scrolling direction while the mouse button is held down. That is, if the user activates the spin button by clicking on its down-triangle, the month value will begin to decrease. If the user now moves the mouse over the up-triangle without releasing the mouse button, the month values begin to increase and the spin button is inverted to indicate the direction change. Also notice that when the mouse cursor is not over the spin button at all, no scrolling occurs, even if the mouse button is held down.

The processing for the *SPNM_SCROLLVALUE* message is responsible for making our spin button behave the same way. First, if the mouse cursor is outside the spin button's window, nothing should happen. The following code accomplishes this:

```
GetCursorPos(&pt);
ScreenToClient(hWnd, &pt);
GetClientRect(hWnd, &rc);
if (!PtInRect(&rc, pt)) break;
```

The *GetCursorPos* function retrieves the current mouse position in screen coordinates. This value must be converted to client coordinates before the *PtInRect* function can determine whether the mouse cursor is within the spin button's client area.

Next, the current value and the valid range of the spin button are retrieved from the window extra bytes:

```
nNewVal = (int) SendMessage(hWnd, SPNM_GETCRNTVALUE, 0, 0l);
nCrntVal = nNewVal;
dwRange = SendMessage(hWnd, SPNM_GETRANGE, 0, 0l);
```

The function also determines whether this particular spin button was created with the *SPNS_WRAP* flag. This data will be used later.

```
fWrap = (BOOL) (GetWindowLong(hWnd, GWL_STYLE) & SPNS_WRAP);
```

To see if the user has changed direction by moving the mouse cursor over a different triangle, we must determine which triangle the mouse was over last and which half it is over now:

```
OldTriangleDown = GetWindowWord(hWnd, GWW_TRIANGLEDOWN);
TriangleDown = (pt.y < rc.bottom / 2) ? TD_UP : TD_DOWN;
```

If the user has changed directions, the window must be inverted to give visual feedback to the user that the spin button has recognized this. Remember that the processing in the *WM_LBUTTONDOWN* message has already inverted half of the window. Inverting the entire window has the effect of restoring the half that was already inverted and inverting the new half:

```
if (OldTriangleDown != TriangleDown) {
   hDC = GetDC(hWnd);
   InvertRect(hDC, &rc);
   ReleaseDC(hWnd, hDC);
}
```

Finally, we can scroll the value:

```
if (TriangleDown == TD_UP) {
   // If value is not at top of range, increment it
   if ((int) HIWORD(dwRange) > nCrntVal) nNewVal++;
   else {
      // If value is at top of range and the "wrap" flag is
      // set, set the value to the bottom of the range
      if (fWrap) nNewVal = (int) LOWORD(dwRange);
   }
} else {
   // If value is not at bottom of range, decrement it
   if ((int) LOWORD(dwRange) < nCrntVal) nNewVal--;
   else {
      // If value is at bottom of range and the "wrap" flag is
      // set, set the value to the top of the range
      if (fWrap) nNewVal = (int) HIWORD(dwRange);
   }
}
```

After the new value has been determined, if it differs from the previous value, the *SPNM_SETCRNTVALUE* message is sent to the spin button telling it the new value:

```
if (nNewVal != nCrntVal)
   SendMessage(hWnd, SPNM_SETCRNTVALUE, nNewVal, 0l);
```

This also notifies the parent window that the spin button's value has changed because the code that processes the *WM_SETCRNTVALUE* message sends a *WM_COMMAND* message with the *SPNN_VALUECHANGE* notification code to the parent.

Just before the processing of the *SPNM_SCROLLVALUE* message terminates, the new triangle that is down must be stored so we will know how to update the window when the next scroll event occurs:

```
SetWindowWord(hWnd, GWW_TRIANGLEDOWN, TriangleDown);
```

The spin button must also maintain the current value. Since this is a relatively small amount of information, it's best to use the window extra bytes.

The Integrating Custom Child Controls with the Dialog Editor section later in this chapter demonstrates how the Spin Button control can be added to dialog boxes with the Dialog Editor and how to manipulate Spin Button controls from your application. Because additional functions are necessary to integrate the Spin Button control with the Dialog Editor, the module definitions file (SPIN.DEF) and the MAKEFILE appear later in this chapter.

Listing 4-3. SPIN.H DLL header module.

```
/***********************************************************
Module name: Spin.H
Programmer : Jeffrey M. Richter
***********************************************************/

// Spin button doesn't send WM_CTLCOLOR message to parent window

// Spin button's class-specific window styles
#define SPNS_WRAP          0x0001L

// Spin button's class-specific window messages
#define SPNM_SETRANGE     (WM_USER + 0)
#define SPNM_GETRANGE     (WM_USER + 1)
#define SPNM_SETCRNTVALUE (WM_USER + 2)
#define SPNM_GETCRNTVALUE (WM_USER + 3)

// Spin button's notification codes sent in HIWORD of
// lParam during a WM_COMMAND message
#define SPNN_VALUECHANGE (1)
```

Listing 4-4. SPIN.C DLL source module.

```
/***********************************************************
Module name: Spin.C
Programmer : Jeffrey M. Richter
***********************************************************/

#include "..\nowindws.h"
#define OEMRESOURCE
#undef NOCOLOR
#undef NOCTLMGR
#undef NOGDI
#undef NOKERNEL
#undef NOLSTRING
#undef NOMEMMGR
#undef NORASTEROPS
#undef NOUSER
#undef NOVIRTUALKEYCODES
#undef NOWINMESSAGES
#undef NOWINOFFSETS
#undef NOWINSTYLES
#include <windows.h>

#include "spin.h"

#define CBWNDEXTRA          (8)
#define GWL_RANGE           (0)
#define GWW_CRNTVALUE       (4)
#define GWW_TRIANGLEDOWN    (6)

#define SPNM_SCROLLVALUE    (WM_USER + 500)

// Time delay between scrolling events in milliseconds
#define TIME_DELAY (150)

typedef enum { TD_NONE, TD_UP, TD_DOWN } TRIANGLEDOWN;

HANDLE _hInstance = NULL;
char _szControlName[] = "Spin";
```

```
static BOOL NEAR PASCAL RegisterControlClass (HANDLE hInstance);
LONG FAR PASCAL SpinWndFn (HWND hWnd, WORD wMsg, WORD wParam,
   LONG lParam);

/**** Windows' Dynamic Link Library Initialization Routines ****/

BOOL FAR PASCAL LibMain (HANDLE hModule, WORD wDataSeg,
     WORD wHeapSize, LPSTR lpszCmdLine) {
  BOOL fOk;
  _hInstance = hModule;
  if (wHeapSize != 0) UnlockData(0);     // Let data segment move
  fOk = RegisterControlClass(hModule);
  return(fOk);    // Return TRUE if initialization is successful
}

int FAR PASCAL WEP (int nSystemExit) {

  switch (nSystemExit) {
     case WEP_SYSTEM_EXIT:     // System is shutting down
        break;
     case WEP_FREE_DLL:        // Usage count is zero
        break;
  }
  UnregisterClass(_szControlName, _hInstance);
  return(1);                   // WEP function successful
}

static BOOL NEAR PASCAL RegisterControlClass (HANDLE hInstance) {
  WNDCLASS wc;
  wc.style          = CS_GLOBALCLASS | CS_HREDRAW | CS_VREDRAW;
  wc.lpfnWndProc    = SpinWndFn;
  wc.cbClsExtra     = 0;
  wc.cbWndExtra     = CBWNDEXTRA;
  wc.hInstance      = hInstance;
  wc.hIcon          = NULL;
  wc.hCursor        = LoadCursor(NULL, IDC_ARROW);
  wc.hbrBackground  = COLOR_BTNFACE + 1;
  wc.lpszMenuName   = NULL;
  wc.lpszClassName  = _szControlName;
  return(RegisterClass(&wc));
}
```

```
static LONG NEAR PASCAL NotifyParent (HWND hWnd, WORD wNotifyCode)
   {
   LONG lResult;
   lResult = SendMessage(GetParent(hWnd), WM_COMMAND,
      GetWindowWord(hWnd, GWW_ID), MAKELONG(hWnd, wNotifyCode));
   return(lResult);
}

LONG FAR PASCAL SpinWndFn (HWND hWnd, WORD wMsg, WORD wParam,
      LONG lParam) {
   LONG lResult = 0;
   HDC hDC;
   POINT pt;
   RECT rc;
   PAINTSTRUCT ps;
   int nCrntVal, nNewVal, x, y;
   TRIANGLEDOWN TriangleDown, OldTriangleDown;
   DWORD dwTime, dwRange;
   BOOL fWrap;

   switch (wMsg) {
      case WM_GETDLGCODE:
         lResult = DLGC_STATIC;
         break;

      case WM_CREATE:       // lParam == &CreateStruct
         SendMessage(hWnd, SPNM_SETRANGE, 0, MAKELONG(0, 0));
         SendMessage(hWnd, SPNM_SETCRNTVALUE, 0, 0);
         break;

      case WM_PAINT:
         // Calling BeginPaint sends a WM_ERASEBKGND message.
         // Because that message is not trapped, DefWindowProc
         // uses the system color COLOR_BTNFACE because it was
         // specified in the hbrBackground member of the WNDCLASS
         // structure when this class was registered.
         hDC = BeginPaint(hWnd, &ps);

         GetClientRect(hWnd, &rc);
         x = rc.right / 2;
         y = rc.bottom / 2;
```

```
    // Draw middle separator bar
    MoveTo(hDC, 0, y);
    LineTo(hDC, rc.right, y);

    // Whenever a DC is retrieved, it is created with a
    // WHITE_BRUSH by default. We must change this to a
    // BLACK_BRUSH so that we can fill the triangles.
    SelectObject(hDC, GetStockObject(BLACK_BRUSH));

    // Draw top triangle and fill it in
    MoveTo(hDC, x, 2);
    LineTo(hDC, rc.right - 2, y - 2);
    LineTo(hDC, 2, y - 2);
    LineTo(hDC, x, 2);
    FloodFill(hDC, x, y - 3, RGB(0, 0, 0));

    // Draw bottom triangle and fill it in
    MoveTo(hDC, 2, y + 2);
    LineTo(hDC, rc.right - 2, y + 2);
    LineTo(hDC, x, rc.bottom - 2);
    LineTo(hDC, 2, y + 2);
    FloodFill(hDC, x, y + 3, RGB(0, 0, 0));
    EndPaint(hWnd, &ps);
    break;

case WM_LBUTTONDOWN:
    // Get coordinates for the spin button's window
    GetClientRect(hWnd, &rc);

    if ((int) HIWORD(lParam) < rc.bottom / 2) { // up arrow
        TriangleDown = TD_UP;
        // Change coordinates so rectangle includes only the
        // top half of the window
        rc.bottom /= 2;
    } else {
        TriangleDown = TD_DOWN;

        // Change coordinates so rectangle includes only the
        // bottom half of the window
        rc.top = rc.bottom / 2;
    }
```

```
    // Save the triangle the mouse was clicked over
    SetWindowWord(hWnd, GWW_TRIANGLEDOWN, TriangleDown);

    // Invert the top or bottom half of the window where the
    // mouse was clicked
    hDC = GetDC(hWnd);
    InvertRect(hDC, &rc);
    ReleaseDC(hWnd, hDC);

    SetCapture(hWnd);

    // Subtract TIME_DELAY so that action is performed at
    // least once
    dwTime = GetTickCount() - TIME_DELAY;

    do {
        // If TIME_DELAY hasn't passed yet, test loop
        // condition
        if (dwTime + TIME_DELAY > GetTickCount())
            continue;

        // Time delay has passed; scroll value in spin button
        SendMessage(hWnd, SPNM_SCROLLVALUE, 0, 0l);

        // Get last time scroll occurred
        dwTime = GetTickCount();

        // See if left mouse button is still down
    } while (GetAsyncKeyState(VK_LBUTTON) & 0x8000);

    ReleaseCapture();

    // Invalidate the entire window. This will force Windows
    // to send a WM_PAINT message restoring the window to its
    // original colors.
    InvalidateRect(hWnd, NULL, TRUE);
    break;

case SPNM_SCROLLVALUE:
    // Get the location of the mouse
    GetCursorPos(&pt);
```

```
// Convert the point from screen coordinates to client
// coordinates
ScreenToClient(hWnd, &pt);

// If the point is NOT in Spin's client area, nothing
// to do
GetClientRect(hWnd, &rc);
if (!PtInRect(&rc, pt)) break;

// Get the spin button's current value and range
nNewVal = (int) SendMessage(hWnd, SPNM_GETCRNTVALUE,
    0, 0l);
nCrntVal = nNewVal;
dwRange = SendMessage(hWnd, SPNM_GETRANGE, 0, 0l);

// Get spin button's styles and test if the "wrap"
// flag is set
fWrap = (BOOL) (GetWindowLong(hWnd, GWL_STYLE) &
    SPNS_WRAP);

// Determine whether the up or down triangle was selected
OldTriangleDown = GetWindowWord(hWnd, GWW_TRIANGLEDOWN);

// Determine whether the mouse is now over the up or
// down triangle
TriangleDown = (pt.y < rc.bottom / 2) ? TD_UP : TD_DOWN;

// If the user has switched triangles, invert the entire
// rectangle. This restores the half that was inverted in
// the WM_LBUTTONDOWN message and inverts the new half.
if (OldTriangleDown != TriangleDown) {
   hDC = GetDC(hWnd);
   InvertRect(hDC, &rc);
   ReleaseDC(hWnd, hDC);
}

if (TriangleDown == TD_UP) {
   // If value is not at top of range, increment it
   if ((int) HIWORD(dwRange) > nCrntVal) nNewVal++;
   else {
```

```
            // If value is at top of range and "wrap" flag is
            // set, set the value to the bottom of the range
            if (fWrap) nNewVal = (int) LOWORD(dwRange);
         }

      } else {
         // If value is not at bottom of range, decrement it
         if ((int) LOWORD(dwRange) < nCrntVal) nNewVal--;
         else {
            // If value is at bottom of range and "wrap" flag
            // is set, set the value to the top of the range
            if (fWrap) nNewVal = (int) HIWORD(dwRange);
         }
      }

      // If the value has been changed, set the new value
      if (nNewVal != nCrntVal)
         SendMessage(hWnd, SPNM_SETCRNTVALUE, nNewVal, 0l);

      // Set new triangle that is down for the next call here
      SetWindowWord(hWnd, GWW_TRIANGLEDOWN, TriangleDown);
      break;

case SPNM_SETRANGE:
   SetWindowLong(hWnd, GWL_RANGE, lParam);
   break;

case SPNM_GETRANGE:
   lResult = GetWindowLong(hWnd, GWL_RANGE);
   break;

case SPNM_SETCRNTVALUE:
   SetWindowWord(hWnd, GWW_CRNTVALUE, wParam);
   NotifyParent(hWnd, SPNN_VALUECHANGE);
   break;

case SPNM_GETCRNTVALUE:
   lResult = (LONG) GetWindowWord(hWnd, GWW_CRNTVALUE);
   break;
```

```
    default:
        lResult = DefWindowProc(hWnd, wMsg, wParam, lParam);
        break;
    }
    return(lResult);
}
```

Integrating Custom Child Controls with the Dialog Editor

This section demonstrates how to add functions to custom child controls so you may use them with the SDK's Dialog Editor application.

The Dialog Editor that comes with the Windows 3.0 SDK lets you design dialog boxes with custom child controls. The custom child control's source code cannot be part of a Windows application; it must be within a DLL. A number of functions must also be contained in this DLL. The source module CNTL-DE.C and its associated header file, CNTL-DE.H, contain functions that make adding Dialog Editor support for custom child controls much easier. These files may be compiled and linked with your own custom child controls.

Preparing the Dialog Editor. To inform the Dialog Editor of a new custom child control, select the "Add Custom Control..." option from the File menu. The dialog box shown in Figure 4-4 will appear.

The "Install control library" option lets you enter the name of the DLL containing the custom child control. Once the Dialog Editor is informed of a custom child control, it adds the name of the control to the *[User Controls]* section of the WIN.INI file. This means the Dialog Editor will always know about these controls and where to find them, making all your own custom child controls available to you whenever you use the Dialog Editor.

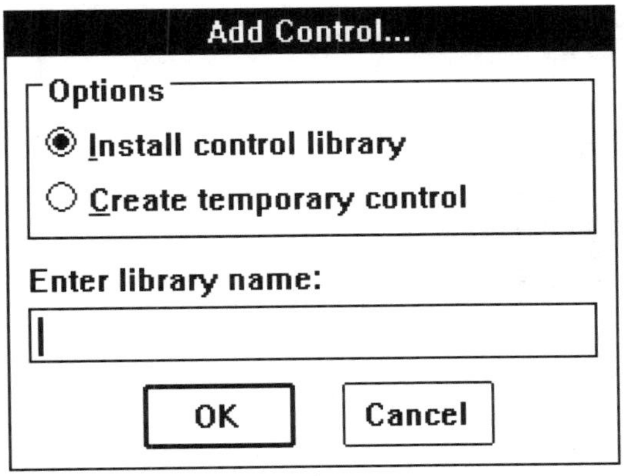

Figure 4-4. Dialog box used to integrate a custom child control with the Dialog Editor.

The "Create temporary control" option in the "Add Control..." dialog box allows you to specify a child control for which you do not have a DLL available. Any controls that you add this way are available only during the current Dialog Editor session and are not added to the WIN.INI file. Because the DLL is not available for the temporary control, the Dialog Editor displays these controls as rectangles with their associated text in the center.

Temporary and custom child controls may be removed from the Dialog Editor by choosing the "Remove custom control..." option from the File menu.

The Dialog Editor maintains a list of all the controls that have been added to a dialog-box template. Controls are added by selecting a name from the Control menu or from the toolbox. To add a temporary or custom child control to the dialog template, choose the "Custom..." option from the Control menu or select the "..." option from the toolbox. Either method will produce a dialog box (shown in Figure 4-5) containing a list of the temporary and custom child controls.

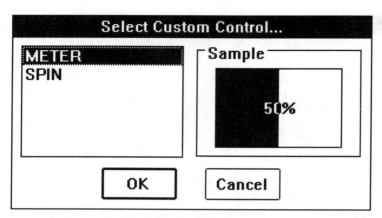

Figure 4-5. Selecting a custom child control to add to a dialog-box template.

In the "Sample" window, the Dialog Editor creates a window of the selected class and displays it so you can see what the control looks like before placing it in the dialog-box template. Once the control is in the template, you may drag and resize it with the mouse as if it were one of the predefined Windows controls.

The ID, text, or style of a custom child control is changed by selecting the "Styles" option from the Edit menu or double-clicking on the desired control. (Double-clicking on a custom child control will display its Styles dialog box only if the *CS_DBLCLKS* style was used when the custom child control's window class was registered. If this style was not specified, the Styles dialog box may be invoked by double-clicking on one of the eight black boxes that surround the control.)

Because the content of the Styles dialog box for each custom child control differs, the DLL for the control is responsible for the dialog box's display and operation. The Styles dialog box for a temporary control looks like the one shown in Figure 4-6.

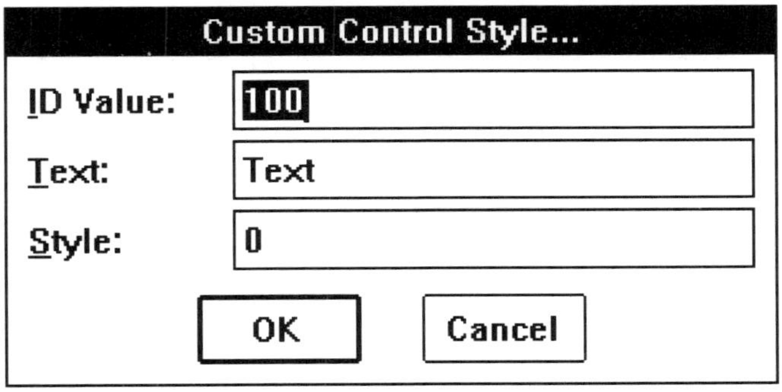

Figure 4-6. Setting style information for a temporary child control.

The "Style:" field contains a numeric value. This means you have to compute the style value based on the desired window and class-specific styles and enter the value directly in this field.

When the Dialog Editor saves your dialog template in the .DLG file, the information about each control is in the following format:

```
CONTROL "ControlText", ControlID, "ControlClassName",
    ControlStyles, X, Y, CX, CY
```

The Dialog Editor knows the *ControlClassName* because that's how you selected a control to add to the template. The *X*, *Y*, *CX*, and *CY* values are determined by how the mouse was used to locate the control in the dialog box. The remaining fields—*ControlText*, *ControlID*, and *ControlStyles*—are changed in the Styles dialog box and are maintained by the Dialog Editor.

Adding the Dialog Editor Support Functions to Custom Controls. The DLL for custom controls must contain seven functions that the Dialog Editor can call to retrieve information about the custom child control. The functions are shown in the following table.

Function name	Description
LibMain	This function is called by Windows when the DLL is first loaded into memory. This function should already be a part of your DLL; it does not need to change.
WEP	This function is called by Windows when the DLL is removed from memory. This function should already be a part of your DLL; it does not need to change.
ClassWndFn	This is the window procedure for the custom child control. It should already be a part of your DLL; it does not need to change.
ClassInfo	This function is called by the Dialog Editor to inform it of the controls supported by this DLL.
ClassFlags	This function is called by the Dialog Editor when the user saves the dialog template. This function interprets the control's styles value and creates a string expanding the class-specific style IDs.
ClassStyle	This function is called by the Dialog Editor when the user wishes to change the ID, text, or styles of the custom control by displaying the Styles dialog box.
ClassDlgFn	This is the dialog-box function used for the Styles dialog box.

In this table, *Class* is a placeholder for the class name of the control. All the functions except *LibMain* and *WEP* must be listed in the *EXPORTS* section of the DLL's .DEF file. In fact, all five functions must be exported by the following ordinal values:

Function name	Ordinal value
ClassWndFn	5
ClassInfo	2
ClassFlags	4
ClassStyle	3
ClassDlgFn	6

The CUSTCNTL.H file that comes with the Windows SDK must be *#include*d in the source files containing the functions that support the Dialog Editor. This file defines a number of data structures and constants that are used when the Dialog Editor interacts with the control's DLL. In addition, CNTL-DE.C and CNTL-DE.H (given later) may be used to simplify the process of adding Dialog Editor support for your own custom child controls. The following examples describe how each *Class* function is implemented for the spin button.

The *ClassInfo* Function. The Dialog Editor calls *ClassInfo* upon initialization. The DLL must allocate a block of memory that is to contain a *CTLINFO* structure and initialize this structure. The *CTLINFO* structure is defined in the CUSTCNTL.H file supplied with the Windows SDK.

```
#define CTLTYPES        12
#define CTLCLASS        20
#define CTLTITLE        94
        .
        .
        .
```

```
typedef struct {
    WORD        wVersion;
    WORD        wCtlTypes;
    char        szClass[CTLCLASS];
    char        szTitle[CTLTITLE];
    char        szReserved[10];
    CTLTYPE Type[CTLTYPES];
} CTLINFO;
```

The source code for the *SpinInfo* function is shown below:

```
GLOBALHANDLE FAR PASCAL SpinInfo (void) {
    GLOBALHANDLE hCtlInfo = NULL;
    hCtlInfo = ControlInfo(0x0100, _szControlName,
        _szControlName);
    if (hCtlInfo == NULL) return(hCtlInfo);
    AddControlType(hCtlInfo, 0, 7, 12, WS_BORDER | WS_CHILD,
        _szControlName);
    return(hCtlInfo);
}
```

This function first calls *ControlInfo,* which allocates a global block of memory to hold a *CTLINFO* structure. The parameters passed to the function describe the control's version, class name, and title. These values are stored in *CTLINFO*. *ControlInfo* returns the handle to the memory block or NULL if the block could not be allocated.

```
GLOBALHANDLE FAR PASCAL ControlInfo
        (WORD wVersion, LPSTR szClass, LPSTR szTitle) {
    GLOBALHANDLE hMem = NULL;
    LPCTLINFO lpCtlInfo;

    hMem = GlobalAlloc(GMEM_MOVEABLE | GMEM_ZEROINIT,
        (DWORD) sizeof(CTLINFO));
    if (hMem == NULL) return(hMem);
    lpCtlInfo = (LPCTLINFO) GlobalLock(hMem);
    lpCtlInfo->wVersion = wVersion;
    lpCtlInfo->wCtlTypes = 0;
```

```
lstrcpy(lpCtlInfo->szClass, szClass);
lstrcpy(lpCtlInfo->szTitle, szTitle);
GlobalUnlock(hMem);
return(hMem);
}
```

CTLINFO also has a member called *wCtlTyles*. This is the number of control types that are supported by the window class. This value must be less than the *CTLTYPES* identifier *#define*d in CUSTCNTL.H. In version 3.0 of Windows, this value is 12. The *ControlInfo* function initializes this value to zero. Every time the *ClassInfo* function calls the *AddControlType* function (described below), the *wCtlTypes* value is incremented.

Once the initial memory block has been prepared, each control type may be added to the block with *AddControlType*. Since only one type of control is supported by the spin button, *AddControlType* is called only once. This function determines the number of individual controls that have already been inserted into the array of *CTLTYPE* structures and adds the new control to the end of the array. A *CTLTYPE* structure has the following members:

```
#define CTLDESCR 22
.
.
.
typedef struct {
    WORD    wType;
    WORD    wWidth;
    WORD    wHeight;
    DWORD   dwStyle;
    char    szDescr[CTLDESCR];
} CTLTYPE;
```

AddControlType accepts the handle to the *CTLINFO* structure returned from *ControlInfo* and a number of parameters that describe the control to be added. *CTLINFO* is checked to see if the maximum number of control types supported by the Dialog Editor have already been added. If so, the new control is not added and FALSE is returned to the caller. Otherwise, the information describing the new control is copied into the array of *CTLTYPE* structures.

The *wType* parameter is not currently used by the Dialog Editor and should always be set to 0. The *wWidth* and *wHeight* parameters describe the default dimensions for the control. If the high bits of the *wWidth* and *wHeight* parameters are 1, the lower 15 bits specify the dimensions in pixels. If the high bit is 0, the lower 15 bits specify the dimensions in dialog-box units.

The *dwStyle* parameter specifies the default styles the control should have. The *szDescr* parameter is not used by the current Dialog Editor but may be used by future development tools.

```
BOOL FAR PASCAL AddControlType (GLOBALHANDLE hMem, WORD wType,
     WORD wWidth, WORD wHeight, DWORD dwStyle, LPSTR szDescr) {
   LPCTLINFO lpCtlInfo; WORD wNumTypes;
   lpCtlInfo = (LPCTLINFO) GlobalLock(hMem);
   wNumTypes = lpCtlInfo->wCtlTypes;
   if (wNumTypes == CTLTYPES) {
      GlobalUnlock(hMem);
      return(FALSE);
   }
   lpCtlInfo->Type[wNumTypes].wType = wType;
   lpCtlInfo->Type[wNumTypes].wWidth = wWidth;
   lpCtlInfo->Type[wNumTypes].wHeight = wHeight;
   lpCtlInfo->Type[wNumTypes].dwStyle = dwStyle;
   lstrcpy(lpCtlInfo->Type[wNumTypes].szDescr, szDescr);
   lpCtlInfo->wCtlTypes++;
   GlobalUnlock(hMem);
   return(TRUE);
}
```

Once all the control types have been added, the handle to the global memory block is returned to the Dialog Editor. If the memory block could not be created, NULL is returned.

The *ClassStyle* and *ClassDlgFn* Functions. The *ClassStyle* function is called by the Dialog Editor whenever the user wants to change any of the style information for a custom control. The user indicates this by double-clicking on the custom control's window. (The user may also change style information by selecting the "Styles..." option from the Edit menu.) The function that processes the dialog box must be called *ClassDlgFn*.

The source code for the *SpinStyle* function is shown below:

```
BOOL FAR PASCAL SpinStyle (HWND hWnd, GLOBALHANDLE hCtlStyle,
   LPFNSTRTOID lpfnStrToId, LPFNIDTOSTR lpfnIdToStr) {

   return(ShowStyleDlg(_hInstance, "StyleDlg", hWnd,
      (FARPROC) SpinDlgFn, 0, hCtlStyle, lpfnStrToId,
      lpfnIdToStr));
}
```

The *ShowStyleDlg* function supplied in CNTL-DE.C does most of the work necessary before presenting the dialog box to the user on behalf of the custom child control. The *hWnd* parameter identifies the handle to the Dialog Editor. This is the window that will own the control's Styles dialog box. The *hCtlStyle* parameter is a handle to a global block of memory. It contains information about the individual custom control the user wishes to change. The memory is in the form of a *CTLSTYLE* structure:

```
#define CTLCLASS 20
#define CTLTITLE 94
.
.
.
typedef struct {
   WORD    wX;
   WORD    wY;
   WORD    wCx;
   WORD    wCy;
   WORD    wId;
   DWORD   dwStyle;
```

```
    char    szClass[CTLCLASS];
    char    szTitle[CTLTITLE];
} CTLSTYLE;
```

The control's upper left corner and dimensions are specified by *wX*, *wY*, *wCx*, and *wCy*. The *wId* member of the structure indicates the ID assigned to this control. The *dwStyle* member specifies the window and class-specific styles assigned to the control. The *szClass* member is the class name of the control. The *szTitle* member stores text for controls that have text associated with them. The spin button has no text associated with it and does not alter this member.

Every control is assigned an ID value. This value is usually a text string defined in a header file. The *CTLSTYLE* structure passes the numeric value of the ID in its *wId* member. However, when the Styles dialog box is displayed, the string equivalent of the ID value should be displayed to the user.

The last two parameters passed to the *ClassStyle* function, *lpfnStrToId* and *lpfnIdToStr*, are addresses of two functions in the Dialog Editor and are called by the control's Styles dialog box. The first function, *lpfnStrToId*, has the following prototype:

```
typedef DWORD   (FAR PASCAL *LPFNSTRTOID)(LPSTR);
```

This function converts the string used for a control's ID to the value for the string. This is possible because the Dialog Editor maintains the header file in memory. The return value indicates whether the ID string is in the header file. If the low-order word is nonzero, the high-order word contains the numeric value of the identifier. If the low-order word is zero, the ID string could not be found.

The second function, *lpfnIdToStr*, performs the opposite operation and has the following prototype:

```
typedef WORD    (FAR PASCAL *LPFNIDTOSTR)(WORD, LPSTR, WORD);
```

This function converts a numeric ID to its string equivalent. The first parameter specifies the numeric ID value of the control. The last two parameters specify the address of the string buffer to receive the string and the maximum size of the string. The return value indicates the number of characters copied into the string buffer. It is zero if the function fails.

The last three values passed to the *ClassStyle* function are really not used by this function at all. They're accessed by the dialog-box procedure for the Styles dialog box. The *ShowStyleDlg* function (in CNTL-DE.C) packages these parameters in a *CTLSTYLEDLG* structure that can be accessed from within the dialog-box procedure. The *CTLSTYLEDLG* structure and the *ShowStyleDlg* function are shown below:

```
typedef struct {
   GLOBALHANDLE hCtlStyle;        // Memory handle holds CTLSTYLE for
                                  // control
   LPFNSTRTOID lpfnStrToId;       // DIALOG function to convert
                                  // string ID to number
   LPFNIDTOSTR lpfnIdToStr;       // DIALOG function to convert
                                  // numeric ID to string
} CTLSTYLEDLG, FAR *LPCTLSTYLEDLG, NEAR *NPCTLSTYLEDLG;
 .
 .
 .
int FAR PASCAL ShowStyleDlg (HANDLE hInstance, LPSTR szTemplate,
     HWND hWndParent, FARPROC fpDlgProc, LONG lParam,
     GLOBALHANDLE hCtlStyle, LPFNSTRTOID lpfnStrToId,
     LPFNIDTOSTR lpfnIdToStr) {

   LOCALHANDLE hCtlStyleDlg; NPCTLSTYLEDLG npCtlStyleDlg;
   int x;
   hCtlStyleDlg = LocalAlloc(LMEM_MOVEABLE | LMEM_ZEROINIT,
      sizeof(CTLSTYLEDLG));
   if (hCtlStyleDlg == NULL) return(FALSE);

   npCtlStyleDlg = (NPCTLSTYLEDLG) LocalLock(hCtlStyleDlg);
   npCtlStyleDlg->hCtlStyle = hCtlStyle;
```

```
npCtlStyleDlg->lpfnStrToId = lpfnStrToId;
npCtlStyleDlg->lpfnIdToStr = lpfnIdToStr;
LocalUnlock(hCtlStyleDlg);

SetProp(hWndParent, _szCtlProp, hCtlStyleDlg);

x = DialogBoxParam(hInstance, szTemplate, hWndParent,
    fpDlgProc, lParam);
RemoveProp(hWndParent, _szCtlProp);
LocalFree(hCtlStyleDlg);
return(x == IDOK);
}
```

ShowStyleDlg allocates a local block of memory large enough to contain a *CTLSTYLEDLG* structure. This structure is declared in CNTL-DE.C and is not part of the standard Dialog Editor interface and the CUSTCNTL.H file. The structure is then filled with three values: the handle to the *CTLSTYLE* memory block, the address of *lpfnStrToId*, and the address of *lpfnIdToStr*. The handle to this local block of memory is then associated with the Dialog Editor's window as a window property.

The dialog box is displayed using the *DialogBoxParam* function. This allows the *ClassStyle* function to pass some value in the *lParam* parameter to the dialog-box procedure if it wants to. When the user closes the dialog box (by selecting the "Ok" or "Cancel" button), the property is removed from the Dialog Editor's window and the local block of memory is freed. The *ClassStyle* function must return TRUE or FALSE to the Dialog Editor, indicating whether the *CTLSTYLE* structure has been changed.

The function that processes messages for the spin button's Styles dialog box is called *SpinDlgFn*. The spin button's Style dialog box appears in Figure 4-7.

While *WM_INITDIALOG* is being processed, the *GetIdString* function is called. This function is in the CNTL-DE.C source module and appears below:

```
WORD FAR PASCAL GetIdString (HWND hDlg, LPSTR szId,
     WORD wIdMaxLen) {
   LOCALHANDLE hCtlStyleDlg;
   NPCTLSTYLEDLG npCtlStyleDlg;
   LPCTLSTYLE lpCtlStyle;
   WORD wIdLen;

   hCtlStyleDlg = GetProp(GetParent(hDlg), _szCtlProp);
   if (hCtlStyleDlg == NULL) return(0);

   npCtlStyleDlg = (NPCTLSTYLEDLG) LocalLock(hCtlStyleDlg);
   lpCtlStyle = (LPCTLSTYLE) GlobalLock(npCtlStyleDlg->hCtlStyle);
   wIdLen = (*npCtlStyleDlg->lpfnIdToStr)
           (lpCtlStyle->wId, szId, wIdMaxLen);
   GlobalUnlock(npCtlStyleDlg->hCtlStyle);
   LocalUnlock(hCtlStyleDlg);
   return(wIdLen);
}
```

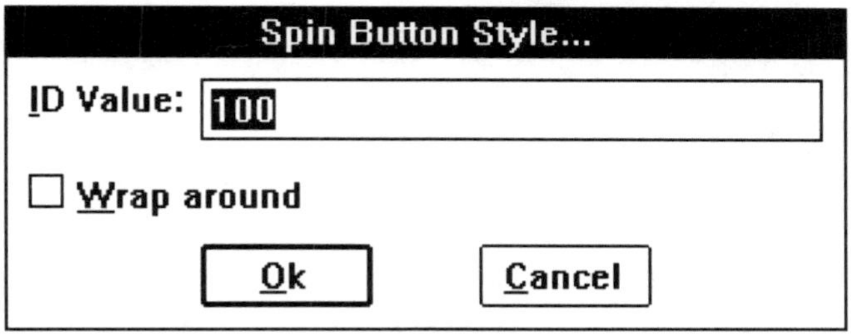

Figure 4-7. Spin Button Style dialog box.

This function is called with the window handle of the dialog box, the address of a buffer where the string equivalent of the control's ID is to go, and the maximum size of this buffer. The function then calls the *GetProp* function to locate the handle of the *CTLSTYLEDLG* memory block. Remember that the window property was associated with the Dialog Editor, not the dialog box itself. This requires that the *GetParent* function be called to get the window handle of the Dialog Editor before calling the *GetProp* function.

Once the handle to the *CTLSTYLEDLG* structure has been obtained, *GetIdString* calls the *lpfnIdToStr* function. This function fills the *szId* parameter with the name of the ID from the header file corresponding to the ID value of the control. The function returns the length of the ID's string or zero if an error occurred. The dialog-box function can then call the *SetDlgItemText* function to place the ID's text value in the EDIT field associated with the "ID Value:" static window.

CNTL-DE.C contains two functions that allow the dialog-box function to retrieve information about the custom control being processed. These functions, *CtlStyleLock* and *CtlStyleUnlock*, both require the window handle of the dialog box. From this window handle, the *GetParent* and *GetProp* functions are used as in *GetIdStr* to retrieve the memory handle of *CTLSTYLEDLG*. With this memory handle, *CtlStyleLock* calls *GlobalLock* to lock the memory block containing *CTLSTYLE*. The address of this block is then returned to the caller. When the caller no longer wishes to access the *CTLSTYLE* structure, the *CtlStyleUnlock* function is called to unlock the block.

WM_INITDIALOG must call *CtlStyleLock* to retrieve the value of the custom control's *dwStyle* member. This value can now be used to activate check boxes or set radio buttons to reflect the current styles of the custom control. The spin button has only one valid style, *SPNS_WRAP*. The complete processing for the *WM_INIT-DIALOG* message appears below:

```
case WM_INITDIALOG:
   GetIdString(hDlg, szId, sizeof(szId));
   SetDlgItemText(hDlg, ID_VALUE, szId);
   lpCtlStyle = CtlStyleLock(hDlg);
   SendDlgItemMessage(hDlg, ID_WRAP, BM_SETCHECK,
      (BOOL) (lpCtlStyle->dwStyle & SPNS_WRAP), 0l);
   CtlStyleUnlock(hDlg);
   break;
```

The only other processing in the dialog-box function that is specific to integrating custom controls with the Dialog Editor is for the *WM_COMMAND* message. The code for this processing appears below:

```
case IDOK:
   GetDlgItemText(hDlg, ID_VALUE, szId, sizeof(szId));
   dwResult = SetIdValue(hDlg, szId);
   if (LOWORD(dwResult) == 0) break;
   lpCtlStyle = CtlStyleLock(hDlg);
   lpCtlStyle->dwStyle &= 0xffff0000;    // Clear control-specific
                                         // styles
   if (SendDlgItemMessage(hDlg, ID_WRAP, BM_GETCHECK, 0, 0l))
      lpCtlStyle->dwStyle |= SPNS_WRAP;
   CtlStyleUnlock(hDlg);
   // Fall through to IDCANCEL case

case IDCANCEL:
   EndDialog(hDlg, wParam);
   break;
```

When the user selects the "Ok" button, the ID value in the EDIT control must be checked to see if the string exists in the header file being used by the Dialog Editor. This is done by calling the *SetIdValue* function in the CNTL-DE.C module:

```
DWORD FAR PASCAL SetIdValue (HWND hDlg, LPSTR szId) {
   LOCALHANDLE hCtlStyleDlg;
   NPCTLSTYLEDLG npCtlStyleDlg;
   LPCTLSTYLE lpCtlStyle;
   DWORD dwResult = 0;

   hCtlStyleDlg = GetProp(GetParent(hDlg), _szCtlProp);
   if (hCtlStyleDlg == NULL) return(dwResult);

   npCtlStyleDlg = (NPCTLSTYLEDLG) LocalLock(hCtlStyleDlg);
   dwResult = (*npCtlStyleDlg->lpfnStrToId)(szId);
   LocalUnlock(hCtlStyleDlg);
   if (LOWORD(dwResult) == 0)
      return(dwResult);
```

```
lpCtlStyle = CtlStyleLock(hDlg);
lpCtlStyle->wId = HIWORD(dwResult);
CtlStyleUnlock(hDlg);
return(dwResult);
}
```

This function calls *lpfnIdToStr* to see whether the ID value string passed in the *szId* parameter is in the header file being used by the Dialog Editor. If the string is not in the header file, the Dialog Editor automatically asks the user if the string should be added. If the user adds the string, *lpfnStrToId* returns nonzero in the high-order word and updates the value in the *CTLSTYLE* structure. If the user does not add the ID to the header file, *lpfnStrToId* returns zero in the low-order word, does not update the *CTLSTYLE* structure, and returns to the caller.

If the dialog-box function sees that the *SetIdValue* function returned zero in the low-order word, the Styles dialog box is not terminated and the user can either cancel the dialog box or enter a different ID value string.

Now the style information for the control must be determined. First, the *dwStyle* member of the *CTLSTYLE* structure is *AND*ed with 0xffff0000. This clears all the bits that represent class-specific styles. Remember that the other bits are for the general window styles, all beginning with *WS_*. Because the spin button does not allow the user to change its window styles, these should not be reset.

Next, we check all radio buttons and check boxes to determine which class-specific styles should be turned on. Because the spin button has only one style, only one check box has to be examined. If the call to *SendDlgItemMessage* using the *BM_GETCHECK* message returned TRUE, the *SPNS_WRAP* flag is set in the *dwStyle* member. Otherwise, no class-specific style bits are set.

Finally, the *CTLSTYLE* structure is updated to reflect the changes. At this point, the *IDOK* case falls through to *IDCANCEL*. This case calls the *EndDialog* function, returning the value of the *wParam* parameter (*IDOK* or *IDCANCEL*).

The *ClassFlags* Function. The last function in SPINDLG.C is *SpinFlags*. This function is called by the Dialog Editor when the user saves the dialog box. The Dialog Editor creates a .DLG file that contains *CONTROL* statements for every control the user added to the dialog-box template. In each line is a list of identifiers representing the styles chosen for the particular control. For custom child controls, the Dialog Editor doesn't know the names associated with the class-specific styles. *SpinFlags* retrieves the names so they can be included in the .DLG file:

```
WORD FAR PASCAL SpinFlags (DWORD dwFlags, LPSTR szString,
    WORD wMaxString) {
  WORD x;
  *szString = 0;
  if (dwFlags & SPNS_WRAP) lstrcat(szString, "SPNS_WRAP | ");
  x = lstrlen(szString);
  if (x > 0) { x -= sizeof(" | ") - 1; *(szString + x) = 0; }
  return(x);
}
```

This function is passed the *dwFlags* parameter, which contains the window and class-specific style bits for the control. It is also passed the address of a buffer, *szString*, where the expanded string identifiers are to be placed. The last parameter, *wMaxString,* specifies the maximum number of characters that may be placed in the buffer.

The function places a zero in the first byte of the string buffer. It then appends the text (and symbol representing C's Boolean *OR* operation) for each style that has a style bit set in the *dwFlags* parameter to the buffer. When the string buffer has been filled, the trailing *OR* symbol is removed and the number of characters in the string is returned to the Dialog Editor. The Dialog Editor then appends the text for the generic window styles to this buffer and outputs the completed line to the .DLG file.

The source code for SPINDLG.C contains all the functions necessary to interface the spin button with the Dialog Editor. Although we have not discussed the functions to access the Meter control with the Dialog Editor, the functions appear in METERDLG.C. This completes the interface required for the Dialog Editor to access custom child controls.

Listing 4-5. SPINDLG.C Spin and Dialog Editor source module.

```
/*************************************************************
Module name: SpinDlg.C
Programmer : Jeffrey M. Richter
*************************************************************/

#include "..\nowindws.h"
#define  OEMRESOURCE
#undef   NOCOLOR
#undef   NOCTLMGR
#undef   NOGDI
#undef   NOKERNEL
#undef   NOLSTRING
#undef   NOMEMMGR
#undef   NORASTEROPS
#undef   NOUSER
#undef   NOVIRTUALKEYCODES
#undef   NOWINMESSAGES
#undef   NOWINOFFSETS
#undef   NOWINSTYLES
#include <windows.h>
#include <custcntl.h>

#include "cntl-de.h"

#include "spin.h"
#include "dialog.h"

extern HANDLE _hInstance;
extern char _szControlName[];
```

```
BOOL FAR PASCAL SpinDlgFn (HWND hDlg, WORD wMessage, WORD wParam,
   LONG lParam);

GLOBALHANDLE FAR PASCAL SpinInfo (void) {
   GLOBALHANDLE hCtlInfo = NULL;

   hCtlInfo = ControlInfo(0x0100, _szControlName, _szControlName);
   if (hCtlInfo == NULL) return(hCtlInfo);
   AddControlType(hCtlInfo, 0, 7, 12, WS_BORDER | WS_CHILD,
      _szControlName);
   return(hCtlInfo);
}


BOOL FAR PASCAL SpinStyle (HWND hWnd, GLOBALHANDLE hCtlStyle,
      LPFNSTRTOID lpfnStrToId, LPFNIDTOSTR lpfnIdToStr) {
   return(ShowStyleDlg(_hInstance, "StyleDlg", hWnd, (FARPROC)
      SpinDlgFn, 0, hCtlStyle, lpfnStrToId, lpfnIdToStr));
}

BOOL FAR PASCAL SpinDlgFn (HWND hDlg, WORD wMsg, WORD wParam,
      LONG lParam) {
   BOOL fProcessed = TRUE;
   char szId[20];
   DWORD dwResult;
   LPCTLSTYLE lpCtlStyle;

   switch (wMsg) {
      case WM_INITDIALOG:
         // Fill the EDIT control with the name of this
         // control's ID
         GetIdString(hDlg, szId, sizeof(szId));
         SetDlgItemText(hDlg, ID_VALUE, szId);

         // Initialize check box reflecting Spin control's styles
         lpCtlStyle = CtlStyleLock(hDlg);
         SendDlgItemMessage(hDlg, ID_WRAP, BM_SETCHECK,
            (BOOL) (lpCtlStyle->dwStyle & SPNS_WRAP), 0l);
         CtlStyleUnlock(hDlg);
         break;
```

```
case WM_COMMAND:
    switch(wParam) {
        case IDOK:

            // Convert the string ID value to its numeric
            // equivalent
            GetDlgItemText(hDlg, ID_VALUE, szId, sizeof(szId));
            dwResult = SetIdValue(hDlg, szId);

            // If string ID not found or added, do NOT end
            // dialog box
            if (LOWORD(dwResult) == 0) break;

            // Calculate the new control's styles
            lpCtlStyle = CtlStyleLock(hDlg);

            // Clear control-specific flags
            lpCtlStyle->dwStyle &= 0xffff0000L;

            if (SendDlgItemMessage(hDlg, ID_WRAP, BM_GETCHECK,
                    0, 0l))
                lpCtlStyle->dwStyle |= SPNS_WRAP;

            CtlStyleUnlock(hDlg);

            // Fall through to IDCANCEL case

        case IDCANCEL:
            // Terminate dialog box, returning IDOK or IDCANCEL
            EndDialog(hDlg, wParam);
            break;

        case ID_VALUE:
            // Disable IDOK button if no text exists in
            // ID_VALUE box
            if (HIWORD(lParam) == EN_CHANGE)
                EnableWindow(GetDlgItem(hDlg, IDOK),
                    SendMessage(LOWORD(lParam), WM_GETTEXTLENGTH,
                    0, 0L) ? TRUE : FALSE);
            break;
```

```
            default: fProcessed = FALSE; break;
         }
         break;

     default: fProcessed = FALSE; break;
   }
   return(fProcessed);
}

WORD FAR PASCAL SpinFlags (DWORD dwFlags, LPSTR szString,
     WORD wMaxString) {
   WORD x;
   *szString = 0;
   if (dwFlags & SPNS_WRAP) lstrcat(szString, "SPNS_WRAP | ");
   x = lstrlen(szString);
   if (x > 0) { x -= sizeof(" | ") - 1; *(szString + x) = 0; }
   return(x);
}
```

Listing 4-6. SPIN.DEF DLL definitions file.

```
; Module name: Spin.DEF
; Programmer : Jeffrey M. Richter

LIBRARY        SPIN
DESCRIPTION    'Spin Button Custom Control Library'
EXETYPE        WINDOWS
STUB           'WinStub.Exe'
CODE           MOVEABLE PRELOAD DISCARDABLE
DATA           MOVEABLE PRELOAD SINGLE
HEAPSIZE       1024
EXPORTS
   WEP          @1      RESIDENTNAME
   SpinInfo     @2
   SpinStyle    @3
   SpinFlags    @4
   SpinWndFn    @5
   pinDlgFn     @6
```

Listing 4-7. SPIN.RC DLL resource file.

```
/************************************************************
Module name: Spin.RC
Programmer : Jeffrey M. Richter
************************************************************/

#include <windows.h>

#include "spin.h"
#include "dialog.h"
#include "spin.dlg"
```

Listing 4-8. DIALOG.H (dialog-box templates) for Spin.

```
#define IDOK        1
#define IDCANCEL    2

#define ID_VALUE    100
#define ID_WRAP     101
```

Listing 4-9. SPIN.DLG dialog-box templates.

```
STYLEDLG DIALOG LOADONCALL MOVEABLE DISCARDABLE 83, 73, 156, 52
CAPTION "Spin Button Style..."
STYLE WS_BORDER | WS_CAPTION | WS_DLGFRAME | WS_POPUP
BEGIN
   CONTROL "&ID Value:", -1, "static", SS_LEFT | WS_CHILD, 4, 4,
      32, 12
   CONTROL "", ID_VALUE, "edit", ES_LEFT | WS_BORDER | WS_TABSTOP
      | WS_CHILD, 36, 4, 116, 12
   CONTROL "&Wrap around", ID_WRAP, "button", BS_AUTOCHECKBOX |
      WS_TABSTOP | WS_CHILD, 4, 20, 56, 12
   CONTROL "&Ok", IDOK, "button", BS_DEFPUSHBUTTON | WS_TABSTOP |
      WS_CHILD, 36, 36, 32, 12
   CONTROL "&Cancel", IDCANCEL, "button", BS_PUSHBUTTON |
      WS_TABSTOP | WS_CHILD, 88, 36, 32, 12
END
```

Listing 4-10. MAKEFILE for Spin custom control DLL.

```
#****************************************************************
#Module name: MAKEFILE
#Programmer : Jeffrey M. Richter
#****************************************************************

PROG = Spin
MODEL = S
CFLAGS = -A$(MODEL)w -D_WINDOWS -D_WINDLL -Gcsw2 -W4 -Zlepid -Od
LFLAGS = /NOE/BA/A:16/M/CO/LI/F
LIBS = $(MODEL)nocrtd + $(MODEL)dllcew + libw

M1 = $(PROG).obj $(PROG)Dlg.obj Cntl-DE.obj

ICONS =
BITMAPS =
CURSORS =
RESOURCES = $(ICONS) $(BITMAPS) $(CURSORS)

.SUFFIXES: .rc

.rc.res:
   rc -r $*.rc

$(PROG).DLL: $(M1) $(PROG).Def $(PROG).Res
   link $(LFLAGS) @<<$(PROG).Lnk
D:\MSC\LibEntry.obj $(M1)
$(PROG).DLL, $(PROG), $(LIBS), $(PROG)
<<
   rc -Fe$(PROG).DLL $(PROG).Res
   copy $(PROG).dll ..\custcntl.04

$(PROG).obj:    $*.c $*.h
$(PROG)Dlg.obj: $*.c $(PROG).h  dialog.h
Cntl-DE.obj:    $*.c $*.h

$(PROG).res:    $*.rc $*.h $*.dlg dialog.h $(RESOURCES)
```

Listing 4-11. METERDLG.C Meter and Dialog Editor source module.

```
/******************************************************************
Module name: MeterDlg.C
Programmer : Jeffrey M. Richter
******************************************************************/

#include "..\nowindws.h"
#define  OEMRESOURCE
#undef   NOCOLOR
#undef   NOCTLMGR
#undef   NOGDI
#undef   NOKERNEL
#undef   NOLSTRING
#undef   NOMEMMGR
#undef   NORASTEROPS
#undef   NOUSER
#undef   NOVIRTUALKEYCODES
#undef   NOWINMESSAGES
#undef   NOWINOFFSETS
#undef   NOWINSTYLES
#include <windows.h>
#include <custcntl.h>

#include "cntl-de.h"

#include "meter.h"
#include "dialog.h"

extern HANDLE _hInstance;
extern char _szControlName[];

BOOL FAR PASCAL MeterDlgFn (HWND hDlg, WORD wMessage, WORD wParam,
   LONG lParam);

GLOBALHANDLE FAR PASCAL MeterInfo (void) {
   GLOBALHANDLE hCtlInfo = NULL;

   hCtlInfo = ControlInfo(0x0100, _szControlName, _szControlName);
   if (hCtlInfo == NULL) return(hCtlInfo);
```

```
        AddControlType(hCtlInfo, 0, 40, 12, WS_BORDER | WS_CHILD,
          _szControlName);
        return(hCtlInfo);

}

BOOL FAR PASCAL MeterStyle (HWND hWnd, GLOBALHANDLE hCtlStyle,
        LPFNSTRTOID lpfnStrToId, LPFNIDTOSTR lpfnIdToStr) {
    return(ShowStyleDlg(_hInstance, MAKEINTRESOURCE(DLG_STYLEDLG),
        hWnd, (FARPROC) MeterDlgFn, 0, hCtlStyle, lpfnStrToId,
        lpfnIdToStr));
}

BOOL FAR PASCAL MeterDlgFn (HWND hDlg, WORD wMsg, WORD wParam,
        LONG lParam) {
    BOOL fResult = TRUE;
    char szId[20];
    DWORD dwResult;

    switch (wMsg) {
        case WM_INITDIALOG:
            GetIdString(hDlg, szId, sizeof(szId));
            SetDlgItemText(hDlg, ID_VALUE, szId);
            break;

        case WM_COMMAND:
            switch (wParam) {
                case IDOK:
                    GetDlgItemText(hDlg, ID_VALUE, szId, sizeof(szId));
                    dwResult = SetIdValue(hDlg, szId);
                    if (LOWORD(dwResult) == 0) break;
                    // Fall through to IDCANCEL case

                case IDCANCEL:
                    EndDialog(hDlg, wParam);
                    break;

                case ID_VALUE:
                    if (HIWORD(lParam) == EN_CHANGE)
                        EnableWindow(GetDlgItem(hDlg, IDOK),
```

```
                        SendMessage(LOWORD(lParam), WM_GETTEXTLENGTH,
                            0, OL) ? TRUE : FALSE);
                    break;

                default: fResult = FALSE; break;
            }
            break;

        default: fResult = FALSE; break;
    }
    return(fResult);
}


WORD FAR PASCAL MeterFlags (DWORD dwFlags, LPSTR szString,
        WORD wMaxString) {
    WORD x;
    *szString = 0;
    x = lstrlen(szString);
    if (x > 0) { x -= sizeof(" | ") - 1; *(szString + x) = 0; }
    return(x);
}
```

Listing 4-12. METER.DEF DLL definitions file.

```
; Module name: Meter.DEF
; Programmer : Jeffrey M. Richter

LIBRARY      METER
DESCRIPTION  'Meter Custom Control Library'
EXETYPE      WINDOWS
STUB         'WinStub.Exe'

;The code segment is marked as PRELOAD FIXED NONDISCARDABLE
;because this module is used by the Setup application presented in
;Chapter 8. In a DLL, Windows allows code segments to be discarded
;if FIXED is not specified. This is why FIXED appears below.
CODE         PRELOAD FIXED NONDISCARDABLE
DATA         MOVEABLE PRELOAD SINGLE
```

```
HEAPSIZE    1024
EXPORTS
   WEP         @1     RESIDENTNAME
   MeterInfo   @2
   MeterStyle  @3
   MeterFlags  @4
   MeterWndFn  @5
   MeterDlgFn  @6
```

Listing 4-13. METER.RC DLL resource file.

```
/***************************************************************
Module name: Meter.RC
Programmer : Jeffrey M. Richter
***************************************************************/

#include <windows.h>

#include "meter.h"
#include "dialog.h"
#include "meter.dlg"
```

Listing 4-14. DIALOG.H (dialog-box template defines) for Meter.

```
#define DLG_STYLEDLG   1000
#define ID_VALUE        100

#define IDOK              1
#define IDCANCEL          2
```

Listing 4-15. METER.DLG dialog-box templates.

```
DLG_STYLEDLG DIALOG LOADONCALL MOVEABLE DISCARDABLE 83, 73,
   156, 36
CAPTION "Meter Style..."
```

```
STYLE WS_BORDER | WS_CAPTION | WS_DLGFRAME | WS_POPUP
BEGIN
   CONTROL "&ID Value:", -1, "static", SS_LEFT | WS_CHILD, 4, 4,
      32, 12
   CONTROL "", ID_VALUE, "edit", ES_LEFT | WS_BORDER | WS_TABSTOP
      | WS_CHILD, 36, 4, 116, 12
   CONTROL "&Ok", IDOK, "button", BS_DEFPUSHBUTTON | WS_TABSTOP |
      WS_CHILD, 36, 20, 32, 12
   CONTROL "&Cancel", IDCANCEL, "button", BS_PUSHBUTTON |
      WS_TABSTOP | WS_CHILD, 88, 20, 32, 12
END
```

Listing 4-16. MAKEFILE for Meter custom control DLL.

```
#******************************************************************
#Module name: MAKEFILE
#Programmer : Jeffrey M. Richter
#******************************************************************

PROG = Meter
MODEL = S
CFLAGS = -A$(MODEL)w -D_WINDOWS -D_WINDLL -Gcsw2 -W4 -Zlepid -Od
LFLAGS = /NOE/BA/A:16/M/CO/LI/F
LIBS = $(MODEL)nocrtd + $(MODEL)dllcew + libw

M1 = $(PROG).obj $(PROG)Dlg.obj Cntl-DE.obj

ICONS =
BITMAPS =
CURSORS =
RESOURCES = $(ICONS) $(BITMAPS) $(CURSORS)

.SUFFIXES: .rc

.rc.res:
   rc -r $*.rc

$(PROG).DLL: $(M1) $(PROG).Def $(PROG).Res
```

```
   link $(LFLAGS) @<<$(PROG).Lnk
D:\MSC\LibEntry.obj $(M1)
$(PROG).DLL, $(PROG), $(LIBS), $(PROG)
<<
   rc -Fe$(PROG).DLL $(PROG).Res
   copy $(PROG).dll ..\custcntl.04

$(PROG).obj:     $*.c $*.h
$(PROG)Dlg.obj: $*.c $(PROG).h  dialog.h
Cntl-DE.obj:     $*.c $*.h

$(PROG).res:     $*.rc $*.h $*.dlg dialog.h $(RESOURCES)
```

Listing 4-17. CNTL-DE.C Custom Control and Dialog Editor source module.

```c
/*****************************************************************
Module name: Cntl-DE.C
Programmer : Jeffrey M. Richter
*****************************************************************/

#include "..\nowindws.h"
#undef NOCTLMGR
#undef NOKERNEL
#undef NOLSTRING
#undef NOMEMMGR
#undef NOUSER
#include <windows.h>
#include <custcntl.h>

#include "cntl-de.h"


// Property string used internally to store local handle of
// CTLSTYLEDLG data structure
static char _szCtlProp[] = "CtlDlgStyleData";

// Data structure used internally to get information on the
// style dialog-box function
```

281

```
typedef struct {
    GLOBALHANDLE hCtlStyle;         // Memory handle holds CTLSTYLE
                                    // for control
    LPFNSTRTOID lpfnStrToId;        // DIALOG function to convert
                                    // string ID to number
    LPFNIDTOSTR lpfnIdToStr;        // DIALOG function to convert
                                    // numeric ID to string
} CTLSTYLEDLG, FAR *LPCTLSTYLEDLG, NEAR *NPCTLSTYLEDLG;

// This function should be called first in the ClassInfo function
// to initialize the new control
GLOBALHANDLE FAR PASCAL ControlInfo (WORD wVersion, LPSTR szClass,
        LPSTR szTitle) {
    GLOBALHANDLE hMem = NULL;
    LPCTLINFO lpCtlInfo;

    hMem = GlobalAlloc(GMEM_MOVEABLE | GMEM_ZEROINIT,
        (DWORD) sizeof(CTLINFO));
    if (hMem == NULL) return(hMem);
    lpCtlInfo = (LPCTLINFO) GlobalLock(hMem);
    lpCtlInfo->wVersion = wVersion;

    // Initialize wCtlTypes to zero, incremented by AddControlType
    // function
    lpCtlInfo->wCtlTypes = 0;
    lstrcpy(lpCtlInfo->szClass, szClass);
    lstrcpy(lpCtlInfo->szTitle, szTitle);
    GlobalUnlock(hMem);
    return(hMem);
}

// This function should be called repeatedly to add new control
// types to the structure returned by the ControlInfo function.
// This function should be called in the ClassInfo function.
BOOL FAR PASCAL AddControlType (GLOBALHANDLE hMem, WORD wType,
        WORD wWidth, WORD wHeight, DWORD dwStyle, LPSTR szDescr) {
    LPCTLINFO lpCtlInfo; WORD wNumTypes;
    lpCtlInfo = (LPCTLINFO) GlobalLock(hMem);
    wNumTypes = lpCtlInfo->wCtlTypes;
    if (wNumTypes == CTLTYPES) {
```

```
      GlobalUnlock(hMem);
      return(FALSE);
   }
   lpCtlInfo->Type[wNumTypes].wType = wType;
   lpCtlInfo->Type[wNumTypes].wWidth = wWidth;
   lpCtlInfo->Type[wNumTypes].wHeight = wHeight;
   lpCtlInfo->Type[wNumTypes].dwStyle = dwStyle;
   lstrcpy(lpCtlInfo->Type[wNumTypes].szDescr, szDescr);
   lpCtlInfo->wCtlTypes++;
   GlobalUnlock(hMem);
   return(TRUE);
}


// This function displays the control's style dialog box and
// should be called from the ClassStyle function
int FAR PASCAL ShowStyleDlg (HANDLE hInstance, LPSTR szTemplate,
      HWND hWndParent, FARPROC fpDlgProc, LONG lParam,
      GLOBALHANDLE hCtlStyle, LPFNSTRTOID lpfnStrToId,
      LPFNIDTOSTR lpfnIdToStr) {
   LOCALHANDLE hCtlStyleDlg;
   NPCTLSTYLEDLG npCtlStyleDlg;
   int x;

   hCtlStyleDlg =
      LocalAlloc(LMEM_MOVEABLE | LMEM_ZEROINIT,
      sizeof(CTLSTYLEDLG));
   if (hCtlStyleDlg == NULL) return(FALSE);

   npCtlStyleDlg = (NPCTLSTYLEDLG) LocalLock(hCtlStyleDlg);
   npCtlStyleDlg->hCtlStyle = hCtlStyle;
   npCtlStyleDlg->lpfnStrToId = lpfnStrToId;
   npCtlStyleDlg->lpfnIdToStr = lpfnIdToStr;
   LocalUnlock(hCtlStyleDlg);

   // Associate property with Dialog Editor's window
   SetProp(hWndParent, _szCtlProp, hCtlStyleDlg);

   // Display control's Styles dialog box
   x = DialogBoxParam(hInstance, szTemplate, hWndParent,
      fpDlgProc, lParam);
```

```
    // Remove property associated with Dialog Editor's window
    RemoveProp(hWndParent, _szCtlProp);

    LocalFree(hCtlStyleDlg);
    return(x == IDOK);          // Return whether CTLSTYLE structure has
                                // been changed
}


// This function should only be called from the ClassDlgFn
// function. It locks the memory block containing the CTLSTYLE
// structure for the selected control and returns the FAR address
// to that structure.
LPCTLSTYLE FAR PASCAL CtlStyleLock (HWND hDlg) {
    LOCALHANDLE hCtlStyleDlg;
    NPCTLSTYLEDLG npCtlStyleDlg;
    LPCTLSTYLE lpCtlStyle = NULL;

    // Property is associated with Dialog Editor's window.
    // Parent of the dialog box is the Dialog Editor.
    hCtlStyleDlg = GetProp(GetParent(hDlg), _szCtlProp);

    if (hCtlStyleDlg == NULL) return(lpCtlStyle);
    npCtlStyleDlg = (NPCTLSTYLEDLG) LocalLock(hCtlStyleDlg);
    lpCtlStyle = (LPCTLSTYLE) GlobalLock(npCtlStyleDlg->hCtlStyle);
    LocalUnlock(hCtlStyleDlg);
    return(lpCtlStyle);
}


// This function should only be called from the ClassDlgFn
// function. It unlocks the memory block containing the CTLSTYLE
// structure for the selected control and returns whether the
// block was successfully unlocked.
BOOL FAR PASCAL CtlStyleUnlock (HWND hDlg) {
    LOCALHANDLE hCtlStyleDlg;
    NPCTLSTYLEDLG npCtlStyleDlg;
    BOOL fOk = FALSE;

    // Property is associated with the Dialog Editor's window.
    // The parent of the dialog box is the Dialog Editor.
    hCtlStyleDlg = GetProp(GetParent(hDlg), _szCtlProp);
```

```
     if (hCtlStyleDlg == NULL) return(fOk);
     npCtlStyleDlg = (NPCTLSTYLEDLG) LocalLock(hCtlStyleDlg);
     fOk = GlobalUnlock(npCtlStyleDlg->hCtlStyle);
     LocalUnlock(hCtlStyleDlg);
     return(fOk);
}


// This function should only be called from the ClassDlgFn
// function. It converts the ID value for the control into an
// identifier string and stores the string in the address passed
// in. The number of characters in the string is returned.
WORD FAR PASCAL GetIdString (HWND hDlg, LPSTR szId,
       WORD wIdMaxLen) {
     LOCALHANDLE hCtlStyleDlg;
     NPCTLSTYLEDLG npCtlStyleDlg;
     LPCTLSTYLE lpCtlStyle;
     WORD wIdLen;

     // Property is associated with the Dialog Editor's window.
     // The parent of the dialog box is the Dialog Editor.
     hCtlStyleDlg = GetProp(GetParent(hDlg), _szCtlProp);
     if (hCtlStyleDlg == NULL) return(0);

     npCtlStyleDlg = (NPCTLSTYLEDLG) LocalLock(hCtlStyleDlg);
     lpCtlStyle = (LPCTLSTYLE) GlobalLock(npCtlStyleDlg->hCtlStyle);

     // Call the lpfnIdToStr function to convert the numeric ID to
     // its string equivalent
     wIdLen = (*npCtlStyleDlg->lpfnIdToStr)(lpCtlStyle->wId, szId,
        wIdMaxLen);

     GlobalUnlock(npCtlStyleDlg->hCtlStyle);
     LocalUnlock(hCtlStyleDlg);
     return(wIdLen);
}


// This function should only be called from the ClassDlgFn
// function. It converts an ID string value into its numeric
// equivalent and stores the numeric value in the CTLSTYLE
// structure for the control. If the LOWORD of the result is 0,
```

```
// the ID is invalid; otherwise, the HIWORD contains the numeric
// value of the ID.
DWORD FAR PASCAL SetIdValue (HWND hDlg, LPSTR szId) {
   LOCALHANDLE hCtlStyleDlg;
   NPCTLSTYLEDLG npCtlStyleDlg;
   LPCTLSTYLE lpCtlStyle;
   DWORD dwResult = 0;

   hCtlStyleDlg = GetProp(GetParent(hDlg), _szCtlProp);
   if (hCtlStyleDlg == NULL) return(dwResult);

   npCtlStyleDlg = (NPCTLSTYLEDLG) LocalLock(hCtlStyleDlg);

   // Call the lpfnStrToId function to convert the string ID to
   // its numeric equivalent
   dwResult = (*npCtlStyleDlg->lpfnStrToId)(szId);

   LocalUnlock(hCtlStyleDlg);

   // If LOWORD is zero, string NOT found
   if (LOWORD(dwResult) == 0)
      return(dwResult);

   // LOWORD is not zero; numeric ID is in the HIWORD
   lpCtlStyle = CtlStyleLock(hDlg);
   lpCtlStyle->wId = HIWORD(dwResult);
   CtlStyleUnlock(hDlg);
   return(dwResult);
}
```

Listing 4-18. CNTL-DE.H Custom Control and Dialog Editor header module.

```
/****************************************************************
Module name: Cntl-DE.H
Programmer : Jeffrey M. Richter
****************************************************************/

// This function should be called first in the ClassInfo function
// to initialize the new control
```

```
GLOBALHANDLE FAR PASCAL ControlInfo (WORD wVersion, LPSTR szClass,
   LPSTR szTitle);

// This function should be called repeatedly to add new control
// types to the structure returned by the ControlInfo function.
// This function should be called in the ClassInfo function.
BOOL FAR PASCAL AddControlType (GLOBALHANDLE hMem, WORD wType,
   WORD wWidth, WORD wHeight, DWORD dwStyle, LPSTR szDescr);

// This function displays the control's style dialog box and
// should be called from the ClassStyle function
int FAR PASCAL ShowStyleDlg (HANDLE hInstance, LPSTR szTemplate,
   HWND hWndParent, FARPROC fpDlgProc, LONG lParam, GLOBALHANDLE
   hCtlStyle, LPFNSTRTOID lpfnStrToId, LPFNIDTOSTR lpfnIdToStr);

// This function should only be called from the ClassDlgFn
// function. It locks the memory block containing the CTLSTYLE
// structure for the selected control and returns the FAR address
// to that structure.
LPCTLSTYLE FAR PASCAL CtlStyleLock (HWND hDlg);

// This function should only be called from the ClassDlgFn
// function. It unlocks the memory block containing the CTLSTYLE
// structure for the selected control and returns whether the
// block was successfully unlocked.
BOOL FAR PASCAL CtlStyleUnlock (HWND hDlg);

// This function should only be called from the ClassDlgFn
// function. It converts the ID value for the control into an
// identifier string and stores the string in the address passed
// in. The number of characters in the string is returned.
WORD FAR PASCAL GetIdString (HWND hDlg, LPSTR szId,
   WORD wIdMaxLen);

// This function should only be called from the ClassDlgFn
// function. It converts an ID string value into its numeric
// equivalent and stores the numeric value in the CTLSTYLE
// structure for the control. If the LOWORD of the result is 0,
// the ID is invalid; otherwise, the HIWORD contains the
// numeric value of the ID.
DWORD FAR PASCAL SetIdValue (HWND hDlg, LPSTR szId);
```

287

Using Custom Controls in an Application

This section describes the steps necessary to use custom child controls in your own applications. Keep in mind that all the DLLs for your custom child controls must be distributed with your application's executable file. The sample application, CUSTCNTL.EXE, demonstrates the use of the Meter and Spin Button controls in a dialog box. The Meter control is also used in Chapter 8, Installing Commercial Applications.

When your application is executed, each custom control's class must be registered. This is done by calling the *LoadLibrary* function to load each custom control's DLL. The *LoadLibrary* function locates the .DLL file and its *LibEntry* function. *LibEntry* is a small assembly language function in the LIBENTRY.ASM file included with the Windows SDK. The object file is also included.

LibEntry calls the *LibMain* function you wrote for the DLL. This function registers the window class for the custom child control. Once the class has been registered, the application may create dialog boxes or windows of the class. The following is an example of how an application that uses the Meter and Spin Button controls might perform its initialization:

```
int PASCAL WinMain (HANDLE hInstance, HANDLE hPrevInstance,
     LPSTR lpszCmdLine, int nCmdShow) {
  HANDLE hLibMeter, hLibSpin;
  hLibMeter = LoadLibrary("METER.DLL");
  if (hLibMeter < 32)
     return(0);
  hLibSpin = LoadLibrary("SPIN.DLL");
  if (hLibSpin < 32) {
     FreeLibrary(hLibMeter);
     return(0);
  }
  .
  .
  .
```

```
// Perform any other initialization and start message loop
.
.
.

FreeLibrary(hLibSpin);
FreeLibrary(hLibMeter);
return(0);
}
```

Before the application terminates, it must call *FreeLibrary* to subtract 1 from the reference count of the library. When the reference count reaches zero, the *WEP* function is called. This function calls the *UnregisterClass* function to remove the custom child control class from Windows.

Once the custom child control's library has been loaded, the control class can be used like any other window class. This means windows may be created by calling *CreateWindow* or *CreateWindowEx*, or by creating dialog boxes if the custom child class name is referenced in the dialog box's template.

Figure 4-8. CUSTCNTL.ICO.

Listing 4-19. CUSTCNTL.C application source module.

```
/****************************************************************
Module name: CustCntl.C
Programmer : Jeffrey M. Richter
****************************************************************/

#include "..\nowindws.h"
#undef NOCOLOR
#undef NOCTLMGR
#undef NOGDI
#undef NOKERNEL
#undef NOLSTRING
#undef NOMB
#undef NOMENUS
#undef NOMINMAX
#undef NOMSG
#undef NORASTEROPS
#undef NOSHOWWINDOW
#undef NOSYSMETRICS
#undef NOUSER
#undef NOWINOFFSETS
#undef NOWINMESSAGES
#undef NOWINSTYLES
#include <windows.h>

#include "custcntl.h"

char _szAppName[] = "CustCntl";

HANDLE _hInstance = NULL;        // our instance handle

#define IDM_DEMO     (0x0110)    // Must be < 0xF000 (GetSystemMenu)
#define IDM_ABOUT    (0x0120)    // Must be < 0xF000

BOOL NEAR PASCAL RegisterAppWndClass (HANDLE hInstance);
BOOL FAR PASCAL AboutProc (HWND hDlg, WORD wMsg, WORD wParam,
    LONG lParam);
```

```
BOOL FAR PASCAL CustCntlDlgProc (HWND hDlg, WORD wMsg,
   WORD wParam, LONG lParam);
LONG FAR PASCAL AppWndProc (HWND hWnd, WORD wMsg, WORD wParam,
   LONG lParam);

// ***************************************************************
int PASCAL WinMain (HANDLE hInstance, HANDLE hPrevInstance,
     LPSTR lpszCmdLine, int nCmdShow) {
   MSG msg;
   HWND hWnd;
   HMENU hMenu;
   HANDLE hLibMeter, hLibSpin;

   _hInstance = hInstance;

   if (hPrevInstance == NULL)
     if (!RegisterAppWndClass(hInstance))
         return(0);

   hWnd = CreateWindow(_szAppName, _szAppName,
     WS_OVERLAPPEDWINDOW | WS_VISIBLE,
     CW_USEDEFAULT, nCmdShow, CW_USEDEFAULT, CW_USEDEFAULT,
     NULL, NULL, hInstance, 0);
   if (hWnd == NULL) return(0);

   // Get handle to application's System menu
   hMenu = GetSystemMenu(hWnd, 0);

   // Append separator bar and two options
   AppendMenu(hMenu, MF_SEPARATOR, 0, 0);
   AppendMenu(hMenu, MF_STRING,
     IDM_DEMO, "&Custom control demo...");
   AppendMenu(hMenu, MF_STRING, IDM_ABOUT, "A&bout...");
   DrawMenuBar(hWnd);

   hLibMeter = LoadLibrary("METER.DLL");
   if (hLibMeter < 32) return(0);
   hLibSpin = LoadLibrary("SPIN.DLL");
   if (hLibSpin < 32) {
```

```
        FreeLibrary(hLibMeter);
        return(0);
    }

    while (GetMessage(&msg, NULL, 0, 0)) {
        TranslateMessage(&msg);
        DispatchMessage(&msg);
    }

    FreeLibrary(hLibMeter);
    FreeLibrary(hLibSpin);
    return(0);
}

// *************************************************************
// This function registers the application's main window

BOOL NEAR PASCAL RegisterAppWndClass (HANDLE hInstance) {
    WNDCLASS WndClass;

    WndClass.style          = 0;
    WndClass.lpfnWndProc    = AppWndProc;
    WndClass.cbClsExtra     = 0;
    WndClass.cbWndExtra     = 0;
    WndClass.hInstance      = hInstance;
    WndClass.hIcon          = LoadIcon(hInstance, _szAppName);
    WndClass.hCursor        = LoadCursor(NULL, IDC_ARROW);
    WndClass.hbrBackground  = COLOR_WINDOW + 1;
    WndClass.lpszMenuName   = NULL;
    WndClass.lpszClassName  = _szAppName;
    return(RegisterClass(&WndClass));
}

// *************************************************************
// This function processes all messages sent to the modeless
// dialog box

BOOL FAR PASCAL CustCntlDlgProc (HWND hDlg, WORD wMsg,
        WORD wParam, LONG lParam) {
    BOOL fProcessed = TRUE;
    int x;
```

```
switch (wMsg) {
    case WM_INITDIALOG:
        // Tell Meter control that the job consists of 25 parts
        SendDlgItemMessage(hDlg, ID_METER, MM_SETPARTSINJOB,
            25, 0);

        // Tell Meter control that the zero parts of the job are
        // complete
        SendDlgItemMessage(hDlg, ID_METER, MM_SETPARTSCOMPLETE,
            0, 0);

        // Tell spin button that the valid range is 0 to 25
        SendDlgItemMessage(hDlg, ID_SPIN, SPNM_SETRANGE, 0,
            MAKELONG(0, 25));

        // Tell spin button that the current value is 0
        SendDlgItemMessage(hDlg, ID_SPIN, SPNM_SETCRNTVALUE,
            0, 0);
        break;

    case WM_COMMAND:
        switch (wParam) {
            case ID_SPIN:
                switch (HIWORD(lParam)) {
                    case SPNN_VALUECHANGE:
                        // User has changed the current value of the
                        // spin button

                        // Request current value from the spin button
                        x = (int) SendMessage(LOWORD(lParam),
                            SPNM_GETCRNTVALUE, 0, 0);

                        // Tells the Meter control the new number of
                        // parts that are complete. This is an
                        // example of the Meter control allowing for
                        // the "parts-complete" value to go both up
                        // and down.
                        SendDlgItemMessage(hDlg, ID_METER,
                            MM_SETPARTSCOMPLETE, x, 0);
```

```
                        // Update the static window to reflect the
                        // current value in the spin button
                        SetDlgItemInt(hDlg, ID_SPINVALUE, x, FALSE);
                        break;
                    }
                    break;

                case IDOK:
                case IDCANCEL:
                    EndDialog(hDlg, wParam);
                    break;

                default: break;
            }
            break;

        default:
            fProcessed = FALSE;
            break;
    }

    return(fProcessed);
}

// ***********************************************************
// This function processes all messages sent to the app's main
// window

LONG FAR PASCAL AppWndProc (HWND hWnd, WORD wMsg, WORD wParam,
        LONG lParam) {
    BOOL fCallDefProc = FALSE;
    LONG lResult = 0;
    FARPROC fpProc;

    switch (wMsg) {
        case WM_DESTROY:
            PostQuitMessage(0);
            break;

        case WM_SYSCOMMAND:
```

```
        // Any menu option selected from CustCntl's System menu

        // Any options that we appended to System menu should be
        // processed by CustCntl and NOT passed to DefWindowProc

        switch (wParam & 0xfff0) {

        case IDM_ABOUT:
           // Display About box
           fpProc = MakeProcInstance(AboutProc, _hInstance);
           DialogBox(_hInstance, "About", hWnd, fpProc);
           FreeProcInstance(fpProc);
           break;

        case IDM_DEMO:
           // Display About box
           fpProc = MakeProcInstance(CustCntlDlgProc,
              _hInstance);
           DialogBox(_hInstance, "CustCntl", hWnd, fpProc);
           FreeProcInstance(fpProc);
           break;

        default:
           // Any options that we do not process should be passed
           // to DefWindowProc
           fCallDefProc = TRUE;
           break;
        }

        break;

     default:
        fCallDefProc = TRUE; break;
   }

   if (fCallDefProc)
      lResult = DefWindowProc(hWnd, wMsg, wParam, lParam);

   return(lResult);
}
```

```
// ************************************************************
// This function processes all messages sent to About dialog box

BOOL FAR PASCAL AboutProc (HWND hDlg, WORD wMsg, WORD wParam,
     LONG lParam) {
   char szBuffer[100];
   BOOL fProcessed = TRUE;

   switch (wMsg) {

      case WM_INITDIALOG:
         // Set version static window to have date and time of
         // compilation
         wsprintf(szBuffer, "%s at %s", (LPSTR) __DATE__, (LPSTR)
            __TIME__);
         SetWindowText(GetDlgItem(hDlg, ID_VERSION), szBuffer);
         break;

      case WM_COMMAND:
         switch (wParam) {
            case IDOK:
            case IDCANCEL:
               if (HIWORD(lParam) == BN_CLICKED)
                  EndDialog(hDlg, wParam);
               break;

            default:
               break;
         }
         break;

      default:
         fProcessed = FALSE; break;
   }
   return(fProcessed);
}
```

Listing 4-20. CUSTCNTL.H application header module.

```
/******************************************************************
Module name: CustCntl.H
Programmer : Jeffrey M. Richter
******************************************************************/

#include "..\spin.04\spin.h"
#include "..\meter.04\meter.h"

#include "dialog.h"
```

Listing 4-21. CUSTCNTL.DEF Custom Control application definitions file.

```
; Module name: CustCntl.DEF
; Programmer : Jeffrey M. Richter

NAME            CustCntl
DESCRIPTION     'CustCntl: Custom Child Control Application'
STUB            'WinStub.exe'
EXETYPE         WINDOWS
CODE            MOVEABLE DISCARDABLE PRELOAD
DATA            MOVEABLE MULTIPLE PRELOAD
HEAPSIZE        1024
STACKSIZE       4096
EXPORTS
   AppWndProc
   CustCntlDlgProc
   AboutProc
```

Listing 4-22. CUSTCNTL.RC application resource file.

```
/*****************************************************************
Module name: CustCntl.RC
Programmer : Jeffrey M. Richter
*****************************************************************/

#include <windows.h>

#include "custcntl.h"
#include "dialog.h"
#include "custcntl.dlg"

CustCntl ICON    MOVEABLE DISCARDABLE CustCntl.Ico
```

Listing 4-23. DIALOG.H (dialog-box template defines) for Custom Control.

```
#define ID_SPINVALUE   100
#define ID_SPIN        101
#define ID_METER       102
#define ID_VERSION     200
#define IDCANCEL       2
```

Listing 4-24. CUSTCNTL.DLG dialog-box templates.

```
ABOUT DIALOG LOADONCALL MOVEABLE DISCARDABLE 16, 20, 126, 92
CAPTION "About CustCntl Demo"
STYLE WS_BORDER | WS_CAPTION | WS_DLGFRAME | WS_SYSMENU |
    WS_VISIBLE | WS_POPUP
BEGIN
   CONTROL "CustCntl", -1, "static", SS_ICON | WS_CHILD, 4, 16,
      18, 21
   CONTROL "CustCntl", -1, "static", SS_CENTER | WS_CHILD, 22, 8,
      100, 12
   CONTROL "Written by:", -1, "static", SS_CENTER | WS_CHILD, 22,
      20, 100, 12
   CONTROL "Jeffrey M. Richter", -1, "static", SS_CENTER |
      WS_CHILD, 22, 32, 100, 12
```

```
   CONTROL "Version date:", -1, "static", SS_CENTER | WS_CHILD,
      22, 48, 100, 12
   CONTROL "", ID_VERSION, "static", SS_CENTER | WS_CHILD, 22, 60,
      100, 12
   CONTROL "&OK", 1, "button", BS_DEFPUSHBUTTON | WS_TABSTOP |
      WS_CHILD, 40, 76, 44, 12
END

CUSTCNTL DIALOG LOADONCALL MOVEABLE DISCARDABLE 11, 22, 144, 36
CAPTION "Custom control demonstration"
STYLE WS_BORDER | WS_CAPTION | WS_DLGFRAME | WS_SYSMENU |
      WS_VISIBLE | WS_POPUP
BEGIN
   CONTROL "&Spin value:", -1, "static", SS_LEFT | WS_CHILD, 4, 4,
      40, 12
   CONTROL "", ID_SPINVALUE, "static", SS_LEFT | WS_BORDER |
      WS_CHILD, 44, 4, 32, 12
   CONTROL "Text", ID_SPIN, "spin", WS_BORDER | WS_CHILD, 76, 4,
      8, 12
   CONTROL "Text", ID_METER, "meter", WS_BORDER | WS_CHILD, 4, 20,
      96, 12
   CONTROL "&Cancel", IDCANCEL, "button", BS_DEFPUSHBUTTON |
      WS_TABSTOP | WS_CHILD, 104, 4, 36, 12
END
```

Listing 4-25. MAKEFILE for Custom Control application.

```
#******************************************************************
#Module name: MAKEFILE
#Programmer : Jeffrey M. Richter
#******************************************************************

PROG = CustCntl
MODEL = S
CFLAGS = -A$(MODEL) -D_WINDOWS -Gcsw2 -W4 -Zlepid -Od
LFLAGS = /NOE/BA/A:16/M/CO/LI/F
LIBS = $(MODEL)nocrt + libw

M1 = $(PROG).obj
```

```
ICONS = $(PROG).ico
BITMAPS =
CURSORS =
RESOURCES = $(ICONS) $(BITMAPS) $(CURSORS)

.SUFFIXES: .rc

.rc.res:
   rc -r $*.rc

$(PROG).Exe: $(M1) $(PROG).Def $(PROG).Res
   link $(LFLAGS) @<<$(PROG).lnk
$(M1)
$(PROG), $(PROG), $(LIBS), $(PROG)
<<
   rc $(PROG).Res

$(PROG).obj:   $*.c $*.h dialog.h

$(PROG).res:   $*.rc $*.h $*.dlg dialog.h $(RESOURCES)
```

CHAPTER 5

Setting Up Printers

Windows version 3.0 gives your applications much greater control over printer settings than previous versions of Windows. In previous versions, settings were systemwide. When the user changed the settings, the new settings affected all the applications running under Windows. For example, if the user changed the printer's settings so that it would print in landscape mode for a spreadsheet application, the printer would remain in landscape mode when printing from a word-processing application.

With version 3.0 of Windows, each application can maintain its own print settings. In fact, an application may maintain several different print settings at once. This allows a word-processing application to remember the settings for a particular document. For example, the user may desire that interoffice memos always print from the laser printer's paper bin 1 and that corporate correspondence always print from bin 2.

This chapter explains how Windows manages printers and how applications can access various printer settings. It concludes with an example of a Printer Setup dialog box. This dialog box is common to Windows applications that allow printing and can usually be seen by selecting the "Printer setup..." option under the File menu.

How Windows Manages Printers

Users install, configure, set up, and remove printers from the Windows environment using the Printers dialog box in the Control Panel (Figure 5-1).

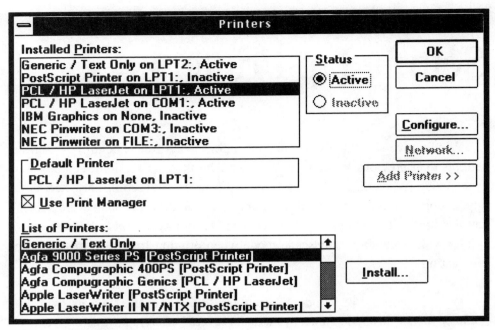

Figure 5-1. Printers dialog box.

When the user selects the "Add Printer >>" pushbutton, the list of available printers appears in the "List of Printers:" list box. This list is obtained from the *[io.device]* section of the SETUP.INF file distributed with Windows. Each line in this section contains the information necessary to install a single printer. The entire *[io.device]* section is far too long to be reproduced here, so only the beginning of it is shown:

```
[io.device]
; (printers, plotters, etc.)
; The file name is followed by
;
; — the descriptive string that will appear in Control Panel and
;   in WIN.INI
; — 1 or 2 strings indicating the scaling for this device
;
```

```
; There may be more than one line for a driver, corresponding to
; different printers.

5:TTY.DRV,"Generic / Text Only","DEVICESPECIFIC"
5:PSCRIPT.DRV,"Agfa 9000 Series PS [PostScript Printer]",
   "DEVICESPECIFIC"
5:PSCRIPT.DRV,"Agfa Compugraphic 400PS [PostScript Printer]",
   "DEVICESPECIFIC"
5:HPPCL.DRV,"Agfa Compugraphic Genics [PCL / HP LaserJet]",
   "DEVICESPECIFIC"
5:PSCRIPT.DRV,"Apple LaserWriter [PostScript Printer]",
   "DEVICESPECIFIC"
5:PSCRIPT.DRV,"Apple LaserWriter II NT/NTX [PostScript Printer]",
   "DEVICESPECIFIC"
5:PSCRIPT.DRV,"Apple LaserWriter Plus [PostScript Printer]",
   "DEVICESPECIFIC"
5:HPPCL.DRV,"Apricot Laser [PCL / HP LaserJet]","DEVICESPECIFIC"
5:PSCRIPT.DRV,"AST TurboLaser/PS - R4081 [PostScript Printer]",
   "DEVICESPECIFIC"
5:HPPLOT.DRV,"AT&T 435","CONTINUOUSSCALING"
5:CITOH.DRV,"AT&T 470/475","133,96,72","75,72,96"
5:IBMGRX.DRV,"AT&T 473/478","167,120,72","60,72,120"
5:CITOH.DRV,"C-Itoh 8510","133,96,72","75,72,96"
5:LBP8II.DRV,"Canon LBP-8II","DEVICESPECIFIC"
5:CANONIII.DRV,"Canon LBP-8III/LBP-4","DEVICESPECIFIC"
5:PSCRIPT.DRV,"Dataproducts LZR-2665 [PostScript Printer]",
   "DEVICESPECIFIC"
5:PSCRIPT.DRV,"Digital LN03R ScriptPrinter [PostScript Printer]",
   "DEVICESPECIFIC"
   .
   .
   .
```

Each line contains a diskette number, the name of the printer's device driver file, text indicating the specific printer's model and its device name, and one or two strings specifying device scaling information.

The diskette number specifies which of the distribution diskettes contains the printer's device driver file. When the user wishes to install a new printer, the Control

Panel first determines if the specified device driver is already installed. If it is, the Control Panel asks the user if it should use the current printer driver or replace it with a new one.

The third field is the line of text the Control Panel places in the "List of Printers:" list box. Some lines contain the printer's type, which is enclosed in square brackets.

PSCRIPT.DRV is used for many different printers. If you examine the complete SETUP.INF file on your computer, you will notice that several other drivers are used for a variety of printers. For example, the EPSON9.DRV file is used for all nine-pin Epson printers and the NEC24PIN.DRV file is used for all 24-pin NEC printers. Although the features and capabilities of PostScript printers vary, the actual translation of data for the particular printer remains the same.

After the user has installed a new printer, the printer's device name is inserted in the "Installed Printers:" list box at the upper left of the dialog box. The Control Panel shows only the type of printer that has been installed or the printer's name if the type was not indicated within square brackets. For example, if the "Apricot Laser [PCL/HP LaserJet]" printer has been installed, the "Installed Printers:" list box will only show that a "PCL/HP LaserJet" printer has been installed. However, if the "AT&T 435" printer is installed, the printer's full name will appear.

Each printer must be assigned a port. The *[ports]* section of the WIN.INI file defines the ports Windows should recognize. By default, the following ports exist:

```
[ports]
LPT1:=
LPT2:=
LPT3:=
COM1:=9600,n,8,1
COM2:=9600,n,8,1
COM3:=9600,n,8,1
COM4:=9600,n,8,1
EPT:=
```

```
FILE:=
LPT1.OS2=
LPT2.OS2=
```

The table below briefly explains the default ports:

Printer	Description
LPT1:, LPT2:, LPT3:	The printer is connected to one of the line-printer ports and may be used for printing.
COM1:, COM2:, COM3:, COM4:	The printer is connected to one of the communications ports and may be used for printing.
EPT:	The printer is connected to the EPT port and may be used for printing.
FILE:	Printing to this printer will cause all output to be sent to a file. When printing begins, the user will be prompted for a file name.
LPT1.OS2, LPT2.OS2	Printing to this printer will cause all output to be sent to the path name specified. These ports are used when Windows is running in a DOS compatibility box under OS/2.

In addition to these ports, Windows defines a NullPort. It indicates that a printer is not connected to any physical port and, consequently, cannot be used for output. The name of this port is specified in the *[windows]* section of the WIN.INI file and is initialized to "None" when Windows is installed:

```
[windows]
  .
  .
  .
```

```
NullPort=None
    .
    .
    .
```

The user can change the name of this port by using the Notepad application or some other text editor. When new printers are installed, the Control Panel assigns them to the NullPort by default.

The Control Panel allows more than one printer to be assigned to the same port. For this reason, the Control Panel allows the user to select which printers are active and which are inactive. Only active printers can be used for sending output.

Suppose your computer has an HP LaserJet and an Epson dot-matrix printer connected via an A-B switch to LPT1:. You would install both the HPPCL.DRV and EPSON9.DRV printer drivers from the Windows distribution diskettes. Using the "Configure..." pushbutton, you would then assign the LPT1: port to both printers. The "Status" box indicates whether the currently selected printer is active or inactive. When an inactive printer is made active, all other printers connected to that port are automatically made inactive. Whenever you decide to use the other printer by switching the A-B switch, the active printer must also be changed in the Control Panel.

A printer assigned to the NullPort is always inactive and can only be printed to after its port has been changed and the printer is made active.

Every time the user exits the "Printers" dialog box, the Control Panel saves the printer information in the *[PrinterPorts]* section of the WIN.INI file:

```
[PrinterPorts]
Generic / Text Only=TTY,LPT2:,15,45
PostScript Printer=PSCRIPT,LPT1:,15,45
PCL / HP LaserJet=HPPCL,LPT1:,15,45,COM1:,15,45
IBM Graphics=IBMGRX,None,15,45
NEC Pinwriter=NEC24PIN,COM3:,15,45,FILE:,15,45
```

On the left of the equal sign is the text describing the printer that has been installed. Following the equal sign is the name of the device driver, not including its extension, used to access that printer. The remainder of the line specifies the port the printer is connected to, the "Device Not Selected:" timeout, and the "Transmission Retry:" timeout. If more than one printer of this type has been installed, these last three fields are repeated for each printer installed. For example, the *[PrinterPorts]* section shows that two HP LaserJet printers have been installed:

Port	Device not selected	Transmission retry
LPT1:	15	45
COM1:	15	45

Although an application may refer to the information in *[PrinterPorts]* to determine which printers are available, this section is usually used only by the Control Panel. Applications should reference the *[devices]* section (also updated by the Control Panel) of the WIN.INI file to determine which printers are available:

```
[devices]
Generic / Text Only=TTY,LPT2:
PostScript Printer=PSCRIPT,None
PCL / HP LaserJet=HPPCL,LPT1:
IBM Graphics=IBMGRX,None
NEC Pinwriter=NEC24PIN,FILE:
```

As in the *[PrinterPorts]* section of the WIN.INI file, the item to the left of the equal sign is the device name of the installed printer. Immediately following the equal sign is the name of the printer device driver. The remainder of the line specifies which port the printer is connected to. This section does not contain the "Device Not Selected" and "Transmission Retry" fields. The Control Panel changes the port of any inactive printers to the NullPort. For example, the line describing the PostScript printer in the *[PrinterPorts]* section indicates that this printer is connected to the LPT1: port. However, this printer is inactive and is therefore assigned to the NullPort ("None") in the *[devices]* section of the WIN.INI file.

The Control Panel also does not list the NullPort for printers that are actively connected to another port. In other words, if the same type of printer is listed on an active port and an inactive port, only the active port listing will appear. Because the HP LaserJet on the LPT1: port is active, the inactive HP LaserJet on the COM1: port is not appended to the PCL/HP LaserJet line.

In addition to assigning printers to various ports, Windows lets the user select a default printer. The "Default Printer" box in the Control Panel shows the default printer. Applications use this printer if the user has not explicitly chosen a different printer. The default printer is selected by double-clicking the mouse on the desired printer in the "Installed Printers:" list box or by selecting the desired printer and pressing Alt-D. The Control Panel will not allow an inactive printer to become the default printer. If the default printer is made inactive, the new active printer becomes the default. The Control Panel also removes any default printer if the user changes its port to the NullPort.

The Control Panel saves this information in the *[windows]* section of the WIN.INI file:

```
[windows]
.
.
.
device=PCL / HP LaserJet,HPPCL,LPT1:
.
.
.
```

Following the equal sign is the text describing the device name of the printer, the printer's device driver file, and the port to which the printer is connected. When no default printer is selected, the line has the following appearance:

```
device=
```

When an application finds that no default printer has been selected, any options that would allow the user to print should be disabled. In addition, if an application requires some knowledge of a printer's capabilities before it can perform some actions, these actions should also be disabled. For example, a word-processing program might not be able to calculate the number of pages in a document if it cannot calculate the paper size for any printer.

Printer Device Drivers. Because there are so many different kinds of printers, it would be impossible for Microsoft to support all of them in Windows itself. For this reason, a special device driver must be developed for each type of printer. Even though Microsoft distributes most of the drivers with Windows, the device drivers are often available directly from the printer manufacturer.

Although the printer device driver file has a .DRV instead of a .DLL extension, it *is* a DLL. The most important responsibility of a printer device driver is to translate device-independent GDI function calls into a series of commands and data that can be sent to the printer. Printer drivers are also responsible for providing device-dependent characteristics such as printer technology (raster, vector, plotter) and horizontal and vertical resolution to an application. Finally, printer drivers let the user and applications change printer settings, such as paper orientation.

When the user selects the "Setup..." button from the "Printer - Configure" dialog box in the Control Panel, another dialog box appears. It contains all the settings applicable to the selected printer. Because each printer supports different settings, the template for the settings dialog box and the code to process it are contained in the printer's device driver file. The settings dialog box for a PCL/HP LaserJet printer is shown in Figure 5-2.

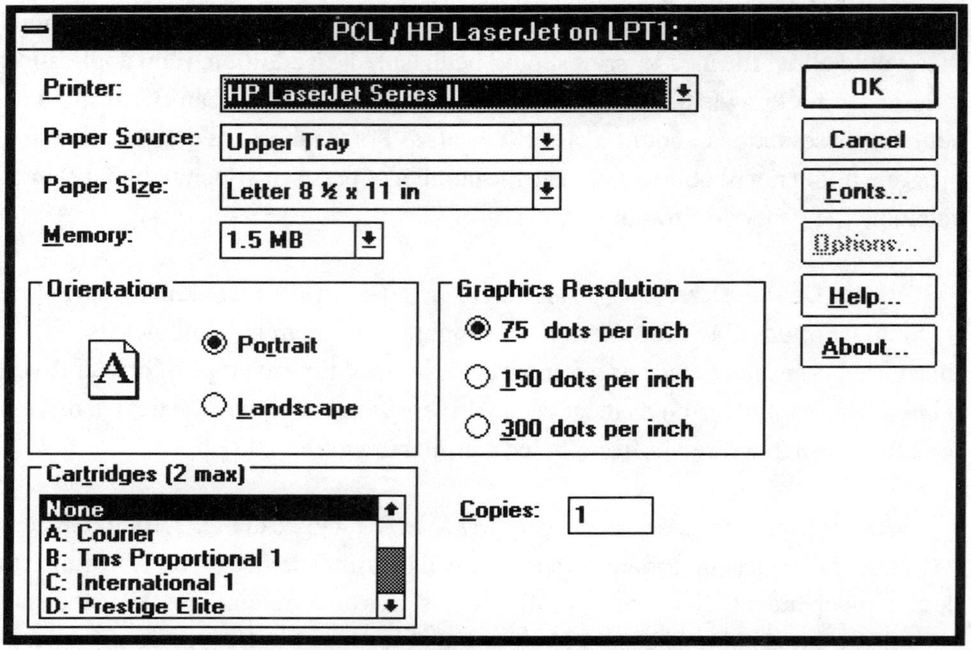

Figure 5-2. Settings dialog box for PCL/HP LaserJet.

The settings dialog box for an NEC Pinwriter is shown in Figure 5-3.

When the Control Panel changes these settings, the printer device driver saves the new settings in WIN.INI. For example, each of the installed PCL/HP LaserJet printers has an entry in WIN.INI:

```
[HPPCL,LPT1]
paper=1
duplex=0
FontSummary=C:\WINDOWS\FSLPT1.PCL


[HPPCL,COM1]
paper=1
prtindex=8
duplex=0
```

```
prtcaps=-13432
paperind=1
FontSummary=C:\WINDOWS\FSCOM1.PCL
```

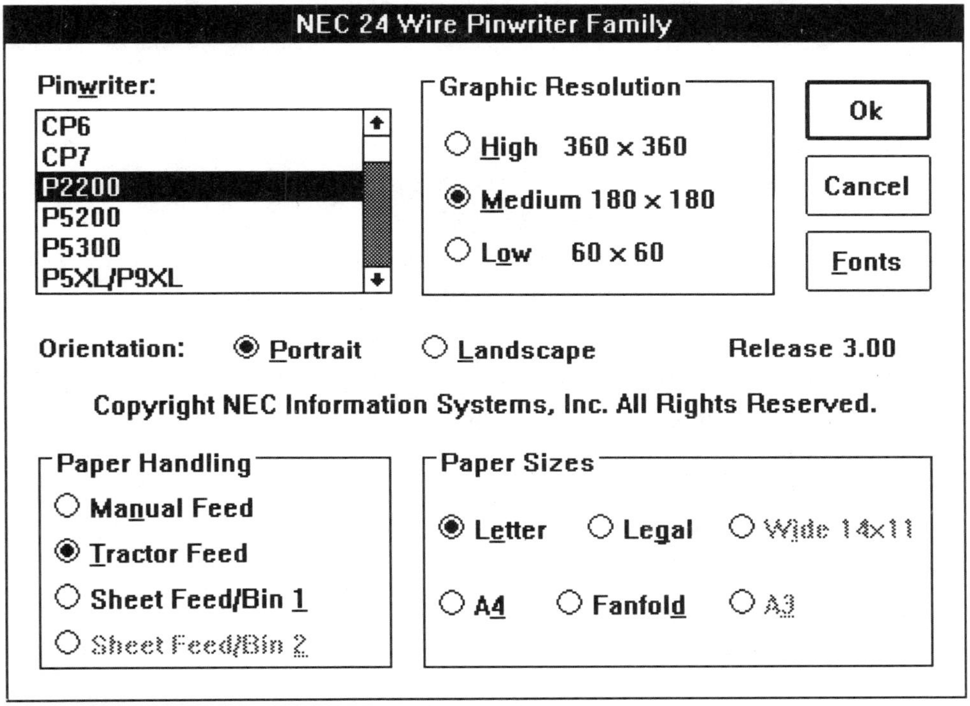

Figure 5-3. Settings dialog box for NEC Pinwriter.

While the PCL/HP LaserJet driver maintains a different configuration for each port a LaserJet printer is connected to, some printer drivers only save the most recent printer configuration. The driver for NEC Pinwriter printers operates this way:

```
[NEC Pinwriter]
Pinwriter=2
Orientation=10
Paper=20
Feed=95
Resolution=17
Font1=24
```

```
Font2=19
Font3=13
Font4=0
Font5=0
Font6=0
Font7=0
Font8=0
```

Because some printer drivers support many different printers, the user must explicitly choose the exact printer model connected to the port. This is done from the printer driver's settings dialog box. The PCL/HP LaserJet dialog box contains a "Printer:" combo box listing all the printer models it supports. The NEC Pinwriter dialog box shows a "Pinwriter:" list box with its supported models.

This exact specification of the printer model allows the printer driver to fine-tune its capabilities. For example, the list box showing the installed cartridges allows the user to select which font cartridges are installed in the printer. When the "HP LaserJet Series II" printer is selected, the user may install two cartridges. However, when the "Tandy LP-1000" printer is selected, the driver doesn't allow any cartridges to be installed.

Applications present a printer's settings dialog box to the user by calling *DeviceMode*. This function is contained in the printer's device driver and is not part of Windows. The prototype for this function is the same for all printer drivers:

```
void FAR PASCAL DeviceMode(HWND hWnd, HANDLE hLibrary,
    LPSTR szDeviceName, LPSTR szPort);
```

Because this function is in a DLL, the library must be loaded before the function can be called. The following code fragment demonstrates how to call *DeviceMode*:

```
typedef void FAR PASCAL FNDEVICEMODE(HWND, HANDLE, LPSTR, LPSTR);
typedef FNDEVICEMODE FAR *LPFNDEVICEMODE;
  .
  .
  .
```

```
BOOL FAR PASCAL CallDeviceModeFunc (HWND hWnd, LPSTR szDriver,
    LPSTR szDeviceName, LPSTR szPort) {
  HANDLE hLibrary;
  LPFNDEVICEMODE lpfnDeviceMode;
  BOOL fOk = FALSE;

  hLibrary = LoadLibrary(szDriver);
  if (hLibrary < 32) {
    // Library could not be loaded
    return(fOk);
  }
  lpfnDeviceMode = (LPFNDEVICEMODE)
    GetProcAddress(hLibrary, "DeviceMode");
  if (lpfnDeviceMode != NULL) {
    lpfnDeviceMode(hWnd, hLibrary, szDeviceName, szPort);
    fOk = TRUE;
  } else {
    // DeviceMode function not in library
  }
  FreeLibrary(hLibrary);
  return(fOk);
}
```

Because this function displays a dialog box to the user, a window handle that will own the dialog box must be passed as the first parameter. The second parameter to *CallDeviceModeFunc* is the name of the printer device driver file to be loaded. The third parameter is the device name of the printer driver. This is the same text that appears in the *[PrinterPorts]* and *[devices]* sections of the WIN.INI file. The last parameter is the null-terminated string representing the output port (for instance, LPT1: or FILE:).

CallDeviceModeFunc attempts to load the DLL using the *LoadLibrary* function. If the library could not be loaded, *LoadLibrary* returns a value of less than 32 identifying the reason. Once the handle to the library has been obtained, *GetProcAddress* can locate the address of *DeviceMode* in the DLL. This line could also appear as follows:

```
lpfnDeviceMode = GetProcAddress(hLibrary, PROC_OLDDEVICEMODE);
```

The *PROC_OLDDEVICEMODE* identifier can be found in the DRIVINIT.H file included with the Windows SDK.

If *GetProcAddress* returns NULL, the library does not contain a *DeviceMode* function. Otherwise, this function is called with all the parameters passed to *CallDeviceModeFunc* (except that it gets the handle to the library instead of the library's name). This causes the library or printer device driver to present the settings dialog box to the user.

When the *DeviceMode* function returns, the *FreeLibrary* function releases the memory used by the library. *CallDeviceModeFunc* returns TRUE or FALSE, indicating whether the call to the *DeviceMode* function was successful.

Although *DeviceMode* is declared as returning no value (*void*), most printer drivers have implemented their *DeviceMode* functions so that they return TRUE or FALSE. However, this is not a rule that developers of device drivers must follow; don't rely on it unless you're sure that the printer drivers your applications access implement this feature.

The *DEVMODE* Structure and Printer Environments. When the user selects the "Ok" button from the printer settings dialog box, the device driver gathers all the settings and places them in a *DEVMODE* structure. This structure is defined in the DRIVINIT.H file included with the Windows SDK:

```
#define CCHDEVICENAME           32
 .
 .
 .
typedef struct _devicemode {
    char    dmDeviceName[CCHDEVICENAME];
    WORD    dmSpecVersion;
    WORD    dmDriverVersion;
    WORD    dmSize;
    WORD    dmDriverExtra;
    DWORD   dmFields;
```

```
    short   dmOrientation;
    short   dmPaperSize;
    short   dmPaperLength;
    short   dmPaperWidth;
    short   dmScale;
    short   dmCopies;
    short   dmDefaultSource;
    short   dmPrintQuality;
    short   dmColor;
    short   dmDuplex;
    BYTE    dmDriverData[];
} DEVMODE;
```

The *DEVMODE* structure consists of three distinct parts:

Part	Description	Members in *DEVMODE* structure
Header	Specifies information about the device driver that initialized the *DEVMODE* structure.	*dmDeviceName, dmSpecVersion, dmDriverVersion, dmSize, dmDriverExtra*
Device-independent	These members specify information that may apply to any printer.	*dmFields, dmOrientation, dmPaperSize, dmPaperLength, dmPaperWidth, dmScale, dmCopies, dmDefaultSource, dmPrintQuality, dmColor, dmDuplex*
Device-dependent	These members specify information specific to this printer driver.	These members begin at the *dmDriverData* member in the structure; their length is specified by the *dmDriverExtra* member.

The table below describes each of the *DEVMODE* structure's members:

Member	Description
dmDriverName	Null-terminated string specifying the printer that the remainder of the structure describes. May be up to 32 characters including the zero byte.
dmSpecVersion	Specifies the version of the *DEVMODE* specification. This value is the same as the version of Windows and therefore is currently 0x0300.
dmDriverSpec	Specifies the version of the printer driver. This value is assigned by the printer driver.
dmSize	Specifies the number of bytes in the device-independent part of the *DEVMODE* structure. This value may change with future versions of Windows. It is safer for applications to use this field than *sizeof(DEVMODE)*.
dmDriverExtra	Specifies the number of bytes in the device-dependent part of the *DEVMODE* structure.
dmFields	Specifies which of the structure members are recognized by the printer's device driver. The following identifiers may be *AND*ed with this member to determine which of the remaining members contain useful information: *DM_ORIENTATION* *DM_PAPERSIZE* *DM_PAPERLENGTH* *DM_PAPERWIDTH* *DM_SCALE* *DM_COPIES* *DM_DEFAULTSOURCE* *DM_PRINTQUALITY* *DM_COLOR* *DM_DUPLEX*

Member	Description
dmOrientation	Specifies the orientation of the paper. It is one of the following identifiers: *DMORIENT_PORTRAIT* *DMORIENT_LANDSCAPE*
dmPaperSize	Specifies the size of the paper. It is one of the following identifiers:

DMPAPER_LETTER	(8 1/2 x 11 in)
DMPAPER_LETTERSMALL	(8 1/2 x 11 in)
DMPAPER_TABLOID	(11 x 17 in)
DMPAPER_LEDGER	(17 x 11 in)
DMPAPER_LEGAL	(8 1/2 x 14 in)
DMPAPER_STATEMENT	(5 1/2 x 8 1/2 in)
DMPAPER_EXECUTIVE	(7 1/2 x 10 in)
DMPAPER_A3	(297 x 420 mm)
DMPAPER_A4	(210 x 297 mm)
DMPAPER_A4SMALL	(210 x 297 mm)
DMPAPER_A5	(148 x 210 mm)
DMPAPER_B4	(250 x 354 mm)
DMPAPER_B5	(182 x 257 mm)
DMPAPER_FOLIO	(8 1/2 x 13 in)
DMPAPER_QUARTO	(215 x 275 mm)
DMPAPER_10X14	(10 x 14 in)
DMPAPER_11X17	(11 x 17 in)
DMPAPER_NOTE	(8 1/2 x 11 in)
DMPAPER_ENV_9	(3 7/8 x 8 7/8 in)
DMPAPER_ENV_10	(4 1/8 x 9 in)
DMPAPER_ENV_11	(4 1/2 x 10 3/8 in)
DMPAPER_ENV_12	(4 3/4 x 11 in)
DMPAPER_ENV_14	(5 x 11 1/2 in)

Member	Description	
	DMPAPER_CSHEET	(17 x 22 in)
	DMPAPER_DSHEET	(22 x 34 in)
	DMPAPER_ESHEET	(34 x 44 in)
dmPaperLength	Overrides the paper length specified in *dmPaperSize* member. Length of paper is specified in tenths of millimeters. If *dmPaperLength* and *dmPaperWidth* are both specified, *dmPaperSize* may be zero.	
dmPaperWidth	Overrides the paper width specified in *dmPaperSize* member. Width of paper is specified in tenths of millimeters. If *dmPaperLength* and *dmPaperWidth* are both specified, *dmPaperSize* may be zero.	
dmScale	Specifies the percentage by which the page is scaled. A value of 50 will cause printed output to be half its width and height.	
dmCopies	Specifies the number of copies to be printed for each page.	
dmDefaultSource	Specifies the paper bin to use when printing. It is one of the following identifiers:	

DMBIN_ONLYONE   *DMBIN_UPPER*
DMBIN_LOWER   *DMBIN_MIDDLE*
DMBIN_MANUAL   *DMBIN_ENVELOPE*
DMBIN_ENVMANUAL   *DMBIN_AUTO*
DMBIN_TRACTOR   *DMBIN_SMALLFMT*
DMBIN_LARGEFMT   *DMBIN_LARGECAPACITY*
DMBIN_CASSETTE

Member	Description
dmPrintQuality	Specifies the resolution to be used when printing. If it is a positive value, it specifies the number of dots per inch, making this member device-dependent. This member may also be one of the following negative identifiers: *DMRES_HIGH* *DMRES_MEDIUM* *DMRES_LOW* *DMRES_DRAFT*
dmColor	Specifies whether the printer should print in color or monochrome. It is one of the following identifiers: *DMCOLOR_COLOR* *DMCOLOR_MONOCHROME*
dmDuplex	Specifies duplex printing. Only one of the following identifiers: *DMDUP_SIMPLEX* *DMDUP_HORIZONTAL* *DMDUP_VERTICAL*
dmDriverData	Specifies device-dependent information. A block of memory whose length is specified by the *dmDriverExtra* member of this structure.

Once the printer driver has filled in the *DEVMODE* structure, it uses the values in the structure to write settings to the user's WIN.INI file (like the *[HPPCL,LPT1]* entry shown earlier). This *DEVMODE* structure is also saved in a printer environment, a block of memory maintained by Windows that retains the most recent settings for a particular printer port.

When Windows is first invoked, no printer environments are in memory. As the user changes settings for various printers, each printer's device driver saves its printer environment. There can only be one printer environment for each printer port.

When the user selects the "Ok" button in *DeviceMode*'s dialog box, the device driver calls *SetEnvironment* to store the current printer settings in memory. The prototype for this function is:

```
int SetEnvironment(LPSTR lpPortName, LPSTR lpEnviron,
  WORD nCount);
```

The first parameter is the name of the port. If an environment already exists for this port, it is deleted. The second parameter is the address of the *DEVMODE* structure that contains the user's printer settings. The last parameter specifies the number of bytes in the complete *DEVMODE* structure. After the environment is set, *SetEnvironment* returns the number of bytes copied into the environment or zero if an error occurred.

You can delete a printer environment by specifying the *nCount* parameter to *SetEnvironment* as zero. In this case, *SetEnvironment* returns -1 if the printer environment has been successfully deleted.

Once the new environment is set, the printer driver's *DeviceMode* function calls the *SendMessage* function as follows:

```
SendMessage(-1, WM_DEVMODECHANGE, 0, (LONG) (LPSTR)
  DevMode->dmDeviceName);
```

This causes the *WM_DEVMODECHANGE* message to be sent to all overlapped and pop-up windows in the Windows system. The message notifies them that the printer environment has changed for the device whose name is specified by the *lParam* parameter. This allows applications that are using the default settings for a particular printer to retrieve the new settings by calling *GetEnvironment*. The prototype for this function is:

```
int GetEnvironment(LPSTR lpPortName, LPSTR lpEnviron,
   WORD nMaxCount);
```

The first parameter specifies the port for which an environment should be retrieved. The second parameter is the address of a *DEVMODE* structure where the environment information is to be copied. The last parameter specifies the maximum number of bytes to copy into the *DEVMODE* structure pointed to by the *lpEnviron* parameter. The *GetEnvironment* function returns the number of bytes copied to the memory block pointed to by *lpEnviron*. If the printer environment cannot be located for the specified port, the return value is zero.

An application can determine the number of bytes required to contain the complete *DEVMODE* structure by calling *GetEnvironment* and passing NULL as the *lpEnviron* parameter. An application can call this function once to retrieve the size of the *DEVMODE* structure, allocate a block of memory that size, then call *GetEnvironment* again to fill the memory block.

If the *lpPortName* parameter to *GetEnvironment* is the NullPort, Windows searches for the environment by matching the *dmDeviceName* member of the *DEVMODE* structure pointed to by the *lpEnviron* parameter. If multiple port environments exist for the same device name, Windows returns the environment for the first one it finds in memory.

The following outline describes the actions performed by *DeviceMode*:

A. *DeviceMode* fills a *DEVMODE* structure.

  1. The *GetEnvironment* function is called to retrieve the most recent printer settings.

  2. If the printer environment could not be found (*GetEnvironment* returned zero), the driver tries to fill a *DEVMODE* structure from entries in the WIN.INI file.

321

3. If no entry exists in the WIN.INI file, the driver fills the *DEVMODE* structure with default values.

B. The printer settings dialog box is displayed to the user, and the controls within it are set to reflect the values in the *DEVMODE* structure.

C. User changes settings in the dialog box until the "Ok" or "Cancel" button is selected.

   1. If the "Cancel" button is selected:

      a. The dialog box is removed.
      b. Control is returned to the application.

   2. If the "Ok" button is selected:

      a. The *DEVMODE* structure is updated with the new settings in the dialog box.
      b. The new settings are written to the WIN.INI file (like the *[HPPCL,LPT1]* entry shown earlier).
      c. The *SetEnvironment* function is called to save the new settings in memory.
      d. The *SendMessage* function is called to send the *WM_DEVMODE-CHANGE* message to all applications.
      e. The dialog box is removed.
      f. Control is returned to the application.

The *ExtDeviceMode* Function. Version 3.0 of Windows defines a new function that should be included in printer device drivers. This function, *ExtDeviceMode*, allows an application to have greater control over the processing of printer settings. As with *DeviceMode*, an application gains access to *ExtDeviceMode* by loading the printer driver's DLL and retrieving the address of the function with *GetProcAddress*:

```
lpfnExtDeviceMode =
  (LPFNDEVMODE) GetProcAddress(hLibrary, "ExtDeviceMode");
```

or

```
lpfnExtDeviceMode =
  (LPFNDEVMODE) GetProcAddress(hLibrary, PROC_EXTDEVICEMODE);
```

The DRIVINIT.H file contains the following definitions to help you work with the *ExtDeviceMode* function:

```
#define PROC_EXTDEVICEMODE MAKEINTRESOURCE(90)
.
.
.
typedef WORD FAR PASCAL FNDEVMODE(HWND, HANDLE, LPDEVMODE, LPSTR,
   LPSTR, LPDEVMODE, LPSTR, WORD);
typedef FNDEVMODE FAR * LPFNDEVMODE;
```

Although all printer device drivers must include *DeviceMode*, it is not guaranteed that any printer driver will include *ExtDeviceMode*. In fact, most of the printer drivers included with Windows 3.0 do not contain *ExtDeviceMode*. Of course, printer drivers are continuously being updated, and many of the drivers may add support for *ExtDeviceMode*.

The list below shows which of the drivers distributed with the Windows run-time system and the Windows supplemental driver library contain *ExtDeviceMode*:

BROHL	BROTH24	BROTH9	CANON10E
CANONBJ	CITOH	DESKJET	HPPCL
HPPCL5A	IBMCOLOR	IBMGRX	LBP8II
PAINTJET	PSCRIPT	STARM24	STARM9
THINKJET	TI850	TOSHIBA	TTY

The following are the drivers distributed with the Windows run-time system and the Windows supplemental driver library that do *not* contain the *ExtDeviceMode* function:

CANONIII	CH5500	DCNX150	DCNX150P
DM309	DM600	EPSON24	EPSON9
FLEX	FUJIMTRX	HPPLOT	IBM4019
IBM5204	JDL850	LBPIII	NEC24PIN
OKI24	OKI24PLS	OKI9	OKI9IBM
OL820	OLIPRIN2	OLIPRINT	PROPRINT
PROPRN24	QWIII	TH760	

The prototype for *ExtDeviceMode* is:

```
int ExtDeviceMode(HWND hWnd, HANDLE hLibrary, LPDEVMODE
    lpDevModeOutput, LPSTR lpDeviceName, LPSTR lpPort, LPDEVMODE
    lpDevModeInput, LPSTR lpProfile, WORD wMode);
```

The meanings of the *hWnd*, *hLibrary*, *lpDeviceName*, and *lpPort* parameters are identical to those used by *DeviceMode*. The *wMode* parameter specifies the action or actions *ExtDeviceMode* is to take. The table below lists the possible actions:

Values in *wMode* (may be *OR*ed together)	Action
DM_MODIFY	Modifies the current printer settings to reflect the changes specified by the *DEVMODE* structure pointed to by the *lpDevModeInput* parameter.
DM_PROMPT	Allows the user to change any of the printer's settings by presenting the printer settings dialog box to the user.

Values in *wMode* (may be *OR*ed together)	Action
DM_COPY	Causes the printer settings to be copied to the *DEVMODE* structure pointed to by the *lpDevModeOutput* parameter.
DM_UPDATE	Writes the new printer settings to the environment and file specified by the *lpProfile* parameter.

If the *wMode* parameter is zero, the *ExtDeviceMode* function returns the number of bytes required to contain a complete *DEVMODE* structure. Otherwise, if the *DM_PROMPT* identifier is specified, the return value is either *IDOK* or *IDCANCEL*, depending on which button the user selected. If *DM_PROMPT* is not specified, the return value is *IDOK* if the function is successful or a negative value if the function fails.

An application may modify a printer's settings by specifying *DM_MODIFY*. This identifier instructs *ExtDeviceMode* to take the *DEVMODE* structure representing the current printer's settings and change some of its members. The *DEVMODE* structure pointed to by *lpDevModeInput* must have its five header members initialized and should contain in its *dmFields* member the list of fields to be changed.

The *dmFields* member of *DEVMODE* identifies the fields supported by the particular printer. However, *dmFields* has a slightly different meaning when used in the *DEVMODE* structure pointed to by the *lpDevModeInput* parameter. In this case, *dmFields* specifies which fields of the current printer settings you wish to change. For example, if an application wants to change the *dmOrientation* and *dmCopies* values of the current printer's settings, it should initialize the following members before calling *ExtDeviceMode*:

```
// Initialize DEVMODE header fields
lstrcpy(DevMode->dmDeviceName, szDeviceName);
DevMode->dmSpecVersion = DM_SPECVERSION;
DevMode->dmDriverVersion = 0;
DevMode->dmSize = sizeof(DEVMODE);
DevMode->dmDriverExtra = 0;

// Specify which fields we wish to change
DevMode->dmFields = DM_ORIENTATION | DM_COPIES

// Set the new, desired values
DevMode->dmOrientation = DM_LANDSCAPE;
DevMode->dmCopies = 2;

// Call the ExtDeviceMode function using DM_MODIFY and
// any other desired DM_ flags
```

Because the code won't modify any of the driver's device-dependent information, the *dmDriverVersion* member and the *dmDriverExtra* member may be set to zero.

Initializing the *dmOrientation* and *dmCopies* members tells *ExtDeviceMode* to use the current *DEVMODE* structure for the printer, changing its orientation to landscape and the number of copies to two. No other fields will be altered. Because some of the device-independent information does not apply to all printers, Windows printer drivers ignore any settings in this structure that do not apply. For example, the driver for a printer that does not support color will ignore any values set in the *dmColor* member, even if the *DM_COLOR* identifier is *OR*ed in the *dmFields* member.

Specifying the *DM_PROMPT* identifier forces the *ExtDeviceMode* function to display the printer settings dialog box to the user. If the *DM_MODIFY* identifier was also specified, the *DEVMODE* structure is modified before the dialog box appears. The user may now change any of the settings in the dialog box. When the user selects the "Ok" button, the *DEVMODE* structure maintained by *ExtDeviceMode* contains the new information.

Unless the *DM_COPY* or *DM_UPDATE* identifier is included with the *wMode* parameter, this updated *DEVMODE* structure will be destroyed, having no effect, when the *ExtDeviceMode* function terminates. *DM_COPY* makes *ExtDeviceMode* copy the updated *DEVMODE* structure to the *DEVMODE* structure pointed to by the *lpDevModeOutput* parameter.

The *DM_UPDATE* identifier causes the *ExtDeviceMode* function to perform the same actions as the *DeviceMode* function:

1. Call *SetEnvironment,* passing it the updated *DEVMODE* structure.

2. Call *SendMessage* using the *WM_DEVMODECHANGE* message to notify all windows of the printer environment change.

3. Save the updated settings in the file specified by the *lpProfile* parameter. If *lpProfile* is NULL, the updated settings are saved in the WIN.INI file.

Calling the *ExtDeviceMode* function with

```
ExtDeviceMode(hWnd, hLibrary, NULL, szDeviceName, lpPort,
  NULL, NULL, DM_PROMPT | DM_UPDATE);
```

has the same effect as calling the *DeviceMode* function. In fact, many printer drivers implement their *DeviceMode* functions using this exact syntax. This line causes the *ExtDeviceMode* function to perform the following actions:

1. It retrieves the printer's current settings by calling *GetEnvironment.* If the environment is not found, the initialization file specified by the *lpProfile* parameter is used. This is WIN.INI because *lpProfile* is NULL. Finally, if the settings cannot be found there, the driver uses built-in default settings.

2. Because *DM_MODIFY* is not specified, *lpDevModeInput* may be NULL and the current printer settings are not changed.

3. The printer settings dialog box is displayed because the *DM_PROMPT* identifier is specified.

4. Since the *DM_COPY* identifier is not specified, the updated settings are not copied to the *DEVMODE* structure pointed to by the *lpDevModeOutput* parameter. Therefore, the *lpDevModeOutput* parameter may be NULL.

5. The *DM_UPDATE* identifier causes the updated settings to be saved in a printer environment and changed in WIN.INI. Again, the WIN.INI file is used because *lpProfile* is NULL.

Sending Output to a Printer. Before sending information to a printer, a Windows application must create a device context for the printer. This is done with the *CreateDC* function. The prototype for this function is:

```
HDC CreateDC(LPSTR szDriverName, LPSTR szDeviceName, LPSTR szPort,
    LPDEVMODE lpDevMode);
```

The *szDriverName* parameter is the name of the printer device driver file and must not include the extension. The *szDeviceName* parameter specifies the device name of the printer driver. The *szPort* parameter is the name of the port to which the printer is connected. The port name uses standard DOS conventions and should be suffixed with a colon (though this is not mandatory). If *szPort* is FILE:, the user will be requested to enter a file name when printing begins. This *szPort* parameter may also specify the full path name of a file where the information is to be sent. If you specify a path name directly, do not terminate it with a colon.

The *lpDevMode* parameter is a pointer to a *DEVMODE* structure. If this parameter is NULL, *CreateDC* will call *GetEnvironment* to retrieve the default printer settings for the specified port. If, on the other hand, *lpDevMode* points to a *DEVMODE* structure, the structure must be complete, including both device-independent and device-dependent information. Although you can create a complete *DEVMODE* structure manually, the structure should be filled by a call to *GetEnvironment* or

ExtDeviceMode. Once the device context has been created, standard GDI functions may be used to send information to the printer.

Getting Printer-Specific Information. Applications often need to query a printer device driver for device-dependent information. For example, a program may call *EnumFonts* to retrieve a list of fonts and sizes supported by the printer. The *GetDeviceCaps* function can be used to determine device-specific information about the printer.

Printer device drivers that support *ExtDeviceMode* also support *Device-Capabilities*. This function is contained in the printer's device driver file, just like *DeviceMode* and *ExtDeviceMode*. An application that wishes to use *Device-Capabilities* must retrieve its address from the DLL the same way the *DeviceMode* and *ExtDeviceMode* functions are retrieved:

```
lpfnDevCaps = (LPFNDEVCAPS) GetProcAddress(hLibrary,
   "ExtDeviceMode");
```

or

```
lpfnDevCaps = (LPFNDEVCAPS) GetProcAddress(hLibrary,
   PROC_DEVICECAPABILITIES);
```

The DRIVINIT.H file contains the following definitions to help you work with *DeviceCapabilities*:

```
#define PROC_DEVICECAPABILTIES        MAKEINTRESOURCE(91)
.
.
.
typedef DWORD FAR PASCAL FNDEVCAPS(LPSTR, LPSTR, WORD, LPSTR,
   LPDEVMODE);
typedef FNDEVCAPS FAR * LPFNDEVCAPS;
```

The prototype for *DeviceCapabilities* is:

```
DWORD DeviceCapabilities(LPSTR lpDeviceName, LPSTR lpPort,
   int nIndex, LPSTR lpOutput, LPDEVMODE lpDevMode);
```

The *lpDeviceName* parameter specifies the device name of the printer driver for which information is requested. The *lpPort* parameter is the name of the port to which the device is connected. The *nIndex* parameter specifies the type of information that is requested. The possible values are listed in the SDK's DRIVINIT.H file and are shown below:

DC_BINS	*DC_DRIVER*	*DC_DUPLEX*	*DC_EXTRA*
DC_FIELDS	*DC_MAXEXTENT*	*DC_MINEXTENT*	*DC_PAPERS*
DC_PAPERSIZE	*DC_SIZE*	*DC_VERSION*	

The *lpOutput* parameter is a pointer to a buffer that is to receive data corresponding to the type of information requested. For example, the *DC_PAPERS* index causes *DeviceCapabilities* to treat the *lpOutput* parameter as a far pointer to an array of *WORD*s. It then fills the array with the paper sizes supported by this driver. The return value indicates the number of entries copied into the array.

The *lpDevMode* parameter specifies where *DeviceCapabilities* should look for values. If *lpDevMode* is NULL, the device driver examines the current default settings for the printer. If *lpDevMode* points to a *DEVMODE* structure, *DeviceCapabilities* returns information about the *DEVMODE* structure. For example, calling *DeviceCapabilities* with the *nIndex* parameter set to *DC_EXTRA* will return the number of extra bytes used for the current default settings if *lpDevMode* is NULL. If *lpDevMode* is not NULL, *DeviceCapabilities* returns the value in the *dmDriverExtra* member of the *DEVMODE* structure pointed to by the *lpDevMode* parameter.

Printer Driver Caveats. Earlier versions of Windows offered insufficient support for controlling printers from applications. Microsoft noticed this need and has begun addressing improved printer support by standardizing a data structure to hold printer settings (*DEVMODE*) and defining functions that can be called from our own applications to alter these settings.

However, much work remains to be done. This is demonstrated by the number of printer drivers that do not support the *ExtDeviceMode* and *DeviceCapabilities* functions. The lack of these functions limits the features a programmer can add to an application.

Some printer drivers that do not support the *ExtDeviceMode* function also do not support the *DEVMODE* structure. *DEVMODE* was defined for version 3.0 of Windows and did not exist prior to it. Because of this, Windows 2.x printer device drivers used a proprietary data structure for saving the printer's settings. This structure was then saved and retrieved using the *SetEnvironment* and *GetEnvironment* functions. Both functions ignore the actual data structure passed in their *lpEnviron* parameters and just store the data in memory. The only requirement of this data structure was that the first member had to be the name of the device that created the structure. This way, a driver could tell if the data retrieved by a call to *GetEnvironment* was created by the same driver.

When an application calls *CreateDC*, a function is called in the printer driver. If the *lpInitData* parameter to *CreateDC* is NULL, the device driver calls the *GetEnvironment* function to retrieve the most current settings for the printer and creates the device context using these settings. If the *lpInitData* parameter is not NULL, it must point to a data structure that was retrieved by a call to *GetEnvironment*. This means the printer device driver was the only program that processed the data structure used to store the particular printer's settings.

Until updated printer drivers are available, programmers will have to be very cautious when it comes to manipulating printer environments and *DEVMODE* structures.

Selecting Printers in Applications

Almost all applications that perform printing offer the user a "Printer setup" dialog box. This dialog box usually has the appearance shown in Figure 5-4.

```
┌──────────────────────────────────────────────────────────────┐
│ ▬                        Printer setup                         │
├──────────────────────────────────────────────────────────────┤
│  Printer:                                    ┌──────────────┐  │
│  ┌────────────────────────────────────────┐  │     Ok       │  │
│  │ Generic / Text Only on LPT2:           │  └──────────────┘  │
│  │ IBM Graphics on None                   │  ┌──────────────┐  │
│  │ NEC Pinwriter on None                  │  │   Cancel     │  │
│  │ PCL / HP LaserJet on COM1:             │  └──────────────┘  │
│  │ PCL / HP LaserJet on LPT1:             │                    │
│  │ PostScript Printer on None             │  ┌──────────────┐  │
│  └────────────────────────────────────────┘  │   Setup...   │  │
│                                              └──────────────┘  │
└──────────────────────────────────────────────────────────────┘
```

Figure 5-4. Printer setup dialog box.

This dialog box allows the user to select the printer to be used for printing. The list box contains only printers that have been installed using the Control Panel application. The "Setup..." pushbutton presents the user with the printer's settings dialog box.

PRINTSTP.C and PRINTSTP.H contain all the code you need to add the "Printer setup" dialog box to your own applications. PRINT.C and PRINT.H create a small application, PRINT.EXE, that demonstrates how to use the functions in PRINTSTP.C.

This application defines two independent printer settings, PS1 and PS2. The user can then change the settings for either one and print a sample line of text specifying the printer settings to be used. For example, the user may set up PS1 and PS2 as follows:

HP LaserJet connected to LPT1: in portrait orientation
HP LaserJet connected to LPT1: in landscape orientation

The application remembers these settings. When the user prints using PS1, the output is in portrait orientation. Using PS2, the output is in landscape orientation. Changing a setting from PRINT.EXE does not alter the default settings for the printer. This is in contrast to the Control Panel, which changes a printer's settings systemwide.

PRINT is written to work with all printer drivers, including those that do not support *ExtDeviceMode* and even those that do not support the *DEVMODE* structure. Of course, some of the capabilities of this system are restricted when drivers that do not support these features are used.

The *PSSTRUCT* Data Structure. To maintain the current printer settings, the functions in PRINTSTP.C use a number of *#define*s and data types. These types are defined in PRINTSTP.H, which must be included in all the modules that reference any functions within PRINTSTP.C. The *#define*s and data types are shown below:

```
#define MAXPORTLEN          (25)
#define MAXDRIVERLEN        (50)
#define MAXDEVICELEN        (CCHDEVICENAME)      // From DRIVINIT.H
#define MAXPRINTINFOLEN     (MAXDEVICELEN + 1 + MAXDRIVERLEN + 1 \
    + MAXPORTLEN)
#define offsetof(s,m)       ((size_t) &(((s *) 0)->m))
#define PSOVERHEAD          offsetof(PSSTRUCT, DevMode)

typedef enum {
  PSSTAT_UNKNOWN, PSSTAT_EXTDEVMODE, PSSTAT_DEVMODEONLY
} PSSTAT;
```

```
typedef struct {
    char szPort[MAXPORTLEN], szDriver[MAXDRIVERLEN];
    PSSTAT PSStat;
    int nEnvSize;
    DEVMODE DevMode;
} PSSTRUCT, FAR *LPPSSTRUCT;
```

The *szPort* and *szDriver* members of *PSSTRUCT* contain the port and driver file name for the selected printer. The *PSStat* member specifies the amount of support offered by the selected printer's device driver. This value is one of the following:

PSSTAT_UNKNOWN	It is currently unknown whether the printer driver supports the *DeviceMode* function or the *ExtDeviceMode* function.
PSSTAT_DEVICEMODEONLY	This printer driver only supports the *DeviceMode* function. It does not support the *ExtDeviceMode* function.
PSSTAT_EXTDEVICEMODE	This driver supports the *ExtDeviceMode* function as well as the *DeviceMode* function.

The *nEnvSize* member is only used if the printer driver does not support the *ExtDeviceMode* function. This member specifies the number of bytes used by the printer environment.

The last member, *DevMode*, specifies the beginning of the printer's settings. Its length will vary from one printer driver to another. If the printer driver does not support the *ExtDeviceMode* function, this member points to the beginning of the printer's environment data.

This data structure is allocated from the global heap by functions in PRINTSTP.C and returned to the calling application.

334

Initially, the Print application creates two printer structures by calling the *SetupDefPrinter* function (in PRINTSTP.C). This function retrieves the name of the default printer as specified in the WIN.INI file. If no default printer exists, NULL is returned to the application. If a default printer does exist, *SetupDefPrinter* allocates a block of memory large enough to hold a *PSSTRUCT* structure and copies the default printer's driver name, port, and device name into the memory block. It also sets the *nEnvSize* member to zero and the *PSStat* member to *PSSTAT_UNKNOWN*. The handle of the block is then returned to the caller.

Print saves the memory block handles in two global variables, *_hMemPS1* and *_hMemPS2*. If a default printer did not exist or there was insufficient memory, the menu options for printing using the *PSSTRUCT*s are disabled. All of this is done while the *WM_CREATE* message is being processed, as shown below:

```
case WM_CREATE:
   _hMemPS1 = SetupDefPrinter();
   if (_hMemPS1 == NULL)
      EnableMenuItem(GetMenu(hWnd), IDM_PRINT1,
         MF_GRAYED | MF_BYCOMMAND);

   _hMemPS2 = SetupDefPrinter();
   if (_hMemPS2 == NULL)
      EnableMenuItem(GetMenu(hWnd), IDM_PRINT2,
         MF_GRAYED | MF_BYCOMMAND);
   break;
```

During a session with the Print application, the user may choose to set up either of the printers by selecting the "Printer setup 1..." or "Printer setup 2..." option from the menu. The code to process both of these menu options appears below:

```
case WM_COMMAND:
.
.
.
   switch (wParam) {
      case IDM_PS1:
```

```
case IDM_PS2:
  if (wParam == IDM_PS1) {
    hMemNewPS =
       PrinterSetup(hWnd, _hMemPS1, PSMODE_ACTIVEONLY);
    if (hMemNewPS == NULL) break;
      GlobalFree(_hMemPS1);
      _hMemPS1 = hMemNewPS;
    } else {
      hMemNewPS = PrinterSetup(hWnd, _hMemPS2, 0);
      if (hMemNewPS == NULL) break;
      GlobalFree(_hMemPS2);
      _hMemPS2 = hMemNewPS;
    }

    lpPS = (LPPSSTRUCT) GlobalLock(hMemNewPS);
    GetProfileString("windows", "NullPort", "",
      szNullPort, sizeof(szNullPort));

    // Gray menu item if print is on NullPort
    EnableMenuItem(GetMenu(hWnd),
      (wParam == IDM_PS1) ? IDM_PRINT1 : IDM_PRINT2,
      MF_BYCOMMAND | (lstrcmpi(szNullPort, lpPS->szPort)
      ? MF_ENABLED : MF_GRAYED));
    GlobalUnlock(hMemNewPS);
    break;
```

When the user selects an option, the *PrinterSetup* function in PRINTSTP.C is called. The first parameter is the handle to the window that is to own the dialog box. The second parameter specifies the global memory handle of the current printer information. The final parameter specifies which of the installed printers should appear in the list box.

Some applications, like Windows Write and Paintbrush, fill their "Printer setup" dialog boxes with only the active printers. Other applications, like Notepad, Cardfile, and Calendar, fill their "Printer setup" dialog boxes with the list of all installed printers.

The "Printer setup" dialog box implemented in PRINTSTP.C supports both types of dialog boxes. When the application calls the *PrinterSetup* function, the last parameter may be zero or *PSMODE_ACTIVEONLY*. If the application specifies *PSMODE_ACTIVEONLY*, the "Printer setup" dialog box will contain only active printers. Although most applications would not use both types of dialog boxes, the sample Print application given at the end of this chapter demonstrates how this feature would be accessed. When the user sets up the PS1, only the active printers are listed. When the user sets up the PS2, all installed printers are listed.

If *PrinterSetup* returns a NULL value, the user did not change the selected printer. If a non-NULL value is returned, this value represents the global memory handle containing the settings of the printer that the user selected.

The application is responsible for freeing the memory block for the old printer. If you do not specify the *PSMODE_ACTIVEONLY* flag when calling the *PrinterSetup* function, the user could select an inactive printer. If this happens, the printer will be connected to the NullPort. Your application should check this and disable any menu options that would allow printing to occur. This process is also demonstrated by the code fragment above.

This scheme works exceptionally well with MDI applications. The application would have only one "Printer setup..." option from the File menu. This option would let the user alter the printer settings for the currently active document. Printer settings could then be saved in the same file as the rest of the document's data. With this method, one document could remember that it is printed in portrait orientation and another document could remember that it is printed in landscape orientation.

The "Print using PS1" and "Print using PS2" options send *WM_COMMAND* messages with the *wParam* parameter equal to *IDM_PRINT1* and *IDM_PRINT2*, respectively. The code fragment to handle these options follows:

```
case IDM_PRINT1:
case IDM_PRINT2:
   hDC = CreatePrinterDC(
      (wParam == IDM_PRINT1) ? _hMemPS1 : _hMemPS2);

   if (hDC == NULL) {
      MessageBox(hWnd, "Cannot print.", _szAppName,
         MB_OK | MB_ICONEXCLAMATION);
      break;
   }
   Escape(hDC, STARTDOC, lstrlen(_szAppName), _szAppName, 0);
   TextOut(hDC, 10, 10, _szText, lstrlen(_szText));
   Escape(hDC, NEWFRAME, 0, 0, 0);
   Escape(hDC, ENDDOC, 0, 0, 0);
   DeleteDC(hDC);
   break;
```

The call to the *CreatePrinterDC* function (in PRINTSTP.C) accepts a global handle to a *PSSTRUCT* structure. This function calls the *CreateDC* function and passes the address of the *DevMode* member of the *PSSTRUCT* structure so that a device context with the appropriate printer settings is created. If a valid device context is returned, the line of text indicated by the *_szText* variable is sent to the printer. The actual mechanics of printing under Windows are beyond the scope of this chapter.

The PRINTSTP.C File

The bulk of the work for this demonstration application lies in the PRINTSTP.C file. This file is responsible for the entire "Printer setup" dialog box and for calling the *DeviceMode* and *ExtDeviceMode* functions, which allow the user to alter a printer's settings.

Let's begin by looking at how the "Printer setup" dialog box is displayed. When the application calls *PrinterSetup*, this function calls *DialogBoxParam*. *PrinterSetup* allows a *LONG* value to be passed to the dialog box when it processes the *WM_INITDIALOG* message. It constructs the *lParam* value by using the *MAKELONG* macro to pass the mode and the global memory handle to the currently selected printer:

```
GLOBALHANDLE FAR PASCAL PrinterSetup
    (HWND hWnd, GLOBALHANDLE hMem, WORD wMode) {
  GLOBALHANDLE hNewMem; FARPROC fpProc;
  fpProc = MakeProcInstance(PrinterSetupProc, _hInstance);
  hNewMem = DialogBoxParam(_hInstance, "PrinterSetup", hWnd,
    fpProc, MAKELONG(wMode, hMem));
  FreeProcInstance(fpProc);
  return(hNewMem);
}
```

When the dialog-box function finally calls the *EndDialog* function, the return value is the memory handle of the newly selected printer or NULL if the user did not select a new printer. This value is returned to the application.

The dialog-box function, *PrinterSetupProc*, first processes the *WM_INITDIALOG* message. The code for this message is shown below:

```
case WM_INITDIALOG:
  // lParam: LOWORD = wMode, HIWORD = GLOBALHANDLE to PSSTRUCT

  if (HIWORD(lParam) != NULL) {       // A printer has been set up
    // Create second memory block of the same size as the first
    hMem = GlobalAlloc(GMEM_MOVEABLE | GMEM_ZEROINIT,
      GlobalSize(HIWORD(lParam)));
  } else {
    // No printer has been set up
    hMem = GlobalAlloc(GMEM_MOVEABLE | GMEM_ZEROINIT,
      sizeof(PSSTRUCT));
  }

  if (hMem == NULL) {                 // Not enough memory
    MessageBox(hDlg, "Insufficient memory.", NULL,
      MB_OK | MB_ICONEXCLAMATION);
    // Terminate dialog box and notify caller of no change
    // in printer
    EndDialog(hDlg, NULL);
    break;
  }
```

```
if (HIWORD(lParam) != NULL) {      // A Printer has been set up
    // Copy original printer information into new block so that
    // we do not alter the original block in any way
    lpPSOrig = (LPPSSTRUCT) GlobalLock(HIWORD(lParam));
    lpPS = (LPPSSTRUCT) GlobalLock(hMem);
    _fmemcpy(lpPS, lpPSOrig, (WORD) GlobalSize(hMem));
    GlobalUnlock(hMem);
    GlobalUnlock(HIWORD(lParam));
}

// Set tab stop in list box to right edge of its window
hWndList = GetDlgItem(hDlg, ID_PRINTERBOX);
GetClientRect(hWndList, &rc);
x = (rc.right * LOWORD(GetDialogBaseUnits())) / 4;
SendMessage(hWndList, LB_SETTABSTOPS, 1,
    (LONG) (int FAR *) &x);

// Save the PSSTRUCT block as a window property
SetProp(hDlg, _szPSSTRUCTProp, hMem);
// Save the dialog box's mode settings as a window property
SetProp(hDlg, _szPSModeProp, LOWORD(lParam));

// Fill the list box with the installed printer information
SendMessage(hDlg, PSM_FILLPRINTERBOX, 0, 0l);
break;
```

The processing begins with the creation of a new global block of memory that will contain the printer being worked on by the "Printer setup" dialog box. If a valid handle to a previous *PSSTRUCT* structure is passed, a new memory block of the same size is created and all the information from the first block is copied into the new block. If a previous printer was not selected, a memory block the size of a *PSSTRUCT* is created. This would occur if the application called the *SetupDefPrinter* function and no default printer was specified in the WIN.INI file.

It is often convenient in Windows to associate some additional information with entries in a list box. I do this by setting a tab stop at the right edge of the list box. Then, before entries are inserted in the list box, I append a tab (\t) character followed by the additional text. When the list box displays the entries, the tab character causes the remainder of the entry to appear to the right of the list box. Since the list box clips all text that would appear outside of it, the user never sees this additional information. For example, the list box will show entries of the following form:

```
PCL / HP LaserJet on LPT1:
```

However, when the user selects an entry from the list box, the function must be able to separate the device name and the port. The function also needs the name of the printer's device driver. To make this information more accessible to the function, give the line actually inserted into the list box the following form:

```
PCL / HP LaserJet on LPT1:\tPCL / HP LaserJet=HPPCL.DRV,LPT1:
```

Because a tab stop is set at the right edge of the list box, the *PCL / HP LaserJet=HPPCL.DRV,LPT1:* part of the entry is clipped. When the program needs this information, it simply retrieves the entire line from the list box using the *LB_GETTEXT* message and then uses the C run-time's *_fstrchr* function to look for the tab character. Don't forget that any list box that is to process tab stops must be created with the *LBS_USETABSTOPS* style in the dialog-box template.

Several of the messages processed by the dialog-box function require the handle to the *PSSTRUCT* structure and the value of the mode parameter, so these values are associated with the dialog box using window properties.

To fill the list box, send the *PSM_FILLPRINTERBOX* message to the dialog-box function. This user-defined message is declared at the top of the PRINTSTP.C file:

```
// User-defined messages for the PrinterSetupProc dialog-box
// function
#define PSM_FILLPRINTERBOX              (WM_USER + 500)
#define PSM_SETDEFAULTPRINTER           (WM_USER + 501)
```

If you examine the WINDOWS.H file, you will notice that Microsoft has already provided two user-defined messages for dialog boxes:

```
#define DM_GETDEFID    (WM_USER+0)
#define DM_SETDEFID    (WM_USER+1)
```

Any user-defined messages of your own must not conflict with Microsoft's. Because you don't know what messages, if any, Microsoft will define in the future, it is much safer to define your own messages for a dialog box using the *RegisterWindowMessage* function explained in Chapter 1. However, for this demonstration, this method is simpler.

The processing for the *PSM_FILLPRINTERBOX* message begins by determining all the printers installed in the system. This is done as follows:

```
x = GetProfileString("devices", NULL, "", szAllPrinters,
  sizeof(szAllPrinters));
```

When NULL is passed as the second parameter to the *GetProfileString* function, the buffer indicated by *szAllPrinters* fills with all the keywords in the *[devices]* section of the WIN.INI file. For example, the buffer might look like this:

```
Generic / Text Only\0
PostScript Printer\0
PCL / HP LaserJet\0
IBM Graphics\0
NEC Pinwriter\0
\0
```

Each device name is terminated by a zero byte. (Each keyword is placed on a separate line above to make the text more readable; the actual buffer does not contain any new-line or carriage-return characters.) The end of the list is marked by the extra zero byte.

Now that the list of installed printers has been obtained, a loop is started that adds each printer in turn to the list box. For each printer in the *szAllPrinters* buffer, the rest of the printer's information is retrieved by calling the *GetProfileString* function again. But instead of NULL being passed for the second parameter, the address of a single device name from the *szAllPrinters* buffer is used. For example, calling

```
GetProfileString("devices", szAllPrinters, "", szPrintInfo,
    sizeof(szPrintInfo));
```

causes the buffer pointed to by the *szPrintInfo* parameter to retrieve the string "*TTY,LPT2:*." If the second parameter to the *GetProfileString* function pointed to the "PCL/HP LaserJet" printer, the *szPrintInfo* buffer would retrieve the string "*HPPCL,LPT1:,COM1:*."

A second loop is now started to cycle through all the ports listed in the *szPrintInfo* string. With each iteration of the loop, the printer port is compared with the NullPort and the mode is checked to see if the *PSMODE_ACTIVEONLY* flag was set. If this flag was set and the port is the NullPort, this printer entry is not inserted into the list box and the next port is checked.

If the printer entry is to be inserted into the list box, the string is built as described in the *WM_INITDIALOG* message and added to the list box using the *LB_ADDSTRING* message. When all the printers have been added to the list box, the *LB_GETCOUNT* message is sent to retrieve the number of items in the list box. If no items are in the list box, the "Printer setup" dialog box must terminate.

If the list box is not empty, the user-defined *PSM_SETDEFAULTPRINTER* message is sent to the dialog-box function. This message sets the entry in the list box that should be initially selected. If an entry in the list box matches the printer described in the *PSSTRUCT* structure, that printer is initially selected. If no printers in the list box match the *PSSTRUCT* printer, the default printer in the WIN.INI file is used for the initial selection. Finally, if neither printer can be located in the list box, the first entry in the list box is selected.

The processing begins with retrieval of the default printer information from the WIN.INI file:

```
GetProfileString("windows", "device", "",
  szPrintInfoDef, sizeof(szPrintInfoDef));

if (*szPrintInfoDef != 0) {
  ParsePrintInfo(szPrintInfoDef, FALSE, szDriverDef,
    szDeviceDef, szPortDef);
} else { *szDeviceDef = *szDriverDef = *szPortDef = 0; }
```

If *szPrintInfoDef* is not empty, the *ParsePrintInfo* function (in PRINTSTP.C) is called. This function accepts a string containing a device name, driver name, and port and separates it into its various components. The first parameter specifies the string containing all three fields. This string may be in the form

```
device name,driver name,port
```

or

```
device name=driver name,port
```

The second parameter is a Boolean value that specifies whether the .DRV extension should be appended to the device driver's name. If this value is TRUE, the extension is appended. The last three parameters specify the address of the buffer where the driver name, device name, and port information should be placed.

A loop is now started that examines each entry in the list box. For each entry, the *LB_GETTEXT* message is sent to the list box to retrieve the full text of the entry. The *ParsePrintInfo* function is called again to separate the individual fields of the string:

```
SendMessage(hWndList, LB_GETTEXT, x, (LONG) (LPSTR) szPrintInfo);

// Printer information string is after the tab ('\t') character
ParsePrintInfo(_fstrchr(szPrintInfo, '\t') + 1, FALSE,
  szDriver, szDevice, szPort);
```

Remember that the part of the string we're interested in follows the tab character.

We now have the three fields for the default printer and a printer in the list box. By comparing the default printer's device names and ports with the device name and port of the printer in the list box, we can determine if they are the same printer. The same comparison can be done for the printer specified in the *PSSTRUCT* structure. When a match is found, the appropriate printer is selected.

As you can see, much work must be done before the dialog box can be displayed to the user. However, this is not the only time the list box needs to be refilled. If the "Printer setup" dialog box is visible and the user installs, removes, activates, inactivates, or changes a printer port by using the Control Panel application, the contents of the "Printer setup" list box must change to reflect that. Fortunately, the Control Panel application sends a *WM_WININICHANGE* message to all overlapped and pop-up windows when it changes the *[devices]* section of the WIN.INI file. This notifies these windows that the information has changed. The "Printer setup" dialog box processes this message as follows:

```
case WM_WININICHANGE:
    // See if user changed the list of printers from another
    // application (most likely Control Panel)
    if (lstrcmpi((LPSTR) lParam, "devices") !=
        0 && lParam != NULL)
      break;

    // If printer information has changed, refill the list box
    SendMessage(hDlg, PSM_FILLPRINTERBOX, 0, 0l);
    break;
```

The *lParam* parameter for a *WM_WININICHANGE* message points to a zero-terminated string identifying the section in the WIN.INI file that has been changed. Although improper procedure, some applications set the *lParam* parameter to NULL when sending the *WM_WININICHANGE* message. In either case, the "Printer setup" dialog box sends the *PSM_FILLPRINTERBOX* message to itself to update its list box with the changes made to the WIN.INI file.

It is possible for the user to remove printers from the Control Panel. This might cause the list box in the "Printer setup" dialog box to have no entries. If this occurs, the dialog box will display a message box to the user indicating that no printers are in the list box and terminate the "Printer setup" dialog box. This is done while the *PSM_FILLPRINTERBOX* message is being processed.

Selecting the "Setup..." or "Ok" Pushbutton. When the user selects either the "Setup..." or "Ok" pushbutton from the "Printer setup" dialog box, the current selection in the list box is retrieved and the *SetupNewPrinter* function is called. *SetupNewPrinter* has the following prototype:

```
int NEAR PASCAL SetupNewPrinter (GLOBALHANDLE FAR *hPSOld,
    HWND hWnd, LPSTR szPrintInfo);
```

SetupNewPrinter first takes the device-independent settings for the current printer and tries to transfer them to the newly selected printer. It then displays the dialog box that allows the user to change the newly selected printer's settings. The new settings for the printer are saved in a new memory block containing a *PSSTRUCT* structure. If everything was successful, the *PSSTRUCT* for the previously selected printer is freed and the new memory block becomes the working *PSSTRUCT*. The return value indicates whether an error occurred and is one of the following values:

SNP_SUCCESS	The function ran to completion.
SNP_NODRIVER	The printer's device driver could not be loaded.
SNP_INVALIDDRIVER	The printer's device driver does not contain the *DeviceMode* or *ExtDeviceMode* function.
SNP_NOMEMORY	Insufficient memory exists to complete the operation.

The *hPSOld* parameter is a far pointer to the global memory handle where the *PSSTRUCT* structure is stored. If the new printer is set up successfully, the *SetupNewPrinter* function will call *GlobalFree* to release this block and then set this variable to contain the handle of the new *PSSTRUCT* memory block. The *hWnd* parameter specifies the handle of the window that is to own the printer settings dialog box. This will be the handle of the "Printer setup" dialog box. The *szPrintInfo* parameter identifies the printer the user wishes to set up and has the following form:

```
device name=driver name,port
```

Once the *SetupNewPrinter* function has loaded the printer driver, it retrieves the address of the *DeviceMode* and *ExtDeviceMode* functions:

```
ExtDeviceMode = GetProcAddress(hDriver, PROC_EXTDEVICEMODE);
DeviceMode = GetProcAddress(hDriver, PROC_OLDDEVICEMODE);
```

How the *SetupNewPrinter* function continues processing is determined by whether the *ExtDeviceMode* function is supported by the printer's device driver. If it is, setting up the selected printer is guaranteed to result in a *DEVMODE* structure. A memory block must be allocated to hold the new *PSSTRUCT* information (which includes this *DEVMODE* structure). The size of the memory block is determined by calling the *ExtDeviceMode* function and passing zero as the *wMode* parameter:

```
nDevModeSize = ExtDeviceMode(hWnd, hDriver, NULL, szDevice,
    szPort, NULL, NULL, 0);

hPSNew = GlobalAlloc(GMEM_MOVEABLE, PSOVERHEAD + nDevModeSize);
if (hPSNew == NULL) {
    FreeLibrary(hDriver);
    return(SNP_NOMEMORY);
}
```

The *szPort*, *szDriver*, *PSStat*, and *nEnvSize* members of the new *PSSTRUCT* structure are initialized as follows:

```
lpPSNew = (LPPSSTRUCT) GlobalLock(hPSNew);

lstrcpy(lpPSNew->szPort, szPort);
lstrcpy(lpPSNew->szDriver, szDriver);
lpPSNew->PSStat = PSSTAT_EXTDEVMODE;
lpPSNew->nEnvSize = 0;
```

If the previously selected printer also supports the *ExtDeviceMode* function, the *SetupNewPrinter* function can transfer the device-independent settings from the old printer to the new printer before displaying the settings dialog box to the user. For example, if the previously selected printer had been set up to print in landscape orientation, the settings dialog box will appear for the new printer with landscape orientation set as the default. In fact, if the currently selected printer is the same as the previously selected printer, the device-dependent settings can be transferred over as well. The following code fragment from the *SetupNewPrinter* function shows how all of this is accomplished:

```
if (lpPSOld->PSStat == PSSTAT_EXTDEVMODE) {

   if (lstrcmpi(lpPSOld->szDriver, szDriver)) {
      // setting up a different printer

      // Reset device- and driver-specific fields in DEVMODE
      lstrcpy(lpPSOld->DevMode.dmDeviceName, szDevice);
      lpPSOld->DevMode.dmDriverVersion = 0;
      lpPSOld->DevMode.dmDriverExtra = 0;
   }

   // Return value is IDOK if successful
   nDlgBoxResult = ExtDeviceMode(hWnd, hDriver,
      &lpPSNew->DevMode, szDevice, szPort,
      &lpPSOld->DevMode, NULL,
      DM_MODIFY | ((hWnd == NULL) ? 0 : DM_PROMPT) | DM_COPY);
} else {
```

```
// Return value is IDOK if successful
nDlgBoxResult = ExtDeviceMode(hWnd, hDriver,
    &lpPSNew->DevMode, szDevice, szPort, NULL, NULL,
    ((hWnd == NULL) ? 0 : DM_PROMPT) | DM_COPY);
}
```

This code also shows the processing if the previously selected printer does not support the *ExtDeviceMode* function. In this case, the *DM_MODIFY* flag cannot be used with the call to *ExtDeviceMode* because we cannot be sure if the printer driver for the previous printer used a *DEVMODE* structure to store its information. The printer settings dialog box will appear, and the systemwide default settings (as set in the Control Panel application) for the printer will be reflected in the dialog box.

Notice that neither of the calls to *ExtDeviceMode* uses the *DM_UPDATE* flag. Because this flag is not specified, the new printer settings are not made systemwide defaults. The *DM_COPY* flag causes the settings to be copied into the *DevMode* member of the *PSSTRUCT* structure.

The *DM_PROMPT* flag is only *OR*ed with the other flags if the *hWnd* parameter is not NULL. The *SetupNewPrinter* function is called with the *hWnd* parameter equal to NULL when the user selects the "Ok" pushbutton from the "Printer setup" dialog box. Imagine that the user had selected the "PCL/HP LaserJet" printer and pressed the "Setup..." pushbutton to change the paper size to A4. The user selects the "Ok" button from the settings dialog box, then "PostScript Printer" from the "Printer setup" dialog box. If the user now presses the "Ok" button, it would be desirable to return to the application a *PSSTRUCT* for the "PostScript Printer" that specified a paper size of A4 instead of the default paper size for that printer. The *SetupNewPrinter* function does this by performing the same operations for the "Ok" button as for the "Setup..." pushbutton. The only difference is that the settings dialog box does not appear when the "Ok" button is pressed.

This applies only when the newly selected printer supports the *ExtDeviceMode* function. If this function does not exist in the printer's device driver, the *DeviceMode* function must be used to set up the printer. Because *DEVMODE* structures are not necessarily used by device drivers that only support the *DeviceMode* function, device-independent information cannot be transferred from one driver to another. However, if the new printer being set up is the same type as the previous printer, its settings can be initialized by calling the *SetEnvironment* function:

```
if ((lpPSOld->nEnvSize > 0) &&
    (lstrcmpi(szDriver, lpPSOld->szDriver) == 0)) {
  SetEnvironment(szPort, (LPSTR) &lpPSOld->DevMode,
    lpPSOld->nEnvSize);
}
```

If the *nEnvSize* member of the previous printer's *PSSTRUCT* structure is greater than zero and the previous printer and the new printer are of the same type, the printer environment's data can be associated with the port to which the new printer is connected. When a printer driver is about to display its settings dialog box, it retrieves the printer environment for the port to which the printer is connected and sets the defaults in the settings dialog box to reflect these settings.

The *DeviceMode* function is now called so that the printer settings dialog box is displayed to the user:

```
if (hWnd != NULL)
  DeviceMode(hWnd, hDriver, szDevice, szPort);
// A valid return value is NOT guaranteed from the DeviceMode
// function, so we will assume that it is IDOK
nDlgBoxResult = IDOK;
```

This function is only called if the *hWnd* parameter to *SetupNewPrinter* is not NULL. If *hWnd* is NULL, the user selected the "Ok" pushbutton instead of "Setup..." from the "Printer setup" dialog box. You may recall that the *DevMode* function sometimes returns TRUE if the user has changed any of the printer's settings. This is not guaranteed, however, so we must assume the user has changed the printer's settings.

The *DeviceMode* function saves the new printer settings in the printer environment. Since the number of bytes in the printer environment is device driver-dependent, an initial call to *GetEnvironment* determines the size of the environment. It is also possible that a printer environment won't exist for the printer just set up. This can happen if the port for the printer is the NullPort. This information can be retrieved by calling *GetEnvironment* and storing the data in a *PSSTRUCT* structure. After the required size is determined, a new memory block is allocated to hold the new *PSSTRUCT* structure and the *szPort*, *szDriver*, *PSStat*, and *nEnvSize* members of this structure are initialized:

```
nEnvSize = GetEnvironment(szPort, NULL, 0);

// Allocate a PSSTRUCT large enough to contain the printer
// environment
hPSNew = GlobalAlloc(GMEM_MOVEABLE,
   (nEnvSize == 0) ? sizeof(PSSTRUCT) : nEnvSize + PSOVERHEAD);
if (hPSNew == NULL) {
   FreeLibrary(hDriver);
   return(SNP_NOMEMORY);
}

lpPSNew = (LPPSSTRUCT) GlobalLock(hPSNew);
lstrcpy(lpPSNew->szPort, szPort);
lstrcpy(lpPSNew->szDriver, szDriver);
lpPSNew->PSStat = PSSTAT_DEVMODEONLY;
lpPSNew->nEnvSize = nEnvSize;
```

If a printer environment does exist for the selected printer, it must be copied into *PSSTRUCT*. If not, we still must save the printer's device name because *CreatePrinterDC* (in PRINTSTP.C) requires this device name to be passed to *CreateDC*.

```
if (nEnvSize > 0) {
   GetEnvironment(szPort, (LPSTR) &lpPSNew->DevMode, nEnvSize);
} else {
   lstrcpy(lpPSNew->DevMode.dmDeviceName, szDevice);
}
```

351

Before the *SetupNewPrinter* function terminates, the old and new *PSSTRUCTs* are unlocked and the device driver is freed. If all the operations were successful, the memory containing the previous *PSSTRUCT* is freed and the new *PSSTRUCT* will be used by the "Printer setup" dialog box. On the other hand, if there was a problem or the user pressed "Cancel" from the *ExtDeviceMode*'s settings dialog box, the memory allocated for the new *PSSTRUCT* is freed and the "Printer setup" dialog box will continue to use the *PSSTRUCT* it had before calling the *SetupNewPrinter* function. The code below shows the termination sequence for the *SetupNewPrinter* function:

```
    .
    .
    .
    GlobalUnlock(*hPSOld);
    FreeLibrary(hDriver);
    GlobalUnlock(hPSNew);

    if (nDlgBoxResult == IDOK) {
       GlobalFree(*hPSOld);
       *hPSOld = hPSNew;
    } else
       GlobalFree(hPSNew);

    return(SNP_SUCCESS);
}
```

Changing the Default Pushbutton

When the user selects the "Setup..." pushbutton, this button becomes the default in the dialog box. After the printer settings dialog box is removed, the "Ok" pushbutton should become the default pushbutton again. This is accomplished by the code that appears in the processing of the *ID_SETUP* and *IDOK* cases in the *WM_COMMAND* message:

```
// Set the "Ok" button back to the default button
SendMessage(hDlg, DM_SETDEFID, IDOK, 0);
SendDlgItemMessage(hDlg, ID_SETUP, BM_SETSTYLE,
    (int) BS_PUSHBUTTON, TRUE);
SendDlgItemMessage(hDlg, IDOK, BM_SETSTYLE,
    (int) BS_DEFPUSHBUTTON, TRUE);

// Set the focus back to the list box
SetFocus(GetDlgItem(hDlg, ID_PRINTERBOX));
```

This code first notifies the dialog-box manager that the "Ok" button is the default. This tells the dialog-box manager what ID value to send if the user presses the Enter key. However, this is not enough. The *ID_SETUP* and *IDOK* buttons' styles must be changed so they paint themselves properly when they process a *WM_PAINT* message. Default pushbuttons have a thicker border. The style of a button is changed by sending a *BM_SETSTYLE* message to the control. When the button control processes this message, it forces a repaint; therefore, the style change is immediate.

As another convenience to the user, input focus is given to the printer list box. This is done by calling *SetFocus* as shown above.

The following listings are part of the printer setup application, Print, which shows how to use window hooks by sensing when the user has been idle for a given period of time and blanking the computer screen.

Figure 5-5. PRINT.ICO.

Listing 5-1. PRINT.C application source module.

```
/*****************************************************************
Module name: Print.C
Programmer : Jeffrey M. Richter
*****************************************************************/

#include "..\nowindws.h"
#undef NOCOLOR
#undef NOCTLMGR
#undef NOGDI
#undef NOKERNEL
#undef NOLSTRING
#undef NOMB
#undef NOMEMMGR
#undef NOMENUS
#undef NOMSG
#undef NOSHOWWINDOW
#undef NOUSER
#undef NOWINMESSAGES
#undef NOWINSTYLES
#include <windows.h>
#include <drivinit.h>

#include "print.h"
#include "printstp.h"

char _szAppName[] = "Print";
char _szText[] = "This is a text line!";
HANDLE _hInstance = NULL;

LONG FAR PASCAL WndProc (HWND hWnd, WORD wMsg, WORD wParam,
   LONG lParam);
BOOL FAR PASCAL AboutProc (HWND hDlg, WORD wMsg, WORD wParam,
   LONG lParam);

int PASCAL WinMain (HANDLE hInstance, HANDLE hPrevInstance,
     LPSTR lpszCmdLine, int nCmdShow) {
   HWND hWnd;
   MSG msg;
   WNDCLASS wc;
```

```
   _hInstance = hInstance;
   if (!hPrevInstance) {
      wc.style          = 0;
      wc.lpfnWndProc = WndProc;
      wc.cbClsExtra  = 0;
      wc.cbWndExtra  = 0;
      wc.hInstance   = hInstance;
      wc.hIcon       = LoadIcon(hInstance, _szAppName);
      wc.hCursor     = LoadCursor(NULL, IDC_ARROW);
      wc.hbrBackground    = COLOR_WINDOW + 1;
      wc.lpszMenuName     = _szAppName;
      wc.lpszClassName    = _szAppName;
      if (!RegisterClass(&wc)) return(0);
   }

   hWnd = CreateWindow(_szAppName, _szAppName,
      WS_OVERLAPPED | WS_VISIBLE | WS_CAPTION | WS_SYSMENU |
      WS_MINIMIZEBOX | WS_MAXIMIZEBOX | WS_THICKFRAME,
      CW_USEDEFAULT, nCmdShow, CW_USEDEFAULT, CW_USEDEFAULT,
      NULL, NULL, hInstance, 0);
   if (hWnd == NULL) return(0);

   while (GetMessage(&msg, NULL, 0, 0)) {
      TranslateMessage(&msg);
      DispatchMessage(&msg);
   }

   return(0);
}

GLOBALHANDLE _hMemPS1 = NULL, _hMemPS2 = NULL;

LONG FAR PASCAL WndProc (HWND hWnd, WORD wMsg, WORD wParam,
      LONG lParam) {
   BOOL fCallDefProc = FALSE;
   LONG lResult = 0;
   GLOBALHANDLE hMemNewPS;
   HDC hDC;
   LPPSSTRUCT lpPS;
   FARPROC fpProc;
   char szNullPort[MAXPORTLEN];
```

```
switch (wMsg) {
  case WM_CREATE:
    _hMemPS1 = SetupDefPrinter();
    if (_hMemPS1 == NULL)
      EnableMenuItem(GetMenu(hWnd), IDM_PRINT1,
        MF_GRAYED | MF_BYCOMMAND);

    _hMemPS2 = SetupDefPrinter();
    if (_hMemPS2 == NULL)
      EnableMenuItem(GetMenu(hWnd), IDM_PRINT2,
        MF_GRAYED | MF_BYCOMMAND);
    break;

  case WM_DESTROY:
    GlobalFree(_hMemPS1);
    GlobalFree(_hMemPS2);
    PostQuitMessage(0);
    break;

  case WM_COMMAND:
    switch (wParam) {
      case IDM_ABOUT:
        fpProc = MakeProcInstance(AboutProc, _hInstance);
        DialogBox(_hInstance, "About", hWnd, fpProc);
        FreeProcInstance(fpProc);
        break;

      case IDM_PS1:
      case IDM_PS2:
        if (wParam == IDM_PS1) {
          hMemNewPS = PrinterSetup(hWnd, _hMemPS1,
            PSMODE_ACTIVEONLY);
          if (hMemNewPS == NULL) break;
          GlobalFree(_hMemPS1);
          _hMemPS1 = hMemNewPS;
        } else {
          hMemNewPS = PrinterSetup(hWnd, _hMemPS2, 0);
          if (hMemNewPS == NULL) break;
          GlobalFree(_hMemPS2);
          _hMemPS2 = hMemNewPS;
        }
```

```
            lpPS = (LPPSSTRUCT) GlobalLock(hMemNewPS);
            GetProfileString("windows", "NullPort", "",
               szNullPort, sizeof(szNullPort));

            // Gray menu item if print is on NullPort
            EnableMenuItem(GetMenu(hWnd),
               (wParam == IDM_PS1) ? IDM_PRINT1 : IDM_PRINT2,
               MF_BYCOMMAND | (lstrcmpi(szNullPort,
               lpPS->szPort) ? MF_ENABLED : MF_GRAYED));
            GlobalUnlock(hMemNewPS);
            break;

         case IDM_PRINT1:
         case IDM_PRINT2:
            hDC = CreatePrinterDC(
               (wParam == IDM_PRINT1) ? _hMemPS1 : _hMemPS2);

            if (hDC == NULL) {
               MessageBox(hWnd, "Cannot print.", _szAppName,
                  MB_OK | MB_ICONEXCLAMATION);
               break;
            }
            Escape(hDC, STARTDOC, lstrlen(_szAppName),
               _szAppName, 0);
            TextOut(hDC, 10, 10, _szText, lstrlen(_szText));
            Escape(hDC, NEWFRAME, 0, 0, 0);
            Escape(hDC, ENDDOC, 0, 0, 0);
            DeleteDC(hDC);
            break;
         }
         break;

      default:
         fCallDefProc = TRUE;
         break;
   }
   if (fCallDefProc)
      lResult = DefWindowProc(hWnd, wMsg, wParam, lParam);
   return(lResult);
}
```

```
// ****************************************************************
// This function processes all messages sent to About dialog box

BOOL FAR PASCAL AboutProc (HWND hDlg, WORD wMsg, WORD wParam,
      LONG lParam) {
   char szBuffer[100];
   BOOL fProcessed = TRUE;

   switch (wMsg) {

      case WM_INITDIALOG:
         // Set version static window to have date and time of
         // compilation
         wsprintf(szBuffer, "%s at %s", (LPSTR) __DATE__,
            (LPSTR) __TIME__);
         SetWindowText(GetDlgItem(hDlg, ID_VERSION), szBuffer);
         break;

      case WM_COMMAND:
         switch (wParam) {
            case IDOK:
            case IDCANCEL:
               if (HIWORD(lParam) == BN_CLICKED)
                  EndDialog(hDlg, wParam);
               break;

            default:
               break;
         }
         break;

      default:
         fProcessed = FALSE; break;
   }
   return(fProcessed);
}
```

Listing 5-2. PRINT.H application header module.

```
/*******************************************************************
Module name: Print.H
Programmer : Jeffrey M. Richter
*******************************************************************/

#include "dialog.h"

#define IDM_PS1       (100)
#define IDM_PS2       (101)
#define IDM_PRINT1    (102)
#define IDM_PRINT2    (103)
#define IDM_ABOUT     (104)
#define IDM_EXIT      (105)
```

Listing 5-3. PRINTSTP.H printer setup dialog box header module.

```
/*******************************************************************
Module name: PrintStp.H
Programmer : Jeffrey M. Richter
*******************************************************************/


#define MAXPORTLEN       (25)
#define MAXDRIVERLEN     (50)
#define MAXDEVICELEN     (CCHDEVICENAME)   // From DRIVINIT.H
#define MAXPRINTINFOLEN  (MAXDEVICELEN + 1 + MAXDRIVERLEN + 1 + \
   MAXPORTLEN)
#define offsetof(s,m)    ((size_t) &(((s *) 0)->m))
#define PSOVERHEAD       offsetof(PSSTRUCT, DevMode)

typedef enum {
  PSSTAT_UNKNOWN, PSSTAT_EXTDEVMODE, PSSTAT_DEVMODEONLY
} PSSTAT;
```

```
typedef struct {
    char szPort[MAXPORTLEN], szDriver[MAXDRIVERLEN];
    PSSTAT PSStat;
    int nEnvSize;
    DEVMODE DevMode;
} PSSTRUCT, FAR *LPPSSTRUCT;

#define PSMODE_ACTIVEONLY (1)
GLOBALHANDLE FAR PASCAL PrinterSetup
    (HWND hWnd, GLOBALHANDLE hMem, WORD wMode);

HDC FAR PASCAL CreatePrinterDC (GLOBALHANDLE hMem);

// Returns handle to PSSTRUCT block or NULL if insufficient memory
GLOBALHANDLE FAR PASCAL SetupDefPrinter (void);

void FAR PASCAL ParsePrintInfo (LPSTR szPrintInfo,
    BOOL fAppendDriverExt, LPSTR szDriver, LPSTR szDevice,
    LPSTR szPort);
```

Listing 5-4. PRINTSTP.C printer setup dialog box source module.

```
/*****************************************************************
Module name: PrintStp.C
Programmer : Jeffrey M. Richter
*****************************************************************/

#include "..\nowindws.h"
#undef NOCTLMGR
#undef NOGDI
#undef NOKERNEL
#undef NOLSTRING
#undef NOMB
#undef NOMEMMGR
#undef NOMINMAX
#undef NOMSG
#undef NOSHOWWINDOW
#undef NOUSER
```

```
#undef NOWH
#undef NOWINMESSAGES
#undef NOWINOFFSETS
#undef NOWINSTYLES
#include <windows.h>
#include <drivinit.h>
#include <string.h>

#include "dialog.h"
#include "printstp.h"

extern HANDLE _hInstance;
char _szPSSTRUCTProp[] = "PSSTRUCT";
char _szPSModeProp[] = "PSMode";


// User-defined messages for the PrinterSetupProc dialog box
// function
#define PSM_FILLPRINTERBOX (WM_USER + 500)
#define PSM_SETDEFAULTPRINTER (WM_USER + 501)

// DRIVINIT.H doesn't define types for use with the old DeviceMode
// function, so we have to
typedef void FAR PASCAL FNDEVICEMODE (HWND, HANDLE, LPSTR, LPSTR);
typedef FNDEVICEMODE FAR *LPFNDEVICEMODE;

// Possible return values from the SetupNewPrinter function
#define SNP_SUCCESS (0)
#define SNP_NODRIVER (1)
#define SNP_INVALIDDRIVER (2)
#define SNP_NOMEMORY (3)
int NEAR PASCAL SetupNewPrinter (GLOBALHANDLE FAR *hPSOld,
   HWND hWnd, LPSTR szPrintInfo);

BOOL FAR PASCAL PrinterSetupProc (HWND hDlg, WORD wMsg,
   WORD wParam, LONG lParam);

// Function called from application to present "Printer setup"
// box. Returns handle to PSSTRUCT block for new printer or NULL
// if no change.
```

```
GLOBALHANDLE FAR PASCAL PrinterSetup (HWND hWnd,
      GLOBALHANDLE hMem, WORD wMode) {
   GLOBALHANDLE hNewMem;
   FARPROC fpProc;
   fpProc = MakeProcInstance(PrinterSetupProc, _hInstance);
   hNewMem = DialogBoxParam(_hInstance, "PrinterSetup", hWnd,
      fpProc, MAKELONG(wMode, hMem));
   FreeProcInstance(fpProc);
   return(hNewMem);
}


// Dialog function for use by "Printer setup" box. EndDialog
// returns handle of new PSSTRUCT block or NULL if no change.
BOOL FAR PASCAL PrinterSetupProc (HWND hDlg, WORD wMsg,
      WORD wParam, LONG lParam) {
   HWND hWndList;
   RECT rc;
   char szNullPort[MAXPORTLEN],
      szAllPrinters[5 * MAXPRINTINFOLEN];
   char szPrintInfo[MAXPRINTINFOLEN], szBuf[2 * MAXPRINTINFOLEN];
   char szPrintInfoDef[MAXPRINTINFOLEN],
      szDriverDef[MAXDRIVERLEN];
   char szDeviceDef[MAXDEVICELEN], szPortDef[MAXPORTLEN];
   char szDevice[MAXDEVICELEN], szDriver[MAXDRIVERLEN],
      szPort[MAXPORTLEN];
   BOOL fProcessed = TRUE;
   GLOBALHANDLE hMem;
   LPPSSTRUCT lpPSOrig, lpPS;
   WORD wMode;
   LPSTR lpszCrntPort, lpszTemp, lpszPrinter, lpszError;
   int nDefPrint, nNumPrinters, nSNPError, x, nDefID;

   switch (wMsg) {

   case WM_INITDIALOG:
      // lParam: LOWORD = wMode, HIWORD = GLOBALHANDLE to PSSTRUCT

      if (HIWORD(lParam) != NULL) {   // A printer has been set up
         // Create second memory block same size as first
         hMem = GlobalAlloc(GMEM_MOVEABLE | GMEM_ZEROINIT,
            GlobalSize(HIWORD(lParam)));
```

```
} else {
  // No printer has been set up
  hMem = GlobalAlloc(GMEM_MOVEABLE | GMEM_ZEROINIT,
    sizeof(PSSTRUCT));
}

if (hMem == NULL) {              // Not enough memory
  MessageBox(hDlg, "Insufficient memory.", NULL,
    MB_OK | MB_ICONEXCLAMATION);
  // Terminate dialog box; notify caller of no change
  // in printer
  EndDialog(hDlg, NULL);
  break;
}

if (HIWORD(lParam) != NULL) {  // A printer has been set up
  // Copy original printer information into new block so
  // that we do not alter the original block in any way
  lpPSOrig = (LPPSSTRUCT) GlobalLock(HIWORD(lParam));
  lpPS = (LPPSSTRUCT) GlobalLock(hMem);
  _fmemcpy(lpPS, lpPSOrig, (WORD) GlobalSize(hMem));
  GlobalUnlock(hMem);
  GlobalUnlock(HIWORD(lParam));
}

// Set tab stop in list box to right edge of its window
hWndList = GetDlgItem(hDlg, ID_PRINTERBOX);
GetClientRect(hWndList, &rc);
x = (rc.right * LOWORD(GetDialogBaseUnits())) / 4;
SendMessage(hWndList, LB_SETTABSTOPS, 1,
  (LONG) (int FAR *) &x);

// Save the PSSTRUCT block as a window property
SetProp(hDlg, _szPSSTRUCTProp, hMem);
// Save the dialog box's mode settings as a window property
SetProp(hDlg, _szPSModeProp, LOWORD(lParam));

// Fill the list box with the installed printer information
SendMessage(hDlg, PSM_FILLPRINTERBOX, 0, 0l);
break;
```

363

```
case WM_DESTROY:
    // Remove the two properties from the window
    RemoveProp(hDlg, _szPSSTRUCTProp);
    RemoveProp(hDlg, _szPSModeProp);
    break;

case WM_WININICHANGE:
    // See if user changed the list of printers from another
    // application (most likely Control Panel)
    if (lstrcmpi((LPSTR) lParam, "devices") != 0 && lParam !=
            NULL)
        break;

    // If printers have changes, refill the list box
    SendMessage(hDlg, PSM_FILLPRINTERBOX, 0, 01);
    break;

case PSM_FILLPRINTERBOX:
    // Retrieve the mode value from the window property
    wMode = GetProp(hDlg, _szPSModeProp);

    // Get the list of all printers installed by the user
    x = GetProfileString("devices", NULL, "", szAllPrinters,
        sizeof(szAllPrinters));
    if (x == sizeof(szAllPrinters) - 2) { // Buffer too small
        MessageBox(hDlg,
            "Too many printers installed.\tList truncated.", NULL,
            MB_OK | MB_ICONEXCLAMATION);
        lpszPrinter = szAllPrinters + sizeof(szAllPrinters) - 3;
        while (lpszPrinter > szAllPrinters && *lpszPrinter != 0)
            *lpszPrinter- = 0;
    }

    // Retrieve the name of the NullPort (usually "None")
    GetProfileString("windows", "NullPort", "",
        szNullPort, sizeof(szNullPort));

    hWndList = GetDlgItem(hDlg, ID_PRINTERBOX);
    // Tell the list box NOT to update its display and empty it
```

```
SendMessage(hWndList, WM_SETREDRAW, FALSE, 0);
SendMessage(hWndList, LB_RESETCONTENT, 0, 0L);

// Fill the list box with printers from [devices] section of
// WIN.INI
lpszPrinter = szAllPrinters;

for (; *lpszPrinter != 0; lpszPrinter =
  _fstrchr(lpszPrinter, 0) + 1) {

   // Get the driver name and port for the printer
   GetProfileString("devices", lpszPrinter, "", szPrintInfo,
      sizeof(szPrintInfo));
   // lpszPrinter = "IBM Graphics"
   // szPrintInfo = "IBMGRX,LPT1:,COM2:"

   lpszCrntPort = _fstrchr(szPrintInfo, ',');
   *lpszCrntPort++ = 0;
   // szPrintInfo = "IBMGRX"
   // lpszCrntPort = "LPT1:,COM2:"

   while (lpszCrntPort != NULL) {
      // If another port exists, terminate string at comma
      lpszTemp = _fstrchr(lpszCrntPort, ',');
      if (lpszTemp != NULL) *lpszTemp = 0;
      // lpszCrntPort = "LPT1:"

      // If active only && printer NOT active, don't add
      // to list box
      if ((wMode & PSMODE_ACTIVEONLY) &&
         lstrcmpi(lpszCrntPort, szNullPort) == 0) {
         ;                                  // Do nothing
      } else {
         // Build string that has the following form:
         // "(device) ON (port)\t(device)=(driver),(port)"
         // Example: "IBM Graphics on LPT1:\tIBM
         // Graphics=IBMGRX,LPT1:"
         wsprintf(szBuf, "%s on %s\t%s=%s,%s",
            (LPSTR) lpszPrinter, (LPSTR) lpszCrntPort,
            (LPSTR) lpszPrinter, (LPSTR) szPrintInfo,
            (LPSTR) lpszCrntPort);
```

```
                    // Add string to list box. Note: the list box sorts
                    // the printers in alpha order because LBS_SORT
                    // style used in dlg template.
                    SendMessage(hWndList, LB_ADDSTRING, 0,
                        (LONG) (LPSTR) szBuf);
                }

                // Find next port if it exists
                lpszCrntPort = lpszTemp;
                if (lpszCrntPort != NULL) lpszCrntPort++;
                // lpszCrntPort = "COM2:"
            }
        }

        nNumPrinters = (int) SendMessage(hWndList, LB_GETCOUNT,
            0, 0);
        if (nNumPrinters == 0) {
            MessageBox(hDlg, "No printers installed.", NULL,
                MB_OK | MB_ICONEXCLAMATION);

            // Sending the WM_COMMAND with IDCANCEL to terminate the
            // dialog box will free the memory allocated during the
            // processing of WM_INITDIALOG message
            SendMessage(hDlg, WM_COMMAND, IDCANCEL,
                MAKELONG(GetDlgItem(hDlg, IDCANCEL), BN_CLICKED));
            break;
        }

        // List box is filled; determine which printer to
        // select initially
        SendMessage(hDlg, PSM_SETDEFAULTPRINTER, 0, 0);

        // Tell the list box it is now OK to update its display
        SendMessage(hWndList, WM_SETREDRAW, TRUE, 0);

        // Force the list box to be completely redrawn
        InvalidateRect(hWndList, NULL, TRUE);
        break;
```

```
case PSM_SETDEFAULTPRINTER:
   // Set up the default selection in the list box
   hWndList = GetDlgItem(hDlg, ID_PRINTERBOX);

   // Retrieve handle to printer memory block from window
   // property
   hMem = GetProp(hDlg, _szPSSTRUCTProp);

   // Get the information for the default printer selected by
   // the user
   GetProfileString("windows", "device", "",
      szPrintInfoDef, sizeof(szPrintInfoDef));

   if (*szPrintInfoDef != 0) {
      ParsePrintInfo(szPrintInfoDef, FALSE, szDriverDef,
         szDeviceDef, szPortDef);
   } else { *szDeviceDef = *szDriverDef = *szPortDef = 0; }

   nDefPrint = -1;
   nNumPrinters = (int) SendMessage(hWndList, LB_GETCOUNT,
      0, 0);
   // Cannot be zero because of check in PSM_FILLPRINTERBOX
   // message

   lpPS = (LPPSSTRUCT) GlobalLock(hMem);
   for (x = 0; x < nNumPrinters; x++) {
      // Get line 'x' from the list box
      SendMessage(hWndList, LB_GETTEXT, x,
         (LONG) (LPSTR) szPrintInfo);

      // PrintInfo string is after the Tab ('\t') character
      ParsePrintInfo(_fstrchr(szPrintInfo, '\t') + 1, FALSE,
         szDriver, szDevice, szPort);

      // Remember index in list box where the "default printer"
      // is located
      if (lstrcmpi(szDevice, szDeviceDef) == 0 &&
         lstrcmpi(szPort, szPortDef) == 0) nDefPrint = x;
```

```
           // If device and port of list-box entry and printer in
           // PSSTRUCT block match, set that printer as the default
           // and stop the "for" loop
           if (lstrcmpi(szDevice, lpPS->DevMode.dmDeviceName) ==
               0 && lstrcmpi(szPort, lpPS->szPort) == 0) {
               SendMessage(hWndList, LB_SETCURSEL, x, 0);
               break;
           }
       }
       GlobalUnlock(hMem);

       if (x == nNumPrinters) {
           // Printer in memory block didn't match any printer
           // in list box

           // Set selection to "default printer" if it was found
           SendMessage(hWndList, LB_SETCURSEL,
               (nDefPrint == -1) ? 0 : nDefPrint, 0);
       }
       break;

   case WM_COMMAND:
       switch (wParam) {
       case ID_PRINTERBOX:
           if (HIWORD(lParam) != LBN_DBLCLK) break;

           // Get the ID of the default pushbutton. Note: assume
           // the HIWORD from sending DM_GETDEFID is DC_HASDEFID.
           nDefID = LOWORD(SendMessage(hDlg, DM_GETDEFID, 0, 0));

           // Simulate the user selecting the default pushbutton
           SendMessage(hDlg, WM_COMMAND, nDefID,
               MAKELONG(GetDlgItem(hDlg, nDefID), BN_CLICKED));
           break;

       case ID_SETUP:
       case IDOK:
           if (HIWORD(lParam) != BN_CLICKED) break;

           hWndList = GetDlgItem(hDlg, ID_PRINTERBOX);
```

```
// Get information about currently selected printer
x = (int) SendMessage(hWndList, LB_GETCURSEL, 0, 0L);
SendMessage(hWndList, LB_GETTEXT, x,
    (LONG) (LPSTR) szPrintInfo);
// szPrintInfo = "Generic / Text Only on FILE:\tGeneric /
// Text Only=TTY,FILE:"

// Get memory handle of current selected printer
hMem = GetProp(hDlg, _szPSSTRUCTProp);

// If Ok button pressed, do setup without displaying the
// printer settings dialog box
nSNPError = SetupNewPrinter(&hMem,
    (wParam == IDOK) ? NULL : hDlg,
    _fstrchr(szPrintInfo, '\t') + 1);

// New printer setup block returned; save it in the
// window property
if (nSNPError == SNP_SUCCESS)
    SetProp(hDlg, _szPSSTRUCTProp, hMem);
else {
    switch (nSNPError) {
        case SNP_NODRIVER:
            lpszError = "Cannot find printer driver.";
            break;
        case SNP_INVALIDDRIVER:
            lpszError = "Invalid printer driver.";
            break;
        case SNP_NOMEMORY:
            lpszError = "Insufficient memory.";
            break;
    }
    MessageBox(hDlg, lpszError,
        NULL, MB_OK | MB_ICONEXCLAMATION);
}

if (wParam == IDOK) {
    // Terminate the dialog box and return handle to new
    // printer setup
    EndDialog(hDlg, hMem);
} else {
```

369

```
                    // Set the "Ok" button back to the default button
                    SendMessage(hDlg, DM_SETDEFID, IDOK, 0);
                    SendDlgItemMessage(hDlg, ID_SETUP, BM_SETSTYLE,
                       (int) BS_PUSHBUTTON, TRUE);
                    SendDlgItemMessage(hDlg, IDOK, BM_SETSTYLE,
                       (int) BS_DEFPUSHBUTTON, TRUE);

                    // Set the focus back to the list box
                    SetFocus(GetDlgItem(hDlg, ID_PRINTERBOX));
                  }
                  break;

            case IDCANCEL:
               // Free memory block allocated by WM_INITDIALOG message
               GlobalFree(GetProp(hDlg, _szPSSTRUCTProp));

               // Return NULL to caller stating no change to
               // selected printer
               EndDialog(hDlg, NULL);
               break;
            }
            break;

      default: fProcessed = FALSE; break;
      }
      return(fProcessed);
}


// Function accepts string in a PrintInfo format. This format is:
// (device name)[= | ,](driver name),(port). It then fills the
// buffers passed in with parsed fields. If fAppendDriverExt is
// TRUE, ".DRV" is appended to the driver's name.
void FAR PASCAL ParsePrintInfo (LPSTR szPrintInfo,
   BOOL fAppendDriverExt, LPSTR szDriver, LPSTR szDevice,
   LPSTR szPort) {
   LPSTR p;
   while (('=' != *szPrintInfo) && (',' != *szPrintInfo))
      *szDevice++ = *szPrintInfo++;
   *szDevice = 0;
   szPrintInfo++;
   p = szDriver;
```

```
    while (*szPrintInfo != ',') *szDriver++ = *szPrintInfo++;
    *szDriver = 0;
    if (_fstrchr(p, '.') == NULL && fAppendDriverExt)
        lstrcpy(szDriver, ".DRV");
    szPrintInfo++;

    while (*szPrintInfo != 0) *szPort++ = *szPrintInfo++;
    *szPort = 0;
}


// Function is called when user selects "Ok" or "Setup..." button
// from "Printer setup" dialog box. This function prepares a new
// PSSTRUCT memory block with information about the selected
// printer. If hWnd is NOT NULL, the user is presented the
// printer settings dialog box to change any settings. The hWnd
// parameter is NULL when the user selects the "Ok" button from
// the "Printer setup" dialog box.
int NEAR PASCAL SetupNewPrinter (GLOBALHANDLE FAR *hPSOld,
        HWND hWnd, LPSTR szPrintInfo) {
    char szDriver[MAXDRIVERLEN], szDevice[MAXDEVICELEN],
        szPort[MAXPORTLEN];
    int nDevModeSize, nEnvSize, nDlgBoxResult;
    LPPSSTRUCT lpPSOld, lpPSNew;
    GLOBALHANDLE hPSNew;
    HANDLE hDriver;
    LPFNDEVMODE ExtDeviceMode;
    LPFNDEVICEMODE DeviceMode;

    ParsePrintInfo(szPrintInfo, TRUE, szDriver, szDevice, szPort);
    hDriver = LoadLibrary(szDriver);
    if (hDriver < 32) return(SNP_NODRIVER);

    ExtDeviceMode = (LPFNDEVMODE) GetProcAddress(hDriver,
        PROC_EXTDEVICEMODE);
    DeviceMode = (LPFNDEVICEMODE) GetProcAddress(hDriver,
        PROC_OLDDEVICEMODE);

    if (ExtDeviceMode == NULL && DeviceMode == NULL) {
        FreeLibrary(hDriver);
        return(SNP_INVALIDDRIVER);
    }
```

```
lpPSOld = (LPPSSTRUCT) GlobalLock(*hPSOld);

if (ExtDeviceMode != NULL) {

    // Get size of complete DEVMODE structure
    nDevModeSize = ExtDeviceMode(hWnd, hDriver, NULL, szDevice,
        szPort, NULL, NULL, 0);

    hPSNew = GlobalAlloc(GMEM_MOVEABLE,
        PSOVERHEAD + nDevModeSize);
    if (hPSNew == NULL) {
        FreeLibrary(hDriver);
        return(SNP_NOMEMORY);
    }

    lpPSNew = (LPPSSTRUCT) GlobalLock(hPSNew);
    // Copy over our port and driver names to new memory block
    lstrcpy(lpPSNew->szPort, szPort);
    lstrcpy(lpPSNew->szDriver, szDriver);
    lpPSNew->PSStat = PSSTAT_EXTDEVMODE;
    lpPSNew->nEnvSize = 0;

    if (lpPSOld->PSStat == PSSTAT_EXTDEVMODE) {

        if (lstrcmpi(lpPSOld->szDriver, szDriver)) {
            // Setting up a different printer

            // Reset device-specific and driver-specific fields
            // in DEVMODE
            lstrcpy(lpPSOld->DevMode.dmDeviceName, szDevice);
            lpPSOld->DevMode.dmDriverVersion = 0;
            lpPSOld->DevMode.dmDriverExtra = 0;
        }

        // Return value is IDOK if successful
        nDlgBoxResult = ExtDeviceMode(hWnd, hDriver,
            &lpPSNew->DevMode, szDevice, szPort,
            &lpPSOld->DevMode, NULL, DM_MODIFY |
            ((hWnd == NULL) ? 0 : DM_PROMPT) | DM_COPY);
```

```
   } else {

      // Return value is IDOK if successful
      nDlgBoxResult = ExtDeviceMode(hWnd, hDriver,
         &lpPSNew->DevMode, szDevice, szPort, NULL, NULL,
         ((hWnd == NULL) ? 0 : DM_PROMPT) | DM_COPY);
   }

} else {

   // For all other cases, DeviceMode function must be called

   // If the old PSSTRUCT has a valid printer environment, set
   // the printer environment
   if (lpPSOld->nEnvSize > 0) {
      SetEnvironment(szPort, (LPSTR) &lpPSOld->DevMode,
         lpPSOld->nEnvSize);
   }

   if (hWnd != NULL)
      DeviceMode(hWnd, hDriver, szDevice, szPort);

   // A valid return value is NOT guaranteed from the
   // DeviceMode function, so we will assume that it is IDOK
   nDlgBoxResult = IDOK;

   // nEnvSize is the size of the printer environment
   nEnvSize = GetEnvironment(szPort, NULL, 0);

   // Allocate a PSSTRUCT large enough to contain the printer
   // environment
   hPSNew = GlobalAlloc(GMEM_MOVEABLE,
      (nEnvSize == 0) ? sizeof(PSSTRUCT) :
      nEnvSize + PSOVERHEAD);
   if (hPSNew == NULL) {
      FreeLibrary(hDriver);
      return(SNP_NOMEMORY);
   }
```

```
        lpPSNew = (LPPSSTRUCT) GlobalLock(hPSNew);
        // Copy over our port and driver names to new memory block
        lstrcpy(lpPSNew->szPort, szPort);
        lstrcpy(lpPSNew->szDriver, szDriver);
        lpPSNew->PSStat = PSSTAT_DEVMODEONLY;
        lpPSNew->nEnvSize = nEnvSize;

        if (nEnvSize > 0) {
           // If a printer environment exists, save it
           GetEnvironment(szPort, (LPSTR) &lpPSNew->DevMode,
              nEnvSize);
        } else {
           lstrcpy(lpPSNew->DevMode.dmDeviceName, szDevice);
        }
    }

    GlobalUnlock(*hPSOld);
    FreeLibrary(hDriver);
    GlobalUnlock(hPSNew);

    // nDlgBoxResult == IDOK if ExtDeviceMode or DeviceMode
    // is successful
    if (nDlgBoxResult == IDOK) {
       GlobalFree(*hPSOld);
       *hPSOld = hPSNew;
    } else
       GlobalFree(hPSNew);

    return(SNP_SUCCESS);
}


// This function accepts a PSSTRUCT and creates a device
// context for the printer described in the structure. If
// fUseDefaultSettings is TRUE, the default settings are used
// for the DC and not any settings that may exist in the PSSTRUCT
// set by a call to PrinterSetup.
HDC FAR PASCAL CreatePrinterDC (GLOBALHANDLE hMem) {
   LPPSSTRUCT lpPS;
   HDC hDC;
```

```
   LPSTR p;
   LPDEVMODE lpDM = NULL;

   lpPS = (LPPSSTRUCT) GlobalLock(hMem);

   if (lpPS->PSStat == PSSTAT_EXTDEVMODE) {
      // Set lpDM to point to valid DEVMODE structure
      lpDM = &lpPS->DevMode;
   } else {
      // lpPS->PSStat must be PSSTAT_DEVMODEONLY or PSSTAT_UNKNOWN
      if (lpPS->nEnvSize > 0) {
         // If a printer environment exists for this printer,
         // use it
         lpDM = &lpPS->DevMode;
      }
   }

   // Remove extension from driver file name if it exists
   p = _fstrchr(lpPS->szDriver, '.');
   if (p != NULL) *p = 0;

   // Create the device context
   hDC = CreateDC(lpPS->szDriver, lpPS->DevMode.dmDeviceName,
      lpPS->szPort, (LPSTR) lpDM);

   // Restore the driver's extension if it was removed
   if (p != NULL) *p = '.';

   GlobalUnlock(hMem);
   return(hDC);
}


// This function is called when an application initializes so that
// the information about the default printer is loaded into a
// PSSTRUCT. Returns handle to PSSTRUCT block or NULL if
// insufficient memory.
GLOBALHANDLE FAR PASCAL SetupDefPrinter (void) {
   GLOBALHANDLE hMem = NULL; LPPSSTRUCT lpPS;
   char szPrintInfo[MAXPRINTINFOLEN];
   char szDriver[MAXDRIVERLEN], szDevice[MAXDEVICELEN],
      szPort[MAXPORTLEN];
```

```
    GetProfileString("windows", "device", "", szPrintInfo,
        sizeof(szPrintInfo));
    if (*szPrintInfo == 0) return(hMem); // No default printer
                                         //  selected
    // szPrintInfo="Generic / Text Only,TTY,FILE:"

    ParsePrintInfo(szPrintInfo, FALSE, szDriver, szDevice, szPort);
    hMem = GlobalAlloc(GMEM_MOVEABLE, sizeof(PSSTRUCT));
    if (hMem == NULL) return(hMem);
    lpPS = (LPPSSTRUCT) GlobalLock(hMem);
    lstrcpy(lpPS->szPort, szPort);
    lstrcpy(lpPS->szDriver, szDriver);
    lstrcpy(lpPS->DevMode.dmDeviceName, szDevice);
    lpPS->PSStat = PSSTAT_UNKNOWN;
    lpPS->nEnvSize = 0;
    GlobalUnlock(hMem);
    return(hMem);
}
```

Listing 5-5. MAKEFILE for printer setup application.

```
#********************************************************************
#Module name: MAKEFILE
#Programmer : Jeffrey M. Richter
#********************************************************************

PROG = Print
MODEL = S
CFLAGS = -A$(MODEL) -D_WINDOWS -Gcsw2 -W4 -Zlepid -Od
LFLAGS = /NOE/BA/A:16/M/CO/LI/F
LIBS = $(MODEL)nocrt + $(MODEL)libcew + libw

M1 = $(PROG).obj PrintStp.obj

ICONS = $(PROG).ico
BITMAPS =
CURSORS =
```

```
RESOURCES = $(ICONS) $(BITMAPS) $(CURSORS)

.SUFFIXES: .rc

.rc.res:
    rc -r $*.rc

$(PROG).Exe: $(M1) $(PROG).Def $(PROG).Res
    link $(LFLAGS) @<<$(PROG).lnk
$(M1)
$(PROG), $(PROG), $(LIBS), $(PROG)
<<
    rc $(PROG).Res

$(PROG).obj:  $*.c $*.h dialog.h
PrintStp.obj: $*.c $(PROG).h dialog.h

$(PROG).res:  $*.rc $*.h $*.dlg dialog.h $(RESOURCES)
```

Listing 5-6. PRINT.DEF Print definitions file.

```
; Module name: Print.DEF
; Programmer : Jeffrey M. Richter

NAME            Print
DESCRIPTION     'Print: Printer Setup Application'
STUB            'WinStub.exe'
EXETYPE         WINDOWS          ▬
CODE            MOVEABLE DISCARDABLE PRELOAD
DATA            MOVEABLE MULTIPLE PRELOAD
HEAPSIZE        1024
STACKSIZE       4096
EXPORTS
    WndProc
    PrinterSetupProc
    AboutProc
```

Listing 5-7. PRINT.RC application resource file.

```
/****************************************************************
Module name: Print.RC
Programmer : Jeffrey M. Richter
****************************************************************/


#include <windows.h>

#include "print.h"
#include "print.dlg"

Print ICON     MOVEABLE DISCARDABLE Print.Ico

Print MENU
BEGIN
   POPUP    "&Examples"
      BEGIN
      MENUITEM "Printer setup &1...",     IDM_PS1
      MENUITEM "Printer setup &2...",     IDM_PS2
      MENUITEM "&Print using PS1",        IDM_PRINT1
      MENUITEM "P&rint using PS2",        IDM_PRINT2
      MENUITEM SEPARATOR
      MENUITEM "A&bout Printer Setup...", IDM_ABOUT
      END
END
```

Listing 5-8. PRINT.DLG dialog-box templates.

```
ABOUT DIALOG LOADONCALL MOVEABLE DISCARDABLE 16, 20, 126, 92
CAPTION "About Print"
STYLE WS_BORDER | WS_CAPTION | WS_DLGFRAME | WS_SYSMENU |
   WS_VISIBLE | WS_POPUP
BEGIN
   CONTROL "Print", -1, "static", SS_ICON | WS_CHILD, 4, 16,
      18, 21
   CONTROL "Print", -1, "static", SS_CENTER | WS_CHILD, 22, 8,
      100, 12
```

```
    CONTROL "Written by:", -1, "static", SS_CENTER | WS_CHILD, 22,
        20, 100, 12
    CONTROL "Jeffrey M. Richter", -1, "static", SS_CENTER |
        WS_CHILD, 22, 32, 100, 12
    CONTROL "Version date:", -1, "static", SS_CENTER | WS_CHILD,
        22, 48, 100, 12
    CONTROL "", ID_VERSION, "static", SS_CENTER | WS_CHILD, 22, 60,
        100, 12
    CONTROL "&Ok", IDOK, "button", BS_DEFPUSHBUTTON | WS_TABSTOP |
        WS_CHILD, 40, 76, 44, 12
END

PRINTERSETUP DIALOG LOADONCALL MOVEABLE DISCARDABLE 8, 28, 180, 68
CAPTION "Printer setup"
STYLE WS_BORDER | WS_CAPTION | WS_DLGFRAME | WS_SYSMENU |
    WS_VISIBLE | WS_POPUP
BEGIN
    CONTROL "&Printer:", -1, "static", SS_LEFT | WS_CHILD, 4, 4,
        36, 8
    CONTROL "", ID_PRINTERBOX, "listbox", LBS_SORT | LBS_NOTIFY |
        LBS_USETABSTOPS | WS_BORDER | WS_VSCROLL | WS_GROUP |
        WS_TABSTOP | WS_CHILD, 4, 14, 125, 49
    CONTROL "&Ok", 1, "button", BS_DEFPUSHBUTTON | WS_GROUP |
        WS_TABSTOP | WS_CHILD, 132, 8, 44, 12
    CONTROL "&Cancel", 2, "button", BS_PUSHBUTTON | WS_GROUP |
        WS_TABSTOP | WS_CHILD, 132, 24, 44, 12
    CONTROL "&Setup...", ID_SETUP, "button", BS_PUSHBUTTON |
        WS_GROUP | WS_TABSTOP | WS_CHILD, 132, 50, 44, 12
END
```

Listing 5-9. DIALOG.H (dialog-box template defines) for Print application.

```
#define IDOK              1
#define IDCANCEL          2
#define ID_PRINTERBOX     120
#define ID_SETUP          121
#define ID_VERSION        200
```

CHAPTER 6

Tasks, Queues, and Hooks

By now, you are familiar with many of the different types of handles used to manipulate data in Microsoft Windows. Handles are used to keep track of windows, local memory blocks, global memory blocks, brushes, pens, and much more. In this chapter we discuss three more types of handles and how Windows uses them to manage the most important of system resources: your applications. We discuss how Windows uses system and application queues to synchronize applications. Finally, we discuss ways that your application can intercept messages from any task by using hooks.

Tasks and Their Handles

Windows maintains three handles for each running application: the data-instance handle, the module-instance handle, and the task-instance handle.

The data-instance handle is the most familiar. This is the handle that is passed as the first parameter to your application's *WinMain* function. Windows uses this handle to identify the data segment for the current instance of the application.

When an application is executed, Windows creates a data segment for the new instance of the application and assigns it a data-instance handle. Windows then calls the application's *WinMain* function and passes the data-instance handle as the *hInstance* parameter. The second parameter, *hPrevInstance*, contains the data-instance handle for another instance of the application if one is running. Otherwise, *hPrevInstance* contains NULL.

Applications use *hPrevInstance* in the following ways:

1. To allow only one instance of your application to run at a time, check the value of the *hPrevInstance* parameter. If the value is not NULL, the application can immediately return to Windows, terminating the new instance of the executing application:

```
int PASCAL WinMain (HANDLE hInstance, HANDLE hPrevInstance,
    LPSTR lpszCmdLine, int nCmdShow) {
    .
    .
    .
    if (hPrevInstance != NULL) return(0);
    .
    .
    .
```

2. Because applications should only register window classes when the first instance of the application is started, the code for registering window classes should only be executed if *hPrevInstance* is NULL:

```
int PASCAL WinMain (HANDLE hInstance, HANDLE hPrevInstance,
    LPSTR lpszCmdLine, int nCmdShow) {
    .
    .
    .
    if (hPrevInstance == NULL) {
       // Register window classes used by this application
    }
    .
    .
    .
```

3. An application can copy data from the other instance's data segment into its own data segment by using the *GetInstanceData* function. This function is described in the discussion of superclassing in Chapter 2.

Although a new data segment is created for each instance of a running application, Windows allows all the instances to share the same code segments. Also, when a new application is invoked, it must register any window classes used by the application. If additional instances of the same application are executed, the new instances should not attempt to register the window classes again, but should assume that the classes have already been registered.

Windows maintains a single module-instance handle for all instances of a particular application. When an application registers a window class, it must initialize a *WNDCLASS* structure and call the *RegisterClass* function. The *hInstance* member of the *WNDCLASS* structure must be initialized to the data-instance handle that was passed as the *hInstance* parameter to *WinMain*. *RegisterClass* examines the *hInstance* member of *WNDCLASS* and determines the module-instance handle associated with it. *RegisterClass* then registers the new window class using the module-instance handle.

The Voyeur application presented in Chapter 1 is a useful tool for studying this scheme. Try executing an instance of the Clock application supplied with Windows, then use Voyeur to peer into the Clock's window. Voyeur's window is shown in Figure 6-1.

The *Owner* field in the *Class Information* section identifies the module-instance handle associated with the registered window class (0x1855). This isn't the same as the value associated with the *Creator* field in the *Window Information* section (0x1886). The *Creator* field identifies the data-instance handle passed to *CreateWindow* or *CreateWindowEx* when the window was created.

When a window is being created, Windows first determines the module-instance handle associated with the *hInstance* parameter passed to *CreateWindow* or *CreateWindowEx*. It then scans all the registered window classes that have the same module-instance handle and class name. This explains why window classes do not have to be registered for each instance of an application.

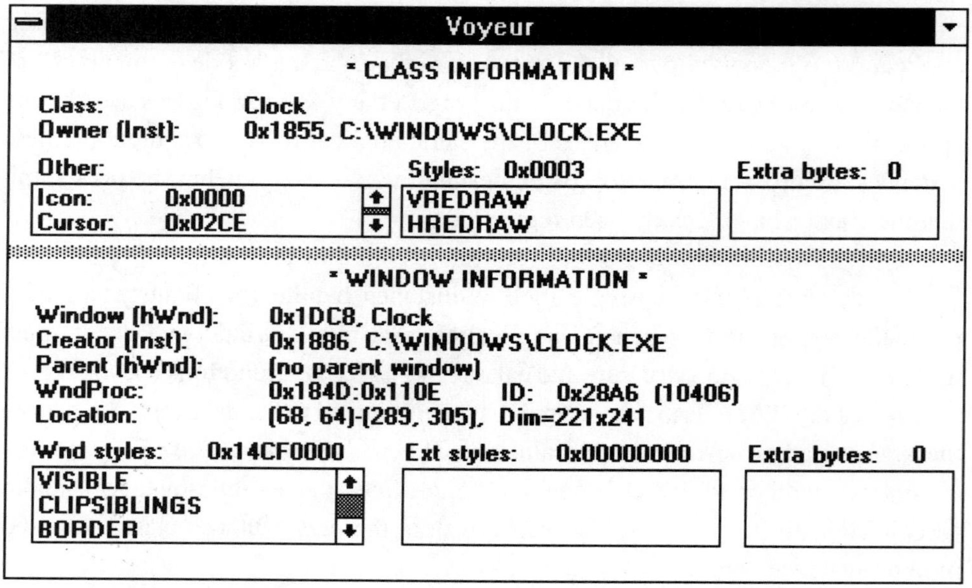

```
┌──────────────────────────────────────────────────────────────────┐
│ ▬                            Voyeur                              ▼ │
├──────────────────────────────────────────────────────────────────┤
│                    * CLASS INFORMATION *                           │
│  Class:            Clock                                           │
│  Owner (Inst):     0x1855, C:\WINDOWS\CLOCK.EXE                    │
│  Other:                          Styles:  0x0003     Extra bytes: 0│
│  ┌──────────────────────┬──┐ ┌──────────────┐ ┌─────────────────┐ │
│  │ Icon:     0x0000     │▲ │ │ VREDRAW      │ │                 │ │
│  │ Cursor:   0x02CE     │▼ │ │ HREDRAW      │ │                 │ │
│  └──────────────────────┴──┘ └──────────────┘ └─────────────────┘ │
│                    * WINDOW INFORMATION *                          │
│  Window (hWnd):    0x1DC8, Clock                                   │
│  Creator (Inst):   0x1886, C:\WINDOWS\CLOCK.EXE                    │
│  Parent (hWnd):    (no parent window)                             │
│  WndProc:          0x184D:0x110E     ID:  0x28A6  (10406)          │
│  Location:         (68, 64)-(289, 305), Dim=221x241               │
│  Wnd styles:   0x14CF0000    Ext styles:  0x00000000  Extra bytes: 0│
│  ┌──────────────────────┬──┐ ┌──────────────┐ ┌─────────────────┐ │
│  │ VISIBLE              │▲ │ │              │ │                 │ │
│  │ CLIPSIBLINGS         │▓ │ │              │ │                 │ │
│  │ BORDER               │▼ │ │              │ │                 │ │
│  └──────────────────────┴──┘ └──────────────┘ └─────────────────┘ │
└──────────────────────────────────────────────────────────────────┘
```

Figure 6-1. Voyeur window.

To reinforce this concept, perform the following experiment. Without terminating the Clock application, start another instance of Clock. Use Voyeur again to peer into the new Clock's window. You will see that the *Owner* field in Voyeur's *Class Information* section is identical to the *Owner* field in the first instance of Clock.

In Voyeur, the data-instance handle for the window is retrieved by calling *GetWindowWord* and passing it the *GWW_HINSTANCE* identifier. The module-instance handle is retrieved by calling *GetClassWord* and passing it the *GCW_HMODULE* identifier. *GetModuleFileName* accepts a data-instance handle or a module-instance handle and fills a buffer with the full path name of the application associated with the handle. When Voyeur calls *GetModuleFileName*, it supplies the handle of the module that registered the subject window or the handle to the data instance that was used to create the subject window. In either case, *GetModuleFileName* fills the data buffer with the same path name, so Voyeur displays the same path name for the *Owner* field and the *Creator* field.

In addition to module- and data-instance handles, applications have task-instance handles. Windows creates a task-instance handle for every instance of an executing application.

To help put all these handles into perspective, let's assume Program Manager, Voyeur, and two instances of Clock are running. This means that Windows is maintaining three module instances (one for each different application), four data instances (one for each running application), and four task instances (one for each running application).

There is always exactly one active task in Windows. The active task is the application that is processing a message. For example, when an application retrieves a message from its application queue, Windows makes that application the active task. When an application sends a message to a window that was registered by another application, Windows performs a task switch during the *SendMessage* function before calling the window's window procedure. When the window procedure returns, Windows performs another task switch so that the first application can resume.

Windows does not consider DLLs tasks. That's why DLLs are only assigned module- and data-instance handles, not task-instance handles. In addition, only one instance of any DLL can ever be loaded into Windows at one time, so exactly one module- and one data-instance handle is assigned to a DLL.

Understanding what happens when a task switch occurs requires exploration of how expanded memory (EMS) is managed under Windows. If Windows is running in real mode and using expanded memory, only the active task's code and data are banked into the real-mode addressing space. All the code and data belonging to inactive tasks are banked out of the real-mode addressing space.

This has some important ramifications for the programmer. Let's say Application A has a memory block that is to be filled by sending a message to a window whose window procedure is in Application B. Application A calls the *SendMessage* function and passes the address of the memory block as the *lParam* parameter. Windows performs a task switch and banks out the code and data associated with Application A. When the window procedure in Application B writes to the address pointed to by the *lParam* parameter, it will actually write over data belonging to Application B...*not* Application A.

The correct way to pass large amounts of information between applications is by using dynamic data exchange. After a DDE session is begun, Application B should allocate a memory block using the *GlobalAlloc* function with the *GMEM_DDESHARE* flag. When a memory block is allocated this way, Windows creates the block above the EMS bank line. Then Application B sends a DDE message identifying the memory block's handle to Application A. When Application A calls the *GlobalLock* function, Windows notices that the block has the *GMEM_DDESHARE* flag set and allocates a new block of memory above the EMS bank line, where Application A is now located. Windows then copies the data from the first memory block to the new memory block. When Application A calls the *GlobalUnlock* function, Windows frees the newly allocated block, leaving the original with Application B.

Global memory blocks allocated by functions within DLLs are owned by the current task, not the library. This means that if a DLL function allocated a block of memory on behalf of an application, that memory block will be freed when the application terminates, not when the DLL terminates. Another example will help explain this.

Application A and Application B use the same DLL. Application A calls a function in the DLL, which in turn calls *GlobalAlloc*. If Application A now terminates, the memory block is freed. However, the DLL continues to exist in memory because Application B is still using it.

There is one exception to this rule. Memory blocks allocated with the *GMEM_DDESHARE* flag are owned by the module (not task) that called *GlobalAlloc*. Let's look at how this affects the lifetime of the data in the memory block.

When an instance of an application terminates, any global memory allocated explicitly by the application is freed. However, if any of those blocks have the *GMEM_DDESHARE* flag, Windows does not free the block until all the instances of the application have been freed. If the *GMEM_DDESHARE* block was allocated by a DLL, Windows does not free the block until the DLL is no longer needed and is removed from memory.

Since we have already diverged from our discussion slightly, let's discuss the *GMEM_NOT_BANKED* flag. When this flag is used with *GlobalAlloc*, Windows allocates memory below the EMS bank line. However, Microsoft recommends that blocks allocated this way not be used for transferring data between applications. The *GMEM_NOT_BANKED* flag should be used by DLLs.

Since memory allocated by a DLL is really owned by the active task, the memory is normally allocated above the EMS bank line. If the DLL is called by different applications, it is possible that the memory block will be unavailable to the DLL. The *GMEM_NOT_BANKED* flag guarantees that the memory block will be available. This method is used by many Windows printer device drivers.

Let's look at another example using the Program Manager Restore application presented in Chapter 2. This application subclasses a window whose class was registered by another application. When a message is sent to Program Manager, Program Manager becomes the active task. This means that it is banked into memory. It also means that the code and data for the Program Manager Restore application are banked out of memory. When Windows calls the window procedure for Program Manager's main window, it tries to call the address of the subclass procedure contained in Program Manager Restore's code segment. Because this code is banked out, Windows will surely crash.

To solve this problem, the code for the subclassing function must be contained in a fixed-code segment within a DLL. Because Windows forces all fixed-code segments in a DLL to be below the EMS bank line, the code is never banked out and is available to all executing tasks. You make a code segment in a DLL fixed by specifying *FIXED* in the segments section of the DLL's .DEF file.

Another function that must reside in a fixed-code segment of a DLL is the callback function specified by *GlobalNotify*. If an application wishes to be informed when a global block of memory it created is discarded, it calls *GlobalNotify*, specifying the address of a callback function. Because Windows may be executing any application when memory needs to be discarded, this callback function must reside in a fixed-code segment of a DLL.

All the code to handle the *GlobalNotify* callback function must be within the DLL's fixed-code segment. Windows will crash if *GlobalNotify* attempts to call a function that is in an inactive task's code segment. *GlobalNotify* can, however, use *SendMessage* to request information from a window. If this happens, *SendMessage* causes a task switch. The task that includes the window procedure for the destination window will become the active task. At this point, the window procedure could call a function in its own task. After the message has been processed, *SendMessage* performs another task switch, making the original task active.

Windows supplies the following functions for working with tasks:

- *GetNumTasks* retrieves the number of tasks that are currently running under Windows.

- *GetCurrentTask* retrieves the task-instance handle of the currently executing task.

- *GetWindowTask* retrieves the task-instance handle of the task associated with the specified window handle.

You may recall that the Voyeur application presented in Chapter 1 will not allow the user to peer into any of the windows that were created by Voyeur. The program determines the task-instance handle of the task that created the window under the mouse cursor by calling *GetWindowTask* and passing it the handle of a window. If the task-instance handle matches that returned by *GetCurrentTask*, the window was created by Voyeur. Voyeur can now ignore this window. Because *GetCurrentTask* is called from within the processing of the *WM_MOUSEMOVE* message, the current task will always be Voyeur.

Looking Toward the Future. Anyone who has written a Windows application is familiar with the Global Protection Violation error. This error occurs when your application tries to access a memory address that contains no data. However, if your application creates a pointer that references memory in another application's data segment, a Global Protection Violation will *not* occur.

The 80286, 80386, and 80486 processors can protect various code from executing and data from being accessed. For example, the processor can be instructed to "hide" the code and data segments of inactive tasks from the currently active task. This level of protection would not allow an application to inadvertently retrieve or modify data belonging to another application. This greater level of "protection" will most likely be built into future versions of Windows.

If future versions of Windows do support this ability, Windows memory management in protected mode will be similar to Windows running in real mode with expanded memory. A task switch will cause Windows to protect the memory segments of the current task and to make segments accessible to the new task. Windows will, of course, make code and data segments of DLLs unprotected so they may be accessed by any application at any time.

Application Queues

Windows creates a message queue for each application when it is started. By default, the queue is large enough to hold eight messages. This may seem like a small number, but the queue is actually used infrequently. If an application requires a queue that is capable of holding more than eight messages, it can simply call *SetMessageQueue*:

```
BOOL SetMessageQueue (int cMsg);
```

This function deletes the current queue for the application and attempts to allocate a new one. The size of the queue is set by the *cMsg* parameter, which specifies the maximum number of messages the queue should hold.

Attempting to allocate a queue could result in insufficient memory. If this happens, *SetMessageQueue* returns zero; the application can try to create a queue of a smaller size. The application must decide whether it can execute with the finally allocated queue size and, if not, immediately return to Windows. The *SetMessageQueue* function should be called before any windows are created because messages in the queue are destroyed when the function is called.

Three functions can append messages to the end of the application queue: *PostMessage*, *PostQuitMessage*, and *PostAppMessage*.

PostMessage has the following prototype:

```
BOOL PostMessage (HWND hWnd, WORD wMsg, WORD wParam, LONG lParam);
```

This function determines which application queue to post the message to by examining the *hWnd* parameter. The message is then appended to the queue. If the queue is full, *PostMessage* returns a zero, indicating that the message could not be posted. Note that the *PostMessage* function does not wait for the message to be processed; it returns immediately after the message has been appended to the application's queue.

PostQuitMessage has the following prototype:

```
void PostQuitMessage (nExitCode);
```

This function causes a *WM_QUIT* message to be inserted into the queue used by the currently executing task. The *nExitCode* parameter may be used by the application to determine what steps to take upon termination. Most applications ignore this value. When this message is retrieved from the application's queue, the *hWnd* and *lParam* members of the *MSG* structure contain zeros. The *wParam* member contains the value that was passed to *PostQuitMessage*.

The last function, *PostAppMessage*, has the following prototype:

```
BOOL PostAppMessage (HANDLE hTask, WORD wMsg, WORD wParam,
    LONG lParam);
```

This function can be used to send a message to an application that did not create any windows. It's identical to *PostMessage* except that the first parameter specifies a task handle instead of a window handle. The return value is nonzero if the message was successfully posted to the application's queue. When a message is retrieved from the queue that was placed there by a call to *PostAppMessage*, the *hWnd* member of the *MSG* structure is zero. Since the *hWnd* member is zero, an application can determine the actions it wants to take by examining the *message* member. This test should be performed in the application's message loop immediately after *GetMessage* returns. The Program Manager Restore application presented in the window subclassing section of Chapter 2 demonstrates the use of *PostAppMessage*.

Some other Windows API functions, like *TranslateMessage*, can alter the application's queue. *TranslateMessage* examines the message being passed to it and, if the message is *WM_KEYDOWN* or *WM_SYSKEYDOWN*, posts a *WM_CHAR* or *WM_SYSCHAR* message to the application's queue. However, this message is not appended; it is inserted at the front of the queue, where it will be retrieved by the next call to *GetMessage* or *PeekMessage*.

391

Whenever an application calls *InvalidateRect* or *InvalidateRgn*, Windows places a *WM_PAINT* message in the queue. But Windows treats *WM_PAINT* messages differently from most other messages. When an application calls *GetMessage*, Windows will only return the *WM_PAINT* message if no other messages are in the queue. Because repainting the screen is one of the slowest operations under Windows, holding *WM_PAINT* messages until all other messages are processed makes Windows run much faster than if it updated the screen after every change. To force a *WM_PAINT* message to be sent to a window, use *UpdateWindow*. This function looks directly into the application's queue and checks for a *WM_PAINT* message. If one exists, Windows sends the *WM_PAINT* message to the window's window procedure.

The *WM_PAINT* message has another unusual attribute. When Windows sends *WM_PAINT* to a window procedure, it does not remove the message from the application's queue. The only way a *WM_PAINT* message can be removed from the queue is by calling *ValidateRect* or *ValidateRgn*. These functions tell Windows that all or part of the window's client area is up to date. If Windows sees that all of the area is up to date, the *WM_PAINT* message is removed. Because the *BeginPaint* function calls the *ValidateRect* function, Windows will remove the *WM_PAINT* message from your application's queue.

If you do not use *BeginPaint* and *EndPaint* or *ValidateRect* and *ValidateRgn* during the *WM_PAINT* message processing in your window procedure, Windows will start an infinite loop. Imagine that your window needs to be painted and is sent the *WM_PAINT* message. This message is processed as follows:

```
case WM_PAINT
  hDC = GetDC(hWnd);
  TextOut(hDC,0,0,"Some text",9);
  ReleaseDC(hWnd,hDC);
  break;
```

In this example, the invalid client area has never been validated. This means that the *WM_PAINT* message will still exist in the application's queue and Windows will again send the *WM_PAINT* message to the window's procedure. Windows will continue to loop in this fashion until your application is terminated.

The *WM_TIMER* message is also handled distinctively. Windows places a *WM_TIMER* message in your application's queue whenever the time specified in the call to *SetTimer* has expired. However, like *WM_PAINT*, *GetMessage* returns a *WM_TIMER* message only when the application's queue contains no other messages (except *WM_PAINT*). In addition, Windows will not put more than one *WM_TIMER* message for a given window in an application's queue.

Suppose your application creates a timer that goes off every 100 milliseconds. If another application starts a printing process that requires 15 seconds, Windows does not put 150 *WM_TIMER* messages in your application's queue. Instead, when control is returned to your application, only one *WM_TIMER* message will be retrieved from the queue. You can imagine how quickly your application's queue would fill up if every *WM_TIMER* message were placed in it.

The System Queue

Although each instance of an application has its own application queue, Windows maintains a single system queue. The system queue stores all keyboard and mouse events.

Each event in the system queue is in the form of an *EVENTMSG* structure (defined in WINDOWS.H):

```
typedef struct tagEVENTMSG {
    WORD message;
    WORD paramL;
    WORD paramH;
    DWORD time;
} EVENTMSG;
```

The *message* member contains one of the following keyboard or mouse messages:

```
WM_MOUSEMOVE
WM_LBUTTONDOWN      WM_MBUTTONDOWN      WM_RBUTTONDOWN
WM_LBUTTONUP        WM_MBUTTONUP        WM_RBUTTONDOWN
WM_KEYDOWN          WM_SYSKEYDOWN
WM_KEYUP            WM_SYSKEYUP
```

The *paramL* and *paramH* members contain additional information about the message. The last member, *time*, contains the time the event occurred. This time is measured in milliseconds since the Windows session began. The current system time can be retrieved by calling *GetTickCount* or *GetCurrentTime*.

The *WM_MOUSEMOVE* event is treated differently from other events stored in the system queue. Windows only stores the most recent *WM_MOUSEMOVE* message in the system queue. An example will explain why Windows behaves this way.

Let's assume your application is covering most of the screen and the user is just moving the mouse back and forth over your application's window area. If another application is processing a lengthy job, Windows does not have a chance to send the *WM_MOUSEMOVE* messages to your application. It's not until your application regains control that Windows sends the last *WM_MOUSEMOVE* message identifying the most recent position of the mouse.

When Windows initializes, it creates a system queue of a fixed size that is not changed during the Windows session. If Windows placed every mouse-movement event in the system queue, the queue would fill up very quickly. The queue can still become saturated with events if the user presses keys or mouse buttons while an application is in the middle of a lengthy process. When this happens, Windows indicates to the user that the system queue is full by beeping the speaker.

When an application calls *GetMessage*, Windows returns an event from the system queue or a message from the application's queue. If Windows returns an event from the system queue, it converts the system-queue event from an *EVENTMSG* structure to a *MSG* structure:

```
typedef struct tagMSG {
    HWND    hwnd;
    WORD    message;
    WORD    wParam;
    LONG    lParam;
    DWORD   time;
    POINT   pt;
} MSG;
```

Once *GetMessage* returns, *DispatchMessage* sends the message to the appropriate window. This function accepts the *MSG* structure containing the message, determines the address of the window procedure used for the window specified by the *hwnd* member, and calls the function, passing it the values in the *message*, *wParam*, and *lParam* members. The window procedure does not receive the *time* and *pt* members of the *MSG* structure. These members contain the system time when the message was posted to the application's queue and the position of the mouse cursor (in screen coordinates) when the message was posted. If the window procedure needs this information, the *GetMessageTime* and *GetMessagePos* functions may be used.

Our discussion wouldn't be complete if we didn't discuss *SendMessage*. When this function is called, a new message is *not* inserted into an application's queue. Instead, Windows immediately sends the message to the window procedure associated with the *hWnd* parameter. *SendMessage* does not return until the message has been processed by the window's window procedure, unlike *PostMessage,* which simply appends the message to the queue and returns directly.

The application's queue is used infrequently. This is because Windows does not allow events from the system queue to accumulate in this queue and because most Windows functions, like *SetFocus*, send *WM_SETFOCUS* and *WM_KILLFOCUS* messages instead of posting them.

395

Windows Hooks

Hooks allow an application to monitor and modify the Windows system. They are very powerful; take extra care when using them.

When you set a hook, you are installing a filter function. Windows calls the filter function before performing the normal processing for an event. This gives your application the opportunity to monitor events and to modify some of them, altering Windows' behavior.

Most hooks affect the entire Windows system, not just the application that installed the hook. This has several ramifications for the programmer.

Because Windows calls the hook filter functions whenever an event occurs, these functions tend to slow down the entire system. Hooks should be installed when needed and removed when they are no longer necessary. Don't install a hook function when your application starts and leave it in place until your application terminates unless you must.

Windows can call hook filter functions regardless of the active task, so your Windows hook function must be in a fixed-code segment of a DLL. The one exception to this rule is the *WH_MSGFILTER* hook. Windows will only call this task-specific hook function when your application is the active task. The filter function for this hook may appear in the application's code instead of a DLL.

Hook Basics. Although Windows offers seven hooks, the methods used for installing and removing them are identical. Later in this chapter, we will discuss the details of each hook and when to use them.

An application installs a hook by calling *SetWindowsHook*. The prototype for this function appears below:

```
FARPROC SetWindowsHook (int nFilterType, FARPROC lpFilterFunc);
```

The first parameter, *nFilterType*, specifies the type of hook the application wishes to install. This is one of the values listed in the following table:

Hook identifier	Description
WH_CALLWNDPROC	When this hook is installed, Windows calls the associated hook function every time a message is sent to a window using the *SendMessage* function.
WH_GETMESSAGE	When this hook is installed, Windows calls the associated hook function every time a message is retrieved by a call to the *GetMessage* or *PeekMessage* function.
WH_KEYBOARD	When this hook is installed, Windows calls the associated hook function every time an application calls the *GetMessage* or *PeekMessage* function and a *WM_KEYDOWN* or *WM_KEYUP* message is retrieved.
WH_SYSMSGFILTER	When this hook is installed, Windows calls the associated hook function every time a dialog box, message box, menu, or scroll bar is about to process a message.
WH_MSGFILTER	When this hook is installed, Windows calls the associated hook function every time a dialog box, message box, menu, or scroll bar belonging to the application that installed the hook is about to process a message.
WH_JOURNALRECORD	When this hook is installed, Windows calls the associated hook function every time an event is processed from the Windows system queue.

Hook identifier	Description
WH_JOURNALPLAYBACK	When this hook is installed, Windows calls the associated hook function every time an event is requested from the Windows system queue.

The second parameter, *lpFilterFunc*, is a procedural-instance address of the filter function. The following rules apply to this second parameter:

1. If the call to *SetWindowsHook* is in the same DLL as the hook function being installed, the *lpFilterFunc* parameter should simply be the name of the filter function. Because DLLs have only one instance, there is no need to create a procedural instance for the filter function by calling *MakeProcInstance*. In fact, calling *MakeProcInstance* and passing it the address of a function within a DLL can occasionally cause Windows to crash.

2. If the call to *SetWindowsHook* is in an application (as opposed to a DLL) and the filter function is in a DLL, the *lpFilterFunc* parameter can simply be the name of the filter function. In this case, the function is usually prototyped in a header file for the DLL and the application must be linked with the .LIB file associated with the DLL containing the filter function. Alternatively, an application can call *GetProcAddress* to retrieve the address of the filter function from the DLL and pass this value to the *SetWindowsHook* function.

3. If the call to *SetWindowsHook* is in an application and the filter function is in the same application, the *lpFilterFunc* parameter must be the procedural-instance address of the filter function. This address is obtained by calling *MakeProcInstance* and passing it the name of the filter function.

Whenever an event occurs that is associated with the type of hook you have installed, Windows calls the filter function specified during the call to *SetWindowsHook*. The filter function must have the following prototype, no matter which of the seven hooks was installed:

```
DWORD FAR PASCAL FilterFunc (int nCode, WORD wParam, LONG lParam);
```

The name of the function, *FilterFunc*, is a placeholder for your own function's name. The first parameter, *nCode*, specifies the hook code. The domain of values for this parameter depends on the type of hook installed. The values of the *wParam* and *lParam* parameters depend on the type of value passed in the *nCode* parameter.

A hook filter function's structure is similar to that of a window procedure. That is, the *nCode* parameter identifies the type of action (or message) that is to be performed by the filter function. The meanings of the *wParam* and *lParam* parameters depend on the type of action specified in *nCode*. We will examine the specific values of *nCode* and its associated values for *wParam* and *lParam* later in this chapter.

The code fragment below shows a possible function skeleton for a *WH_KEYBOARD* hook:

```
// The "_NextFilterFunc" global variable will be initialized to
// the return value from the call to the SetWindowsHook function
static FARPROC _NextFilterFunc = NULL;
 .
 .
 .
DWORD FAR PASCAL KybdHook (int nCode, WORD wParam, LONG lParam) {
   BOOL fCallDefProc = FALSE;
   DWORD dwResult = 0;

   switch (nCode) {

      case HC_ACTION:
         // Do HC_ACTION processing
         break;

      case HC_NOREMOVE:
         // Do HC_NOREMOVE processing
         break;
```

```
    default:
        fCallDefProc = TRUE;
        break;
}
if ((nCode < 0) || (fCallDefProc && (_NextFilterFunc != NULL)))
    dwResult = DefHookProc(nCode, wParam, lParam,
        &_NextFilterFunc);
return(dwResult);
}
```

A filter-function chain is formed when many applications install hooks of a particular type. Windows remembers the address of the most recently installed filter function for a specific hook. For example, if Application A installs a *WH_KEYBOARD* hook, Windows will call this filter function whenever a keyboard message is retrieved. If Application B also installs a *WH_KEYBOARD* hook, Windows will forget all about the filter function installed by Application A and only call the one installed by Application B. It is the responsibility of each filter function to make sure any previously installed filter functions are called.

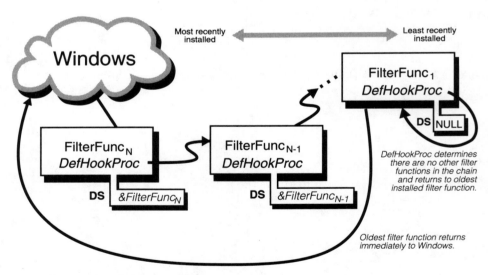

Figure 6-2. Processing for hook codes.

The *SetWindowsHook* function returns the procedural-instance address of the previous filter function installed for the specified hook. The function that is installing the new filter function must save this address in a global variable:

```
static FARPROC _NextFilterFunc = NULL;
.
.
.
_NextFilterFunc = SetWindowsHook(WH_KEYBOARD, KybdHook);
.
.
.
```

If no other filter function has been installed for the specified hook, *SetWindowsHook* returns NULL.

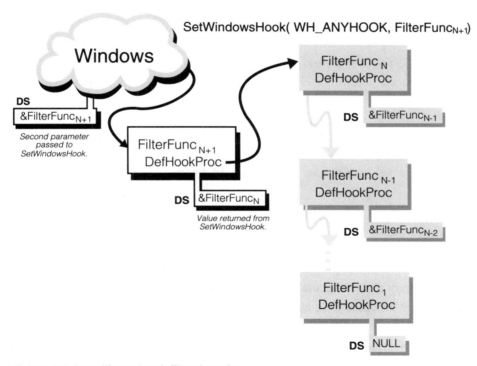

Figure 6-3. Installing a hook filter function.

Toward the end of every filter function is a call to *DefHookProc*. This function calls the next filter function in the chain and passes it the same *nCode*, *wParam*, and *lParam* parameters as it received. Before the next filter function terminates, it also calls *DefHookProc,* passing it the address of the next filter function. This cooperation among filter functions is crucial to the continued operation of Windows and all the applications that have installed hooks.

The last filter function in the chain (*_NextFilterFunc* == NULL) should not call *DefHookProc* but should simply return a value in the *dwResult* variable. *DefHookProc* does not operate like a normal function. When *DefHookProc* is called, it alters the contents of the stack so that it does not return to your function but directly to Windows. That's why you shouldn't write a filter function expecting to do any cleanup after the call to *DefHookProc*.

The code fragment below demonstrates an incorrect coding practice:

```
GLOBALHANDLE hMem = GlobalAlloc(GMEM_MOVEABLE, 100);
 .
 .
 .
dwResult = DefHookProc(nCode, wParam, lParam,
   &_NextFilterFunc);
// Control may not return to this filter function and
// therefore no important lines should be placed here
 .
 .
 .
GlobalFree(hMem);
```

DefHookProc is not guaranteed to return to this filter function, so the call to *GlobalFree* may never execute. Because Windows calls hook filter functions so frequently, it won't take long before Windows runs out of free memory.

The return value expected from a filter function depends on the type of hook installed and the value of the *nCode* parameter. If your application requires that a certain value be returned from the filter function, your filter function must not call *DefHookProc*. On the other hand, if the return value from your filter function does not affect your application, *DefHookProc* may be called.

Sometimes a hook filter function should not call any of the other filter functions in the chain. Let's say an application copies the window under the mouse cursor to the clipboard whenever the F9 key is pressed. The application must install a *WH_KEYBOARD* hook that examines each keystroke for an F9 key. For each keystroke that is not an F9, the next filter function in the chain should be called. However, once the filter function detects the F9 key, it performs the operations necessary to copy the window to the clipboard and immediately returns—without calling the next filter function in the chain. In fact, the *WH_KEYBOARD* filter function should return 1 to Windows, telling it to discard the keystroke event and not pass it to the application.

Removing a Filter Function from the Chain. When an application no longer needs its hooks, they are removed by calling *UnhookWindowsHook*:

```
BOOL UnhookWindowsHook (int nFilterType, FARPROC lpFilterFunc);
```

The *nFilterType* parameter specifies the type of hook being removed; the *lpFilterFunc* parameter specifies the procedural-instance address of the filter function being removed. These parameters are identical to the ones used when *SetWindowsHook* installed the hook.

The return value from *UnhookWindowsHook* indicates whether the filter function has been successfully removed from the chain. If so, a nonzero value is returned.

Windows does not require that hook filter functions be removed in the reverse of the order in which they were installed. However, removing a filter function from the middle of the chain causes the links in the chain to be incorrect. Windows must execute a procedure to ensure that the links of the chain are updated correctly.

Two special values for *nCode* apply to all hook filter functions: *HC_LPFNNEXT* (defined as -1) and *HC_LPLPFNNEXT* (defined as -2). All the other possible hook codes that are sent to filter functions have positive values. Windows uses these two negative codes to update the filter-function chain.

When you install a filter function, Windows stores its address in memory and returns the address of the previously installed filter function. This address must be saved in a global variable. At the end of your filter function is a call to *DefHookProc*. Note that the last parameter to *DefHookProc* is not really the address of the next filter function in the chain. Instead, this is the address in memory where the address to the next filter function can be found.

Now, let's say an application is removing a filter function but that this function is in the middle of the chain. Somehow, Windows has to change the value of the global variable containing the address of the next filter function and set it to the address of the filter function that is now next in the chain. This is how Windows does it:

1. An application calls *UnhookWindowsHook* to remove the filter function from the chain.

2. Windows calls the filter function being removed from the chain with the *nCode* parameter set to *HC_LPFNNEXT* (see Figure 6-4). Windows knows the address of this function because it is the second parameter passed to *UnhookWindowsHook*. *DefHookProc* sees that *nCode* is *HC_LPFNNEXT* and returns the address of the "next" filter function.

3. Windows now calls the first filter function in the chain with the *nCode* parameter set to *HC_LPLPFNNEXT* and the *lParam* parameter set to the address of the filter function being removed (Figure 6-5). *DefHookProc* sees that *nCode* is *HC_LPLPFNNEXT* and compares the value in *lParam* to the address of the next filter function stored in the filter function's data segment. If a match is not found, *DefHookProc* calls the next filter function and tries again.

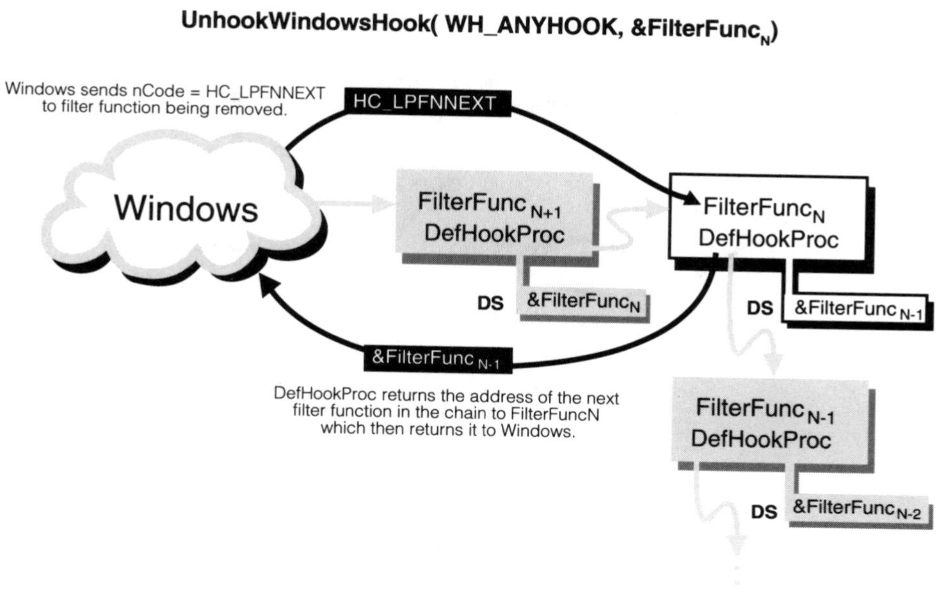

UnhookWindowsHook(WH_ANYHOOK, &FilterFunc$_N$)

Figure 6-4. Sending HC_LPFNNEXT to the filter function being removed.

4. When a match is found, *DefHookProc* returns its address (Figure 6-6). Windows changes the address of the next filter function in your data segment to the value returned in step 2 above.

The *WH_CALLWNDPROC* and *WH_GETMESSAGE* Hooks. One of the most useful utilities for debugging Windows programs is the Spy application supplied with the SDK. This application allows you to monitor the messages sent to a particular window (or to all windows). By using the *WH_CALLWNDPROC* and *WH_GETMESSAGE* hooks, Spy can intercept all messages being sent to a window and display that information in its own client area.

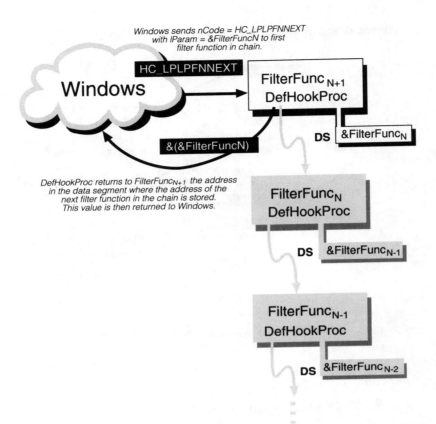

Figure 6-5. Sending DC_LPLPFNNEXT through the filter chain.

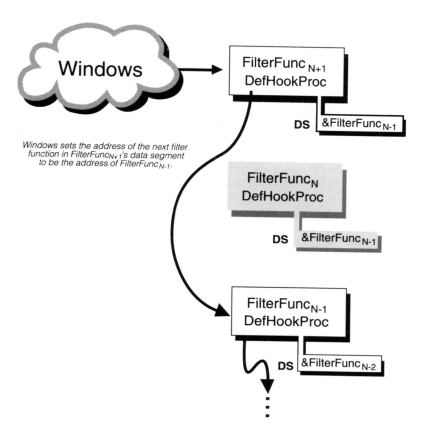

Windows sets the address of the next filter function in FilterFunc$_{N+1}$'s data segment to be the address of FilterFunc$_{N-1}$.

Figure 6-6. The new chain after a *FilterFunc$_N$* has been removed.

When an application calls *SendMessage*, Windows checks to see whether a *WH_CALLWNDPROC* hook filter function has been installed. If it has, Windows calls the first *WH_CALLWNDPROC* filter function in the chain. The table below summarizes the values that should be expected by the filter function and the return values expected by Windows:

nCode	wParam	lParam	Return value
HC_ACTION	The message is being sent by the current task if *wParam* is nonzero.	Points to a *CALLWNDPROC* structure.	Not used.
HC_LPFNNEXT	Not used.	Not used.	Address of the next filter function in the chain.
HC_LPLPFNNEXT	Not used.	Address of the filter function being removed.	Address into filter function's data segment containing the address of the next filter function in the chain.

Because we discussed the *HC_LPFNNEXT* and *HC_LPLPFNNEXT* hook codes earlier in this section, we will only discuss the *HC_ACTION* hook code here.

The *HC_ACTION* hook code notifies the filter function that a message has been sent to a window. The *lParam* parameter points to a *CALLWNDPROC* structure that has the following prototype:

```
typedef struct {
    WORD hlParam;      // high-order word of lParam
    WORD llParam;      // low-order word of lParam
    WORD wParam;
```

```
    WORD wMsg;
    HWND hWnd;
} CALLWNDPROC;
```

The filter function can examine the contents of this structure and modify any or all of its members. At the end of the filter function, *DefHookProc* may be called so that any other functions in the chain have a chance to monitor or modify the structure. When all the filter functions have had a chance to process the message, Windows will send the modified message to the proper window.

Because messages are sent so frequently in Windows to carry out operations, installing a *WH_CALLWNDPROC* hook filter function will hurt Windows' performance dramatically. For this reason, the *WH_CALLWNDPROC* hook function is usually only used for debugging purposes.

The *WH_CALLWNDPROC* hook intercepts messages being sent to a window procedure by calling *SendMessage*. To intercept messages retrieved from the application's queue (by calls to the *GetMessage* and *PeekMessage* functions), you must install a *WH_GETMESSAGE* hook filter function.

A *WH_GETMESSAGE* hook operates identically to the *WH_CALLWNDPROC* hook function. That is, all the parameters passed to a *WH_GETMESSAGE* hook filter function have the same meaning as those passed to a *WH_CALLWNDPROC* hook filter function except that the *lParam* parameter passed during an *HC_ACTION* hook code to a *WH_GETMESSAGE* filter function is a pointer to a *MSG* structure instead of a *CALLWNDPROC* structure.

The *WH_KEYBOARD* Hook. The *WH_KEYBOARD* hook is used by an application when it wants to examine keystrokes, even when it does not have the input focus. For example, the Recorder application supplied with Windows uses this hook. The Recorder allows the user to define a specific keystroke that activates a prerecorded sequence of events. While the Recorder is running, it watches the

409

keyboard messages to see if the user presses a key that initiates a macro. The Recorder watches all keystrokes, even when it is not the active application.

When the user presses or releases a key, this event is placed in the Windows system queue. This event is retrieved when an application makes a call to *GetMessage* or *PeekMessage*. Just before Windows returns the keystroke event, it calls the first *WH_KEYBOARD* filter function in the chain. The table below summarizes the values that should be expected by the filter function and the return value expected by Windows:

nCode	*wParam*	*lParam*	**Return value**
HC_ACTION	Specifies the virtual key code of the key.	Specifies the same information as sent in *lParam* to a window procedure when it receives a *WM_KEYDOWN* message.	Zero if message should be processed, one if the message should be discarded.
HC_NOREMOVE	Specifies the virtual key code of the key.	Specifies the same information as sent in *lParam* parameter to a window procedure when it receives a *WM_KEYDOWN* message.	Zero if message should be processed, one if the message should be discarded.
HC_LPFNNEXT	Not used.	Not used.	Address of the next filter function in the chain.
HC_LPLPFNNEXT	Not used.	Address of the filter function being removed.	Address into filter function's data segment containing address of next filter function in chain.

If the keystroke event is being retrieved from the system queue because the application called the *PeekMessage* function with the *PM_NOREMOVE* flag, the filter function will receive a hook code of *HC_NOREMOVE*. Any other time a keystroke event occurs, the *HC_ACTION* hook code is received.

When the hook code is *HC_ACTION* or *HC_NOREMOVE*, the *wParam* parameter identifies the virtual key code representing the pressed or released key. The list of virtual key codes supported by Windows is in Appendix A of the *Microsoft Windows SDK Programmer's Reference*, Volume 2.

The *lParam* parameter contains additional information about the keystroke event:

Bits in *lParam*	Description
0 through 15	Repeat count (number of times the keystroke is repeated as a result of the user holding down the key).
16 through 23	Scan code of key.
24	This bit is on if the key is extended. Extended keys are function keys or keys on the numeric keypad.
25 through 26	Not used.
27 through 28	Used internally by Windows.
29	This bit is on if the Alt key was held down while the key was pressed.
30	This bit is on if the key is down before the message is sent.
31	This bit is on if the key is being released.

Windows does not allow a *WH_KEYBOARD* filter function to change the values in the *wParam* or *lParam* parameter before sending messages to an application. If you want to write a hook filter function that converts all occurrences of one keystroke to another, you have to use *WH_CALLWNDPROC* and *WH_GETMESSAGE* because these hooks allow their filter functions to modify messages.

The *WH_SYSMSGFILTER* and *WH_MSGFILTER* Hooks. Windows calls the *WH_SYSMSGFILTER* and *WH_MSGFILTER* hook filter-function chains whenever a message is about to be processed by a dialog box, message box, menu, or scroll bar. While the *WH_SYSMSGFILTER* hook can be used to monitor messages being sent to any application, the *WH_MSGFILTER* hook can only be used to monitor messages being sent to dialog boxes, messages boxes, and so on that were created by the application that installed the hook. Because a *WH_MSGFILTER* hook applies only to the task that installed the hook, the filter function does not need to be placed in a fixed-code segment of a DLL.

The *lParam* parameter for *WH_SYSMSGFILTER* and *WH_MSGFILTER* points to a *MSG* structure identifying the message to be processed. The table below summarizes the values expected by the filter function and the return values expected by Windows:

nCode	*wParam*	*lParam*	**Return value**
MSGF_DIALOGBOX	Not used	Points to a *MSG* structure.	Nonzero if the filter function processes the message.
MSGF_MENU	Not used	Points to a *MSG* structure.	Nonzero if the filter function processes the message.
MSGF_SCROLLBAR	Not used	Points to a *MSG* structure.	Nonzero if the filter function processes the message.
MSGF_NEXTWINDOW	Not used	Points to a *MSG* structure.	Nonzero if the filter function processes the message.
HC_LPFNNEXT	Not used	Not used.	Address of next filter function in the chain.
HC_LPLPFNNEXT	Not used	Address of the filter function being removed.	Address into filter function's data segment containing address of next filter function in chain.

If you read about the *SetWindowsHook* function in the *Windows Programmer's Reference*, you will notice that it mentions a *MSGF_MESSAGEBOX* hook code that can be sent to the *WH_SYSMSGFILTER* hook's filter function. Windows will never send this code to your filter function because message boxes in version 3.0 of Windows are dialog boxes. If you wish to trap events that occur in a message box, you should process the event when a *MSGF_DIALOGBOX* hook code is retrieved.

The *MSGF_NEXTWINDOW* hook code arrives at a *WM_SYSMSGFILTER* hook's filter function whenever the user presses the Alt-Tab or Alt-Esc keys to make another application active. The *MSGF_NEXTWINDOW* hook code is received by a *WH_MSGFILTER* hook function only if the user presses the Alt-Tab or Alt-Esc key combination when the application that installed the hook is the active task.

The *WH_MSGFILTER* hook is useful if your application displays a message box to the user and you wish to allow the user to press the F1 key to display help information about the message box. By installing a *WH_MSGFILTER*, you can test the value of the *nCode* parameter to see if it is *MSGF_DIALOGBOX*. If it is, your filter function could call the Windows *WinHelp* function to display help text to the user.

At first, you would probably think about implementing the filter function as a *WH_KEYBOARD* hook instead of a *WH_MSGFILTER* hook. The advantage of using a *WH_MSGFILTER* hook is that it is task-specific. Applications written for Windows should always try to avoid interfering with other applications as much as possible. By implementing a task-specific hook instead of a systemwide hook, you prevent Windows from calling your filter function when your application is inactive. If you did decide to implement this code by using a *WH_KEYBOARD* hook, the hook filter function would have to verify that your application was the active task. It would be undesirable to have the help text for your message box appear to the user if he pressed the F1 key while another application was active.

The *WH_JOURNALRECORD* and *WH_JOURNALPLAYBACK* Hooks. Perhaps the most commonly used hooks are *WH_JOURNALRECORD* and *WH_JOURNALPLAYBACK*, which are used to add a macro recording facility to applications such as the Windows Recorder.

When a *WH_JOURNALRECORD* hook is installed, Windows calls the *WH_JOURNALRECORD* hook filter-function chain whenever a message is retrieved from the Windows system queue. Recall that the Windows system queue is used to store all the user's input (mouse and keyboard events). The table below summarizes the values that should be expected by the filter function and the return values expected by Windows:

nCode	*wParam*	*lParam*	**Return value**
HC_ACTION	Not used.	Points to an *EVENTMSG* structure.	Nonzero if the filter function processes the message.
HC_SYSMODALON	Not used.	Not used.	Not used.
HC_SYSMODALOFF	Not used.	Not used.	Not used.
HC_LPFNNEXT	Not used.	Not used.	Address of next filter function in the chain.
HC_LPLPFNNEXT	Not used.	Address of the filter function being removed.	Address into filter function's data segment containing address of the next filter function in the chain.

When the hook code to a *WH_JOURNALRECORD* hook filter function is *HC_ACTION*, the *lParam* parameter points to an *EVENTMSG* structure. This structure is not in the *Windows Programmer's Reference* but can be found in the WINDOWS.H file included with the SDK:

```
typedef struct tagEVENTMSG {
    WORD message;
    WORD paramL;
    WORD paramH;
    DWORD time;
} EVENTMSG;
typedef EVENTMSG *PEVENTMSGMSG;
typedef EVENTMSG NEAR *NPEVENTMSGMSG;
typedef EVENTMSG FAR *LPEVENTMSGMSG;
```

For macro recording to be implemented in an application, a *WH_JOURNAL-RECORD* filter function should append each *EVENTMSG* structure to a block of memory. This technique is demonstrated by the Echo application discussed later.

The *HC_SYSMODALON* and *HC_SYSMODALOFF* hook codes are used to notify a *WH_JOURNALRECORD* filter function when a system modal dialog box appears or is removed, respectively. The filter function should watch for the *HC_SYSMODALON* hook code and temporarily stop appending *EVENTMSG* structures to the memory block. Depending on the application, it might be even better to turn the recording off completely and notify the user that a system modal dialog box has appeared. The user should not be notified until after that dialog box has been removed. The Echo application shows how to implement this logic. You may also want to experiment with the Recorder application supplied with Windows to see how it operates.

While the recorded sequence of events is being played back, Windows stops calling *WH_JOURNALPLAYBACK* when a system modal dialog box appears on the screen. Once the dialog box has been removed, Windows resumes calling the *WH_JOURNALPLAYBACK* filter function.

After the *WH_JOURNALRECORD* hook has been removed, *WH_JOURNAL-PLAYBACK* is used to play back the sequence of events. When a *WH_JOURNAL-PLAYBACK* hook is installed, Windows ignores all mouse and keyboard input from the user and retrieves system events by calling the *WH_JOURNALPLAYBACK* filter function. While a *WH_JOURNALPLAYBACK* hook is installed, the mouse will have no effect on the position of the mouse cursor on the screen. The table below summarizes the values that should be expected by the filter function and the return values expected by Windows:

nCode	*wParam*	*lParam*	**Return value**
HC_GETNEXT	Not used.	Points to an *EVENTMSG* structure.	Number of clock ticks Windows should wait before processing the message.
HC_SKIP	Not used.	Not used.	Not used.
HC_SYSMODALON	Not used.	Not used.	Not used.
HC_SYSMODALOFF	Not used.	Not used.	Not used.
HC_LPFNNEXT	Not used.	Not used.	Address of the next filter function in the chain.
HC_LPLPFNNEXT	Not used.	Address of the filter function being removed.	Address into filter function's data segment containing address of the next filter function in the chain.

HC_SYSMODALON and *HC_SYSMODALOFF* notify the *WH_JOURNAL-PLAYBACK* filter function that a system modal dialog box has appeared or been removed. Windows stops calling the filter function while the dialog box is on the screen. Because a system modal dialog box usually means that some serious action must be taken, a *WH_JOURNALPLAYBACK* hook can watch for the *HC_SYS-MODALON* hook code and unhook itself. It would not be wise to continue playing the events after the dialog box was removed.

When the filter function receives the *HC_GETNEXT* hook code, the next *EVENTMSG* structure in the memory block should be copied to the *EVENTMSG* structure pointed to by the *lParam* parameter.

The *HC_SKIP* hook code notifies the *WH_JOURNALPLAYBACK* filter function that Windows is done processing the current event and to prepare the next one. This means that the filter function should continue to return the first event in the sequence every time Windows sends the *HC_GETNEXT* hook code. When Windows sends the *HC_SKIP* hook code, the filter function should prepare to send the next event in the sequence the next time Windows sends the *HC_GETNEXT* hook code. When the filter function receives the *HC_SKIP* hook code and determines that all the saved events have been played, the filter function can call the *UnhookWindowsHook* function to remove itself from the chain. A *WH_JOURNALPLAYBACK* filter function should not unhook itself during the processing of a *HC_GETNEXT* hook code.

When the filter function returns from processing *HC_GETNEXT*, the *time* member of the *EVENTMSG* structure (pointed to by the *lParam* parameter) must contain the system time when the message should occur. To accomplish this, I recommend updating the *time* member of all the saved events immediately after the *WH_JOURNALRECORD* hook's filter function is removed. The result should have the *time* member in each *EVENTMSG* structure, reflecting the number of clock ticks that have elapsed since recording started. The following code fragment shows how to calculate this:

```
LPEVENTMSGMSG lpEventMsg;
WORD wNumEvents;
 .
 .
 .
while (wNumEvents-)
   lpEventMsg[wNumEvents].time -= lpEventMsg[0].time;
 .
 .
 .
```

The *lpEventMsg* variable points to an array of saved *EVENTMSG* structures, and the *wNumEvents* variable contains the number of events that have been recorded.

When the *WH_JOURNALPLAYBACK* hook is installed, the application should save the current system time:

```
FARPROC _fnNextFilterFunc;
DWORD _dwStartPlaybackTime;
  .
  .
  .
_fnNextFilterFunc = SetWindowsHook(WH_JOURNALPLAYBACK,
   (FARPROC) JrnlPlayBackHook);
_dwStartPlaybackTime = GetTickCount();
  .
  .
  .
```

Then, when the *HC_GETNEXT* hook code is passed to the filter function, the function can copy the current *EVENTMSG* to the location pointed to by the *lParam* parameter and change that copy's *time* member to the proper playback time:

```
((LPEVENTMSGMSG) lParam)->time += _dwStartPlaybackTime;
```

The return value from the filter function indicates the number of milliseconds Windows should wait before playing back the event. If the playback time has passed, the function should return zero. The code fragment below shows how to calculate this value:

```
DWORD dwResult;
  .
  .
  .
switch (nCode) {
   case HC_GETNEXT:
      // Copy current event to EVENTMSG structure pointed to
      // by lParam
      *((LPEVENTMSGMSG) lParam) = lpEventMsg[wCurrentEvent];

      // Update time member in copy to system playback time
      ((LPEVENTMSGMSG) lParam)->time += _dwStartPlaybackTime;
```

```
      // Return # of milliseconds Windows should wait before
      // processing event
      dwResult = ((LPEVENTMSGMSG) lParam)->time - GetTickCount();
      if ((signed long) dwResult < 0) dwResult = 0;
      break;
    .
    .
    .
}
.
.
.
return(dwResult);
```

If you would like to have the recorded macros played back at full speed instead of recorded speed, the filter function should change the *time* member in the copied structure to the current system time and return zero:

```
DWORD dwResult;
.
.
.
switch (nCode) {
  case HC_GETNEXT:
      // Copy current event to EVENTMSG structure pointed to
      // by lParam
      *((LPEVENTMSGMSG) lParam) = lpEventMsg[wCurrentEvent];

      // Update time member in copy to system playback time
      ((LPEVENTMSGMSG) lParam)->time = GetTickCount();

      // Return # of milliseconds Windows should wait before
      // processing event
      dwResult = 0;
      break;
    .
    .
    .
}
```

.
.
.

```
return(dwResult);
```

There are some issues to keep in mind when recording and playing back macros. Use of the mouse should be kept to a minimum. The *EVENTMSG* structures that *WH_JOURNALRECORD* receives contain the position of the mouse in screen coordinates. When a macro is played back, the windows on the screen may be in different locations or different sizes than when the macro was recorded. This may cause the mouse events to be sent to a window other than the original one. In addition, macros could be played back on a monitor having a different screen resolution from that of the monitor used when the events were recorded. Finally, incompatibilities could result when a macro recorded on one keyboard is played back on a machine connected to a keyboard with a different country setting.

The Screen-Blanker Utility

Ever since Windows was introduced, company after company has written some type of screen-blanking program. You know the kind I mean: The computer sits idle for a while, the screen turns black, and some animated design moves across it. The sample application SCRNBLNK.EXE demonstrates how to implement one of these screen blankers. It uses the *WH_JOURNALRECORD* hook to monitor input from the user. When no user input has been detected after five minutes, the application blanks the user's screen and draws some multicolored circles. To continue working with Windows, the user can press any key or the mouse button.

Figure 6-7. SCRNBLNK.ICO.

420

Listing 6-1. SCRNBLNK.C application source module.

```
/****************************************************************
Module name: ScrnBlnk.C
Programmer : Jeffrey M. Richter
****************************************************************/

#include "..\nowindws.h"
#undef NOCOLOR
#undef NOCTLMGR
#undef NOGDI
#undef NOHELP
#undef NOKERNEL
#undef NOLSTRING
#undef NOMB
#undef NOMENUS
#undef NOMINMAX
#undef NOMSG
#undef NORASTEROPS
#undef NOSHOWWINDOW
#undef NOSYSMETRICS
#undef NOUSER
#undef NOWH
#undef NOWINOFFSETS
#undef NOWINMESSAGES
#undef NOWINSTYLES
#include <windows.h>
#include <stdlib.h>
#include <math.h>

#include "dialog.h"
#include "SB-DLL.h"

char _szAppName[] = "ScrnBlnk";
char _szBlnkClass[] = "ScrnBlnkPopup";

HANDLE _hInstance = NULL;              // our instance handle

#define IDM_PREFERENCES    (0x0110)   // Must be < 0xF000
#define IDM_ABOUT          (0x0120)   // Must be < 0xF000
```

```
static WORD _wMinutes = 5;        // Default to 5-minute idle time
static HWND _hWnd, _hWndBlnk;

BOOL NEAR PASCAL RegisterWndClasses (HANDLE hInstance);
LONG FAR PASCAL AppWndProc (HWND hWnd, WORD wMsg, WORD wParam,
    LONG lParam);
LONG FAR PASCAL BlnkWndProc (HWND hWnd, WORD wMsg, WORD wParam,
    LONG lParam);
DWORD FAR PASCAL JrnlRcrdHookFunc (int nCode, WORD wParam,
    LPEVENTMSGMSG lpEventMsg);
BOOL FAR PASCAL PrefProc (HWND hDlg, WORD wMsg, WORD wParam,
    LONG lParam);
BOOL FAR PASCAL AboutProc (HWND hDlg, WORD wMsg, WORD wParam,
    LONG lParam);

// ****************************************************************
int PASCAL WinMain (HANDLE hInstance, HANDLE hPrevInstance,
    LPSTR lpszCmdLine, int nCmdShow) {
  MSG msg;

  _hInstance = hInstance;

  if (hPrevInstance != NULL) return(0);

  if (!RegisterWndClasses(hInstance)) return(0);

  // Create application's main window. Show only as icon
  // (WS_MINIMIZE).
  _hWnd = CreateWindow(_szAppName, _szAppName, WS_OVERLAPPED |
    WS_CAPTION | WS_SYSMENU | WS_MINIMIZE, 0, 0,
    0, 0, NULL, NULL, hInstance, 0);

  if (_hWnd == NULL) return(0);

  ShowWindow(_hWnd, SW_MINIMIZE);
  UpdateWindow(_hWnd);

  // Create hidden unowned pop-up window that covers user's
  // entire screen
```

```
  _hWndBlnk = CreateWindow(_szBlnkClass, NULL,
     WS_POPUP, 0, 0, GetSystemMetrics(SM_CXSCREEN),
     GetSystemMetrics(SM_CYSCREEN), NULL, NULL, hInstance, 0);

  if (_hWndBlnk == NULL) return(0);

  // Send WM_TIMER messages to unowned pop-up window every second
  if (0 == SetTimer(_hWndBlnk, 1, 1000, NULL)) {
     MessageBox(_hWnd, "Not enough timers!", _szAppName, MB_OK);
     return(0);
  }

  while (GetMessage(&msg, NULL, 0, 0)) {
     TranslateMessage(&msg);
     DispatchMessage(&msg);
  }

  KillTimer(_hWndBlnk, 1);
  DestroyWindow(_hWndBlnk);

  return(0);
}

// ******************************************************************

BOOL NEAR PASCAL RegisterWndClasses (HANDLE hInstance) {
  WNDCLASS WndClass;

  WndClass.style        = 0;
  WndClass.lpfnWndProc  = AppWndProc;
  WndClass.cbClsExtra   = 0;
  WndClass.cbWndExtra   = 0;
  WndClass.hInstance    = hInstance;
  WndClass.hIcon        = LoadIcon(hInstance, _szAppName);
  WndClass.hCursor      = NULL;
  WndClass.hbrBackground = NULL;
  WndClass.lpszMenuName = NULL;
  WndClass.lpszClassName = _szAppName;
  if (!RegisterClass(&WndClass)) return(0);
```

```
   WndClass.style          = 0;
   WndClass.lpfnWndProc    = BlnkWndProc;
   WndClass.cbClsExtra     = 0;
   WndClass.cbWndExtra     = 0;
   WndClass.hInstance      = hInstance;
   WndClass.hIcon          = LoadIcon(hInstance, _szAppName);
   WndClass.hCursor        = NULL;

   // Unowned pop-up window's background is always BLACK so that
   // contents of screen are removed
   WndClass.hbrBackground  = GetStockObject(BLACK_BRUSH);

   WndClass.lpszMenuName   = NULL;
   WndClass.lpszClassName  = _szBlnkClass;
   return(RegisterClass(&WndClass));
}
// ****************************************************************
// This function processes all messages sent to ScrnBlnk's main
// window

LONG FAR PASCAL AppWndProc (HWND hWnd, WORD wMsg, WORD wParam,
      LONG lParam) {
   BOOL fCallDefProc = FALSE;
   LONG lResult = 0;
   HMENU hMenu;
   FARPROC fpProc;
   WORD wIdleTime;

   switch (wMsg) {
      case WM_CREATE:
         // Append the "Preferences" and "About" options to
         // the system menu
         hMenu = GetSystemMenu(hWnd, 0);
         AppendMenu(hMenu, MF_SEPARATOR, 0, 0);
         AppendMenu(hMenu, MF_STRING, IDM_PREFERENCES,
            "&Preferences...");
         AppendMenu(hMenu, MF_STRING, IDM_ABOUT, "A&bout...");
         DrawMenuBar(hWnd);
```

```
      // Install the WH_JOURNALRECORD hook filter function
      InstallJrnlHook(TRUE);
      break;

case WM_DESTROY:
      // Remove the WH_JOURNALRECORD hook filter function
      InstallJrnlHook(FALSE);

      PostQuitMessage(0);
      break;

case WM_QUERYOPEN:
      // Do not allow application to open; show only as icon
      lResult = 0;
      break;

case WM_SYSCOMMAND:
      switch (wParam & 0xfff0) {
         case IDM_PREFERENCES:
            // Prompt user for idle time in minutes
            fpProc = MakeProcInstance(PrefProc, _hInstance);

            // The last parameter is the current setting of
            // _wMinutes
            wIdleTime = DialogBoxParam(_hInstance,
               "Preferences", hWnd, fpProc, _wMinutes);
            FreeProcInstance(fpProc);

            // If wIdleTime == -1, the user pressed "Cancel"
            // else wIdleTime is the idle time
            if ((int) wIdleTime != -1) _wMinutes = wIdleTime;
            break;

         case IDM_ABOUT:
            fpProc = MakeProcInstance(AboutProc, _hInstance);
            DialogBox(_hInstance, "About", hWnd, fpProc);
            FreeProcInstance(fpProc);
            break;
```

```
            default:
                fCallDefProc = TRUE; break;
        }
        break;

    default:
        fCallDefProc = TRUE; break;
    }

    if (fCallDefProc)
        lResult = DefWindowProc(hWnd, wMsg, wParam, lParam);

    return(lResult);
}

// ****************************************************************

#define GETRANDOM(Min, Max) ((rand() % (int)(((Max)+1) -
    (Min))) + (Min))

#define DEGTORAD(Deg) ((Deg * 3.14159) / 180)

LONG FAR PASCAL BlnkWndProc (HWND hWnd, WORD wMsg, WORD wParam,
        LONG lParam) {
    BOOL fCallDefProc = FALSE, fForceStop = FALSE;
    LONG lResult = 0;
    WORD wXCenter, wYCenter, wCircle, wRadius, wTheta, wInc;
    WORD wRed, wGreen, wBlue;
    RECT rc;
    HPEN hPen, hOldPen;
    HDC hDC;
    MSG msg;

    switch (wMsg) {
        case WM_TIMER:

            // If windows is already visible, animate drawing
            if (!IsWindowVisible(hWnd)) {
```

```
      // Every second, check if the idle time has elapsed.
      // Is system time minus the time of the last user
      // event greater than the number of minutes the user
      // specified?
      if (GetTickCount() - GetLastEventTime() > _wMinutes *
            60000ul) {
         ShowWindow(hWnd, SW_SHOW);
         ShowCursor(0);
      }
      break;
}

// Animate the circle drawing in the blank window
GetWindowRect(hWnd, &rc);

// Select random center point for circle
wXCenter = GETRANDOM(0, rc.right - 1);
wYCenter = GETRANDOM(0, rc.bottom - 1);

// Select random radius length for circle
wRadius = GETRANDOM(rc.right / 20, rc.right - 1);

// Select random theta angle
wInc = GETRANDOM(1, 5);

hDC = GetDC(hWnd);
SetBkMode(hDC, TRANSPARENT);

// Draw circle twice:
// 1st time: Circle is drawn in multicolors
// 2nd time: Circle is draw in all black, effectively
// removing it
for (wCircle = 0; !fForceStop && wCircle < 2; wCircle++)
{
   for (wTheta = 0; wTheta < 360; wTheta += wInc) {

      // Drawing takes a long time, so see if user
      // becomes active again by pressing a mouse button
      // or key on the keyboard
```

```
fForceStop =
    PeekMessage(&msg, hWnd, WM_KEYFIRST, WM_KEYLAST,
        PM_NOYIELD | PM_NOREMOVE) ||
    PeekMessage(&msg, hWnd, WM_LBUTTONDOWN,
        WM_MOUSELAST, PM_NOYIELD | PM_NOREMOVE);

// If either type of event (mouse or keyboard) in
// queue, stop drawing the circle prematurely
if (fForceStop) break;

// Select a random color for spoke of the circle.
// Do not allow a spoke to be BLACK (RGB(0, 0, 0)).
do {
    wRed = GETRANDOM(0, 32);
    wGreen = GETRANDOM(0, 32);
    wBlue = GETRANDOM(0, 32);
} while (wRed == 0 && wGreen == 0 && wBlue == 0);

// Create a pen using a cycling style and the
// random color
hPen = CreatePen((wTheta % 3), 1,
    RGB(wRed * 7, wGreen * 7, wBlue * 7));
hOldPen = SelectObject(hDC, hPen);

// Start at center of the circle and draw the spoke
MoveTo(hDC, wXCenter, wYCenter);
LineTo(hDC,
    (int) (wRadius * cos(DEGTORAD(wTheta))) +
        wXCenter,
    (int) (wRadius * sin(DEGTORAD(wTheta))) +
        wYCenter);

// Restore original pen in hDC and delete the
// created pen
SelectObject(hDC, hOldPen);
DeleteObject(hPen);
}
```

```
            // For the 2nd time the circle is drawn, set the ROP2
            // code R2_BLACK. This causes all of the spokes to be
            // painted black no matter what colors were used to
            // create the pen.
            SetROP2(hDC, R2_BLACK);
         }
         ReleaseDC(hWnd, hDC);
         break;

      case WM_LBUTTONDOWN:
      case WM_MBUTTONDOWN:
      case WM_RBUTTONDOWN:
      case WM_KEYDOWN:
      case WM_SYSKEYDOWN:
         // If any of the above events occur, the user is active
         // and we must show the mouse cursor and hide ourselves
         ShowCursor(1);
         ShowWindow(hWnd, SW_HIDE);
         break;

      default:
         fCallDefProc = TRUE; break;
   }

   if (fCallDefProc)
      lResult = DefWindowProc(hWnd, wMsg, wParam, lParam);

   return(lResult);
}

// ****************************************************************
// This function processes all messages sent to the Preferences
// dialog box

BOOL FAR PASCAL PrefProc (HWND hDlg, WORD wMsg, WORD wParam,
      LONG lParam) {
   BOOL fProcessed = TRUE, fTranslated;
   WORD wMinutes;
```

```
switch (wMsg) {

    case WM_INITDIALOG:
        // The lParam parameter contains the current settings of
        // the _wMinutes variable. This should be shown as the
        // default value.
        SetDlgItemInt(hDlg, ID_MINUTES, (WORD) lParam, FALSE);
        break;

    case WM_COMMAND:
        switch (wParam) {
            case IDOK:
                if (HIWORD(lParam) != BN_CLICKED) break;
                wMinutes =
                    GetDlgItemInt(hDlg, ID_MINUTES, &fTranslated,
                        FALSE);
                if (!fTranslated || wMinutes == 0) {
                    MessageBox(hDlg, "Invalid value for minutes.",
                        _szAppName, MB_OK); break;
                 }
                // Return the new value the user entered
                EndDialog(hDlg, wMinutes);
                break;

            case IDCANCEL:
                if (HIWORD(lParam) != BN_CLICKED) break;
                // Return -1 indicating the user pressed "Cancel"
                EndDialog(hDlg, -1);
                break;

            default:
                break;
        }
        break;

    default:
        fProcessed = FALSE; break;
    }
    return(fProcessed);
}
```

```
// ****************************************************************
// This function processes all messages sent to About dialog box

BOOL FAR PASCAL AboutProc (HWND hDlg, WORD wMsg, WORD wParam,
      LONG lParam) {
   BOOL fProcessed = TRUE;
   char szBuffer[100];

   switch (wMsg) {

      case WM_INITDIALOG:
         // Set version static window to have date and time of
         // compilation
         wsprintf(szBuffer, "%s at %s", (LPSTR) __DATE__,
            (LPSTR) __TIME__);
         SetWindowText(GetDlgItem(hDlg, ID_VERSION), szBuffer);
         break;

      case WM_COMMAND:
         switch (wParam) {
            case IDOK: case IDCANCEL:
               if (HIWORD(lParam) == BN_CLICKED)
                  EndDialog(hDlg, wParam);
               break;

            default:
               break;
         }
         break;

      default:
         fProcessed = FALSE; break;
   }
   return(fProcessed);
}
```

Listing 6-2. SCRNBLNK.DLG dialog-box templates.

```
ABOUT DIALOG LOADONCALL MOVEABLE DISCARDABLE 16, 20, 126, 106
CAPTION "About ScrnBlnk"
STYLE WS_BORDER | WS_CAPTION | WS_DLGFRAME | WS_SYSMENU |
   WS_VISIBLE | WS_POPUP
BEGIN
   CONTROL "ScrnBlnk", -1, "static", SS_ICON | WS_CHILD, 4, 38,
      18, 21
   CONTROL "Screen Blanker", -1, "static", SS_CENTER | WS_CHILD,
      22, 8, 100, 12
   CONTROL "Written by:", -1, "static", SS_CENTER | WS_CHILD, 22,
      20, 100, 12
   CONTROL "Jeffrey M. Richter", -1, "static", SS_CENTER |
      WS_CHILD, 22, 32, 100, 12
   CONTROL "and", -1, "static", SS_CENTER | WS_CHILD, 22, 40,
      100, 8
   CONTROL "Susan Ramee", -1, "static", SS_CENTER | WS_CHILD, 20,
      48, 100, 12
   CONTROL "Version date:", -1, "static", SS_CENTER | WS_CHILD,
      22, 64, 100, 12
   CONTROL "", ID_VERSION, "static", SS_CENTER | WS_CHILD, 22, 76,
      100, 12
   CONTROL "&Ok", 1, "button", BS_DEFPUSHBUTTON | WS_TABSTOP |
      WS_CHILD, 40, 92, 44, 12
END

PREFERENCES DIALOG LOADONCALL MOVEABLE DISCARDABLE 7, 20, 88, 36
CAPTION "Preferences"
STYLE WS_BORDER | WS_CAPTION | WS_DLGFRAME | WS_SYSMENU |
   WS_VISIBLE | WS_POPUP
BEGIN
   CONTROL "&Minutes til blank:", -1, "static", SS_LEFT |
      WS_CHILD, 4, 4, 60, 12
   CONTROL "", ID_MINUTES, "edit", ES_LEFT | WS_BORDER |
      WS_TABSTOP | WS_CHILD, 64, 4, 20, 12
   CONTROL "&Ok", IDOK, "button", BS_DEFPUSHBUTTON | WS_TABSTOP |
      WS_CHILD, 8, 20, 32, 12
   CONTROL "&Cancel", IDCANCEL, "button", BS_PUSHBUTTON |
      WS_TABSTOP | WS_CHILD, 48, 20, 32, 12
END
```

432

Listing 6-3. SCRNBLNK.H application header module.

```
/****************************************************************
Module name: ScrnBlnk.H
Programmer : Jeffrey M. Richter
****************************************************************/

#include "dialog.h"
```

Listing 6-4. SCRNBLNK.DEF ScrnBlnk application definitions file.

```
; Module name: ScrnBlnk.DEF
; Programmer : Jeffrey M. Richter

NAME        ScrnBlnk
DESCRIPTION 'ScrnBlnk: Windows Screen Blanking Application'
STUB        'WinStub.exe'
EXETYPE     WINDOWS
CODE        MOVEABLE DISCARDABLE PRELOAD
DATA        MOVEABLE MULTIPLE PRELOAD
HEAPSIZE    1024
STACKSIZE   4096
EXPORTS
   AppWndProc
   PrefProc
   AboutProc
```

Listing 6-5. DIALOG.H (dialog-box template defines) for ScrnBlnk.

```
#define ID_VERSION 200
#define ID_MINUTES 100
```

Listing 6-6. SCRNBLNK.RC application resource file.

```
/******************************************************************
Module name: ScrnBlnk.RC
Programmer : Jeffrey M. Richter
******************************************************************/

#include <windows.h>

#include "dialog.h"
#include "scrnblnk.dlg"

ScrnBlnk ICON MOVEABLE DISCARDABLE ScrnBlnk.Ico
```

Listing 6-7. MAKEFILE for screen-blanking application.

```
#******************************************************************
#Module name: MAKEFILE
#Programmer : Jeffrey M. Richter
#******************************************************************

PROG = ScrnBlnk
MODEL = S
CFLAGS = -A$(MODEL) -D_WINDOWS -Gcsw2 -W4 -Zlepid -Od
LFLAGS = /NOE/BA/A:16/M/CO/LI/F
LIBS = SB-DLL + $(MODEL)libcew + libw

M1 = $(PROG).obj

ICONS = $(PROG).ico
BITMAPS =
CURSORS =
RESOURCES = $(ICONS) $(BITMAPS) $(CURSORS)

.SUFFIXES: .rc

.rc.res:
    rc -r $*.rc
```

```
$(PROG).Exe: $(M1) $(PROG).Def $(PROG).Res
   link $(LFLAGS) @<<$(PROG).lnk
$(M1)
$(PROG), $(PROG), $(LIBS), $(PROG)
<<
   rc $(PROG).Res

$(PROG).obj:    $*.c dialog.h

$(PROG).res:    $*.rc $*.dlg dialog.h $(RESOURCES)
```

Listing 6-8. SB-DLL.C DLL source module.

```
/****************************************************************
Module name: SB-DLL.C
Programmer : Jeffrey M. Richter
****************************************************************/

#include "..\nowindws.h"
#undef NOHELP
#undef NOKERNEL
#undef NOMEMMGR
#undef NOUSER
#undef NOWH
#include <windows.h>

#include "SB-DLL.h"

static HANDLE _hInstance = NULL;      // our instance handle

static FARPROC _fnNextJrnlRcrdHookFunc = NULL;
static DWORD _dwLastEventTime = 0;

DWORD FAR PASCAL JrnlRcrdHookFunc (int nCode, WORD wParam,
   LPEVENTMSGMSG lpEventMsg);

BOOL FAR PASCAL LibMain (HANDLE hModule, WORD wDataSeg,
     WORD cbHeapSize, LPSTR lpCmdLine) {
   _hInstance = hModule;
```

```
      if (cbHeapSize != 0) UnlockData(0);    // Let data segment move
      return(TRUE);    // return TRUE if initialization is successful
}

int FAR PASCAL WEP (int nSystemExit) {
   switch (nSystemExit) {
      case WEP_SYSTEM_EXIT:    // System is shutting down
         break;
      case WEP_FREE_DLL:       // Usage count is zero
         break;
   }
   return(1);                            // WEP function successful
}

void FAR PASCAL InstallJrnlHook (BOOL fInstall) {
   if (fInstall) {
      _fnNextJrnlRcrdHookFunc =
         SetWindowsHook(WH_JOURNALRECORD,
            (FARPROC) JrnlRcrdHookFunc);
      _dwLastEventTime = GetTickCount();
   } else {
      UnhookWindowsHook(WH_JOURNALRECORD,
         (FARPROC) JrnlRcrdHookFunc);
      _fnNextJrnlRcrdHookFunc = NULL;
      _dwLastEventTime = NULL;
   }
}

DWORD FAR PASCAL GetLastEventTime (void) {
   return(_dwLastEventTime); }

DWORD FAR PASCAL JrnlRcrdHookFunc (int nCode, WORD wParam,
      LPEVENTMSGMSG lpEventMsg) {
   BOOL fCallDefProc = FALSE;
   DWORD dwResult = 0;
   switch (nCode) {

      case HC_ACTION:
         _dwLastEventTime = lpEventMsg->time;
         fCallDefProc = TRUE;
         break;
```

```
    case HC_SYSMODALON:
    case HC_SYSMODALOFF:
    default:
        fCallDefProc = TRUE;
        break;
}

if ((nCode < 0) || (fCallDefProc && (_fnNextJrnlRcrdHookFunc !=
        NULL)))
    dwResult = DefHookProc(nCode, wParam, (LONG) lpEventMsg,
        &_fnNextJrnlRcrdHookFunc);

return(dwResult);
}
```

Listing 6-9. SB-DLL.H DLL header module.

```
/****************************************************************
Module name: SB-DLL.H
Programmer : Jeffrey M. Richter
****************************************************************/

void FAR PASCAL  InstallJrnlHook (BOOL fInstall);

DWORD FAR PASCAL GetLastEventTime (void);
```

Listing 6-10. SB-DLL.DEF DLL definitions file.

```
; Module name: SB-DLL.DEF
; Programmer : Jeffrey M. Richter

LIBRARY     SB-DLL
DESCRIPTION 'Screen Blanker Dynamic-link library'
EXETYPE     WINDOWS
STUB        'WinStub.Exe'
CODE        NONDISCARDABLE FIXED PRELOAD
DATA        MOVEABLE PRELOAD SINGLE
```

437

```
HEAPSIZE    0
EXPORTS
   WEP     @1     RESIDENTNAME
   JrnlRcrdHookFunc
   InstallJrnlHook
   GetLastEventTime
```

Listing 6-11. SB-DLL.RC DLL resource file.

```
// No resources
```

Listing 6-12. SB-DLL.MKF (MAKEFILE for screen-blanking DLL).

```
#********************************************************************
#Module name: SB-DLL.MKF
#Programmer : Jeffrey M. Richter
#********************************************************************

PROG = SB-DLL
MODEL = S
CFLAGS = -A$(MODEL)w -D_WINDOWS -D_WINDLL -Gcsw2 -W4 -Zlepid -Od
LFLAGS = /NOE/BA/A:16/M/CO/LI/F
#LIBS = $(MODEL)nocrtd + $(MODEL)dllcew + libw
LIBS = $(MODEL)dllcew + libw

M1 = $(PROG).obj

ICONS =
BITMAPS =
CURSORS =
RESOURCES = $(ICONS) $(BITMAPS) $(CURSORS)

.SUFFIXES: .rc

.rc.res:
   rc -r $*.rc
```

```
$(PROG).DLL: $(M1) $(PROG).Def
   link $(LFLAGS) @<<$(PROG).lnk
\MSC\LibEntry.obj $(M1)
$(PROG).DLL, $(PROG), $(LIBS), $(PROG)
<<
   rc $(PROG).DLL
   implib $(PROG).LIB $(PROG).DEF

$(PROG).obj:    $*.c $*.h

$(PROG).res:    $*.rc $*.h $(RESOURCES)
```

The Screen Blanker initializes by registering two window classes, *ScrnBlnk* and *ScrnBlnkPopup*. The ScrnBlnk class is the application's main window. This window is created as an icon and refuses to be opened by the user. (This is done by intercepting *WM_QUERYOPEN* and returning zero.) The main window serves as an indicator to the user that the Screen Blanker is loaded and allows the user to select options from the application's system menu. During *WM_CREATE* message processing, two menu items are added to the system menu: "Preferences" and "About." The "Preferences" menu presents a dialog box that allows the user to change the number of minutes that Windows must be idle before blanking the screen (the default is five minutes). After the menu items have been appended, the *InstallJrnlHook* function is called, passing TRUE as its parameter. This function is in the SB-DLL.C file:

```
static FARPROC _fnNextJrnlRcrdHookFunc = NULL;
static DWORD _dwLastEventTime = NULL;
.
.
.
void FAR PASCAL InstallJrnlHook (BOOL fInstall) {
   if (fInstall) {
     _fnNextJrnlRcrdHookFunc =
        SetWindowsHook(WH_JOURNALRECORD, (FARPROC)
           JrnlRcrdHookFunc);
     _dwLastEventTime = GetTickCount();
   } else {
```

439

```
        UnhookWindowsHook(WH_JOURNALRECORD, (FARPROC)
            JrnlRcrdHookFunc);
        _fnNextJrnlRcrdHookFunc = NULL;
        _dwLastEventTime = NULL;
    }
}
```

Because the hook is being installed (*fInstall* is TRUE), this function sets the *WH_JOURNALRECORD* hook into the chain and initializes the *_dwLastEventTime* variable equal to the current system time. This global variable is updated every time a system event is passed to the *WH_JOURNALRECORD* filter function. This function is shown below:

```
DWORD FAR PASCAL JrnlRcrdHookFunc (int nCode, WORD wParam,
    LPEVENTMSGMSG lpEventMsg) {
  BOOL fCallDefProc = FALSE; DWORD dwResult = 0;
  switch (nCode) {

    case HC_ACTION:
        _dwLastEventTime = lpEventMsg->time;
        fCallDefProc = TRUE;
        break;

    case HC_SYSMODALON:
    case HC_SYSMODALOFF:
    default:
        fCallDefProc = TRUE;
        break;
    }
  if ((nCode < 0) || (fCallDefProc && _fnNextJrnlRcrdHookFunc !=
        NULL)))
     dwResult = DefHookProc(nCode, wParam, (LONG) lpEventMsg,
        (FARPROC FAR *) &_fnNextJrnlRcrdHookFunc);
  return(dwResult);
}
```

Notice that the last parameter to the filter function is of the *LPEVENTMSGMSG* type instead of *LONG*. This is just to make the coding of the function a little simpler.

440

After the hook has been installed, the Screen Blanker creates a *ScrnBlnkPopup* window with the following call:

```
_hWndBlnk = CreateWindow(_szBlnkClass, NULL,
    WS_POPUP, 0, 0, GetSystemMetrics(SM_CXSCREEN),
    GetSystemMetrics(SM_CYSCREEN), NULL, NULL, hInstance, 0);
```

As you can see, the window created has the dimension of the entire screen. You will also notice that the *WS_POPUP* style is used and that no parent window is specified (this is called an unowned pop-up window). The following discussion explains why the Screen Blanker needs an unowned pop-up.

The logic that controls when the Screen Blanker should blank the screen is in the processing of the *WM_TIMER* messages in the *BlnkWndProc* window procedure:

```
switch (wMsg) {
    case WM_TIMER:
        if (!IsWindowVisible(hWnd)) {
            if (GetTickCount() - GetLastEventTime() > _wMinutes *
                    60000ul) {
                ShowWindow(hWnd, SW_SHOW);
                ShowCursor(0);
            }
            break;
        }
        // Draw in the blank window
        .
        .
        .
```

We can determine whether the *ScrnBlnkPopup* window is already visible by calling *IsWindowVisible*. If this function returns TRUE, we draw some circles in the blank window. But if *IsWindowVisible* returns FALSE, we have to see if the user has been idle for at least the number of minutes specified in the *_wMinutes* variable. We examine the last time an event occurred by calling the *GetLastEventTime* function in SB-DLL.C. This function simply returns the value of the *_dwLastEventTime* variable contained in the data segment of the DLL.

441

If the user has been idle for the requested period, the *ScrnBlnkPopup* window is made visible via a call to *ShowWindow* and the mouse cursor is hidden. When the window appears, Windows sends a *WM_ERASEBKGND* message to its window procedure. Because this message is not intercepted, it is passed to *DefWindowProc*, which examines the value of the *hbrBackground* member for the registered class and paints the window's background in that color. *ScrnBlnkPopup* sets the *hbrBackground* member of the *WNDCLASS* structure as follows:

```
WndClass.hbrBackground = GetStockObject(BLACK_BRUSH);
```

Windows will make the entire screen black when the window is visible.

Now we can study why the window had to be an unowned pop-up. When a window is a child or an owned pop-up, Windows prohibits that window from being visible when its parent or owner is an icon. Since the application's main window is always an icon, Windows would never allow the *ScrnBlnkPopup* window to be seen if it weren't an unowned pop-up.

The user can continue to work with Windows by pressing a key or mouse button. When one of these events occurs, the following code fragment executes:

```
case WM_LBUTTONDOWN:
case WM_MBUTTONDOWN:
case WM_RBUTTONDOWN:
case WM_KEYDOWN:
case WM_SYSKEYDOWN:
   ShowCursor(1);
   ShowWindow(hWnd, SW_HIDE);
   break;
```

This causes the mouse cursor to be shown again and hides the *ScrnBlnkPopup* window. When this window is hidden, the windows beneath it are no longer obscured and Windows automatically sends *WM_PAINT* messages to all the visible windows.

You may have noticed that the *PeekMessage* function is called twice during the processing of the *WM_TIMER* message. If the user presses a mouse button while the drawing algorithm is still drawing, the pop-up window won't be hidden until the drawing cycle is complete. To solve this problem, the *PeekMessage* function is called in the drawing loop:

```
fForceStop =
   PeekMessage(&msg, hWnd, WM_KEYFIRST, WM_KEYLAST,
      PM_NOYIELD | PM_NOREMOVE) ||
   PeekMessage(&msg, hWnd, WM_LBUTTONDOWN, WM_MOUSELAST,
      PM_NOYIELD | PM_NOREMOVE);
if (fForceStop) break;
```

If a keyboard or mouse event is found, *fForceStop* is set to TRUE and the drawing algorithm is prematurely terminated.

The Echo Application (a Macro Recorder)

The Echo sample application discussed here shows how to implement an input event recorder using the *WH_JOURNALRECORD* and *WH_JOURNAL-PLAYBACK* hooks. The user starts recording events by choosing the "Record" option from the application's Macro menu. At this point, every mouse movement and keystroke is recorded until the user selects the "Stop" option. When the user has stopped the recorder, the "Playback" option will play back the recorded events.

This application also shows how the F1 key can be intercepted when it is sent to a dialog box so that help information can be displayed using a *WH_MSGFILTER* hook. When the user presses the F1 key while the About dialog box is displayed, the Echo application calls up the Windows help engine.

Recording and Playing Events. All the procedures for recording and playing back events can be found in the RECORDER.C file. This module consists of three functions: *Recorder*, *JrnlRecHookFunc*, and *JrnlPlybkHookFunc*. The Recorder function is the controlling function for all the recorder's operations. The following table shows the values that may be passed to the Recorder:

Record mode	*wParam*	*lParam*	Return value
RM_STARTRECORD	Not used.	The low-order word contains the window handle that will be notified when the recording stops. The high-order word contains the message that should be sent to this window.	*REC_ACTIVE* if the recorder is currently recording or playing. *REC_NOMEMORY* if insufficient memory exists to begin recording. *REC_OK* if recording has started successfully.
RM_STOPRECORD	Not used.	Not used.	*REC_INACTIVE* if the recorder was not recording. *REC_OK* if recording stopped successfully.
RM_STARTPLAY	Global memory handle containing recorded events.	The low-order word contains the window handle that will be notified when the playback stops. The high-order word contains the message that should be sent to this window.	*REC_ACTIVE* if recorder is currently recording or playing. *REC_NOEVENTS* if there are no events in the memory block. *REC_OK* if playback started successfully.
RM_STOPPLAY	Not used.	Not used.	*REC_INACTIVE* if recording is not currently playing. *REC_OK* if playback stopped successfully.

Notice that the *RM_STARTRECORD* and *RM_STARTPLAY* modes expect a window handle and a message number passed in as the *lParam* parameter. The Recorder saves this information in static variables. When the Recorder stops recording or playing, it sends the specified message to the specified window to notify it that it has stopped. The *wParam* parameter of the message will then contain the global memory handle containing the recorded events. The *lParam* parameter contains either *REC_OK*, *REC_TOOMANY*, or *REC_SYSMODALON*.

The table below shows the four ways journal recording can be stopped and the value that will be sent to the specified window in the *lParam* parameter:

Method of stopping the Recorder while recording	Value in *lParam* parameter
When the user chooses the "Stop" option from the Macro menu in the application.	*REC_OK*
When the *HC_ACTION* hook code is sent to the *JrnlRecHookFunc* function, the *GlobalReAlloc* function is called to increase the size of the memory block. If there is insufficient memory, the Recorder is stopped.	*REC_NOMEMORY*
When the *HC_ACTION* hook code is sent to the *JrnlRecHookFunc* function, a check is made to see if more than 65,535 events have been placed in the memory block. If so, the Recorder is stopped.	*REC_TOOMANY*
When the *HC_SYSMODALOFF* hook code is sent to the *JrnlRecHookFunc* function, the Recorder is stopped.	*REC_SYSMODALON*

If the *JrnlRecHookFunc* function receives the *HC_SYSMODALON* hook code, it sets a static variable, *fPause,* to TRUE. When this variable is TRUE, the *JrnlRecHookFunc* function ignores all *HC_ACTION* hook codes. Once the system modal dialog box is removed, an *HC_SYSMODALOFF* hook code is sent to the filter function. This stops the Recorder and sends the *REC_SYSMODALON* identifier to the window handle specified when recording started.

To notify the user that Echo has stopped recording events, a message box is displayed. However, the appearance of a system modal dialog box usually means that something critical has happened to the Windows system. Echo should not display its message box until the user has dealt with the system modal dialog box. This is why the Recorder notifies the application that it has stopped recording after the system modal dialog box has been destroyed. This same approach is used when a system modal dialog box appears during playback.

When the Recorder stops playing, it sends the specified message to the specified window to notify it that it has stopped. If the Recorder has stopped playing, the *wParam* parameter of the message will contain zero. The *lParam* parameter contains either *REC_OK* or *REC_SYSMODALON*. The table below shows the two methods used to stop playing back the events and the value that will be sent to the specified window in the *lParam* parameter:

Method of stopping the Recorder during playback	Value in *lParam* parameter
When the *HC_SKIP* hook code is sent to the *JrnlPlybkHookFunc* function and all the events in the memory block have been played, the player is stopped.	*REC_OK*
When the *HC_SYSMODALOFF* hook code is sent to the *JrnlPlybkHookFunc* function, the player is stopped.	*REC_SYSMODALON*

The user-defined message that Echo passes to the Recorder function is *USER_RECORDER*. Echo monitors this message so it can set the static *fRecording* and *fPlaying* flags, which are used to determine which menu items should be disabled in the Macro menu. The processing for this message is also used to display message boxes telling the user why recording or playing has been halted.

Requesting Help. Aside from recording and playing back input events, the Echo application also shows how to detect when the user has pressed a key during the processing of a dialog box. After this has been detected, the Windows *WinHelp* function can be called to display help information to the user.

In the Echo application, this is demonstrated when the user selects the "About..." option from the File menu. The code to display the About box appears below:

```
case WM_COMMAND:
    switch (wParam) {
        .
        .
        .
        case IDM_ABOUT:
            fpMsgFilter = MakeProcInstance(
                (FARPROC) MsgFilterHookFunc, _hInstance);
            SetWindowsHook(WH_MSGFILTER, fpMsgFilter);

            fpDlgProc =
                MakeProcInstance(AboutProc, _hInstance);
            DialogBox(_hInstance, "About", hWnd, fpDlgProc);
            FreeProcInstance(fpDlgProc);

            UnhookWindowsHook(WH_MSGFILTER, fpMsgFilter);
            FreeProcInstance(fpMsgFilter);

            break;
```

This code installs a *WH_MSGFILTER* function just before the dialog box is displayed and removes the hook immediately after the dialog box is destroyed. Because the *WH_MSGFILTER* hook is task-specific, the filter function exists in the application's code and is not required to be in a fixed-code segment of a DLL. However, when the filter function is in an application, we must use *MakeProcInstance* to create a procedural instance for the function and then pass this address into *SetWindowsHook* and *UnhookWindowsHook* when installing and removing the hook. After the hook is installed, Windows will call *MsgFilterHookFunc* whenever

447

a message is about to be processed by the About dialog box. The code for the
WH_MSGFILTER filter function is shown below:

```
static FARPROC _fnNextMsgFilterHookFunc = NULL;

DWORD FAR PASCAL MsgFilterHookFunc (int nCode, WORD wParam,
        LPMSG lpMsg) {
    BOOL fCallDefProc = FALSE;
    DWORD dwResult = 0;

    switch (nCode) {

        case MSGF_DIALOGBOX:
            if ((lpMsg->message != WM_KEYDOWN) ||
                (lpMsg->wParam != VK_F1)) {
                fCallDefProc = TRUE;
                break;
            }

            // WM_KEYDOWN and key is the F1 key
            WinHelp(_hWndApp, NULL, HELP_HELPONHELP, NULL);
            dwResult = 1;
            break;

        case MSGF_MENU:
        case MSGF_SCROLLBAR:
        case MSGF_NEXTWINDOW:
        default:
            fCallDefProc = TRUE;
            break;
    }

    if ((nCode < 0) || (fCallDefProc &&
        (_fnNextMsgFilterHookFunc != NULL)))
        dwResult = DefHookProc(nCode, wParam, (LONG) lpMsg,
            &_fnNextMsgFilterHookFunc);

    return(dwResult);
}
```

Since we are only interested in doing any work when the *MSGF_DIALOGBOX* hook code is received, the remainder of the hook codes are simply processed by calling *DefHookProc*. If the hook code is *MSGF_DIALOGBOX*, we must ensure that the message about to be processed by the dialog box is *WM_KEYDOWN* and that the virtual key code is *VK_F1*. If these conditions are met, the filter function calls the *WinHelp* function.

Because this is only a simulation, no useful help is displayed; only the help information on how to use help is displayed. The Windows help engine identifies the application requesting help by the window handle that is passed to the *WinHelp* function as the first parameter. The first parameter to *WinHelp* is therefore the handle to the application's main window and not the handle to the dialog box, *lpMsg->hwnd*. When the Echo application terminates, the processing for the *WM_CLOSE* message calls the *WinHelp* function again:

```
case WM_CLOSE:
    WinHelp(hWnd, NULL, HELP_QUIT, NULL);
```

The first parameter to this call to *WinHelp* is the window handle that was used in the filter function. All applications that use the Windows help engine should call *WinHelp* when they terminate and pass it the *HELP_QUIT* identifier. This informs the help engine that the application will no longer require help and instructs it to terminate itself along with the application.

Figure 6-8. ECHO.ICO.

449

Listing 6-13. ECHO.C application source module.

```
/*****************************************************************
Module name: Echo.C
Programmer : Jeffrey M. Richter
*****************************************************************/

#include "..\nowindws.h"
#undef NOCOLOR
#undef NOCTLMGR
#undef NOHELP
#undef NOKERNEL
#undef NOMB
#undef NOMEMMGR
#undef NOMENUS
#undef NOMSG
#undef NOSHOWWINDOW
#undef NOUSER
#undef NOVIRTUALKEYCODES
#undef NOWH
#undef NOWINMESSAGES
#undef NOWINSTYLES
#include <windows.h>

#include "Echo.h"
#include "Recorder.h"


//***************************************************************
char _szAppName[] = "Echo";

HANDLE _hInstance = NULL;  // our instance handle
HWND _hWndApp = NULL;      // main application's window handle

LONG FAR PASCAL AppWndProc (HWND hWnd, WORD wMsg, WORD wParam,
   LONG lParam);
BOOL FAR PASCAL AboutProc (HWND hDlg, WORD wMsg, WORD wParam,
   LONG lParam);
DWORD FAR PASCAL MsgFilterHookFunc (int nCode, WORD wParam,
   LPMSG lpMsg);
```

```
int PASCAL WinMain (HANDLE hInstance, HANDLE hPrevInstance,
      LPSTR lpszCmdLine, int nCmdShow) {
  WNDCLASS WndClass;
  MSG msg;

  _hInstance = hInstance;

  WndClass.style          = 0;
  WndClass.lpfnWndProc    = AppWndProc;
  WndClass.cbClsExtra     = 0;
  WndClass.cbWndExtra     = 0;
  WndClass.hInstance      = hInstance;
  WndClass.hIcon          = LoadIcon(hInstance, _szAppName);
  WndClass.hCursor        = LoadCursor(NULL, IDC_ARROW);
  WndClass.hbrBackground  = COLOR_WINDOW + 1;
  WndClass.lpszMenuName   = _szAppName;
  WndClass.lpszClassName  = _szAppName;
  RegisterClass(&WndClass);

  // Create application window; store in global variable
  _hWndApp = CreateWindow(_szAppName, _szAppName,
    WS_OVERLAPPEDWINDOW, CW_USEDEFAULT, SW_SHOW, CW_USEDEFAULT,
    CW_USEDEFAULT, NULL, NULL, hInstance, 0);

  if (_hWndApp == NULL) return(0);
  ShowWindow(_hWndApp, nCmdShow);
  UpdateWindow(_hWndApp);

  while (GetMessage(&msg, NULL, 0, 0)) {
     TranslateMessage(&msg);
     DispatchMessage(&msg);
  }
  return(0);
}

// Window-defined message sent by the Recorder function in the
// RECORDER.C DLL when recording or playing of events is stopped
#define USER_RECORDER (WM_USER + 0)

LONG FAR PASCAL AppWndProc (HWND hWnd, WORD wMsg, WORD wParam,
      LONG lParam) {
```

```
static BOOL fRecording = FALSE, fPlaying = FALSE;
static GLOBALHANDLE hMacro;  // Global handle containing
                 // recorded events
BOOL fCallDefProc = FALSE;
LONG lResult = 0;
FARPROC fpMsgFilter, fpDlgProc;
RECRESULT RecResult = REC_OK;
char *szRecMsg = NULL;

switch (wMsg) {

   case WM_DESTROY:
      // Close the Windows help engine
      WinHelp(hWnd, NULL, HELP_QUIT, NULL);
      PostQuitMessage(0);
      break;

   case USER_RECORDER:
      // Message sent when recording or playing is stopped
      if (wParam == 0) {      // Playing stopped
         fPlaying = FALSE;
         if ((RECRESULT) lParam == REC_SYSMODALON)
            MessageBox(hWnd, "System Modal Dialog Box - Playing
               Halted", _szAppName, MB_SYSTEMMODAL |
               MB_ICONHAND | MB_OK);
         break;
      }

      // Recording stopped
      // wParam = GLOBALHANDLE of block, lParam = RECRESULT
      fRecording = FALSE;
      hMacro = wParam;

      if ((RECRESULT) lParam == REC_TOOMANY)
         MessageBox(NULL, "Out of memory", _szAppName,
            MB_SYSTEMMODAL | MB_ICONHAND | MB_OK);

      if ((RECRESULT) lParam == REC_SYSMODALON)
         MessageBox(hWnd, "System Modal Dialog Box - Recording
            Halted", _szAppName, MB_SYSTEMMODAL | MB_ICONHAND |
            MB_OK);
```

```
        break;

case WM_INITMENU:
    // User is working with the menu; enable/disable options
    EnableMenuItem(GetMenu(hWnd), IDM_STARTRECORD,
        MF_BYCOMMAND | ((fRecording || fPlaying) ? MF_GRAYED :
            MF_ENABLED));
    EnableMenuItem(GetMenu(hWnd), IDM_STOPRECORD,
        MF_BYCOMMAND | (fRecording ? MF_ENABLED : MF_GRAYED));
    EnableMenuItem(GetMenu(hWnd), IDM_STARTPLAYBACK,
        MF_BYCOMMAND | ((fRecording || fPlaying || hMacro ==
        NULL) ? MF_GRAYED : MF_ENABLED));
    break;

case WM_COMMAND:
    switch (wParam) {

    case IDM_EXIT:
        SendMessage(hWnd, WM_CLOSE, 0, 0);
        break;

    case IDM_ABOUT:
        // Create procedural instance for task-specific filter
        // function
        fpMsgFilter =
            MakeProcInstance((FARPROC) MsgFilterHookFunc,
                _hInstance);
        SetWindowsHook(WH_MSGFILTER, fpMsgFilter);

        fpDlgProc = MakeProcInstance(AboutProc, _hInstance);
        DialogBox(_hInstance, "About", hWnd, fpDlgProc);
        FreeProcInstance(fpDlgProc);

        // Remove the filter function from the chain
        UnhookWindowsHook(WH_MSGFILTER, fpMsgFilter);
        FreeProcInstance(fpMsgFilter);

        break;
```

453

```
  case IDM_STARTRECORD:
     // If a macro was already recorded, free it
     if (hMacro != NULL) GlobalFree(hMacro);

     fRecording = TRUE;

     // Last parameter is handle to this window and message
     // that should be sent when recording is stopped
     RecResult = Recorder(RM_STARTRECORD, 0,
        MAKELONG(hWnd, USER_RECORDER));
     break;

  case IDM_STOPRECORD:
     RecResult = Recorder(RM_STOPRECORD, 0, 0);
     break;

  case IDM_STARTPLAYBACK:
     fPlaying = TRUE;

     // Last parameter is handle to this window and message
     // that should be sent when playing is stopped
     RecResult = Recorder(RM_STARTPLAY, hMacro,
        MAKELONG(hWnd, USER_RECORDER));
     break;

  default:
     break;
  }

// Inform user if an error occurred with the recorder
switch (RecResult) {
  case REC_ACTIVE:
     szRecMsg = "Recorder already recording/playing.";
     break;

  case REC_INACTIVE:
     szRecMsg = "Recorder already stopped.";
     break;

  case REC_NOMEMORY:
```

```
                szRecMsg =
                  "Insufficient memory to start recording.";
                break;

              case REC_NOEVENTS:
                szRecMsg = "No events to playback.";
                break;
          }

          if (szRecMsg != NULL)
            MessageBox(hWnd, szRecMsg, _szAppName,
              MB_OK | MB_ICONINFORMATION);

          break;

        default:
          fCallDefProc = TRUE; break;
    }

    if (fCallDefProc)
      lResult = DefWindowProc(hWnd, wMsg, wParam, lParam);

    return(lResult);
}

// *******************************************************************

static FARPROC _fnNextMsgFilterHookFunc = NULL;

DWORD FAR PASCAL MsgFilterHookFunc (int nCode, WORD wParam,
      LPMSG lpMsg) {
  BOOL fCallDefProc = FALSE;
  DWORD dwResult = 0;

  switch (nCode) {

    case MSGF_DIALOGBOX:
      // Message is for the About dialog box because we know
      // that this is the only dialog box created by this
      // application
```

```
            if (lpMsg->message != WM_KEYDOWN || lpMsg->wParam !=
                VK_F1) {
              fCallDefProc = TRUE;
              break;
            }

            // Message is WM_KEYDOWN and key is the F1 key;
            // display help
            WinHelp(_hWndApp, NULL, HELP_HELPONHELP, NULL);
            dwResult = 1;      // Tell Windows we processed the message
            break;

         case MSGF_MENU:
         case MSGF_SCROLLBAR:
         case MSGF_NEXTWINDOW:
         default:
            fCallDefProc = TRUE;
            break;
      }

      if ((nCode < 0) || (fCallDefProc &&
          (_fnNextMsgFilterHookFunc != NULL)))
         dwResult = DefHookProc(nCode, wParam, (LONG) lpMsg,
            &_fnNextMsgFilterHookFunc);

      return (dwResult);
}

// *************************************************************
// This function processes all messages sent to About dialog box

BOOL FAR PASCAL AboutProc (HWND hDlg, WORD wMsg, WORD wParam,
      LONG lParam) {
   BOOL fProcessed = TRUE;
   char szBuffer[100];

   switch (wMsg) {

      case WM_INITDIALOG:
         // Set version static window to have date and time of
         // compilation
```

```
        wsprintf(szBuffer, "%s at %s", (LPSTR) __DATE__,
          (LPSTR) __TIME__);
        SetWindowText(GetDlgItem(hDlg, ID_VERSION), szBuffer);
        break;

    case WM_COMMAND:
      switch (wParam) {
        case IDOK:
        case IDCANCEL:
          if (HIWORD(lParam) == BN_CLICKED)
            EndDialog(hDlg, wParam);
          break;

        default:
          break;
      }
      break;

    default:
      fProcessed = FALSE; break;
  }
  return(fProcessed);
}
```

Listing 6-14. ECHO.H application header module.

```
/******************************************************************
Module name: Echo.H
Programmer : Jeffrey M. Richter
******************************************************************/

#include "dialog.h"

#define IDM_ABOUT          100
#define IDM_EXIT           101
#define IDM_STARTRECORD    102
#define IDM_STOPRECORD     103
#define IDM_STARTPLAYBACK  104
```

Listing 6-15. ECHO.DLG dialog-box templates.

```
ABOUT DIALOG LOADONCALL MOVEABLE DISCARDABLE 16, 20, 126, 92
CAPTION "About Echo"
STYLE WS_BORDER | WS_CAPTION | WS_DLGFRAME | WS_SYSMENU |
   WS_VISIBLE | WS_POPUP
BEGIN
   CONTROL "Echo", -1, "static", SS_ICON | WS_CHILD, 4, 16, 18, 21
   CONTROL "Echo", -1, "static", SS_CENTER | WS_CHILD, 22, 8,
      100, 12
   CONTROL "Written by:", -1, "static", SS_CENTER | WS_CHILD, 22,
      20, 100, 12
   CONTROL "Jeffrey M. Richter", -1, "static", SS_CENTER |
      WS_CHILD, 22, 32, 100, 12
   CONTROL "Version date:", -1, "static", SS_CENTER | WS_CHILD,
      22, 48, 100, 12
   CONTROL "", ID_VERSION, "static", SS_CENTER | WS_CHILD, 22, 60,
      100, 12
   CONTROL "&OK", 1, "button", BS_DEFPUSHBUTTON | WS_TABSTOP |
      WS_CHILD, 40, 76, 44, 12
END
```

Listing 6-16. ECHO.DEF application definitions file.

```
; Module name: Echo.DEF
; Programmer : Jeffrey M. Richter

NAME         Echo
DESCRIPTION  'Echo: Windows Recorder Application'
STUB         'WinStub.exe'
EXETYPE      WINDOWS
CODE         MOVEABLE DISCARDABLE PRELOAD
DATA         MOVEABLE MULTIPLE PRELOAD
HEAPSIZE     1024
STACKSIZE    4096
EXPORTS
   AppWndProc
   AboutProc
   MsgFilterHookFunc
```

Listing 6-17. DIALOG.H (dialog-box template defines).

```
#define ID_VERSION    100
```

Listing 6-18. ECHO.RC application resource file.

```
/*******************************************************************
Module name: Echo.RC
Programmer : Jeffrey M. Richter
*******************************************************************/

#include <windows.h>

#include "echo.h"
#include "echo.dlg"

Echo ICON MOVEABLE DISCARDABLE Echo.Ico

Echo MENU
BEGIN
   POPUP "&File"
   BEGIN
     MENUITEM "&About...",      IDM_ABOUT
     MENUITEM "E&xit",          IDM_EXIT
   END

   POPUP "&Macro"
   BEGIN
     MENUITEM "&Record",        IDM_STARTRECORD
     MENUITEM "&Stop",          IDM_STOPRECORD
     MENUITEM "&Playback",      IDM_STARTPLAYBACK
   END
END
```

Listing 6-19. MAKEFILE for Echo application.

```
#************************************************************
#Module name : MAKEFILE
#Programmer : Jeffrey M. Richter
#************************************************************

PROG = Echo
MODEL = S
CFLAGS = -A$(MODEL) -D_WINDOWS -Gcsw2 -W4 -Zlepid -Od
LFLAGS = /NOE/BA/A:16/M/CO/LI/F
LIBS = $(MODEL)libcew + libw + Recorder

M1 = $(PROG).obj

ICONS = $(PROG).ico
BITMAPS =
CURSORS =
RESOURCES = $(ICONS) $(BITMAPS) $(CURSORS)

.SUFFIXES: .rc

.rc.res:
   rc -r $*.rc

$(PROG).Exe: $(M1) $(PROG).Def $(PROG).Res
   link $(LFLAGS) @<<$(PROG).lnk
$(M1)
$(PROG), $(PROG), $(LIBS), $(PROG)
<<
   rc $(PROG).Res

$(PROG).obj:   $*.c $*.h dialog.h

$(PROG).res:   $*.rc $*.h $*.dlg dialog.h $(RESOURCES)
```

Listing 6-20. RECORDER.C DLL source module.

```c
/*******************************************************************
Module name: Recorder.C
Programmer : Jeffrey M. Richter
*******************************************************************/

#include "..\nowindws.h"
#undef NOCOLOR
#undef NOKERNEL
#undef NOMEMMGR
#undef NOMSG
#undef NOSHOWWINDOW
#undef NOUSER
#undef NOWH
#undef NOWINMESSAGES
#undef NOWINSTYLES
#include <windows.h>
#include "Recorder.h"

//*****************************************************************
static FARPROC _fnNextJrnlHookFunc = NULL;
static GLOBALHANDLE _hMemEvents = NULL;
static RECRESULT _PrematureHalt = REC_OK;

DWORD FAR PASCAL JrnlRecHookFunc (int nCode, WORD wParam,
   LPEVENTMSGMSG lpEventMsg);
DWORD FAR PASCAL JrnlPlybkHookFunc (int nCode, WORD wParam,
   LPEVENTMSGMSG lpEventMsg);

// Statistical information that appears at the beginning of the
// memory block
typedef struct {
   WORD wNumEvents, wNumEventsPlayed;
   DWORD dwStartTime;
} RECORDSTAT, FAR *LPRECORDSTAT;
```

```
BOOL FAR PASCAL LibMain (HANDLE hModule, WORD wDataSeg,
      WORD cbHeapSize, LPSTR lpCmdLine) {
   if (cbHeapSize != 0) UnlockData(0);     // Let data segment move
   return(TRUE);     // Return TRUE if initialization is successful
}

int FAR PASCAL WEP (int nSystemExit) {
   switch (nSystemExit) {
      case WEP_SYSTEM_EXIT:       // System is shutting down
         break;
      case WEP_FREE_DLL:       // Usage count is zero
         break;
   }
   return(1);                       // WEP function successful
}

RECRESULT FAR PASCAL Recorder (RECORDMODE RecordMode, WORD wParam,
      LONG lParam) {
   static HWND hWndNotify = NULL;
   static WORD wMsgNotify = WM_NULL;
   static RECORDMODE LastRecordMode = -1;
   RECRESULT RecResult = REC_OK;
   WORD wNumEvents;
   LPRECORDSTAT lpRecordStat;
   LPEVENTMSGMSG lpEvent;

   switch (RecordMode) {

      case RM_STARTRECORD:
         // wParam: Not used
         // LOWORD(lParam): hWnd to send stop msg to
         // HIWORD(lParam): Message to send to hWnd
         // Returns: REC_ACTIVE, REC_NOMEMORY, REC_OK

         if (_hMemEvents) { RecResult = REC_ACTIVE;
            break; }

         // Save information so it can be used by RM_STOPRECORD
         hWndNotify = (HWND) LOWORD(lParam);
         wMsgNotify = (WORD) HIWORD(lParam);
```

```
    // Assume the recording will be stopped by the user
    _PrematureHalt = REC_OK;

    // Allocate memory block to hold the statistical data
    _hMemEvents = GlobalAlloc(GMEM_MOVEABLE,
        sizeof(RECORDSTAT));
    if (_hMemEvents == NULL) { RecResult = REC_NOMEMORY;
        break; }

    // Initialize the statistical data
    lpRecordStat = (LPRECORDSTAT) GlobalLock(_hMemEvents);
    lpRecordStat->wNumEvents = lpRecordStat->wNumEventsPlayed
        = 0;
    GlobalUnlock(_hMemEvents);

    // Turn on the event recording
    _fnNextJrnlHookFunc =
        SetWindowsHook(WH_JOURNALRECORD,
            (FARPROC) JrnlRecHookFunc);

    RecResult = REC_OK;
    break;

case RM_STOPRECORD:
    // wParam: Not used
    // lParam: Not used
    // Returns: REC_INACTIVE, REC_OK

    if (_hMemEvents == NULL) { RecResult = REC_INACTIVE;
        break; }

    if (LastRecordMode == RM_STARTPLAY) { break; }

    // Stop the recording of events
    UnhookWindowsHook(WH_JOURNALRECORD,
        (FARPROC) JrnlRecHookFunc);

    // Modify all 'time' members in the EVENTMSG structures
    lpRecordStat = (LPRECORDSTAT) GlobalLock(_hMemEvents);
    lpEvent = (LPEVENTMSGMSG) &lpRecordStat[1];
```

```
    wNumEvents = lpRecordStat->wNumEvents;
    while (wNumEvents > 1)
        lpEvent[-wNumEvents].time -= lpEvent[0].time;

    lpEvent[0].time = 0;
    GlobalUnlock(_hMemEvents);
    RecResult = REC_OK;

    // Send message to specified window to notify it that
    // recording has stopped
    SendMessage(hWndNotify, wMsgNotify, _hMemEvents,
        _PrematureHalt);

    _hMemEvents = NULL;
    break;

case RM_STARTPLAY:
    // wParam: GLOBALHANDLE to macro
    // lParam: LOWORD(lParam) = hWnd to send stop msg to
    // lParam: HIWORD(lParam) = Message to send to hWnd
    // Returns: REC_ACTIVE, REC_OK, REC_NOEVENTS

    if (_hMemEvents != NULL) { RecResult = REC_ACTIVE;
        break; }

    // Save information so it can be used by RM_STOPRECORD
    hWndNotify = (HWND) LOWORD(lParam);
    wMsgNotify = (WORD) HIWORD(lParam);

    // Assume the playing will be stopped after all events
    // have been played
    _PrematureHalt = REC_OK;

    _hMemEvents = (GLOBALHANDLE) wParam;

    // Initialize statistical data
    lpRecordStat = (LPRECORDSTAT) GlobalLock(_hMemEvents);
    wNumEvents = lpRecordStat->wNumEvents;
    lpRecordStat->wNumEventsPlayed = 0;
```

```
        // Save the time playback is started
        lpRecordStat->dwStartTime = GetTickCount();

        GlobalUnlock(_hMemEvents);
        if (wNumEvents == 0) { RecResult = REC_NOEVENTS; break; }

        _fnNextJrnlHookFunc =
           SetWindowsHook(WH_JOURNALPLAYBACK,
              (FARPROC) JrnlPlybkHookFunc);

        break;

   case RM_STOPPLAY:
      // Stop playing the recorded events
      UnhookWindowsHook(WH_JOURNALPLAYBACK,
         (FARPROC) JrnlPlybkHookFunc);
      _hMemEvents = NULL;
      RecResult = REC_OK;

      // Send message to specified window to notify it that
      // playing has stopped
      SendMessage(hWndNotify, wMsgNotify, 0, _PrematureHalt);
      break;
   }

   LastRecordMode = RecordMode;
   return(RecResult);
}

DWORD FAR PASCAL JrnlRecHookFunc (int nCode, WORD wParam,
      LPEVENTMSGMSG lpEventMsg) {
   static BOOL fPause = FALSE;
   LPRECORDSTAT lpRecordStat;
   LPEVENTMSGMSG lpEvent;
   BOOL fCallDefProc = FALSE;
   DWORD dwResult = 0;
   WORD wNumEvents;
   GLOBALHANDLE hMemTemp;
```

```
switch (nCode) {

    case HC_ACTION:
        fCallDefProc = TRUE;

        // If a system modal dialog box is up, don't record event
        if (fPause) break;

        // Determine the number of events in the memory block now
        lpRecordStat = (LPRECORDSTAT) GlobalLock(_hMemEvents);
        wNumEvents = lpRecordStat->wNumEvents + 1;
        GlobalUnlock(_hMemEvents);
        if (wNumEvents == 0xffff) {
            // Too many events recorded; stop recording
            _PrematureHalt = REC_TOOMANY;
            Recorder(RM_STOPRECORD, 0, 0);
            break;
        }

        // Increase size of memory block to hold the new event
        hMemTemp = GlobalReAlloc(_hMemEvents,
            sizeof(RECORDSTAT) + wNumEvents * sizeof(EVENTMSG),
            GMEM_MOVEABLE);
        if (hMemTemp == NULL) {
            // Insufficient memory; stop recording
            _PrematureHalt = REC_NOMEMORY;
            Recorder(RM_STOPRECORD, 0, 0);
            break;
        }

        _hMemEvents = hMemTemp;

        // Append the new event to the end of the memory block
        lpRecordStat = (LPRECORDSTAT) GlobalLock(_hMemEvents);
        lpEvent = (LPEVENTMSGMSG) &lpRecordStat[1];
        lpEvent[lpRecordStat->wNumEvents] = *lpEventMsg;
        lpRecordStat->wNumEvents++;
        GlobalUnlock(_hMemEvents);
        break;
```

```
      case HC_SYSMODALON:
         // Stop recording events while the system modal dialog
         // box is up
         fPause = TRUE;
         fCallDefProc = TRUE;
         break;

      case HC_SYSMODALOFF:
         // The system modal dialog box is gone; stop recording
         // and notify the user that recording has stopped
         fPause = FALSE;
         _PrematureHalt = REC_SYSMODALON;
         Recorder(RM_STOPRECORD, 0, 0);
         break;

      default:
         fCallDefProc = TRUE;
         break;
   }

   if (fCallDefProc)
      dwResult = DefHookProc(nCode, wParam, (LONG) lpEventMsg,
         (FARPROC FAR *) &_fnNextJrnlHookFunc);

   return(dwResult);
}

DWORD FAR PASCAL JrnlPlybkHookFunc (int nCode, WORD wParam,
      LPEVENTMSGMSG lpEventMsg) {
   BOOL fCallDefProc = FALSE;
   DWORD dwResult = 0;
   LPRECORDSTAT lpRecordStat;
   LPEVENTMSGMSG lpEvent;

   lpRecordStat = (LPRECORDSTAT) GlobalLock(_hMemEvents);
   switch (nCode) {

      case HC_SKIP:
         // Prepare to return the next event the next time the
         // hook code is HC_GETNEXT. If all events have been
         // played, stop playing.
```

```
        if (++lpRecordStat->wNumEventsPlayed ==
              lpRecordStat->wNumEvents)
          Recorder(RM_STOPPLAY, 0, 0);
        break;

    case HC_GETNEXT:
        // Copy the current event to the EVENTMSG structure
        // pointed to by lParam
        lpEvent = (LPEVENTMSGMSG) &lpRecordStat[1];
        *lpEventMsg = lpEvent[lpRecordStat->wNumEventsPlayed];

        // Adjust the 'time' by adding the time playback started
        lpEventMsg->time += lpRecordStat->dwStartTime;

        // Return the number of milliseconds Windows should wait
        // before processing the event
        dwResult = lpEventMsg->time - GetTickCount();

        // If the event occurred in the past, have Windows
        // process it now
        if ((signed long) dwResult < 0) dwResult = 0;
        break;

    case HC_SYSMODALOFF:
        // When the system modal dialog box is removed, stop
        // playing the events and notify the application
        _PrematureHalt = REC_SYSMODALON;
        Recorder(RM_STOPPLAY, 0, 0);
        fCallDefProc = TRUE;
        break;

    case HC_SYSMODALON:
    default:
        fCallDefProc = TRUE;
        break;

}
GlobalUnlock(_hMemEvents);
```

```
   if (fCallDefProc)
      dwResult = DefHookProc(nCode, wParam, (LONG) lpEventMsg,
         (FARPROC FAR *) &_fnNextJrnlHookFunc);

   return(dwResult);
}
```

Listing 6-21. RECORDER.H DLL header module.

```
/*****************************************************************
Module name: Recorder.H
Programmer : Jeffrey M. Richter
*****************************************************************/

typedef enum {
   REC_OK,           // Operation was successful
   REC_ACTIVE,       // Attempt to start recording while already
                     // recording
                     // Attempt to start play while already playing
   REC_INACTIVE,     // Attempt to stop recording while NOT
                     // recording
   REC_NOMEMORY,     // When attempting to start recording or
                     // during recording
   REC_NOEVENTS,     // Attempt playback with no events in memory
                     // block
   REC_TOOMANY,      // Attempt to record more than 65,535 events
   REC_SYSMODALON,   // Recording/playing halted because a
                     // system modal dialog box appeared
} RECRESULT;

typedef enum {
   RM_STARTRECORD, RM_STOPRECORD, RM_STARTPLAY, RM_STOPPLAY
} RECORDMODE;

RECRESULT FAR PASCAL Recorder (RECORDMODE RecordMode,
   WORD wParam, LONG lParam);
```

Listing 6-22. RECORDER.DEF DLL definitions file.

```
; Module name: Recorder.DEF
; Programmer : Jeffrey M. Richter

LIBRARY      RECORDER
DESCRIPTION 'Recorder: Journal hook routines for Echo'
STUB        'WinStub.exe'
EXETYPE     WINDOWS
CODE        FIXED PRELOAD
DATA        MOVEABLE SINGLE PRELOAD
HEAPSIZE    0
EXPORTS
    WEP              @1    RESIDENTNAME
    Recorder         @2
    JrnlRecHookFunc  @3
    JrnlPlybkHookFunc @4
```

Listing 6-23. RECORDER.MKF MAKEFILE for Recorder DLL.

```
#****************************************************************
#Module name: RECORDER.MKF
#Programmer : Jeffrey M. Richter
#****************************************************************

PROG = Recorder
MODEL = S
CFLAGS = -A$(MODEL)w -D_WINDOWS -D_WINDLL -Gcsw2 -W4 -Zlepid -Od
LFLAGS = /NOE/BA/A:16/M/CO/LI/F
LIBS = $(MODEL)dllcew + libw

M1 = $(PROG).obj

ICONS =
BITMAPS =
CURSORS =
RESOURCES = $(ICONS) $(BITMAPS) $(CURSORS)
```

```
.SUFFIXES: .rc

$(PROG).DLL: $(M1) $(PROG).Def
   link $(LFLAGS) @<<$(PROG).lnk
\MSC\LibEntry.obj $(M1)
$(PROG).DLL, $(PROG), $(LIBS), $(PROG)
<<
   rc $(PROG).DLL
   implib $(PROG).LIB $(PROG).DEF

$(PROG).obj:   $*.c $*.h
```

CHAPTER 7

MDI Application Techniques

The Multiple Document Interface standard is not new to Windows, but its implementation in Windows 3.0 makes developing MDI applications much simpler. This chapter explains how to design and implement extensions to MDI applications.

For a description of how a user interacts with an MDI application, see Chapter 11 of the *IBM SAA Common User Access Advanced Interface Design Guide*. To learn the mechanics of implementing an MDI application under Windows, see Chapter 21 of the *Microsoft Windows Guide to Programming*.

MDI Application Basics

Every MDI application consists of a Frame window, an MDICLIENT window, and multiple MDI Child windows. The application registers the Frame window's class and MDI Child window classes. If the application allows the user to work on three types of documents (spreadsheets, charts, and macros, for instance), three MDI Child window classes must be registered. Instances of these windows are created as children of the MDICLIENT window, which was itself created as a child of the Frame window. The MDICLIENT window class is a system global class that is registered by Windows when the session begins.

The Frame window is like the main overlapped window used by non-MDI applications. All windows created by the MDI application are descendants of this Frame window. One of the first duties of the Frame window is to create an instance of an MDICLIENT window class during the processing of the *WM_CREATE* message. The MDICLIENT window is responsible for maintaining all of the MDI Child windows.

MDI applications behave differently because the Frame window calls *DefFrameProc* instead of *DefWindowProc* when default processing for a message is desired. The parameters that would normally be passed to *DefWindowProc* are passed to *DefFrameProc*. The pseudo-C code below shows the messages processed by *DefFrameProc* and their default actions:

```
LONG FAR PASCAL DefFrameProc (HWND hWnd, HWND hWndMDIClient,
    WORD wMsg, WORD wParam, LONG lParam) {
  DWORD dwResult = 0;
  BOOL fCallDefProc = FALSE;

  if (hWndMDIClient == NULL)
    return(DefWindowProc(hWnd, wMsg, wParam, lParam));

  switch (wMsg) {

    case WM_COMMAND:
      if (User Selected An MDI Child From the "Window" Menu) {
        hWndSelectedChild = GetChildhWndFromMenuId(wParam);
        SendMessage(hWndMDIClient, WM_MDIACTIVATE,
          hWndSelectedChild, 0);
        break;
      }

      if (User Selected The "More Windows..." Option From The
          "Window" Menu) {
        DialogBoxParam("More Windows..." Dialog Box);
      }

      switch (wParam & 0xFFF0) {
        case SC_RESTORE:
        case SC_CLOSE:
        case SC_NEXTWINDOW:
        case SC_MINIMIZE:
```

```
        if (An MDI Child Is Maximized)
           dwResult = SendMessage(hWndMaximizedChild,
               WM_SYSCOMMAND, wParam, lParam);
        break;
   }
   break;

case WM_GETTEXT:
   if (!(An MDI Child Is Maximized) ||
       (MDI Child Has No Caption)) {
      fCallDefProc = TRUE;
   } else {
      Put The Frame Window's Caption In A Buffer;
      Append The MDI Child's Caption To The Buffer;
      dwResult = Address Of The Buffer;
   }
   break;

case WM_MENUCHAR:
   if (User Pressed Dash) {
      if (An MDI Child Is Maximized)
         dwResult = MAKELONG(0, 2);
      else
         if (An MDI Child Is Active) {
            PostMessage(hWndActiveChild, WM_SYSCOMMAND,
               SC_KEYMENU, MAKELONG('-', 0));
            dwResult = MAKELONG(0, 1);
         }
   }
   fCallDefProc = TRUE;
   break;

case WM_NCACTIVATE:
   SendMessage(hWndMDIClient, WM_NCACTIVATE, wParam,
      lParam);
   fCallDefProc = TRUE;
   break;

case WM_NEXTMENU:
   if ((Frame Window Is Maximized) &&
```

```
            (An MDI Child Is Active) &&
            !(An MDI Child Is Maximized)) {
         if ((((Left Arrow Pressed) && (Frame Menu Is Active))
              || ((Right Arrow Pressed) &&
              (Frame's System Menu Is Active))) {
            dwResult = MAKELONG(hMenuOfActiveChildsSysMenu,
               hWndOfActiveChild);
            break;
         }
      }
      dwResult = 0;
      break;

   case WM_SETFOCUS:
      SetFocus(hWndMDIClient);
      break;

   case WM_SIZE:
      MoveWindow(hWndMDIClient, 0, 0, LOWORD(lParam),
         HIWORD(lParam), TRUE);
      fCallDefProc = TRUE;
      break;

   default:
      fCallDefProc = TRUE;
      break;
   }
   if (fCallDefProc)
      dwResult = DefWindowProc(hWnd, wMsg, wParam, lParam);
   return(dwResult);
}
```

Actions that occur within MDI Child windows are communicated to the MDICLIENT window by calling *DefMDIChildProc* in each MDI Child's window procedure. The parameters expected by *DefMDIChildProc* are identical to those expected by *DefWindowProc*. The pseudo-C code below shows the messages processed by the *DefMDIChildProc* function and their default actions:

```
LONG FAR PASCAL DefMDIChildProc (HWND hWndMDIChild, WORD wMsg,
     WORD wParam, LONG lParam) {
  DWORD dwResult = 0;
  BOOL fCallDefProc = FALSE;

  switch (wMsg) {

    case WM_CHILDACTIVATE:
       Notify hWndMDIClient That Child Became Active;
       break;

    case WM_CLOSE:
       SendMessage(hWndMDIClient, WM_MDIDESTROY, hWndChild, 0);
       break;

    case WM_GETMINMAXINFO:
       DoNormalProcessingForChildren;
       break;

    case WM_ICONERASEBKGND:
       if (An MDI Child Is Maximized) dwResult = 0;
       else fCallDefProc = TRUE;
       break;

    case WM_MENUCHAR:
       SendMessage(hWndFrame, WM_SYSCOMMAND, SC_KEYMENU,
          wParam);
       dwResult = MAKELONG(0, 1);
       break;

    case WM_MOVE:
       if (!(hWndMDIChild Is Maximized)) {
          Calculate New Scroll Bar Ranges For hWndMDIClient;
       fCallDefProc = TRUE;
       break;

    case WM_NEXTMENU:
       if (Left Arrow Pressed)
          dwResult = MAKELONG(hMenuFramesSysMenu, hWndFrame);
       else
```

```
              dwResult = MAKELONG(hMenuFramesTopLevelMenu,
                  hWndFrame);
          break;

      case WM_SETTEXT:
          DefWindowProc(hWndMDIChild, wMsg, wParam, lParam);
          Modify Menu Item In Frame's "Window" Menu;
          if (hWndMDIChild Is Maximized)
              Redraw Frame's Non-Client Area;
          break;

      case WM_SIZE:
          Do Normal Processing For MDI Child;
          // This includes determining if scroll bars are necessary
          // in MDI Client's window
          break;

      case WM_SYSCOMMAND:
          switch (wParam & 0xFFF0) {
              case SC_NEXTWINDOW:
                  SendMessage(hWndMDIClient, WM_MDINEXT,
                      hWndMDIChild, 0);
                  break;

              default:
                  fCallDefProc = TRUE;
          }
          break;
  }

  if (fCallDefProc)
      dwResult = DefWindowProc(hWndMDIChild, wMsg, wParam,
          lParam);

  return(dwResult);
}
```

478

The MDI Sample Application

The MDI sample application shows how to implement various features in your own MDI programs. The initialization code for the MDI application can be found in the MDI.C module. This module creates the Frame window and the ribbon that may appear under the Frame's menu bar. The dialog-box procedure for the ribbon is also in MDI.C.

FRAME.C contains the function that registers the Frame window class and the window procedure that processes messages for this window. The application registers two MDI Child classes, Sheet and Chart. The functions that register the MDI Child classes and the window procedures required to process messages for these classes can be found in SHEET.C and CHART.C, presented later in this chapter.

MDI.H contains a number of values that are used for menu resources and string tables throughout the application. The *#define:*

```
#define GETFRAME(hWnd)   GetParent(GetParent(hWnd))
```

is frequently used in the window procedures for the two MDI Child classes. It returns the handle of the application's Frame window.

Several user-defined messages are also established in MDI.H. The prefix used for each message identifies the window class that processes the message. The table below shows each message prefix and its meaning:

Message prefix	Window class that processes the message
FW	Processed by the Frame window.
AC	Processed by all the MDI Child windows.
AW	Processed by the Frame window and the MDI Child windows.

At the bottom of MDI.H are macro definitions that access class and window extra bytes. These macros are explained in Appendix C.

The remainder of this chapter discusses the various features that have been implemented in the MDI sample application.

Closing MDI Child Windows

Like applications, MDI Child windows can be closed by selecting the "Close" option from the Child's system menu. As a convenience to the user, Windows allows applications to be closed by double-clicking on the system menu. In fact, the bitmap used to represent the application's system menu is sometimes called the *Close Box*. Windows allows MDI Child windows to be closed when the user double-clicks on the MDI Child's Close Box. However, a bug in the Windows 3.0 implementation of MDI prevents a maximized MDI Child from being closed this way.

The code below shows how you can correct this bug in your own MDI applications. It must appear in the processing of the *WM_NCLBUTTONDBLCLK* message in the Frame's window procedure:

```
case WM_NCLBUTTONDBLCLK:
  fCallDefProc = TRUE;
  if (wParam != HTMENU)
    break;

  // If the active Child is not maximized, break;
  dwResult = SendMessage(_hWndMDIClient, WM_MDIGETACTIVE, 0, 0);
  if (HIWORD(dwResult) != 1)
    break;

  GetWindowRect(hWnd, &rc);
  rc.top += GetSystemMetrics(SM_CYCAPTION) +
    GetSystemMetrics(SM_CYFRAME);
  rc.left += GetSystemMetrics(SM_CXFRAME);
  hBitmap = LoadBitmap(NULL, MAKEINTRESOURCE(OBM_CLOSE));
  GetObject(hBitmap, sizeof(BITMAP), (LPSTR) (LPBITMAP) &Bitmap);
```

```
rc.bottom = rc.top + Bitmap.bmHeight;
rc.right = rc.left + Bitmap.bmWidth / 2;
if (!PtInRect(&rc, MAKEPOINT(lParam)))
    break;
SendMessage(LOWORD(dwResult), WM_SYSCOMMAND, SC_CLOSE, lParam);
fCallDefProc = FALSE;
break;
```

When an MDI Child window is maximized, *DefMDIChildProc* alters the Frame window's menu bar by placing the MDI Child's system menu at the beginning and its "Restore" button at the end. Figure 7-1 shows how the menu bar is changed.

When the user double-clicks on a window outside the client area, Windows sends the *WM_NCLBUTTONDBLCLK* message to the window. The *wParam* parameter contains the hit code that identifies the region of the window that the mouse was over. (For a complete list of hit codes, see the *WM_NCHITTEST* message on page 6-85 of the *Windows Programmer's Reference*.) To determine whether the MDI Child's Close Box was clicked, we need to examine the location of the mouse only if the *wParam* parameter is *HTMENU*. Otherwise, we should call *DefFrameProc* for normal message processing.

Once we know that the mouse was double-clicked in the Frame window's menu bar and there is a maximized MDI Child window, we must determine if the mouse is over the rectangular area occupied by the MDI Child's Close Box.

GetWindowRect returns the screen coordinates of the Frame window. This includes the window's caption bar and resizing borders. By adding the height of a caption bar and the height of the thickframe to *rc.top*, we get the y-coordinate (in screen units) of the top of the menu bar. We can store this value in *rc.top*. Then we add the width of the thickframe to *rc.left* to get the x-coordinate where the left of the menu bar starts. We'll store this value in *rc.left*.

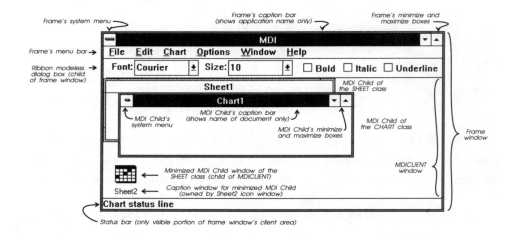

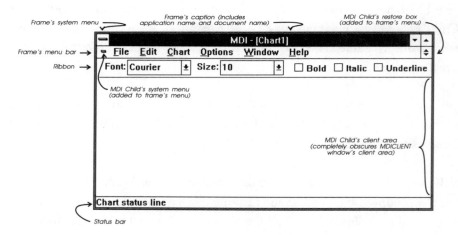

Figure 7-1. MDI applications before and after an MDI Child is maximized.

Now we must calculate the width and height of the bitmap used to represent an MDI Child's Close Box. The *LoadBitmap* function is used to retrieve a handle to this bitmap. Windows has several bitmaps that any application can access. The *LoadBitmap* function uses the data-instance handle to determine which .EXE file (or .DLL file) to retrieve bitmaps from. If this value is NULL, *LoadBitmap* retrieves one of the predefined bitmaps. A list of these bitmaps appears in Appendix C.

We use *OBM_CLOSE* to retrieve the handle of the Close Box bitmap. To finish defining the rectangular area, we must calculate the bottom coordinate:

```
rc.bottom = rc.top + Bitmap.bmHeight;
```

The right edge is equal to the left edge's coordinate plus half the width of the bitmap:

```
rc.right = rc.left + Bitmap.bmWidth / 2;
```

We have to divide the width of the Close Box bitmap by two because it contains the images for application Close Boxes (on the left) and MDI Child Close Boxes (on the right).

With the *rc* variable set to the screen coordinates of the MDI Child's Close Box, the *PtInRect* function can now be used to determine if the mouse cursor is within the rectangle. If it is, a *WM_SYSCOMMAND* message is sent to the active MDI Child window with the *wParam* parameter set to *SC_CLOSE*, telling the window that the user has tried to close it.

Eating Mouse Messages

When the user clicks the left button of the mouse over a window that is currently inactive, Windows activates the window and sends the *WM_LBUTTONDOWN* message to its window procedure. However, some applications may prefer that Windows activate the window without sending the *WM_LBUTTONDOWN* message. Let's perform an experiment using Microsoft's Word for Windows.

In Word for Windows, open two document windows. Only one window is active; select a region of text in that window. Make the other document window active by clicking the left mouse button within its client area. If you now click the mouse button over the client area of the first document's window, Word for Windows simply activates the document window. The text in the window remains selected. It isn't until you press the mouse button again that Word deselects the text and positions the caret at the mouse cursor's location.

The developers of Word for Windows had to make a deliberate effort for Word to behave this way. Normally, when an MDI Child window is activated by the mouse, a *WM_MOUSEACTIVATE* message is sent to the MDI Child, followed by a *WM_LBUTTONDOWN* message. Word ignores the *WM_LBUTTONDOWN* message when it is associated with the activation of an MDI Child window.

Whenever a click of the mouse activates a window, Windows sends a *WM_MOUSEACTIVATE* message to the window procedure. The *wParam* parameter contains the handle to the topmost parent window of the window being activated. The *lParam* parameter contains the hit test code in the low-order word and the mouse message (*WM_?BUTTONDOWN* or *WM_NC?BUTTONDOWN*) in the high-order word. The value returned while a *WM_MOUSEACTIVATE* message is being processed tells Windows how it should handle the *WM_?BUTTONDOWN* or *WM_NC?BUTTONDOWN* message. The possible return values are:

Identifier	Meaning
MA_ACTIVATE	Activate the window and send the mouse message.
MA_NOACTIVATE	Do not activate the window.
MA_ACTIVATEANDEAT	Activate the window but do not send the mouse message.

The documentation for this can be found in the README.WRI file distributed on the Windows SDK diskettes.

You might expect that your MDI Child's window procedure could simply intercept the *WM_MOUSEACTIVATE* message and return *MA_ACTIVATEAND-EAT* to cause the mouse event to be thrown away. However, there is a catch. Windows never considers a window with the *WS_CHILD* style active. That is, the *GetActiveWindow* function will never return a handle to a child window. Instead, Windows goes up the family tree until it finds a window that does not have the *WS_CHILD* style and makes it the active window. In an MDI application, this is always the application's Frame window. When an MDI Child window is active, it just means that the window has the input focus and that its caption bar should be painted using the *COLOR_ACTIVECAPTION* color.

All of this means that a *WM_MOUSEACTIVATE* message is sent every time a mouse button is clicked over an MDI Child window. If the return value from this message were always *MA_ACTIVATEANDEAT*, the MDI Child's window procedure would never receive any *WM_?BUTTONDOWN* or *WM_NC?BUTTONDOWN* messages. The code below shows the proper way to disable the *WM_?BUTTONDOWN* side-effect for MDI Child windows:

```
LONG FAR PASCAL MDIChildProc (HWND hWnd, WORD wMsg, WORD wParam,
    LONG lParam) {
  static HWND hWndPrevChild = NULL;
  .
  .
  .
  case WM_MDIACTIVATE:
    if (wParam == FALSE) {      // Deactivating this window
      hWndPrevChild = NULL;
      break;
    }

    // Save handle of window losing activity
    hWndPrevChild = HIWORD(lParam);
```

```
        // If this window is being activated when no other MDI
        // Children exist, always accept mouse presses
        if (hWndPrevChild == NULL) hWndPrevChild = hWnd;
        break;

    case WM_MOUSEACTIVATE:
        // Throw away mouse message if this MDI Child is just being
        // activated and mouse is NOT over the Child's client area
        if (hWnd != hWndPrevChild && HTCLIENT == LOWORD(lParam))
            dwResult = MA_ACTIVATEANDEAT;
        else dwResult = MA_ACTIVATE;
        break;

    case WM_SETCURSOR:
        // Message occurs after WM_ACTIVATE and WM_MOUSEACTIVATE.
        // Use this to reset hWndPrevChild.
        fCallDefProc = TRUE;
        hWndPrevChild = hWnd;
        break;
        .
        .
        .

}
```

When an inactive MDI Child window is activated by a mouse click, Windows sends a series of messages to that window: *WM_MDIACTIVATE*, *WM_MOUSE-ACTIVATE*, and *WM_SETCURSOR*. *WM_MDIACTIVATE* notifies the MDI Child window that is being activated (*wParam* is 1). The high word of the *lParam* parameter contains the handle of the window that is being deactivated. The MDI Child saves this handle in a static variable, *hWndPrevChild*. When the *WM_MOUSEACTIVATE* message is received, the value of *hWndPrevChild* is compared to the window handle that is processing the message. If the handles are different, the mouse message should be eaten. However, we also test to see if the mouse is within the MDI Child's client area (*HTCLIENT == LOWORD(lParam)*). If the mouse is not in the client area, we do not want to eat the mouse message.

Whether the MDI Child is activated by the mouse or by some other means, Windows sends a *WM_SETCURSOR* message after the MDI Child has been activated. The *hWndPrevChild* variable is set to the handle of the newly activated window. This prevents future mouse messages from being eaten.

CHART.C (presented at the end of the chapter) demonstrates how mouse messages are eaten by displaying a dialog box whenever the window procedure receives a *WM_LBUTTONDOWN* message.

Status Bars

Many MDI applications have status bars. A status bar is a line of text (usually consisting of statistical information about the document the user is working on). MDI.EXE demonstrates how to implement a status bar as part of the Frame window's client area. When the user chooses to display the status bar, the MDICLIENT is resized (by calling the *MoveWindow* function) so that its height does not cause the Frame's client area to be completely obscured.

The Frame window maintains a Boolean value in its class extra bytes that reflects the current state (on or off) of the status bar. When the Frame window is created, this value is initialized to TRUE:

```
case WM_CREATE:
    .
    .
    .
    SETCLSEB(hWnd, CLSEB, fStatusBarOn, TRUE);
```

This makes the status bar visible by default when the application is started. A complete description of the macros that store and retrieve class extra bytes can be found in Appendix C.

487

The application must know the dimensions of the status bar. The user-defined message *FW_GETSTATBARRECT* was created to make this information accessible. The Frame window's window procedure processes this message as follows:

```
case FW_GETSTATBARRECT:
    // lParam is a far pointer to a RECT structure
    // to be initialized by this message
    GetClientRect(hWnd, (LPRECT) lParam);
    if (!GETCLSEB(hWnd, CLSEB, fStatsBarOn)) {
        // User has turned off the status bar
        ((LPRECT) lParam)->top = ((LPRECT) lParam)->bottom;
        break;
    }
    wTemp = GetDC(hWnd);
    GetTextMetrics((HDC) wTemp, &tm);
    ReleaseDC((HDC) wTemp);
    ((LPRECT) lParam->top = ((LPRECT) lParam)->bottom -
        tm.tmHeight - GetSystemMetrics(SM_CYBORDER);
    break;
```

If the user has turned off the status bar, the rectangle will simply be a rectangle of zero height that spans the width of the Frame window's client area. If the status bar is not turned off, the height of the bar is calculated as the height of a line of text plus the height of a window frame that cannot be sized. *GetSystem-Metrics(SM_CYBORDER)* allows the application to draw a horizontal line that separates the MDICLIENT window from the status bar. Because this type of horizontal line is drawn so frequently, the *FW_DRAWSTATUSDIVIDE* message was defined so that the processing for drawing this line would not have to be duplicated in all MDI Child window procedures. The code for this message appears below:

```
case FW_DRAWSTATUSDIVIDE:
    // lParam is a far pointer to a PAINTSTRUCT structure that
    // allows this message to write on the Frame's client area
    // occupied by the status bar
    dwResult = GetSystemMetrics(SM_CYBORDER);
```

```
hPen = CreatePen(PS_SOLID, (int) dwResult, RGB(0, 0, 0));
hPen = SelectObject(((LPPAINTSTRUCT) lParam)->hdc, hPen);
MoveTo(((LPPAINTSTRUCT) lParam)->hdc, 0,
      ((LPPAINTSTRUCT) lParam)->rcPaint.top);
LineTo(((LPPAINTSTRUCT) lParam)->hdc,
      ((LPPAINTSTRUCT) lParam)->rcPaint.right,
      ((LPPAINTSTRUCT) lParam)->rcPaint.top);
hPen = SelectObject(((LPPAINTSTRUCT) lParam)->hdc, hPen);
DeleteObject(hPen);
break;
```

The most important thing to note here is the use of *GetSystemMetrics (SM_CYBORDER)*. Because the application uses this value instead of hard-coding a one- or two-pixel line, the dividing line should be visible on any monitor. This message returns the height of the nonsizeable border so that the calling procedure can take this value into account before it does any additional painting.

Drawing information in the status bar is simply a matter of intercepting the *WM_PAINT* message when it is sent to the Frame's window procedure. Because the only visible part of the Frame's client area is the status bar, this message indicates that the status bar needs to be repainted. Each MDI Child window class may wish to display different information in the status bar, so painting this information should be the responsibility of the MDI Child window. The processing for the paint message determines whether any MDI Child windows exist, then sends the user-defined *AC_PAINTSTATBAR* message to the active MDI Child window.

If an MDI Child does not exist, the Frame window can paint any information it desires in the status bar.

While a user is working in an MDI Child window, that Child window may wish to update the information in the status bar. It can do this by executing the following statements:

```
RECT rc;
.
.
.
SendMessage(GETFRAME(hWndMDIChild),
   FW_GETSTATBARRECT, 0, (LONG) (LPRECT) &rc);
InvalidateRect(GETFRAME(hWndMDIChild), &rc, TRUE);
```

These statements inform Windows that the status-bar area of the Frame window needs repainting. However, some MDI Child windows update their status bars frequently. For example, Word for Windows' status bar shows the column containing the cursor. If the user is typing quickly, Word won't be able to keep up. Word invalidates the status bar's area so Windows doesn't send the *WM_PAINT* message to the Frame window until the queue holds no other messages. This has the effect of updating the status bar when the user has momentarily stopped typing.

If it is absolutely necessary for the status bar to be updated as changes occur, the MDI Child can add the following line after the code shown above:

```
UpdateWindow(GETFRAME(hWndMDIChild));
```

Each Child window receives the *AC_PAINTSTATBAR* message. This message includes the *wParam* parameter containing the handle to the device context that must be used for painting and the *lParam* parameter pointing to the *PAINTSTRUCT* structure initialized by the call to the *BeginPaint* function.

Menu Option Help

Because it is not always obvious to a user what a particular menu item does, some applications display help text at the bottom of the window as the user highlights menu options. This section discusses a method of adding menu help text to applications. Although the technique discussed here applies to MDI applications, it could also apply to non-MDI applications.

Menu option help is displayed in the area used by an application's status bar. If the user has elected to hide the status bar, the menu help text is not displayed.

When the user highlights menu options, help text for the highlighted menu item is painted in the application's status bar. After the user has selected a menu option or exited from the menu system, the menu help text is replaced by the normal statistical information.

As the user navigates through the application's menu system, Windows sends *WM_MENUSELECT* messages to the window that owns the active menu. The low-order word of the *lParam* parameter associated with the *WM_MENUSELECT* message is used to determine what type of item the user has highlighted. The table below lists the identifiers that may be *AND*ed with the low-order word of *lParam* to determine the status of the highlighted menu item:

Identifier	Value	Description
MF_GRAYED	0x0001	The highlighted menu item is grayed.
MF_DISABLED	0x0002	The highlighted menu item is disabled.
MF_BITMAP	0x0004	The highlighted menu item is a bitmap.
MD_CHECKED	0x0008	The highlighted menu item is checked.
MF_POPUP	0x0010	The highlighted menu item is a pop-up menu and has no menu ID.
MF_OWNERDRAW	0x0100	The highlighted menu item is an owner-drawn item.
MF_SYSMENU	0x2000	The highlighted menu item is an item in the window's system menu or is the system menu's pop-up (if the *MF_POPUP* bit is on).
MF_MOUSESELECT	0x8000	The highlighted menu item was selected with the mouse.

Before deciding what help text to display, the window procedure processing the *WM_MENUSELECT* message must know if a menu item is highlighted or if a pop-up menu is highlighted. The window procedure performs a bitwise *AND* operation on the low-order word of the *lParam* parameter and the *MF_POPUP* identifier. If the *MF_POPUP* bit is on, the user has highlighted a pop-up menu and the *wParam* parameter is the menu handle of the highlighted menu. If the *MF_POPUP* bit is off, the user has highlighted a menu item and the *wParam* parameter is its menu item ID.

The window procedure must also determine whether the highlighted item is part of the window's system menu. To do this, the procedure performs another bitwise *AND* operation between the low-order word of the *lParam* parameter and the *MF_SYSMENU* identifier. If the *MF_SYSMENU* bit is on, the user has highlighted the window's system menu or an item in the window's system menu.

Now it's time to add MDI Child windows to our discussion. When an MDI Child window is maximized, the Child's system menu is appended to the beginning of the Frame window's menu. Because the menu is part of the Frame's menu, highlighting options in the MDI Child's system menu causes *WM_MENUSELECT* messages to be sent to the Frame's window procedure. The *MF_SYSMENU* bit will be off because this menu is not the Frame window's system menu.

A restore box is appended to the end of the Frame's menu when the MDI Child window is maximized. This menu item is not a pop-up but a bitmap menu item. A user can enter the Frame's menu system and, using the right and left arrows, scroll through the menus until the restore box is the highlighted option. When this happens, Windows sends the *WM_MENUSELECT* message to the Frame's window procedure. The low-order word of the *lParam* parameter will have the *MF_POPUP* and *MF_SYSMENU* bits turned off and the *MF_BITMAP* bit turned on.

When an MDI Child window is not maximized, the MDI Child's system menu is not part of the Frame's menu but is the system menu for the MDI Child window. When menu items are highlighted in the nonmaximized MDI Child's system menu, the *WM_MENUSELECT* message is sent to the MDI Child's window procedure because it owns the active menu. In addition, since this menu is the Child's system menu, the *lParam* parameter for this message will always have the *MF_SYSMENU* bit turned on.

Whenever a *WM_MENUSELECT* message is retrieved by a window procedure, the procedure must determine what help text to paint in the status bar. Let's examine the simplest situation first. When no MDI Child windows exist, all *WM_MENU-SELECT* messages are sent to the Frame's window procedure. The Frame window can use the values in the *lParam* and *wParam* parameters to determine what text should be displayed. The template below shows the skeleton code to set this up:

```
case WM_MENUSELECT:
   switch (LOWORD(lParam) & (MF_POPUP | MF_SYSMENU)) {
      case 0:
         // wParam is a menu ID from a nonsystem menu
         break;

      case MF_POPUP:
         // wParam is handle to a nonsystem pop-up menu
         break;

      case MF_SYSMENU:
         // wParam is a menu ID from the system menu
         break;

      case MF_POPUP | MF_SYSMENU:
         // wParam is the handle to the system menu
         break;
   }
   .
   .
   .
```

In each case, the window procedure can examine the status of bits in the *lParam* parameter to modify the help text displayed to the user. For example, if the user has highlighted the "Copy" option in the Edit menu when this option is grayed (*(LOWORD(lParam) & MF_GRAYED) != FALSE*), the help text could tell the user that an object in the window needs to be selected before this option can be chosen.

This is a good method to use when implementing menu help text in a non-MDI application, but in an MDI application some additional work is necessary. Because the menu in the Frame window was placed there by the active MDI Child, that Child should be responsible for determining what help text is displayed. However, the *WM_MENUSELECT* message is sent to the Frame window for all highlighted menu options (except the nonmaximized MDI Child's system menu).

When the MDI sample application's Frame window receives the *WM_MENUSELECT* message, it determines whether an MDI Child exists and sends the message to the MDI Child directly:

```
switch (LOWORD(lParam) & (MF_POPUP | MF_SYSMENU)) {

    case 0:
        // wParam is a menu item ID NOT on the app's system menu

        if (hWndActiveMDIChild != NULL) {
            // An MDI Child exists
            if (fMDIChildIsMaximized) {
                // If menu item is from the MDI Child's system menu,
                // set the MF_SYSMENU bit in the lParam parameter
                wTemp = GetSubMenu(GetMenu(hWnd), 0);
                if (GetMenuState(wTemp, wParam, MF_BYCOMMAND) != -1)
                    lParam |= MF_SYSMENU;
            }

            // Make active MDI Child think that it received the
            // WM_MENUSELECT message
            SendMessage(hWndActiveMDIChild, wMsg, wParam, lParam);
            wTemp = 0;      // MDI Child handled the message
            break;
```

```
        }
        wTemp = IDS_FRAMEMENUID + wParam;
        break;

    case MF_POPUP:
        // wParam is handle to pop-up menu
        if (hWndActiveMDIChild != NULL) {
            // An MDI Child exists
            if (fMDIChildIsMaximized) {
                // If pop-up menu is first top-level menu, it is
                // the MDI Child's system menu; set MF_SYSMENU flag
                if (wParam == GetSubMenu(GetMenu(hWnd), 0))
                    lParam |= MF_SYSMENU;
            }

            // Make active MDI Child think that it received the
            // WM_MENUSELECT message
            SendMessage(hWndActiveMDIChild, wMsg, wParam, lParam);
            wTemp = 0;    // MDI Child handled the message
            break;
        }

        // Calculate the index of the top-level menu
        hMenu = GetMenu(hWnd);
        wTemp = GetMenuItemCount(hMenu);
        while (wTemp—)
            if (GetSubMenu(hMenu, wTemp) == (HMENU) wParam) break;
        wTemp += IDS_FRAMEPOPUPID + 1;    // Jump over system menu
        break;

    case MF_SYSMENU:
        // wParam is menu item ID from system menu
        wTemp = IDS_FRAMEMENUID + ((wParam & 0x0FFF) >> 4);
        break;

    case MF_POPUP | MF_SYSMENU:
        // wParam is handle to app's sys menu
        wTemp = IDS_FRAMEPOPUPID;
        break;
}
```

If the *MF_SYSMENU* bit is on, the *WM_MENUSELECT* message is for a menu item on the Frame's system menu and must be processed by the Frame. If the *MF_SYSMENU* bit is off, the *WM_MENUSELECT* message is passed to the active MDI Child window (if one exists). First we check to ensure that the MDI Child window is maximized. If so, and if the highlighted menu item is from the first pop-up menu of the Frame's window, the *MF_SYSMENU* bit is turned on before the message is sent to the MDI Child. This indicates to the MDI Child window that an option on the Child's system menu is highlighted.

This lets the MDI Child window process *WM_MENUSELECT* messages just as the Frame window procedure does. The table below shows what the Frame's window procedure should expect to receive in the *lParam* parameter for a *WM_MENU-SELECT* message:

Highlighted item	*MF_POPUP* bit	*MF_SYSMENU* bit
Application's system menu item	off	on
Application's system menu pop-up	on	on
Maximized MDI Child's system menu item	off	off
Maximized MDI Child's system menu pop-up	on	off
Maximized MDI Child's restore box	off	off
Application's nonsystem menu item	off	off
Application's nonsystem menu pop-up	on	off

The table below shows what an MDI Child window procedure should expect to receive in the *lParam* parameter for a *WM_MENUSELECT* message:

Highlighted item	*MF_POPUP* bit	*MF_SYSMENU* bit
MDI Child's system menu item	off	on
MDI Child's system menu pop-up	on	on
Frame's nonsystem menu item	off	off
Frame's nonsystem menu pop-up	on	off

By examining the *lParam* and *wParam* parameters of the *WM_MENUSELECT* message, the Frame and MDI Child window procedures find a string-table identifier representing a line of help text in the MDI sample application's resource file. This will be used later when the help text needs to be displayed in the status bar.

If the *MF_POPUP* bit is turned on, the procedure must determine which pop-up menu is highlighted. This is done by the following loop:

```
hMenu = GetMenu(hWnd);
wTemp = GetMenuItemCount(hMenu);
while (wTemp—)
   if (GetSubMenu(hMenu, wTemp) == (HMENU) wParam) break;
```

At the end of this loop, *wTemp* will contain the index (based at zero) of the highlighted pop-up menu. If there are any menu items (not pop-up menus) in the Frame window's top-level menu, the loop will still work correctly. This is because the *GetSubMenu* function returns NULL if the item at the specified index is not a pop-up menu.

If the *wParam* parameter indicates a handle to a cascading menu, this loop will not locate it. To locate the handle of a cascading menu, use the menu item ID for the first option in the cascading menu and compare it to what the first item should be in that menu:

```
if (GetMenuItemID(wParam, 0) == IDM_FIRSTOPTIONINCASCADINGMENU) {
   // Pop-up menu is the cascading menu pop-up
}
```

Now that we have determined the string-table ID for the help text, the window that received the *WM_MENUSELECT* message sends the user-defined *FW_SET-MENUHELP* message to the Frame's window procedure. The *wParam* parameter is the handle to the window that received the *WM_MENUSELECT* message, and the *lParam* parameter is the menu help code or string table's ID value, in this case.

The Frame window saves the window handle and the menu help code in its extra bytes:

```
case FW_SETMENUHELP:
   // Save the handle of the window sending the message
   SETCLSEB(hWnd, CLSEB, hWndMenuHelp, (HWND) wParam);

   // Save the menu help code that the window sent to
   SETCLSEB(hWnd, CLSEB, dwMenuHelp, lParam);
   .
   .
   .
   break;
```

Displaying help text as the user highlights each menu option requires a lot of painting. Painting is a slow operation that degrades Windows' performance. To alleviate this problem, we can take advantage of the *WM_ENTERIDLE* message. This message is sent to a window procedure when a message was just processed by a menu or dialog box and no other messages are waiting in the queue.

For our discussion, this means that as long as the user holds down the arrow key, *WM_KEYDOWN* messages are appended to the queue and processed by the menu system. When the user releases the arrow key, Windows sends the *WM_ENTERIDLE* message to the window procedure. It is at this point that the help text for the last highlighted menu option should be painted.

498

When the MDI sample application's Frame window receives the *WM_ENTERIDLE* message, the *wParam* parameter is either *MSGF_DIALOGBOX* or *MSGF_MENU*. These identifiers reveal whether the user was just using a dialog box or the application's menu system. Upon receiving a *WM_ENTERIDLE* message, the Frame window executes the following code:

```
case WM_ENTERIDLE:
   if (wParam != MSGF_MENU) break;

   // Display new menu help; invalidate the status bar
   SendMessage(hWnd, FW_GETSTATBARRECT, 0, (LONG) (LPRECT) &rc);
   InvalidateRect(hWnd, &rc, TRUE);

   // BeginPaint is OK because an invalid rectangle must exist due
   // to the call to InvalidateRect above. This causes the
   // background for the Frame's client area to be drawn
   //_correctly.
   BeginPaint(hWnd, &ps);
   SetBkMode(ps.hdc, TRANSPARENT);

   // Send message to window that last received a WM_MENUSELECT
   // message to tell it to paint the status bar with the
   // appropriate menu help text
   SendMessage((HWND) GETCLSEB(hWnd, CLSEB, hWndMenuHelp),
      AW_PAINTMENUHELP, 0, (LONG) (LPPAINTSTRUCT) &ps);
   EndPaint(hWnd, &ps);
   .
   .
   .
```

This code tells Windows that the area occupied by the Frame's status bar needs to have its background and text repainted. *BeginPaint* and *EndPaint* are usually not called except in response to a *WM_PAINT* message. However, calling the *BeginPaint* function here has the side-effect of having Windows automatically send the *WM_ERASEBKGND* message to the Frame's window procedure to make sure that the background is drawn in the correct color. Once the device context gives us permission to write on the status-bar area of the Frame, the background mode is changed to *TRANSPARENT* so that painting the menu help text does not change the Frame's background color.

   Finally, we're ready to paint the menu help text. The Frame window sends the user-defined *AW_PAINTMENUHELP* message to the window specified by *wParam* the last time the Frame window processed a *FW_SETMENUHELP* message. This window may be the Frame window or an MDI Child window. The code for processing the *AW_PAINTMENUHELP* message is almost identical in either case. Here's how an MDI Child processes the message:

```
case AW_PAINTMENUHELP:
    // Message sent from Frame window to notify Child that it
    // should paint the status bar text for the last highlighted
    // menu item.
    // lParam = LPPAINTSTRUCT of Frame's status bar.

    // Ask the Frame window what the last selected menu ID was.
    // This value was sent to the frame by this window during the
    // processing for the WM_MENUSELECT message.
    dwResult = SendMessage(GETFRAME(hWnd), FW_GETMENUHELP, 0, 0);

    // Draw the horizontal dividing line separating the status bar
    // from the MDICLIENT window
    ((LPPAINTSTRUCT) lParam)->rcPaint.top +=
        SendMessage(GETFRAME(hWnd), FW_DRAWSTATUSDIVIDE, 0,
            (LONG) (LPPAINTSTRUCT) lParam);

    // Construct the string that is to be displayed
    LoadString(_hInstance, LOWORD(dwResult), szString,
        sizeof(szString));
    GetWindowText(hWnd, szCaption, sizeof(szCaption));
    wsprintf(szBuf, szString, (LPSTR) szCaption);

    // Paint the menu help text in the status bar
    TextOut((((LPPAINTSTRUCT) lParam)->hdc, 0, ((LPPAINTSTRUCT)
        lParam)->rcPaint.top, szBuf, lstrlen(szBuf));
    break;
```

Because a message can only pass *WORD* and *DWORD* parameters, the Frame window cannot pass the menu help code. Instead, the code that processes the *AW_PAINTMENUHELP* message must send the *FW_GETMENUHELP* message back to the Frame to retrieve the help code. The *FW_GETMENUHELP* message simply returns the value that was stored in the Frame window's class extra bytes the last time the *FW_SETMENUHELP* message was processed:

```
case FW_GETMENUHELP:
   // Sent by the Frame or MDI Child when they receive
   // a AW_PAINTMENUHELP message
   dwResult = GETCLSEB(hWnd, CLSEB, dwMenuHelp);
   break;
```

Let's tie up some loose ends.

We've assumed that Windows sends the *WM_ENTERIDLE* message to the Frame's window procedure. This is not always true in an MDI application. If the user is scrolling through options and passes through a nonmaximized MDI Child's system menu, Windows sends the *WM_ENTERIDLE* message to the MDI Child. The MDI Child window must tell the Frame window when it has received a *WM_ENTERIDLE* message:

```
case WM_ENTERIDLE:
   SendMessage(GETFRAME(hWnd), wMsg, wParam, lParam);
   break;
```

Windows sends the *WM_ENTERIDLE* message when a message has been processed and the application's queue is empty. Let's say the user has opened a menu and its help text appears at the bottom of the Frame window. The user starts moving the mouse across the screen and then stops. This causes several *WM_MOUSEMOVE* messages to be sent to the window procedure. After the last one is processed, Windows sends a *WM_ENTERIDLE* message. Our procedure would erase the status bar and repaint the help text. To prevent this flashing, we must add the following lines to the processing of the *WM_ENTERIDLE* message in the Frame's window procedure:

```
case WM_ENTERIDLE:
   .
   .
   .

   if (GETCLSEB(hWnd, CLSEB, hWndMenuHelp) == -1)
     break;
   .
   .
   .

   SETCLSEB(hWnd, CLSEB, hWndMenuHelp, (HWND) -1);
```

A final loose end: If the menu system is closed (because the user selected a menu item or pressed the Esc key), the area occupied by the status bar must be invalidated so Windows will send a *WM_PAINT* message to the Frame window and restore the statistical information. Fortunately, Windows notifies the window procedure that the menu system has been closed by sending the *WM_MENUSELECT* message with the low-order word of *lParam* equal to negative one and the high-order word equal to zero. The Frame and the MDI Children check for this and send a *FW_SETMENUHELP* message to the Frame window with *wParam* equal to zero:

```
case WM_MENUSELECT:
   if (lParam == MAKELONG(-1, 0)) {
      // User has stopped using the menu system. Notify Frame
      // window so that the status bar will be invalidated.
      SendMessage(GETFRAME(hWnd), FW_SETMENUHELP, NULL, 0);
      break;
   }
   .
   .
   .
```

When the Frame window gets this message, it executes the following code to invalidate the status-bar area:

```
case FW_SETMENUHELP:
   .
   .
   .
```

502

```
if (wParam == NULL) {
   SendMessage(hWnd, FW_GETSTATBARRECT, 0, (LONG) (LPRECT)
      &rc);
   InvalidateRect(hWnd, &rc, TRUE);
}
break;
```

Custom Tiling

Almost all MDI applications contain a Window menu that allows the user to manipulate MDI Child windows. Usually the first options to appear in this menu are "Cascade" and "Tile." "Cascade" organizes MDI Child windows so that only the caption bar of each is visible. The active MDI Child is positioned on the top of the stack. The "Tile" option organizes the MDI Child windows side by side so none of the windows overlap and all of the area in the MDICLIENT window is occupied. The active MDI Child is the upper left window.

The window procedure for the MDICLIENT window contains all the code required to arrange the MDI Child windows. The *WM_MDICASCADE* and *WM_MDITILE* messages make the MDICLIENT window rearrange the MDI Children. The programmer does not have to write any additional code. A third message, *WM_MDIICONARRANGE*, causes the MDICLIENT window to arrange any MDI Children that have been reduced to icons. The MDICLIENT window organizes the icons so that they are lined up at the bottom of the MDICLIENT window's area. Whenever the MDICLIENT receives a *WM_MDICASCADE* or *WM_MDITILE* message, the iconic MDI Children are automatically arranged and the non-iconic windows are positioned so that only the bottom row of icons is visible.

The method of tiling implemented by the MDICLIENT window causes windows to be tiled horizontally. That is, if two windows exist, tiling places the active one on the left and the inactive one on the right. In many applications it would be better if a form of vertical tiling were used. For example, Word for Windows tiles its MDI Children so that the active window is above the inactive window. Fewer lines of text are displayed, but each line is seen in its entirety.

FRAME.C includes a function called *TileVertically* that shows how to design a custom tiling scheme for MDI Child windows. The only parameter is the window handle of the MDICLIENT window, *hWndMDIClient*.

This function starts by calculating the area occupied by the MDICLIENT window. Assuming that all of the MDI Child windows will be completely contained within this window after tiling, the size of the MDICLIENT window without scroll bars must be calculated. This can be done by hiding the scroll bars before calling *GetClientRect*:

```
ShowScrollBar(hWndMDIClient, SB_BOTH, 0);
```

As with *WM_MDICASCADE* and *WM_MDITILE*, we want to arrange the iconic MDI Children too. We do this by sending the *WM_MDIICONARRANGE* message to the MDICLIENT window. It is important to do this after the scroll bars have been hidden and before adjusting the position of any of the other MDI Children. When MDI Children are iconic, the MDICLIENT window ensures that the other MDI Children are positioned so that the bottom row of icons is visible. This means that the usable area in the MDICLIENT window is smaller if any MDI Children are iconic. To calculate the amount of usable space, the iconic Children must be arranged first and the y-coordinate that represents the top of the bottom row of icons must be calculated.

This is done by creating a loop that cycles through all the Child windows of the MDICLIENT window:

```
int nTopOfBottomIconRow = 0, nOpenMDIChildren = 0;
HWND hWndChild;
RECT rc;
.
.
.
hWndChild = GetWindow(hWndMDIClient, GW_CHILD);
do {
```

```
if (GetWindow(hWndChild, GW_OWNER) != NULL) continue;

if (IsIconic(hWndChild)) {
    // Window is iconic and is NOT an icon's caption.
    // Get the area of the iconic window.
    GetWindowRect(hWndChild, &rc);
    // rc.top is top of icon in screen coordinates
    nTopOfBottomIconRow = max(nTopOfBottomIconRow, rc.top);
} else nOpenMDIChildren++;

} while (hWndChild = GetWindow(hWndChild, GW_HWNDNEXT));
```

When a window is iconic, Windows creates another window (of a system global class) that displays the icon's caption. This window's parent and owner is the icon window. The non-iconic MDI Children will not have explicit owners; therefore, *GetWindow(hWndChild, GW_OWNER)* will return NULL. The icon caption bar windows should not be taken into account when the loop is processing children of the MDICLIENT window.

The loop calculates the y-coordinate of the bottom row of icons by getting the window coordinates for each iconic window and setting *nTopOfBottomIconRow* to the largest *y* value. If the Child window is not an icon, *nOpenMDIChildren* is incremented by one. When the Children have been enumerated, *GetWindow(hWndChild, GW_HWNDNEXT)* returns NULL and the loop terminates.

Finally, the height of the usable area can be computed:

```
GetClientRect(hWndMDIClient, &rc);
if (nTopOfBottomIconRow) {
    Point.x = 0; Point.y = nTopOfBottomIconRow;
    ScreenToClient(hWndMDIClient, &Point);
    // Point.y is top of bottom icon row in client coordinates
    rc.bottom = Point.y;
}
```

If *nTopOfBottomIconRow* is not zero, the y-coordinate is converted to client coordinates and the usable area identified by the *rc* variable is updated to reflect the appropriate dimensions.

MDI Child windows can't be repositioned if any MDI Child is maximized. Here's the code that restores any maximized MDI Children:

```
dwChildInfo = SendMessage(hWndMDIClient, WM_MDIGETACTIVE, 0, 0);
if (HIWORD(dwChildInfo) == 1)
  ShowWindow(LOWORD(dwChildInfo), SW_RESTORE);
```

The tiling algorithm positions the MDI Child windows on top of each other. However, if several MDI Children are open and tiled in this way, each of the windows will be extremely short. For this reason, the algorithm selects a desired minimum height for the MDI Child windows as five times the height of a caption bar:

```
nMinWndHeight = max(1, rc.bottom /
  (5 * GetSystemMetrics(SM_CYCAPTION)));
```

If the usable region in the MDICLIENT area is so short that one window does not fit, the windows will be tiled in one row. The number of rows and the height of each row that will appear in the MDICLIENT is now calculated:

```
nNumRows = min(nOpenMDIChildren, nMinWndHeight);
nRowHeight = rc.bottom / nNumRows;
```

The tiling algorithm is designed so that each row has at least (number of windows) divided by (number of rows) MDI Children in it. If the result of this division yields a remainder, the remaining MDI Children are distributed evenly among the rows closest to the bottom. This formula determines the number of MDI Children to be placed on each row:

```
nNumWndsOnRow = nOpenMDIChildren / nNumRows +
  (((nOpenMDIChildren % nNumRows) > (nNumRows - (nCrntRow + 1)))
  ? 1 : 0);
```

506

Now that the initial calculations have been done, the loop cycles through the rows and columns to tile the open MDI Children:

```
hWndChild = GetWindow(hWndMDIClient, GW_CHILD);

hWinPosInfo = BeginDeferWindowPos(nOpenMDIChildren);

for (nCrntRow = 0; nCrntRow < nNumRows; nCrntRow++) {

   nNumWndsOnRow = nOpenMDIChildren / nNumRows +
      ((nOpenMDIChildren % nNumRows > (nNumRows - (nCrntRow + 1)))
      ? 1 : 0);

   nColWidth = rc.right / nNumWndsOnRow;
   for (nCrntCol = 0; nCrntCol < nNumWndsOnRow; ) {
      if (!IsIconic(hWndChild) && GetWindow(hWndChild,
            GW_OWNER) == NULL) {
         hWinPosInfo = DeferWindowPos(hWinPosInfo, hWndChild,
         NULL, nCrntCol * nColWidth, nCrntRow * nRowHeight,
         nColWidth, nRowHeight, SWP_NOACTIVATE | SWP_NOZORDER);
         nCrntCol++;
      }
      hWndChild = GetWindow(hWndChild, GW_HWNDNEXT);
   }
}
EndDeferWindowPos(hWinPosInfo);
```

The MDI Child windows are repositioned by making calls to *DeferWindowPos*. We must call *BeginDeferWindowPos* first. This function allocates a block of memory that holds the repositioning information set by calls to the *DeferWindowPos* function. The parameter passed to the *BeginDeferWindowPos* function specifies the number of windows to be repositioned. If the *DeferWindowPos* function is called more often than this number, Windows automatically increases the size of the memory block to contain the additional information. The new block of memory is returned by *DeferWindowPos*. After all the position information has been set, we call *EndDeferWindowPos*. This function instructs Windows to repaint all the MDI Child windows at once.

507

It is possible to call *SetWindowPos* instead of *BeginDeferWindowPos*, *DeferWindowPos*, and *EndDeferWindowPos*, but this would cause an annoying amount of screen updating, and repositioning all the windows would take much longer.

When tiling occurs, the active MDI Child window should be positioned in the upper left corner of the MDICLIENT window. In the *TileVertically* function, this is done for us automatically. Whenever a window is active, it appears closest to the top of the window manager's list. Therefore, the call to *GetWindow(hWndMDIClient, GW_CHILD)* always returns the active MDI Child window. Since the tiling algorithm places the first child in the upper left corner, everything works out fine.

Implementing a Ribbon

A ribbon is a set of controls that appears just under an MDI application's menu bar. It allows easy access to options that affect an area in an MDI Child window. For example, the ribbon in Word for Windows allows the user to alter the character attributes of selected text. Microsoft Excel and Project for Windows also use ribbons that allow the user to enter text or select miniature icons to perform operations.

Most applications let the user show or hide the ribbon. When the ribbon is hidden, more screen real estate is available for the MDI Child windows. The MDI sample application implements a ribbon using a modeless dialog box. This dialog box is created in the *WinMain* function in MDI.C as a child of the Frame window. For a dialog box to be created as a child window, *WS_CHILD* must appear on the *STYLE* line in the template.

If you examine MDI.DLG, you will notice that *WS_CLIPSIBLINGS* also appears on the *STYLE* line. This is necessary for Windows to update the screen correctly. Because the MDICLIENT window and the ribbon can occupy the same area of the screen, Windows might allow either window to paint over the other's area. The *WS_CLIPSIBLINGS* style prevents windows from painting areas occupied by their siblings. The MDICLIENT window is also created with the *WS_CLIPSIBLINGS* style.

Because the Dialog Editor application that comes with the Windows SDK does not allow you to set either of these styles, you must edit the .DLG file with a text editor to alter the *STYLE* line and recompile the application's resources. If you later edit the .DLG file with the Dialog Editor, the .DLG file will have to be edited again because the Dialog Editor strips out the *WS_CLIPSIBLINGS* style when it writes the new .DLG file.

Although ribbons affect the contents of the active MDI Child window, the ribbon implemented in the MDI sample application does not demonstrate this.

The user turns the ribbon on and off by selecting the "Ribbon" option from the Options menu. When the Frame's window procedure receives this message, it toggles the visible state of the ribbon and sends the user-defined *FW_RESIZE-MDICLIENT* message to the Frame window:

```
case WM_COMMAND:
   switch (wParam) {
      .
      .
      .
      case IDM_OPTIONSRIBBON:
         ShowWindow(_hDlgRibbon,
            IsWindowVisible(_hDlgRibbon) ? SW_HIDE : SW_SHOW);
         SendMessage(hWnd, FW_RESIZEMDICLIENT, 0, 0);
         break;
      .
      .
      .
```

The *FW_RESIZEMDICLIENT* message is received by the Frame's window procedure whenever the user resizes the Frame window, toggles the status bar on or off, or toggles the ribbon on or off. This message calculates the new height and position of the MDICLIENT window:

```
case FW_RESIZEMDICLIENT:
  GetClientRect(hWnd, &rc);
  if (IsWindowVisible(_hDlgRibbon)) {
    GetClientRect(_hDlgRibbon, &rcTemp);
    rc.top += rcTemp.bottom:
    rc.bottom -= rcTemp.bottom;
  }
  SendMessage(hWnd, FW_GETSTATBARRECT, 0, (LONG) (LPRECT)
    &rcTemp);
  rc.bottom -= rcTemp.bottom - rcTemp.top;
  MoveWindow(_hWndMDIClient, 0, rc.top, rc.right, rc.bottom,
    TRUE);
  break;
```

Once the user turns the ribbon on, it stays on until the user explicitly turns it off. If the user closes all the MDI Child windows, the ribbon should be disabled and all of its controls should appear gray. You do this by having each MDI Child's window procedure post the *FW_MDICHILDDESTROY* message to the Frame window when the child processes the *WM_DESTROY* message. When the Frame window receives the *FW_MDICHILDDESTROY* message from the last MDI Child, it disables the ribbon dialog box:

```
case FW_MDICHILDDESTROY:
  if (hWndActiveMDIChild != NULL) break;
  EnableWindow(_hDlgRibbon, FALSE);
  break;
```

When the user selects "Open sheet" or "Open chart" from the File menu in the MDI sample application, the Frame window creates a new MDI Child window and enables the ribbon.

When a window is disabled, Windows won't send it mouse or keyboard messages. Children of the disabled window don't receive mouse or keyboard input either. This means child controls don't receive input when the ribbon is disabled. However, when a child control is drawn, the control's window procedure determines if the *WS_DISABLE* style is on for the particular control. If this style is on, the control

510

is drawn using grayed text. Although the child controls won't receive input, disabling the ribbon doesn't change the *WS_DISABLE* style bit for the controls. To make the controls paint themselves using gray text, the individual controls must be disabled by placing the following code in the ribbon's dialog-box procedure, *RibbonDlgProc* (in the MDI.C module):

```
case WM_ENABLE:
    hWndChild = GetWindow(hWnd, GW_CHILD);
    while (hWndChild != NULL) {
        EnableWindow(hWndChild, wParam);
        hWndChild = GetWindow(hWndChild, GW_HWNDNEXT);
    }
    break;
```

The value in *wParam* for a *WM_ENABLE* message indicates whether the window is being enabled (*wParam* is nonzero) or disabled (*wParam* is zero). This loop simply makes all the children of the dialog box have the same state as the dialog box itself.

The *WM_PAINT* message is also intercepted in the ribbon's dialog-box procedure. This message is used to draw a dividing line between the dialog box and the MDICLIENT window. Like the dividing line drawn for the status bar, this line is painted with a pen that has a thickness of *GetSystemMetrics(SM_CYBORDER)*.

Child controls in a ribbon should retain focus for a short time. Once the user has selected the desired option, the control should set the focus back to the MDI application's Frame window. This allows the user to work fluidly with the document, perform some operation by selecting a control in the ribbon, and continue to work. The code fragment below shows how focus is set to the Frame window after a ribbon control has performed its operation:

```
case WM_COMMAND:
    // Make sure focus is given back to the Frame after an
    // option is chosen by the user
```

```
switch (wParam) {
   case ID_FONT:
   case ID_SIZE:
      // Do whatever work is necessary
      if (HIWORD(dwParam) != CBN_SELCHANGE) break;
      SetFocus(GetParent(hDlg));
      break;

   case ID_BOLD:
   case ID_ITALIC:
   case ID_UNDERLINE:
      // Do whatever work is necessary
      if (HIWORD(dwParam) != BN_CLICKED) break;
      SetFocus(GetParent(hDlg));
      break;

   case IDOK:
   case IDCANCEL:
      SetFocus(GetParent(hDlg));
      break;
}
break;
```

When the ribbon's dialog-box procedure receives the *WM_COMMAND* message, focus is sent back to the Frame window. The Frame window sets focus to the MDICLIENT window, and the MDICLIENT window sets focus to the active MDI Child window.

Some controls, like list boxes, combo boxes, and scroll bars, keep the input focus for a longer period than buttons so that a user can scroll through a list of choices. If the user is working with one of these controls in the ribbon, the Enter and Esc keys should set the focus back to the active MDI Child window. When either of these keys is pressed, Windows sends a *WM_COMMAND* message with *wParam* set to *IDOK* or *IDCANCEL*. Windows sends these identifiers regardless of whether "Ok" and "Cancel" buttons exist in the dialog box. The dialog-box procedure can call *SetFocus* when either of these events occurs.

Closing an MDI Application

An MDI application allows the user to work with many documents at once. Because several windows are displayed, it's easy for the user to lose track of which documents have been updated and not saved. For this reason, it is important that an MDI application be forgiving and take extra precautions so that no work is accidentally destroyed. Of course, this is important for non-MDI applications as well.

An MDI application should see if any data could be lost when the user attempts one of the following actions:

- Closing an MDI Child window.

- Terminating the MDI application.

- Terminating the Windows session.

Most MDI Child windows maintain a Boolean value (called a *dirty flag*) in the window's extra bytes to indicate whether the document has been updated since it was last saved. Whenever an action takes place that changes the document, this value is set to TRUE. After the file has been successfully written to disk, the value is changed to FALSE.

Let's examine the situation where the user is terminating the Windows session first. When the user closes Program Manager, a system modal message box is presented to verify that the Windows session should be terminated. If the user answers affirmatively, Windows sends the *WM_QUERYENDSESSION* message to all running applications. Each application has an opportunity to determine whether any data would be lost if the application were terminated and may prompt the user to take some action. If an application finds that the dirty flag is set, it presents a message box similar to the one in Figure 7-2.

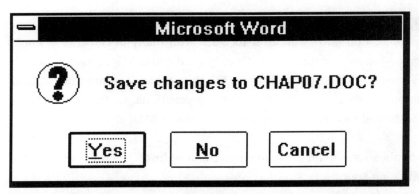

Figure 7-2. Dialog box presented to user when application terminates and documents have not been saved.

The caption of the message box should indicate the name of the application that is presenting it. Remember that every application is going to get a chance to present a message box, and the user may not remember which application a particular file belongs to. The name of the file should also appear in the message box. In MDI applications, this message box may appear several times, once for every document window the user has opened. The options in the box allow the user to do one of the following:

Option	Description
Yes	Save the updated document. Continue terminating the Windows session.
No	Do not save the updated document. Continue terminating the Windows session.
Cancel	Do not save the updated document. Stop terminating the Windows session.

If the user presses the "Yes" or "No" button, the application should return TRUE in response to *WM_QUERYENDSESSION*. Windows will send the *WM_QUERY-ENDSESSION* message to the next application.

If the user selected "Cancel," the window procedure should return FALSE. Windows will stop sending *WM_QUERYENDSESSION* messages and start sending *WM_ENDSESSION* messages to the applications that previously received *WM_QUERYENDSESSION* messages.

The *WM_ENDSESSION* message notifies applications of whether or not the Windows session is actually being terminated. The value of the *wParam* parameter is TRUE if the session is terminating. If an application responded TRUE to the *WM_QUERYENDSESSION* message (notifying Windows that it didn't mind being terminated) but another application responded FALSE (notifying Windows that it did not want the session to terminate), Windows would send the *WM_ENDSESSION* message to the first application with the *wParam* parameter set to FALSE. If all applications returned TRUE, Windows would send the *WM_ENDSESSION* message with *wParam* set to TRUE and then terminate the Windows session.

For an MDI application, this processing should be extended so that when the MDI Frame window receives a *WM_QUERYENDSESSION* message, it sends this message to each of the MDI Child windows. Similarly, the Frame window should forward all *WM_ENDSESSION* messages to the MDI Children.

In the MDI sample application, the code in the Frame's window procedure for sending the *WM_QUERYENDSESSION* message to the MDI Children looks like this:

```
case WM_QUERYENDSESSION:
   dwResult = TRUE;
   hWndChild = GetWindow(_hWndMDIClient, GW_CHILD);
   if (hWndChild == NULL) break;

   do {
      // Do not ask caption bars of iconic MDI Children
      if (GetWindow(hWndChild, GW_OWNER) != NULL) continue;
         dwResult = SendMessage(hWndChild, WM_QUERYENDSESSION,
            wParam, lParam);
```

```
    // If the MDI Child says that it is NOT OK, don't ask the
    // rest of the MDI Children
    if (dwResult == FALSE) break;

} while (hWndChild = GetWindow(hWndChild, GW_HWNDNEXT));

// dwResult is TRUE; terminate the session
if (dwResult == TRUE) break;

wTemp = hWndChild;
hWndChild = GetWindow(_hWndMDIClient, GW_CHILD);
do {
    // If this Child is the one that said NO, stop
    if (wTemp == hWndChild) break;
    // Do not send to caption bars of iconic MDI Children
    if (GetWindow(hWndChild, GW_OWNER) != NULL) continue;
    // Tell Child we are not ending session (wParam is FALSE)
    SendMessage(hWndChild, WM_ENDSESSION, FALSE, 0);
} while (hWndChild = GetWindow(hWndChild, GW_HWNDNEXT));
// dwResult is FALSE; don't terminate the session
break;
```

The first loop enumerates all the MDI Child windows and sends the *WM_QUERYENDSESSION* message to each. If all the MDI Children return TRUE, TRUE is returned to Windows and the next application gets the *WM_QUERY-ENDSESSION* message. If any of the MDI Children return FALSE, however, the loop is immediately stopped and a new loop is started. The second loop sends the *WM_ENDSESSION* message (with the *wParam* parameter set to FALSE) to each of the MDI Children that responded TRUE. When the loop completes, FALSE is returned to Windows so the session will not be terminated.

The MDI Child window procedures for the Sheet and Chart classes process the *WM_QUERYENDSESSION* message in the following way:

```
case WM_QUERYENDSESSION:
    // Construct string including the document's name
    lstrcpy(szBuf, "Save changes to ");
```

```
wTemp = lstrlen(szBuf);
GetWindowText(hWnd, szBuf + wTemp, sizeof(szBuf) - wTemp);
lstrcat(szBuf, "?");

wTemp = MessageBox(hWnd, szBuf, _szAppName,
    MB_ICONQUESTION | MB_YESNOCANCEL |
    (wParam ? MB_APPLMODAL : MB_SYSTEMMODAL));

switch (wTemp) {
    case IDYES:
        // Save the document and it's OK to quit
        dwResult = TRUE;
        break;

    case IDNO:
        // Don't save the document and it's OK to quit
        dwResult = TRUE;
        break;

    case IDCANCEL:
        // Don't save the document and it's NOT OK to quit
        dwResult = FALSE;
        break;
}
break;
```

The MDI sample application does not maintain a dirty flag for each of the created windows; therefore, the code above always prompts the user to save the updated document to disk. You will also notice that the call to *MessageBox* tests the value of *wParam*. Whenever Windows sends the *WM_QUERYENDSESSION* message, both *wParam* and *lParam* are zero. When this message is sent from the Frame window's procedure, the values of *wParam* and *lParam* are also passed to the MDI Child window. Since *wParam* is FALSE, a system modal message box will be displayed to the user. The message box must be system modal so the user cannot close Program Manager a second time.

You may be wondering when *wParam* will ever be TRUE. Well, when the user wants to close the MDI application without terminating the Windows session, a *WM_CLOSE* message is sent to the Frame's window procedure. The processing for this message appears below:

```
case WM_CLOSE:
   fCallDefProc = (BOOL) SendMessage(hWnd, WM_QUERYENDSESSION,
      TRUE, 0);
   if (fCallDefProc) SendMessage(hWnd, WM_ENDSESSION, TRUE, 0);
   break;
```

This makes the application believe that the Windows session is terminating. The *wParam* sent with the *WM_QUERYENDSESSION* message is TRUE. This indicates to the MDI Child window that a system modal message box is not necessary and that an application modal message box should be displayed instead.

Normally, the *DefFrameProc* function destroys the window when it processes a *WM_CLOSE* message. Therefore, setting the *fCallDefProc* variable equal to the result of sending the *WM_QUERYENDSESSION* message determines whether or not the window is destroyed.

If any of the MDI Child windows return FALSE, the processing in the Frame window's procedure automatically sends the *WM_ENDSESSION* message (*wParam* is FALSE) to all the MDI Children that had returned TRUE. However, if the application is going to terminate, we must send the *WM_ENDSESSION* message to the Frame window so that the MDI Children will be notified. The processing of the *WM_ENDSESSION* message in the Frame's window procedure is shown below:

```
case WM_ENDSESSION:
   hWndChild = GetWindow(_hWndMDIClient, GW_CHILD);
   if (hWndChild == NULL) break;

   do {
      // Do not send to caption bars of iconic MDI Children
      if (GetWindow(hWndChild, GW_OWNER) != NULL) continue;
```

```
    SendMessage(hWndChild, WM_ENDSESSION, wParam, 0);
} while (hWndChild = GetWindow(hWndChild, GW_HWNDNEXT));
break;
```

Since none of the MDI Children have any processing to do when the *WM_ENDSESSION* message is processed, they simply return:

```
case WM_ENDSESSION:
    // Do any last-minute cleanup during this message
    break;
```

So far, we have discussed two occasions when the application should test for possible loss of data. The third occasion is when the user simply closes a single MDI Child window. In this case, the window receives a *WM_CLOSE* message and processes it as follows:

```
case WM_CLOSE:
  fCallDefProc = (BOOL) SendMessage(hWnd, WM_QUERYENDSESSION,
      TRUE, 0);
  if (fCallDefProc) SendMessage(hWnd, WM_ENDSESSION, TRUE, 0);
  break;
```

The *WM_QUERYENDSESSION* message is only sent to the MDI Child window that is being closed. The *wParam* parameter is TRUE, so an application modal message box will appear instead of a system modal message box. If the user indicated that the MDI Child could be closed, the *WM_ENDSESSION* message is sent so the Child can do last-minute cleanup; the *DefMDIChildProc* function is allowed to process the *WM_CLOSE* message, destroying the Child window.

Figure 7-3. MDI.ICO.

Figure 7-4. SHEET.ICO.

Figure 7-5. CHART.ICO.

Listing 7-1. MAKEFILE for MDI application.

```
#*********************************************************************
#Module name: MAKEFILE
#Programmer : Jeffrey M. Richter
#*********************************************************************

PROG = MDI
MODEL = M
CFLAGS = -A$(MODEL) -D_WINDOWS -Gcsw2 -W4 -Zlepid -Od -NT _$*
LFLAGS = /NOE/BA/A:16/M/CO/LI/F
LIBS = $(MODEL)nocrt + libw

M1 = $(PROG).obj Frame.obj Sheet.obj Chart.obj

ICONS = $(PROG).ico
BITMAPS =
```

```
CURSORS =
RESOURCES = $(ICONS) $(BITMAPS) $(CURSORS)

.SUFFIXES: .rc

.rc.res:
    rc -r $*.rc

$(PROG).Exe: $(M1) $(PROG).Def $(PROG).Res
    link $(LFLAGS) @<<$(PROG).lnk
$(M1)
$(PROG), $(PROG), $(LIBS), $(PROG)
<<
    rc $(PROG).Res

$(PROG).obj:    $*.c $*.h
Frame.obj:      $*.c $(PROG).h
Sheet.obj:      $*.c $(PROG).h
Chart.obj:      $*.c $(PROG).h

$(PROG).res:    $*.rc $*.h $*.dlg dialog.h $(RESOURCES)
```

Listing 7-2. MDI.H application header module.

```
/*****************************************************************
Module name: MDI.H
Programmer : Jeffrey M. Richter & Elvira Peretsman
*****************************************************************/
#include "dialog.h"

extern char    _szAppName[];    // The name of the application
extern HANDLE _hInstance;       // Data instance of the application
extern HANDLE _hAccelTable;     // Handle to active accelerator table
extern HWND _hWndMDIClient;     // Handle to MDICLIENT window
extern HWND _hDlgRibbon;        // Handle to Ribbon modeless dialog
                                // box

BOOL FAR PASCAL RegisterFrameWndClass (void);
BOOL FAR PASCAL RegisterSheetWndClass (void);
```

```
BOOL FAR PASCAL RegisterChartWndClass (void);
BOOL FAR PASCAL RibbonDlgProc (HWND hDlg, WORD wMsg, WORD wParam,
    DWORD dwParam);

#define GETFRAME(hWnd) ((HWND) (GetParent(GetParent(hWnd))))

// User-defined messages processed by Frame Window class
#define FW_MDICHILDDESTROY (WM_USER + 0)
#define FW_RESIZEMDICLIENT (WM_USER + 1)
#define FW_GETSTATBARRECT (WM_USER + 2)
#define FW_SETMENUHELP (WM_USER + 3)
#define FW_GETMENUHELP (WM_USER + 4)
#define FW_DRAWSTATUSDIVIDE (WM_USER + 5)

// User-defined messages processed by all window classes
#define AW_PAINTMENUHELP (WM_USER + 100)

// User-defined messages processed by all MDI Child window classes
#define AC_PAINTSTATBAR (WM_USER + 200)

// FILE MENU
#define IDM_FILEOPENSHEET 101
#define IDM_FILEOPENCHART 102
#define IDM_FILESAVE 104
#define IDM_FILESAVEAS 105
#define IDM_FILEPRINT 106
#define IDM_FILEPRINTERSETUP 107
#define IDM_EXIT 108

// EDIT MENU
#define IDM_EDITCUT 110
#define IDM_EDITCOPY 111
#define IDM_EDITPASTE 112

// SHEET MENU
#define IDM_SHEETOPTION 120

// CHART MENU
#define IDM_CHARTOPTION 130
```

```
// OPTIONS MENU
#define IDM_OPTIONSSTATUS 140
#define IDM_OPTIONSRIBBON 141

// HELP MENU
#define IDM_HELPINDEX 150
#define IDM_HELPKEYBOARD 151
#define IDM_HELPCOMMANDS 152
#define IDM_HELPPROCEDURES 153
#define IDM_HELPUSINGHELP 154
#define IDM_ABOUT 155

// WINDOW MENU
#define IDM_WINDOWTILEVERT 160
#define IDM_WINDOWTILEHORIZ 161
#define IDM_WINDOWCASCADE 162
#define IDM_WINDOWARRANGEICONS 163
#define IDM_WINDOWCHILD 164


//************ String Table Constants ************

// String table used to fill the font and size comboboxes
/ in the Ribbon
#define IDS_FONT 100
#define IDS_SIZE 200

// String table for Frame window's menu
#define IDS_FRAMEPOPUPID 1000
#define IDS_FRAMEMENUID 2000

// String table for Sheet window's menu
#define IDS_SHEETPOPUPID 3000
#define IDS_SHEETMENUID 4000

// String table for Chart window's menu
#define IDS_CHARTPOPUPID 5000
#define IDS_CHARTMENUID 6000
```

```
// String table for contents of status bar when no menu is open
#define IDS_FRAMESTATUSBAR 7000
#define IDS_SHEETSTATUSBAR 7001
#define IDS_CHARTSTATUSBAR 7002


// Identifiers to help use string tables for menu help
// descriptions for menu items in the Application and MDI
// Child system menus
#define IDM_SYSMENUSIZE 0x00        // ((SC_SIZE & 0x0FFF) >> 4)
#define IDM_SYSMENUMOVE 0x01        // ((SC_MOVE & 0x0FFF) >> 4)
#define IDM_SYSMENUMINIMIZE 0x02    // ((SC_MINIMIZE & 0x0FFF) >> 4)
#define IDM_SYSMENUMAXIMIZE 0x03    // ((SC_MAXIMIZE & 0x0FFF) >> 4)
#define IDM_SYSMENUNEXTWINDOW 0x04  // ((SC_NEXTWINDOW & 0x0FFF)
                                    // >> 4)
#define IDM_SYSMENUCLOSE 0x06       // ((SC_CLOSE & 0x0FFF) >> 4)
#define IDM_SYSMENURESTORE 0x12     // ((SC_RESTORE & 0x0FFF) >> 4)
#define IDM_SYSMENUTASKLIST 0x13    // ((SC_TASKLIST & 0x0FFF) >> 4)

void FAR PASCAL ChangeMDIMenu (HWND hWndFrame, HWND hWndClient,
   HMENU hTopLevelMenu, WORD wMenuID);

HWND FAR PASCAL CreateMDIChild (LPSTR szClassName,
   LPSTR szWindowName, DWORD dwStyle, short x, short y,
   short nWidth, short nHeight, HWND hWndMDIClient,
   HANDLE hInstance, LONG lParam);

//******* Macros for Use by Window and Class Extra Bytes ********

#define offsetof(Struct, Member) \
   ((unsigned int) &(((Struct NEAR *) 0)->Member))

#define GETWNDEB(hWnd, Struct, Member) \
   ((sizeof((((Struct FAR *)0)->Member) == sizeof(DWORD)) ? \
      GetWindowLong(hWnd, offsetof(Struct, Member)) : \
      GetWindowWord(hWnd, offsetof(Struct, Member)))

#define SETWNDEB(hWnd, Struct, Member, Value) \
   ((sizeof((((Struct FAR *)0)->Member) == sizeof(DWORD)) ? \
      SetWindowLong(hWnd, offsetof(Struct, Member), Value) : \
      SetWindowWord(hWnd, offsetof(Struct, Member), (WORD) Value))
```

```
#define GETCLSEB(hWnd, Struct, Member) \
  ((sizeof(((Struct FAR *)0)->Member) == sizeof(DWORD)) ? \
    GetClassLong(hWnd, offsetof(Struct, Member)) : \
    GetClassWord(hWnd, offsetof(Struct, Member)))

#define SETCLSEB(hWnd, Struct, Member, Value) \
  ((sizeof(((Struct FAR *)0)->Member) == sizeof(DWORD)) ? \
    SetClassLong(hWnd, offsetof(Struct, Member), Value) : \
    SetClassWord(hWnd, offsetof(Struct, Member), (WORD) Value))
```

Listing 7-3. MDI.C application source module.

```
/*******************************************************************
Module name: MDI.C
Programmer : Jeffrey M. Richter & Elvira Peretsman
*******************************************************************/

#include "..\nowindws.h"
#undef NOCTLMGR
#undef NOGDI
#undef NOKERNEL
#undef NOMB
#undef NOMDI
#undef NOMENUS
#undef NOMSG
#undef NOSYSMETRICS
#undef NOUSER
#undef NOWINMESSAGES
#undef NOWINSTYLES
#include <windows.h>

#include "mdi.h"


// Application global variables
char  _szAppName[] = "MDI";    // The name of the application
HANDLE _hInstance = NULL;      // Data instance of the application
HANDLE _hAccelTable = NULL;    // Handle to active accelerator
                               // table
```

```
HWND    _hWndMDIClient = NULL;   // Handle to MDICLIENT window
HWND    _hDlgRibbon = NULL;      // Handle to Ribbon modeless dialog
                                 // box


/**************** Main Application Loop ****************/

// NEAR or FAR dependent on compilation model S or M respectively
int PASCAL WinMain (HANDLE hInstance, HANDLE hPrevInstance,
     LPSTR lpszCmdLine, int nCmdShow) {
  MSG msg;
  FARPROC fpProc;
  HWND hWndFrame;

  if (hPrevInstance != NULL) {
    // Only allow one instance of the application to run
    MessageBox(NULL, "MDI application is already running.",
      _szAppName, MB_OK | MB_ICONINFORMATION);
    return(0);
  }

  _hInstance = hInstance;

  // Register the Frame window class
  if (!RegisterFrameWndClass()) return(0);

  // Register the MDI Child window classes
  if (!RegisterSheetWndClass()) return(0);
  if (!RegisterChartWndClass()) return(0);

  // Create the Frame window
  hWndFrame = CreateWindow("Frame", _szAppName,
    WS_OVERLAPPEDWINDOW | WS_CLIPCHILDREN | WS_MAXIMIZE |
    WS_VISIBLE | WS_MAXIMIZEBOX | WS_MINIMIZEBOX, CW_USEDEFAULT,
    nCmdShow, CW_USEDEFAULT, CW_USEDEFAULT, NULL, NULL,
    _hInstance, NULL);
  if (hWndFrame == NULL) return(0);

  // Create the Ribbon dialog box with Frame as owner
  fpProc = MakeProcInstance(RibbonDlgProc, _hInstance);
```

```
   _hDlgRibbon = CreateDialog(_hInstance, "RIBBON", hWndFrame,
      fpProc);
   if (_hDlgRibbon == NULL) {
      FreeProcInstance(fpProc);
      return(0);
   }

   while (GetMessage(&msg, NULL, 0, 0)) {
      if (!TranslateMDISysAccel(_hWndMDIClient, &msg)) {
         if (_hAccelTable == NULL ||
               !TranslateAccelerator(hWndFrame, _hAccelTable,
               &msg)) {
            if (!IsDialogMessage(_hDlgRibbon, &msg)) {
               TranslateMessage(&msg);
               DispatchMessage(&msg);
            }
         }
      }
   }

   FreeProcInstance(fpProc);
   return(msg.wParam);
}

// Function to make creating MDI Child as easy as creating any
// other kind of window
HWND FAR PASCAL CreateMDIChild (LPSTR szClassName,
      LPSTR szWindowName, DWORD dwStyle, short x, short y,
      short nWidth, short nHeight, HWND hWndMDIClient,
      HANDLE hInstance, LONG lParam) {
   MDICREATESTRUCT cs;
   HWND hWndChild;

   cs.szClass = szClassName;
   cs.szTitle = szWindowName;
   cs.hOwner  = hInstance;
   cs.x       = x;
   cs.y       = y;
   cs.cx      = nWidth;
```

```
   cs.cy        = nHeight;
   cs.style     = dwStyle;
   cs.lParam    = lParam;
   hWndChild = (HWND) SendMessage(hWndMDIClient, WM_MDICREATE,
      0, (LONG) (LPMDICREATESTRUCT) &cs);
   return(hWndChild);
}


// Function to change the menu in the Frame window whenever a new
// MDI Child becomes active
void FAR PASCAL ChangeMDIMenu (HWND hWndFrame, HWND hWndClient,
      HMENU hMenuNew, WORD wMenuID) {
  WORD wCount;
  HMENU hSubMenu = 0;

   // Get number of top-level menu items in the menu used by the
   // window being activated
   wCount = GetMenuItemCount(hMenuNew);

   // Locate the pop-up menu that contains the menu option with
   // the 'wMenuID' identifier in it. This must be an identifier
   // for an option in the new menu's "Window" pop-up menu.
   while (wCount) {
      hSubMenu = GetSubMenu(hMenuNew, wCount - 1);
      if ((int) GetMenuState(hSubMenu, wMenuID, MF_BYCOMMAND) !=
            -1)
         break;
      wCount—;
   }

   // Tell the MDICLIENT window to set up the new menu
   SendMessage(hWndClient, WM_MDISETMENU, 0, MAKELONG(hMenuNew,
      hSubMenu));

   DrawMenuBar(hWndFrame);
}


// *************************************************************
// This function processes all messages sent to About dialog box
```

```
BOOL FAR PASCAL AboutProc (HWND hDlg, WORD wMsg, WORD wParam,
      LONG lParam) {
   char szBuffer[100];
   BOOL fProcessed = TRUE;

   switch (wMsg) {

      case WM_INITDIALOG:
         // Set version static window to have date and time of
         // compilation
         wsprintf(szBuffer, "%s at %s", (LPSTR) __DATE__,
            (LPSTR) __TIME__);
        SetWindowText(GetDlgItem(hDlg, ID_VERSION), szBuffer);
         break;

      case WM_COMMAND:
         switch (wParam) {
            case IDOK: case IDCANCEL:
               if (HIWORD(lParam) == BN_CLICKED)
                  EndDialog(hDlg, wParam);
               break;

            default:
               break;
         }
         break;

      default:
         fProcessed = FALSE; break;
   }
   return(fProcessed);
}

BOOL FAR PASCAL RibbonDlgProc (HWND hDlg, WORD wMsg, WORD wParam,
      DWORD dwParam) {
   BOOL fProcessed = TRUE;
   HPEN hPen;
   RECT rc;
   PAINTSTRUCT ps;
   HWND hCtl;
```

```
int i;
char szBuf[25];

switch (wMsg) {

    case WM_INITDIALOG:
        // Add strings to the font combobox
        hCtl = GetDlgItem(hDlg, ID_FONT);
        i = IDS_FONT;
        while (LoadString(_hInstance, i++, szBuf, sizeof(szBuf))
                != 0)
        SendMessage(hCtl, CB_ADDSTRING, 0, (LONG) (LPSTR) szBuf);
        SendMessage(hCtl, CB_SETCURSEL, 0, 0);

        // Add strings to the font-size combobox
        hCtl = GetDlgItem(hDlg, ID_SIZE);
        i = IDS_SIZE;
        while (LoadString(_hInstance, i++, szBuf, sizeof(szBuf))
                != 0)
        SendMessage(hCtl, CB_ADDSTRING, 0, (LONG) (LPSTR) szBuf);
        SendMessage(hCtl, CB_SETCURSEL, 0, 0);
        break;

    case WM_ENABLE:
        // Make all child windows have the same status as the
        // dialog box
        hCtl = GetWindow(hDlg, GW_CHILD);
        while (hCtl != NULL) {
            EnableWindow(hCtl, wParam);
            hCtl = GetWindow(hCtl, GW_HWNDNEXT);
        }
        break;

    case WM_PAINT:
        // Paint a horizontal dividing line between the Ribbon
        // and the MDICLIENT window
        BeginPaint(hDlg, &ps);
        hPen = CreatePen(PS_SOLID, GetSystemMetrics(SM_CYBORDER),
            RGB(0, 0, 0));
        SelectObject(ps.hdc, hPen);
```

530

```
        GetClientRect(hDlg, &rc);
        MoveTo(ps.hdc, 0, rc.bottom -
            GetSystemMetrics(SM_CYBORDER));
        LineTo(ps.hdc, rc.right, rc.bottom -
            GetSystemMetrics(SM_CYBORDER));
        EndPaint(hDlg, &ps);
        DeleteObject(hPen);
        break;

    case WM_COMMAND:
        // Make sure focus is given back to the Frame after
        // an option is chosen by the user

        switch (wParam) {
            case ID_FONT:
            case ID_SIZE:
                if (HIWORD(dwParam) != CBN_SELCHANGE) break;
                SetFocus(GetParent(hDlg));
                break;

            case ID_BOLD:
            case ID_ITALIC:
            case ID_UNDERLINE:
                if (HIWORD(dwParam) != BN_CLICKED) break;
                SetFocus(GetParent(hDlg));
                break;

            case IDOK:
            case IDCANCEL:
                SetFocus(GetParent(hDlg));
                break;
        }
        break;

    default:
        fProcessed = FALSE;
        break;
    }
    return(fProcessed);
}
```

Listing 7-4. FRAME.C Frame window source module.

```
/**************************************************************
Module name: Frame.C
Programmer : Jeffrey M. Richter & Elvira Peretsman
**************************************************************/

#include "..\nowindws.h"
#undef NOCOLOR
#undef NOCTLMGR
#undef NODEFERWINDOWPOS
#undef NOGDI
#undef NOKERNEL
#undef NOLSTRING
#undef NOMB
#undef NOMDI
#undef NOMENUS
#undef NOMINMAX
#undef NONCMESSAGES
#undef NOSCROLL
#undef NOSHOWWINDOW
#undef NOSYSCOMMANDS
#undef NOSYSMETRICS
#undef NOTEXTMETRIC
#undef NOUSER
#undef NOWH
#undef NOWINMESSAGES
#undef NOWINOFFSETS
#undef NOWINSTYLES
#define OEMRESOURCE
#include <windows.h>

#include "mdi.h"

static char _szClassName[] = "Frame";

// Structure for use with class extra bytes
typedef struct {
    WORD   wNumSheets;      // Number of Sheet windows created
    WORD   wNumCharts;      // Number of Chart windows created
```

```
    HMENU hMenu;              // Menu used when no MDI Children are
                             // active
    BOOL   fStatusBarOn;      // Is the status bar showing?
    HWND   hWndMenuHelp;      // Window that last received a
                             // WM_MENUSELECT message
    DWORD dwMenuHelp;         // Menu help code placed here by
                             // hWndMenuHelp window
} CLSEB;

void NEAR PASCAL TileVertically (HWND hWndMDIClient);
BOOL FAR PASCAL AboutProc (HWND hDlg, WORD wMsg, WORD wParam,
    LONG lParam);

LONG FAR PASCAL FrameWndProc (HWND hWnd, WORD wMsg, WORD wParam,
        LONG lParam) {
    BOOL fCallDefProc = FALSE;
    DWORD dwResult = 0;

    CLIENTCREATESTRUCT ccs;
    HMENU hMenu;
    RECT rc, rcTemp;
    WORD wTemp = 0;
    FARPROC fpProc;
    char szBuf[100];
    PAINTSTRUCT ps;
    TEXTMETRIC tm;
    HPEN hPen;
    BITMAP Bitmap;
    HWND hWndActiveMDIChild, hWndChild;
    BOOL fMDIChildIsMaximized;

    if (IsWindow(_hWndMDIClient))
        dwResult = SendMessage(_hWndMDIClient, WM_MDIGETACTIVE,
            0, 0);

    // Get the window handle of the active MDI Child. This is NULL
    // if no MDI Children exist.
    hWndActiveMDIChild = (HWND) LOWORD(dwResult);
```

```
// Determine if the MDI Child is maximized
fMDIChildIsMaximized = HIWORD(dwResult);
dwResult = 0;

switch (wMsg) {

    case WM_CREATE:
        // Initialize default values in the class extra bytes
        hMenu = LoadMenu(_hInstance, _szClassName);
        SETCLSEB(hWnd, CLSEB, hMenu, hMenu);
        SETCLSEB(hWnd, CLSEB, fStatusBarOn, TRUE);

        // Create the MDICLIENT window as a child of the Frame
        ccs.hWindowMenu = GetSubMenu(GetMenu(hWnd), 1);
        ccs.idFirstChild = IDM_WINDOWCHILD;

        _hWndMDIClient = CreateWindow("MDIClient", "",
            WS_CHILD | WS_CLIPCHILDREN | WS_VSCROLL | WS_HSCROLL |
            WS_VISIBLE | WS_CLIPSIBLINGS, 0, 0, 0, 0, hWnd, NULL,
            _hInstance, (LPSTR) (LPCLIENTCREATESTRUCT) &ccs);
        break;

    case WM_CLOSE:
        // Before closing the application, ask the MDI Children
        // if it is OK. wParam is TRUE because the Windows
        // session is NOT being ended.
        fCallDefProc = (BOOL) SendMessage(hWnd,
            WM_QUERYENDSESSION, TRUE, 0);
        if (fCallDefProc) SendMessage(hWnd, WM_ENDSESSION,
            TRUE, 0);
        break;

    case WM_QUERYENDSESSION:
        // If called by Windows, wParam is zero. Otherwise,
        // wParam is TRUE.

        // Assume that it is OK to end the session
        dwResult = TRUE;

        // Get the handle of the first MDI Child
        hWndChild = GetWindow(_hWndMDIClient, GW_CHILD);
```

534

```
// If no MDI Children exist, it is OK to terminate
if (hWndChild == NULL) break;

// Ask each child if it is OK to terminate
do {
   // Do not ask caption bars of iconic MDI Children
   if (GetWindow(hWndChild, GW_OWNER) != NULL) continue;

   dwResult = SendMessage(hWndChild, WM_QUERYENDSESSION,
      wParam, 0);

   // If the MDI Child says that it is NOT OK, don't ask
   // the rest of the MDI Children
   if (dwResult == FALSE) break;

} while ((hWndChild = GetWindow(hWndChild, GW_HWNDNEXT))
   != NULL);

// If any MDI Child said NO, tell the other children that
// the session is NOT being terminated
if (dwResult == FALSE) {
   wTemp = hWndChild;
   hWndChild = GetWindow(_hWndMDIClient, GW_CHILD);
   do {
      // If this child is the one that said NO, stop
      if (wTemp == hWndChild) break;

      // Do not send to caption bars of iconic MDI
      // Children
      if (GetWindow(hWndChild, GW_OWNER) != NULL)
         continue;

      // Tell child we are not ending the session
      // (wParam is FALSE)
      SendMessage(hWndChild, WM_ENDSESSION, FALSE, 0);
   } while ((hWndChild = GetWindow(hWndChild,
      GW_HWNDNEXT)) != NULL);
}
// dwResult is TRUE if OK, FALSE if not OK
break;
```

```
case WM_ENDSESSION:
    // wParam != FALSE if shutting down

    // Get handle of first MDI Child window
    hWndChild = GetWindow(_hWndMDIClient, GW_CHILD);

    // If no MDI Children exist, we are done
    if (hWndChild == NULL) break;

    // Tell each MDI Child whether the session is ending
    do {
        // Do not send to caption bars of iconic MDI Children
        if (GetWindow(hWndChild, GW_OWNER) != NULL) continue;

        SendMessage(hWndChild, WM_ENDSESSION, wParam, 0);
    } while ((hWndChild = GetWindow(hWndChild, GW_HWNDNEXT))
        != NULL);
    break;

case WM_DESTROY:
    PostQuitMessage(0);
    break;

case WM_SYSCOMMAND:
    // Set focus to Frame window. This causes any comboboxes
    // in the ribbon to be closed.
    SetFocus(hWnd);
    fCallDefProc = TRUE;
    break;

case WM_NCLBUTTONDBLCLK:
    // Code to allow double-clicking the MDI Child's system
    // menu to close the MDI Child window
    fCallDefProc = TRUE;

    // If mouse wasn't clicked in the application's menu,
    // nothing to do
    if (wParam != HTMENU) break;
```

```
// If the active child is not maximized, nothing to do
dwResult = SendMessage(_hWndMDIClient, WM_MDIGETACTIVE,
    0, 0);
if (HIWORD(dwResult) != 1) break;

// Get position and dimensions of the MDI Child's system
// menu in the Frame's menu bar

// Get position and dimensions of the Frame window
GetWindowRect(hWnd, &rc);

// Get handle to the CLOSE BOX bitmaps
wTemp = LoadBitmap(NULL, MAKEINTRESOURCE(OBM_CLOSE));

// Get dimensions of the bitmaps
GetObject((HBITMAP) wTemp, sizeof(BITMAP), (LPSTR)
    (LPBITMAP) &Bitmap);
DeleteObject((HBITMAP) wTemp);

// Adjust the rectangle
rc.top += GetSystemMetrics(SM_CYCAPTION) +
    GetSystemMetrics(SM_CYFRAME);
rc.bottom = rc.top + Bitmap.bmHeight;
rc.left += GetSystemMetrics(SM_CXFRAME);

// The close bitmap includes the Application and MDI
// Child close boxes, so we only want half of the
// bitmap's width
rc.right = rc.left + Bitmap.bmWidth / 2;

// If the mouse cursor is within this rectangle, tell the
// MDI Child window to close
if (!PtInRect(&rc, MAKEPOINT(lParam))) break;
SendMessage(LOWORD(dwResult), WM_SYSCOMMAND, SC_CLOSE,
    lParam);
fCallDefProc = FALSE;
break;
```

```
case FW_MDICHILDDESTROY:
    // Message is posted by an MDI Child just before it is
    // destroyed

    // If another MDI Child exists, nothing to do
    if (hWndActiveMDIChild != NULL) break;

    // Set the menu bar and accelerator table to the Frame's
    // defaults
    ChangeMDIMenu(hWnd, _hWndMDIClient,
        (HMENU) GETCLSEB(hWnd, CLSEB, hMenu),
        IDM_WINDOWTILEVERT);
    _hAccelTable = NULL;

    // Force the status bar to be updated
    InvalidateRect(hWnd, NULL, TRUE);

    // Disable the Ribbon
    EnableWindow(_hDlgRibbon, FALSE);
    break;

case FW_GETSTATBARRECT:
    // lParam = LPRECT.
    // Get the client area of the Frame window.
    GetClientRect(hWnd, (LPRECT) lParam);

    // If the status bar is OFF, set the status bar to have
    // no height
    if (!GETCLSEB(hWnd, CLSEB, fStatusBarOn)) {
        ((LPRECT) lParam)->top = ((LPRECT) lParam)->bottom;
        break;
    }

    // Change the dimensions so that the status bar is the
    // height of one line of text plus a small border
    wTemp = GetDC(hWnd);
    GetTextMetrics((HDC) wTemp, &tm);
    ReleaseDC(hWnd, (HDC) wTemp);
    ((LPRECT) lParam)->top = ((LPRECT) lParam)->bottom -
        tm.tmHeight - GetSystemMetrics(SM_CYBORDER);
    break;
```

```
case FW_DRAWSTATUSDIVIDE:
    // lParam = (LPPAINTSTRUCT) &ps.
    // Draw a line separating the status bar from the
    // MDICLIENT window.
    dwResult = GetSystemMetrics(SM_CYBORDER);
    hPen = CreatePen(PS_SOLID, (int) dwResult, RGB(0, 0, 0));
    hPen = SelectObject(((LPPAINTSTRUCT) lParam)->hdc, hPen);
    MoveTo(((LPPAINTSTRUCT) lParam)->hdc, 0,
        ((LPPAINTSTRUCT) lParam)->rcPaint.top);
    LineTo(((LPPAINTSTRUCT) lParam)->hdc,
        ((LPPAINTSTRUCT) lParam)->rcPaint.right,
        ((LPPAINTSTRUCT) lParam)->rcPaint.top);
    hPen = SelectObject(((LPPAINTSTRUCT) lParam)->hdc, hPen);
    DeleteObject(hPen);
    break;

case FW_RESIZEMDICLIENT:
    // Sent when the Frame window is resized or when the
    // status bar and ribbon are toggled
    GetClientRect(hWnd, &rc);

    if (IsWindow(_hDlgRibbon) &&
        IsWindowVisible(_hDlgRibbon)) {
        // Ribbon is displayed; adjust rectangle
        GetClientRect(_hDlgRibbon, &rcTemp); rc.top +=
            rcTemp.bottom; rc.bottom -= rcTemp.bottom;
    }

    // Get the dimensions of the status bar rectangle and
    // adjust the dimensions of the MDICLIENT window
    SendMessage(hWnd, FW_GETSTATBARRECT, 0,
        (LONG) (LPRECT) &rcTemp);
    rc.bottom -= rcTemp.bottom - rcTemp.top;
    MoveWindow(_hWndMDIClient, 0, rc.top, rc.right,
        rc.bottom, TRUE);
    break;

case WM_SIZE:
    // Force MDICHILD window to be resized
    SendMessage(hWnd, FW_RESIZEMDICLIENT, 0, 0);
    break;
```

```
  case WM_PAINT:
    // Since the only visible portion of the Frame's client
    // area is the status bar when it is ON, this must mean
    // that the status bar needs to be repainted

    // Set up the device context
    BeginPaint(hWnd, &ps);
    SendMessage(hWnd, FW_GETSTATBARRECT, 0, (LONG) (LPRECT)
        &ps.rcPaint);
    SetBkMode(ps.hdc, TRANSPARENT);

    // If an MDI Child exists, the status bar must be updated
    // by it
    if (hWndActiveMDIChild) {
      SendMessage(hWndActiveMDIChild, AC_PAINTSTATBAR,
          ps.hdc, (LONG) (LPPAINTSTRUCT) &ps);
    } else {
      // No MDI Child exists; the Frame can do whatever it
      // wants here
      ps.rcPaint.top += (int) SendMessage(hWnd,
          FW_DRAWSTATUSDIVIDE, 0, (LONG) (LPPAINTSTRUCT)
          &ps);
      LoadString(_hInstance, IDS_FRAMESTATUSBAR, szBuf,
          sizeof(szBuf));
      TextOut(ps.hdc, 0, ps.rcPaint.top, szBuf,
          lstrlen(szBuf));
    }
    EndPaint(hWnd, &ps);
    break;

  case WM_INITMENU:
    // The user has entered the menu system; set any options
    CheckMenuItem(wParam, IDM_OPTIONSSTATUS, MF_BYCOMMAND |
        (GETCLSEB(hWnd, CLSEB, fStatusBarOn) ? MF_CHECKED :
        MF_UNCHECKED));

    CheckMenuItem(wParam, IDM_OPTIONSRIBBON, MF_BYCOMMAND |
        (IsWindowVisible(_hDlgRibbon) ? MF_CHECKED :
        MF_UNCHECKED));
    break;
```

```
case FW_SETMENUHELP:
   // Called by the Frame and MDI Children whenever a
   // WM_MENUSELECT message is received.
   // wParam = HWND of sender.
   // lParam = Menu description code.

   // Save the handle of the window sending the message
   SETCLSEB(hWnd, CLSEB, hWndMenuHelp, (HWND) wParam);

   // Save the menu help code that the window sent to
   SETCLSEB(hWnd, CLSEB, dwMenuHelp, lParam);

   // When the Frame or MDI Child receives a WM_MENUSELECT
   // message specifying that the menu system is closed
   // (lParam == MAKELONG(-1, 0)), the menu help should
   // disappear and be replaced by the proper information on
   // the status bar

   if (wParam == NULL) {
      SendMessage(hWnd, FW_GETSTATBARRECT, 0,
         (LONG) (LPRECT) &rc);
      // Force status bar to be updated
      InvalidateRect(hWnd, &rc, TRUE);
   }
   break;

case FW_GETMENUHELP:
   // Sent by the Frame or MDI Child when they receive an
   // AW_PAINTMENUHELP message
   dwResult = GETCLSEB(hWnd, CLSEB, dwMenuHelp);
   break;

case WM_MENUSELECT:
   // The user has highlighted a menu item

   if (lParam == MAKELONG(-1, 0)) {
      // User has stopped using the menu system
      SendMessage(hWnd, FW_SETMENUHELP, 0, 0);
      break;
   }
```

```
// If wTemp == 0, at end of switch, MDI Child handled
// the message
wTemp = 0;

switch (LOWORD(lParam) & (MF_POPUP | MF_SYSMENU)) {

    case 0:
        // wParam is a menu item ID NOT on the app's system
        // menu

        if (hWndActiveMDIChild != NULL) {
            // An MDI Child exists
            if (fMDIChildIsMaximized) {

                // If menu item from the MDI Child's system
                // menu, set the MF_SYSMENU bit in the lParam
                // parameter
                wTemp = GetSubMenu(GetMenu(hWnd), 0);
                if ((int) GetMenuState(wTemp, wParam,
                    MF_BYCOMMAND) != -1) lParam |= MF_SYSMENU;
            }

            // Make active MDI Child think that it received
            // the WM_MENUSELECT message
            SendMessage(hWndActiveMDIChild, wMsg, wParam,
                lParam);
            wTemp = 0;     // MDI Child handled the message
            break;
        }

        wTemp = IDS_FRAMEMENUID + wParam;
        break;

    case MF_POPUP:
        // wParam is handle to pop-up menu

        if (hWndActiveMDIChild != NULL) {
            // An MDI Child exists
            if (fMDIChildIsMaximized) {
```

```
                    // If pop-up menu is first top-level menu, it
                    // is the MDI Child's system menu. Set the
                    // MF_SYSMENU flag.
                    if (wParam == GetSubMenu(GetMenu(hWnd), 0))
                        lParam |= MF_SYSMENU;
                }

                // Make active MDI Child think that it received
                // the WM_MENUSELECT message
                SendMessage(hWndActiveMDIChild, wMsg, wParam,
                    lParam);
                wTemp = 0;       // MDI Child handled the message
                break;
            }

            // Calculate the index of the top-level menu
            hMenu = GetMenu(hWnd);
            wTemp = GetMenuItemCount(hMenu);
            while (wTemp-)
            if (GetSubMenu(hMenu, wTemp) == (HMENU) wParam)
                break;
            wTemp += IDS_FRAMEPOPUPID + 1;  // Jump over system
                                            // menu
            break;

        case MF_SYSMENU:
            // wParam is menu item ID from system menu
            wTemp = IDS_FRAMEMENUID + ((wParam & 0x0FFF) >> 4);
            break;

        case MF_POPUP | MF_SYSMENU:
            // wParam is handle to app's sys menu
            wTemp = IDS_FRAMEPOPUPID;
            break;
    }

// If message handled by MDI Child, nothing more to do
if (wTemp == 0) break;
```

```
        // Tell the Frame that the Frame window should display
        // the help text and the identifier for the help text
        SendMessage(hWnd, FW_SETMENUHELP, hWnd, wTemp);
        break;

    case WM_ENTERIDLE:
        if (wParam != MSGF_MENU) break;

        // User has stopped scrolling through menu items

        // If menu help already displayed, nothing more to do.
        // This is signaled by hWndMenu help being -1.
        if (GETCLSEB(hWnd, CLSEB, hWndMenuHelp) == -1)
            break;

        // Display new menu help; invalidate the status bar
        SendMessage(hWnd, FW_GETSTATBARRECT, 0, (LONG) (LPRECT)
            &rc);
        InvalidateRect(hWnd, &rc, TRUE);

        // BeginPaint is OK; an invalid rectangle must exist
        // because of the call to InvalidateRect above. This
        // causes the background for the Frame's client area
        // to be drawn correctly.
        BeginPaint(hWnd, &ps);

        // Set up the device context
        SetBkMode(ps.hdc, TRANSPARENT);

        // Send message to window that last received a
        // WM_MENUSELECT message to tell it to paint the status
        // bar with the appropriate menu help text
        SendMessage((HWND) GETCLSEB(hWnd, CLSEB, hWndMenuHelp),
            AW_PAINTMENUHELP, 0, (LONG) (LPPAINTSTRUCT) &ps);

        EndPaint(hWnd, &ps);

        // Set flag notifying this message that the most recently
        // selected menu item has had its help text painted. This
        // stops unsightly screen flicker.
```

```
        SETCLSEB(hWnd, CLSEB, hWndMenuHelp, (HWND) -1);
        break;

    case AW_PAINTMENUHELP:
        // Message sent from Frame window to notify Frame that it
        // should paint the status bar text for the last
        // highlighted menu item.
        // lParam = LPPAINTSTRUCT of Frame's status bar.

        // Ask the Frame window what the last selected menu ID
        // was. This value was sent to the frame by this window
        // during the processing for the WM_MENUSELECT message.
        dwResult = SendMessage(hWnd, FW_GETMENUHELP, 0, 0);

        // Draw the horizontal dividing line separating the
        // status bar from the MDICLIENT window
        ((LPPAINTSTRUCT) lParam)->rcPaint.top += (int)
            SendMessage(hWnd, FW_DRAWSTATUSDIVIDE, 0,
            (LONG) (LPPAINTSTRUCT) lParam);

        // Construct the string that is to be displayed
        LoadString(_hInstance, LOWORD(dwResult), szBuf,
            sizeof(szBuf));

        // Paint the menu help text in the status bar
        TextOut((((LPPAINTSTRUCT) lParam)->hdc,0, ((LPPAINTSTRUCT)
            lParam)->rcPaint.top, szBuf, lstrlen(szBuf));
        break;

    case WM_COMMAND:
        // If a child is being activated via the "Window" menu,
        // let the DefFrameProc handle it
        if (wParam >= IDM_WINDOWCHILD) {
            fCallDefProc = TRUE;
            break;
        }

        switch (wParam) {
```

```
case IDM_FILEOPENSHEET:
    // Get the # of sheets already created and
    // increment by 1
    wTemp = GETCLSEB(hWnd, CLSEB, wNumSheets) + 1;
    SETCLSEB(hWnd, CLSEB, wNumSheets, wTemp);

    // The sheet's caption should display sheet number
    wsprintf(szBuf, "Sheet%d", wTemp);

    // Create the MDI Child window
    CreateMDIChild("Sheet", szBuf, 0, CW_USEDEFAULT,
        CW_USEDEFAULT, CW_USEDEFAULT, CW_USEDEFAULT,
        _hWndMDIClient, _hInstance, 0);

    // Make sure the ribbon is enabled when any
    // children exist
    EnableWindow(_hDlgRibbon, TRUE);
    break;

case IDM_FILEOPENCHART:
    // Get the # of charts already created and
    // increment by 1
    wTemp = GETCLSEB(hWnd, CLSEB, wNumCharts) + 1;
    SETCLSEB(hWnd, CLSEB, wNumCharts, wTemp);

    // The chart's caption should display the chart
    // number
    wsprintf(szBuf, "Chart%d", wTemp);

    // Create the MDI Child window
    CreateMDIChild("Chart", szBuf, 0, CW_USEDEFAULT,
        CW_USEDEFAULT, CW_USEDEFAULT, CW_USEDEFAULT,
        _hWndMDIClient, _hInstance, 0);

    // Make sure the ribbon is enabled when any
    // children exist
    EnableWindow(_hDlgRibbon, TRUE);
    break;
```

```
case IDM_OPTIONSSTATUS:
   // Toggle status of status bar; resize MDICLIENT
   wTemp = !GETCLSEB(hWnd, CLSEB, fStatusBarOn);
   SETCLSEB(hWnd, CLSEB, fStatusBarOn, wTemp);
   SendMessage(hWnd, FW_RESIZEMDICLIENT, 0, 0);
   break;

case IDM_OPTIONSRIBBON:
   // Toggle status of ribbon; resize MDICLIENT
   ShowWindow(_hDlgRibbon,
      IsWindowVisible(_hDlgRibbon) ? SW_HIDE :
      SW_SHOW);
   SendMessage(hWnd, FW_RESIZEMDICLIENT, 0, 0);
   break;

case IDM_EXIT:
   SendMessage(hWnd, WM_CLOSE, 0, 0L);
   break;

case IDM_HELPINDEX:
case IDM_HELPKEYBOARD:
case IDM_HELPCOMMANDS:
case IDM_HELPPROCEDURES:
case IDM_HELPUSINGHELP:
   MessageBox(hWnd, "Option not implemented.",
      _szAppName, MB_OK);
   break;

case IDM_ABOUT:
   fpProc = MakeProcInstance(AboutProc, _hInstance);
   DialogBox(_hInstance, "About", hWnd, fpProc);
   FreeProcInstance(fpProc);
   break;

case IDM_WINDOWTILEVERT:
   // Call our own function to perform vertical tiling
   TileVertically(_hWndMDIClient);
   break;
```

```
              case IDM_WINDOWTILEHORIZ:
                  // Let the MDICLIENT window do the repositioning
                  SendMessage(_hWndMDIClient, WM_MDITILE, 0, 0);
                  break;

              case IDM_WINDOWCASCADE:
                  // Let the MDICLIENT window do the repositioning
                  SendMessage(_hWndMDIClient, WM_MDICASCADE, 0, 0);
                  break;

              case IDM_WINDOWARRANGEICONS:
                  // Let the MDICLIENT window do the repositioning
                  SendMessage(_hWndMDIClient, WM_MDIICONARRANGE,
                      0, 0);
                  break;

              default:
                  // Menu options not processed by the Frame window
                  // must be passed to MDI Children for processing
                  SendMessage(hWndActiveMDIChild, wMsg, wParam,
                      lParam);
                  break;
          }
          break;

      default:
          fCallDefProc = TRUE;
          break;
    }

    if (fCallDefProc)
        dwResult = DefFrameProc(hWnd, _hWndMDIClient, wMsg, wParam,
            lParam);
    return(dwResult);
}

BOOL FAR PASCAL RegisterFrameWndClass (void) {
    WNDCLASS wc;
```

```
    wc.style            = CS_HREDRAW | CS_VREDRAW;
    wc.lpfnWndProc      = FrameWndProc;

    // Number of class extra bytes used by structure
    wc.cbClsExtra       = sizeof(CLSEB);

    wc.cbWndExtra       = 0;
    wc.hInstance        = _hInstance;
    wc.hIcon            = LoadIcon(_hInstance, _szClassName);
    wc.hCursor          = LoadCursor(NULL, IDC_ARROW);
    wc.hbrBackground    = COLOR_WINDOW + 1;
    wc.lpszMenuName     = _szClassName;
    wc.lpszClassName    = _szClassName;
    return(RegisterClass(&wc));
}


void NEAR PASCAL TileVertically (HWND hWndMDIClient) {
    int nNumWndsOnRow, nOpenMDIChildren = 0,
        nTopOfBottomIconRow = 0;
    int nCrntCol, nColWidth, nCrntRow, nNumRows, nRowHeight,
        nMinWndHeight;
    HWND hWndChild;
    HANDLE hWinPosInfo;
    RECT rc;
    POINT Point;
    DWORD dwChildInfo;

    // Assume that scroll bars will be off after windows are tiled.
    // By forcing them off now, GetClientRect will return the
    // correct size.
    ShowScrollBar(hWndMDIClient, SB_BOTH, 0);

    // The WM_MDICASCADE and WM_MDITILE messages cause the icons to
    // be arranged, so we will too. In fact, this is necessary to
    // locate the top of the bottom icon row in the next step of
    // this function.
    SendMessage(hWndMDIClient, WM_MDIICONARRANGE, 0, 0);

    // Get handle to first MDI Child window
    hWndChild = GetWindow(hWndMDIClient, GW_CHILD);
```

549

```
do {
  if (IsIconic(hWndChild) && GetWindow(hWndChild, GW_OWNER) ==
      NULL) {
    // Window is iconic and window is NOT an icon's caption

    // Get client area of the icon window
    GetWindowRect(hWndChild, &rc);

    // rc.top is in screen coordinates
    nTopOfBottomIconRow = max(nTopOfBottomIconRow, rc.top);
  }

  if (!IsIconic(hWndChild) && GetWindow(hWndChild, GW_OWNER)
      == NULL)
    ++nOpenMDIChildren;

} while ((hWndChild = GetWindow(hWndChild, GW_HWNDNEXT)) !=
    NULL);

// All MDI Children are icons; no tiling is necessary
if (nOpenMDIChildren == 0) return;

// Find height of usable client area for tiling
GetClientRect(hWndMDIClient, &rc);

if (nTopOfBottomIconRow) {
  // At least one MDI Child is iconic

  // Convert coordinates from screen to client
  Point.x = 0;
  Point.y = nTopOfBottomIconRow;
  ScreenToClient(hWndMDIClient, &Point);
  // Point.y is top of bottom icon row in client coordinates
  rc.bottom = Point.y;
}

// Restore the active MDI child if it's maximized
dwChildInfo = SendMessage(hWndMDIClient, WM_MDIGETACTIVE,
    0, 0);
if (HIWORD(dwChildInfo) == 1)
  ShowWindow(LOWORD(dwChildInfo), SW_RESTORE);
```

```
// Calculate the minimum desired height of each MDI Child
nMinWndHeight = max(1, rc.bottom /
   (5 * GetSystemMetrics(SM_CYCAPTION)));

// Calculate the number of rows that will be tiled
nNumRows = min(nOpenMDIChildren, nMinWndHeight);

// Calculate the height of each row
nRowHeight = rc.bottom / nNumRows;

// Get the handle to the first MDI Child window
hWndChild = GetWindow(hWndMDIClient, GW_CHILD);

// Prime the storage of positioning information
hWinPosInfo = BeginDeferWindowPos(nOpenMDIChildren);

// Execute the loop for each row
for (nCrntRow = 0; nCrntRow < nNumRows; nCrntRow++) {

   // Calculate the number of MDI Children that will appear
   // on this row
   nNumWndsOnRow = nOpenMDIChildren / nNumRows +
      ((nOpenMDIChildren % nNumRows >
      (nNumRows - (nCrntRow + 1))) ? 1 : 0);

   // Calculate the width of each of these children
   nColWidth = rc.right / nNumWndsOnRow;

   // Fill each column with an MDI Child window
   for (nCrntCol = 0; nCrntCol < nNumWndsOnRow; ) {

      if (!IsIconic(hWndChild) && GetWindow(hWndChild,
         GW_OWNER) == NULL) {
         // Child is NOT iconic and not an icon's caption bar

         // Tell windows what the new position and dimensions
         // of this MDI Child should be
         hWinPosInfo = DeferWindowPos(hWinPosInfo, hWndChild,
            NULL, nCrntCol * nColWidth, nCrntRow * nRowHeight,
            nColWidth, nRowHeight, SWP_NOACTIVATE |
            SWP_NOZORDER);
```

```
        // Go to the next column
        nCrntCol++;
      }

      // Get handle to the next MDI Child window
      hWndChild = GetWindow(hWndChild, GW_HWNDNEXT);
    }
  }

  // All of the positioning has been set. Now tell Windows to
  // update all the windows at once.
  EndDeferWindowPos(hWinPosInfo);
}
```

Listing 7-5. SHEET.C MDI Child source module.

```
/*******************************************************************
Module name: Sheet.C
Programmer : Jeffrey M. Richter & Elvira Peretsman
*******************************************************************/

#include "..\nowindws.h"
#undef NOCOLOR
#undef NOGDI
#undef NOKERNEL
#undef NOLSTRING
#undef NOMB
#undef NOMDI
#undef NOMENUS
#undef NOUSER
#undef NOWINMESSAGES
#undef NOWINOFFSETS
#include <windows.h>

#include "mdi.h"

static char _szClassName[] = "Sheet";
```

```
typedef struct {
  HMENU hMenu;
  HANDLE hAccelTable;
} CLSEB;

LONG FAR PASCAL SheetProc (HWND hWnd, WORD wMsg, WORD wParam,
      LONG lParam) {
  BOOL fCallDefProc = FALSE;
  DWORD dwResult = 0;
  WORD wTemp = 0;
  HMENU hMenu;
  char szBuf[100], szString[100], szCaption[25];

  switch (wMsg) {
    case WM_CREATE:
      // If this window is first instance created of this class
      if (GETCLSEB(hWnd, CLSEB, hMenu) == NULL) {

        // Initialize the menu and accelerator handles for
        // this class
        wTemp = LoadMenu(_hInstance, _szClassName);
        SETCLSEB(hWnd, CLSEB, hMenu, (HMENU) wTemp);
        wTemp = LoadAccelerators(_hInstance, _szClassName);
        SETCLSEB(hWnd, CLSEB, hAccelTable, (HANDLE) wTemp);
      }
      break;

    case WM_MDIACTIVATE:
      if (wParam == FALSE) break;

      // Child is being activated

      // Set the menu bar and the accelerators to the
      // appropriate ones for this window class
      ChangeMDIMenu(GETFRAME(hWnd), GetParent(hWnd), (HMENU)
        GETCLSEB(hWnd, CLSEB, hMenu), IDM_WINDOWTILEVERT);
      _hAccelTable = (HANDLE) GETCLSEB(hWnd, CLSEB,
        hAccelTable);
```

553

```
        // For the status bar at the bottom of the Frame window
        // to be updated for this child's information
        InvalidateRect(GETFRAME(hWnd), NULL, TRUE);
        break;

    case WM_CLOSE:
        // Make sure it's OK to close this child window
        fCallDefProc = (BOOL) SendMessage(hWnd,
            WM_QUERYENDSESSION, TRUE, 0);
        if (fCallDefProc) SendMessage(hWnd, WM_ENDSESSION,
            TRUE, 0);
        break;

    case WM_QUERYENDSESSION:
        // Prompt user whether to save changes to this document.
        // Usually a dirty flag (stored in the window's extra
        // bytes) is used to determine if it is necessary to ask
        // this question.

        // Construct string including the document's name
        lstrcpy(szBuf, "Save changes to ");
        wTemp = lstrlen(szBuf);
        GetWindowText(hWnd, szBuf + wTemp,
            sizeof(szBuf) - wTemp);
        lstrcat(szBuf, "?");

        // Display message box to user. The message box should be
        // system modal if the entire Windows session is being
        // terminated (wParam is FALSE).
        wTemp = MessageBox(hWnd, szBuf, _szAppName,
            MB_ICONQUESTION | MB_YESNOCANCEL |
            (wParam ? MB_APPLMODAL : MB_SYSTEMMODAL));

        switch (wTemp) {
            case IDYES:
                // Save the document and it's OK to quit
                dwResult = TRUE;
                break;
```

```
        case IDNO:
           // Don't save the document and it's OK to quit
           dwResult = TRUE;
           break;

         case IDCANCEL:
           // Don't save the document and it's NOT OK to quit
           dwResult = FALSE;
           break;
     }
     break;

case WM_ENDSESSION:
   // Do any last-minute cleanup during this message
   break;

case WM_DESTROY:
   // Notify the Frame window that a child has been
   // destroyed after the child is actually destroyed.
   // (That's why we use PostMessage instead of SendMessage
   // here.)
   PostMessage(GETFRAME(hWnd), FW_MDICHILDDESTROY, hWnd, 0);
   fCallDefProc = TRUE;
   break;

case AC_PAINTSTATBAR:
   // Message sent by the Frame window when the status bar
   // needs to be repainted
   // wParam = HDC, lParam = LPPAINTSTRUCT to status area
   // in frame

   // Construct status bar string for display
   LoadString(_hInstance, IDS_SHEETSTATUSBAR, szBuf,
      sizeof(szBuf));

   // Draw the horizontal dividing line separating the
   // status bar from the MDICLIENT window
   ((LPPAINTSTRUCT) lParam)->rcPaint.top += (int)
      SendMessage(GETFRAME(hWnd), FW_DRAWSTATUSDIVIDE, 0,
      (LONG) (LPPAINTSTRUCT) lParam);
```

555

```
        // Paint the text in the status bar
        TextOut((HDC) wParam, 0,
            ((LPPAINTSTRUCT) lParam)->rcPaint.top,
            szBuf, lstrlen(szBuf));
        break;

    case WM_MENUSELECT:
        // Normally only MDI Child system menu options could
        // appear in this message, but the Frame window forces
        // WM_MENUSELECT messages to appear here whenever a menu
        // selection occurs

        if (lParam == MAKELONG(-1, 0)) {
            // User has stopped using the menu system. Notify
            // Frame window so the status bar will be invalidated.
            SendMessage(GETFRAME(hWnd), FW_SETMENUHELP, 0, 0);
            break;
        }

        switch (LOWORD(lParam) & (MF_POPUP | MF_SYSMENU)) {

            case 0:
                // wParam is a menu item ID NOT on the Child's
                // system menu

                // If wParam is any of the MDI Children listed in
                // the "Window" menu, display the same help text
                if ((wParam > IDM_WINDOWCHILD) && (wParam <=
                        IDM_WINDOWCHILD + 9))
                    wParam = IDM_WINDOWCHILD;

                // Tell the Frame that this window should display
                // the help text and identifier for the help text
                wTemp = IDS_SHEETMENUID + wParam;
                break;

            case MF_POPUP:
                // wParam is handle to pop-up menu. Calculate the
                // index of the top-level menu.
                hMenu = GetMenu(GETFRAME(hWnd));
```

```
      wTemp = GetMenuItemCount(hMenu);
      while (wTemp—)
         if (GetSubMenu(hMenu, wTemp) ==
            (HMENU) wParam) break;
      wTemp += IDS_SHEETPOPUPID;
      if (!IsZoomed(hWnd)) wTemp++;
      break;

   case MF_SYSMENU:
      // wParam is menu item ID from MDI Child's system
      // menu
      wTemp = IDS_SHEETMENUID + ((wParam & 0x0FFF) >> 4);
      break;

   case MF_POPUP | MF_SYSMENU:
      // wParam is handle to MDI Child's system menu
      wTemp = IDS_SHEETPOPUPID;
      break;
   }
   // Tell the Frame that this window should display the
   // help text and the identifier for the help text
   SendMessage(GETFRAME(hWnd), FW_SETMENUHELP, hWnd, wTemp);
   break;

case WM_ENTERIDLE:
   // User stopped moving around in the help system; make
   // the Frame believe it received this message directly
   SendMessage(GETFRAME(hWnd), wMsg, wParam, lParam);
   break;

case AW_PAINTMENUHELP:
   // Message sent from Frame window to notify child that it
   // should paint the status bar text for the last
   // highlighted menu item.
   // lParam = LPPAINTSTRUCT of Frame's status bar.

   // Ask the Frame window what the last selected menu ID
   // was. This value was sent to the frame by this window
   // during the processing for the WM_MENUSELECT message.
   dwResult = SendMessage(GETFRAME(hWnd), FW_GETMENUHELP,
      0, 0);
```

```
        // Draw the horizontal dividing line separating the
        // status bar from the MDICLIENT window
        ((LPPAINTSTRUCT) lParam)->rcPaint.top += (int)
            SendMessage(GETFRAME(hWnd), FW_DRAWSTATUSDIVIDE, 0,
            (LONG) (LPPAINTSTRUCT) lParam);

        // Construct the string to be displayed
        LoadString(_hInstance, LOWORD(dwResult), szString,
            sizeof(szString));
        GetWindowText(hWnd, szCaption, sizeof(szCaption));
        wsprintf(szBuf, szString, (LPSTR) szCaption);

        // Paint the menu help text in the status bar
        TextOut(((LPPAINTSTRUCT) lParam)->hdc, 0,
            ((LPPAINTSTRUCT) lParam)->rcPaint.top, szBuf,
            lstrlen(szBuf));
        break;

    case WM_COMMAND:
        // Any menu options NOT processed by the Frame are passed
        // to the active child
        MessageBox(hWnd, "Option not implemented.", _szAppName,
            MB_OK);
        break;

    default: fCallDefProc = TRUE; break;
    }

    if (fCallDefProc)
        dwResult = DefMDIChildProc(hWnd, wMsg, wParam, lParam);

    return(dwResult);
}

BOOL FAR PASCAL RegisterSheetWndClass (void) {
    WNDCLASS wc;

    wc.style           = 0;
    wc.lpfnWndProc     = SheetProc;
```

```
        // Number of class extra bytes used by structure
        wc.cbClsExtra      = sizeof(CLSEB);

        wc.cbWndExtra      = 0;
        wc.hInstance       = _hInstance;
        wc.hIcon           = LoadIcon(_hInstance, _szClassName);
        wc.hCursor         = LoadCursor(NULL, IDC_ARROW);
        wc.hbrBackground   = COLOR_WINDOW + 1;
        wc.lpszMenuName    = NULL;
        wc.lpszClassName   = _szClassName;
        return(RegisterClass(&wc));
}
```

Listing 7-6. CHART.C MDI Child window source module.

```
/*******************************************************************
Module name: Chart.C
Programmer : Jeffrey M. Richter & Elvira Peretsman
*******************************************************************/

#include "..\nowindws.h"
#undef NOCOLOR
#undef NOGDI
#undef NOKERNEL
#undef NOLSTRING
#undef NOMB
#undef NOMDI
#undef NOMENUS
#undef NONCMESSAGES
#undef NOUSER
#undef NOWINMESSAGES
#undef NOWINOFFSETS
#include <windows.h>

#include "mdi.h"

static char _szClassName[] = "Chart";
```

```
// Structure for use with class extra bytes
typedef struct {
    HMENU hMenu;
    HANDLE hAccelTable;
} CLSEB;

LONG FAR PASCAL ChartProc (HWND hWnd, WORD wMsg, WORD wParam,
        LONG lParam) {
    static HWND hWndPrevChild = NULL;
    BOOL fCallDefProc = FALSE;
    DWORD dwResult = 0;
    HMENU hMenu;
    WORD wTemp = 0;
    char szBuf[100], szString[100], szCaption[25];

    switch (wMsg) {

        case WM_CREATE:
            // If this window is first instance created of this class
            if (GETCLSEB(hWnd, CLSEB, hMenu) == NULL) {

                // Initialize the menu and accelerator handles for
                // this class
                wTemp = LoadMenu(_hInstance, _szClassName);
                SETCLSEB(hWnd, CLSEB, hMenu, (HMENU) wTemp);
                wTemp = LoadAccelerators(_hInstance, _szClassName);
                SETCLSEB(hWnd, CLSEB, hAccelTable, (HANDLE) wTemp);
            }
            break;

        case WM_MDIACTIVATE:
            if (wParam == FALSE) {
                // Child is being deactivated. Reset the previous
                // child so WM_MOUSEACTIVATE will work OK.
                hWndPrevChild = NULL;
                break;
            }

            // Child is being activated
```

```
    // Set handle of child being deactivated
    hWndPrevChild = HIWORD(lParam);

    // If this child is being activated and no other child
    // exists, pretend this child was the last one activated
    if (hWndPrevChild == NULL) hWndPrevChild = hWnd;

    // Set the menu bar and the accelerators to the
    // appropriate ones for this window class
    ChangeMDIMenu(GETFRAME(hWnd), GetParent(hWnd),
        (HMENU) GETCLSEB(hWnd, CLSEB, hMenu),
        IDM_WINDOWTILEVERT);
    _hAccelTable = (HANDLE) GETCLSEB(hWnd, CLSEB,
        hAccelTable);

    // For the status bar at the bottom of the Frame window
    // to be updated for this child's information
    InvalidateRect(GETFRAME(hWnd), NULL, TRUE);
    break;

case WM_CLOSE:
    // Make sure it's OK to close this child window
    fCallDefProc = (BOOL) SendMessage(hWnd,
        WM_QUERYENDSESSION, TRUE, 0);
    if (fCallDefProc) SendMessage(hWnd, WM_ENDSESSION,
        TRUE, 0);
    break;

case WM_QUERYENDSESSION:
    // Prompt user whether to save changes to this document.
    // Usually a dirty flag (stored in the window's extra
    // bytes) is used to determine if it is necessary to ask
    // this question.

    // Construct string including the document's name
    lstrcpy(szBuf, "Save changes to ");
    wTemp = lstrlen(szBuf);
    GetWindowText(hWnd, szBuf + wTemp,
        sizeof(szBuf) - wTemp);
    lstrcat(szBuf, "?");
```

```
        // Display message box to user. The message box should be
        // system modal if the entire Windows session is being
        // terminated (wParam is FALSE).
        wTemp = MessageBox(hWnd, szBuf, _szAppName,
            MB_ICONQUESTION | MB_YESNOCANCEL | (wParam ?
            MB_APPLMODAL : MB_SYSTEMMODAL));

        switch (wTemp) {
            case IDYES:
                // Save the document and it's OK to quit
                dwResult = TRUE;
                break;

            case IDNO:
                // Don't save the document and it's OK to quit
                dwResult = TRUE;
                break;

            case IDCANCEL:
                // Don't save the document and it's NOT OK to quit
                dwResult = FALSE;
                break;
        }
        break;

case WM_ENDSESSION:
    // Do any last-minute cleanup during this message
    break;

case WM_DESTROY:
    // Notify the Frame window that a child has been
    // destroyed after the child is actually destroyed.
    // (That's why we use PostMessage instead of SendMessage
    // here.)
    PostMessage(GETFRAME(hWnd), FW_MDICHILDDESTROY, hWnd, 0);
    fCallDefProc = TRUE;
    break;
```

```
case WM_MOUSEACTIVATE:
    // User clicked the mouse of the Child window. If the
    // mouse is clicked in the window's client area and the
    // previously active child was NOT this child, the mouse
    // message should be eaten.
    if ((HTCLIENT == LOWORD(lParam)) &&
        (hWnd != hWndPrevChild))
        dwResult = MA_ACTIVATEANDEAT;
    else dwResult = MA_ACTIVATE;
    break;

case WM_SETCURSOR:
    // After an MDI Child becomes active, set the previously
    // active child to this window so that mouse messages
    // will NOT be eaten
    hWndPrevChild = hWnd;
    fCallDefProc = TRUE;
    break;

case WM_LBUTTONDOWN:
    // Just to let you know when the WM_LBUTTONDOWN message
    // is received
    MessageBox(hWnd, "WM_LBUTTONDOWN", "Chart", MB_OK);
    break;

case AC_PAINTSTATBAR:
    // Message sent by the Frame window when the status bar
    // needs to be repainted
    // wParam = HDC, lParam = LPPAINTSTRUCT to status area
    // in frame

    // Construct status bar string for display
    LoadString(_hInstance, IDS_CHARTSTATUSBAR, szBuf,
        sizeof(szBuf));

    // Draw the horizontal dividing line separating the
    // status bar from the MDICLIENT window
    ((LPPAINTSTRUCT) lParam)->rcPaint.top += (int)
        SendMessage(GETFRAME(hWnd), FW_DRAWSTATUSDIVIDE, 0,
        (LONG) (LPPAINTSTRUCT) lParam);
```

```
            // Paint the text in the status bar
            TextOut((HDC) wParam, 0,
                ((LPPAINTSTRUCT) lParam)->rcPaint.top,
                szBuf, lstrlen(szBuf));
            break;

    case WM_MENUSELECT:
        // Normally only MDI Child system menu options could
        // appear in this message, but the Frame window forces
        // WM_MENUSELECT messages to appear here whenever a menu
        // selection occurs

        if (lParam == MAKELONG(-1, 0)) {
            // User has stopped using the menu system. Notify
            // Frame window so the status bar will be invalidated.
            SendMessage(GETFRAME(hWnd), FW_SETMENUHELP, 0, 0);
            break;
        }

        switch (LOWORD(lParam) & (MF_POPUP | MF_SYSMENU)) {

            case 0:
                // wParam is a menu item ID NOT on the Child's
                // system menu

                // If wParam is any of the MDI Children listed in
                // the "Window" menu, display the same help text
                if ((wParam > IDM_WINDOWCHILD) &&
                    (wParam <= IDM_WINDOWCHILD + 9))
                    wParam = IDM_WINDOWCHILD;

                wTemp = IDS_CHARTMENUID + wParam;
                break;

            case MF_POPUP:
                // wParam is handle to pop-up menu. Calculate the
                // index of the top-level menu.
                hMenu = GetMenu(GETFRAME(hWnd));
                wTemp = GetMenuItemCount(hMenu);
                while (wTemp-)
```

```
            if (GetSubMenu(hMenu, wTemp) == (HMENU) wParam)
                break;
        wTemp += IDS_CHARTPOPUPID;
        if (!IsZoomed(hWnd)) wTemp++;
        break;

    case MF_SYSMENU:
        // wParam is menu item ID from MDI Child's system
        // menu
        wTemp = IDS_CHARTMENUID + ((wParam & 0x0FFF) >> 4);
        break;

    case MF_POPUP | MF_SYSMENU:
        // wParam is handle to MDI Child's sys menu
        wTemp = IDS_CHARTPOPUPID;
        break;
    }
    // Tell the Frame that this window should display the
    // help text and the identifier for the help text
    SendMessage(GETFRAME(hWnd), FW_SETMENUHELP, hWnd, wTemp);
    break;

case WM_ENTERIDLE:
    // User stopped moving around in the help system; make
    // the Frame believe it received this message directly
    SendMessage(GETFRAME(hWnd), wMsg, wParam, lParam);
    break;

case AW_PAINTMENUHELP:
    // Message sent from Frame window to notify child that it
    // should paint the status bar text for the last
    // highlighted menu item.
    // lParam = LPPAINTSTRUCT of Frame's status bar.

    // Ask the Frame window what the last selected menu ID
    // was. This value was sent to the frame by this window
    // during the processing for the WM_MENUSELECT message.
    dwResult = SendMessage(GETFRAME(hWnd), FW_GETMENUHELP,
        0, 0);
```

```
            // Draw the horizontal dividing line separating the
            // status bar from the MDICLIENT window
            ((LPPAINTSTRUCT) lParam)->rcPaint.top += (int)
                SendMessage(GETFRAME(hWnd), FW_DRAWSTATUSDIVIDE, 0,
                (LONG) (LPPAINTSTRUCT) lParam);

            // Construct the string that is to be displayed
            LoadString(_hInstance, LOWORD(dwResult), szString,
                sizeof(szString));
            GetWindowText(hWnd, szCaption, sizeof(szCaption));
            wsprintf(szBuf, szString, (LPSTR) szCaption);

            // Paint the menu help text in the status bar
            TextOut(((LPPAINTSTRUCT) lParam)->hdc, 0,
                ((LPPAINTSTRUCT) lParam)->rcPaint.top, szBuf,
                lstrlen(szBuf));
            break;

        case WM_COMMAND:
            // Any menu options NOT processed by the Frame are passed
            // to the active child
            MessageBox(hWnd, "Option not implemented.", _szAppName,
                MB_OK);
            break;

        default: fCallDefProc = TRUE; break;
    }

    if (fCallDefProc)
        dwResult = DefMDIChildProc(hWnd, wMsg, wParam, lParam);

    return(dwResult);
}

BOOL FAR PASCAL RegisterChartWndClass (void) {
    WNDCLASS wc;

    wc.style        = 0;
    wc.lpfnWndProc  = ChartProc;
```

```
    // Number of class extra bytes used by structure
    wc.cbClsExtra      = sizeof(CLSEB);

    wc.cbWndExtra      = 0;
    wc.hInstance       = _hInstance;
    wc.hIcon           = LoadIcon(_hInstance, _szClassName);
    wc.hCursor         = LoadCursor(NULL, IDC_ARROW);
    wc.hbrBackground   = COLOR_WINDOW + 1;
    wc.lpszMenuName    = NULL;
    wc.lpszClassName   = _szClassName;
    return(RegisterClass(&wc));
}
```

Listing 7-7. DIALOG.H dialog-box template defines.

```
#define ID_VERSION   200
#define ID_BOLD      105
#define ID_FONT      101
#define ID_FONTTEXT  102
#define ID_ITALIC    106
#define ID_SIZE      104
#define ID_SIZETEXT  103
#define ID_UNDERLINE 107
```

Listing 7-8. MDI.RC application resource file.

```
/*******************************************************************
Module name: MDI.RC
Programmer : Jeffrey M. Richter & Elvira Peretsman
*******************************************************************/

#include <windows.h>
#include "mdi.h"
#include "mdi.dlg"

Sheet ICON Sheet.ico
Chart ICON Chart.ico
Frame ICON MDI.ico
```

```
/********** Frame Menu Setup (No open documents) **********/
Frame MENU
BEGIN
   POPUP "&File"
      BEGIN
      MENUITEM "Open &sheet",     IDM_FILEOPENSHEET
      MENUITEM "Open &chart",     IDM_FILEOPENCHART
      MENUITEM SEPARATOR
      MENUITEM "E&xit",           IDM_EXIT
      END

   POPUP "&Help"
      BEGIN
      MENUITEM "&Index",          IDM_HELPINDEX
      MENUITEM "&Keyboard",       IDM_HELPKEYBOARD
      MENUITEM "&Commands",       IDM_HELPCOMMANDS
      MENUITEM "&Procedures",     IDM_HELPPROCEDURES
      MENUITEM "&Using Help",     IDM_HELPUSINGHELP
      MENUITEM SEPARATOR
      MENUITEM "&About...",       IDM_ABOUT
      END
END

// Menu help descriptions for Frame's top-level menu
STRINGTABLE LOADONCALL MOVEABLE DISCARDABLE
BEGIN
   IDS_FRAMEPOPUPID + 0,
      "Move, size, or close the application window"
   IDS_FRAMEPOPUPID + 1,
      "Open, print or save documents; quit MDI Application"
   IDS_FRAMEPOPUPID + 2,   "Get help"
END

// Menu help descriptions for Frame's menu items
STRINGTABLE LOADONCALL MOVEABLE DISCARDABLE
BEGIN
   IDS_FRAMEMENUID + IDM_SYSMENUSIZE,   "Changes window size"
   IDS_FRAMEMENUID + IDM_SYSMENUMOVE,   "Changes window position"
   IDS_FRAMEMENUID + IDM_SYSMENUMINIMIZE,
      "Reduces window to an icon"
```

```
    IDS_FRAMEMENUID + IDM_SYSMENUMAXIMIZE,
        "Enlarges the window to full size"
    IDS_FRAMEMENUID + IDM_SYSMENUCLOSE, "Quit MDI Application;
        prompts to save documents"
    IDS_FRAMEMENUID + IDM_SYSMENURESTORE,
        "Restores window to normal size"
    IDS_FRAMEMENUID + IDM_SYSMENUTASKLIST,
        "Make another application active"

    IDS_FRAMEMENUID + IDM_FILEOPENSHEET, "Open new sheet"
    IDS_FRAMEMENUID + IDM_FILEOPENCHART, "Open new chart"
    IDS_FRAMEMENUID + IDM_EXIT,
        "Quit MDI Application; prompts to save documents"

    IDS_FRAMEMENUID + IDM_HELPINDEX, "Lists Help topics"
    IDS_FRAMEMENUID + IDM_HELPKEYBOARD,
        "Lists keys and their actions"
    IDS_FRAMEMENUID + IDM_HELPCOMMANDS, "Lists help on commands"
    IDS_FRAMEMENUID + IDM_HELPPROCEDURES,
        "Lists help on various procedures"
    IDS_FRAMEMENUID + IDM_HELPUSINGHELP,
        "How to use the help system"
    IDS_FRAMEMENUID + IDM_ABOUT,
        "Displays program information"
END

/*********************** Sheet Menu ***********************/
Sheet ACCELERATORS
BEGIN
    VK_DELETE, IDM_EDITCUT,   VIRTKEY, SHIFT
    VK_INSERT, IDM_EDITCOPY,  VIRTKEY, CONTROL
    VK_INSERT, IDM_EDITPASTE, VIRTKEY, SHIFT
END

Sheet MENU
BEGIN
    POPUP "&File"
        BEGIN
        MENUITEM "Open &sheet",         IDM_FILEOPENSHEET
        MENUITEM "Open &chart",         IDM_FILEOPENCHART
```

```
        MENUITEM SEPARATOR
        MENUITEM "&Save",                  IDM_FILESAVE
        MENUITEM "Save &as...",            IDM_FILESAVEAS
        MENUITEM SEPARATOR
        MENUITEM "&Print",                 IDM_FILEPRINT
        MENUITEM "P&rinter setup...",      IDM_FILEPRINTERSETUP
        MENUITEM SEPARATOR
        MENUITEM "E&xit",                  IDM_EXIT
        END

    POPUP "&Edit"
        BEGIN
        MENUITEM "Cu&t\tShift+Del",        IDM_EDITCUT
        MENUITEM "&Copy\tCtrl+Ins",        IDM_EDITCOPY
        MENUITEM "&Paste\tShift+Ins",      IDM_EDITPASTE
        END

    POPUP "&Sheet"
        BEGIN
        MENUITEM "Sheet option",           IDM_SHEETOPTION
        END

    POPUP "&Options"
        BEGIN
        MENUITEM "&Status",                IDM_OPTIONSSTATUS
        MENUITEM "&Ribbon",                IDM_OPTIONSRIBBON
        END

    POPUP "&Window"
        BEGIN
        MENUITEM "Tile &vertically",       IDM_WINDOWTILEVERT
        MENUITEM "Tile &horizontally",     IDM_WINDOWTILEHORIZ
        MENUITEM "&Cascade",               IDM_WINDOWCASCADE
        MENUITEM "&Arrange icons",         IDM_WINDOWARRANGEICONS
        END

    POPUP "&Help"
        BEGIN
        MENUITEM "&Index",                 IDM_HELPINDEX
        MENUITEM "&Keyboard",              IDM_HELPKEYBOARD
```

```
        MENUITEM "&Commands",              IDM_HELPCOMMANDS
        MENUITEM "&Procedures",            IDM_HELPPROCEDURES
        MENUITEM "&Using Help",            IDM_HELPUSINGHELP
        MENUITEM SEPARATOR
        MENUITEM "&About...",              IDM_ABOUT
        END
END


// Menu help descriptions for Sheet's top-level menu
STRINGTABLE LOADONCALL MOVEABLE DISCARDABLE
BEGIN
    IDS_SHEETPOPUPID + 0, "Move, size, or close the active sheet"
    IDS_SHEETPOPUPID + 1,
        "Open, print or save the sheet; quit MDI Application"
    IDS_SHEETPOPUPID + 2, "Cut, copy, and paste"
    IDS_SHEETPOPUPID + 3, "Perform sheet specific operations"
    IDS_SHEETPOPUPID + 4,
        "Toggle visibility of status bar and ribbon"
    IDS_SHEETPOPUPID + 5,
        "Rearrange windows or activate specified window"
    IDS_SHEETPOPUPID + 6, "Get help"
END


// Menu help descriptions for Sheet's menu items
STRINGTABLE LOADONCALL MOVEABLE DISCARDABLE
BEGIN
    IDS_SHEETMENUID + IDM_SYSMENUSIZE, "Changes sheet's size"
    IDS_SHEETMENUID + IDM_SYSMENUMOVE, "Changes sheet's
        position"
    IDS_SHEETMENUID + IDM_SYSMENUMINIMIZE,
        "Reduces sheet to an icon"
    IDS_SHEETMENUID + IDM_SYSMENUMAXIMIZE,
        "Enlarges sheet to full size"
    IDS_SHEETMENUID + IDM_SYSMENUCLOSE,
        "Closes the sheet; prompts to save"
    IDS_SHEETMENUID + IDM_SYSMENURESTORE,
        "Restores sheet to normal size"
    IDS_SHEETMENUID + IDM_SYSMENUNEXTWINDOW,
        "Switches to the next sheet or chart document"
```

```
IDS_SHEETMENUID + IDM_FILEOPENSHEET, "Open new sheet"
IDS_SHEETMENUID + IDM_FILEOPENCHART, "Open new chart"
IDS_SHEETMENUID + IDM_FILESAVE,
    "Save the active sheet (%s)"
IDS_SHEETMENUID + IDM_FILESAVEAS,
    "Save the active sheet with a new name"
IDS_SHEETMENUID + IDM_FILEPRINT,
    "Print the active sheet (%s)"
IDS_SHEETMENUID + IDM_FILEPRINTERSETUP,
    "Changes the printer and printing options"
IDS_SHEETMENUID + IDM_EXIT,
    "Quit MDI Application; prompts to save documents"

IDS_SHEETMENUID + IDM_EDITCUT,
    "Cuts the selection from %s and puts it on the Clipboard"
IDS_SHEETMENUID + IDM_EDITCOPY,
    "Copies the selection from %s and puts it on the Clipboard"
IDS_SHEETMENUID + IDM_EDITPASTE,
    "Inserts Clipboard contents into %s"

IDS_SHEETMENUID + IDM_SHEETOPTION,
    "Perform some sheet related operation on %s"

IDS_SHEETMENUID + IDM_OPTIONSSTATUS,
    "Toggles the status bar on/off"
IDS_SHEETMENUID + IDM_OPTIONSRIBBON,
    "Toggles the ribbon on/off"

IDS_SHEETMENUID + IDM_WINDOWTILEVERT,
    "Tiles windows vertically"
IDS_SHEETMENUID + IDM_WINDOWTILEHORIZ
    "Tiles windows horizontally"
IDS_SHEETMENUID + IDM_WINDOWCASCADE,
    "Arranges windows in a cascading fashion"
IDS_SHEETMENUID + IDM_WINDOWARRANGEICONS,
    "Arranges iconic windows"

IDS_SHEETMENUID + IDM_HELPINDEX, "Lists Help topics"
IDS_SHEETMENUID + IDM_HELPKEYBOARD,
    "Lists keys and their actions"
```

```
    IDS_SHEETMENUID + IDM_HELPCOMMANDS, "Lists help on commands"
    IDS_SHEETMENUID + IDM_HELPPROCEDURES,
        "Lists help on various procedures"
    IDS_SHEETMENUID + IDM_HELPUSINGHELP,
        "How to use the help system"
    IDS_SHEETMENUID + IDM_ABOUT,
        "Displays program information"

    IDS_SHEETMENUID + IDM_WINDOWCHILD,
        "Switches to the window containing this document"
END

/*********************** Chart Menu ***********************/
Chart ACCELERATORS
BEGIN
    VK_DELETE, IDM_EDITCUT,   VIRTKEY, SHIFT
    VK_INSERT, IDM_EDITCOPY,  VIRTKEY, CONTROL
    VK_INSERT, IDM_EDITPASTE, VIRTKEY, SHIFT
END

Chart MENU
BEGIN
    POPUP "&File"
      BEGIN
      MENUITEM "Open &sheet",     IDM_FILEOPENSHEET
      MENUITEM "Open &chart",     IDM_FILEOPENCHART
      MENUITEM SEPARATOR
      MENUITEM "&Save",           IDM_FILESAVE
      MENUITEM "Save &as...",     IDM_FILESAVEAS
      MENUITEM SEPARATOR
      MENUITEM "&Print",          IDM_FILEPRINT
      MENUITEM "P&rinter setup",  IDM_FILEPRINTERSETUP
      MENUITEM SEPARATOR
      MENUITEM "E&xit",           IDM_EXIT
      END

    POPUP "&Edit"
      BEGIN
      MENUITEM "Cu&t\tShift+Del",    IDM_EDITCUT
```

```
        MENUITEM "&Copy\tCtrl+Ins",     IDM_EDITCOPY
        MENUITEM "&Paste\tShift+Ins",   IDM_EDITPASTE
        END

    POPUP "&Chart"
       BEGIN
        MENUITEM "Chart option",        IDM_CHARTOPTION
        END

    POPUP "&Options"
       BEGIN
        MENUITEM "&Status",             IDM_OPTIONSSTATUS
        MENUITEM "&Ribbon",             IDM_OPTIONSRIBBON
        END

    POPUP "&Window"
       BEGIN
        MENUITEM "Tile &vertically",    IDM_WINDOWTILEVERT
        MENUITEM "Tile &horizontally",  IDM_WINDOWTILEHORIZ
        MENUITEM "&Cascade",            IDM_WINDOWCASCADE
        MENUITEM "&Arrange icons",      IDM_WINDOWARRANGEICONS
        END

    POPUP "&Help"
       BEGIN
        MENUITEM "&Index",              IDM_HELPINDEX
        MENUITEM "&Keyboard",           IDM_HELPKEYBOARD
        MENUITEM "&Commands",           IDM_HELPCOMMANDS
        MENUITEM "&Procedures",         IDM_HELPPROCEDURES
        MENUITEM "&Using Help",         IDM_HELPUSINGHELP
        MENUITEM SEPARATOR
        MENUITEM "&About...",           IDM_ABOUT
        END
END

// Menu help descriptions for Chart's top-level menu
STRINGTABLE LOADONCALL MOVEABLE DISCARDABLE
BEGIN
   IDS_CHARTPOPUPID + 0, "Move, size, or close the active chart"
   IDS_CHARTPOPUPID + 1,
      "Open, print or save the chart; quit MDI Application"
```

```
    IDS_CHARTPOPUPID + 2, "Cut, copy, and paste"
    IDS_CHARTPOPUPID + 3, "Perform chart specific operations"
    IDS_CHARTPOPUPID + 4,
        "Toggle visibility of status bar and ribbon"
    IDS_CHARTPOPUPID + 5,
        "Rearrange windows or activate specified window"
    IDS_CHARTPOPUPID + 6, "Get help"
END


// Menu help descriptions for Chart's menu items
STRINGTABLE LOADONCALL MOVEABLE DISCARDABLE
BEGIN
    IDS_CHARTMENUID + IDM_SYSMENUSIZE, "Changes chart's size"
    IDS_CHARTMENUID + IDM_SYSMENUMOVE, "Changes chart's position"
    IDS_CHARTMENUID + IDM_SYSMENUMINIMIZE,
        "Reduces chart to an icon"
    IDS_CHARTMENUID + IDM_SYSMENUMAXIMIZE,
        "Enlarges chart to full size"
    IDS_CHARTMENUID + IDM_SYSMENUCLOSE,
        "Closes the chart; prompts to save"
    IDS_CHARTMENUID + IDM_SYSMENURESTORE,
        "Restores chart to normal size"
    IDS_CHARTMENUID + IDM_SYSMENUNEXTWINDOW,
        "Switches to the next sheet or chart document"

    IDS_CHARTMENUID + IDM_FILEOPENSHEET, "Open new sheet"
    IDS_CHARTMENUID + IDM_FILEOPENCHART, "Open new chart"
    IDS_CHARTMENUID + IDM_FILESAVE, "Save the active chart (%s)"
    IDS_CHARTMENUID + IDM_FILESAVEAS,
        "Save the active chart with a new name"
    IDS_CHARTMENUID + IDM_FILEPRINT, "Print the active chart (%s)"
    IDS_CHARTMENUID + IDM_FILEPRINTERSETUP,
        "Changes the printer and printing options"
    IDS_CHARTMENUID + IDM_EXIT,
        "Quit MDI Application; prompts to save documents"

    IDS_CHARTMENUID + IDM_EDITCUT,
        "Cuts the selection from %s and puts it on the Clipboard"
    IDS_CHARTMENUID + IDM_EDITCOPY,
        "Copies the selection from %s and puts it on the Clipboard"
```

```
    IDS_CHARTMENUID + IDM_EDITPASTE,
       "Inserts Clipboard contents into %s"

    IDS_CHARTMENUID + IDM_CHARTOPTION,
       "Perform some chart related operation on %s"

    IDS_CHARTMENUID + IDM_OPTIONSSTATUS,
       "Toggles the status bar on/off"
    IDS_CHARTMENUID + IDM_OPTIONSRIBBON,
       "Toggles the ribbon on/off"

    IDS_CHARTMENUID + IDM_WINDOWTILEVERT,
       "Tiles windows vertically"
    IDS_CHARTMENUID + IDM_WINDOWTILEHORIZ,
       "Tiles windows horizontally"
    IDS_CHARTMENUID + IDM_WINDOWCASCADE,
       "Arranges windows in a cascading fashion"
    IDS_CHARTMENUID + IDM_WINDOWARRANGEICONS,
       "Arranges iconic windows"

    IDS_CHARTMENUID + IDM_HELPINDEX,  "Lists Help topics"
    IDS_CHARTMENUID + IDM_HELPKEYBOARD,
       "Lists keys and their actions"
    IDS_CHARTMENUID + IDM_HELPCOMMANDS, "Lists help on commands"
    IDS_CHARTMENUID + IDM_HELPPROCEDURES,
       "Lists help on various procedures"
    IDS_CHARTMENUID + IDM_HELPUSINGHELP,
       "How to use the help system"
    IDS_CHARTMENUID + IDM_ABOUT, "Displays program information"

    IDS_CHARTMENUID + IDM_WINDOWCHILD,
       "Switches to the window containing this document"
END

/********* String tables to fill comboboxes in Ribbon *********/
STRINGTABLE LOADONCALL MOVEABLE DISCARDABLE
BEGIN
    IDS_FONT + 0, "Courier"
    IDS_FONT + 1, "Helv"
    IDS_FONT + 2, "Modern"
    IDS_FONT + 3, "Roman"
```

```
   IDS_FONT + 4, "Script"
   IDS_FONT + 5, "Symbol"
   IDS_FONT + 6, "System"
   IDS_FONT + 7, "Terminal"
END


STRINGTABLE LOADONCALL MOVEABLE DISCARDABLE
BEGIN
   IDS_SIZE + 0, "10"
   IDS_SIZE + 1, "12"
   IDS_SIZE + 2, "15"
   IDS_SIZE + 3, "18"
   IDS_SIZE + 4, "22"
   IDS_SIZE + 5, "28"
END


// Status bar statistics line for Frame and MDI Children windows
STRINGTABLE LOADONCALL MOVEABLE DISCARDABLE
BEGIN
   IDS_FRAMESTATUSBAR,     "Frame status line"
   IDS_SHEETSTATUSBAR,     "Sheet status line"
   IDS_CHARTSTATUSBAR,     "Chart status line"
END
```

Listing 7-9. MDI.DLG dialog-box templates.

```
RIBBON DIALOG LOADONCALL MOVEABLE DISCARDABLE 0, 0, 600, 15
STYLE WS_CHILD | WS_CLIPSIBLINGS
BEGIN
   CONTROL "Font:", ID_FONTTEXT, "static", SS_RIGHT | WS_CHILD, 4,
      2, 16, 8
   CONTROL "", ID_FONT, "combobox", CBS_DROPDOWNLIST | WS_VSCROLL
      | WS_TABSTOP | WS_CHILD, 21, 1, 48, 51
   CONTROL "Size:", ID_SIZETEXT, "static", SS_RIGHT | WS_CHILD,
      74, 2, 16, 8
   CONTROL "", ID_SIZE, "combobox", CBS_DROPDOWNLIST | WS_VSCROLL
      | WS_TABSTOP | WS_CHILD, 91, 1, 48, 51
   CONTROL "Bold", ID_BOLD, "button", BS_AUTOCHECKBOX | WS_TABSTOP
      | WS_CHILD, 147, 1, 28, 12
```

```
    CONTROL "Italic", ID_ITALIC, "button", BS_AUTOCHECKBOX |
        WS_TABSTOP | WS_CHILD, 177, 1, 28, 12
    CONTROL "Underline", ID_UNDERLINE, "button", BS_AUTOCHECKBOX |
        WS_TABSTOP | WS_CHILD, 207, 1, 42, 12
END


ABOUT DIALOG LOADONCALL MOVEABLE DISCARDABLE 16, 20, 126, 106
CAPTION "About MDI"
STYLE WS_BORDER | WS_CAPTION | WS_DLGFRAME | WS_SYSMENU |
    WS_VISIBLE | WS_POPUP
BEGIN
    CONTROL "Frame", -1, "static", SS_ICON | WS_CHILD, 4, 38,
        18, 21
    CONTROL "MDI Sample Application", -1, "static", SS_CENTER |
        WS_CHILD, 22, 8, 100, 12
    CONTROL "Written by:", -1, "static", SS_CENTER | WS_CHILD, 22,
        20, 100, 12
    CONTROL "Elvira Peretsman", -1, "static", SS_CENTER | WS_CHILD,
        22, 32, 100, 12
    CONTROL "and", -1, "static", SS_CENTER | WS_CHILD, 22, 40,
        100, 8
    CONTROL "Jeffrey M. Richter", -1, "static", SS_CENTER |
        WS_CHILD, 20, 48, 100, 12
    CONTROL "Version date:", -1, "static", SS_CENTER | WS_CHILD,
        22, 64, 100, 12
    CONTROL "", ID_VERSION, "static", SS_CENTER | WS_CHILD, 22, 76,
        100, 12
    CONTROL "&OK", 1, "button", BS_DEFPUSHBUTTON | WS_TABSTOP |
        WS_CHILD, 40, 92, 44, 12
END
```

Listing 7-10. MDI.DEF application definitions file.

```
; Module name: MDI.DEF
; Programmer : Jeffrey M. Richter & Elvira Peretsman

NAME          MDI
DESCRIPTION   'MDI: Multiple Document Interface Sample Application'
STUB          'WinStub.exe'
```

```
EXETYPE      WINDOWS
DATA         MOVEABLE MULTIPLE PRELOAD
SEGMENTS
  _TEXT      MOVABLE DISCARDABLE PRELOAD
  _MDI       MOVABLE DISCARDABLE PRELOAD
  _Frame     MOVABLE DISCARDABLE PRELOAD
  _Sheet     MOVABLE DISCARDABLE LOADONCALL
  _Chart     MOVABLE DISCARDABLE LOADONCALL
CODE         MOVEABLE DISCARDABLE
HEAPSIZE     1024
STACKSIZE    10240
EXPORTS
  FrameWndProc
  RibbonDlgProc
  AboutProc
  SheetProc
  ChartProc
```

CHAPTER 8

Installing Commercial Applications

When your application is complete, you will need to organize the files so they can be distributed. Most applications are distributed on floppy disks and contain an installation or setup program. The setup program introduces the application, prompts the user for any information that is required before installation can begin, and copies the files from the distribution disks onto the user's drive.

This chapter explains how to design and implement a software installation program for your Windows applications. The SETUP.EXE program described demonstrates the concepts discussed. You may distribute it with your own software.

The setup program usually gives the user a first impression of the software. For this reason, the program should be easy to use, should ask very few questions, and should get the user up and running as quickly as possible. Until recently, Windows applications were installed with DOS-based rather than Windows-based setup programs. I recommend that you use a Windows-based setup program because it has the same interface as all other Windows applications, making it easier for the user.

To execute the installation program, the user should only be required to insert the first distribution disk into the desired floppy drive, select "Run..." from the Program Manager's File menu, and type *A:\SETUP*. The setup program should not require command-line parameters. If the user can fine-tune the installation procedure, the setup program should prompt the user with dialog boxes once it is running.

Keep in mind that the setup program is being executed from a floppy disk. This means that disk operations execute more slowly than if they were being performed from the hard drive. The mouse cursor should be turned into an hourglass while any lengthy operations are executing. In addition, progress meters should be displayed to inform the user of the current operation's status. The SETUP.EXE program presented in this chapter uses the Meter custom child control discussed in Chapter 4. As files are being copied from the floppy to the hard disk, the Meter custom child control is updated.

A setup program should always keep the user abreast of the installation process by presenting windows that report which operations are being performed. These windows should always appear in a consistent location on the monitor. The first window should welcome the user to the installation program. This window contains the name of the application being installed. It lets the user enter a destination directory where the application's files will be placed. If the application software requires several directories, they should be created as subdirectories of the destination directory. Any windows that contain questions for the user should be accompanied by a reasonable default value.

When the user has entered the desired destination directory, the setup program should immediately verify that there is enough available disk space to hold the files that need to be copied. If the desired drive does not contain sufficient disk space, the user should be notified of the space requirements of the new application and how much space is available on the desired drive. At this point, the user can easily delete some unneeded files using the File Manager. The File Manager could also be used to determine if there is another drive that has sufficient free space to install the application.

Once the setup program has started copying files, the user should be interrupted only to insert new distribution disks. If the software package allows the user to select portions of an application to install, the user should be able to choose those options before the setup program begins copying files. For example, if the application comes with an on-line tutorial or filter DLLs that allow the user to convert data from one application to another, the user should be able to decide whether the tutorial should be installed and which conversion DLLs are to be installed.

Sometimes the setup program needs to ask the user questions that require some knowledge of the application. You should write a help file for users to access with the Windows help engine. The .HLP file supplied with your application can include descriptions of installation options and define terms that have specific meaning for your application.

Now that all the installation options have been specified, the setup program can begin copying files. The files on the distribution floppies should be organized so that a minimum of disk swapping is necessary. Of course, the placement of files depends on the distribution media. A user who is installing your application from low-density 3.5-inch disks will need to perform more swapping than a user installing from high-density 5.25-inch disks.

The SETUP.EXE program presented in this chapter allows you to create a SETUP.INF file that contains the layout of files on the distribution disks. This lets you support different media simply by modifying SETUP.INF.

Another way to speed installation is to perform data compression on the distributed files. This has many advantages. Fewer floppies are required, making the package less expensive to produce. Fewer floppies also means fewer disk swaps during installation. And since the compressed files are smaller than their decompressed counterparts, less data is read from the floppy for each file. The time necessary to decompress files is relatively small, speeding the installation process.

The only disadvantage to compressing files is that a user cannot go directly to a distribution disk and copy a desired file from the disk to the hard drive. If this would be desirable with your application, you must supply an additional program for the user or document some procedure that a user could follow. For example, the

README.TXT file included with Windows states that individual files may be copied and decompressed by using the supplied EXPAND.EXE utility.

Finally, the setup program can add a new program group to the Windows Program Manager. This new program group should contain a program item for each of the executable files that have been installed. The setup program can now display a window to the user stating that the installation has been completed successfully.

Many applications use initialization files for saving information between invocations. An application should not use the WIN.INI file to save information about the application, but should create a private profile file for its own use. There are several good reasons for doing this. If every application used WIN.INI, the file would become extremely large. The larger this file gets, the longer it takes to retrieve information from it. Second, if a new version of Windows becomes available, installing the new version may destroy the current WIN.INI file and all the information saved in it.

The best way to create an initialization file is to have your application do it instead of your setup program. When your application is first invoked, have it check for the existence of the initialization file and, if it does not exist, create it with reasonable default values. If this file should somehow be destroyed, the file can be re-created simply by having the user execute the application. If re-creating the file is necessary, all of the user's settings have been lost. A message box should be displayed notifying the user that the application must be configured again.

Special Considerations for Resources

Remember: The setup program is executed from a disk, and the disk may be switched during installation. This means Windows can't load a program segment or resource from the .EXE after the setup process has started. To ensure that the code is always available, set the *PRELOAD* and *NONDISCARDABLE* flags in the SETUP.DEF file. If the setup application uses any DLLs, the code segments in them must include the *PRELOAD*, *NONDISCARDABLE*, and *FIXED* flags. The *FIXED* flag is necessary because Windows will not make a DLL's code segment nondiscardable without it.

All the resources (icons, dialog boxes, string tables, and so on) must be marked as *PRELOAD* and *FIXED*. Windows treats all resources as discardable unless they have the *FIXED* flag specified. In addition, any resources in the setup program must be referenced by number. Many applications use the following method to declare an icon in the application's resource file:

```
Setup  ICON SETUP.ICO
```

Then the application references the icon with the following syntax:

```
LoadIcon(hInstance, "Setup");
```

When you declare resources this way, Windows creates a *NameTable* in memory. The *NameTable* is a list of all the resource's string names. When the application references a resource by name, Windows must scan the *NameTable* for the desired string and determine where the resource is in the executable file. The problem here is that Windows always creates an application's *NameTable* in a discardable block of memory and reloads the table from the executable file when it is needed. This is unsatisfactory for a setup program. We must access resources differently. Here's how we can declare and access an icon.

First, in a header file that is included by both the application and the resource file, define an identifier that represents the icon:

```
#define ICON_SETUP   1
```

Declare the icon in the application's resource file:

```
ICON_SETUP    ICON    SETUP.ICO
```

The application then references the icon using the following syntax:

```
LoadIcon(hInstance, MAKEINTRESOURCE(ICON_SETUP));
```

This method of accessing resources is better because it requires less disk and memory space. It's also faster than the first approach.

When SETUP.EXE is first executed, a dialog-box template (*DLG_INSERTDISK*) is loaded into memory. When it's time for the second disk, Windows locks the memory block containing the template and creates the *DLG_INSERTDISK* dialog box. Windows then unlocks and frees the memory block containing the dialog-box template. When it's time to prompt the user to swap disks again, Windows must reload *DLG_INSERTDISK* from the SETUP.EXE file. However, Windows no longer has access to this file because it is on the first disk. This causes SETUP.EXE to fail.

The workaround: The memory block containing *DLG_INSERTDISK* must be locked before it is used to create the dialog box. The lock will prevent Windows from freeing the block after the dialog box is created. Windows will always be able to find the dialog-box template in memory.

The code for locking the memory block can be found at the beginning of the *CopyAllFiles* function in the SETUP.C source module:

```
HANDLE hDlgRes;

// Get the handle of the "InsertDisk" dialog box from the
// EXEcutable file
hDlgRes = FindResource(_hInstance,
   MAKEINTRESOURCE(DLG_INSERTDISK), RT_DIALOG);

// Get the memory handle of the "InsertDisk" dialog box in memory.
// The block is already in memory because the dialog box is marked
// as PRELOAD FIXED.
hDlgRes = LoadResource(_hInstance, hDlgRes);
```

```
// Force the memory block to be locked down. This prohibits
// Windows from discarding the dialog-box template from memory.
LockResource(hDlgRes);
```

FindResource searches through the module associated with the *_hInstance* parameter. The second parameter is the name of the resource. If the resource is identified by a numeric value, the *MAKEINTRESOURCE* macro (defined in WINDOWS.H) should be used as above. If the resource is identified by name, the name may be used as the second parameter. The third parameter indicates the type of resource *FindResource* should attempt to locate. The table below shows the values that can be used:

Value (defined in WINDOWS.H)	Meaning
RT_ACCELERATOR	Accelerator table resource
RT_BITMAP	Bitmap resource
RT_DIALOG	Dialog-box template resource
RT_FONT	Font resource
RT_FONTDIR	Font directory resource
RT_MENU	Menu resource
RT_RCDATA	User-defined resource

Since *DLG_INSERTDISK* is a dialog-box template, *RT_DIALOG* must be used.

The value returned by *FindResource* is a handle that identifies the resource's location in the executable file. If the resource could not be found, NULL is returned.

Now that we have the location of the resource in the executable file, we call *LoadResource* to allocate a memory handle for the dialog-box template. Windows won't load a resource until *LockResource* is called. In the case of SETUP.EXE, the dialog-box template is already in memory because the template had the *PRELOAD* and *FIXED* flags specified in SETUP.DLG. *LoadResource* will ascertain this and return the handle of the existing memory block.

Finally, we call *LockResource*. This forces Windows to place a lock on the memory block. As long as at least one lock is outstanding, Windows will not free the memory.

At the end of the *CopyAllFiles* function, the dialog-box template will no longer be needed. We execute the following code to free the memory block:

```
// The dialog-box template is no longer necessary, so
// it may be unlocked and removed from memory
UnlockResource(hDlgRes);
FreeResource(hDlgRes);
```

UnlockResource removes the outstanding lock placed on the memory block by *LockResource*. *UnlockResource* is a macro, not a function, and is defined in WINDOWS.H as follows:

```
#define UnlockResource(h) GlobalUnlock(h)
```

Although the dialog template's memory block is now unlocked, blocks are not usually freed until the application terminates. We call *FreeResource* to free the block immediately.

Resources are shared among different instances of the same application. If two instances of an application load the same icon into memory, *LoadIcon* will return the same value to both applications. The advantage is that memory is conserved when several instances of the application are running. However, this method can cause some problems for the software developer. Let's look at one possible scenario:

Application APP.EXE contains a dialog-box template marked *PRELOAD* and *FIXED*. When this application is executed, Windows creates a memory block for the dialog-box template and loads the template into memory. At this point, APP.EXE has *not* created a dialog box based on this template.

588

The user now executes a second instance of APP.EXE. When this second instance is loaded, Windows sees that the dialog-box template is already in memory and does not create another memory block. The two instances will share the block of memory containing the template.

Now the second instance of APP.EXE creates a dialog box based on the template. Windows creates the dialog box, unlocks the memory block containing the template, and frees the block. When the first instance of APP.EXE needs to create the dialog box, the template will not be in memory and Windows must reload it from the APP.EXE file on disk.

This could be quite a problem. If APP.EXE requires that a particular resource (a dialog-box template, in this example) be in memory, the program will most likely fail. Guaranteeing that a particular resource resides in memory requires that the resource have at least one outstanding lock before its use. This is accomplished by using the *FindResource*, *LoadResource*, and *LockResource* functions, as demonstrated earlier.

The Setup Application

The application discussed in this section is a complete setup program that you can use without modification to install your own applications. The program reads and analyzes a SETUP.INF file (Listing 8-1) that contains information describing how the files are laid out on the distribution floppy disks. To prepare your application for distribution, simply change this file to reflect information about your program.

SETUP.EXE also shows how to use the Meter custom child control presented in Chapter 4.

The SETUP.INF File. SETUP.INF describes how files are arranged on the distribution disks. If you have ordered this book with the companion disks, you will find SETUP.INF on the first disk. This file describes the directories and files necessary to compile and link all the sample applications presented throughout the book.

Listing 8-1. SETUP.INF Setup information file.

```
; Module name: Setup.Inf
; Programmer : Jeffrey M. Richter

[Application]
;Application global information
AppName=Win3: A Developer's Guide Installation
DefDir=C:\DevGuide
SpaceNeeded=1500
DefPMGroup=DevGuide.GRP, A Developer's Guide

[Disks]
;List of diskettes needed to install the product and the name
;of each diskette
1=Setup, Chapters 1 to 3
2=Chapters 4 to 6
3=Chapters 7 to 8

[Dirs]
;Lists of directories that must be created from the destination
;directory. Files to be copied are in the same directory structure
;on the floppy (by default).
1=.
2=Voyeur.01
3=PMRest.02
4=NoAlpha.02
5=DlgTech.03
6=Spin.04
7=Meter.04
8=CustCntl.04
9=Print.05
10=ScrnBlnk.06
11=Echo.06
12=MDI.07
13=Setup.08
```

```
[Files]
;description, name, (dir #), (diskette #), (Compressed)
Read Me Text File,    README.TXT, 1, 1, N
Make All Batch File, MAKEALL.BAT, 1, 1, N
Make Dist. Disks,     MAKEDD.BAT,  1, 1, N
Copy Dir Batch File, COPYDIR.BAT, 1, 1, N
No Windows Header,    NOWINDWS.H,  1, 1, N

Voyeur Files (Chapter 1), VOYEUR.EXE, 2, 1, N
Voyeur Files (Chapter 1), MAKEFILE,   2, 1, N
Voyeur Files (Chapter 1), VOYEUR.C,   2, 1, N
Voyeur Files (Chapter 1), VOYEUR.H,   2, 1, N
Voyeur Files (Chapter 1), DIALOG.H,   2, 1, N
Voyeur Files (Chapter 1), VOYEUR.DLG, 2, 1, N
Voyeur Files (Chapter 1), VOYEUR.DEF, 2, 1, N
Voyeur Files (Chapter 1), EYES.CUR,   2, 1, N
Voyeur Files (Chapter 1), VOYEUR.ICO, 2, 1, N
Voyeur Files (Chapter 1), VOYEUR.RC,  2, 1, N

PM Restore Files (Chapter 2), PMREST.EXE, 3, 1, N
PM Restore Files (Chapter 2), MAKEFILE,   3, 1, N
PM Restore Files (Chapter 2), PMREST.C,   3, 1, N
PM Restore Files (Chapter 2), PMREST.DEF, 3, 1, N
PM Restore Files (Chapter 2), PMREST.DLG, 3, 1, N
PM Restore Files (Chapter 2), DIALOG.H,   3, 1, N
PM Restore Files (Chapter 2), PMREST.H,   3, 1, N
PM Restore Files (Chapter 2), PMREST.ICO, 3, 1, N
PM Restore Files (Chapter 2), PMREST.RC,  3, 1, N

No Alpha Files (Chapter 2), NOALPHA.EXE, 4, 1, N
No Alpha Files (Chapter 2), MAKEFILE,    4, 1, N
No Alpha Files (Chapter 2), NOALPHA.C,   4, 1, N
No Alpha Files (Chapter 2), SUPERCLS.C,  4, 1, N
No Alpha Files (Chapter 2), NOALPHA.DEF, 4, 1, N
No Alpha Files (Chapter 2), NOALPHA.DLG, 4, 1, N
No Alpha Files (Chapter 2), DIALOG.H,    4, 1, N
No Alpha Files (Chapter 2), NOALPHA.H,   4, 1, N
No Alpha Files (Chapter 2), SUPERCLS.H,  4, 1, N
No Alpha Files (Chapter 2), NOALPHA.ICO, 4, 1, N
No Alpha Files (Chapter 2), NOALPHA.RC,  4, 1, N
```

```
Dialog Tech Files (Chapter 3), DLGTECH.EXE, 5, 1, N
Dialog Tech Files (Chapter 3), MAKEFILE,    5, 1, N
Dialog Tech Files (Chapter 3), DLG-DYNA.C, 5, 1, N
Dialog Tech Files (Chapter 3), DLG-MDLS.C, 5, 1, N
Dialog Tech Files (Chapter 3), DLG-OPTS.C, 5, 1, N
Dialog Tech Files (Chapter 3), DLGTECH.C,   5, 1, N
Dialog Tech Files (Chapter 3), DLGTECH.DEF, 5, 1, N
Dialog Tech Files (Chapter 3), DLGTECH.DLG, 5, 1, N
Dialog Tech Files (Chapter 3), DIALOG.H,    5, 1, N
Dialog Tech Files (Chapter 3), DLG-DYNA.H, 5, 1, N
Dialog Tech Files (Chapter 3), DLG-MDLS.H, 5, 1, N
Dialog Tech Files (Chapter 3), DLG-OPTS.H, 5, 1, N
Dialog Tech Files (Chapter 3), DLGTECH.H,   5, 1, N
Dialog Tech Files (Chapter 3), DLGTECH.ICO, 5, 1, N
Dialog Tech Files (Chapter 3), DLGTECH.RC,  5, 1, N

Meter Control Files (Chapter 4), MAKEFILE,    7, 2, N
Meter Control Files (Chapter 4), CNTL-DE.C,  7, 2, N
Meter Control Files (Chapter 4), METER.C,     7, 2, N
Meter Control Files (Chapter 4), METERDLG.C, 7, 2, N
Meter Control Files (Chapter 4), METER.DEF,  7, 2, N
Meter Control Files (Chapter 4), METER.DLG,  7, 2, N
Meter Control Files (Chapter 4), METER.DLL,  7, 2, N
Meter Control Files (Chapter 4), CNTL-DE.H,  7, 2, N
Meter Control Files (Chapter 4), DIALOG.H,   7, 2, N
Meter Control Files (Chapter 4), METER.H,     7, 2, N
Meter Control Files (Chapter 4), METER.RC,   7, 2, N

Spin Control Files (Chapter 4), MAKEFILE, 6, 2, N
Spin Control Files (Chapter 4), CNTL-DE.C, 6, 2, N
Spin Control Files (Chapter 4), SPIN.C,    6, 2, N
Spin Control Files (Chapter 4), SPINDLG.C, 6, 2, N
Spin Control Files (Chapter 4), SPIN.DEF,  6, 2, N
Spin Control Files (Chapter 4), SPIN.DLG,  6, 2, N
Spin Control Files (Chapter 4), SPIN.DLL,  6, 2, N
Spin Control Files (Chapter 4), CNTL-DE.H, 6, 2, N
Spin Control Files (Chapter 4), DIALOG.H,  6, 2, N
Spin Control Files (Chapter 4), SPIN.H,    6, 2, N
Spin Control Files (Chapter 4), SPIN.RC,   6, 2, N
```

```
Custom Control Files (Chapter 4), CUSTCNTL.EXE, 8, 2, N
Custom Control Files (Chapter 4), MAKEFILE,     8, 2, N
Custom Control Files (Chapter 4), CUSTCNTL.C,   8, 2, N
Custom Control Files (Chapter 4), CUSTCNTL.DEF, 8, 2, N
Custom Control Files (Chapter 4), CUSTCNTL.DLG, 8, 2, N
Custom Control Files (Chapter 4), METER.DLL,    8, 2, N
Custom Control Files (Chapter 4), SPIN.DLL,     8, 2, N
Custom Control Files (Chapter 4), CUSTCNTL.H,   8, 2, N
Custom Control Files (Chapter 4), DIALOG.H,     8, 2, N
Custom Control Files (Chapter 4), CUSTCNTL.ICO, 8, 2, N
Custom Control Files (Chapter 4), CUSTCNTL.RC,  8, 2, N

Printer Setup Files (Chapter 5), PRINT.EXE,  9, 2, N
Printer Setup Files (Chapter 5), MAKEFILE,   9, 2, N
Printer Setup Files (Chapter 5), PRINT.C,    9, 2, N
Printer Setup Files (Chapter 5), PRINTSTP.C, 9, 2, N
Printer Setup Files (Chapter 5), PRINT.DEF,  9, 2, N
Printer Setup Files (Chapter 5), PRINT.DLG,  9, 2, N
Printer Setup Files (Chapter 5), DIALOG.H,   9, 2, N
Printer Setup Files (Chapter 5), PRINT.H,    9, 2, N
Printer Setup Files (Chapter 5), PRINTSTP.H, 9, 2, N
Printer Setup Files (Chapter 5), PRINT.ICO,  9, 2, N
Printer Setup Files (Chapter 5), PRINT.RC,   9, 2, N

Screen Blanker Files (Chapter 6), SCRNBLNK.EXE, 10, 2, N
Screen Blanker Files (Chapter 6), MAKEFILE,     10, 2, N
Screen Blanker Files (Chapter 6), SB-DLL.C,     10, 2, N
Screen Blanker Files (Chapter 6), SCRNBLNK.C,   10, 2, N
Screen Blanker Files (Chapter 6), SB-DLL.DEF,   10, 2, N
Screen Blanker Files (Chapter 6), SCRNBLNK.DEF, 10, 2, N
Screen Blanker Files (Chapter 6), SB-DLL.DLG,   10, 2, N
Screen Blanker Files (Chapter 6), SCRNBLNK.DLG, 10, 2, N
Screen Blanker Files (Chapter 6), SB-DLL.DLL,   10, 2, N
Screen Blanker Files (Chapter 6), DIALOG.H,     10, 2, N
Screen Blanker Files (Chapter 6), SB-DLL.H,     10, 2, N
Screen Blanker Files (Chapter 6), SCRNBLNK.H,   10, 2, N
Screen Blanker Files (Chapter 6), SCRNBLNK.ICO, 10, 2, N
Screen Blanker Files (Chapter 6), SB-DLL.LIB,   10, 2, N
Screen Blanker Files (Chapter 6), SB-DLL.MKF,   10, 2, N
```

Screen Blanker Files (Chapter 6), SB-DLL.RC,   10, 2, N
Screen Blanker Files (Chapter 6), SCRNBLNK.RC, 10, 2, N

Echo Files (Chapter 6), ECHO.EXE,   11, 2, N
Echo Files (Chapter 6), MAKEFILE,   11, 2, N
Echo Files (Chapter 6), ECHO.C,   11, 2, N
Echo Files (Chapter 6), RECORDER.C,   11, 2, N
Echo Files (Chapter 6), ECHO.DEF,   11, 2, N
Echo Files (Chapter 6), RECORDER.DEF, 11, 2, N
Echo Files (Chapter 6), ECHO.DLG,   11, 2, N
Echo Files (Chapter 6), RECORDER.DLL, 11, 2, N
Echo Files (Chapter 6), DIALOG.H,   11, 2, N
Echo Files (Chapter 6), ECHO.H,   11, 2, N
Echo Files (Chapter 6), RECORDER.H,   11, 2, N
Echo Files (Chapter 6), ECHO.ICO,   11, 2, N
Echo Files (Chapter 6), RECORDER.LIB, 11, 2, N
Echo Files (Chapter 6), RECORDER.MKF, 11, 2, N
Echo Files (Chapter 6), ECHO.RC,   11, 2, N

MDI Files (Chapter 7), MDI.EXE,   12, 3, N
MDI Files (Chapter 7), MAKEFILE,   12, 3, N
MDI Files (Chapter 7), FRAME.C,   12, 3, N
MDI Files (Chapter 7), SHEET.C,   12, 3, N
MDI Files (Chapter 7), MDI.C,   12, 3, N
MDI Files (Chapter 7), MDI.DEF,   12, 3, N
MDI Files (Chapter 7), MDI.DLG,   12, 3, N
MDI Files (Chapter 7), DIALOG.H,   12, 3, N
MDI Files (Chapter 7), MDI.H,   12, 3, N
MDI Files (Chapter 7), CHART.ICO, 12, 3, N
MDI Files (Chapter 7), MDI.ICO,   12, 3, N
MDI Files (Chapter 7), SHEET.ICO, 12, 3, N
MDI Files (Chapter 7), MDI.RC,   12, 3, N
MDI Files (Chapter 7), CHART.C,   12, 3, N

Setup Files (Chapter 8), SETUP.EXE, 13, 3, N
Setup Files (Chapter 8), SETUP.DEF, 13, 3, N
Setup Files (Chapter 8), SETUP.H,   13, 3, N
Setup Files (Chapter 8), SETUP.C,   13, 3, N

```
Setup Files (Chapter 8), SETUP.INF,  13, 3, N
Setup Files (Chapter 8), DISK.ICO,   13, 3, N
Setup Files (Chapter 8), SETUP.ICO,  13, 3, N
Setup Files (Chapter 8), SETUP.DLG,  13, 3, N
Setup Files (Chapter 8), SETUP.RC,   13, 3, N
Setup Files (Chapter 8), DIALOG.H,   13, 3, N
Setup Files (Chapter 8), MAKEFILE,   13, 3, N
Setup Files (Chapter 8), SETUPDLG.C, 13, 3, N
Setup Files (Chapter 8), SETUPINF.H, 13, 3, N
Setup Files (Chapter 8), SETUPINF.C, 13, 3, N
Setup Files (Chapter 8), SETUPPM.C,  13, 3, N

[PM Info]
;File Name,    App Description, Icon file #, Icon #
VOYEUR.EXE,    Voyeur
PMREST.EXE,    PM Restore
NOALPHA.EXE,   No Alpha
DLGTECH.EXE,   Dlg Tech
CUSTCNTL.EXE,  Child Controls
PRINT.EXE,     Printer Setup
SCRNBLNK.EXE,  Screen Blanker
ECHO.EXE,      Echo
MDI.EXE,       MDI, MDI.EXE, 2
SETUP.EXE,     Setup

[End]
```

Any blank lines or lines beginning with a semicolon are not parsed by the setup program. The sections appearing in the SETUP.INF file are discussed in the following paragraphs:

The *[Application]* section. This section contains information that is global to the application being installed. The following table discusses each of the fields in this section:

Field	Description
AppName	Specifies the name of the program that is being installed. The name appears in the caption of every dialog box.
DefDir	Specifies the default destination directory. The user is allowed to select a different drive or directory.
SpaceNeeded	Specifies the amount of hard disk space required to contain the files that will be installed. The value is specified in kilobytes.
DefPMGroup	Specifies the name of the program group that will be created in Program Manager at the end of the installation.

The *[Disks]* section. This section tells Setup how many disks are in the distribution package and the name of each disk. Each line consists of a number, an equal sign, and the name of a distribution disk. The numbers are used only internally to let Setup determine where to locate a particular file. The numbers are arbitrary; they needn't start at one and they needn't be contiguous.

When Setup cannot find a file, a dialog box requests that the user insert the appropriate disk. The name of this disk is retrieved from the *[Disks]* section.

The *[Dirs]* section. This section lists all the subdirectories Setup should create. Each line consists of a number, an equal sign, and the subdirectory's path. The number is for internal use only. Setup uses this information to determine which directory on the distribution disk contains the file to be copied and the directory, relative to the destination directory, where the file should be copied. The path is always relative to the destination and source paths, which can be specified or overridden by the user.

If Setup is about to create a subdirectory and notices that it already exists, an error does not occur; Setup simply tries to create the next subdirectory in the list. It tries to create subdirectories in the order in which they appear in the *[Dirs]* section. If you need to create subdirectories that are more than one level deep, make sure the subdirectories closer to the root are listed first. For example, if you need to create a D:\DESTDIR\LEVEL1\LEVEL2 directory, SETUP.INF must list the entries in the following order:

```
[Dirs]
.
.
.
6=LEVEL1
7=LEVEL1\LEVEL2
```

The *[Files]* section. This section notifies Setup of the files that need to be installed. Each line in this section consists of five fields separated by commas:

Field	Description
File description	This text is displayed in the Progress dialog box as Setup copies the file.
File name	This is the name of the file to be copied.
Directory number	Tells Setup which directory contains the file to be copied. Setup constructs the source file's path name by appending the subdirectory and file name to the source directory's path. The same procedure is used to construct the destination path name.
Disk number	Tells Setup which distribution disk contains the file to be copied. Setup first tries to open the file on the distribution disk. If the file cannot be found, it prompts the user to insert the disk (represented by this number) containing the file to be copied.
Compressed	Tells Setup whether the file is compressed or not. If the value of this field is Y, Setup copies the file from the distribution disk using a decompression algorithm. If the value is N, Setup simply copies the file. At present, the Setup program contains no logic to deal with compressed files.

The *[PM Info]* section. This section tells Setup what application files should be added to the newly created group in Program Manager. The name of the group is specified by the *DefPMGroup* line that appears in the *[Application]* section of the SETUP.INF file. Each line in the *[PM Info]* section consists of four fields separated by commas:

Field	Description
File name	This is the file that should be invoked when the user chooses this icon from Program Manager. When Setup adds this program to the group, it searches through the files listed in the *[Files]* section. When a match is found, Setup constructs the complete path name using the destination directory and subdirectory specified for the file. Program Manager uses this path name to access the program. Because the complete path is specified, there is no need for Setup to modify the *PATH=* line in the user's AUTOEXEC.BAT file.
File description	This is the text Program Manager will display under the icon for the newly installed application.
Icon file name	This is an optional field. If this field is specified, Setup will instruct Program Manager to display an icon from this file instead of the file specified by the File name field. If this field is not specified, Setup will instruct Program Manager to display an icon from the file specified by the File name field.
Icon position	This is an optional field. If you wish to use it, the Icon file name field must also be specified. By default, Program Manager will display the first icon that appears in the file specified by the Icon file name field. If you specify a value in this field, Setup will instruct Program Manager to use a different icon from the file. If the value is zero, the first icon is used; if the value is one, the second icon is used; and so on.

The *[End]* section. This must be the last section. When Setup parses the line containing *[End]*, the SETUP.INF file is closed and Setup's Welcome window is presented. Any text appearing after this line is ignored.

SETUPINF.C contains all the code that processes SETUP.INF. The *SetupInfoSys* function has been designed analogously to a window procedure. Its prototype is shown below:

```
DWORD FAR PASCAL SetupInfoSys (SETUPINFOMSG Msg, WORD wParam,
  LPSTR lpBuffer);
```

The first parameter is the message to be processed. The meanings of the remaining two parameters, *wParam* and *lpBuffer*, depend on the message being sent. SETUPINF.H includes the prototype for this function and an enumerated type that lists all the messages that are processed by *SetupInfoSys*. Any module that needs to gain access to the information in SETUP.INF must include this header file.

When Setup begins, it opens SETUP.INF and calls the *SetupInfoSys* function, passing it the *SIM_INITIALIZE* message. The *lParam* parameter is a far pointer to the complete path name of the SETUP.INF file. The Setup program assumes that this file can be located in the root directory of the drive from which the Setup program was executed. The path is constructed as follows:

```
char _szSrcDir[MAXDIR] = "x:\\";

int PASCAL WinMain (HANDLE hInstance, HANDLE hPrevInstance,
  LPSTR lpszCmdLine, int nCmdShow) {

  char szBuf[100];
  .
  .
  .
```

```
// Initialize the default source path so it uses the same drive
// letter that the SETUP.EXE application was executed from
GetModuleFileName(hInstance, szBuf, sizeof(szBuf));
_szSrcDir[0] = *szBuf;

// Read the SETUP.INF file into memory
wsprintf(szBuf, "%s%sSETUP.INF", (LPSTR) _szSrcDir, (LPSTR)
    ((*(_fstrrchr(_szSrcDir, '\\') + 1) == 0) ? "" : "\\"));

nResult = (SIM_INITIALIZE_ERROR) SetupInfoSys(SIM_INITIALIZE,
    0, szBuf);
```

Calling *SetupInfoSys* with the *SIM_INITIALIZE* message makes Setup open, read, and parse SETUP.INF. After the file has been read, it is closed; it won't be needed again. This is important because the user may switch disks during the installation process, and the setup program cannot guarantee that SETUP.INF will always be accessible.

The rest of the messages listed in SETUPINF.H are sent by various parts of the setup program when information about the installation is necessary.

SETUP.C and SETUPDLG.C contain all the code for user prompts and dialog boxes. None of the code in these modules should be new to you by now.

Dynamic Data Exchange With Program Manager

SETUPPM.C adds the new program group and files to Program Manager. This is accomplished via a dynamic data exchange (DDE) conversation with Program Manager. Starting on page 22-19 of the *Microsoft Windows Guide to Programming* is a description of what commands may be sent to Program Manager. The following table describes each command:

Command	Description
CreateGroup	Instructs Program Manager to create a new group window.
AddItem	Instructs Program Manager to add a new program item to the active group.
DeleteGroup	Instructs Program Manager to delete a group, including its contents and associated data file.
ShowGroup	Instructs Program Manager to alter the appearance of a group window. (A window may be maximized, minimized, restored, etc.)
ExitProgman	Instructs Program Manager to terminate and (optionally) save its current state.

The first step is to initiate a DDE conversation. This is most easily managed by creating a window class whose job is to handle DDE communications. Setup registers a window class called DDEClient for this purpose.

A program starts a DDE conversation by informing all running applications that it wants to communicate with a particular application about a particular topic. Setup wishes to communicate with PROGMAN, and the topic is also PROGMAN. Here's how Setup initiates the DDE conversation with Program Manager:

```
char szProgMan[] = "PROGMAN";
.
.
.
// Create the Application and Topic atoms
aApp = GlobalAddAtom(szProgMan);
aTopic = GlobalAddAtom(szProgMan);

// Initiate a conversation with Program Manager.
// The last parameter contains the Application and Topic atoms.
hWndDDEClient = CreateWindow("DDEClient", "", 0, 0, 0, 0, 0,
    NULL, NULL, hInstance, (LPSTR) MAKELONG(aApp, aTopic));
```

601

```
// Delete the Application and Topic atoms
GlobalDeleteAtom(aApp);
GlobalDeleteAtom(aTopic);

if (hWndDDEClient == NULL) {
   // If the DDE conversation could not be initiated, the
   // "DDEClient" would not allow itself to be created.
   // This causes NULL to be returned from CreateWindow above.
   return(FALSE);
}
```

When Windows tries to create a DDEClient window, the *WM_NCCREATE*
message is sent to the window procedure. The code to process this message is shown
below:

```
case WM_NCCREATE:
   dwResult = DefWindowProc(hWnd, wMsg, wParam, lParam);
   if (dwResult == NULL) break;

   // Tell all applications that we are looking for a server.
   // A window handle of -1 causes this message to be broadcast
   // to all top-level windows.
   SendMessage(-1, WM_DDE_INITIATE, hWnd,
      (LONG) ((LPCREATESTRUCT) lParam)->lpCreateParams);

   // By the time SendMessage returns, we have a server if the
   // server's window handle is not NULL
   if (GETWNDEB(hWnd, WNDEB, hWndServer) != NULL)
      break;

   // A conversation was not established. Usually this is because
   // the application is not running. Attempt to execute the
   // desired application.
   GlobalGetAtomName(LOWORD((LONG) ((LPCREATESTRUCT)
      lParam)->lpCreateParams), szBuf, sizeof(szBuf));
   WinExec(szBuf, SW_RESTORE);

   // Try again to locate a server
   SendMessage(-1, WM_DDE_INITIATE, hWnd,
      (LONG) ((LPCREATESTRUCT) lParam)->lpCreateParams);
```

```
// If a server still could not be found, this DDEClient should
// not be created
if (GETWNDEB(hWnd, WNDEB, hWndServer) == NULL) {
  DefWindowProc(hWnd, WM_NCDESTROY, wParam, lParam);
  dwResult = FALSE;
}

break;
```

If a running application matches the specification and knows how to talk about the topic, it will send a *WM_DDE_ACK* message to the DDEClient window. The DDEClient window processes *WM_DDE_ACK* as follows:

```
case WM_DDE_ACK:
  if (GETWNDEB(hWnd, WNDEB, hWndServer) == NULL) {
    // No conversation initiated; WM_DDE_ACK must be from a
    // potential server that just received my WM_DDE_INITIATE
    // message
    SETWNDEB(hWnd, WNDEB, hWndServer, (HWND) wParam);
    break;
  }

  // WM_DDE_ACK message received from a potential server, but we
  // have already established a conversation with another server.
  // Tell the server that we do not wish to continue our
  // conversation with it.
  PostMessage((HWND) wParam, WM_DDE_TERMINATE, hWnd, 0);
  break;
```

When a DDEClient window is created, two extra window bytes are reserved. These store the window handle of the server. They are NULL if a conversation is not established. The window extra bytes are accessed with *GETWNDEB* and *SETWNDEB*, as explained in Appendix C.

After all the potential servers have responded to our broadcast, *WM_NCCREATE* checks the contents of the extra bytes to see if a conversation has been started. If not, it may be because Program Manager isn't running, so the DDEClient window attempts to execute Program Manager by calling *WinExec*. The process of trying to initiate a DDE conversation is started again. If a conversation is not established this time, the *WM_NCDESTROY* message is passed to *DefWindowProc* so that the window's data is cleaned up. We set *dwResult* to FALSE, and Windows returns a NULL window handle to the application to notify it that a conversation could not be established.

Sending Commands to Program Manager. Setup uses code like the following to send commands to Program Manager:

```
// Create a string containing the command to be executed by
// Program Manager
wsprintf(szCmd, "[CreateGroup(%s,%s)]",
   (LPSTR) szPMGroup, (LPSTR) szPMGroupFileName);

// Allocate a block of memory large enough to contain the
// desired command. Memory blocks used in DDE conversations
// must be created with the GMEM_DDESHARE flag.
hMem = GlobalAlloc(GMEM_MOVEABLE | GMEM_DDESHARE,
   lstrlen(szCmd) + 1);

// Copy the command into the memory block
lpCommand = GlobalLock(hMem);
lstrcpy(lpCommand, szCmd);
GlobalUnlock(hMem);

// Tell the DDEClient window that we wish it to send the
// command to the server
fOk = (BOOL) SendMessage(hWndDDEClient, WM_DDE_EXECUTE, 0,
   MAKELONG(0, hMem));

// A DDE server does not free a memory block used in a
// WM_DDE_EXECUTE message, so we must do it
GlobalFree(hMem);
```

This code creates the command string to be sent and allocates a block of memory large enough to contain the string. The block of memory must be allocated using the *GMEM_DDESHARE* flag. The command string is then copied into the memory block. Setup sends the *WM_DDE_EXECUTE* message to the DDEClient window that is communicating with Program Manager. The result will be TRUE or FALSE, indicating whether Program Manager successfully processed the command.

A DDEClient window sends a *WM_DDE_EXECUTE* message to its server when it wants the server to process commands. Ordinarily, only a Server window would receive *WM_DDE_EXECUTE*. However, Setup sends *WM_DDE_EXECUTE* messages to the DDEClient window. The DDEClient window procedure forwards the message to Program Manager. Here's how the DDEClient window procedure processes *WM_DDE_EXECUTE*:

```
case WM_DDE_EXECUTE:
    // Because this is a client and NOT a server, this message was
    // sent to this window from the Setup application. The lParam
    // parameter contains the handle of the memory containing the
    // commands to be executed by the server.

    // Verify that a conversation was started and hasn't been
    // terminated
    if (hWndServer == NULL) break;

    // Tell the server to execute the command
    PostMessage(hWndServer, WM_DDE_EXECUTE, hWnd, lParam);

    // Wait for response from the server
    GetMessage(&Msg, hWnd, WM_DDE_ACK, WM_DDE_ACK);

    // Return whether the command was acknowledged successfully
    wParam = LOWORD(Msg.lParam);
    dwResult = ((DDEACK *) &wParam)->fAck;
    break;
```

This code first ensures that neither application has terminated the DDE conversation. The *WM_DDE_EXECUTE* message is then posted to Program Manager's window, and the DDEClient window waits for Program Manager to respond by calling *GetMessage* and telling it to wait for *WM_DDE_ACK*. When *WM_DDE_ACK* is retrieved from the application's queue, the low-order word of the *lParam* parameter contains a *DDEACK* bit-field structure. This structure is declared in the DDE.H file included with the Windows SDK:

```
typedef struct {
   unsigned bAppReturnCode:8;
   unsigned reserved:6,
   unsigned fBusy:1,
   unsigned fAck:1;
} DDEACK;
```

The *fAck* member of this structure indicates whether the message was processed successfully (*fAck* is nonzero) or not (*fAck* is zero).

Terminating the DDE Conversation. After Setup has sent all the commands to Program Manager, it is no longer necessary to continue the conversation. Setup terminates the DDE conversation by destroying the DDEClient window:

```
DestroyWindow(hWndDDEClient);
```

The processing of the *WM_DESTROY* message in the DDEClient's window procedure is shown below:

```
case WM_DESTROY:
   // Tell server that we are terminating the conversation
   PostMessage(GETWNDEB(hWnd, WNDEB, hWndServer),
      WM_DDE_TERMINATE, hWnd, 0);

   // Tell ourselves we are no longer communicating with a server
   SETWNDEB(hWnd, WNDEB, hWndServer, NULL)

   // From now on, do not send a WM_DDE_ACK message to the server
   // in response to any messages sent from the server
```

```
// Wait for response from the server. If a response is not
// received in DDE_WAITTIME timer ticks, assume that the server
// has also terminated the conversation.
dwStopTime = GetTickCount() + DDE_WAITTIME;
do {
    // Check the application queue for a WM_DDE_TERMINATE
    // message for this "DDEClient" window
    if (PeekMessage(&Msg, hWnd, WM_DDE_TERMINATE,
        WM_DDE_TERMINATE, PM_REMOVE)) break;

} while (GetTickCount() < dwStopTime);
break;
```

This code posts the *WM_DDE_TERMINATE* message to the Server window, informing it that we wish to terminate the conversation. We then set the extra bytes in the DDEClient window to NULL, indicating that a conversation is no longer active.

Once the server has received the *WM_DDE_TERMINATE* message from the client, it should immediately respond by posting a *WM_DDE_TERMINATE* message. The *do...while* loop waits for the *WM_DDE_TERMINATE* message to appear in the application's queue.

It's a good idea to set a maximum time limit for responses whenever DDE communication is in effect. Otherwise, the server's failure to send a *WM_DDE_TERMINATE* confirmation message could leave the DDEClient in an endless loop, prohibiting Setup from regaining control.

Figure 8-1. SETUP.ICO.

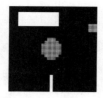

Figure 8-2. DISK.ICO.

Listing 8-2. DIALOG.H (dialog-box template defines) for Setup application.

```
#define DLG_WELCOME     1
#define DLG_INSERTDISK      2
#define DLG_STATUS      3

#define ICN_SETUP       10
#define ICN_DISK        11

#define ID_METER        100
#define ID_DESTPATH     101
#define ID_DISKNAME     102
#define ID_STATLINE1    103
#define ID_STATLINE2    104
#define ID_SRCPATH      105

#define IDABORT 3
#define IDCANCEL        2
#define IDIGNORE        5
#define IDNO    7
#define IDOK    1
#define IDRETRY 4
#define IDYES   6
```

Listing 8-3. MAKEFILE for Setup application.

```
#*******************************************************************
#Module name: MAKEFILE
#Programmer : Jeffrey M. Richter
#*******************************************************************

PROG = Setup
MODEL = S
CFLAGS = -A$(MODEL) -D_WINDOWS -Gcsw2 -W4 -Zlepid -Od
LFLAGS = /NOE/BA/A:16/M/CO/LI/F
LIBS = $(MODEL)libcew + libw

M1 = $(PROG).obj SetupInf.obj SetupDlg.obj SetupPM.obj

ICONS = $(PROG).ico
BITMAPS =
CURSORS =
RESOURCES = $(ICONS) $(BITMAPS) $(CURSORS)

.SUFFIXES: .rc

.rc.res:
   rc -r $*.rc

$(PROG).Exe: $(M1) $(PROG).Def $(PROG).Res
   link $(LFLAGS) @<<$(PROG).lnk
$(M1)
$(PROG), $(PROG), $(LIBS), $(PROG)
<<KEEP
   rc $(PROG).Res

$(PROG).obj:    $*.c $*.h dialog.h
SetupInf.obj:   $*.c $*.h $(PROG).h
SetupDlg.obj:   $*.c SetupInf.h $(PROG).h
SetupPM.obj:    $*.c $(PROG).h

$(PROG).res:    $*.rc $*.h $*.dlg dialog.h $(RESOURCES)
```

Listing 8-4. SETUP.C application source module.

```
/******************************************************************
Module name: Setup.C
Programmer : Jeffrey M. Richter
******************************************************************/

#include "..\nowindws.h"
#undef NOATOM
#undef NOCTLMGR
#undef NOKERNEL
#undef NOLFILEIO
#undef NOLSTRING
#undef NOMB
#undef NOMEMMGR
#undef NOMINMAX
#undef NOMSG
#undef NOOPENFILE
#undef NORESOURCE
#undef NOSHOWWINDOW
#undef NOSYSMETRICS
#undef NOUSER
#undef NOWINMESSAGES
#undef NOWINOFFSETS
#undef NOWINSTYLES
#include <windows.h>
#include <dde.h>

#include <dos.h>
#include <direct.h>
#include <string.h>

#include "Setup.H"
#include "SetupInf.H"
#include "..\Meter.04\Meter.H"

BOOL NEAR PASCAL CreateDstDirTree (HWND hDlgStatus);
BOOL NEAR PASCAL CopyAllFiles (HWND hDlgStatus);
BOOL NEAR PASCAL CreatePMInfo (HANDLE hInstance);
```

```
#define WasCancelled(hDlg) (!IsWindowEnabled(GetDlgItem(hDlg, \
   IDCANCEL)))

char _szAppName[] = "Setup";
HANDLE _hInstance;
char _szSrcDir[MAXDIR] = "x:\\";    // Where SETUP.EXE was run from
char _szDstDir[MAXDIR];

int PASCAL WinMain (HANDLE hInstance, HANDLE hPrevInstance,
      LPSTR lpszCmdLine, int nCmdShow) {
   int nResult;
   HWND hDlgStatus;
   FARPROC fpStatDlgProc, fpProc;
   HANDLE hLibMeter;
   DWORD dwDiskSpaceNeeded, dwFreeDiskSpace;
   struct diskfree_t DiskFreeSpace;
   char szBuf[100];

   // Don't let another instance of this application execute
   if (hPrevInstance != NULL) return(0);

   // Prepare the DDEClient window class so we can use it later
   if (!RegisterDDEClient(hInstance)) return(0);

   // Initialize the default source path so it uses the same drive
   // letter from which the SETUP.EXE application was executed
   GetModuleFileName(hInstance, _szSrcDir, sizeof(_szSrcDir));
   *(_fstrrchr(_szSrcDir, '\\') + 1) = 0;

   _hInstance = hInstance;

   // Ensure that the METER.DLL is available at the beginning
   wsprintf(szBuf, "%sMETER.DLL", (LPSTR) _szSrcDir);
   hLibMeter = LoadLibrary(szBuf);
   if (hLibMeter < 32) {
     MsgBox(hInstance, NULL, IDS_NOMETERLIB, _szAppName,
       MB_ICONINFORMATION | MB_OK | MB_TASKMODAL);
      return(0);
   }
```

```
// Read the SETUP.INF file into memory
wsprintf(szBuf, "%s%sSETUP.INF", (LPSTR) _szSrcDir, (LPSTR)
   ((*(_fstrrchr(_szSrcDir, '\\') + 1) == 0) ? "" : "\\"));

nResult = (SIM_INITIALIZE_ERROR) SetupInfoSys(SIM_INITIALIZE,
   0, szBuf);
if (nResult != SIM_INIT_NOERROR) {
   MsgBox(hInstance, NULL,
      (nResult == SIM_INIT_NOMEM) ? IDS_NOMEMORY :
      IDS_NOSETUPINFOFILE, _szAppName, MB_ICONINFORMATION |
      MB_OK | MB_TASKMODAL, (LPSTR) szBuf);
   FreeLibrary(hLibMeter);
   return(0);
}

// Get the amount of memory (in K) needed for the installation
dwDiskSpaceNeeded = SetupInfoSys(SIM_GETSPACENEEDED, 0, 0);

// Create the Status dialog box
fpStatDlgProc = MakeProcInstance(StatusDlgProc, hInstance);
hDlgStatus = CreateDialog(hInstance,
   MAKEINTRESOURCE(DLG_STATUS), NULL, fpStatDlgProc);

do {
   // Welcome user to setup program and prompt for destination
   // directory
   fpProc = MakeProcInstance(WelcomeDlgProc, hInstance);
   nResult = DialogBox(hInstance, MAKEINTRESOURCE(DLG_WELCOME),
      NULL, fpProc);
   FreeProcInstance(fpProc);
   if (nResult == IDCANCEL) break;

   // See if sufficient disk space exists on destination drive
   _dos_getdiskfree(_szDstDir[0] - 'A' + 1, &DiskFreeSpace);
   dwFreeDiskSpace = ((DWORD) DiskFreeSpace.avail_clusters *
      (DWORD) DiskFreeSpace.sectors_per_cluster *
      (DWORD) DiskFreeSpace.bytes_per_sector) / 1024UL;

   if (dwFreeDiskSpace < dwDiskSpaceNeeded) {
      MsgBox(hInstance, NULL, IDS_NODISKSPACE, _szAppName,
```

```
         MB_OK | MB_ICONINFORMATION | MB_TASKMODAL,
         _szDstDir[0], dwFreeDiskSpace, dwDiskSpaceNeeded);
      continue;
   }

   // Try to create the destination directory tree
   ShowWindow(hDlgStatus, SW_SHOW);
   UpdateWindow(hDlgStatus);
   nResult = CreateDstDirTree(hDlgStatus);
   ShowWindow(hDlgStatus, SW_HIDE);

   if (nResult == FALSE) {
      // If the directory tree cannot be created, force loop
      // to repeat
      dwFreeDiskSpace = 0;
   }

} while (dwFreeDiskSpace < dwDiskSpaceNeeded);

if (nResult == IDCANCEL) {
   DestroyWindow(hDlgStatus);
   FreeProcInstance(fpStatDlgProc);
   FreeLibrary(hLibMeter);
   return(0);
}

// Make the destination directory the current directory
chdir(_szDstDir);

// Try to copy the files
ShowWindow(hDlgStatus, SW_SHOW);
UpdateWindow(hDlgStatus);
nResult = CopyAllFiles(hDlgStatus);
ShowWindow(hDlgStatus, SW_HIDE);

// Clean up the things we no longer need
DestroyWindow(hDlgStatus);
FreeProcInstance(fpStatDlgProc);
FreeLibrary(hLibMeter);
```

613

```
    if (nResult == FALSE) {
       // Installation not complete
       MsgBox(hInstance, NULL, IDS_SETUPNOGOOD, _szAppName,
          MB_OK | MB_ICONINFORMATION | MB_TASKMODAL);
       return(0);
    }

    MsgBox(hInstance, NULL,
       CreatePMInfo(hInstance) ? IDS_PMADDOK : IDS_PMADDNOGOOD,
       _szAppName, MB_OK | MB_ICONINFORMATION | MB_TASKMODAL);
       return(0);
}

// **** Functions for Creating the Destination Directory Tree ****
BOOL NEAR PASCAL CreateDstDirTree (HWND hDlgStatus) {
   int nResult, nMaxDirs, nDirNum;
   char szBuf[MAXDIR]; MSG Msg;

   SetDlgItemText(hDlgStatus, ID_STATLINE1,
      "Creating destination directory tree...");
   nMaxDirs = (int) SetupInfoSys(SIM_GETNUMDIRS, 0, 0);
   SendDlgItemMessage(hDlgStatus, ID_METER, MM_SETPARTSCOMPLETE,
      0, 0);
   SendDlgItemMessage(hDlgStatus, ID_METER, MM_SETPARTSINJOB,
      nMaxDirs + 1, 0);
   SetDlgItemText(hDlgStatus, ID_STATLINE2, _szDstDir);

   // Create the destination directory
   nResult = chdir(_szDstDir);
   if (nResult != 0) {
      nResult = mkdir(_szDstDir);
      if (nResult != 0) {
         MsgBox(_hInstance, hDlgStatus, IDS_CANTMAKEDIR,
            _szAppName, MB_ICONINFORMATION | MB_OK,
            (LPSTR) _szDstDir);
         return(FALSE);
      } else chdir(_szDstDir);
   }
   SendDlgItemMessage(hDlgStatus, ID_METER, MM_SETPARTSCOMPLETE,
      1, 0);
```

```
// Create any subdirectories under the destination directory
for (nDirNum = 0; nDirNum < nMaxDirs; nDirNum++) {
    // Let some other applications execute
    while (PeekMessage(&Msg, NULL, NULL, NULL, PM_REMOVE)) {
        TranslateMessage(&Msg);
        DispatchMessage(&Msg);
    }

    if (WasCancelled(hDlgStatus)) {
        nResult = IDCANCEL;
        break;
    }

    wsprintf(szBuf, "%s%s", (LPSTR) _szDstDir,
        (LPSTR) ((*(_fstrrchr(_szDstDir,
        '\\') + 1) == 0) ? "" : "\\"));
    SetupInfoSys(SIM_GETDIR, nDirNum, _fstrchr(szBuf, 0));
    SetDlgItemText(hDlgStatus, ID_STATLINE2, szBuf);

    nResult = chdir(szBuf);
    if (nResult != 0) {
        nResult = mkdir(szBuf);
        if (nResult != 0) {
            MsgBox(_hInstance, hDlgStatus, IDS_CANTMAKEDIR,
                _szAppName, MB_ICONINFORMATION | MB_OK,
                (LPSTR) szBuf);
            nResult = IDCANCEL;
            break;
        } else chdir(szBuf);
    }
    nResult = IDOK;
    SendDlgItemMessage(hDlgStatus, ID_METER,
        MM_SETPARTSCOMPLETE, nDirNum + 2, 0);
}
return(nResult != IDCANCEL);
}
```

```
// ************** Functions for Copying Files *****************

typedef enum {
   CFE_NOERROR,
   CFE_NOMEMORY,
   CFE_CANTOPENSRC,
   CFE_CANTOPENDST,
} COPYFILE_ERROR;

COPYFILE_ERROR NEAR PASCAL CopyFile (LPSTR szSrcPath,
      LPSTR szDstPath) {
   const WORD wBufferSize = 65535u;
   int nSrcFile, nDstFile;
   WORD wBytesRead, wDate, wTime;
   OFSTRUCT ofSrc, ofDst;
   LPSTR lpBuffer;
   GLOBALHANDLE hMem;

   nSrcFile = OpenFile(szSrcPath, &ofSrc, OF_READ);
   if (nSrcFile == -1) return(CFE_CANTOPENSRC);

   hMem = GlobalAlloc(GMEM_MOVEABLE, wBufferSize);
   if (hMem == NULL) {
      _lclose(nSrcFile);
      return(CFE_NOMEMORY);
   }

   nDstFile = OpenFile(szDstPath, &ofDst, OF_CREATE | OF_WRITE);
   if (nDstFile == -1) {
      _lclose(nSrcFile);
      GlobalFree(hMem);
      return(CFE_CANTOPENDST);
   }

   lpBuffer = GlobalLock(hMem);
   do {
      wBytesRead = _lread(nSrcFile, lpBuffer, wBufferSize);
      _lwrite(nDstFile, lpBuffer, wBytesRead);
   } while (wBytesRead == wBufferSize);
   GlobalUnlock(hMem);
```

```
    // Make the destination file have the same time stamp as the
    // source file
    _dos_getftime(nSrcFile, &wDate, &wTime);
    _dos_setftime(nDstFile, wDate, wTime);
    _lclose(nDstFile);

    GlobalFree(hMem);
    _lclose(nSrcFile);
    return(CFE_NOERROR);
}

BOOL NEAR PASCAL CopyAllFiles (HWND hDlgStatus) {
    int nMaxFiles, nFileNum, nResult; COPYFILE_ERROR CFE;
    char szSrcPath[MAXPATH], szDstPath[MAXPATH],
        szFileName[MAXFILENAME];
    char szFileDesc[MAXFILEDESC], szDir[MAXDIRDESC],
        szDiskDesc[MAXDISKDESC];
    MSG Msg; FARPROC fpProc;

    HANDLE hDlgRes;

    // Get the handle of the "InsertDisk" dialog box from the
    // EXEcutable file
    hDlgRes = FindResource(_hInstance,
        MAKEINTRESOURCE(DLG_INSERTDISK), RT_DIALOG);

    // Get the memory handle of the "InsertDisk" dialog box in
    // memory. The block is already in memory because the dialog
    // box is marked as PRELOAD FIXED.
    hDlgRes = LoadResource(_hInstance, hDlgRes);

    // Force the memory block to be locked down. This prohibits
    // Windows from discarding the dialog-box template from memory.
    LockResource(hDlgRes);

    SetDlgItemText(hDlgStatus, ID_STATLINE1, "Copying files...");
    nMaxFiles = (int) SetupInfoSys(SIM_GETNUMFILES, 0, 0);
    SendDlgItemMessage(hDlgStatus, ID_METER, MM_SETPARTSCOMPLETE,
        0, 0);
```

```
SendDlgItemMessage(hDlgStatus, ID_METER, MM_SETPARTSINJOB,
   nMaxFiles, 0);

fpProc = MakeProcInstance(InsertDiskDlgProc, _hInstance);
for (nFileNum = 0; nFileNum < nMaxFiles; nFileNum++) {
   SetupInfoSys(SIM_GETFILEDESC, nFileNum, szFileDesc);
   SetupInfoSys(SIM_GETFILENAME, nFileNum, szFileName);
   SetupInfoSys(SIM_GETFILEDIR, nFileNum, szDir);
   SetupInfoSys(SIM_GETFILEDISK, nFileNum, szDiskDesc);
   SetDlgItemText(hDlgStatus, ID_STATLINE2, szFileDesc);

   wsprintf(szDstPath, "%s%s%s\\%s", (LPSTR) _szDstDir, (LPSTR)
      ((*(_fstrrchr(_szDstDir, '\\') + 1) == 0) ? "" : "\\"),
      (LPSTR) szDir, (LPSTR) szFileName);

  do {
     // Let other applications execute
     while (PeekMessage(&Msg, NULL, NULL, NULL, PM_REMOVE)) {
        TranslateMessage(&Msg);
        DispatchMessage(&Msg);
     }

     if (WasCancelled(hDlgStatus)) {
        nResult = IDCANCEL;
        break;
     }

     wsprintf(szSrcPath, "%s%s%s\\%s", (LPSTR) _szSrcDir,
        (LPSTR) ((*(_fstrrchr(_szSrcDir, '\\') + 1) == 0) ? ""
        : "\\"), (LPSTR) szDir, (LPSTR) szFileName);

     nResult = IDOK;
     if (!SetupInfoSys(SIM_ISFILECOMPRESSED, nFileNum, 0)) {
        CFE = CopyFile(szSrcPath, szDstPath);

        switch (CFE) {

           case CFE_NOERROR:
              nResult = IDOK;
              break;
```

```
        case CFE_NOMEMORY:
          nResult = MsgBox(_hInstance, hDlgStatus,
            IDS_NOMEMORYCOPY, _szAppName,
            MB_ICONINFORMATION | MB_RETRYCANCEL);
          break;

        case CFE_CANTOPENSRC:
          nResult = DialogBoxParam(_hInstance,
            MAKEINTRESOURCE(DLG_INSERTDISK), hDlgStatus,
            fpProc, (LONG) (LPSTR) szDiskDesc);

          // Normally, Windows would have discarded the
          // dialog-box template from memory after the
          // dialog box had been created. Because the call
          // to LockResource() above forced the memory
          // block to be locked, the template will NOT
          // be discarded. If the template were discarded,
          // the next time this dialog box needed to be
          // created Windows would have to load the
          // template from the EXEcutable file. However,
          // the SETUP.EXE file is probably not on the
          // diskette currently in the drive. This would
          // cause the program to behave erratically.
          break;

      case CFE_CANTOPENDST:
          nResult = MsgBox(_hInstance, hDlgStatus,
            IDS_CANTOPENDST, _szAppName,
            MB_ICONINFORMATION | MB_RETRYCANCEL);
          break;
    }
  } else {
    // Use decompression function to copy the file
  }

// Make sure the user really wants to cancel Setup
if (nResult == IDCANCEL) {
  nResult = MsgBox(_hInstance, hDlgStatus,
    IDS_QUERYABORT, _szAppName,
    MB_ICONQUESTION | MB_YESNO);
```

619

```
            if (nResult == IDYES) {
                nResult = IDCANCEL;
                break;
            }
        }

    } while (nResult != IDCANCEL && CFE != CFE_NOERROR);
    if (nResult == IDCANCEL) break;

    SendDlgItemMessage(hDlgStatus, ID_METER,
        MM_SETPARTSCOMPLETE, nFileNum + 1, 0);
    }

    // The dialog-box template is no longer needed, so it may be
    // unlocked and removed from memory
    UnlockResource(hDlgRes);
    FreeResource(hDlgRes);

    FreeProcInstance(fpProc);
    return(nResult != IDCANCEL);
}


// **************** Miscellaneous Function ********************
int FAR cdecl MsgBox (HANDLE hInstance, HWND hWnd, WORD wID,
        LPSTR szCaption, WORD wType, ...) {
    char szResString[200], szText[200];
    void FAR *VarArgList = (WORD FAR *) &wType + 1;
    LoadString(hInstance, wID, szResString,
        sizeof(szResString) - 1);
    wvsprintf(szText, szResString, VarArgList);
    return(MessageBox(hWnd, szText, szCaption, wType));
}
```

Listing 8-5. SETUP.DEF application definitions file.

```
; Module name: Setup.DEF
; Programmer : Jeffrey M. Richter

NAME          Setup
DESCRIPTION   'Setup: Window Application installation Application'
STUB          'WinStub.exe'
EXETYPE       WINDOWS

;Segments must be NONDISCARDABLE so that Windows will not attempt
;to load a segment after the user has swapped diskettes
CODE          MOVEABLE PRELOAD NONDISCARDABLE
DATA          MOVEABLE MULTIPLE PRELOAD
HEAPSIZE      1024
STACKSIZE     4096
EXPORTS
   StatusDlgProc      @1
   WelcomeDlgProc     @2
   InsertDiskDlgProc  @3
   DDEClientWndProc   @4
```

Listing 8-6. SETUP.DLG dialog-box templates.

```
DLG_WELCOME DIALOG PRELOAD FIXED 0, 0, 192, 100
CAPTION "Caption"
FONT 8, "Helv"
STYLE WS_BORDER | WS_CAPTION | WS_DLGFRAME | WS_SYSMENU |
   DS_MODALFRAME | WS_POPUP
BEGIN
   CONTROL "Setup will install this application into the following
      directory, which it will create on your hard disk.", -1,
      "static ", SS_LEFT | WS_CHILD, 8, 8, 180, 20
   CONTROL "If you want to install the application in a different
      directory and/or drive. Type the name of the directory
      below:", - 1, "static", SS_LEFT | WS_CHILD, 8, 32, 180, 28
   CONTROL "Copy to:", -1, "static", SS_LEFT | WS_CHILD, 32, 60,
      32, 12
```

```
      CONTROL "", ID_DESTPATH, "edit", ES_LEFT | ES_UPPERCASE |
         WS_BORDER | WS_TABSTOP | WS_CHILD, 64, 60, 84, 12
      CONTROL "&Ok", IDOK, "button", BS_DEFPUSHBUTTON | WS_TABSTOP |
         WS_CHILD, 48, 80, 32, 16
      CONTROL "&Cancel", IDCANCEL, "button", BS_PUSHBUTTON |
         WS_TABSTOP | WS_CHILD, 108, 80, 32, 16
END

DLG_INSERTDISK DIALOG PRELOAD FIXED 0, 0, 192, 72
CAPTION "Caption"
FONT 8, "Helv"
STYLE WS_BORDER | WS_CAPTION | WS_DLGFRAME | WS_SYSMENU |
   DS_MODALFRAME | WS_POPUP
BEGIN
      CONTROL "#11", -1, "static", SS_ICON | WS_CHILD, 4, 4, 16, 16
      CONTROL "Setup needs the following disk:", -1, "static",
         SS_LEFT | WS_CHILD, 40, 4, 112, 8
      CONTROL "Application Diskette", ID_DISKNAME, "static",
         SS_LEFT | WS_CHILD, 40, 12, 112, 12
      CONTROL "", ID_SRCPATH, "edit", ES_LEFT | ES_UPPERCASE |
         WS_BORDER | WS_TABSTOP | WS_CHILD, 16, 32, 160, 12
      CONTROL "&Ok", IDOK, "button", BS_DEFPUSHBUTTON | WS_TABSTOP |
         WS_CHILD, 48, 52, 32, 16
      CONTROL "&Cancel", IDCANCEL, "button", BS_PUSHBUTTON |
         WS_TABSTOP | WS_CHILD, 112, 52, 32, 16
END

DLG_STATUS DIALOG PRELOAD FIXED 0, 0, 188, 68
CAPTION "Caption"
FONT 8, "Helv"
STYLE WS_BORDER | WS_CAPTION | WS_DLGFRAME | WS_SYSMENU |
   DS_MODALFRAME | WS_POPUP
BEGIN
      CONTROL "", ID_STATLINE1, "static", SS_LEFT | WS_CHILD, 4, 4,
         144, 8
      CONTROL "", ID_STATLINE2, "static", SS_LEFT | WS_CHILD, 4, 16,
         144, 12
      CONTROL "", ID_METER, "meter", WS_BORDER | WS_CHILD, 16, 28,
         156, 12
```

```
    CONTROL "&Cancel", IDCANCEL, "button", BS_DEFPUSHBUTTON |
        WS_TABSTOP | WS_CHILD, 76, 48, 32, 16
END
```

Listing 8-7. SETUP.H application header module.

```
/*****************************************************************
Module name: Setup.H
Programmer : Jeffrey M. Richter
*****************************************************************/

#include "dialog.h"

// Defines used by the Setup program
#define MAXPATH 80
#define MAXDRIVE 3
#define MAXDIR 66
#define MAXFILE 9
#define MAXEXT 5
#define MAXFILENAME (MAXFILE + MAXEXT)

extern char _szAppName[];
extern HANDLE _hInstance;
extern char _szSrcDir[MAXDIR];
extern char _szDstDir[MAXDIR];

// Prototypes for various functions
BOOL FAR PASCAL RegisterDDEClient (HANDLE hInstance);
BOOL FAR PASCAL WelcomeDlgProc (HWND hDlg, WORD wMsg, WORD wParam,
    LONG lParam);
BOOL FAR PASCAL StatusDlgProc (HWND hDlg, WORD wMsg, WORD wParam,
    LONG lParam);
BOOL FAR PASCAL InsertDiskDlgProc (HWND hDlg, WORD wMsg,
    WORD wParam, LONG lParam);

int FAR cdecl MsgBox (HANDLE hInstance, HWND hWnd, WORD wID,
    LPSTR szCaption, WORD wType, ...);
```

```
// Defines for use with Setup's string table
#define IDS_NOMETERLIB 1000
#define IDS_NOMEMORY 1001
#define IDS_NOSETUPINFOFILE 1002
#define IDS_NODISKSPACE 1003
#define IDS_CANTMAKEDIR 1004
#define IDS_QUERYABORT 1005
#define IDS_SETUPNOGOOD 1006
#define IDS_SETUPOKNOPM 1007
#define IDS_SETUPDONE 1008
#define IDS_PMADDOK 1009
#define IDS_PMADDNOGOOD 1010
#define IDS_NOMEMORYCOPY 1011
#define IDS_CANTOPENDST 1012


//****** Macros for use by Window and Class Extra Bytes ********

#define offsetof(Struct, Member) \
    ((unsigned int) &(((Struct NEAR *) 0)->Member))

#define GETWNDEB(hWnd, Struct, Member) \
    ((sizeof(((Struct FAR *)0)->Member) == sizeof(DWORD)) ? \
        GetWindowLong(hWnd, offsetof(Struct, Member)) : \
        GetWindowWord(hWnd, offsetof(Struct, Member)))

#define SETWNDEB(hWnd, Struct, Member, Value) \
    ((sizeof(((Struct FAR *)0)->Member) == sizeof(DWORD)) ? \
        SetWindowLong(hWnd, offsetof(Struct, Member), Value) : \
        SetWindowWord(hWnd, offsetof(Struct, Member), (WORD) Value))

#define GETCLSEB(hWnd, Struct, Member) \
    ((sizeof(((Struct FAR *)0)->Member) == sizeof(DWORD)) ? \
        GetClassLong(hWnd, offsetof(Struct, Member)) : \
        GetClassWord(hWnd, offsetof(Struct, Member)))

#define SETCLSEB(hWnd, Struct, Member, Value) \
    ((sizeof(((Struct FAR *)0)->Member) == sizeof(DWORD)) ? \
        SetClassLong(hWnd, offsetof(Struct, Member), Value) : \
        SetClassWord(hWnd, offsetof(Struct, Member), (WORD) Value))
```

624

Listing 8-8. SETUP.RC application resource file. Note that the strings are broken here to accommodate the narrow page width and would not normally be allowed to break.

```
/******************************************************************
Module name: Setup.RC
Programmer : Jeffrey M. Richter
******************************************************************/

#include <windows.h>
#include "setup.h"

#include "dialog.h"
#include "setup.dlg"


ICN_SETUP    ICON      PRELOAD FIXED Setup.Ico
ICN_DISK     ICON      PRELOAD FIXED Disk.Ico

STRINGTABLE PRELOAD FIXED
BEGIN
IDS_NOMETERLIB, "Setup cannot find the METER.DLL file.\nPlease
   verify the distribution diskette."
IDS_NOMEMORY, "Insufficient memory to run Setup.\nClose some
   applications and try again."
IDS_NOSETUPINFOFILE, "The %s file cannot be found.\nPlease verify
   the distribution diskette."
IDS_NODISKSPACE, "Drive %c: contains %ldK of free disk
   space.\nSetup requires a minimum of %ldK.\nPlease select
   another drive."
IDS_CANTMAKEDIR, "The %s directory cannot be created.\nEnter
   another directory or try another drive."
IDS_QUERYABORT, "Setup has not completed installing the
   software.\nAre you sure you want to cancel?"
IDS_SETUPNOGOOD, "The software has not been successfully
   installed.\nYou must run Setup again before using the
   software."
IDS_PMADDOK, "Setup has installed the software successfully\nand
   added the application(s) to the Program Manager."
IDS_PMADDNOGOOD, "Setup has installed the software
   successfully\nbut could not add the application(s) to the
   Program Manager."
```

```
IDS_NOMEMORYCOPY, "Insufficient memory to copy file.\nClose
    another application or cancel Setup."
IDS_CANTOPENDST, "Cannot create destination file.\nTry again or
    cancel Setup."
END
```

Listing 8-9. SETUPDLG.C dialog-box source module.

```
/******************************************************************
Module name: SetupDlg.C
Programmer : Jeffrey M. Richter
******************************************************************/

#include "..\nowindws.h"
#undef NOCTLMGR
#undef NOKERNEL
#undef NOLSTRING
#undef NOMB
#undef NOOPENFILE
#undef NOSYSMETRICS
#undef NOUSER
#undef NOWINMESSAGES
#include <windows.h>

#include "..\Meter.04\Meter.H"
#include "Setup.h"
#include "SetupInf.h"

// Setup's initial sign on screen. Asks user for destination
// directory.
BOOL FAR PASCAL WelcomeDlgProc (HWND hDlg, WORD wMsg, WORD wParam,
        LONG lParam) {
    BOOL fProcessed = TRUE;
    char szBuf[MAXDIR];
    OFSTRUCT ofStruct;
    RECT rc;
```

```
switch (wMsg) {
   case WM_INITDIALOG:
      SetupInfoSys(SIM_GETAPPNAME, 0, szBuf);
      SetWindowText(hDlg, szBuf);
      GetWindowRect(hDlg, &rc);
      SetWindowPos(hDlg, NULL,
         (GetSystemMetrics(SM_CXSCREEN) - (rc.right - rc.left))
         / 2, (GetSystemMetrics(SM_CYSCREEN) - (rc.bottom -
         rc.top)) / 3, 0, 0, SWP_NOSIZE | SWP_NOZORDER);

      SetupInfoSys(SIM_GETDEFDIR, 0, szBuf);
      SetDlgItemText(hDlg, ID_DESTPATH, szBuf);
      break;

   case WM_COMMAND:
      switch (wParam) {
         case ID_DESTPATH:
            EnableWindow(GetDlgItem(hDlg, IDOK),
               (BOOL) SendMessage(LOWORD(lParam),
               EM_LINELENGTH, 0, 0));
            break;

         case IDOK:
            GetDlgItemText(hDlg, ID_DESTPATH, szBuf,
               sizeof(szBuf));
            OpenFile(szBuf, &ofStruct, OF_PARSE);
            lstrcpy(_szDstDir, (LPSTR) ofStruct.szPathName);
            // Do IDCANCEL case

         case IDCANCEL:
            EndDialog(hDlg, wParam);
            break;
      }
      break;

   default:
      fProcessed = FALSE;
      break;
}
return(fProcessed);
}
```

```
// Display copying status. Let user cancel the installation.
BOOL FAR PASCAL StatusDlgProc (HWND hDlg, WORD wMsg, WORD wParam,
     LONG lParam) {
  BOOL fProcessed = TRUE;
  int nResult;
  char szBuf[100];
  RECT rc;

  switch (wMsg) {
    case WM_INITDIALOG:
       SetupInfoSys(SIM_GETAPPNAME, 0, szBuf);
       SetWindowText(hDlg, szBuf);
       GetWindowRect(hDlg, &rc);
       SetWindowPos(hDlg, NULL,
          (GetSystemMetrics(SM_CXSCREEN) - (rc.right -
          rc.left)) / 2, (GetSystemMetrics(SM_CYSCREEN) -
          (rc.bottom - rc.top)) / 3, 0, 0, SWP_NOSIZE |
          SWP_NOZORDER);
       break;

    case WM_SHOWWINDOW:
       fProcessed = FALSE;
       if (!wParam) break;
       EnableWindow(GetDlgItem(hDlg, IDCANCEL), TRUE);
       SetDlgItemText(hDlg, ID_STATLINE1, "");
       SetDlgItemText(hDlg, ID_STATLINE2, "");
       SendDlgItemMessage(hDlg, ID_METER, MM_SETPARTSCOMPLETE,
          0, 0);
       SendDlgItemMessage(hDlg, ID_METER, MM_SETPARTSINJOB,
          0, 0);
       break;

    case WM_COMMAND:
       switch (wParam) {
          case IDOK:
             // User pressed ENTER. Do IDCANCEL case.
          case IDCANCEL:
             nResult = MsgBox(_hInstance, hDlg,
                IDS_QUERYABORT, _szAppName,
                MB_ICONQUESTION | MB_YESNO);
```

```
                  if (nResult == IDYES)
                     EnableWindow(GetDlgItem(hDlg, IDCANCEL), FALSE);
                  break;
            }
            break;

      default:
         fProcessed = FALSE;
         break;
   }
   return(fProcessed);
}

// Prompt user to insert a different diskette
BOOL FAR PASCAL InsertDiskDlgProc (HWND hDlg, WORD wMsg,
      WORD wParam, LONG lParam) {
   BOOL fProcessed = TRUE;
   char szBuf[100];
   RECT rc;

   switch (wMsg) {
      case WM_INITDIALOG:
         // lParam is address of diskette description
         SetupInfoSys(SIM_GETAPPNAME, 0, szBuf);
         SetWindowText(hDlg, szBuf);
         GetWindowRect(hDlg, &rc);
         SetWindowPos(hDlg, NULL,
            (GetSystemMetrics(SM_CXSCREEN) - (rc.right - rc.left))
            / 2, (GetSystemMetrics(SM_CYSCREEN) - (rc.bottom -
            rc.top)) / 3, 0, 0, SWP_NOSIZE | SWP_NOZORDER);

         // Throw away the data segment and use the new one.
         // This is in case the data segment has moved.
         SetDlgItemText(hDlg, ID_DISKNAME, (LPSTR) (char NEAR *)
            lParam);
         SetDlgItemText(hDlg, ID_SRCPATH, _szSrcDir);
         SendDlgItemMessage(hDlg, ID_SRCPATH, EM_LIMITTEXT,
            sizeof(_szSrcDir), 0);
         MessageBeep(0);
         break;
```

```
    case WM_COMMAND:
       switch (wParam) {
          case ID_SRCPATH:
             EnableWindow(GetDlgItem(hDlg, IDOK),
                (BOOL) SendMessage(LOWORD(lParam),
                EM_LINELENGTH, 0, 0));
             break;

          case IDOK:
             GetDlgItemText(hDlg, ID_SRCPATH, _szSrcDir,
                sizeof(_szSrcDir));
             // Do IDCANCEL case

          case IDCANCEL:
             EndDialog(hDlg, wParam);
             break;
       }
       break;

    default:
       fProcessed = FALSE;
       break;
  }
  return(fProcessed);
}
```

Listing 8-10. SETUPINF.C file-handling source module.

```
/*******************************************************************
Module name: SetupInf.C
Programmer : Jeffrey M. Richter
*******************************************************************/

#include "..\nowindws.h"
#undef NOCTLMGR
#undef NOKERNEL
#undef NOLFILEIO
#undef NOLSTRING
```

```
#undef NOMB
#undef NOMEMMGR
#undef NOMSG
#undef NOOPENFILE
#undef NOSHOWWINDOW
#undef NOUSER
#undef NOWINMESSAGES
#undef NOWINOFFSETS
#undef NOWINSTYLES
#include <windows.h>

#include <string.h>
#include <stdlib.h>

#include "Setup.H"
#include "SetupInf.H"

#define MAXSETUPINFOSIZE   10240

struct {
    char szAppName[MAXAPPNAME];
    char szDefDir[MAXDIR];
    WORD wSpaceNeeded;
    char szPMGroupFileName[MAXFILENAME];
    char szPMGroupName[MAXPMDESC];
    WORD wNumDisks, wNumDirs, wNumFiles, wNumPMFiles;
} SetupInfo;

struct {
    WORD wNum;
    char szDesc[MAXDISKDESC];
} DiskInfo[10];

struct {
    WORD wNum;
    char szDesc[MAXDIRDESC];
} DirInfo[25];
```

```
struct {
   char szDesc[MAXFILEDESC];
   char szFileName[MAXFILENAME];
   WORD wDirNum, wDiskNum;
   BOOL fCompressed;
} FileInfo[200];

struct {
   char szFileName[MAXFILENAME];
   char szDesc[MAXPMDESC];
   char szIconFileName[MAXFILENAME];
   WORD wIconPos;
} PMInfo[20];

typedef enum {
   RS_UNDEFINED,
   RS_APPLICATION,
   RS_DISKS,
   RS_DIRS,
   RS_FILES,
   RS_PMINFO,
   RS_TERMINATE
} READSTATE;

static WORD NEAR PASCAL latoi (LPSTR szString) {
   WORD wNum = 0;
   while (*szString >= '0' && *szString <= '9')
      wNum = (wNum * 10) + (*szString++ - '0');
   return(wNum);
}

LPSTR NEAR PASCAL StripEndBlanks (LPSTR szString) {
   LPSTR p = szString, q = szString;

   while (*p == ' ' || *p == '\t') p++;
   while (*p) *szString++ = *p++;
   *szString- = 0;
   while (szString >= q && (*szString == ' ' ||
      *szString == '\t')) *szString- = 0;
   return(q);
}
```

```
static int NEAR PASCAL PrepareSetupInfo (LPSTR szInfoFile) {
   READSTATE State = RS_UNDEFINED;
   WORD wResult = TRUE;
   char szLine[100];
   LPSTR p, szData;
   HCURSOR hCursor;

   hCursor = SetCursor(LoadCursor(NULL, IDC_WAIT));
   // Initialize application global information
   SetupInfo.szAppName[0] = 0;
   SetupInfo.szDefDir[0] = 0;
   SetupInfo.wSpaceNeeded = 0;
   SetupInfo.szPMGroupFileName[0] = 0;
   SetupInfo.szPMGroupName[0] = 0;
   SetupInfo.wNumDisks = SetupInfo.wNumDirs = 0;
   SetupInfo.wNumFiles = SetupInfo.wNumPMFiles = 0;

   while (State != RS_TERMINATE) {

      // Read next line from data buffer
      p = _fstrchr(szInfoFile, '\r');
      if (p != NULL) *p = 0;
      lstrcpy(szLine, szInfoFile);
      if (p != NULL) szInfoFile = p + 2;

      // Remove leading white space
      StripEndBlanks(szLine);

      // See if the state has changed
      if (*szLine == '[') {
         State = RS_UNDEFINED;

         if (lstrcmpi(szLine, "[End]") == 0)
            State = RS_TERMINATE;
         if (lstrcmpi(szLine, "[Application]") == 0)
            State = RS_APPLICATION;
         if (lstrcmpi(szLine, "[Disks]") == 0)
            State = RS_DISKS;
         if (lstrcmpi(szLine, "[Dirs]") == 0)
            State = RS_DIRS;
```

633

```
        if (lstrcmpi(szLine, "[Files]") == 0)
            State = RS_FILES;
        if (lstrcmpi(szLine, "[PM Info]") == 0)
            State = RS_PMINFO;

        if (State == RS_UNDEFINED) {
            // Unrecognized section in SETUP.INF file
        }
        continue;
    }

    // Line is part of the current state
    if (*szLine == ';') continue;
    if (*szLine == 0) continue;

    if (State == RS_APPLICATION || State == RS_DISKS ||
            State == RS_DIRS) {
        szData = _fstrchr(szLine, '=');
        if (szData != NULL) *szData++ = 0;
    } else szData = szLine;

    StripEndBlanks(szLine);
    if (szData != szLine) StripEndBlanks(szData);

    switch (State) {
        case RS_APPLICATION:
            if (lstrcmpi(szLine, "AppName") == 0)
                lstrcpy(SetupInfo.szAppName, szData);

            if (lstrcmpi(szLine, "DefDir") == 0)
                lstrcpy(SetupInfo.szDefDir, szData);

            if (lstrcmpi(szLine, "SpaceNeeded") == 0)
                SetupInfo.wSpaceNeeded = latoi(szData);

            if (lstrcmpi(szLine, "DefPMGroup") == 0) {
                p = _fstrchr(szData, ','); *p = 0;
                lstrcpy(SetupInfo.szPMGroupFileName,
                    StripEndBlanks(szData));
```

```
        lstrcpy(SetupInfo.szPMGroupName,
            StripEndBlanks(p + 1));
     }
     break;

case RS_DISKS:
   DiskInfo[SetupInfo.wNumDisks].wNum = latoi(szLine);
   lstrcpy(DiskInfo[SetupInfo.wNumDisks++].szDesc,
        szData);
   break;

case RS_DIRS:
   DirInfo[SetupInfo.wNumDirs].wNum = latoi(szLine);
   lstrcpy(DirInfo[SetupInfo.wNumDirs++].szDesc, szData);
   break;

case RS_FILES:
   p = _fstrchr(szData, ','); *p++ = 0;
   lstrcpy(FileInfo[SetupInfo.wNumFiles].szDesc,
        StripEndBlanks(szData));

   szData = p; p = _fstrchr(szData, ','); *p++ = 0;
   lstrcpy(FileInfo[SetupInfo.wNumFiles].szFileName,
        StripEndBlanks(szData));

   szData = p; p = _fstrchr(szData, ','); *p++ = 0;
   FileInfo[SetupInfo.wNumFiles].wDirNum =
        latoi(StripEndBlanks(szData));

   szData = p; p = _fstrchr(szData, ','); *p++ = 0;
   FileInfo[SetupInfo.wNumFiles].wDiskNum =
        latoi(StripEndBlanks(szData));

   StripEndBlanks(p);
   FileInfo[SetupInfo.wNumFiles++].fCompressed =
        (*p == 'Y' || *p == 'y');
   break;
```

```
        case RS_PMINFO:
            p = _fstrchr(szData, ','); *p++ = 0;
            lstrcpy(PMInfo[SetupInfo.wNumPMFiles].szFileName,
                StripEndBlanks(szData));
            szData = p; p = _fstrchr(szData, ',');
            if (p != NULL) *p++ = 0;
            lstrcpy(PMInfo[SetupInfo.wNumPMFiles].szDesc,
                StripEndBlanks(szData));

          if (p == NULL) {
            PMInfo[SetupInfo.wNumPMFiles].szIconFileName[0] = 0;
            PMInfo[SetupInfo.wNumPMFiles].wIconPos = 0;
          } else {
            szData = p; p = _fstrchr(szData, ',');
            if (p != NULL) *p++ = 0;

            lstrcpy(PMInfo[SetupInfo.wNumPMFiles].szIconFileName,
                StripEndBlanks(szData));
            PMInfo[SetupInfo.wNumPMFiles].wIconPos =
                latoi(StripEndBlanks(p));
          }
        SetupInfo.wNumPMFiles++;
         break;
      }
   }
   SetCursor(hCursor);
   return(wResult);
}

DWORD FAR PASCAL SetupInfoSys (SETUPINFOMSG Msg, WORD wParam,
      LPSTR lpBuffer) {
   DWORD dwResult = 0;
   GLOBALHANDLE hMem;
   int nFile;
   OFSTRUCT of;
   LPSTR p;
   WORD x;

   switch (Msg) {
      case SIM_INITIALIZE:
```

```
   // wParam = NU, lpBuffer = pathname
   dwResult = SIM_INIT_NOERROR;
   hMem = GlobalAlloc(GMEM_MOVEABLE | GMEM_ZEROINIT,
      MAXSETUPINFOSIZE);
   if (hMem == NULL) {
      dwResult = SIM_INIT_NOMEM;
      break;
   }
   nFile = OpenFile(lpBuffer, &of, OF_READ);
   if (nFile == -1) {
      dwResult = SIM_INIT_NOFILE;
      break;
   }
   p = GlobalLock(hMem);
   // Put a terminating zero byte at the end of the buffer
   *(p + _lread(nFile, p, MAXSETUPINFOSIZE)) = 0;
   _lclose(nFile); PrepareSetupInfo(p);
   GlobalUnlock(hMem); GlobalFree(hMem);
   break;

case SIM_GETAPPNAME:
   // wParam: NU, lpBuffer: to buffer
   lstrcpy(lpBuffer, SetupInfo.szAppName);
   break;

case SIM_GETDEFDIR:
   // wParam: NU, lpBuffer: to buffer
   lstrcpy(lpBuffer, SetupInfo.szDefDir);
   break;

case SIM_GETSPACENEEDED:
   // wParam = NU, lpBuffer = NU
   dwResult = SetupInfo.wSpaceNeeded
   break;

case SIM_GETNUMDISKS:
   // wParam: NU, lpBuffer = NU
   dwResult = SetupInfo.wNumDisks;
   break;
```

```
case SIM_GETDISKDESC:
   // wParam: Disk #, lpBuffer: LPSTR
   lstrcpy(lpBuffer, DiskInfo[wParam].szDesc);
   break;

case SIM_FINDDISKNUM:
   // wParam: Dir#, lpBuffer: NU
   dwResult = SetupInfoSys(SIM_GETNUMDISKS, 0, 0);
   while (dwResult-)
      if (wParam == DiskInfo[(WORD) dwResult].wNum) break;
   break;

case SIM_GETNUMDIRS:
   // wParam: NU, lpBuffer: NU
   dwResult = SetupInfo.wNumDirs;
   break;

case SIM_GETDIR:
   // wParam: Dir#, lpBuffer = to buffer
   lstrcpy(lpBuffer, DirInfo[wParam].szDesc);
   break;

case SIM_FINDDIRNUM:
   // wParam: Dir#, lpBuffer: NU
   dwResult = SetupInfoSys(SIM_GETNUMDIRS, 0, 0);
   while (dwResult-)
      if (wParam == DirInfo[(WORD) dwResult].wNum) break;
   break;

case SIM_GETNUMFILES:
   // wParam: NU, lpBuffer: NU
   dwResult = SetupInfo.wNumFiles;
   break;

case SIM_GETFILEDESC:
   // wParam: File#, lpBuffer: to buffer
   lstrcpy(lpBuffer, FileInfo[wParam].szDesc);
   break;
```

```
case SIM_GETFILENAME:
   // wParam: File#, lpBuffer: to buffer
   lstrcpy(lpBuffer, FileInfo[wParam].szFileName);
    break;

case SIM_GETFILEDISK:
   // wParam: File#, lpBuffer: to buffer 4 DESC. Returns #.
   dwResult = FileInfo[wParam].wDiskNum;
   x = (WORD) SetupInfoSys(SIM_FINDDISKNUM,
       (WORD) dwResult, 0);
   lstrcpy(lpBuffer, DiskInfo[x].szDesc);
    break;

case SIM_GETFILEDIR:
   // wParam: File#, lpBuffer: to buffer. Returns #.
   dwResult = FileInfo[wParam].wDirNum;
   x = (WORD) SetupInfoSys(SIM_FINDDIRNUM,
       (WORD) dwResult, 0);
   lstrcpy(lpBuffer, DirInfo[x].szDesc);
    break;

case SIM_ISFILECOMPRESSED:
    // wParam: File#, lpBuffer: NU
   dwResult = FileInfo[wParam].fCompressed;
    break;

case SIM_GETPMGROUP:
   // wParam: NU, lpBuffer: buffer
   lstrcpy(lpBuffer, SetupInfo.szPMGroupName);
    break;

case SIM_GETPMGROUPFILENAME:
   // wParam: NU, lpBuffer: buffer
   lstrcpy(lpBuffer, SetupInfo.szPMGroupFileName);
    break;

case SIM_GETNUMPMPROGS:
   // wParam: NU, lpBuffer: NU
   dwResult = SetupInfo.wNumPMFiles;
    break;
```

639

```
case SIM_FINDDIRFORFILE:
   // wParam: NU, lpBuffer: filename
   for (dwResult = 0; dwResult < SetupInfo.wNumFiles;
         dwResult++)
      if (lstrcmpi(lpBuffer, FileInfo[(WORD)
            dwResult].szFileName) == 0)
         break;
   if (dwResult == SetupInfo.wNumFiles) dwResult = -1;
   else {
      dwResult =
         SetupInfoSys(SIM_FINDDIRNUM, FileInfo[(WORD)
         dwResult].wDirNum, 0);
   }
   break;

case SIM_GETPMPROGNAME:
   // wParam: PMProg#, lpBuffer: buffer
   lstrcpy(lpBuffer, PMInfo[wParam].szFileName);
   // Return directory index
   dwResult = SetupInfoSys(SIM_FINDDIRFORFILE, 0, lpBuffer);
   break;

case SIM_GETPMPROGDESC:
   // wParam: PMProg#, lpBuffer: buffer
   lstrcpy(lpBuffer, PMInfo[wParam].szDesc);
   break;

case SIM_GETPMICONINFO:
   // wParam: PMProg#, lpBuffer: buffer. Returns icon #.
   if (PMInfo[wParam].szIconFileName[0] == 0) {
      lstrcpy(lpBuffer, PMInfo[wParam].szFileName);
   } else {
      lstrcpy(lpBuffer, PMInfo[wParam].szIconFileName);
   }
   dwResult = MAKELONG(
      (WORD) SetupInfoSys(SIM_FINDDIRFORFILE, 0, lpBuffer),
      PMInfo[wParam].wIconPos);
   break;
```

```
    }
    return(dwResult);
}
```

Listing 8-11. SETUPINF.H file-handling header.

```
/****************************************************************
Module name: SetupInf.H
Programmer : Jeffrey M. Richter
****************************************************************/

typedef enum {
    SIM_INITIALIZE,         // wParam: NU, lpBuffer: SETUP.INF
                            // file's pathname

    SIM_GETAPPNAME,         // wParam: NU, lpBuffer: buffer
    SIM_GETDEFDIR,          // wParam: NU, lpBuffer: buffer
    SIM_GETSPACENEEDED,     // wParam: NU, lpBuffer: NU

    SIM_GETNUMDISKS,        // wParam: NU, lpBuffer: NU
    SIM_GETDISKDESC,        // wParam: Disk#, lpBuffer: NU
    SIM_FINDDISKNUM,        // wParam: Disk#, lpBuffer: NU

    SIM_GETNUMDIRS,         // wParam: NU, lpBuffer: NU
    SIM_GETDIR,             // wParam: Dir#, lpBuffer: buffer
    SIM_FINDDIRNUM,         // wParam: Dir#, lpBuffer: NU

    SIM_GETNUMFILES,        // wParam: NU, lpBuffer: NU
    SIM_GETFILEDESC,        // wParam: File#, lpBuffer: buffer
    SIM_GETFILENAME,        // wParam: File#, lpBuffer: buffer
    SIM_GETFILEDIR,         // wParam: File#, lpBuffer: buffer.
                            // Returns #.
    SIM_GETFILEDISK,        // wParam: File#, lpBuffer: buffer 4
                            // DESC. Returns #.
    SIM_ISFILECOMPRESSED,   // wParam: File#, lpBuffer: NU
    SIM_FINDDIRFORFILE,     // wParam: NU, lpBuffer: Filename
```

```
    SIM_GETPMGROUP,           // wParam: NU, lpBuffer: buffer
    SIM_GETPMGROUPFILENAME, // wParam: NU, lpBuffer: buffer
    SIM_GETNUMPMPROGS,        // wParam: NU, lpBuffer: NU
    SIM_GETPMPROGNAME,        // wParam: PMProg#, lpBuffer: buffer
    SIM_GETPMPROGDESC,        // wParam: PMProg#, lpBuffer: buffer
    SIM_GETPMICONINFO         // wParam: PMProg#, lpBuffer: buffer.
                              // Returns icon #.
} SETUPINFOMSG;

// Possible return values from sending the SIM_INITIALIZE message
typedef enum {
    SIM_INIT_NOERROR,
    SIM_INIT_NOMEM,
    SIM_INIT_NOFILE
} SIM_INITIALIZE_ERROR;

DWORD FAR PASCAL SetupInfoSys (SETUPINFOMSG Msg, WORD wParam,
    LPSTR lpBuffer);

// Defines used by the Setup program
#define MAXDISKDESC 50
#define MAXDIRDESC 30
#define MAXFILEDESC 50
#define MAXPMDESC 30
#define MAXAPPNAME 40
```

Listing 8-12. SETUPPM.C Program Manager DDE conversation.

```
/****************************************************************
Module name: SetupPM.C
Programmer : Jeffrey M. Richter
****************************************************************/

#include "..\nowindws.h"
#undef NOATOM
#undef NOKERNEL
#undef NOLSTRING
#undef NOMEMMGR
```

```
#undef NOMSG
#undef NOSHOWWINDOW
#undef NOUSER
#undef NOWINMESSAGES
#undef NOWINOFFSETS
#include <windows.h>
#include <dde.h>

#include <string.h>

#include "Setup.h"
#include "SetupInf.h"

char _szClassName[] = "DDEClient";

typedef struct {
   HWND hWndServer;
} WNDEB;

#define DDE_WAITTIME    3000

LONG FAR PASCAL DDEClientWndProc (HWND hWnd, WORD wMsg,
      WORD wParam, LONG lParam) {
   DWORD dwResult = 0, dwStopTime;
   BOOL fCallDefProc = FALSE;
   HWND hWndServer = (HWND) GETWNDEB(hWnd, WNDEB, hWndServer);
   char szBuf[100]; MSG Msg;

   switch (wMsg) {

      case WM_NCCREATE:
         dwResult = DefWindowProc(hWnd, wMsg, wParam, lParam);
         if (dwResult == NULL) break;

         SendMessage(-1, WM_DDE_INITIATE, hWnd,
            (LONG) ((LPCREATESTRUCT) lParam)->lpCreateParams);

         if (GETWNDEB(hWnd, WNDEB, hWndServer) != NULL)
            break;
```

```
        // A conversation could not be established. Attempt
        // to execute the desired application.
        GlobalGetAtomName(LOWORD((LONG) ((LPCREATESTRUCT)
           lParam)->lpCreateParams), szBuf, sizeof(szBuf));
        WinExec(szBuf, SW_RESTORE);

        SendMessage(-1, WM_DDE_INITIATE, hWnd,
           (LONG) ((LPCREATESTRUCT) lParam)->lpCreateParams);

        if (GETWNDEB(hWnd, WNDEB, hWndServer) == NULL)
           DefWindowProc(hWnd, WM_NCDESTROY, wParam, lParam);

        break;

    case WM_DESTROY:
        PostMessage(hWndServer, WM_DDE_TERMINATE, hWnd, 0);
        SETWNDEB(hWnd, WNDEB, hWndServer, NULL);
        // From now on, do not send a WM_DDE_ACK message to the
        // server in response to any message sent from the server

        // Wait for response from the server
        dwStopTime = GetTickCount() + DDE_WAITTIME;
        do {
           if (PeekMessage(&Msg, hWnd, WM_DDE_TERMINATE,
              WM_DDE_TERMINATE, PM_REMOVE)) break;

        } while (GetTickCount() < dwStopTime);
        break;

    case WM_DDE_DATA:
        if (hWndServer != (HWND) wParam) {
           // Conversation not initiated with this server or
           // server sent after we terminated the conversation
           if (HIWORD(lParam) != NULL) {
              // Data handle is not. If it were NULL, a link was
              // set using the WM_DDE_ADVISE message.
              GlobalFree(HIWORD(lParam));
           }
           GlobalDeleteAtom(LOWORD(lParam));
        }
        break;
```

```
case WM_DDE_EXECUTE:
   // Because this is a client and NOT a server, this
   // message was sent to this window from the Setup
   // application. The lParam parameter contains the handle
   // of the memory containing the commands to be executed
   // by the server.

   // Verify that a conversation was started and hasn't been
   // terminated
   if (hWndServer == NULL) break;

   PostMessage(hWndServer, wMsg, hWnd, lParam);

   // Wait for response from the server
   GetMessage(&Msg, hWnd, WM_DDE_ACK, WM_DDE_ACK);

   // Return whether command was acknowledged successfully
   wParam = LOWORD(Msg.lParam);
   dwResult = ((DDEACK *) &wParam)->fAck;
   break;

case WM_DDE_TERMINATE:
   if (hWndServer == NULL) break;
   // The server has terminated the conversation with us.
   // We must send the WM_DDE_TERMINATE message back to
   // the server.
   PostMessage(hWndServer, WM_DDE_TERMINATE, hWnd, 0);
   SETWNDEB(hWnd, WNDEB, hWndServer, (HWND) NULL);
   break;

case WM_DDE_ACK:
   if (hWndServer == NULL) {
      // No conversation initiated. WM_DDE_ACK must be from
      // a potential server that just received my
      // WM_DDE_INITIATE message.
      SETWNDEB(hWnd, WNDEB, hWndServer, (HWND) wParam);
      break;
   }
```

```
              // WM_DDE_ACK message was received from a potential
              // server, but we have already established a conversation
              // with another server. Tell the server that we do not
              // wish to continue our conversation with it.
              PostMessage((HWND) wParam, WM_DDE_TERMINATE, hWnd, 0);
              break;

         default:
            fCallDefProc = TRUE;
         break;
      }

      if (fCallDefProc)
         dwResult = DefWindowProc(hWnd, wMsg, wParam, lParam);

      return(dwResult);
}

BOOL FAR PASCAL RegisterDDEClient (HANDLE hInstance) {
   WNDCLASS wc;
   wc.style = 0;
   wc.cbClsExtra = 0;
   wc.cbWndExtra = sizeof(WNDEB);
   wc.lpfnWndProc = DDEClientWndProc;
   wc.hInstance = hInstance;
   wc.hIcon = NULL;
   wc.hCursor = NULL;
   wc.hbrBackground = NULL;
   wc.lpszMenuName = NULL;
   wc.lpszClassName = _szClassName;
   return(RegisterClass(&wc));
}


// ***** Functions for Adding Files to Program Manager ******

BOOL NEAR PASCAL CreatePMInfo (HANDLE hInstance) {
   int nDirIndex, nPMProg, nMaxPMProgs;
   DWORD dwTemp;
   BOOL fOk;
   char szPMGroup[100], szPMGroupFileName[100];
```

```
char szPMProgName[100], szPMProgDesc[100],
   szPMIconFileName[100];
char szBuf[100], szBuf2[100], szCmd[100],
   szProgMan[] = "PROGMAN";
HWND hWndDDEClient, hWndPM;
ATOM aApp, aTopic;
GLOBALHANDLE hMem;
LPSTR lpCommand;

// Initiate a conversation with Program Manager
aApp = GlobalAddAtom(szProgMan);
aTopic = GlobalAddAtom(szProgMan);
hWndDDEClient = CreateWindow("DDEClient", "", 0, 0, 0, 0, 0,
   NULL, NULL, hInstance, (LPSTR) MAKELONG(aApp, aTopic));
GlobalDeleteAtom(aApp);
GlobalDeleteAtom(aTopic);

if (hWndDDEClient == NULL) {
   // Conversation could not be initiated
   return(FALSE);
}

// Force Program Manager to open so that the user can see what
// group and applications we are adding

// Notice that I use the FindWindow function here. I cannot use
// the window handle of the DDE Server window because Program
// Manager could acknowledge our DDE conversation by creating a
// DDEServer window. Calling the ShowWindow function and
// using this handle would make the DDEServer window visible;
// this is definitely NOT desirable.
ShowWindow(hWndPM = FindWindow(szProgMan, NULL), SW_RESTORE);

// Disable Program Manager so the user can't work with it while
// we are doing our stuff
EnableWindow(FindWindow(szProgMan, NULL), FALSE);

// Create the PM Group box
SetupInfoSys(SIM_GETPMGROUP, 0, szPMGroup);
SetupInfoSys(SIM_GETPMGROUPFILENAME, 0, szPMGroupFileName);
```

```
wsprintf(szCmd, "[CreateGroup(%s%s%s)]",
   (LPSTR) szPMGroup, (LPSTR) (*szPMGroupFileName == 0 ? "" :
   ","), (LPSTR) szPMGroupFileName);

hMem = GlobalAlloc(GMEM_MOVEABLE | GMEM_DDESHARE,
   lstrlen(szCmd) + 1);
lpCommand = GlobalLock(hMem);
lstrcpy(lpCommand, szCmd);
GlobalUnlock(hMem);

fOk = (BOOL) SendMessage(hWndDDEClient, WM_DDE_EXECUTE, 0,
   MAKELONG(0, hMem));
GlobalFree(hMem);

// Add the individual PM files to the Group box
nMaxPMProgs = (int) SetupInfoSys(SIM_GETNUMPMPROGS, 0, 0);
for (nPMProg = 0; fOk && (nPMProg < nMaxPMProgs); nPMProg++) {
   SetupInfoSys(SIM_GETPMPROGDESC, nPMProg, szPMProgDesc);
   nDirIndex = (int) SetupInfoSys(SIM_GETPMPROGNAME, nPMProg,
      szPMProgName);

   // Calculate the top of the destination directory path
   wsprintf(szBuf, "%s%s", (LPSTR) _szDstDir, (LPSTR)
      ((*(_fstrrchr(_szDstDir, '\\') + 1) == 0) ? "" : "\\"));
   lstrcpy(szBuf2, szBuf);

   // Append subdirectory where the file is and the file's name
   SetupInfoSys(SIM_GETDIR, nDirIndex, _fstrchr(szBuf, 0));
   lstrcat(szBuf, "\\");
   lstrcat(szBuf, szPMProgName);

   // Append the subdirectory where the icon file is and the
   // icon file's name
   dwTemp = SetupInfoSys(SIM_GETPMICONINFO, nPMProg,
      szPMIconFileName);
   SetupInfoSys(SIM_GETDIR, LOWORD(dwTemp),
      _fstrchr(szBuf2, 0));
   lstrcat(szBuf2, "\\");
   lstrcat(szBuf2, szPMIconFileName);
```

```
   // Add the new file to the already created PM Group
   wsprintf(szCmd, "[AddItem(%s,%s,%s,%d)]", (LPSTR) szBuf,
       (LPSTR) szPMProgDesc, (LPSTR) szBuf2, HIWORD(dwTemp));
   hMem = GlobalAlloc(GMEM_MOVEABLE | GMEM_DDESHARE,
       lstrlen(szCmd) + 1);
   lpCommand = GlobalLock(hMem);
   lstrcpy(lpCommand, szCmd);
   GlobalUnlock(hMem);

   fOk = (BOOL) SendMessage(hWndDDEClient, WM_DDE_EXECUTE, 0,
       MAKELONG(0, hMem));
   GlobalFree(hMem);
 }
 // Terminate the DDE conversation with Program Manager
 DestroyWindow(hWndDDEClient);
 EnableWindow(hWndPM, TRUE);
 return(fOk);
}
```

The NOWINDWS.H File

All the sample applications in this book include the NOWINDWS.H header file (see Listing A-1). The WINDOWS.H file included with the Windows SDK contains a number of data structure and macro definitions. For any single application, most of these are not required. When the C compiler processes a file, however, all the symbols must be placed in the symbol table. This uses an enormous amount of memory, limiting the size of the source file that can compiled. NOWINDWS.H prevents most of the unneeded symbols from being added to the compiler's symbol table. When your source file requires the symbols associated with a particular Windows capability, simply add the *#undef* preprocessor directive. For example, if the file processes nonclient window messages, it should look like this:

```
#include <nowindws.h>
#undef NONCMESSAGES
#undef NOUSER
#undef NOWINMESSAGES
#include <windows.h>
    .
    .
    .
```

The order of the *#undef*s is not significant; I always place them in alphabetical order.

The indention scheme used in NOWINDWS.H indicates which other identifiers must also be *#undef*ed. In the example above, *NOWINMESSAGES* and *NOUSER* must be *#undef*ed if you want to use *NCMESSAGES*.

651

Listing A-1. NOWINDWS.H.

```
/******************************************************************
Module name:     NOWINDWS.H
Programmer :     Jeffrey M. Richter
Description:     Header file to NOT include things in WINDOWS.H.
This file MUST be included BEFORE WINDOWS.H. If you desire some-
thing from WINDOWS.H, use an #undef between this file and the
WINDOWS.H file.
******************************************************************/

#define NOGDI
   #define NODRAWTEXT
   #define NOGDICAPMASKS
   #define NOMETAFILE
   #define NORASTEROPS
   #define NOTEXTMETRIC

#define NOKERNEL
   #define NOATOM
   #define NOKEYBOARDINFO
   #define NOLANGUAGE
   #define NOMEMMGR
   #define NOOPENFILE
   #define NORESOURCE

#define NOHELP

#define NOMINMAX

#define NOPROFILER

#define NOUSER
   #define NOCLIPBOARD
   #define NOCOLOR
   #define NOCOMM
   #define NOCTLMGR
   #define NODEFERWINDOWPOS
   #define NOICONS
   #define NOKANJI
```

```
#define NOLSTRING
#define NOLFILEIO
#define NOMB
#define NOMDI
#define NOMENUS
#define NOMSG
#define NOSCROLL
#define NOSHOWWINDOW
#define NOSOUND
#define NOSYSCOMMANDS
#define NOSYSMETRICS
#define NOVIRTUALKEYCODES
#define NOWH
#define NOWINMESSAGES
    #define NOKEYSTATES
    #define NONCMESSAGES
#define NOWINOFFSETS
#define NOWINSTYLES
```

Windows Bitmaps

The Microsoft Windows Device Driver Kit specifies that all video device drivers include a set of bitmaps that are accessible to any Windows application. An application gains access to these bitmaps by calling *LoadBitmap* and specifying NULL as the first parameter. The second parameter specifies an identifier, defined in WINDOWS.H, that represents the bitmap to be retrieved. *LoadBitmap* returns a handle to the desired bitmap.

The chart on the following pages lists the predefined bitmaps. Many contain several images. The images are of identical size and may be isolated by dividing the bitmap's width and height by the number of images in its rows or columns. For example, to retrieve the image representing a selected radio button, you would perform the following steps:

```
BITMAP BitmapInfo;
HBITMAP hBitmap;
RECT rc;

hBitmap = LoadBitmap(NULL, OBM_CHECKBOXES);
GetObject(hBitmap, sizeof(BITMAP) &BitmapInfo);

// Calculate the rectangle bounding the desired image
// (row 1, column 1). For reference: the unchecked check
// box is in row 0, column 0.
rc.top = (BitmapInfo.bmWidth / 4) * 1;
rc.right = (BitmapInfo.bmWidth / 4) * 2 - 1;
rc.left = (BitmapInfo.bmHeight / 3) * 1;
rc.bottom = (BitmapInfo.bmHeight / 3) * 2 - 1;
```

This information can be used in calls to *BitBlt* or *StretchBlt*.

Identifier	Description	Appearance
OBM_CHECK	Check mark used to check menu items.	
OBM_CHECKBOXES	Used for radio buttons and check boxes.	
OBM_CLOSE	Used to represent the system menus for applications and MDI Children.	
OBM_COMBO	Used in combo boxes.	
OBM_DNARROW	Down arrow in vertical scroll bars.	
OBM_DNARROWD	Depressed down arrow in vertical scroll bars.	
OBM_LFARROW	Left arrow in horizontal scroll bars.	
OBM_LFARROWD	Depressed left arrow in horizontal scroll bars.	
OBM_MNARROW	Used to represent cascading menus.	
OBM_REDUCE	Triangle used for minimize box in window's caption.	
OBM_REDUCED	Depressed triangle used for minimize box in window's caption.	

Identifier	Description	Appearance
OBM_RESTORE	Double triangles used for restore box in window's caption.	
OBM_RESTORED	Depressed double triangles used for restore box in window's caption.	
OBM_RGARROW	Right arrow in horizontal scroll bars.	
OBM_RGARROWD	Depressed right arrow in horizontal scroll bars.	
OBM_UPARROW	Up arrow in vertical scroll bars.	
OBM_UPARROWD	Depressed up arrow in vertical scroll bars.	
OBM_ZOOM	Triangle used for maximize box in window's caption.	
OBM_ZOOMD	Depressed triangle used for maximize box in window's caption.	

The following bitmaps are supplied for compatibility with versions of Windows prior to 3.0:

Identifier	Description	Appearance
OBM_BTNCORNERS	Circles used to draw rounded corners of pushbuttons.	
OBM_SIZE	Size box used on tiled windows.	
OBM_BTSIZE	Size box used at intersection of horizontal and vertical scroll bars.	
OBM_OLD_CLOSE	Used to represent the system menus for both applications and MDI Children.	
OBM_OLD_DNARROW	Down arrow used in vertical scroll bars.	
OBM_OLD_REDUCE	Down arrow used for minimize box in window's caption.	
OBM_OLD_RESTORE	Double arrows used for restore box in window's caption.	
OBM_OLD_RGARROW	Right arrow used in horizontal scroll bars.	
OBM_OLD_UPARROW	Up arrow used in vertical scroll bars.	

Identifier	Description	Appearance
OBM_OLD_ZOOM	Up arrow used for maximize box in window's caption.	⬆

APPENDIX C

Accessing Class and Window Extra Bytes

This appendix introduces macros that give Windows developers a convenient method for storing and retrieving data associated with class and window extra bytes. For a complete description of how class and window extra bytes are used, refer to Chapter 1.

To use these macros to access a window's extra bytes, the application must declare a data structure enumerating the elements to be stored and their types. Each element should be a two- or four-byte entity. For example, a window class that needs to store a window handle and a *DWORD* value might declare a structure like this:

```
typedef struct {
   HWND hWndChild;
   DWORD dwLastEventTime;
} WNDEXTRABYTES;
```

When the application is initializing the *WNDCLASS* structure to pass to *RegisterClass*, the *cbWndExtra* member of this structure should be initialized as follows:

```
WndClass.cbWndExtra = sizeof(WNDEXTRABYTES);
```

This will guarantee that the proper number of extra bytes is always allocated. If the programmer later adds, deletes, or changes the type of a member, the *sizeof* operator will return the proper length of the structure when the module is recompiled.

Storing information in the window's extra bytes is accomplished like this:

```
SETWNDEB(hWnd, WNDEXTRABYTES, dwLastEventTime, GetTickCount());
```

The *SETWNDEB* macro is shown below:

```
#define SETWNDEB(hWnd, Struct, Member, Value) \
   ((sizeof(((Struct FAR *)0)->Member) == sizeof(DWORD)) ? \
      SetWindowLong(hWnd, offsetof(Struct, Member), Value) : \
      SetWindowWord(hWnd, offsetof(Struct, Member), (WORD) Value))
```

This macro causes the compiler to determine whether the *SetWindowWord* or *SetWindowLong* function should be called, based on the size of the member being passed. In the example above, the *SetWindowLong* function will be called because the *dwLastEventTime* member of the *WNDEXTRABYTES* structure is the same size as a *DWORD*.

A member's offset into the structure is the same as its offset into the window's extra bytes. Therefore, the offset is also automatically determined at compile time. If members of the structure are added, deleted, moved, or changed, recompiling the module will automatically generate the correct offsets.

Values stored in the window's extra bytes are retrieved by the *GETWNDEB* macro:

```
#define GETWNDEB(hWnd, Struct, Member) \
   ((sizeof(((Struct FAR *)0)->Member) == sizeof(DWORD)) ? \
      GetWindowLong(hWnd, offsetof(Struct, Member)) : \
      GetWindowWord(hWnd, offsetof(Struct, Member)))
```

This macro is similar to *SETWNDEB* except that it calls *GetWindowWord* or *GetWindowLong* and does not require an additional parameter specifying a new value.

To extend this method to work with class extra bytes, the application must declare another data structure enumerating the elements to be stored in the class extra bytes and their types:

```
typedef struct {
  .
  .
  .
} CLSEXTRABYTES;
```

You then modify the function that initializes the *WNDCLASS* structure by adding the following line:

```
WndClass.cbClsExtra = sizeof(CLSEXTRABYTES);
```

To store and retrieve data in the class extra bytes, use the following macros:

```
#define SETCLSEB(hWnd, Struct, Member, Value) \
   ((sizeof(((Struct FAR *)0)->Member) == sizeof(DWORD)) ? \
      SetClassLong(hWnd, offsetof(Struct, Member), Value) : \
      SetClassWord(hWnd, offsetof(Struct, Member), (WORD) Value))

#define GETCLSEB(hWnd, Struct, Member) \
   ((sizeof(((Struct FAR *)0)->Member) == sizeof(DWORD)) ? \
      GetClassLong(hWnd, offsetof(Struct, Member)) : \
      GetClassWord(hWnd, offsetof(Struct, Member)))
```

These are identical to *SETWNDEB* and *GETWNDEB* except that they call *SetClassWord*, *SetClassLong*, *GetClassWord*, and *GetClassLong*.

All of these macros reference *offsetof*. This macro is located in the STDDEF.H file included with the C compiler:

```
#define offsetof(Struct, Member) \
   ((unsigned int) &(((Struct NEAR *) 0)->Member))
```

663

The *offsetof* macro assumes that there is a data structure of type *Struct* at memory address zero. It then references the specified member of the structure, *Member*, and returns the memory address where this member is located.

Index

Voyeur!

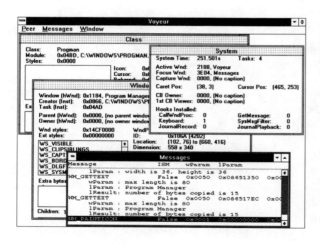

A Library of Technical References from M&T Books

NetWare User's Guide
by Edward Liebing

Endorsed by Novell, this book informs NetWare users of the services and utilities available, and how to effectively put them to use. Contained is a complete task-oriented reference that introduces users to NetWare and guides them through the basics of NetWare menu-driven utilities and command line utilities. Each utility is illustrated, thus providing a visual frame of reference. You will find general information about the utilities, then specific procedures to perform the task in mind. Utilities discussed include NetWare v2.1 through v2.15. For advanced users, a workstation troubleshooting section is included, describing the errors that occur. Two appendixes, describing briefly the services available in each NetWare menu or command line utility are also included.

Book only   **Item #071-0**   **$24.95**

Blueprint of a LAN
by Craig Chaiken

Blueprint of a LAN provides a hands-on introduction to microcomputer networks. For programmers, numerous valuable programming techniques are detailed. Network administrators will learn how to build and install LAN communication cables, configure and troubleshoot network hardware and software, and provide continuing support to users. Included are a very inexpensive zero-slot, star topology network, remote printer and file sharing, remote command execution, electronic mail, parallel processing support, high-level language support, and more. Also contained is the complete Intel 8086 assembly language source code that will help you build an inexpensive to install, local area network. An optional disk containing all source code is available.

Book & Disk (MS-DOS)   **Item #066-4**   **$39.95**
Book only   **Item #052-4**   **$29.95**

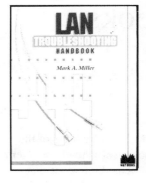

LAN Troubleshooting Handbook
by Mark A. Miller

This book is specifically for users and administrators who need to identify problems and maintain a LAN that is already installed. Topics include LAN standards, the OSI model, network documentation, LAN test equipment, cable system testing, and more. Addressed are specific issues associated with troubleshooting the four most popular LAN architectures: ARCNET, Token Ring, Ethernet, and StarLAN. Each are closely examined to pinpoint the problems unique to its design and the hardware. Handy checklists to assist in solving each architecture's unique network difficulties are also included.

Book & Disk (MS-DOS)	**Item #056-7**	**$39.95**
Book only	**Item #054-0**	**$29.95**

Building Local Area Networks with Novell's NetWare
by Patrick H. Corrigan and Aisling Guy

From the basic components to complete network installation, here is the practical guide that PC system integrators will need to build and implement PC LANs in this rapidly growing market. The specifics of building and maintaining PC LANs, including hardware configurations, software development, cabling, selection criteria, installation, and on-going management are described in a clear "how-to" manner with numerous illustrations and sample LAN management forms. *Building Local Area Networks* gives particular emphasis to Novell's NetWare, Version 2.1. Additional topics covered include the OS/2 LAN manager, Tops, Banyan VINES, internetworking, host computer gateways, and multisystem networks that link PCs, Apples, and mainframes.

Book & Disk (MS-DOS)	**Item #025-7**	**$39.95**
Book only	**Item #010-9**	**$29.95**

1-800-533-4372 (in CA 1-800-356-2002)

NetWare Supervisor's Guide
by John T. McCann, Adam T. Ruef, and Steven L. Guengerich

Written for network administrators, consultants, installers, and power users of all versions of NetWare, including NetWare 386. Where other books provide information on using NetWare at a workstation level, this definitive reference focuses on how to administer NetWare. Contained are numerous examples which include understanding and using NetWare's undocumented commands and utilities, implementing system fault tolerant LANs, refining installation parameters to improve network performance, and more.

Book only   **Item #111-3**   **$29.95**

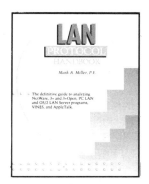

LAN Protocol Handbook
by Mark A. Miller, P.E.

Requisite reading for all network administrators and software developers needing in-depth knowledge of the internal protocols of the most popular network software. It illustrates the techniques of protocol analysis—the step-by-step process of unraveling LAN software failures. Detailed are how Ethernet, IEEE 802.3, IEEE 802.5, and ARCNET networks transmit frames of information between workstations. From that foundation, it presents LAN performnce measurements, protocol analysis methods, and protocol analyzer products. Individual chapters thoroughly discuss Novell's NetWare, 3Com's 3+ and 3+Open, IBM Token-Ring related protocols, and more!

Book only   **Item 099-0**   **$34.95**

1-800-533-4372 (in CA 1-800-356-2002)

NetWare for Macintosh User's Guide
by Kelley J. P. Lindberg

NetWare for Macintosh User's Guide is the definitive reference to using Novell's NetWare on Macintosh computers. Whether a novice or advanced user, this comprehensive text provides the information readers need to get the most from their NetWare network. It includes an overview of network operations and detailed explanations of all NetWare for Macintosh menu and command line utilities. Detailed tutorials cover such tasks as logging in, working with directories and files, and printing over a network. Advanced users will benefit from the information on managing workstation environments and troubleshooting.

Book only   **Item #126-1**   **$29.95**

NetWare 386 User's Guide
by Christine Milligan

NetWare 386 User's Guide is a complete guide to using and understanding Novell's NetWare 386. It is an excellent reference for 386. Detailed tutorials cover tasks such as logging in, working with directories and files, and printing over a network. Complete explanations of the basic concepts underlying NetWare 386, along with a summary of the differences between NetWare 286 and 386, are included. Advanced users will benefit from the information on managing workstation environments and the troubleshooting index that fully examines NetWare 386 error messages.

Book only   **Item #101-6**   **$29.95**

1-800-533-4372 (in CA 1-800-356-2002)

The Complete Kit for Creating Customized NetWare 286 Manuals

The NetWare Manual Makers
Complete Kits for Creating Customized NetWare Manuals

Developed to meet the tremendous demand for customized manuals, The NetWare Manual Makers enables the NetWare supervisor and administrator to create network training manuals specific to their individual sites. Administrators simply fill in the blanks on the template provided on disk and print the file to create customized manuals and command cards. Included are general "how-to" information on using a network, as well as fill-in-the-blank sections that help administrators explain and document procedures unique to a particular site. The disk files are provided in WordPerfect and ASCII formats. The WordPerfect file creates a manual that looks exactly like the one in the book. The ASCII file can be imported into any desktop publishing or word processing software.

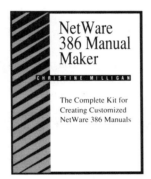

The Complete Kit for Creating Customized NetWare 386 Manuals

The NetWare 286 Manual Maker
The Complete Kit for Creating Customized NetWare 286 Manuals
by Christine Milligan

Book/Disk	Item #119-9	$49.95

The NetWare 386 Manual Maker
The Complete Kit for Creating Customized NetWare 386 Manuals
by Christine Milligan

Book/Disk	Item #120-2	$49.95

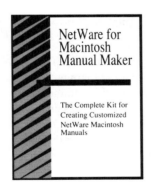

The Complete Kit for Creating Customized NetWare Macintosh Manuals

The NetWare for Macintosh Manual Maker
The Complete Kit for Creating Customized NetWare for Macintosh Manuals
by Kelley J. P. Lindberg

Book/Disk	Item #130-X	$49.95

1-800-533-4372 (in CA 1-800-356-2002)

Running WordPerfect on Netware
by Greg McMurdie and Joni Taylor

Written by NetWare and WordPerfect experts, the book contains practical information for both system administrators and network WordPerfect users. Administrators will learn how to install, maintain, and troubleshoot WordPerfect on the network. Users will find answers to everyday questions such as how to print over the network, how to handle error messages, and how to use WordPerfect's tutorial on NetWare.

Book only	Item #145-8	$29.95

Graphics Programming in C
by Roger T. Stevens

All the information you need to program graphics in C, including source code, is presented. You'll find complete discussions of ROM BIOS, VGA, EGA, and CGA inherent capabilities; methods of displaying points on a screen; improved, faster algorithms for drawing and filling lines, rectangles, rounded polygons, ovals, circles, and arcs; graphic cursors; and much more! Both Turbo C and Microsoft C are supported.

Book/Disk (MS-DOS)	Item #019-4	$36.95
Book only	Item #018-4	$26.95

Object-Oriented Programming for Presentation Manager
by William G. Wong

Written for programmers and developers interested in OS/2 Presentation Manager (PM), as well as DOS programmers who are just beginning to explore Object-Oriented Programming and PM. Topics include a thorough overview of Presentation Manager and Object-Oriented Programming, Object-Oriented Programming languages and techniques, developing Presentation Manager applications using C and OOP techniques, and more.

Book/Disk (MS-DOS)	Item #079-6	$39.95
Book only	Item #074-5	$29.95

Fractal Programming in C
by Roger T. Stevens

If you are a programmer wanting to learn more about fractals, this book is for you. Learn how to create pictures that have both beauty and an underlying mathematical meaning. Included are over 50 black and white pictures and 32 full color fractals. All source code to reproduce these pictures is provided on disk in MS-DOS format and requires an IBM PC or clone with an EGA or VGA card, a color monitor, and a Turbo C, Quick C, or Microsoft C compiler.

Book/Disk (MS-DOS)	**Item #038-9**	**$36.95**
Book only	**Item #037-0**	**$26.95**

Fractal Programming in Turbo Pascal
by Roger T. Stevens

This book equips Turbo pascal programmers with the tools needed to program dynamic fractal curves. It is a reference that gives full attention to developing the reader's understanding of various fractal curves. More than 100 black and white and 32 full color fractals are illustrated throughout the book. All source code to reproduce the fractals is available on disk in MS/PC-DOS format. Requires a PC or clone with EGA or VGA, color monitor, and Turbo Pascal 4.0 or better.

Book/Disk (MS-DOS)	**Item #107-5**	**$39.95**
Book	**Item #106-7**	**$29.95**

Programming the 8514/A
by Jake Richter and Bud Smith

Written for programmers who want to develop software for the 8514/A, this complete reference includes information on both the 8514/A register and adapter Interface. Topics include an introduction to the 8514/A and its architecture, a discussion on programming to the applications interface specification, a complete section on programming the hardware, and more. A sample source code and programs are available on the optional disk in MS-DOS format.

Book/Disk (MS-DOS)	**Item #103-2**	**$39.95**
Book only	**Item #086-9**	**$29.95**

1-800-533-4372 (in CA 1-800-356-2002)

C++ Techniques and Applications
by Scott Robert Ladd

This book guides the professional programmer into the practical use of the C++ programming language—an object-oriented enhancement of the popular C programming language. The book contains three major sections. Part One introduces programmers to the syntax and general usage of C++ features; Part Two covers object-oriented programming goals and techniques; and Part Three focuses on the creation of applications.

Book/Disk (MS-DOS)   Item #076-1 $39.95

Book only   Item #075-3 $29.95

Fractal Programming and Ray Tracing with C++
by Roger T. Stevens

Finally, a book for C and C++ programmers who want to create complex and intriguing graphic designs. By the author of three best-selling graphics books, this new title thoroughly explains ray tracing, discussing how rays are traced, how objects are used to create ray-traced images, and how to create ray tracing programs. A complete ray tracing program, along with all of the source code is included. Contains 16 pages of full-color graphics.

Book/Disk (MS-DOS)   Item 118-0 $39.95

Book only   Item 134-2 $29.95

Advanced Fractal Programming in C
by Roger T. Stevens

Programmers who enjoyed our best-selling *Fractal Programming in C* can move on to the next level of fractal programming with this book. Included are how-to instructions for creating many different types of fractal curves, including source code. Contains 16 pages of full-color fractals. All the source code to generate the fractals is available on an optional disk in MS/PC-DOS format.

Book/Disk (MS-DOS)   Item #097-4 $39.95

Book only   Item #096-6 $29.95

Advanced Graphics Programming in Turbo Pascal
by Roger T. Stevens and Christopher D. Watkins

This new book is must reading for Turbo Pascal programmers who want to create impressive graphic designs on IBM PC's and compatibles. There's 16 pages of full color graphic displays along with the source code to create these dramatic pictures. Complete explanations are provided on how to tailor the graphics to suit the programmer's needs. Covered are algorithms for creating complex 2-D shapes including lines, circles and squares; how to create advanced 3-D shapes, wire-frame graphics, and solid images; numerous tips and techniques for varying pixel intensities to give the appearance or roundness to an object; and more.

Book/Disk (MS-DOS)	Item #132-6	$39.95
Book only	Item #131-8	$29.95

Advanced Graphics Programming in Turbo Pascal

Roger T. Stevens and Christopher D. Watkins

Advanced Graphics Programming in C and C++
by Roger T. Stevens

This book is for all C and C++ programmers who want to create impressive graphic designs on thier IBM PC or compatible. Though in-depth discussions and numerous sample programs, readers will learn how to create advanced 3-D shapes, wire-frame graphics, solid images, and more. All source code is available on disk in MS/PC-DOS format. Contains 16 pages of full color graphics.

Book/Disk (MS-DOS)	Item #173-3	$39.95
Book only	Item #171-7	$29.95

Advanced Graphics Programming in C and C++

Roger T. Stevens

Graphics Programming with Microsoft C 6.0
by Mark Mallet

Written for all C programmrs, this book explores graphics programming with Microsoft C 6.0, including full coverage of Microsoft C's built-in graphics libraries. Sample programs will help readers learn the techniques needed to create spectacular graphic designs, including 3-D figures, solid images, and more. All source code in book is available on disk in MS/PC-DOS format. Includes 16 pages of full-color graphics.

Book/Disk (MS-DOS)	Item #167-9	$39.95
Book only	Item #165-2	$29.95

Graphics Programming with Microsoft C 6.0

Mark Mallet

1-800-533-4372 (in CA 1-800-356-2002)

Using QuarkXPress
by Tim Meehan

Written in an enjoyable, easy-to-read style, this book addresses
the needs of both beginning and intermediate users. It includes
numerous illustrations and screen shots that guide readers through
comprehensive explanations of QuarkXPress, its potential and
real-world applications. Using QuarkXPress contains comprehensive explanations of the concepts, practices, and uses of
QuarkXPress with sample assignments of increasing complexity
that give readers actual hands-on experience using the program.

Book/Disk	Item #129-6	$34.95
Book only	Item #128-8	$24.95

An OPEN LOOK at UNIX
A Developer's Guide to X
by John David Miller

This is the book that explores the look and feel of the OPEN
LOOK graphical user interface, discussing its basic philiosophy,
environment, and user-interface elements. It includes a detailed
summary of the X Window System, introduces readers to object-
oriented programming, and shows how to develop commercial-
grade X applications. Dozens of OPEN LOOK program examples
are presented, along with nearly 13,000 lines of C code. All
source code is available on disk in 1.2 MB UNIX cpio format.

Book/Disk	Item #058-3	$39.95
Book only	Item #057-5	$29.95

Turbo C++ by Example
by Alex Lane

Turbo C++ by Example includes numerous code examples that
teach C programmers new to C++ how to skillfully program with
Borland's powerful Turbo C++. Detailed are key features of
Turbo C++ with code examples. Includes both Turbo Debugger
and Tools 2.0—a collection of tools used to design and debug
Turbo C++ programs, and Turbo Profiler. All listings available on
disk in MS/PC-DOS format.

Book/Disk (MS-DOS)	Item #141-5	$36.95
Book only	Item #123-7	$26.95

1-800-533-4372 (in CA 1-800-356-2002)

FoxPro: A Developer's Guide
Application Programming Techniques
by Pat Adams and Jordan Powell

Picking up where the FoxPro manual leaves off, this book shows programmers how to master the exceptional power of FoxPro. Useful tips and techniques, along with FoxPro's features, commands, and functions are all covered. Special attention is given to networking issues. Contains discussions on running FoxPro applications on both PCs and Macs that are on the same network. All source code is available on disk in MS/PC-DOS format.

Book/Disk (MS-DOS)	Item #084-2	$39.95
Book only	Item #083-4	$29.95

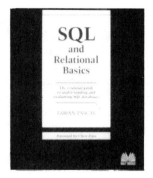

SQL and Relational Basics
by Fabian Pascal

SQL and Relational Basics was written to help PC users apply sound and general objectives to evaluating, selecting, and using database management systems. Misconceptions about relational data management and SQL are addressed and corrected. The book concentrates on the practical objectives of the relational approach as they pertain to the micro environment. Users will be able to design and correctly implement relational databases and applications, and work around product deficiencies to minimize future maintenance.

Book only:	Item #063-X	$28.95

A Small C Compiler, Second Edition
by James Hendrix

This is a solid resource for all programmers who want to learn to program in C. It thoroughly explains Small C's structure, syntax, and features. It succinctly covers the theory of compiler operation and design, discussing Small C's compatibility with C, explaining how to modify the compiler to generate new versions of itself, and more. A full-working Small C compiler, plus all the source code and files are provided on disk in MS/PC-DOS format.

Book/Disk (MS-DOS)	Item #124-5	$29.95

1-800-533-4372 (in CA 1-800-356-2002)

Small-Windows
A Library of Windowing Functions for the C Language
by James Hendrix

Here is an extensive library of C language functions for creating and manipulating display windows. This manual and disk package contains 41 windowing functions, 18 video functions written in assembly, and menu functions that support both static and pop-up menus. Small Windows is available for MS-DOS systems, and Microsoft C Versions 4.0/5.0, Turbo C 1.5, Small C, and Lattice C 3.1 compilers. Documentation and full C source code are included.

Manual & Disk   **Item #35-6**   **$29.95**

Small Assembler
by James Hendrix

Small Assembler is a full macro assembler that was developed primarily for use with the Small C compiler. This manual presents an overview of the Small Assembler, documents the command lines that invoke programs, and provides appendixes and reference materials for the programmer. The accompanying disk includes both the executable assembler and full source code.

Manual & Disk   **Item #024-9**   **$29.95**

Small-Tools User's Manual
by James Hendrix

This package of programs performs specific modular operations on text files such as editing, formatting, sorting, merging, listing, printing, searching, and much more. Small-Tools is supplied in source code form. You can select and adapt these tools to your own purposes. Documentation is included.

Manual & Disk   **Item #02-X**   **$29.95**

The One Minute Memory Manager
Every PC user's Guide to Faster More Efficient Computing
by Phillip Robinson

Readers will learn why memory is important, how and when to install more, and how to wring the most out of their memory. Clear, concise instructions teach users how to manage their computer's memory to multiply its speed and ability to run programs simultaneously. Tips and techniques also show users how to conserve memory when working with popular software programs.

Book only: Item #102-4 $24.95

Windows 3.0:
A Developer's Guide

Jeffrey M. Richter

Windows 3.0: A Developer's Guide
Jeffrey M. Richter

This example-packed guide is for all experienced C programmers developing applications for Windows 3.0. This book describes every feature, function, and components of the Windows Application Programming Interface, teaching programmers how to take full advantage of its many capabilities. Diagrams and source code examples are used to demonstrate advanced topics, including window subclassing, dynamic memory mamagement, and software installation techniques.

Book/Disk (MS-DOS)   Item #164-4 $39.95

Book   Item #162-8 $29.95

Windows 3.0 By Example
by Michael Hearst

Here is a hands-on guide to Windows 3.0. Written for all users new to Windows, this book provides thorough, easy-to-follow explanations of every Windows 3.0 feature and function. Numerous exercises and helpful practice sessions help readers further develop their understanding of Windows 3.0

Book only   Item #180-6 $26.95

1-800-533-4372 (in CA 1-800-356-2002)

ORDER FORM

To Order:

Return this form with your payment to M&T books, 501 Galveston Drive, Redwood City, CA 94063 or **call toll-free 1-800-533-4372 (in California, call 1-800-356-2002).**

ITEM #	DESCRIPTION	DISK	PRICE

Subtotal	
CA residents add sales tax ____%	
Add $3.50 per item for shipping and handling	
TOTAL	

Charge my:

☐ **Visa**

☐ **MasterCard**

☐ **AmExpress**

☐ **Check enclosed, payable to M&T Books.**

CARD NO. _____

SIGNATURE _____   EXP. DATE _____

NAME _____

ADDRESS _____

CITY _____

STATE _____   ZIP _____

M&T GUARANTEE: If your are not satisfied with your order for any reason, return it to us within 25 days of receipt for a full refund. Note: Refunds on disks apply only when returned with book within guarantee period. Disks damaged in transit or defective will be promptly replaced, but cannot be exchanged for a disk from a different title.

8020